PENGUIN BOOKS

LIBERAL FASCISM

Jonah Goldberg is a columnist for the *Los Angeles Times* and contributing editor to *National Review*. A *USA Today* contributor and former
columnist for *The Times*, he has also written for *The New Yorker*,
Commentary, the *Wall Street Journal* and many other publications.
He lives in Washington, D. C.

Liberal FASCISM

· · · · · · · · · · · · · · · · ·

The Secret History of the

LEFT

from

MUSSOLINI

to the

POLITICS OF MEANING

JONAH GOLDBERG

PENGUIN BOOKS

PENGUIN BOOKS

Published by the Penguin Group
Penguin Books Ltd, 80 Strand, London WC2R ORL, England
Penguin Group (USA) Inc., 375 Hudson Street, New York, New York 10014, USA
Penguin Group (Canada), 90 Eglinton Avenue East, Suite 700, Toronto, Ontario, Canada M4P 2Y3
(a division of Pearson Penguin Canada Inc.)
Penguin Ireland, 25 St Stephen's Green, Dublin 2, Ireland
(a division of Penguin Books Ltd)
Penguin Group (Australia), 250 Camberwell Road,
Camberwell, Victoria 3124, Australia (a division of Pearson Australia Group Pty Ltd)
Penguin Books India Pvt Ltd, 11 Community Centre,
Panchsheel Park, New Delhi – 110 017, India
Penguin Group (NZ), 67 Apollo Drive, Rosedale, North Shore 0632, New Zealand
(a division of Pearson New Zealand Ltd)
Penguin Books (South Africa) (Pty) Ltd, 24 Sturdee Avenue, Rosebank, Johannesburg 2196, South Africa

Penguin Books Ltd, Registered Offices: 80 Strand, London WC2R ORL, England

www.penguin.com

First published in the United States of America by Doubleday 2007
First published in Great Britain by Penguin Books 2009

4

Copyright © Jonah Goldberg, 2007
All rights reserved

The moral right of the author has been asserted

Printed in England by Clays Ltd, St Ives plc

978-0-141-03950-3

www.greenpenguin.co.uk

Mixed Sources
Product group from well-managed
forests and other controlled sources
www.fsc.org Cert no. SA-COC-1592
© 1996 Forest Stewardship Council

Penguin Books is committed to a sustainable future
for our business, our readers and our planet.
The book in your hands is made from paper
certified by the Forest Stewardship Council.

For Sidney Goldberg, Hop Bird

· CONTENTS ·

Everything You Know About Fascism Is Wrong

George Carlin: . . . and the poor have been systematically looted in this country. The rich have been made richer under this criminal, fascist president and his government. *[Applause.] [Cheers.]*

Bill Maher: Okay, okay.

James Glassman: You know, George—George, I think you know—do you know what fascism is?

Carlin: Fascism, when it comes to America—

Glassman: Do you know what Nazis are?

Carlin: When fascism comes to America, it will not be in brown and black shirts. It will not be with jack-boots. It will be Nike sneakers and Smiley shirts. Smiley-smiley. Fascism—Germany lost the Second World War. Fascism won it. Believe me, my friend.

Maher: And actually, fascism is when corporations become the government.

Carlin: Yes.[1]

Outside of a few academic seminars, this is about as intelligent as discussions about fascism get in America. Angry left-wingers shout that all those to their right, particularly corporate fat cats and the politicians who love them, are fascists. Meanwhile, besieged conservatives sit dumbfounded by the nastiness of the slander.

Bill Maher to the contrary, fascism is *not* "when corporations become the government." Ironically, however, George Carlin's conclusion is right, though not his reasoning. If fascism does come to America, it will indeed take the form of "smiley-face fascism"—*nice* fascism. In fact, in many respects fascism not only is here but has been here for nearly a century. For what we call liberalism—the refurbished edifice of American Progressivism—is in fact a descendant and manifestation of fascism. This doesn't mean it's the same thing as Nazism. Nor is it the twin of Italian Fascism. But Progressivism was a sister movement of fascism, and today's liberalism is the daughter of Progressivism. One could strain the comparison and say that today's liberalism is the well-intentioned niece of European fascism. She is hardly identical to her uglier relations, but she nonetheless carries an embarrassing family resemblance that few will admit to recognizing.

There is no word in the English language that gets thrown around more freely by people who don't know what it means than "fascism." Indeed, the more someone uses the word "fascist" in everyday conversation, the less likely it is that he knows what he's talking about.

You might think that the exception to this rule would be scholars of fascism. But what really distinguishes the scholarly community is its honesty. Not even the professionals have figured out what exactly fascism is. Countless scholarly investigations begin with this pro forma acknowledgment. "Such is the welter of divergent opinion surrounding the term," writes Roger Griffin in his introduction to *The Nature of Fascism,* "that it is almost *de rigueur* to open contributions to the debate on fascism with some such observation."

The few scholars who have ventured their own definitions provide a glimmer of insight as to why consensus is so elusive. Griffin, a contemporary leading light in the field, defines fascism as "a genus of political ideology whose mythic core in its various permutations is a palingenetic form of populist ultra-nationalism." Roger Eatwell claims that fascism's "essence" is a "form of thought that preaches the need for social rebirth in order to forge a *holistic-national radical Third Way.*" Emilio Gentile suggests, "A mass movement, that combines different classes but is prevalently of the middle classes, which sees itself as having a mission of national regeneration, is in a state of war with its adversaries and seeks a monopoly of power by using terror, parliamentary tactics and compromise to create a new regime, destroying democracy."[2]

While these are perfectly serviceable definitions, what most recommends them over others is that they are short enough to reprint here. For example, the social scientist Ernst Nolte, a key figure in the German "historians' dispute" (*Historikerstreit*) of the 1980s, has a six-point definition called the "Fascist minimum" that tries to define fascism by what it opposes—that is, fascism is both "anti-liberalism" and "anti-conservatism." Other definitional constructs are even more convoluted, requiring that contrary evidence be counted as exceptions that prove the rule.

It's an academic version of Heisenberg's uncertainty principle: the more closely you study the subject, the less clearly defined it becomes. The historian R. A. H. Robinson wrote twenty years ago, "Although enormous amounts of research time and mental energy have been put into the study of it . . . fascism has remained the great conundrum for students of the twentieth century." Meanwhile, the authors of the *Dictionnaire historique des fascismes et du nazisme* flatly assert, "No universally accepted definition of the fascist phenomenon exists, no consensus, however slight, as to its range, its ideological origins, or the modalities of action which characterize it." Stanley G. Payne, considered by many to be the leading living scholar of fascism, wrote in 1995, "At the end of the twentieth century *fascism* remains probably the vaguest of the major political terms." There are even serious scholars who argue that Nazism wasn't fascist, that fascism doesn't exist at all, or that it is primarily a secular religion (this is my own view). "[P]ut simply," writes Gilbert Allardyce, "we have agreed to use the word without agreeing on how to define it."[3]

And yet even though scholars admit that the nature of fascism is vague, complicated, and open to wildly divergent interpretations, many modern liberals and leftists act as if they know *exactly* what fascism is. What's more, they see it everywhere—except when they look in the mirror. Indeed, the left wields the term like a cudgel to beat opponents from the public square like seditious pamphleteers. After all, no one has to take a fascist seriously. You're under no obligation to listen to a fascist's arguments or concern yourself with his feelings or rights. It's why Al Gore and many other environmentalists are so quick to compare global-warming skeptics to Holocaust deniers. Once such an association takes hold, there's no reason to give such people the time of day.

In short, "fascist" is a modern word for "heretic," branding an individual worthy of excommunication from the body politic. The left uses other words—"racist," "sexist," "homophobe," "christianist"—for similar purposes, but these words have less elastic meanings. Fascism, however, is the gift that keeps on giving. George Orwell noted this tendency as early as 1946 in his famous essay "Politics and the English Language": "The word *Fascism* has now no meaning except in so far as it signifies 'something not desirable.' "[4]

Hollywood writers use the words "fascist," "Brownshirt," and "Nazi" as if they mean no more and no less than "anything liberals don't like." On NBC's *West Wing* support for school choice was deemed "fascist" (even though school choice is arguably the most un-fascist public policy ever conceived, after homeschooling). Crash Davis, Kevin Costner's character in the movie *Bull Durham,* explains to his protégé, "Quit trying to strike everybody out. Strikeouts are boring and besides that, they're fascist. Throw some ground balls. They're more democratic." A rude cook on *Seinfeld* is the "Soup Nazi."

The real world is only marginally less absurd. Representative Charlie Rangel claimed that the GOP's 1994 Contract with America was more extreme than Nazism. "Hitler wasn't even talking about doing these things" (this *is* technically accurate in that Hitler wasn't, in fact, pushing term limits for committee chairs and "zero-based" budgeting). In 2000 Bill Clinton called the Texas GOP platform a "fascist tract." The *New York Times* leads a long roster of mainstream publications eager to promote leading academics who raise the possibility that the GOP is a fascist party and that Christian conservatives are the new Nazis.[5]

More recently, the Pulitzer Prize–winning *New York Times* reporter Chris Hedges penned a book called *American Fascists: The Christian Right and the War on America,* which is just one of many current polemics asserting that conservative or fundamentalist Christians are fascists (Rick Perlstein's otherwise quite negative *New York Times* review begins with the declaration: "Of course there are Christian fascists in America"). The Reverend Jesse Jackson ascribes every form of opposition to his race-based agenda as fascist. During the 2000 Florida recount, he proclaimed that survivors of the Holocaust had been targeted "again" because the Florida ballot was too complicated for a few thousand elderly voters. On *Larry King Live,* Jackson absurdly proclaimed, "The Christian Coalition was a strong force in Germany." He continued: "It laid down a suitable, scientific, theological rationale for the tragedy in Germany. The Christian Coalition was very much in evidence there."[6]

Ask the average, reasonably educated person what comes to mind when she hears the word "fascism" and the immediate responses are "dictatorship," "genocide," "anti-Semitism," "racism," and (of course) "right wing." Delve a bit deeper—and move a bit further to the left— and you'll hear a lot about "eugenics," "social Darwinism," "state capitalism," or the sinister rule of big business. War, militarism, and nationalism will also come up a lot. Some of these attributes were indisputably central to what we might call "classical" fascism—the Fascism of Benito Mussolini and the Nazism of Adolf Hitler. Others—like the widely misunderstood term "social Darwinism"— have little to do with fascism.[7] But very few of these things are unique to fascism, and almost none of them are distinctly right-wing or conservative—at least in the American sense.

To begin with, one must be able to distinguish between the symptoms and the disease. Consider militarism, which will come up again and again in the course of this book. Militarism was indisputably central to fascism (and communism) in countless countries. But it has a more nuanced relationship with fascism than one might suppose. For some thinkers in Germany and the United States (such as Teddy Roosevelt and Oliver Wendell Holmes), war was truly the source of important moral values. This was militarism as a social philosophy pure and simple. But for far more people, militarism was a pragmatic expedient: the highest, best means for organizing society in productive ways. Inspired by ideas like those in William James's famous essay "The Moral Equivalent of War," militarism seemed to provide a workable and sensible model for achieving desirable ends. Mussolini, who openly admired and invoked James, used this logic for his famous "Battle of the Grains" and other sweeping social initiatives. Such ideas had an immense following in the United States, with many leading progressives championing the use of "industrial armies" to create the ideal workers' democracy. Later, Franklin Roosevelt's Civilian Conservation Corps—as militaristic a social program as one can imagine—borrowed from these ideas, as did JFK's Peace Corps.

This trope has hardly been purged from contemporary liberalism. Every day we hear about the "war on cancer," the "war on drugs," the "War on Poverty," and exhortations to make this or that social challenge the "moral equivalent of war." From health care to gun control to global warming, liberals insist that we need to "get beyond politics" and "put ideological differences behind us" in order to "do the people's business." The experts and scientists know what to do, we are told; therefore the time for debate is over. This, albeit in a nicer and more benign form, is the logic of fascism—and it was on ample display in the administrations of Woodrow Wilson, Franklin Roosevelt, and yes, even John F. Kennedy.

Then, of course, there's racism. Racism was indisputably central to Nazi ideology. Today we are perfectly comfortable equating racism and Nazism. And in important respects that's absolutely appropriate. But why not equate Nazism and, say, Afrocentrism? Many early Afrocentrists, like Marcus Garvey, were pro-fascist or openly identified themselves as fascists. The Nation of Islam has surprising ties to Nazism, and its theology is Himmleresque. The Black Panthers—a militaristic cadre of young men dedicated to violence, separatism, and racial superiority—are as quintessentially fascist as Hitler's Brownshirts or Mussolini's action squads. The Afrocentrist writer Leonard Jeffries (blacks are "sun people," and whites are "ice people") could easily be mistaken for a Nazi theorist.

Certain quarters of the left assert that "Zionism equals racism" and that Israelis are equivalent to Nazis. As invidious and problematic as those comparisons are, why aren't we hearing similar denunciations of groups ranging from the National Council of La Raza—that is, "The Race"—to the radical Hispanic group MEChA, whose motto—*"Por La Raza todo. Fuera de La Raza nada"*—means "Everything for the race, nothing outside the race"? Why is it that when a white man spouts such sentiments it's "objectively" fascist, but when a person of color says the same thing it's merely an expression of fashionable multiculturalism?

The most important priority for the left is not to offer any answer at all to such questions. They would much prefer to maintain Orwell's definition of fascism as anything not desirable, thus excluding their own fascistic proclivities from inquiring eyes. When they are forced to answer, however, the response is usually more instinctive, visceral, or dismissively mocking than rational or principled. Their logic seems to be that multiculturalism, the Peace Corps, and such are good things—things that liberals approve of—and good things *can't* be fascist by simple virtue of the fact that liberals approve of them. Indeed, this seems to be the irreducible argument of countless writers who glibly use the word "fascist" to describe the "bad guys" based on no other criteria than that liberals think they are bad. Fidel Castro, one could argue, is a textbook fascist. But because the left approves of his resistance to U.S. "imperialism"—and because he uses the abracadabra words of Marxism—it's not just wrong but objectively stupid to call him a fascist. Meanwhile, calling Ronald Reagan, George W. Bush, Rudy Giuliani, and other conservatives fascists is simply what right-thinking, sophisticated people *do.*

The major flaw in all of this is that fascism, properly understood, is not a phenomenon of the right at all. Instead, it is, and always has been, a phenomenon of the left. This fact—an inconvenient truth if there ever was one—is obscured in our time by the equally mistaken belief that fascism and communism are opposites. In reality, they are closely related, historical competitors for the same constituents, seeking to dominate and control the same social space. The fact that they appear as polar opposites is a trick of intellectual history and (more to the point) the result of a concerted propaganda effort on the part of the "Reds" to make the "Browns" appear objectively evil and "other" (ironically, demonization of the "other" is counted as a definitional trait of fascism). But in terms of their theory and practice, the differences are minimal.

It is difficult now, in the light of their massive crimes and failures, to remember that both fascism and communism were, in their time, utopian visions and the bearers of great hopes. What's more, fascism, like communism, was an international movement that attracted adherents in every Western society. Particularly in the aftermath of World War I—but beginning much earlier—a fascist moment arose on the ashes of the old European order. It drew together the various strands of European politics and culture—the rise of ethnic national-ism, the Bismarckian welfare state, and the collapse of Christianity as a source of social and political orthodoxy and universal aspira-tions. In place of Christianity, it offered a new religion of the di-vinized state and the nation as an organic community.

This international movement had many variants and offshoots and went by different names in different countries. Its expression in dif-ferent societies varied depending on national culture. This is one of the reasons it is so hard to define. But in reality, international fas-cism drew from the same intellectual wellsprings as American Progressivism. Indeed, American Progressivism—the moralistic so-cial crusade from which modern liberals proudly claim descent—is in some respects the major source of the fascist ideas applied in Europe by Mussolini and Hitler.

Americans like to think of themselves as being immune to fascism while constantly feeling threatened by it. "It can't happen here" is the common refrain. But fascism definitely has a history in this coun-try, and that is what this book is about. The American fascist tradi-tion is deeply bound up with the effort to "Europeanize" America and give it a "modern" state that can be harnessed to utopian ends. This American fascism seems—and is—very different from its European variants because it was moderated by many special fac-tors—geographical size, ethnic diversity, Jeffersonian individualism, a strong liberal tradition, and so on. As a result, American fascism is milder, more friendly, more "maternal" than its foreign counterparts; it is what George Carlin calls "smiley-face fascism." Nice fascism. The best term to describe it is *"liberal* fascism." And this liberal fas-cism was, and remains, fundamentally left-wing.

This book will present an alternative history of American liberal-ism that not only reveals its roots in, and commonalities with, clas-sical fascism but also shows how the fascist label was projected onto the right by a complex sleight of hand. In fact, conservatives are the more authentic classical liberals, while many so-called liberals are "friendly" fascists.

Now, I am not saying that all liberals are fascists. Nor am I saying that to believe in socialized medicine or smoking bans is evidence that you are a crypto-Nazi. What I am mainly trying to do is to dismantle the granitelike assumption in our political culture that American conservatism is an offshoot or cousin of fascism. Rather, as I will try to show, many of the ideas and impulses that inform what we call liberalism come to us through an intellectual tradition that led directly to fascism. These ideas were embraced by fascism, and remain in important respects fascistic.

We cannot easily recognize these similarities and continuities today, however, let alone speak about them, because this whole realm of historical analysis was foreclosed by the Holocaust. Before the war, fascism was widely viewed as a progressive social movement with many liberal and left-wing adherents in Europe and the United States; the horror of the Holocaust completely changed our view of fascism as something uniquely evil and ineluctably bound up with extreme nationalism, paranoia, and genocidal racism. After the war, the American progressives who had praised Mussolini and even looked sympathetically at Hitler in the 1920s and 1930s had to distance themselves from the horrors of Nazism. Accordingly, leftist intellectuals redefined fascism as "right-wing" and projected their own sins onto conservatives, even as they continued to borrow heavily from fascist and pre-fascist thought.

Much of this alternative history is quite easy to find, if you have eyes to see it. The problem is that the liberal-progressive narrative on which most of us were raised tends to shunt these incongruous and inconvenient facts aside, and to explain away as marginal what is actually central.

For starters, it is simply a fact that, in the 1920s, fascism and fascistic ideas were very popular on the American left. "That Fascism stunk in the nostrils of the *New Masses,*" John Patrick Diggins writes of the legendary hard-left journal, "may have been true after 1930. For the radicals of the twenties the whiff from Italy carried no foul ideological odor."[8] There was a reason for this. In many respects, the founding fathers of modern liberalism, the men and women who laid the intellectual groundwork of the New Deal and the welfare state, thought that fascism sounded like a pretty good idea. Or to be fair: many simply thought (in the spirit of Deweyan Pragmatism) that it sounded like a worthwhile "experiment." Moreover, while the odor of Italian Fascism eventually grew rancid in the nostrils of both the American left and the American right (considerably later than 1930, by the way), the reasons for their revulsion did not for the most part stem from profound ideological differences. Rather, the American left essentially picked a different team—the Red team—and as such swore fealty to communist talking points about fascism. As for the non-communist liberal left, while the *word* "fascism" grew in disrepute, many fascistic ideas and impulses endured.

It was around this time that Stalin stumbled on a brilliant tactic of simply labeling all inconvenient ideas and movements fascist. Socialists and progressives aligned with Moscow were called socialists or progressives, while socialists disloyal or opposed to Moscow were called fascists. Stalin's theory of social fascism rendered even Franklin Roosevelt a fascist according to loyal communists everywhere. And let us recall that Leon Trotsky was marked for death for allegedly plotting a "fascist coup." While this tactic was later deplored by many sane American left-wingers, it is amazing how many useful idiots fell for it at the time, and how long its intellectual half-life has been.

Before the Holocaust and Stalin's doctrine of social fascism, liberals could be more honest about their fondness for fascism. During the "pragmatic" era of the 1920s and early 1930s, a host of Western liberal intellectuals and journalists were quite impressed with Mussolini's "experiment."[9] More than a few progressives were intrigued by Nazism as well. W. E. B. DuBois, for example, had very complex and mixed emotions about the rise of Hitler and the plight of the Jews, believing that National Socialism could be the model for economic organization. The formation of the Nazi dictatorship, he wrote, had been "absolutely necessary to get the state in order." Hewing to the progressive definition of "democracy" as egalitarian statism, DuBois delivered a speech in Harlem in 1937 proclaiming that "there is today, in some respects, more democracy in Germany than there has been in years past."[10]

For years, segments of the so-called Old Right argued that FDR's New Deal was fascistic and/or influenced by fascists. There is ample truth to this, as many mainstream and liberal historians have grudgingly admitted.[11] However, that the New Deal was fascist was hardly a uniquely right-wing criticism in the 1930s. Rather, those who offered this sort of critique, including the Democratic hero Al Smith and the Progressive Republican Herbert Hoover, were beaten back with the charge that they were crazy right-wingers and themselves the real fascists. Norman Thomas, the head of the American Socialist Party, frequently charged that the New Deal was fundamentally fascistic. Only Communists loyal to Moscow—or the useful idiots in Stalin's thrall—could say that Thomas was a right-winger or a fascist. But that is precisely what they did.

Even more telling, FDR's defenders openly admitted their admiration of fascism. Rexford Guy Tugwell, an influential member of FDR's Brain Trust, said of Italian Fascism, "It's the cleanest, neatest most efficiently operating piece of social machinery I've ever seen. It makes me envious." "We are trying out the economics of Fascism without having suffered all its social or political ravages," proclaimed the *New Republic*'s editor George Soule, an enthusiastic supporter of the FDR administration.[12]

But this whole discussion misses a larger and frequently overlooked point. The New Deal *did* emulate a fascistic regime; but Italy and Germany were secondary models, post hoc confirmations that liberals were on the right track. The real inspiration for the New Deal was the Wilson administration during World War I. This is hardly a secret. FDR campaigned on his pledge to re-create the war socialism of the Wilson years; his staff set out with that goal, and it was heartily applauded by the liberal establishment of the 1930s. Countless editorial boards, politicians, and pundits—including the revered Walter Lippmann—called on President Roosevelt to become a "dictator," which was not a dirty word in the early 1930s, and to tackle the Depression the same way Wilson and the progressives had fought World War I.

Indeed, it is my argument that during World War I, America became a fascist country, albeit temporarily. The first appearance of modern totalitarianism in the Western world wasn't in Italy or Germany but in the United States of America. How else would you describe a country where the world's first modern propaganda ministry was established; political prisoners by the thousands were harassed, beaten, spied upon, and thrown in jail simply for expressing private opinions; the national leader accused foreigners and immigrants of injecting treasonous "poison" into the American bloodstream; newspapers and magazines were shut down for criticizing the government; nearly a hundred thousand government propaganda agents were sent out among the people to whip up support for the regime and its war; college professors imposed loyalty oaths on their colleagues; nearly a quarter-million goons were given legal authority to intimidate and beat "slackers" and dissenters; and leading artists and writers dedicated their crafts to proselytizing for the government?

The reason so many progressives were intrigued by both Mussolini's and Lenin's "experiments" is simple: they saw their reflection in the European looking glass. Philosophically, organizationally, and politically the progressives were as close to authentic, homegrown fascists as any movement America has ever produced.[13] Militaristic, fanatically nationalist, imperialist, racist, deeply involved in the promotion of Darwinian eugenics, enamored of the Bismarckian welfare state, statist beyond modern reckoning, the progressives represented the American flowering of a transatlantic movement, a profound reorientation toward the Hegelian and Darwinian collectivism imported from Europe at the end of the nineteenth century.

In this sense, both the Wilson and the FDR administrations were descendants—albeit distant ones—of the first fascist movement: the French Revolution.

Given the benefit of hindsight, it's difficult to understand why anyone doubts the fascist nature of the French Revolution. Few dispute that it was totalitarian, terrorist, nationalist, conspiratorial, and populist. It produced the first modern dictators, Robespierre and Napoleon, and worked on the premise that the nation had to be ruled by an enlightened avant-garde who would serve as the authentic, organic voice of the "general will." The paranoid Jacobin mentality made the revolutionaries more savage and cruel than the king they replaced. Some fifty thousand people ultimately died in the Terror, many in political show trials that Simon Schama describes as the "founding charter of totalitarian justice." Robespierre summed up the totalitarian logic of the Revolution: "There are only two parties in France: the people and its enemies. We must exterminate those miserable villains who are eternally conspiring against the rights of man . . . [W]e must exterminate all our enemies."[14]

But what truly makes the French Revolution the first fascist revolution was its effort to turn politics into a religion. (In this the revolutionaries were inspired by Rousseau, whose concept of the general will divinized *the people* while rendering the *person* an afterthought.) Accordingly, they declared war on Christianity, attempting to purge it from society and replace it with a "secular" faith whose tenets were synonymous with the Jacobin agenda. Hundreds of pagan-themed festivals were launched across the country celebrating Nation, Reason, Brotherhood, Liberty, and other abstractions in order to bathe the state and the general will in an aura of sanctity. As we shall see, the Nazis emulated the Jacobins in minute detail.

It is no longer controversial to say that the French Revolution was disastrous and cruel. But it is deeply controversial to say that it was fascist, because the French Revolution is the *fons et origo* of the left and the "revolutionary tradition." The American right and classical liberals look fondly on the American Revolution, which was essentially conservative, while shuddering at the horrors and follies of Jacobinism. But if the French Revolution was fascist, then its heirs would have to be seen as the fruit of this poisoned tree, and fascism itself would finally and *correctly* be placed where it belongs in the story of the left. This would cause seismic disorder in the leftist worldview; so instead, leftists embrace cognitive dissonance and terminological sleight of hand.

At the same time, it must be noted that scholars have had so much difficulty explaining what fascism is because various fascisms have been so different from each other. For example, the Nazis were genocidal anti-Semites. The Italian Fascists were protectors of the Jews until the Nazis took over Italy. Fascists fought for the side of the Axis, but the Spanish stayed out of the war (and protected Jews as well). The Nazis hated Christianity, the Italians made peace with the Catholic Church (though Mussolini himself despised Christianity with an untrammeled passion), and members of the Romanian Legion of the Archangel Michael styled themselves as Christian crusaders. Some fascists championed "state capitalism," while others, such as the Blue Shirts of Kuomintang China, demanded the immediate seizure of the means of production. The Nazis were officially anti-Bolshevist, but there was a movement of "National Bolshevism" within Nazi ranks, too.

The one thing that unites these movements is that they were all, in their own ways, totalitarian. But what do we mean when we say something is "totalitarian"? The word has certainly taken on an understandably sinister connotation in the last half century. Thanks to work by Hannah Arendt, Zbigniew Brzezinski, and others, it's become a catchall for brutal, soul-killing, Orwellian regimes. But that's not how the word was originally used or intended. Mussolini himself coined the term to describe a society where everybody belonged, where everyone was taken care of, where everything was inside the state and nothing was outside: where truly no child was left behind.

Again, it is my argument that American liberalism is a totalitarian political religion, but not necessarily an Orwellian one. It is nice, not brutal. Nannying, not bullying. But it is definitely totalitarian—or "holistic," if you prefer—in that liberalism today sees no realm of human life that is beyond political significance, from what you eat to what you smoke to what you say. Sex is political. Food is political. Sports, entertainment, your inner motives and outer appearance, all have political salience for liberal fascists. Liberals place their faith in priestly experts who know better, who plan, exhort, badger, and scold. They try to use science to discredit traditional notions of religion and faith, but they speak the language of pluralism and spirituality to defend "nontraditional" beliefs. Just as with classical fascism, liberal fascists speak of a "Third Way" between right and left where all good things go together and all hard choices are "false choices."

The idea that there are no hard choices—that is, choices between competing goods is religious and totalitarian because it assumes that all good things are fundamentally compatible. The conservative or classical liberal vision understands that life is unfair, that man is flawed, and that the only perfect society, the only real utopia, waits for us in the next life.

Liberal fascism differs from classical fascism in many ways. I don't deny this. Indeed, it is central to my point. Fascisms differ from each other because they grow out of different soil. What unites them are their emotional or instinctual impulses, such as the quest for community, the urge to "get beyond" politics, a faith in the perfectibility of man and the authority of experts, and an obsession with the aesthetics of youth, the cult of action, and the need for an all-powerful state to coordinate society at the national or global level. Most of all, they share the belief—what I call the totalitarian temptation—that with the right amount of tinkering we can realize the utopian dream of "creating a better world."

But as with everything in history, time and place matter, and the differences between various fascisms can be profound. Nazism was the product of German culture, grown out of a German context. The Holocaust could not have occurred in Italy, because Italians are not Germans. And in America, where hostility to big government is central to the national character, the case for statism must be made in terms of "pragmatism" and decency. In other words, our fascism must be nice and for your own good.

American Progressivism, from which today's liberalism descended, was a kind of Christian fascism (many called it "Christian socialism"). This is a difficult concept for modern liberals to grasp because they are used to thinking of the progressives as the people who cleaned up the food supply, pushed through the eight-hour workday, and ended child labor. But liberals often forget that the progressives were also imperialists, at home and abroad. They were the authors of Prohibition, the Palmer Raids, eugenics, loyalty oaths, and, in its modern incarnation, what many call "state capitalism."

Many liberals also miss the religious dimension of Progressivism because they tend to view religion and progressive politics as diametrically opposed to each other; thus, while liberals who remember the civil rights movement acknowledge that the churches played a role, they don't see it on a continuum with other religiously inspired progressive crusades like abolition and temperance. Today's liberal fascism eschews talk of Christianity for the most part, except to roll back its influence wherever it can (although a right-wing version often called compassionate conservatism has made inroads in the Republican Party). But while the God talk may have fallen by the wayside, the religious crusader's spirit that powered Progressivism remains as strong as ever. Rather than talk in explicitly religious terms, however, today's liberals use a secularized vocabulary of "hope" and construct explicitly spiritual philosophies like Hillary Clinton's "politics of meaning."

Similarly, the nasty racism that infused the progressive eugenics of Margaret Sanger and others has largely melted away. But liberal fascists are still racist in their own nice way, believing in the inherent numinousness of blacks and the permanence of white sin, and therefore the eternal justification of white guilt. While I would argue that this is bad and undesirable, I would not dream of saying that today's liberals are genocidal or vicious in their racial attitudes the way Nazis were. Still, it should be noted that on the postmodern left, they do speak in terms Nazis could understand. Indeed, notions of "white logic" and the "permanence of race" were not only understood by Nazis but in some cases pioneered by them. The historian Anne Harrington observes that the "key words of the vocabulary of postmodernism (deconstructionism, logocentrism) actually had their origins in antiscience tracts written by Nazi and protofascist writers like Ernst Krieck and Ludwig Klages." The first appearance of the word *Dekonstrucktion* was in a Nazi psychiatry journal edited by Hermann Göring's cousin.[15] Many on the left talk of destroying "whiteness" in a way that is more than superficially reminiscent of the National Socialist effort to "de-Judaize" German society. Indeed, it is telling that the man who oversaw the legal front of this project, Carl Schmitt, is hugely popular among leftist academics. Mainstream liberals don't necessarily agree with these intellectuals, but they do accord them a reverence and respect that often amount to a tacit endorsement.

A simple fact remains: Progressives did many things that we would today call objectively fascist, and fascists did many things we would today call objectively progressive. Teasing apart this seeming contradiction, and showing why it is not in fact a contradiction, are major aims of this book. But that does not mean I am calling liberals Nazis.

Let me put it this way: no serious person can deny that Marxist ideas had a profound impact on what we call liberalism. To point this out doesn't mean that one is calling, say, Barack Obama a Stalinist or a communist. One can go even further and note that many of the most prominent liberals and leftists of the twentieth century assiduously minimized the evils and dangers presented by Soviet Communism; but that doesn't necessarily mean it would be fair to accuse them of actually *favoring* Stalin's genocidal crimes. It's cruel to call someone a Nazi because it unfairly suggests sympathy with the Holocaust. But it is no less inaccurate to assume that fascism was simply the ideology of Jewish genocide. If you need a label for that, call it Hitlerism, for Hitler would not be Hitler without genocidal racism. And while Hitler was a fascist, fascism need not be synonymous with Hitlerism.

For example, it's illuminating to note that Jews were overrepresented in the Italian Fascist Party and remained so from the early 1920s until 1938. Fascist Italy had nothing like a death camp system. Not a single Jew of *any national origin* under Italian control anywhere in the world was handed over to Germany until 1943, when Italy was invaded by the Nazis. Jews in Italy survived the war at a higher rate than anywhere under Axis rule save Denmark, and Jews in Italian-controlled areas of Europe fared almost as well. Mussolini actually sent Italian troops into harm's way to save Jewish lives. Francisco Franco, allegedly a quintessential fascist dictator, also refused Hitler's demand to hand over Spanish Jews, saving tens of thousands of Jews from extermination. It was Franco who signed the document abrogating the 1492 Edict of Expulsion of the Jews from Spain. Meanwhile, the supposedly "liberal" French and Dutch eagerly cooperated with the Nazi deportation program.

At this point I need to make a few statements of a kind that should be obvious, but are necessary in order to prevent any possibility of being misunderstood or having my argument distorted by hostile critics. I love this country and have tremendous faith in its goodness and decency; under no circumstances can I imagine a fascist regime like that of the Nazis coming to power here, let alone an event like the Holocaust. This is because Americans, all Americans—liberals, conservatives, and independents, blacks, whites, Hispanics, and Asians—are shaped by a liberal, democratic, and egalitarian culture strong enough to resist any such totalitarian temptations. So, no, I do not think liberals are evil, villainous, or bigoted in the sense that typical Nazi comparisons suggest. The right-wing shtick of calling Hillary Clinton "Hitlery" is no less sophomoric than the constant drumbeat of "Bushitler" nonsense one finds on the left. The Americans who cheered for Mussolini in the 1920s cannot be held to account for what Hitler did nearly two decades later. And liberals today are not responsible for what their intellectual forefathers believed, though they should account for it.

But at the same time, Hitler's crimes do not erase the similarities between Progressivism—now called liberalism—and the ideologies and attitudes that brought Mussolini and Hitler to power.

For example, it has long been known that the Nazis were economic populists, heavily influenced by the same ideas that motivated American and British populists. And while too often downplayed by liberal historians, American populism had a strong anti-Semitic and conspiratorial streak. A typical cartoon in a populist publication depicted the world grasped in the tentacles of an octopus sitting atop the British Isles. The octopus was labeled "Rothschild." An Associated Press reporter noted of the 1896 Populist convention "the extraordinary hatred of the Jewish race" on display.[16] Father Charles Coughlin, "the Radio Priest," was a left-wing populist rabble-rouser and conspiracy theorist whose anti-Semitism was well-known among establishment liberals even when they defended the pro-Roosevelt demagogue as being "on the side of the angels."

Today, populist conspiracy theories run amok across the left (and are hardly unknown on the right). A full third of Americans believe it is "very" or "somewhat" likely that the government was behind (or allowed) the 9/11 attacks. A particular paranoia about the influence of the "Jewish lobby" has infected significant swaths of the campus and European left—not to mention the poisonous and truly Hitlerian anti-Semitic populism of the Arab "street" under regimes most would recognize as fascist. My point isn't that the left is embracing Hitlerite anti-Semitism. Rather, it is embracing populism and indulging anti-Semites to an extent that is alarming and dangerous. Moreover, it's worth recalling that the success of Nazism in Weimar Germany partially stemmed from the unwillingness of decent men to take it seriously.

There are other similarities between German and Italian Fascist ideas and modern American liberalism. For example, the corporatism at the heart of liberal economics today is seen as a bulwark against right-wing and vaguely fascistic corporate ruling classes. And yet the economic ideas of Bill and Hillary Clinton, John Kerry, Al Gore, and Robert Reich are deeply similar to the corporatist "Third Way" ideologies that spawned fascist economics in the 1920s and 1930s. Indeed, contemporary liberalism's cargo cult over the New Deal is enough to place modern liberalism in the family tree of fascism.

Or consider the explosion of health and New Age crusades in recent years, from the war on smoking, to the obsession with animal rights, to the sanctification of organic foods. No one disputes that these fads are a product of the cultural and political left. But few are willing to grapple with the fact that we've seen this sort of thing before. Heinrich Himmler was a certified animal rights activist and an aggressive promoter of "natural healing." Rudolf Hess, Hitler's deputy, championed homeopathy and herbal remedies. Hitler and his advisers dedicated hours of their time to discussions of the need to move the entire nation to vegetarianism as a response to the unhealthiness promoted by capitalism. Dachau hosted the world's largest alternative and organic medicine research lab and produced its own organic honey.

In profound ways, the Nazi antismoking and public health drives foreshadowed today's crusades against junk food, trans fats, and the like. A Hitler Youth manual proclaimed, "Nutrition is not a private matter!"—a mantra substantially echoed by the public health establishment today. The Nazis' fixation on organic foods and personal health neatly fit their larger understanding of how the world works. Many Nazis were convinced that Christianity, which held that men were intended to conquer nature rather than live in harmony with it, and capitalism, which alienated men from their natural state, conspired to undermine German health. In a widely read book on nutrition, Hugo Kleine blamed "capitalist special interests" (and "masculinized Jewish half-women") for the decline in quality of German foods, which contributed in turn to the rise in cancer (another Nazi obsession). Organic food was inextricably linked to what the Nazis then described—as the left does today—as "social justice" issues.[17]

Are you automatically a fascist if you care about health, nutrition, and the environment? Of course not. What is fascist is the notion that in an organic national community, the individual has no right *not* to be healthy; and the state therefore has the obligation to force us to be healthy for our own good. To the extent that these modern health movements seek to harness the power of the state to their agenda, they flirt with classical fascism. Even culturally, environmentalism gives license to the sort of moral bullying and intrusion that, were it couched in terms of traditional morality, liberals would immediately denounce as fascist.

As of this writing, a legislator in New York wants to ban using iPods when crossing the street.[18] In many parts of the country it is illegal to smoke in your car or even outdoors if other human beings could conceivably be near you. We hear much about how conservatives want to "invade our bedrooms," but as this book went to press, Greenpeace and other groups were launching a major campaign to "educate" people on how they can have environmentally friendly sex. Greenpeace has a whole list of strategies for "getting it on for the good of the planet."[19] You may trust that environmentalists have no desire to translate these voluntary suggestions into law, but I have no such confidence given the track record of similar campaigns in the past. Free speech, too, is under relentless assault where it matters most—around elections—and it is being sanctified where it matters least, around strippers' poles and on terrorist Web sites.

In *Democracy in America,* Alexis de Tocqueville warned: "It must not be forgotten that it is especially dangerous to enslave men in the minor details of life. For my own part, I should be inclined to think freedom less necessary in great things than in little ones."[20] This country seems to have inverted Tocqueville's hierarchy. We must all lose our liberties on the little things so that a handful of people can enjoy their freedoms to the fullest.

For generations our primary vision of a dystopian future has been that of Orwell's *1984.* This was a fundamentally "masculine" nightmare of fascist brutality. But with the demise of the Soviet Union and the vanishing memory of the great twentieth-century fascist and communist dictatorships, the nightmare vision of *1984* is slowly fading away. In its place, Aldous Huxley's *Brave New World* is emerging as the more prophetic book. As we unravel the human genome and master the ability to make people happy with televised entertainment and psychoactive drugs, politics is increasingly a vehicle for delivering prepackaged joy. America's political system used to be about the pursuit of happiness. Now more and more of us want to stop chasing it and have it delivered. And though it has been the subject of high school English essay questions for generations, we have not gotten much closer to answering the question, what exactly was so bad about the Brave New World?

Simply this: it is fool's gold. The idea that we can create a heaven on earth through pharmacology and neuroscience is as utopian as the

Marxist hope that we could create a perfect world by rearranging the means of production. The history of totalitarianism is the history of the quest to transcend the human condition and create a society where our deepest meaning and destiny are realized simply by virtue of the fact that we live in it. It cannot be done, and even if, as often in the case of liberal fascism, the effort is very careful to be humane and decent, it will still result in a kind of benign tyranny where some people get to impose their ideas of goodness and happiness on those who may not share them.

The introduction of a novel term like "liberal fascism" obviously requires an explanation. Many critics will undoubtedly regard it as a crass oxymoron. Actually, however, I am not the first to use the term. That honor falls to H. G. Wells, one of the greatest influences on the progressive mind in the twentieth century (and, it turns out, the inspiration for Huxley's *Brave New World*). Nor did Wells coin the phrase as an indictment, but as a badge of honor. Progressives must become "liberal fascists" and "enlightened Nazis," he told the Young Liberals at Oxford in a speech in July 1932.[21]

Wells was a leading voice in what I have called the fascist moment, when many Western elites were eager to replace Church and Crown with slide rules and industrial armies. Throughout his work he championed the idea that special men—variously identified as scientists, priests, warriors, or "samurai"—must impose progress on the masses in order to create a "New Republic" or a "world theocracy." Only through militant Progressivism—by whatever name—could mankind achieve the fulfillment of the kingdom of God. Wells, simply put, was enthralled by the totalitarian temptation. "I have never been able to escape altogether from its relentless logic," he declared.[22]

Fascism, like Progressivism and communism, is expansionist because it sees no natural boundary to its ambitions. For violent variants, like so-called Islamofascism, this is transparently obvious. But Progressivism, too, envisions a New World Order. World War I was a "crusade" to redeem the whole world, according to Woodrow Wilson. Even Wilson's pacifist secretary of state, William Jennings Bryan, could not shake off his vision of a Christian world order, complete with a global prohibition of alcohol.

One objection to all of this might be: So what? It's interesting in a counterintuitive way to learn that a bunch of dead liberals and progressives thought this or that, but what does it have to do with liberals today? Two responses come to mind. The first is admittedly not fully responsive. Conservatives in America must carry their intellectual history—real and alleged—around their necks like an albatross. The ranks of elite liberal journalism and scholarship swell with intrepid scribblers who point to "hidden histories" and "disturbing echoes" in the conservative historical closet. Connections with dead right-wingers, no matter how tenuous and obscure, are trotted out as proof that today's conservatives are continuing a nefarious project. Why, then, is it so trivial to point out that the liberal closet has its own skeletons, particularly when those skeletons are the architects of the modern welfare state?

Which raises the second response. Liberalism, unlike conservatism, is operationally uninterested in its own intellectual history. But that doesn't make it any less indebted to it. Liberalism stands on the shoulders of its own giants and thinks its feet are planted firmly on the ground. Its assumptions and aspirations can be traced straight back to the Progressive Era, a fact illustrated by the liberal tendency to use the word "progressive" whenever talking about its core convictions and idea-generating institutions (the *Progressive* magazine, the Progressive Policy Institute, the Center for American Progress, and so on). I am simply fighting on a battleground of liberalism's choosing. Liberals are the ones who've insisted that conservatism has connections with fascism. They are the ones who claim free-market economics are fascist and that therefore their own economic theories should be seen as the more virtuous, even though the truth is almost entirely the reverse.

Today's liberalism doesn't seek to conquer the world by force of arms. It is not a nationalist and genocidal project. To the contrary, it is an ideology of good intentions. But we all know where even the best of intentions can take us. I have not written a book about how all liberals are Nazis or fascists. Rather, I have tried to write a book warning that even the best of us are susceptible to the totalitarian temptation.

This includes some self-described conservatives. Compassionate conservatism, in many respects, is a form of Progressivism, a descendant of Christian socialism. Much of George W. Bush's rhetoric about leaving no children behind and how "when somebody hurts, government has got to move" bespeaks a vision of the state that is indeed totalitarian in its aspirations and not particularly conservative in the American sense. Once again, it is a nice totalitarianism, motivated no doubt by sincere Christian love (thankfully tempered by poor implementation); but love, too, can be smothering. In fact, the rage that Bush's tenure has elicited in many of his critics is illustrative. Bush's intentions are decent, but those who don't share his vision find them oppressive. The same works the other way around. Liberals agree with Hillary Clinton's intentions; they just assert that anyone who finds them oppressive is a fascist.

Finally, since we must have a working definition of fascism, here is mine: Fascism is a religion of the state. It assumes the organic unity of the body politic and longs for a national leader attuned to the will of the people. It is *totalitarian* in that it views everything as political and holds that any action by the state is justified to achieve the common good. It takes responsibility for all aspects of life, including our health and well-being, and seeks to impose uniformity of thought and action, whether by force or through regulation and social pressure. Everything, including the economy and religion, must be aligned with its objectives. Any rival identity is part of the "problem" and therefore defined as the enemy. I will argue that contemporary American liberalsim embodies all of these aspects of fascism.

• • •

Before we conclude, some housekeeping issues.

I will follow the standard practice among English-speaking historians of fascism. When referring to generic fascism, I will spell the word with a lowercase *f* (unless at the beginning of a sentence). When referring to Italian Fascism, I will use the uppercase. I have also tried to be clear when I am talking about liberalism as we use the phrase today and classical liberalism, which means, more or less, the exact opposite.

Fascism is an enormous topic with thousands of books covering relevant themes. I have tried to be fair to the academic literature, though this is not an academic book. Indeed, the literature is so fraught with controversy that not only is there no accepted definition of fascism, but there isn't even a consensus that Italian Fascism and

Nazism were kindred phenomena. I have tried to steer clear of such debates whenever possible. But my own view is that despite the profound doctrinal differences between Italian and German fascism, they represent kindred sociological phenomena.

I have also tried to steer clear of the scores of other "fascisms" around the globe. Critics may claim that this is to my advantage, in that this or that fascism was clearly right-wing or conservative or unprogressive. I'll take such criticisms on a case-by-case basis. But I should also note that this practice hurts my case as much as it helps. For example, by excluding Oswald Mosley's British Union of Fascists, I have cut myself off from a wonderful supply of left-wing pro-fascist rhetoric and arguments.

I have tried not to clutter the book with citations, but I have included quite a few explanatory—or discursive—notes. Readers curious about other sources and further reading should consult the Web site for this book, www.liberal-fascism.com, and may also post comments or queries there. I will do my best to engage as many good-faith correspondents as possible.

· 1 ·

Mussolini:
The Father of Fascism

You're the top!
You're the Great Houdini!
You're the top!
You are Mussolini!
—An early version of the Cole Porter song "You're the Top"[1]

IF YOU WENT solely by what you read in the *New York Times*
or the *New York Review of Books,* or what you learned from
Hollywood, you could be forgiven for thinking that Benito
Mussolini came to power around the same time as Adolf Hitler—or
even a little bit later—and that Italian Fascism was merely a tardy,
watered-down version of Nazism. Germany passed its hateful race
policies—the Nuremberg Laws—in 1935, and Mussolini's Italy followed suit in 1938. German Jews were rounded up in 1942, and Jews
in Italy were rounded up in 1943. A few writers will casually mention, in parenthetical asides, that until Italy passed its race laws there
were actually Jews serving in the Italian government and the Fascist
Party. And on occasion you'll notice a nod to historical accuracy in-
dicating that the Jews were rounded up only *after* the Nazis had invaded northern Italy and created a puppet government in Salò. But
such inconvenient facts are usually skipped over as quickly as possible. More likely, your understanding of these issues comes from

such sources as the Oscar-winning film *Life Is Beautiful,*[2] which can be summarized as follows: Fascism arrived in Italy and, a few months later, so did the Nazis, who carted off the Jews. As for Mussolini, he was a bombastic, goofy-looking, but highly effective dictator who made the trains run on time.

All of this amounts to playing the movie backward. By the time Italy reluctantly passed its shameful race laws—which it never enforced with even a fraction of the barbarity shown by the Nazis—over 75 percent of Italian Fascism's reign had already transpired. A full sixteen years elapsed between the March on Rome and the passage of Italy's race laws. To start with the Jews when talking about Mussolini is like starting with FDR's internment of the Japanese: it leaves a lot of the story on the cutting room floor. Throughout the 1920s and well into the 1930s, fascism meant something very different from Auschwitz and Nuremberg. Before Hitler, in fact, it never occurred to anyone that fascism had anything to do with anti-Semitism. Indeed, Mussolini was supported not only by the chief rabbi of Rome but by a substantial portion of the Italian Jewish community (and the world Jewish community). Moreover, Jews were overrepresented in the Italian Fascist movement from its founding in 1919 until they were kicked out in 1938.

Race did help turn the tables of American public opinion on Fascism. But it had nothing to do with the Jews. When Mussolini invaded Ethiopia, Americans finally started to turn on him. In 1934 the hit Cole Porter song "You're the Top" engendered nary a word of controversy over the line "You are Mussolini!" When Mussolini invaded that poor but noble African kingdom the following year, it irrevocably marred his image, and Americans decided they had had enough of his act. It was the first war of conquest by a Western European nation in over a decade, and Americans were distinctly unamused, particularly liberals and blacks. Still, it was a slow process. The *Chicago Tribune* initially supported the invasion, as did reporters like Herbert Matthews. Others claimed it would be hypocritical to condemn it. The *New Republic*—then in the thick of its pro-Soviet phase—believed it would be "naïve" to blame Mussolini when the real culprit was international capitalism. And more than a few prominent Americans continued to support him, although quietly. The poet Wallace Stevens, for example, stayed pro-Fascist. "I am pro-Mussolini, personally," he wrote to a friend. "The Italians," he explained, "have as much right to take Ethiopia from the coons as the coons had to take it from the boa-constrictors."[3] But over time, largely due to his subsequent alliance with Hitler, Mussolini's image never recovered.

That's not to say he didn't have a good ride.

In 1923 the journalist Isaac F. Marcosson wrote admiringly in the *New York Times* that "Mussolini is a Latin [Teddy] Roosevelt who first acts and then inquires if it is legal. He has been of great service to Italy at home."[4] The American Legion, which has been for nearly its entire history a great and generous American institution, was founded the same year as Mussolini's takeover and, in its early years, drew inspiration from the Italian Fascist movement. "Do not forget," the legion's national commander declared that same year, "that the Fascisti are to Italy what the American Legion is to the United States."[5]

In 1926 the American humorist Will Rogers visited Italy and interviewed Mussolini. He told the *New York Times* that Mussolini was "some Wop." "I'm pretty high on that bird." Rogers, whom the National Press Club had informally dubbed "Ambassador-at-Large of the United States," wrote up the interview for the *Saturday Evening Post.* He concluded, "Dictator form of government is the greatest form of government: that is if you have the right Dictator."[6] In 1927 the *Literary Digest* conducted an editorial survey asking the question: "Is there a dearth of great men?" The person named most often to refute the charge was Benito Mussolini—followed by Lenin, Edison, Marconi, and Orville Wright, with Henry Ford and George Bernard Shaw tying for sixth place. In 1928 the *Saturday Evening Post* glorified Mussolini even further, running an eight-part autobiography written by Il Duce himself. The series was gussied up into a book that gained one of the biggest advances ever given by an American publisher.

And why shouldn't the average American think Mussolini was anything but a great man? Winston Churchill had dubbed him the world's greatest living lawgiver. Sigmund Freud sent Mussolini a copy of a book he co-wrote with Albert Einstein, inscribed, "To Benito Mussolini, from an old man who greets in the Ruler, the Hero of Culture." The opera titans Giacomo Puccini and Arturo Toscanini were both pioneering Fascist acolytes of Mussolini. Toscanini was an early member of the Milan circle of Fascists, which conferred an aura of seniority not unlike being a member of the Nazi Party in the days of the Beer Hall Putsch. Toscanini ran for the Italian parliament on a Fascist ticket in 1919 and didn't repudiate Fascism until twelve years later.[7]

Mussolini was a particular hero to the muckrakers—those progressive liberal journalists who famously looked out for the little guy. When Ida Tarbell, the famed reporter whose work helped break up Standard Oil, was sent to Italy in 1926 by *McCall's* to write a series on the Fascist nation, the U.S. State Department feared that this "pretty red radical" would write nothing but "violent anti-Mussolini articles." Their fears were misplaced. Tarbell was wooed by the man she called "a despot with a dimple," praising his progressive attitude toward labor. Similarly smitten was Lincoln Steffens, another famous muckraker, who is today perhaps dimly remembered for being the man who returned from the Soviet Union declaring, "I have been over into the future, and it works." Shortly after that declaration, he made another about Mussolini: God had "formed Mussolini out of the rib of Italy." As we'll see, Steffens saw no contradiction between his fondness for Fascism and his admiration of the Soviet Union. Even Samuel McClure, the founder of *McClure's Magazine,* the home of so much famous muckraking, championed Fascism after visiting Italy. He hailed it as "a great step forward and the first new ideal in government since the founding of the American Republic."[8]

Meanwhile, almost all of Italy's most famous and admired young intellectuals and artists were Fascists or Fascist sympathizers (the most notable exception was the literary critic Benedetto Croce). Giovanni Papini, the "magical pragmatist" so admired by William James, was deeply involved in the various intellectual movements that created Fascism. Papini's *Life of Christ*—a turbulent, almost hysterical tour de force chronicling his acceptance of Christianity—caused a sensation in the United States in the early 1920s. Giuseppe Prezzolini, a frequent contributor to the *New Republic* who would one day become a respected professor at Columbia University, was one of Fascism's earliest literary and ideological architects. F. T. Marinetti, the founder of the Futurist movement—which in America was seen as an artistic companion to Cubism and Expressionism—

was instrumental in making Italian Fascism the world's first success-ful "youth movement." America's education establishment was keenly interested in Italy's "breakthroughs" under the famed "schoolmas-ter" Benito Mussolini, who, after all, had once been a teacher.

Perhaps no elite institution in America was more accommodating to Fascism than Columbia University. In 1926 it established Casa Italiana, a center for the study of Italian culture and a lecture venue for prominent Italian scholars. It was Fascism's "veritable home in America" and a "schoolhouse for budding Fascist ideologues," ac-cording to John Patrick Diggins. Mussolini himself had contributed some ornate Baroque furniture to Casa Italiana and had sent Columbia's president, Nicholas Murray Butler, a signed photo thanking him for his "most valuable contribution" to the promotion of understanding between Fascist Italy and the United States.[9] Butler himself was not an advocate of fascism for America, but he did believe it was in the best interests of the Italian people and that it had been a very real success, well worth studying. This subtle dis-tinction—fascism is good for Italians, but maybe not for America—was held by a vast array of prominent liberal intellectuals in much the same way some liberals defend Castro's communist "experi-ment."

While academics debated the finer points of Mussolini's corpo-ratist state, mainstream America's interest in Mussolini far out-stripped that of any other international figure in the 1920s. From 1925 to 1928 there were more than a hundred articles written on Mussolini in American publications and only fifteen on Stalin.[10] For more than a decade the *New York Times*'s foreign correspondent Anne O'Hare McCormick painted a glowing picture of Mussolini that made the *Times*'s later fawning over Stalin seem *almost* critical. The *New York Tribune* was vexed to answer the question: Was Mussolini Garibaldi or Caesar? Meanwhile, James A. Farrell, the head of U.S. Steel, dubbed the Italian dictator "the greatest living man" in the world.

Hollywood moguls, noting his obvious theatrical gifts, hoped to make Mussolini a star of the big screen, and he appeared in *The Eternal City* (1923), starring Lionel Barrymore. The film recounts the battles between communists and Fascists for control of Italy, and—*mirabile dictu*—Hollywood takes the side of the Fascists. "His deportment on the screen," one reviewer proclaimed, "lends weight to the theory that this is just where he belongs."[11] In 1933 Columbia Pictures released a "documentary" called *Mussolini Speaks*—supervised by Il Duce himself. Lowell Thomas—the legendary American journalist who had made Lawrence of Arabia famous—worked closely on the film and provided fawning commentary throughout. Mussolini was portrayed as a heroic strongman and national savior. When the crescendo builds before Mussolini gives a speech in Naples, Thomas declares breathlessly, "This is his supreme moment. He stands like a modern Caesar!" The film opened to record business at the RKO Palace in New York. Columbia took out an ad in *Variety* proclaiming the film a hit in giant block letters because "it appeals to all RED BLOODED AMERICANS" and "it might be the ANSWER TO AMERICA'S NEEDS."

Fascism certainly had its critics in the 1920s and 1930s. Ernest Hemingway was skeptical of Mussolini almost from the start. Henry Miller disliked Fascism's program but admired Mussolini's will and strength. Some on the so-called Old Right, like the libertarian Albert J. Nock, saw Fascism as just another kind of statism. The nativist Ku Klux Klan—ironically, often called "American fascists" by liberals—tended to despise Mussolini and his American followers (mainly because they were immigrants). Interestingly, the hard left had almost nothing to say about Italian Fascism for most of its first decade. While liberals were split into various unstable factions, the American left remained largely oblivious to Fascism until the Great Depression. When the left did finally start attacking Mussolini in earnest—largely on orders from Moscow—they lumped him in essentially the same category as Franklin Roosevelt, the socialist Norman Thomas, and the progressive Robert La Follette.[12]

We'll be revisiting how American liberals and leftists viewed Fascism in subsequent chapters. But first it seems worth asking, how was this possible? Given everything we've been taught about the evils of fascism, how is it that for more than a decade this country was in significant respects pro-fascist? Even more vexing, how is it—considering that most liberals and leftists believe they were put on this earth to oppose fascism with every breath—that many if not most American liberals either admired Mussolini and his project or simply didn't care much about it one way or the other?

The answer resides in the fact that Fascism was born of a "fascist moment" in Western civilization, when a coalition of intellectuals going by various labels—progressive, communist, socialist, and so forth—believed the era of liberal democracy was drawing to a close. It was time for man to lay aside the anachronisms of natural law, traditional religion, constitutional liberty, capitalism, and the like and rise to the responsibility of remaking the world in his own image. God was long dead, and it was long overdue for men to take His place. Mussolini, a lifelong socialist intellectual, was a warrior in this crusade, and his Fascism—a doctrine he created from the same intellectual material Lenin and Trotsky had built their movements with—was a grand leap into the era of "experimentation" that would sweep aside old dogmas and usher in a new age. This was in every significant way a project of the left as we understand the term today, a fact understood by Mussolini, his admirers, and his detractors. Mussolini declared often that the nineteenth century was the century of liberalism and the twentieth century would be the "century of Fascism." It is only by examining his life and legacy that we can see how right—and left—he was.

• • •

Benito Amilcare Andrea Mussolini was named after three revolutionary heroes. The name Benito—a Spanish name, as opposed to the Italian equivalent, Benedetto—was inspired by Benito Juárez, the Mexican revolutionary turned president who not only toppled the emperor Maximilian but had him executed. The other two names were inspired by now-forgotten heroes of anarchist-socialism, Amilcare Cipriani and Andrea Costa.

Mussolini's father, Alessandro, was a blacksmith and ardent socialist with an anarchist bent who was a member of the First International along with Marx and Engels and served on the local socialist council. Alessandro's "[h]eart and mind were always filled and pulsing with socialistic theories," Mussolini recalled. "His intense sympathies mingled with [socialist] doctrines and causes. He discussed them in the evening with his friends and his eyes filled with light."[13] On other nights Mussolini's father read him passages from *Das Kapital*. When villagers brought their horses to Alessandro's shop to be shod, part of the price came in the form of listening to the blacksmith spout his socialist theories. Mussolini was a congenital rabble-rouser. At the age of ten, young Benito led a demonstration against his school for serving bad food. In high school he called himself a socialist, and at the age of eighteen, while working as a substitute teacher, he became the secretary of a socialist organization and began his career as a left-wing journalist.

Mussolini undoubtedly inherited his father's hatred of traditional religion, particularly the Catholic Church. (His brother Arnaldo was named in homage to Arnaldo da Brescia, a medieval monk, executed in 1155, who was revered as a local hero for rebelling against the wealth and abuses of the Church.) When Mussolini was ten, the priests at his school had to drag him to Mass kicking and screaming. Later in life, as a student activist in Switzerland, he made a name for himself by regularly offending devout Christians. He particularly liked to ridicule Jesus, describing him as an "ignorant Jew" and claiming that he was a pygmy compared to Buddha. One of his favorite tricks was to publicly dare God to strike him dead—if He existed. After returning to Italy as a rising socialist journalist, he repeatedly accused priests of moral turpitude, denounced the Church in sundry ways, and even wrote a bodice ripper called *Claudia Particella, the Cardinal's Mistress,* which dripped with sexual innuendo.

Mussolini's Nietzschean contempt for the "slave morality" of Christianity was sufficiently passionate that he'd sought to purge Christians of all kinds from the ranks of Italian Socialism. In 1910, for example, at a socialist congress in Forlì, he introduced and carried a resolution which held that the Catholic faith—or any other mainstream monotheism—was inconsistent with socialism and that any socialists who practiced religion or even tolerated it in their children should be expelled from the party. Mussolini demanded that party members renounce religious marriage, baptism, and all other Christian rituals. In 1913 he wrote another anti-Church book on Jan Hus, the Czech heretic-nationalist, called *Jan Hus the Truthful.* In it, one could argue, lay the seeds for Mussolini's Fascism to come.

The second major theme in Mussolini's life was sex. At the age of seventeen, in 1900, the same year he joined the Socialist Party, Mussolini lost his virginity to an elderly prostitute "who spilled out lard from all parts of her body." She charged him fifty centesimi. At the age of eighteen, he had an affair with a woman whose husband was away on military duty. He "accustomed her to my exclusive and tyrannical love: she obeyed me blindly, and let me dispose of her just as I wished." Boasting 169 mistresses over the course of his sexual career, Mussolini was also, by contemporary standards, something of a rapist.[14]

Indeed, Mussolini was one of the first modern sex symbols, paving the way for the sexual deification of Che Guevara. The Italian regime's propagandistic celebration of his "manliness" has launched a thousand academic seminars. Countless intellectuals celebrated Mussolini as the ideal representative man of the new age. Prezzolini wrote of him, "This man is a *man* and stands out even more in a world of half-figures and consciences that are finished like worn out rubber bands." Leda Rafanelli, an anarchist intellectual (who later slept with Mussolini), wrote after hearing him speak for the first time, "Benito Mussolini . . . is the socialist of the heroic times. He feels, he still believes, with an enthusiasm full of virility and force. He is a Man."[15]

Mussolini cultivated an impression of being married to all Italian women. The investment paid off when Italy faced sanctions for its invasion of Ethiopia and Mussolini asked Italians to donate their gold to the state. Millions sent in their wedding rings, 250,000 women in Rome alone. Nor were the ladies of high society immune to his charms. Clementine Churchill had been quite smitten with his "beautiful golden brown, piercing eyes" when she met him in 1926. She was delighted to take home a signed photo as a keepsake. Lady Ivy Chamberlain, on the other hand, treasured her Fascist Party badge as a memento.

Because Mussolini trifled with men's wives, owed money, enraged the local authorities, and was approaching the age of conscription, he found it wise to flee Italy in 1902 for Switzerland, then a European Casablanca for socialist radicals and agitators. He had two lire to his name when he arrived, and, he wrote to a friend, the only metal rattling in his pocket was a medallion of Karl Marx. There he fell in with the predictable crowd of Bolshevists, socialists, and anarchists, including such intellectuals as Angelica Balabanoff, a daughter of Ukrainian aristocrats and a longtime colleague of Lenin's. Mussolini and Balabanoff remained friends for two

decades, until she became the secretary of the Comintern and he became a socialist apostate, that is, a fascist.

Whether Mussolini and Lenin actually met is the subject of some
controversy. However, we know that they were mutual admirers. Lenin
would later say that Mussolini was the only true revolutionary in Italy,
and according to Mussolini's first biographer, Margherita Sarfatti
(a Jew and Mussolini's lover), Lenin also later said, "Mussolini? A
great pity he is lost to us! He is a strong man, who would have led our
party to victory."[16]

While in Switzerland, Mussolini worked quickly to develop his
intellectual bona fides. Writing socialist tracts wherever he could,
the future Duce imbibed the lingo of the international European left.
He wrote the first of his many books while in Switzerland, *Man and
Divinity,* in which he railed against the Church and sang the praises
of atheism, declaring that religion was a form of madness. The Swiss
weren't much more amused with the young radical than the Italians
had been. He was regularly arrested and often exiled by various can-
tonal authorities for his troublemaking. In 1904 he was officially labeled an "enemy of society." At one point he considered whether he
should work in Madagascar, take a job at a socialist newspaper in
New York, or join other socialist exiles in the leftist haven of
Vermont (which fills much the same function today).

While Mussolini would become a fairly inept wartime leader, he
was not the bumbling oaf many Anglo-American historians and intellectuals have portrayed. For one thing, he was astoundingly well
read (even more so than the young Adolf Hitler, who was also something of a bibliophile). His fluency in socialist theory was, if not legendary, certainly impressive to everyone who knew him. We know
from his biographers and his own writings that he read Marx, Engels,
Schopenhauer, Kant, Nietzsche, Sorel, and others. From 1902 to
1914 Mussolini wrote countless articles both examining and translating the socialist and philosophical literature of France, Germany, and
Italy. He was famous for his ability to speak on obscure subjects
without notes and in great depth. Indeed, alone among the major
leaders of Europe in the 1930s and 1940s, he could speak, read, and
write intelligently in several languages. Franklin Roosevelt and
Adolf Hitler were undoubtedly the better politicians and command-
ers in chief, largely because of their legendarily keen instincts. But

by the standards that liberal intellectuals apply today, Mussolini was the smartest of the three.[17]

After Mussolini's return to Italy (and a time in Austria) his reputation as a radical grew slowly but steadily until 1911. He became the editor of *La lotta di classe* (*Class War*), which served as the megaphone of the extremist wing of the Italian Socialist Party. "The national flag is for us a rag to be planted in a dunghill," he declared. Mussolini openly opposed the government's war against Turkey for control of Libya, and in a speech in Forlì he called on the Italian people to declare a general strike, block the streets, and blow up the trains. "His eloquence that day was reminiscent of Marat," the socialist leader Pietro Nenni wrote.[18] His eloquence didn't save him from eight counts of seditious behavior. But he wisely exploited his trial—in much the same way that Hitler made use of his time in the dock—delivering a speech that portrayed him as a patriotic martyr fighting the ruling classes.

Mussolini was sentenced to a year in prison, reduced on appeal to five months. He emerged from prison as a socialist star. At his welcoming banquet a leading socialist, Olindo Vernocchi, declared: "From today you, Benito, are not only the representative of the Romagna Socialists but the *Duce* of all revolutionary socialists in Italy."[19] This was the first time he was called "Il Duce" (the leader), making him the Duce of Socialism before he was the Duce of Fascism.

Using his newfound status, Mussolini attended the Socialist congress in 1912 at a time when the national party was bitterly split between moderates who favored incremental reform and radicals who endorsed more violent measures. Throwing in his lot with the radicals, Mussolini accused two leading moderates of heresy. Their sin? They'd congratulated the king on surviving an attempted assassination by an anarchist. Mussolini could not tolerate such squishiness. Besides, "What is a king anyway except by definition a useless citizen?" Mussolini joined the formal leadership of the party and four months later took over the editorship of its national newspaper, *Avanti!*, one of the most plum posts in all of European radicalism. Lenin, monitoring Mussolini's progress from afar, took note approvingly in *Pravda*.

Had he died in 1914, there's little doubt that Marxist theorists would be invoking Mussolini as a heroic martyr to the proletarian struggle. He was one of Europe's leading radical socialists in arguably the most radical socialist party outside of Russia. Under his stewardship, *Avanti!* became close to gospel for a whole generation of socialist intellectuals, including Antonio Gramsci. He also launched a theoretical journal, *Utopia*, named in tribute to Thomas More, whom Mussolini considered the first socialist. *Utopia* clearly reflected the influence of Georges Sorel's syndicalism on Mussolini's thinking.[20]

Sorel's impact on Mussolini is vital to an understanding of fascism because without syndicalism fascism was impossible. Syndicalist theory is hard to penetrate today. It's not quite socialism and it's not quite fascism. Joshua Muravchik calls it "an ill-defined variant of socialism that stressed violent direct action and was simultaneously elitist and anti-statist." Essentially, syndicalists believed in rule by revolutionary trade unions (the word is derived from the French word *syndicat,* while the Italian word *fascio* means "bundle" and was commonly used as a synonym for unions). Syndicalism informed corporatist theory by arguing that society could be divided by professional sectors of the economy, an idea that deeply influenced the New Deals of both FDR and Hitler. But Sorel's greatest contribution to the left—and Mussolini in particular—lay elsewhere: in his concept of "myths," which he defined as "artificial combinations invented to give the appearance of reality to hopes that inspire men in their present activity." For Sorel, the Second Coming of Christ was a quintessential myth because its underlying message—Jesus is coming, look busy—was crucial for organizing men in desirable ways.[21]

For syndicalists at the time and, ultimately, for leftist revolutionaries of all stripes, Sorel's myth of the general strike was the equivalent of the Second Coming. According to this myth, if all workers declared a general strike, it would crush capitalism and render the proletariat—rather than the meek—the inheritors of the earth. Whether the implementation of a general strike would actually have this result didn't matter, according to Sorel. What mattered was mobilizing the masses to understand their power over the capitalist ruling classes. As Mussolini said in an interview in 1932, "It is faith that moves mountains, not reason. Reason is a tool, but it can never be the motive force of the crowd." This kind of thinking has been commonplace on the left ever since. Think of Al Sharpton when allegedly confronted by the fact that the Tawana Brawley "assault" was a fake. "It don't matter," he's reported to have said. "We're building a movement."[22]

Even more impressive was Sorel's application of the idea of myth to Marxism itself. Again, Sorel held that Marxist prophecy didn't need to be true. People just needed to *think* it was true. Even at the turn of the last century it was becoming obvious that Marxism as social science didn't make a whole lot of sense. Taken literally, Marx's *Das Kapital,* according to Sorel, had little merit. But, Sorel asked, what if Marx's nonsensicalness was actually intended? If you looked at "this *apocalyptic text* . . . as a product of the spirit, as an image created for the purpose of molding consciousness, it . . . is a good illustration of the principle on which Marx believed he should base the rules of the socialist action of the proletariat."[23] In other words, Marx should be read as a prophet, not as a policy wonk. That way the masses would absorb Marxism unquestioningly as a religious dogma.

Sorel was deeply influenced by the Pragmatism of William James, who pioneered the notion that all one needs is the "will to believe." It was James's benign hope to make room for religion in a burgeoning age of science, by arguing that any religion that worked for the believer was not merely valid but "true." Sorel was an irrationalist who took this sort of thinking to its logical conclusion: any idea that can be successfully imposed—with violence if necessary—becomes true and good. By marrying James's will to believe with Nietzsche's will to power, Sorel redesigned left-wing revolutionary politics from scientific socialism to a revolutionary religious movement that believed in the utility of the *myth* of scientific socialism. Enlightened revolutionaries would act as if Marxism were gospel in order to bring the masses under their control for the greater good. Today we might call these aspects of this impulse "lying for justice."

Of course, a lie could not become "true"—that is, successful—unless you had good liars. This is where another of Sorel's major contributions comes in: the need for a "revolutionary elite" to impose its will upon the masses. On this point, as many have observed, Mussolini and Lenin held almost identical views. Central to their common outlook was the Sorelian conviction that a small cadre of professional intellectual radicals—who were prepared to reject compromise, parliamentary politics, and anything else that smacked of incremental reform—were indispensable to any successful revolutionary struggle. This avant-garde would shape "revolutionary consciousness" by fomenting violence and undermining liberal institutions. "We must create a proletarian minority sufficiently numerous, sufficiently knowledgeable, sufficiently audacious to substitute itself, at the opportune moment, for the bourgeois minority," Mussolini channeled Lenin in pitch-perfect tones. "The mass will simply follow and submit."[24]

JACOBIN FASCISM

If Mussolini stood on Sorel's shoulders, then in an important respect Sorel stood on Rousseau's and Robespierre's. A brief review of the intellectual origins of fascist thought reveals its roots in the Romantic nationalism of the eighteenth century, and in the philosophy of Jean-Jacques Rousseau, who properly deserves to be called the father of modern fascism.

Historians have debated the meaning of the French Revolution for centuries. In many respects, their contending views of this event embody the fundamental difference between liberal and conservative (compare Wordsworth and Burke, for example). Even our modern distinction between "left" and "right" derives from the seating arrangements in the revolutionary assembly.

Whatever else it may have been, however, one thing is clear: the French Revolution was the first totalitarian revolution, the mother of modern totalitarianism, and the spiritual model for the Italian Fascist, German Nazi, and Russian Communist revolutions. A nationalist-populist uprising, it was led and manipulated by an intellectual vanguard determined to replace Christianity with a political religion that glorified "the people," anointed the revolutionary vanguard as their priests, and abridged the rights of individuals. As Robespierre put it, "The people is always worth more than individuals . . . The people is sublime, but individuals are weak"—or, at any rate, expendable.[25]

Robespierre's ideas were derived from his close study of Rousseau, whose theory of the general will formed the intellectual basis for all modern totalitarianisms. According to Rousseau, individuals who live in accordance with the general will are "free" and "virtuous" while those who defy it are criminals, fools, or heretics. These enemies of the common good must be forced to bend to the general will. He described this state-sanctioned coercion in Orwellian terms as the act of "forcing men to be free." It was Rousseau who originally sanctified the sovereign will of the masses while dismissing the mechanisms of democracy as corrupting and profane. Such mechanics—voting in elections, representative bodies, and so forth—are "hardly ever necessary where the government is well-intentioned," wrote Rousseau in a revealing turn of phrase. "For the rulers well know that the general will is always on the side which is most favorable to the public interest, that is to say, the most equitable; so that it is needful only to act justly to be certain of following the general will."[26]

That fascism and communism promised to be more democratic than democracy itself was axiomatic for their twentieth-century proselytizers in Europe and America. "The movement" represented, variously, the *Volk*, the people, the authentic nation and its providential mission in history, while parliamentary democracy was corrupt, inauthentic, unnatural.[27] But the salience of the general will is more profound than the mere rationalization of legitimacy through populist rhetoric. The idea of the general will created a true secular religion out of the mystic chords of nationalism, a religion in which "the people" in effect worshipped themselves.[28] Just as individuals couldn't be "free" except as part of the group, their existence lacked meaning and purpose except in relation to the collective.

It followed, moreover, that if the people were the new God, there was no room for God Himself. In *The Social Contract*, Rousseau tells us that because of Christianity's distinction between God and Caesar, "men have never known whether they ought to obey the civil ruler or the priest." What Rousseau proposed instead was a society in which religion and politics were perfectly combined. Loyalty to the state and loyalty to the divine must be seen as the same thing.

The philosopher and theologian Johann Gottfried von Herder, credited somewhat unfairly with laying the intellectual foundation for Nazism, took Rousseau's political arguments and made them into cultural ones. The general will was unique in each nation, according to Herder, because of the historic and spiritual distinctiveness of a specific *Volk*. This Romantic emphasis led various intellectuals and artists to champion the distinctiveness or superiority of races, nations, and cultures. But it is Rousseau's divinization of the community under the direction of the most powerful state ever proposed in political philosophy to which the totalitarianisms of the twentieth century were most indebted. Rousseau's community is not defined by ethnicity or geography or custom. Rather, it is bound together by the general will as expressed in the dogmas of what he called a "civil religion" and enforced by the all-powerful God-state. Those who defy the collective spirit of the community live outside the state and have no claim on its protections. Indeed, not only is the state not required to defend antisocial individuals or subcommunities, it is compelled to do away with them.[29]

The French revolutionaries put these precepts into effect. For example, Rousseau had suggested that Poland create nationalistic holidays and symbols to create a new secular faith. Therefore the Jacobins—who had nearly committed Rousseau to memory—immediately set about launching a grand new totalitarian religion. Robespierre argued that only a "religious instinct" could defend the revolution from the acid of skepticism. But the revolutionaries also knew that before such faith could be attached to the state, they had to exterminate every trace of "deceitful" Christianity. So they embarked on a sweeping campaign to dethrone Christianity. They replaced venerated holidays with pagan, nationalistic celebrations. The Cathedral of Notre Dame was renamed a "temple of reason." Hundreds of pagan-themed festivals were launched across the country celebrating such abstractions as Reason, Nation, and Brotherhood.

Mussolini's Italy in turn aped this strategy. The Italian Fascists held pageants and performed elaborate pagan rites in order to convince the masses, and the world, that "Fascism is a religion" (as Mussolini often declared). "Two religions are today contending . . . for sway over the world—the black and the red," Mussolini would write in 1919. "We declare ourselves the heretics." In 1920 he explained, "We worked with alacrity, to . . . give Italians a 'religious concept of the nation' . . . to lay the foundations of Italian greatness. The religious notion of Italianism . . . should become the impulse and fundamental direction of our lives."[30]

Of course, Italy faced a special challenge in that the nation's capital also contained the capital of the worldwide Catholic Church. As such, the battle between secular religion and traditional religion became muddied by parochial power politics and the uniqueness of Italian culture (Germany had no such handicap, as we will see). The Catholic Church understood what Mussolini was up to. In its 1931 encyclical *Non abbiamo bisogno*, the Vatican accused the Fascists of "Statolatry" and denounced their effort "to monopolize completely the young, from their tenderest years up to manhood and womanhood, for the exclusive advantage of a party and of a regime based on an ideology which clearly resolves itself into a true, a real pagan worship of the State."[31]

The idea of priests and leaders representing the spirit or general will of the people is modern to the extent that it dethrones traditional religion. But the impulse to endow certain classes of people or individual rulers with religious authority is very ancient and may even be hardwired into human nature. Louis XIV's (probably fictional) declaration "*L'état, c'est moi*" summarized the idea that the ruler and the state were one. The revolutionaries' accomplishment was to preserve this doctrine while displacing the source of legitimacy from God to the people, the nation, or simply to the idea of progress. Napoleon, the revolutionary general, seized control of France with just such a writ. He was a secular dictator committed to furthering the revolutionary liberation of the peoples of Europe. His victories against the Austro-Hungarian Empire prompted the captive nations of the Hapsburgs to greet him as "the great liberator." He beat back the authority of the Catholic Church, crowning himself Holy Roman Emperor and ordering his troops to use cathedrals to stable their horses. Napoleon's troops carried with them the Rousseauian bacillus of divinized nationalism.

Thus tumbles both the glorious myth of the left and the central indictment of the right: that the French Revolution was a wellspring of rationalism. In fact it was no such thing. The Revolution was a romantic spiritual revolt, an attempt to replace the Christian God with a Jacobin one. Invocations to Reason were thinly veiled appeals to a new personalized God of the Revolution. Robespierre despised atheism and atheists as signs of the moral decay of monarchy, believing instead in an "Eternal Being who intimately affects the destinies of nations and who seems to me personally to watch over the French Revolution in a very special way."[32] For the Revolution to be successful, Robespierre had to force the people to recognize this God who spoke through him and the general will.

Only in this way could Robespierre realize the dream that would later transfix Nazis, communists, and progressives alike: the creation of "New Men." "I am convinced," he proclaimed in a typical statement, "of the necessity of bringing about a complete regeneration, and, if I may express myself so, of creating a new people." (To this end, he pushed through a law requiring that children be taken from their parents and indoctrinated in boarding schools.) The action-priests of the Revolution, wrote Tocqueville, "had a fanatical faith in their vocation—that of transforming the social system, root and branch, and regenerating the whole human race." He later recognized that the French Revolution had become a "religious revival" and the ideology that spewed from it a "species of religion" which "like Islam [has] overrun the whole world with apostles, militants, and martyrs."[33]

Fascism is indebted to the French Revolution in other ways as well. Robespierre appreciated, as did Sorel and his heirs, that violence was a linchpin that kept the masses committed to the ideals of the Revolution: "If the spring of popular government in time of peace is virtue, the springs of popular government in revolution are at once virtue and terror: virtue, without which terror is fatal; terror, without which virtue is powerless. Terror is nothing other than justice, prompt, severe, inflexible; it is therefore an emanation of virtue; it is not so much a special principle as it is a consequence of the general principle of democracy applied to our country's most urgent needs."[34]

"For the first time in history," writes the historian Marisa Linton, "terror became an official government policy, with the stated aim to use violence in order to achieve a higher political goal." The irony seemed lost on the Bolsheviks—self-proclaimed descendants of the French Revolution—who defined fascism, rather than their own system, as an "openly terroristic dictatorship."[35]

The utility of terror was multifaceted, but among its chief benefits was its tendency to maintain a permanent sense of crisis. Crisis is routinely identified as a core mechanism of fascism because it short-circuits debate and democratic deliberation. Hence all fascistic movements commit considerable energy to prolonging a heightened state of emergency. Across the West, this was the most glorious boon of World War I.

WAR: WHAT IS IT GOOD FOR?

Both Mussolini and Lenin are reported to have had the exact same response to the news of the war. "The Socialist International is dead." And they were right. Across Europe (and later America) socialist and other left-leaning parties voted for war, turning their backs on doctrines of international solidarity and the dogma that this was a war for capitalism and imperialism. After a reflexive two-month period of following this party line, Mussolini started moving into what was known as the interventionist camp. In October 1914 he penned an editorial in *Avanti!* explaining his new pro-war stance in terms that mixed Marxism, pragmatism, and adventurism. A party "which wishes to live in history and, in so far as it is allowed, to make history, cannot submit, at the penalty of suicide to a line which is dependent on an unarguable dogma or eternal law, separate from the iron necessity [of change]." He quoted Marx's admonition that "whoever develops a set program for the future is a reactionary." Living up to the letter of the party, he declared, would destroy its spirit.[36]

David Ramsay Steele suggests that Mussolini's switch in favor of war "was as scandalous as though, 50 years later, [Che] Guevara had announced that he was off to Vietnam, to help defend the South against North Vietnamese aggression."[37] It's a good line, but it obscures the fact that socialists throughout Europe and America were rallying to the cause of war, largely because that's where the masses wanted to go. The most shocking example came when the socialists in the German parliament voted in favor of granting credits to fund the war. Even in the United States the vast majority of socialists and progressives supported American intervention with a bloodlust that would embarrass their heirs today—if their heirs actually took the time to learn the history of their own movement.

This is a vital point because, while it is most certainly true that World War I gave birth to Fascism, it also gave birth to anti-Fascist propaganda. From the moment Mussolini declared himself in favor of the war, Italian Socialists smeared him for his heresy. "*Chi paga?*" became the central question of the anti-Mussolini whisper campaign. "Who's paying him?" He was accused of taking money from arms makers, and it was hinted darkly that he was on France's payroll. There's no evidence for any of this. From the beginning, fascism was dubbed as right-wing not because it necessarily *was* right-wing but because the communist left thought this was the best way to punish apostasy (and, even if it was right-wing in some long forgotten doctrinal sense, fascism was still right-wing socialism). It has ever been thus. After all, if support for the war made one objectively right-wing, then Mother Jones was a rabid right-winger, too. This should be a familiar dynamic today, as support for the war in Iraq is all it takes to be a "right-winger" in many circles.

Mussolini on occasion acknowledged that fascism was perceived as a movement of the "right," but he never failed to make it clear that his inspiration and spiritual home was the socialist left. "You hate me today because you love me still," he told Italian Socialists. "Whatever happens, you won't lose me. Twelve years of my life in the party ought to be sufficient guarantee of my socialist faith. Socialism is in my blood." Mussolini resigned his editorship of *Avanti!* but he could never resign his love of the cause. "You think you can turn me out, but you will find I shall come back again. I am and shall remain a socialist and my convictions will never change! They are bred into my very bones."[38]

Nevertheless, Mussolini was forced to quit the party organization. He joined up with a group of pro-war radicals called the Fascio Autonomo d'Azione Rivoluzionaria and quickly became their leader. Again, Mussolini had not moved to the right. His arguments for entering the war were made entirely in the context of the left and mirrored to no small extent the liberal and leftist arguments of American interventionists such as Woodrow Wilson, John Dewey, and Walter Lippmann. The war, he and his fellow apostates insisted, was against the reactionary Germans and the Austro-Hungarian Empire, a war to liberate foreign peoples from the yoke of imperialism and advance the cause of socialist revolution in Italy, a true "proletarian nation."

Mussolini founded a new newspaper, *Il Popolo d'Italia.* The name itself—*The People of Italy*—is instructive because it illustrates the subtle change in Mussolini's thinking and the first key distinction between socialism and fascism. Socialism was predicated on the Marxist view that "workers" as a class were more bound by common interests than any other criteria. Implicit in the slogan "Workers of the world, unite!" was the idea that class was more important than race, nationality, religion, language, culture, or any other "opiate" of the masses. It had become clear to Mussolini that not only was this manifestly not so but it made little sense to pretend otherwise. If Sorel had taught that Marxism was a series of useful myths rather than scientific fact, why not utilize more useful myths if they're available? "I saw that internationalism was crumbling," Mussolini later admitted. It was "utterly foolish" to believe that class consciousness could ever trump the call of nation and culture.[39] "The sentiment of nationality exists and cannot be denied." What was then called socialism was really just a *kind* of socialism: international socialism. Mussolini was interested in creating a new socialism, a socialism in one state, a *national socialism*, which had the added benefit of being achievable. The old Socialist Party stood in the way of this effort, and thus it was "necessary," Mussolini wrote in *Il Popolo,* "to assassinate the Party in order to save Socialism." In another issue he implored, "Proletarians, come into the streets and piazzas with us and cry: 'Down with the corrupt mercantile policy of the Italian bourgeoisie' . . . Long live the war of liberation of the peoples!"[40]

In 1915 Mussolini was called up for service. He fought well, receiving shrapnel in his leg. The war tended to accelerate his thinking. The soldiers had fought as Italians, not as "workers." Their sacrifice was not for the class struggle but for the Italian struggle. He began to formulate the idea—known as *trincerocrazia*—that veterans deserved to run the country because they had sacrificed more and had the discipline to improve Italy's plight (echoes of this conviction can be found in the "chicken hawk" epithet today). "Socialism of the trenches" seemed so much more plausible than socialism of the factory floor, for Mussolini had in effect seen it. On March 23, 1919, Mussolini and a handful of others founded the Fasci di Combattimento in Milan, aiming to form a popular front of pro-war leftists, from socialist veterans groups to Futurist, anarchist, nationalist, and syndicalist intellectuals. Some highlights from their program:

- Lowering the minimum voting age to eighteen, the minimum age for representatives to twenty-five, and universal suffrage, including for women.
- "The abolition of the Senate and the creation of a national technical council on intellectual and manual labor, industry, commerce and culture."
- End of the draft.
- Repeal of titles of nobility.
- "A foreign policy aimed at expanding Italy's will and power in opposition to all foreign imperialisms."
- The prompt enactment of a state law sanctioning a legal workday of eight *actual* hours of work for all workers.
- A minimum wage.
- The creation of various government bodies run by workers' representatives.
- Reform of the old-age and pension system and the establishment of age limits for hazardous work.
- Forcing landowners to cultivate their lands or have them expropriated and given to veterans and farmers' cooperatives.
- The obligation of the state to build "rigidly secular" schools for the raising of "the proletariat's moral and cultural condition."
- "A large progressive tax on capital that would amount to a one-time *partial expropriation* of all riches."
- "The seizure of all goods belonging to religious congregations and the abolition of episcopal revenues."
- The "review" of all military contracts and the "sequestration of 85% of all war profits."
- The nationalization of all arms and explosives industries.[41]

Ah, yes. Those anti-elitist, stock-market-abolishing, child-labor-ending, public-health-promoting, wealth-confiscating, draft-ending, secularist right-wingers!

In November the newly named and explicitly left-wing Fascists ran a slate of candidates in the national elections. They got trounced at the hands of the Socialists. Most historians claim this is what taught Mussolini to move to the "right." Robert O. Paxton writes that Mussolini realized "there was no space in Italian politics for a party that was both nationalist and Left."[42]

This, I think, distorts the picture. Mussolini did not move fascism from left to right; he moved it from socialist to populist. An unwieldy phenomenon, populism had never been known as a conservative or right-wing orientation before, and it is only because so many were determined to label fascism right-wing that populism under Mussolini was redefined as such. After all, the notion that political power is and should be vested in the people was a classical liberal position. Populism was a more radical version of this position. It's still a "power to the people" ideology, but it is skeptical of the parliamentary machinery of conventional liberalism (e.g., checks and balances). In the United States the populists—always a force on the left in the nineteenth and early twentieth centuries—pushed for such reforms as direct elections of senators and the nationalization of industry and banking. Direct democracy and nationalization were two of the main planks of the Fascist agenda. Mussolini also stopped calling *Il Popolo d'Italia* a "socialist daily" in favor of a "producers' daily."

An emphasis on "producers" had everywhere been the hallmark of populist economics and politics. The key distinction for "producerism," as many called it, was between those who created wealth with their own hands and those who merely profited from it. William Jennings Bryan, for example, was keen on distinguishing the good and decent "people" from "the idle holders of idle capital." The populists sought to expand the scope of government in order to smash the "economic royalists" and help the little guy. This was Mussolini's approach in a nutshell (much as it is that of left-wing icons of today, such as Venezuela's Hugo Chávez). Fascist slogans included "The land to him who works it!" and "To every peasant the entire fruit of his sacred labor!" Mussolini still employed warmed-over Marxist theory when convenient—as many populists did—to explain his new fondness for the small landowner. Italy was still a "proletarian nation," he explained, and so needed to develop economically before it could achieve socialism, even if that meant making a pragmatic nod to capitalist expediency in the form of trade. Lenin had made the identical adjustment under his New Economic Policy in 1921, in which peasants were encouraged to grow more food for their own use and profit.

None of this is to say that Mussolini was a deeply consistent ideologue or political theorist. As a pragmatist, he was constantly willing to throw off dogma, theory, and alliances whenever convenient. In the few years immediately following the formation of the Fasci di Combattimento, Mussolini's main governing themes were expediency and opportunism. This was, after all, the age of "experimentation." FDR would later preach a similar gospel, holding that he had no fixed agenda other than to put Americans to work and launch a program of "bold experimentation." "We do not distrust the future," FDR declared. "The people . . . have not failed. In their need they have . . . asked for discipline and direction under leadership. They have made me the present instrument of their wishes. In that spirit I take it." Likewise, the Fasci di Combattimento, Mussolini wrote in May 1920, "do not feel tied to any particular doctrinal form." And much as Roosevelt would later, Mussolini asked the Italian people to trust him now and worry about an actual program down the road. Shortly before he became prime minister, he famously responded to those who wanted specifics from him: "The democrats of *Il Mondo* want to know our program? It is to break the bones of the democrats of *Il Mondo*. And the sooner the better."[43]

From 1919 to 1922, when Mussolini led the March on Rome and became prime minister, his first objective was power and combat. Make no mistake: many Fascists were skull crackers, leg breakers, and all-purpose thugs, particularly among the OVRA, the secret police of the Fascist state modeled after Lenin's secret police, hence the nickname "Cheha." The casualties from the Fascist-initiated "civil war" hover around two thousand, with 35 percent of the dead confirmed leftists and 15 percent Fascists. This may sound like a lot or a little depending on your perspective, but it is worth keeping in mind that more Italians died during this period from traditional Italian Mafia wars. It's also worth noting that many Fascists were actually impressive, respectable men who earned not only the cooperation of the police but the sympathy of both judges and the common man. In a national contest between two broad factions, the Italian people—workers, peasants, small-business men, and professionals, as well as the well-to-do and wealthy—chose the Fascists over avowed international socialists and communists.

Mussolini's style was remarkably similar to Yasir Arafat's (though Arafat was undoubtedly far more murderous). He played the political game of claiming to seek peaceful accords and alliances while straining to contain the more violent elements within his movement. His hands were tied, he'd claim, when squads of Fascist Blackshirts broke the bones of his opponents. Again like Lenin—and Arafat—Mussolini practiced a philosophy of "the worse the better." He celebrated the violence committed by socialists because it gave him the opportunity to commit more violence in retribution. A brawler who'd been in countless fist and knife fights, Mussolini saw physical violence as a redemptive and natural corollary to intellectual combat (in this he was a lot like Teddy Roosevelt). There's no need to defend Mussolini against the charge that he was a practitioner of organized political violence, as some of his more friendly biographers have tried to do. It's easier to concede the points of both defenders and critics. Yes, the socialists and communists he was fighting were often just as bad as the Fascists. And on other occasions the Fascists were much worse. At the end of the day, however, the salient fact was that in a nation torn by economic and social chaos as well as political bitterness in the wake of the Versailles Treaty, Mussolini's message and tactics triumphed. Moreover, his success had less to do with ideology and violence than with populist emotional appeals. Mussolini promised to restore two things in short supply: pride and order.

The precipitating events in his rise are controversial for reasons not worth dwelling on. Suffice it to say that the March on Rome was not a spontaneous, revolutionary event but a staged bit of political theater designed to advance a Sorelian myth. The violence between Fascist and other left-wing parties reached a crescendo in the summer of 1922, when the communists and socialists called for a general strike to protest the government's refusal to clamp down on the Fascists. Mussolini declared that if the government didn't break the strike, his Fascists would do it themselves. He didn't wait for—or expect—a response. When the "Reds" launched their strike on July

31, Mussolini's *squadristi*—made up largely of skilled ex–military troops—broke it within a day. They drove the streetcars, kept the traffic moving, and, most famously, got the "trains running on time."

Mussolini's strikebreaking tactics had a profound effect on the Italian public. At a time when intellectuals all over the world were growing cynical about parliamentary democracy and liberal politics, Mussolini's military efficiency seemed to transcend partisan politics. Just as many today say we need to "get beyond labels" in order to get things done, Mussolini was seen as moving beyond the "tired categories of left and right." Similarly—like certain modern liberals—he promised what he called a "Third Way" that was neither left nor right. He just wanted to get things done. With the public largely behind him, he planned to break a different sort of strike—the parliamentary deadlock that had paralyzed the government and, hence, "progress." He threatened that he and his Blackshirts—so named because Italian special forces wore black turtlenecks, which quickly became a fashion among Fascists—would march on Rome and take the reins of state. Behind the scenes, King Vittorio Emanuele had already asked him to form a new government. But Il Duce marched anyway, reenacting Julius Caesar's march on Rome and giving the new Fascist government a useful "revolutionary myth" that he would artfully exploit in years to come. Mussolini became prime minister and Fascist Italy was born.

How did Mussolini govern? Like the old joke about the gorilla, however he wanted. Mussolini became a dictator, less brutal than most, more brutal than some. But he was also very popular. In 1924 he held reasonably fair elections, and the Fascists won by a landslide. Among his achievements in the 1920s were the passage of women's suffrage (which the *New York Times* hailed as a nod to the pressure of American feminists), a concordat with the Vatican, and the revitalization of the Italian economy. The settlement of the long-simmering schism between Italy and the pope was a monumental accomplishment in terms of Italy's domestic politics. Mussolini succeeded where so many others had failed.

We will deal with many of the ideological issues and policies swirling around Italian Fascism in subsequent chapters. But there are some points that are worth stating here. First, Mussolini successfully cast himself as the leader of the future. Indeed, he was brought to power in part by an artistic movement called Futurism. Throughout the 1920s, even if he implemented some policies that Western intellectuals disliked—anti-press laws, for example—his *method* of governing was regarded as quintessentially *modern*. At a time when many young intellectuals were rejecting the "dogma" of classical liberalism, Mussolini seemed a leader at the forefront of the movement to reject old ways of thinking. This was the dawn of the "fascist century," after all. It was no coincidence that Fascism was the first politically successful, self-styled modern youth movement, and was widely recognized as such. "Yesterday's Italy is not recognizable in today's Italy," Mussolini declared in 1926. "The whole nation is 20 years old and as such it has the courage, the spirit, the intrepidity."[44] No leader in the world was more associated with the cult of technology, particularly aviation, than Mussolini in the 1920s. By the 1930s world leaders were trying to fit into Mussolini's mold as a "modern" statesman.

Part of Mussolini's reputation as a new kind of leader stemmed from his embrace of "modern" ideas, among them American Pragmatism. He claimed in many interviews that William James was one of the three or four most influential philosophers in his life. He surely said this to impress American audiences. But Mussolini really was an admirer of James (and the James-influenced Sorel), who believed that Pragmatism justified and explained his governing philosophy and governed in a pragmatic fashion. He was indeed the "Prophet of the Pragmatic Era in Politics," as a 1926 article in the *Political Science Quarterly* (and subsequent book) dubbed him.[45]

If at times he would adopt, say, free-market policies, as he did to some extent in the early 1920s, that didn't make him a capitalist. Mussolini never conceded the absolute authority of the state to dictate the course of the economy. By the early 1930s he had found it necessary to start putting Fascist ideology down on paper. Before then, it was much more ad hoc. But when he did get around to writing it out, doctrinal Fascist economics looked fairly recognizable as just another left-wing campaign to nationalize industry, or regulate it to the point where the distinction was hardly a difference. These policies fell under the rubric of what was called corporatism, and not only were they admired in America at the time, but they are unknowingly emulated to a staggering degree today.

Pragmatism is the only philosophy that has an everyday word as its corollary with a generally positive connotation. When we call a leader pragmatic, we tend to mean he's realistic, practical, and above all nonideological. But this conventional use of the word obscures some important distinctions. Crudely, Pragmatism is a form of relativism which holds that any belief that is useful is therefore necessarily true. Conversely, any truth that is inconvenient or non-useful is necessarily untrue. Mussolini's useful truth was the concept of a "totalitarian" society—he made up the word—defined by his famous motto: "Everything in the State, nothing outside the State, nothing against the State." The practical consequence of this idea was that everything was "fair game" if it furthered the ends of the state. To be sure, the militarization of society was an important part of fascism's assault on the liberal state, as many anti-fascists assert. But that was the means, not the end. Mussolini's radical lust to make the state an object of religious fervor was born in the French Revolution, and Mussolini, an heir to the Jacobins, sought to rekindle that fire. No project could be less conservative or less right-wing.

In this and many other ways, Mussolini remained a socialist until his last breath, just as he predicted. His reign ended in 1943, when he became little more than a figurehead for the Nazi regime head-quartered at Salò, where he pathetically plotted his comeback. He spent his days issuing proclamations, denouncing the bourgeoisie, promising to nationalize all businesses with more than a hundred employees, and implementing a constitution written by Nicola Bombacci, a communist and longtime friend of Lenin's. He selected a socialist journalist to record his final chapter as Il Duce, according to whom Mussolini declared, "I bequeath the republic to the republicans not to the monarchists, and the work of social reform to the socialists and not to the middle classes." In April 1945 Mussolini fled for his life—back to Switzerland, ironically—with a column of German soldiers (he was disguised as one of them) as well as his aides, his mistress, and his acolyte Bombacci in tow. They were captured by a band of communist partisans, who the next morning were ordered to execute him. Mussolini's mistress allegedly dove in front of her lover. Bombacci merely shouted, "Long live Mussolini! Long live Socialism!"[46]

· 2 ·

Adolf Hitler:
Man of the Left

W AS HITLER'S GERMANY fascist? Many of the leading scholars of fascism and Nazism—Eugen Weber, A. James Gregor, Renzo De Felice, George Mosse, and others—have answered more or less no. For various reasons having to do with different interpretations of fascism, these academics have concluded that Italian Fascism and Nazism, while superficially similar and historically bound up with each other, were in fact very different phenomena. Ultimately, it is probably too confusing to try to separate Nazism and Italian Fascism completely. In other words, Nazism wasn't Fascist with a capital *F,* but it was fascist with a lowercase *f.* But the fact that such an argument exists among high-level scholars should suggest how abysmally misunderstood both phenomena are in the popular mind, and why reflexive rejection of the concept of liberal fascism may be misguided.

The words "fascist" and "fascism" barely appear in *Mein Kampf.* In seven-hundred-plus pages, only two paragraphs make mention of either word. But the reader does get a good sense of what Hitler thought of the Italian experiment and what it had to teach Germany. "The appearance of a new and great idea was the secret of success in the French Revolution. The Russian Revolution owes its triumph to an idea. And it was only the idea that enabled Fascism triumphantly to subject a whole nation to a process of complete renovation."[1]

The passage is revealing. Hitler acknowledges that fascism was invented by Mussolini. It may have been reinvented, reinterpreted, revised, or extended, but its authorship—and, to a lesser extent, its novelty—were never in doubt. Nor did many people doubt for its first fifteen years or so that it was essentially an *Italian* movement or method.

National Socialism likewise predated Hitler. It existed in different forms in many countries.[2] The ideological distinctions between Fascism and National Socialism aren't important right now. What is important is that Hitler didn't get the *idea* for Nazism from Italian Fascism, and at first Mussolini claimed no parentage of Nazism. He even refused to send Hitler an autographed picture of himself when the Nazis requested one from the Italian embassy. Nevertheless, no Nazi ideologue ever seriously claimed that Nazism was an offshoot of Italian Fascism. And during Nazism's early days, Fascist theorists and Nazi theorists often quarreled openly. Indeed, it was Mussolini who threatened a military confrontation with Hitler to save Fascist Austria from a Nazi invasion in 1934.

It's no secret that Mussolini didn't care for Hitler personally. When they met for the first time, Mussolini recounted how "Hitler recited to me from memory his *Mein Kampf,* that brick I was never able to read." Der Führer, according to Mussolini, "was a gramophone with just seven tunes and once he had finished playing them he started all over again." But their differences were hardly just personal. Italian Fascist ideologues went to great lengths to distance themselves from the Nazi strains of racism and anti-Semitism. Even "extremist ultra-Fascists" such as Roberto Farinacci and Giovanni Preziosi (who was a raving anti-Semite personally and later became a Nazi toady) wrote that Nazism, with its emphasis on parochial and exclusivist racism, "was offensive to the conscience of mankind." In May 1934 Mussolini probably penned—and surely approved—an article in *Gerarchia* deriding Nazism as "one hundred per cent racism. Against everything and everyone: yesterday against Christian civilization, today against Latin civilization, tomorrow, who knows, against the civilization of the whole world." Indeed, Mussolini doubted that Germans were a single race at all, arguing instead that they were a mongrel blend of six different peoples. (He also argued that up to 7 percent of Bavarians were dim-witted.) In

September of that same year, Mussolini was still referring to his "sovereign contempt" for Germany's racist policies. "Thirty centuries of history permit us to regard with supreme pity certain doctrines supported beyond the Alps by the descendents of people who did not know how to write, and could not hand down documents recording their own lives, at a time when Rome had Caesar, Virgil, and Augustus."[3] Meanwhile, the Nazi ideologues derided the Italians for practicing "Kosher Fascism."

What Hitler got from Italian Fascism—and, as indicated above, from the French and Russian revolutions—was the importance of having an idea that would arouse the masses. The particular content of the idea was decidedly secondary. The ultimate utility of ideas is not their intrinsic truth but the extent to which they make a desired action possible—in Hitler's case the destruction of your enemies, the attainment of glory, and the triumph of your race. This is important to keep in mind because Hitler's ideological coherence left a great deal to be desired. His opportunism, pragmatism, and megalomania often overpowered any desire on his part to formulate a fixed ideological approach.

Hermann Rauschning, an early Nazi who broke with Hitler, encapsulated this point when he famously dubbed Hitler's movement "The Revolution of Nihilism." According to Rauschning, Hitler was a pure opportunist devoid of loyalty to men or ideas—unless you call hatred of Jews an idea—and willing to break oaths, liquidate people, and say or do anything to achieve and hold power. "This movement is totally without ideals and lacks even the semblance of a program. Its commitment is entirely to action . . . the leaders choose action on a cold, calculating and cunning basis. For National Socialists there was and is no aim they would not take up or drop at a moment's notice, their only criterion being the strengthening of the movement." Rauschning exaggerated the case, but it is perfectly true that Nazi ideology cannot be summarized in a program or platform. It can be better understood as a maelstrom of prejudices, passions, hatreds, emotions, resentments, biases, hopes, and attitudes that, when combined, most often resembled a religious crusade wearing the mask of a political ideology.[4]

Contrary to his relentless assertions in *Mein Kampf,* Hitler had no great foundational ideas or ideological system. His genius lay in the realization that people wanted to rally to ideas and symbols. And so his success lay in the quintessential techniques, technologies, and icons of the twentieth century—marketing, advertising, radio, airplanes, TV (he broadcast the Berlin Olympics), film (think Leni Riefenstahl), and, most of all, oratory to massive, exquisitely staged rallies. Time and again in *Mein Kampf,* Hitler makes it clear that he believed his greatest gift to the party wasn't his ideas but his ability to speak. Conversely, his sharpest criticism of others seems to be that so-and-so was not a good speaker. This was more than simple vanity on Hitler's part. In the 1930s, in Germany and America alike, the ability to sway the masses through oratory was often the key to power. "Without the loudspeaker," Hitler once observed, "we would never have conquered Germany."[5] Note the use of the word "conquered."

However, saying that Hitler had a pragmatic view of ideology is not to say that he didn't use ideology. Hitler had many ideologies. Indeed he was an ideology peddler. Few "great men" were more adept at adopting, triangulating, and blending different ideological poses for different audiences. This was the man, after all, who had campaigned as an ardent anti-Bolshevik, then signed a treaty with Stalin, and convinced Neville Chamberlain as well as Western pacifists that he was a champion of peace while busily (and openly) arming for war.[6]

Nevertheless, the four significant "ideas" we can be sure Hitler treasured in their own right were power concentrated in himself, hatred—and fear—of Jews, faith in the racial superiority of the German *Volk,* and, ultimately, war to demonstrate and secure the other three.

The popular conception that Hitler was a man of the right is grounded in a rich complex of assumptions and misconceptions about what constitutes left and right, terms that get increasingly slippery the more you try to nail them down. This is a problem we will be returning to throughout this book, but we should deal with it here at least as to how it related to Hitler and Nazism.

The conventional story of Hitler's rise to power goes something like this: Hitler and the Nazis exploited popular resentment over Germany's perceived illegitimate defeat in World War I ("the stab in the back" by communists, Jews, and weak politicians) and the unjust "peace" imposed at Versailles. Colluding with capitalists and industrialists eager to defeat the Red menace (including, in some of the more perfervid versions, the Bush family), the Nazis staged a reactionary coup by exploiting patriotic sentiment and mobilizing the "conservative"—often translated as racist and religious—elements in German society. Once in power, the Nazis established "state capitalism" as a reward to the industrialists, who profited further from the Nazis' push to exterminate the Jews.

Obviously, there's a lot of truth here. But it is not the whole truth. And as we all know, the most effective lies are the ones sprinkled with the most actual truths. For decades the left has cherry-picked the facts to form a caricature of what the Third Reich was about. Caricatures do portray a real likeness, but they exaggerate certain features for a desired effect. In the case of the Third Reich, the desired effect was to cast Nazism as the polar opposite of Communism. So, for example, the roles of industrialists and conservatives were grossly exaggerated, while the very large and substantial leftist and socialist aspects of Nazism were shrunk to the status of trivia, the obsession of cranks and Hitler apologists.

Consider William Shirer's classic, *The Rise and Fall of the Third Reich,* which did so much to establish the "official" history of the Nazis. Shirer writes of the challenge facing Hitler when the radicals within his own party, led by the SA founder Ernst Röhm, wanted to carry out a "Second Revolution" that would purge the traditional elements in the German army, the aristocracy, the capitalists, and others. "The Nazis had destroyed the Left," Shirer writes, "but the Right remained: big business and finance, the aristocracy, the Junker landlords and the Prussian generals, who kept tight rein over the Army."[7]

Now, in one sense, this is a perfectly fair version of events. The Nazis had indeed "destroyed the Left," and "the Right" did remain. But ask yourself, how do we normally talk about such things? For example, the right in America was once defined by the so-called country-club Republicans. In the 1950s, starting with the founding of *National Review,* a new breed of self-described conservatives and libertarians slowly set about taking over the Republican Party. From one perspective one could say the conservative movement "destroyed" the Old Right in America. But a more accurate and typical way of describing these events would be to say that the New Right *replaced* the old one, incorporating many of its members in the process. Indeed, that is precisely why we refer to the *rise* of the New Right in the 1970s and early 1980s. Similarly, when a new generation of leftists asserted themselves in the 1960s via such organizations as the Students for a Democratic Society, we called these activists the New Left because they had edged aside the Old Left, who were their elders and in many cases their actual parents. In time the New Left and the New Right took over their respective parties— the Democrats in 1972, the Republicans in 1980—and today they are simply the left and the right. Likewise, the Nazis did indeed take over—and not merely destroy—the German left.

Historians in recent years have revisited the once "settled" question of who supported the Nazis. Ideological biases once required that the "ruling classes" and the "bourgeoisie" be cast as the villains while the lower classes—the "proletariat" and the unemployed—be seen as supporting the communists and/or the liberal Social Democrats. After all, if the left is the voice for the poor, the powerless, and the exploited, it would be terribly inconvenient for those segments of society to support fascists and right-wingers—particularly if Marxist theory *requires* that the downtrodden be left-wing in their orientation.

That's pretty much gone out the window. While there's a big debate about how much of the working and lower classes supported the Nazis, it is now largely settled that very significant chunks of both constituted the Nazi base. Nazism and Fascism were both *popular* movements with support from every stratum of society. Meanwhile, the contention that industrialists and other fat cats were pulling Hitler's strings from behind the scenes has also been banished to the province of aging Marxists, nostalgic for paradigms lost. It's true that Hitler eventually received support from German industry, but it came late and generally tended to follow his successes rather than fund them. But the notion, grounded in Marxist gospel, that Fascism or Nazism was the fighting arm of capitalist reaction crashed with the Berlin Wall. (Indeed, the very notion that corporations are inherently right-wing is itself an ideological vestige of earlier times, as I discuss in a subsequent chapter on economics.)

In Germany the aristocracy and business elite were generally repulsed by Hitler and the Nazis. But when Hitler demonstrated that he wasn't going away, these same elites decided it would be wise to put down some insurance money on the upstarts. This may be reprehensible, but these decisions weren't driven by anything like an ideological alliance between capitalism and Nazism. Corporations in Germany, like their counterparts today, tended to be opportunistic, not ideological.

The Nazis rose to power exploiting anticapitalist rhetoric they indisputably believed. Even if Hitler was the nihilistic cipher many portray him as, it is impossible to deny the sincerity of the Nazi rank and file who saw themselves as mounting a revolutionary assault on the forces of capitalism. Moreover, Nazism also emphasized many of the themes of later New Lefts in other places and times: the primacy of race, the rejection of rationalism, an emphasis on the organic and holistic—including environmentalism, health food, and exercise—and, most of all, the need to "transcend" notions of class.

For these reasons, Hitler deserves to be placed firmly on the left because first and foremost he was a revolutionary. Broadly speaking, the left is the party of change, the right the party of the status quo. On this score, Hitler was in no sense, way, shape, or form a man of the right. There are few things he believed more totally than that he was a revolutionary. And his followers agreed. Yet for more than a generation to call Hitler a revolutionary has been a form of heresy, particularly for Marxist and German historians, since for the left revolution is always good—the inevitable forward motion of the Hegelian wheel of history. Even if their bloody tactics are (sometimes) to be lamented, revolutionaries move history forward. (For conservatives, in contrast, revolutions are almost always bad—unless, as in the case of the United States, you are trying to *conserve* the victories and legacy of a previous revolution.)

You can see why the Marxist left would resist the idea that Hitler was a revolutionary. Because if he was, then either Hitler was a force for good or revolutions can be bad. And yet how can you argue that Hitler wasn't a revolutionary in the leftist mold? Hitler despised the bourgeoisie, traditionalists, aristocrats, monarchists, and all believers in the established order. Early in his political career, he "had become repelled by the traditionalist values of the German bourgeoisie," writes John Lukacs in *The Hitler of History*. The Nazi writer Hanns Johst's play *Der König* centers on a heroic revolutionary who meets a tragic end because he's betrayed by reactionaries and the bourgeoisie. The protagonist takes his own life rather than abandon his revolutionary principles. When Hitler met Johst (whom he later named poet laureate of the Third Reich) in 1923, he told him that he'd seen the play *seventeen times* and that he suspected his own life might end the same way.[8]

As David Schoenbaum has noted, Hitler viewed the bourgeoisie in almost the exact same terms as Lenin did. "Let us not deceive ourselves," Hitler declared. "Our bourgeoisie is already worthless for any noble human endeavor." Several years after he was firmly in power, he explained: "We did not defend Germany against Bolshevism back then because we were not intending to do anything like conserve a bourgeois world or go so far as to freshen it up. Had communism really intended nothing more than a certain purification by eliminating isolated rotten elements from among the ranks of our so-called 'upper ten thousand' or our equally worthless Philistines, one could have sat back quietly and looked on for a while."[9]

A related definition of the right is that it is not merely in favor of preserving the status quo but affirmatively *reactionary*, seeking to restore the old order. This perspective obviously leaves much to be desired since most libertarians are considered members of the right and few would call such activists reactionaries. As we shall see, there is a sense in which Hitler was a reactionary insofar as he was trying to overthrow the entire millennium-old Judeo-Christian order to restore the paganism of antiquity—a mission shared by some on the left but none on the right today.

"Reactionary" is one of those words smuggled in from Marxist talking points that we now accept uncritically. Reactionaries in Marxist and early-twentieth-century progressive parlance were those who wanted to return to either the monarchy or, say, the Manchester Liberalism of the nineteenth century. They wished to restore, variously, the authority of God, Crown, patriotism, or the market—not Wotan and Valhalla. It is for this reason that Hitler saw himself in an existential battle with the forces of reaction. "We had no wish to resurrect the dead from the old Reich which had been ruined through its own blunders, but to build a new State," Hitler wrote in *Mein Kampf*. And elsewhere: "Either the German youth will one day create a new State founded on the racial idea or they will be the last witnesses of the complete breakdown and death of the bourgeois world."[10]

Such radicalism—succeed or destroy it all!—explains why Hitler, the anti-Bolshevik, often spoke with grudging admiration of Stalin and the communists—but never had anything but derision for "reactionaries" who wanted merely to "turn back the clock" to the nineteenth century. Indeed, he considered the German Social Democrats' greatest achievement to be the destruction of the monarchy in 1918.

Consider the symbolism of Horst Wessel, the party's most famous martyr, whose story was transformed into the anthem of the Nazi struggle, played along with "Deutschland über Alles" at all official events. The lyrics of the "Horst Wessel Song" refer to Nazi "comrades" shot at by the "Red Front and *reactionaries.*"

If we put aside for a moment the question of whether Hitlerism was a phenomenon of the right, what is indisputable is that Hitler was in no way *conservative*—a point scholars careful with their words always underscore. Certainly, to suggest that Hitler was a conservative in any sense related to American conservatism is lunacy. American conservatives seek to preserve both traditional values and the classical liberal creed enshrined in the Constitution. American conservatism straddles these two distinct but overlapping libertarian and traditionalist strains, whereas Hitler despised both of them.

THE RISE OF A NATIONAL SOCIALIST

The perception of Hitler and Nazism as right-wing rests on more than a historiographical argument or Hitler's animosity to traditionalists. The left has also used Hitler's racism, his alleged status as a capitalist, and his hatred of Bolshevism to hang the conservative label not only on Hitler and Nazism but on generic fascism as well. We can best address the merits—or lack thereof—of these points by briefly revisiting the story of Hitler's rise. Obviously, Hitler's personal tale has been so thoroughly dissected by historians and Hollywood that it doesn't make sense to repeat it all here. But some essential facts and themes deserve more attention than they usually get.

Hitler was born in Austria, just over the border from Bavaria. Like that of many early Nazis, his youth was marked by a certain amount of envy toward the "true" Germans just across the border. (Many of the first Nazis were men from humble backgrounds in the hinter-lands determined to "prove" their "Germanness" by being more "German" than anyone else.) This attitude flowed easily into anti-Semitism. Who better to hate than the Jews, particularly the success-fully assimilated Germanized ones? Who were they to pretend they were Germans? Still, exactly when and why Hitler became an anti-Semite is unknown. Hitler himself claimed that he didn't hate Jews as a child; yet youthful contemporaries later recalled that he'd been an anti-Semite for as long as they could remember. The only reason Hitler might have been reluctant to admit he was a lifelong Jew hater would be that doing so would undermine his claims to have deduced the evilness of Jews from careful study and mature observation.

This introduces one of the most significant differences between Mussolini and Hitler. For most of his career, Mussolini considered anti-Semitism a silly distraction and, later, a necessary sop to his overbearing German patron. Jews could be good socialists or fascists if they thought and behaved like good socialists or fascists. Because Hitler thought explicitly in terms of what we would today call iden-tity politics, Jews were irredeemably Jews, no matter how well they spoke German. His allegiance, like that of all practitioners of iden-tity politics, was to the iron cage of immutable identity.

In *Mein Kampf,* Hitler declares that he is a nationalist but not a pa-triot, a distinction with profound implications. Patriots revere the ideas, institutions, and traditions of a particular country and its gov-ernment. The watchwords for nationalists are "blood," "soil," "race," *"Volk,"* and so forth. As a revolutionary nationalist, Hitler believed the entire bourgeois edifice of modern German culture was hollowed out by political or spiritual corruption. As a result, he believed Germany needed to rediscover its pre-Christian authenticity. This was the logical extension of identity politics—the idea that experi-ence of a personal quest for meaning in racial conceptions of authen-ticity could be applied to the entire community.

It was this mind-set that made Pan-Germanism so attractive to a young Hitler. Pan-Germanism took many forms, but in Austria the basic animating passion was a decidedly un-conservative antipathy toward the liberal, multiethnic pluralism of the Austro-Hungarian Empire, which accepted Jews, Czechs, and the rest of the non-Teutonic rabble as equal citizens. Some Pan-German "nationalists" wanted to break out of the Empire entirely. Others simply believed that the Germans should be first among equals.

Of course, young Hitler's nationalist inferiority complex had to compete with a host of other resentments swirling around in his psyche. Indeed, no psyche in human history has been so thoroughly mined for various explanatory pathologies, and few subjects have offered a richer lode. "The search for Hitler," writes Ron Rosenbaum in *Explaining Hitler,* "has apprehended not one coherent, consensus image of Hitler but rather many different Hitlers, competing Hitlers, conflicting embodiments of competing visions." Psychologists and historians have argued that Hitler's personality stems from the fact(s) that he was abused by his father, had a history of incest in his family, was a sadomasochist, a coprophiliac, a homosexual, or was part Jewish (or feared that he was). These theories vary in plausibility. But what is certain is that Hitler's megalomania was the product of a rich complex of psychological maladies and impulses. Taken as a whole, they point to a man who felt he had much to compensate for and whose egocentrism knew no bounds. "I have to attain immortality," Hitler once confessed, "even if the whole German nation perishes in the process."[11]

Hitler suffered from an enormous intellectual inferiority complex. A lifelong underachiever, he was eternally bitter about getting poor grades in school. More important, perhaps, he resented his father for any number of perceived offenses. Alois Hitler—born Alois Schicklgruber—worked for the Austrian civil service, which is to say for the Empire and against "German interests." Alois wanted Adolf to be not an artist but a civil servant like himself. Alois may also have been partly Jewish, a possibility that kept Hitler's own racial history a state secret when he became dictator.

Hitler defied his father, moving to Vienna in hopes of attending the Academy of Fine Arts, but his application was rejected. On his second try, his drawings were so bad he wasn't even allowed to apply. Partly thanks to some money he inherited from an aunt, Hitler slowly clawed out a professional life as a tradesman-artist (he was never a housepainter, as his enemies claimed). He mostly copied older paintings and drawings and sold them to merchants as frame fillers, place holders, and postcards. Constantly reading—mostly German mythology and pseudo history—Hitler ignored Vienna's café society, puritanically refusing to drink, smoke, or dance (women in his mind were little more than terrifying syphilis carriers). In one of his few moments of understatement, he wrote in *Mein Kampf,* "I believe that those who knew me in those days took me for an eccentric."

It was in Vienna that Hitler was first introduced to National Socialism. Vienna at the turn of the century was the center of the universe for those eager to learn more about Aryan mumbo jumbo, the mystical powers of the Hindu swastika, and the intricacies of Cosmic Ice Theory. Hitler swam in these bohemian waters, often staying up nights writing plays about pagan Bavarians bravely fighting off invading Christian priests trying to impose foreign beliefs on Teutonic civilization. He also spent days wandering the poorer sections of the city, only to come home to work on grandiose city plans that included more progressive housing for the working class. Indeed, he would rail against the unearned wealth of the city's aristocrats and the need for social justice.

Most of all, Hitler immersed himself in the burgeoning field of "scientific" anti-Semitism. "Once, when passing through the inner City," he wrote in *Mein Kampf,* "I suddenly encountered a phenomenon in a long caftan and wearing black side-locks. My first thought was: Is this a Jew? They certainly did not have this appearance in Linz. I watched the man stealthily and cautiously; but the longer I gazed at the strange countenance and examined it feature by feature, the more the question shaped itself in my brain: Is this a German?" Hitler the scholar continues: "As was always my habit with such experiences, I turned to books for help in removing my doubts. For the first time in my life I bought myself some anti-Semitic pamphlets for a few pence."

After making a careful study of the subject, he concluded in *Mein Kampf,* "I could no longer doubt that there was not a question of Germans who happened to be of a different religion but rather that there was question of an entirely different people. For as soon as I began to investigate the matter and observe the Jews, then Vienna appeared to me in a different light. Wherever I now went I saw Jews, and the more I saw of them the more strikingly and clearly they stood out as a different people from the other citizens."

The leading intellectual in Vienna touting "Teutonomania"—the neo-Romantic "discovery" of German exceptionalism very similar to some forms of Afrocentrism today—was Georg Ritter von Schönerer, whom Hitler followed closely and whom he later called a "profound thinker." A drunk and a brawler, as well as a perfectly loutish anti-Semite and anti-Catholic, von Schönerer was something of a product of Bismarck's Kulturkampf, insisting that Catholics convert to German Lutheranism and even suggesting that parents reject Christian names in favor of purely "Teutonic" ones and calling for a ban on interracial marriages in order to keep Slavs and Jews from spoiling the genetic stock. And if Germans couldn't unify into a single, racially pure German fatherland, the very least that could be done was to adopt a policy of racial preferences and affirmative action for Germans.

But Hitler's true hero in those days was the burgomaster of Vienna himself, Dr. Karl Lueger. The head of the Christian Social Party, Lueger was a master politician-demagogue, a Viennese Huey Long of sorts, who championed—usually in explosive, sweaty tirades—a mixture of "municipal socialism," populism, and anti-Semitism. His infamous calls for anti-Jewish boycotts and his warnings to Vienna's Jews to behave themselves or end up like their co-religionists in Russia were reported in newspapers around the world. Indeed, the emperor had overruled Lueger's election twice, recognizing that he could only mean headaches for those who favored the status quo.

In 1913 Hitler inherited the remainder of his father's estate and moved to Munich, fulfilling his dream of living in a "real" German city and avoiding military service for the Hapsburgs. These were among his happiest days. He spent much of his time studying architecture and delving deeper into pseudo-historical Aryan theories and anti-Semitism (particularly the writings of Houston Stewart Chamberlain). He also renewed his study of Marxism, which both fascinated and repulsed him, appreciating its ideas but becoming utterly convinced that Marx was the architect of a Jewish plot. At the outbreak of World War I, Hitler immediately petitioned King Ludwig III of Bavaria for permission to serve in the Bavarian army, which, after some entanglement with Austrian authorities, was granted. Hitler served honorably during the war. He was promoted to corporal and received the Iron Cross.

As countless others have observed, World War I gave birth to all the horrors of the twentieth century. A host of banshees were let loose upon the Western world, shattering old dogmas of religion, democracy, capitalism, monarchy, and mankind's role in the world. The war fueled widespread hatred, suspicion, and paranoia toward elites and established institutions. For belligerents on both sides, economic planning lent political and intellectual credibility to state-directed war socialism. And, of course, it led to the enthronement of revolutionaries throughout Europe: Lenin in Russia, Mussolini in Italy, and Hitler in Germany.

Not surprisingly, Hitler's experience during the war was very similar to Mussolini's. Hitler witnessed men of high and low station fighting side by side in the trenches. These men experienced the corruption and duplicity—real and perceived—of their own government.

Hitler's hatred of communists was also given new heat and strength during the war, thanks largely to antiwar agitation on the home front. German civilians starved along with the troops. They made bread with sawdust and turned pets into meals. Cats were called "roof rabbits." German Reds fed off this suffering, organizing strikes against the government and demanding peace with the Soviets and the establishment of German socialism. Hitler, who as it would turn out had no problem with German socialism, saw communist antiwar mobilization as treason twice over: it not only betrayed the troops at the front but was done at the behest of a foreign power. Infuriated by the fifth columnists, he railed, "What was the army fighting for if the homeland itself no longer wanted victory? For whom the immense sacrifices and privations? The soldier is expected to fight for victory and the homeland goes on strike against it!"[12]

When the Germans surrendered, Hitler and countless other soldiers famously protested that they had been "stabbed in the back" by a corrupt democratic government—the "November criminals"—that no longer represented the authentic needs or aspirations of the German nation. Hitler was recovering in a hospital, stricken with temporary blindness, when news of the armistice was announced. For him it was a transformative event, a moment of religious vision and divine calling. "During those nights my hatred increased, hatred for those responsible for this dastardly crime," he wrote. The perpetrators in his mind were a diverse coalition of capitalists, communists, and cowards, all of whom were fronts for a Jewish menace. Hitler's hatred for communism was not—as communists themselves have claimed—grounded in a rejection of socialist policies or notions of egalitarianism, progress, or social solidarity. It was bound up inextricably with a sense of betrayal of German honor and pathological anti-Semitism. This is what launched Hitler's political career.

After recovering from his wounds, Corporal Hitler found a post in Munich. His job was to monitor organizations promoting what the army considered to be "dangerous ideas"—pacifism, socialism, communism, and so on. In September 1919 he was ordered to attend a meeting of one of the countless new "workers' parties," which at the time was generally code for some flavor of socialism or communism.

Young Hitler showed up at a meeting of the German Workers' Party ready to dismiss it as just another left-wing fringe group. But one of the speakers was Gottfried Feder, who had impressed Hitler when he'd heard him speak previously. The title of Feder's talk that night: "How and by What Means Is Capitalism to Be Eliminated?" Feder was a populist ideologue who had tried to ingratiate himself with the socialist revolutionaries who briefly turned Munich into a Soviet-style commune in 1919. Like all populists, Feder was obsessed with the distinction between "exploitative" and "productive" finance. Hitler instantly recognized the potential of Feder's ideas, which would appeal to the "little guy" in both cities and small towns. Hitler understood that, just as in America, the increasing power of big banks, corporations, and department stores fostered a sense of powerlessness among blue-collar workers, small farmers, and small-business owners. While Feder's economic proposals were little better than gibberish (as is almost always the case with populist economics), they were perfect for a party seeking to exploit resentment of national elites and, particularly, Jews. Rarely did a day go by that Feder didn't call Jews "parasites."

Although Hitler was impressed by Feder's speech, he recounts in *Mein Kampf* that he remained underwhelmed by the German Workers' Party, considering it just another of those groups that "sprang out of the ground, only to vanish silently after a time." He did take a moment to dress down an attendee who dared to suggest that Bavaria should break from Germany and join Austria—a comment that was bound to horrify a Pan-German like Hitler. Hitler's tirade so impressed some of the officials at the meeting that one of them—a meek-looking fellow named Anton Drexler—stopped him as he was leaving and gave him a copy of a party pamphlet.

At 5:00 a.m. the next morning, Hitler was lying on his cot at the barracks watching the mice eat the bread crumbs he usually left for them. Unable to sleep, he took out the pamphlet and read it straight through. Written by Drexler himself and titled "My Political Awakening," the autobiographical booklet revealed to Hitler that there were others who thought as he did, that his story was not unique, and that there was a ready-made ideology available for him to adopt and exploit.

Even if Hitler's nationalism, populism, anti-Semitism, and non-Marxist socialism took more time to germinate, the relevant point is that what came to be known as Hitlerism or Nazism was already a significant current in Germany and elsewhere in Central Europe (particularly Czechoslovakia). Hitler would give these inchoate passions a name and a focus, but the raw materials were already there. Unlike Mussolini's Fascism, which was mostly a creation of his own intellect, Hitler's ideology came to him largely preassembled. Mussolini's Fascism, moreover, played no discernible role in the formation of early Nazi ideology or Hitler's embryonic political vision. What Hitler would later confess to admiring about Mussolini was Il Duce's success, his tactics, his Sorelian exploitation of political myth, his *salesmanship*. These ideas and movements were swirling all around Europe and Germany. What the masses didn't need was some new doctrine. What they needed was someone who could pull them into *action*. "Action" was the watchword across the Western world. Action got things done. That's what Hitler realized when he read that pamphlet on his cot in the predawn hours: his time had come. He would become National Socialism's greatest salesman, not its creator.

Even while Hitler was still pondering whether he should join the German Workers' Party, he received a membership card in the mail. He'd been recruited! He was given party number 555. Needless to say, it wasn't long before he was running the show. It turned out that this antisocial, autodidactic misanthrope was the consummate party man. He had all the gifts a cultish revolutionary party needed: oratory, propaganda, an eye for intrigue, and an unerring instinct for populist demagoguery. When he joined the party, its treasury was a cigar box with less than twenty marks in it. At the height of his success the party controlled most of Europe and was poised to rule the world.

In 1920 the Nazi Party issued its "unalterable" and "eternal" party platform, co-written by Hitler and Anton Drexler and dedicated to the overarching principle that the "common good must come before self-interest." Aside from the familiar appeals to Germany for the Germans and denunciation of the Treaty of Versailles, the most striking thing about the platform was its concerted appeal to socialistic and populist economics, including providing a livelihood for citizens; abolition of income from interest; the total confiscation of war profits; the nationalization of trusts; shared profits with labor; expanded old-age pensions; "communalization of department stores"; the execution of "usurers" regardless of race; and the outlawing of child labor. (The full platform can be found in the Appendix.)

So, we are supposed to see a party in favor of universal education, guaranteed employment, increased entitlements for the aged, the expropriation of land without compensation, the nationalization of industry, the abolition of market-based lending—a.k.a. "interest slavery"—the expansion of health services, and the abolition of child labor as objectively and obviously right-wing.

What the Nazis pursued was a form of anticapitalist, antiliberal, and anti-conservative communitarianism encapsulated in the concept of *Volksgemeinschaft,* or "people's community." The aim was to transcend class differences, but only within the confines of the community. "We have endeavored," Hitler explained, "to depart from the external, the superficial, endeavored to forget social origin, class, profession, fortune, education, capital and everything that separates men, in order to reach that which binds them together."[13] Again and again, Nazi propaganda, law, and literature insisted that none of the "conservative" or "bourgeois" categories should hold any German back from fulfilling his potential in the new Reich. In a perversely ironic way, the Nazi pitch was often crafted in the same spirit as liberal sentiments like "a mind is a terrible thing to waste" and "the content of their character." This sounds silly in the American context because to us race has always been the more insurmountable barrier than class. But in Germany class was always the crucial dividing line, and Nazi anti-Semitism provided one of many unifying concepts that all "true" Germans, rich and poor, could rally around. The tectonic divide between the National Socialists and the communists wasn't over economics at all—though there were doctrinal differences—but over the question of nationalism. Marx's most offending conviction to Hitler was the idea that the "workingmen have no country."

The Nazis may not have called themselves left-wingers, but that's almost irrelevant. For one thing, the left today—and yesterday—constantly ridicules ideological labels, insisting that words like "liberal" and "left" don't really mean anything. How many times have we heard some prominent leftist insist that he is really a "progressive" or that she "doesn't believe in labels"? For another, the "social space" the Nazis were fighting to control *was on the left.* Not only the conventional analysis typified by Shirer but most Marxist analysis concedes that the Nazis aimed first to "destroy the left" before they went after the traditionalist right. The reason for this was that the Nazis could more easily defeat opponents on the left because they appealed to the same social base, used the same language, and thought in the same categories. A similar phenomenon was on display during the 1960s, when the New Left in the United States—and throughout Europe—attacked the liberal center while largely ignoring the traditionalist right. In American universities, for example, conservative faculty were often left alone, while liberal academics were hounded relentlessly.

The Nazis' ultimate aim was to transcend both left and right, to advance a "Third Way" that broke with both categories. But in the real world the Nazis seized control of the country by dividing, conquering, and then replacing the left.

This is the monumental fact of the Nazi rise to power that has been slowly airbrushed from our collective memories: the Nazis campaigned as *socialists.* Yes, they were also nationalists, which in the context of the 1930s was considered a rightist position, but this was at a time when the "internationalism" of the Soviet Union defined *all* nationalisms as right-wing. Surely we've learned from

the parade of horribles on offer in the twentieth century that nationalism isn't inherently right-wing—unless we're prepared to call
Stalin, Castro, Arafat, Chávez, Guevara, Pol Pot, and, for that matter, Woodrow Wilson, Franklin Roosevelt, and John F. Kennedy,
right-wingers. Stalin himself ruled as a nationalist, invoking
"Mother Russia" and dubbing World War II the "great patriotic war."
By 1943 he had even replaced the old Communist anthem ("The
Internationale") with one that was thoroughly Russian. Moreover,
historically, nationalism was a liberal-left phenomenon. The French
Revolution was a nationalist revolution, but it was also seen as a left-
liberal one for breaking with the Catholic Church and empowering
the people. German Romanticism as championed by Gottfried
Herder and others was seen as both nationalistic and liberal. The
National Socialist movement was part of this revolutionary tradition.

But even if Nazi nationalism was in some ill-defined but fundamental way right-wing, this only meant that Nazism was right-wing
socialism. And right-wing socialists are still socialists. Most of the
Bolshevik revolutionaries Stalin executed were accused of being not
conservatives or monarchists but rightists—that is, right-wing socialists. Any deviation from the Soviet line was automatic proof of
rightism. Ever since, we in the West have apishly mimicked the
Soviet usage of such terms without questioning the propagandistic
baggage attached.

The Nazi ideologist—and Hitler rival—Gregor Strasser put it
quite succinctly: "We are socialists. We are enemies, deadly enemies, of today's capitalist economic system with its exploitation of
the economically weak, its unfair wage system, its immoral way of
judging the worth of human beings in terms of their wealth and their
money, instead of their responsibility and their performance, and we
are determined to destroy this system whatever happens!"[14]

Hitler is just as straightforward in *Mein Kampf*. He dedicates an
entire chapter to the Nazis' deliberate exploitation of socialist and
communist imagery, rhetoric, and ideas and how this marketing confused both liberals and communists. The most basic example is
the Nazi use of the color red, which was firmly associated with
Bolshevism and socialism. "We chose red for our posters after particular and careful deliberation . . . so as to arouse their attention and
tempt them to come to our meetings . . . so that in this way we got a

chance of talking to the people." The Nazi flag—a black swastika inside a white disk in a sea of red—was explicitly aimed at attracting communists. "In *red* we see the social idea of the movement, in *white* the nationalistic idea, in the *swastika* the mission of the struggle for the victory of Aryan man."[15]

The Nazis borrowed whole sections from the communist playbook. Party members—male and female—were referred to as comrades. Hitler recalls how his appeals to "class-conscious proletarians" who wanted to strike out against the "monarchist, reactionary agitation with the fists of the proletariat" were successful in drawing countless communists to their meetings.[16] Sometimes the communists came with orders to smash up the place. But the Reds often refused to riot on command because they had been won over to the National Socialist cause. In short, the battle between the Nazis and the communists was a case of two dogs fighting for the same bone.

Nazism's one-nation politics by its very definition appealed to people from all walks of life. Professors, students, and civil servants were all disproportionately supportive of the Nazi cause. But it's important to get a sense of the kind of person who served as the rank-and-file Nazi, the young, often thuggish true believers who fought in the streets and dedicated themselves to the revolution. Patrick Leigh Fermor, a young Briton traveling in Germany shortly after Hitler came to power, met some of these men in a Rhineland workers' pub, still wearing their night-shift overalls. One of his new drinking buddies offered to let Fermor crash at his house for the night. When Fermor climbed the ladder to the attic to sleep in a guest bed, he found "a shrine to Hitleriana":

The walls were covered with flags, photographs, posters, slogans and emblems. His SA uniforms hung neatly ironed on a hanger . . . When I said that it must be rather claustrophobic with all that stuff on the walls, he laughed and sat down on the bed, and said: "Mensch! You should have seen it last year! You would have laughed! Then it was all red flags, stars, hammers, sickles, pictures of Lenin and Stalin and Workers of the World Unite! . . . Then, suddenly when Hitler came to power, I understood it was all nonsense and lies. I realized Adolf was the man for me. All of a sudden!" He snapped his fingers in the air.

"And here I am!" . . . Had a lot of people done the same, then? "Millions! I tell you, I was astonished how easily they all changed sides!"[17]

Even after Hitler seized power and became more receptive to pleas from businessmen—the demands of his war machine required no less—party propaganda still aimed relentlessly at workers. Hitler always emphasized (and grossly exaggerated) his status as an "ex-worker." He would regularly appear in shirtsleeves and spoke informally to blue-collar Germans: "I was a worker in my youth like you, slowly working my way upward by industry, by study, and I think I can say as well by hunger." As the self-described *Volkskanzler,* or "people's chancellor," he played all the populist notes. One of his first official acts was to refuse to accept an honorary doctorate. A Nazi catechism asked, "What professions has Adolf Hitler had?" The expected reply: "Adolf Hitler was a construction worker, an artist, and a student." In 1939, when the new Chancellery was built, Hitler greeted the construction workers first and gave the stonemasons pictures of himself and fruit baskets. He promised "people's cars" for every worker. He failed to deliver them on time, but they eventually became the Volkswagens we all know today. The Nazis were brilliant at arguing for a one-nation politics in which a farmer and a businessman were valued equally. At Nazi rallies, organizers never allowed an aristocrat to speak unless he was paired with a humble farmer from the sticks.[18]

What distinguished Nazism from other brands of socialism and communism was not so much that it included more aspects from the political right (though there were some). What distinguished Nazism was that it forthrightly included a worldview we now associate almost completely with the political left: identity politics. This was what distinguished Nazism from doctrinaire communism, and it seems hard to argue that the marriage of one leftist vision to another can somehow produce right-wing progeny. If this was how the world worked, we would have to label nationalist-socialist organizations like the PLO and the Cuban Communist Party right-wing.

Insight into the mind-set of early members of the Nazi Party comes in the form of a series of essays written for a contest conducted by Theodore Abel, an impressively clever American sociologist. In 1934 Abel took out an ad in the Nazi Party journal asking "old fighters" to submit essays explaining why they had joined. He restricted his request to "old fighters" because so many opportunists had joined the party after Hitler's rise. The essays were combined in the fascinating book *Why Hitler Came Into Power.* One essayist, a coal miner, explained that he was "puzzled by the denial of race and nation implicit in Marxism. Though I was interested in the betterment of the workingman's plight, I rejected [Marxism] unconditionally. I often asked myself why socialism had to be tied up with internationalism—why it could not work as well or better in conjunction with nationalism." A railroad worker concurred, "I shuddered at the thought of Germany in the grip of Bolshevism. The slogan 'Workers of the World Unite!' made no sense to me. At the same time, however, National Socialism, with its promise of a community . . . barring all class struggle, attracted me profoundly." A third worker wrote that he embraced the Nazis because of their "uncompromising will to stamp out the class struggle, snobberies of caste and party hatreds. The movement bore the true message of socialism to the German workingman."[19]

One of the great ironies of history is that the more similar two groups are, the greater the potential for them to hate each other. God seems to have a particular fondness for contradicting the clichéd notion that increased "understanding" between groups or societies will breed peace. Israelis and Palestinians, Greeks and Turks, Indians and Pakistanis understand each other very well, and yet they would probably take exception to this liberal rule of thumb. Academics who share nearly identical worldviews, incomes, and interests are notoriously capable of despising each other—even as they write learned papers about how increased understanding brings comity. So it was with Communists and Nazis between the two world wars.

The notion that communism and Nazism are polar opposites stems from the deeper truth that they are in fact kindred spirits. Or, as Richard Pipes has written, "Bolshevism and Fascism were heresies of socialism."[20] Both ideologies are reactionary in the sense that they try to re-create tribal impulses. Communists champion class, Nazis race, fascists the nation. All such ideologies—we can call them totalitarian for now—attract the same *types* of people.

Hitler's hatred for communism has been opportunistically exploited to signify ideological distance, when in fact it indicated the exact opposite. Today this maneuver has settled into conventional wisdom. But what Hitler hated about Marxism and communism had almost nothing to do with those aspects of communism that we would consider relevant, such as economic doctrine or the need to destroy the capitalists and bourgeoisie. In these areas Hitler largely saw eye to eye with socialists and communists. His hatred stemmed from his paranoid conviction that the people calling themselves communists were in fact in on a foreign, Jewish conspiracy. He says this over and over again in *Mein Kampf.* He studied the names of communists and socialists, and if they sounded Jewish, that's all he needed to know. It was all a con job, a ruse, to destroy Germany. Only "authentically" German ideas from authentic Germans could be trusted. And when those Germans, like Feder or Strasser, proposed socialist ideas straight out of the Marxist playbook, he had virtually no objection whatsoever. Hitler never cared much about economics anyway. He always considered it "secondary." What mattered to him was German identity politics.

Let me anticipate an objection. The argument goes something like this: Communism and fascism are opposites; therefore, since fascism is fundamentally anti-Semitic, communism must not be. Another version simply reverses the equation: Fascism (or Nazism) was all about anti-Semitism, but communism wasn't; therefore, they are not similar. Other versions fool around with the word "rightwing": anti-Semitism is right-wing; Nazis were anti-Semites; therefore, Nazism was right-wing. You can play these games all day.

Yes, the Nazis were anti-Semites of the first order, but anti-Semitism is by no means a right-wing phenomenon. It is also widely recognized, for example, that Stalin was an anti-Semite and that the Soviet Union was, in effect, officially anti-Semitic (though far less genocidal than Nazi Germany—*when it came to the Jews*). Karl Marx himself—despite his Jewish heritage—was a committed Jew hater, railing in his letters against "dirty Jews" and denouncing his enemies with phrases like "niggerlike Jew." Perhaps more revealing, the German Communists often resorted to nationalistic and anti-Semitic appeals when they found it useful. Leo Schlageter, the young Nazi who was executed by the French in 1923 and subsequently made into a martyr to the German nationalist cause, was also lionized by the communists. The communist ideologue Karl Radek delivered a speech to the Comintern celebrating Schlageter as precisely the sort of man the communists needed. The communist (and half-Jewish) radical Ruth Fischer tried to win over the German proletariat with some Marxist anti-Semitic verbiage: "Whoever cries out against Jewish capitalists is already a class warrior, even when he does not know it . . . Kick down the Jewish capitalists, hang them from the lampposts, and stamp upon them." Fischer later became a high-ranking official in the East German Communist government.[21]

In the early 1920s, noting the similarities between Italian Fascism and Russian Bolshevism was not particularly controversial. Nor was it insulting to communists or fascists. Mussolini's Italy was among the first to recognize Lenin's Russia. And as we've seen, the similarities between the two men were hardly superficial. Radek noted as early as 1923 that "Fascism is middle-class Socialism and we cannot persuade the middle classes to abandon it until we can prove to them that it only makes their condition worse."[22]

But most communist theorists rejected or were ignorant of Radek's fairly accurate understanding of fascism. Leon Trotsky's version was far more influential. According to Trotsky, fascism was the last gasp of capitalism long prophesied in Marxist scripture. Millions of communists and fellow travelers in Europe and America sincerely believed that fascism was a capitalist backlash against the forces of truth and light. As Michael Gold of the *New Masses* put it in response to the poet Ezra Pound's support for fascism: "When a cheese goes putrid, it becomes limburger, and some people like it, smell and all. When the capitalist state starts to decay, it goes fascist."[23]

Many communists probably didn't buy the Trotskyite claim that committed socialists like Norman Thomas were no different from Adolf Hitler, but they were soon under orders to act like they did. In 1928, at Stalin's direction, the Third International advanced the doctrine of "social fascism," which held that there was really no difference between a Social Democrat and a Fascist or a Nazi. Fascism was "a fighting organization of the bourgeoisie, an organization that rests on the active support of social democracy [which] is the moderate wing of fascism." According to the theory of social fascism, a liberal democrat and a Nazi "do not contradict each other," but, in

Stalin's words, "complete each other. They are not antipodes but twins."[24] The strategy behind the doctrine of social fascism was as horribly misguided as the theory behind it. The thinking was that the center would not hold in Western democracies, and in a conflict between fascists and communists the communists would win. This was one reason—aside from a common outlook on most issues—that communists and Nazis tended to vote together in the Reichstag. The German Communists were operating under the Moscow-provided motto *"Nach Hitler, kommen wir"* ("After Hitler, we take over"). Or, "First Brown, then Red."

The doctrine of social fascism had two consequences that are directly relevant to our discussion. The first is that forever afterward, anyone who was against the far left was seen as being in league with the fascist far right. For decades, even after the launch of the Popular Front, if you were against the Soviet Union, you were open to the charge of being a fascist. Even Leon Trotsky—the co-founder of the Soviet state—was labeled a "Nazi agent" and the leader of a failed "fascist coup" the moment Stalin decided to get rid of him. Indeed, charges of rightism, fascism, and Nazism were leveled at countless victims of Stalin's purges. Eventually, the international left simply reserved for itself the absolute right to declare whomever it desired to delegitimize a Nazi or fascist without appeal to reason or fact. In time, as Nazism became synonymous with "ultimate evil," this became an incredibly useful cudgel, which is still wielded today.

The second consequence of the doctrine of social fascism was that it caused Hitler to win.

· 3 ·

Woodrow Wilson and the
Birth of Liberal Fascism

I T CAN'T HAPPEN here."

Any discussion of American fascism must get around this mossiest of political clichés. Most often used by leftists, it is typically also used sarcastically, as in: "George Bush is a crypto-Nazi racist stooge of the big corporations pursuing imperialist wars on the Third World to please his oil-soaked paymasters, but—yeah, right— 'it *can't* happen here' " (though Joe Conason in typically humorless fashion has titled his latest book *It Can Happen Here: Authoritarian Peril in the Age of Bush*).

The phrase, of course, comes from Sinclair Lewis's propagandistic novel of 1935. *It Can't Happen Here* tells the story of a fascist takeover of America, and it is, by general agreement, a terrible read, full of cartoonish characters, purple prose, and long canned speeches reminiscent of Soviet theater. But it wasn't seen that way when it was released. The *New Yorker,* for example, hailed it as "one of the most important books ever produced in this country . . . It is so crucial, so passionate, so honest, so vital that only dogmatists, schismatics, and reactionaries will care to pick flaws in it."[1]

The hero of the dystopian tale is the Vermont newspaperman Doremus Jessup, who describes himself as an "indolent and somewhat sentimental Liberal."[2] The villain, Senator Berzelius "Buzz" Windrip, is a charismatic blowhard—modeled on Senator Huey

Long—who is elected president in 1936. The plot is complicated, with fascist factions staging coups against an already fascist government, but the basic gist should be very appealing to liberals. A good Vermont liberal (a very different thing, however, from a Howard Dean liberal today), Jessup stages an underground insurrection, loses, flees to Canada, and is about to launch a big counterattack when the book ends.

The title derives from a prediction made by Jessup shortly before the fateful election. Jessup warns a friend that a Windrip victory will bring a "real Fascist dictatorship."

"Nonsense! Nonsense!" replies his friend. "That couldn't happen here in America, not possibly! We're a country of freemen . . . [I]t just can't happen here in America."

"The hell it can't," Jessup replies. And he is soon proven right.

The phrase and the phobia captured by *It Can't Happen Here* have been with us ever since. Most recently, Philip Roth's *Plot Against America* offered a better-written version of a similar scenario in which Charles Lindbergh defeats Franklin Roosevelt in 1940. But Roth's was just the latest in a long line of books and films that have played on this theme. Hollywood has been particularly keen on the idea that we must be eternally vigilant about the fascist beast lurking in the swamps of the political right.

The irony, of course, is that it *did* happen here, and Lewis virtually admits as much. In the same scene Jessup unleashes a gassy tirade about how America is ripe for a fascist takeover. His argument hinges on what happened in America during and immediately after World War I:

> Why, there's no country in the world that can get more hysterical—yes, or more obsequious!—than America . . . Remember our war hysteria, when we called sauerkraut "Liberty cabbage" and somebody actually proposed calling German measles "Liberty measles"? And wartime censorship of honest papers? Bad as Russia! . . . Remember our Red scares and our Catholic scares . . . Prohibition—shooting down people just because they *might* be transporting liquor—no, that couldn't happen in *America*! Why, where in all history has there ever been a people so ripe for a dictatorship as ours![3]

Lewis undersold his case. The period of liberty cabbage, wartime censorship, and propaganda wasn't an example of how America might someday be *ripe* for fascism. It was an example of how America had actually *endured* a fascistic dictatorship. If the events that transpired during and immediately after World War I occurred today in any Western nation, few educated people would fail to recognize it for what it was. Indeed, a great many educated people have convinced themselves that America under George W. Bush has nearly become "a thinly veiled military dictatorship," in the words of the writer Andrew Sullivan. The liberty cabbage, the state-sanctioned brutality, the stifling of dissent, the loyalty oaths and enemies lists—all of these things not only happened in America but happened at the hands of liberals. Self-described progressives—as well as the majority of American socialists—were at the forefront of the push for a truly totalitarian state. They applauded every crackdown and questioned the patriotism, intelligence, and decency of every pacifist and classically liberal dissenter.

Fascism, at its core, is the view that every nook and cranny of society should work together in spiritual union toward the same goals overseen by the state. "Everything in the State, nothing outside the State," is how Mussolini defined it. Mussolini coined the word "totalitarian" to describe not a tyrannical society but a humane one in which everyone is taken care of and contributes equally. It was an organic concept where every class, every individual, was part of the larger whole. The militarization of society and politics was considered simply the best available means toward this end. Call it what you like—progressivism, fascism, communism, or totalitarianism—the first true enterprise of this kind was established not in Russia or Italy or Germany but in the United States, and Woodrow Wilson was the twentieth century's first fascist dictator.

This claim may sound outrageous on its face, but consider the evidence. More dissidents were arrested or jailed in a few years under Wilson than under Mussolini during the entire 1920s. Wilson arguably did as much if not more violence to civil liberties in his last three years in office than Mussolini did in his first twelve. Wilson created a better and more effective propaganda ministry than Mussolini ever had. In the 1920s Mussolini's critics harangued him—rightly—for using his semiofficial Fascisti to bully the opposition and for his harassment of the press. Just a few years earlier, Wilson had unleashed literally hundreds of thousands of badge-carrying goons on the American people and prosecuted a vicious campaign against the press that would have made Mussolini envious.

Wilson didn't act alone. Like Mussolini and Hitler, he had an activist ideological movement at his disposal. In Italy they were called Fascists. In Germany they were called National Socialists. In America we called them progressives.

The progressives were the real social Darwinists as we think of the term today—though they reserved the term for their enemies (see Chapter 7). They believed in eugenics. They were imperialists. They were convinced that the state could, through planning and pressure, create a pure race, a society of new men. They were openly and proudly hostile to individualism. Religion was a political tool, while politics was the true religion. The progressives viewed the traditional system of constitutional checks and balances as an outdated imped-iment to progress because such horse-and-buggy institutions were a barrier to their own ambitions. Dogmatic attachment to constitu-tions, democratic practices, and antiquated laws was the enemy of progress for fascists and progressives alike. Indeed, fascists and pro-gressives shared the same intellectual heroes and quoted the same philosophers.

Today, liberals remember the progressives as do-gooders who cleaned up the food supply and agitated for a more generous social welfare state and better working conditions. Fine, the progressives did that. But so did the Nazis and the Italian Fascists. And they did it for the same reasons and in loyalty to roughly the same principles.

Historically, fascism is the product of democracy gone mad. In America we've chosen not to discuss the madness our Republic en-dured at Wilson's hands—even though we live with the conse-quences of it to this day. Like a family that pretends the father never drank too much and the mother never had a nervous breakdown, we've moved on as if it were all a bad dream we don't really remem-ber, even as we carry around the baggage of that dysfunction to this day. The motivation for this selective amnesia is equal parts shame, laziness, and ideology. In a society where Joe McCarthy must be the greatest devil of American history, it would not be convenient to mention that the George Washington of modern liberalism was the far greater inquisitor and that the other founding fathers of American liberalism were far crueler jingoists and warmongers than modern conservatives have ever been.

THE IDEALISM OF POWER WORSHIP

Thomas Woodrow Wilson was born in 1856, and his first memory was of hearing the terrible news that Abraham Lincoln had been elected president and that war was inevitable. The Wilsons were northern transplants from Ohio who lived in Georgia and South Carolina, but they quickly acclimated to southern ways. Joseph Wilson, a Presbyterian minister, served as a chaplain to Confederate troops and volunteered his church as a military hospital. Young Woodrow was a frail boy with terrible dyslexia who was mostly homeschooled and didn't learn how to read until the age of ten. Even after, study always required intense concentration. That he made a career as a prominent academic, let alone president of the United States, is a testament to his extraordinary patience, willpower, and ambition. But it all came at a terrible cost. He had virtually no close friends for most of his adult life, and he suffered from terrible stomach problems, including persistent constipation, nausea, and heartburn.

There's no disputing that a big part of Wilson's appeal, then and now, stemmed from the fact that he was the first Ph.D. to serve in the Oval Office. Of course, the White House was no stranger to great minds and great scholars. But Wilson was the first professional academic at a time when the professionalization of social science was considered a cornerstone of human progress. He was both a practitioner and a priest of the cult of expertise—the notion that human society was just another facet of the natural world and could be mastered by the application of the scientific method. A onetime president of the American Political Science Association, Wilson himself is widely credited with having launched the academic study of public administration, a fancy term for how to modernize and professionalize the state according to one's own personal biases.

Wilson started his academic career at Davidson College, but he was homesick and left before the end of his first year. In 1875, after another year of homeschooling from his father, he tried again. This time he enrolled at the College of New Jersey, which later became Princeton, to study politics and history. Wilson liked his new environment, in part because of the high number of southern Presbyterians, and he excelled there. He launched the Liberal Debating Society and served as editor of the school newspaper and secretary of the football association. Not surprisingly, the young Wilson got a taste for politics as he gained self-confidence and learned to like the sound of his own voice.

After graduating from Princeton, he enrolled at the University of Virginia to study law in hopes of one day entering politics. Homesickness and a lifelong difficulty making friends plagued him once again. He left UVA on Christmas Day of his first year, claiming he had a cold, and never returned. He finished his studies at home. After passing the Georgia bar, he spent a short time as a lawyer but found he didn't have the knack for it and concluded that it was too arduous a course for him to take into politics. Frustrated in his desire to become a statesman, Wilson enrolled at the recently established Johns Hopkins University, where he pursued his Ph.D. After graduating, he landed several teaching posts while he worked on his academic writing, specifically his widely acclaimed eight-hundred-page tome *The State*. Wilson eventually returned to the one institution where he had known some social happiness, Princeton University, where he rose to president.

Wilson's choice to head down an academic path should not be seen as an alternative to a political career. Rather, it was an alternative path to the career he always wanted. The Sage of New Jersey was never a reluctant statesman. Not long after finishing *The State,* Wilson began moving beyond narrow academic writing in favor of more popular commentary, generally geared toward enhancing his political profile. High among his regular themes was the advocacy of progressive imperialism in order to subjugate, and thereby elevate, lesser races. He applauded the annexation of Puerto Rico and the Philippines—"they are children and we are men in these deep matters of government and justice"—and regularly denounced what he called "the anti-imperialist weepings and wailings that came out of Boston."[4] It's a sign of how carefully he cultivated his political profile that four years before he "reluctantly" accepted the "unsolicited" gubernatorial nomination in New Jersey, *Harper's Weekly* had begun running the slogan "For President—Woodrow Wilson" on the cover of *every issue.*

Indeed, from his earliest days as an undergraduate the meek, homeschooled Wilson was infatuated with political power. And as is so common to intellectuals, he let his power worship infect his analysis.

Lord Acton's famous observation that "power tends to corrupt and absolute power corrupts absolutely" has long been misunderstood. Acton was not arguing that power causes powerful leaders to become corrupt (though he probably believed that, too). Rather, he was noting that historians tend to forgive the powerful for transgressions they would never condone by the weak. Wilson is guilty on both counts: he not only fawned over great men but, when he attained real power, was corrupted by it himself. Time and again, his sympathies came down on the side of great men who broke the traditional restraints on their power. Two of his biggest heroes were the Prussian chancellor Otto von Bismarck and Abraham Lincoln. It might seem odd that someone who fervently believed that giving blacks the right to vote was "the foundation of every evil in this country" would celebrate Lincoln. But what appealed to Wilson about the Great Emancipator was Lincoln's ability to impose his will on the entire country. Lincoln was a centralizer, a modernizer who used his power to forge a new, united nation. In other words, Wilson admired Lincoln's means—suspension of habeas corpus, the draft, and the campaigns of the radical Republicans after the war—far more than he liked his ends. "If any trait bubbles up in all one reads about Wilson," writes the historian Walter McDougall, "it is this: he loved, craved, and in a sense glorified power."[5]

Wilson's fascination with power is the leitmotif of his whole career. It informed his understanding of theology and politics, and their intersection. Power was God's instrument on earth and therefore was always to be revered. In *Congressional Government* he admitted, "I cannot imagine power as a thing negative and not positive." Such love of power can be found in many systems and men outside the orbit of fascism, but few ideologies or aesthetics are more directly concerned with the glory of might, will, strength, and action. Some of this was on display in fascist art and architecture, which wallowed in the powerful physical form and the unconquerable might of the nation: strength in unity, the triumph of will, the domination of destiny over decadence and indecision. Doctrinaire fascism, much like communism, sold itself as an unstoppable force of divine or historical inevitability. Those who stood in the way—the bourgeoisie, the "unfit," the "greedy," the "individualist," the traitor, the kulak, the Jew—could be demonized as the "other" because, at the end of the day, they were not merely expendable, nor were they merely reluctant to join the collective, they were by their very existence blocking the will to power that gave the mob and the avant-garde which claimed to speak for it their reason for existence. "Where this age differs from those immediately preceding it is that a liberal intelligentsia is lacking," wrote George Orwell. "Bully-worship, under various disguises, has become a universal religion."[6] For some, like Wilson, God gave a divine writ for bullying. For others the license for organized cruelty came from more impersonal historical forces. But the impulse was the same.

Wilson would later argue when president that he was the right hand of God and that to stand against him was to thwart divine will. Some thought this was simply proof of power corrupting Wilson, but this was his view from the outset. He always took the side of power, believing that power accrued to whoever was truly on God's side. As an undergraduate, Wilson was convinced that Congress was destined to wield the most power in the American system, and so he championed the idea of giving Congress unfettered control of governance. During his senior year, in his first published article, he even argued that America should switch to a parliamentary system, where there are fewer checks on the will of rulers. Wilson was a champion debater, so it's telling that he believed the best debaters should have the most power.

Wilson wrote his most famous and original work, *Congressional Government,* when he was a twenty-nine-year-old graduate student at Johns Hopkins. He set out to argue that America should switch to a centralized parliamentary system, but the work evolved into a sweeping indictment of the fragmentation and diffuseness of power in the American political system. Wilson fully abandoned his faith in congressional government when he witnessed Teddy Roosevelt's success at turning the Oval Office into a bully pulpit. The former advocate of congressional power became an unapologetic champion of the imperial presidency. "The President," he wrote in 1908 in *Constitutional Government in the United States,* "is at liberty, both in law and in conscience, to be as big a man as he can. His capacity will set the limit; and if Congress be overborne by him, it will be no fault of the makers of the Constitution, . . . but only because the President has the nation behind him and Congress has not."[7]

Wilson's view of politics could be summarized by the word "statolatry," or state worship (the same sin with which the Vatican charged Mussolini). Wilson believed that the state was a natural, organic, and spiritual expression of the people themselves. From the outset, he believed that the government and people should have an organic bond that reflected the "true spirit" of the people, or what the Germans called the *Volksgeist.* "Government is not a machine, but a living thing," he wrote in *Congressional Government.* "It falls not under the [Newtonian] theory of the universe, but under the [Darwinian] theory of organic life." From this perspective, the everexpanding power of the state was entirely natural. Wilson, along with the vast majority of progressive intellectuals, believed that the increase in state power was akin to an inevitable evolutionary process. Governmental "experimentation," the watchword of pragmatic liberals from Dewey and Wilson to FDR, was the social analogue to evolutionary adaptation. Constitutional democracy, as the founders understood it, was a momentary phase in this progression. Now it was time for the state to ascend to the next plateau. "Government," Wilson wrote approvingly in *The State,* "does now whatever experience permits or the times demand."[8] Wilson was the first president to speak disparagingly of the Constitution.

Wilson reinforced such attitudes by attacking the very idea of natural and individual rights. If the original, authentic state was a dictatorial family, Wilson argued in the spirit of Darwin, what historical basis was there to believe in individual rights? "No doubt," he wrote, taking dead aim at the Declaration of Independence, "a lot of nonsense has been talked about the inalienable rights of the individual, and a great deal that was mere vague sentiment and pleasing speculation has been put forward as fundamental principle." If a law couldn't be executed, it wasn't a real law, according to Wilson, and "abstract rights" were vexingly difficult to execute.

Wilson, of course, was merely one voice in the progressive chorus of the age. "[W]e must demand that the individual shall be willing to lose the sense of personal achievement, and shall be content to realize his activity only in connection to the activity of the many," declared the progressive social activist Jane Addams. "Now men are free," explained Walter Rauschenbusch, a leading progressive theologian of the Social Gospel movement, in 1896, "but it is often the freedom of grains of sand that are whirled up in a cloud and then dropped in a heap, but neither cloud nor sand-heap have any coherence." The remedy was obvious: "New forms of association must be created. Our disorganized competitive life must pass into an organic cooperative life." Elsewhere Rauschenbusch put it more simply: "Individualism means tyranny."[9] In a sense, the morally inverted nonsense made famous by Herbert Marcuse in the 1960s—"oppressive freedom," "repressive tolerance," "defensive violence"—was launched by the progressives decades earlier. "Work makes you free," the phrase made famous by the Nazis, was anticipated by progressives who believed that collectivism was the new "freedom."

America is today in the midst of an obscene moral panic over the role of Christians in public life. There is a profound irony in the fact that such protests issue most loudly from self-professed "progressives" when the real progressives were dedicated in the most fundamental way to the Christianization of American life. Progressivism, as the title of Washington Gladden's book suggested, was "applied Christianity." The Social Gospel held that the state was the right arm of God and was the means by which the whole nation and world would be redeemed. But while Christianity was being made into a true state religion, its transcendent and theological elements became corrupted.

These two visions—Darwinian organicism and Christian messianism—seem contradictory today because they reside on different sides of the culture war. But in the Progressive Era, these visions complemented each other perfectly. And Wilson embodied this synthesis. The totalitarian flavor of such a worldview should be obvious. Unlike classical liberalism, which saw the government as a necessary evil, or simply a benign but voluntary social contract for free men to enter into willingly, the belief that the entire society was one organic whole left no room for those who didn't want to behave, let alone "evolve." Your home, your private thoughts, everything was part of the organic body politic, which the state was charged with redeeming.

Hence a phalanx of progressive reformers saw the home as the front line in the war to transform men into compliant social organs. Often the answer was to get children out of the home as quickly as possible. An archipelago of agencies, commissions, and bureaus sprang up overnight to take the place of the anti-organic, contra-evolutionary influences of the family. The home could no longer be seen as an island, separate and sovereign from the rest of society. John Dewey helped create kindergartens in America for precisely this purpose—to shape the apples before they fell from the tree—while at the other end of the educational process stood reformers like Wilson, who summarized the progressive attitude perfectly when, as president of Princeton, he told an audience, "Our problem is not merely to help the students to adjust themselves to world life . . . [but] to make them as unlike their fathers as we can."[10]

If the age of parliamentary democracy was coming to an end—as progressives and fascists alike proclaimed—and the day of the organic redeemer state was dawning, then the Constitution must evolve or be thrown into the dustbin of history. Wilson's writings are chock-ablock with demands that the "artificial" barriers established in our "antiquated" eighteenth-century system of checks and balances be smashed. He mocked the "Fourth of July sentiments" of those who still invoked the founding fathers as a source for constitutional guidance. He believed the system of governmental checks and balances had "proven mischievous just to the extent to which they have succeeded in establishing themselves as realities."[11] Indeed, the ink from Wilson's pen regularly exudes the odor of what we today call the living Constitution. On the campaign trail in 1912, Wilson explained that "living political constitutions must be Darwinian in structure and in practice. Society is a living organism and must obey the laws of Life . . . it must develop." Hence "all that progressives ask or desire is permission—in an era when 'development,' 'evolution,' is the scientific word—to interpret the Constitution according to the Darwinian principle."[12] As we've seen, this interpretation leads to a system where the Constitution means whatever the reigning interpreters of "evolution" say it means.

A more authentic form of leadership was needed: a great man who could serve both as the natural expression of the people's will and as a guide and master checking their darker impulses. The leader needed to be like a brain, which both regulates the body and depends on it for protection. To this end, the masses had to be subservient to the will of the leader. In his unintentionally chilling 1890 essay, *Leaders of Men,* Wilson explained that the "true leader" uses the masses like "tools." He must not traffic in subtleties and nuance, as literary men do. Rather, he must speak to stir their passions, not their intellects. In short, he must be a skillful demagogue.

"Only a very gross substance of concrete conception can make any impression on the minds of the masses," Wilson wrote. "They must get their ideas very absolutely put, and are much readier to receive a half truth which they can promptly understand than a whole truth which has too many sides to be seen all at once. The competent leader of men cares little for the internal niceties of other people's characters: he cares much—everything—for the external uses to which they may be put . . . He supplies the power; others supply only the materials upon which that power operates . . . It is the power which dictates, dominates; the materials yield. Men are as clay in the hands of the consummate leader."[13] A cynic might concede that there is much truth in Wilson's interpretation, but he would at least acknowledge his own cynicism. Wilson believed he was an idealist.

Many believed, including Wilson, that they had found just such a figure in Theodore Roosevelt. More than a popular leader, he was the designated idol of a true leadership cult. William Allen White, the famed progressive writer, recalled in 1934 that he'd been "a young arrogant protagonist of the divine rule of the plutocracy" until Roosevelt "shattered the foundations of my political ideals. As they crumbled then and there, politically, I put his heel on my neck and I became his man."[14] Roosevelt was the first to translate *"L'état, c'est moi"* into the American argot, often claiming that the nation's sovereignty was indistinguishable from his own august personage. As president, he regularly exceeded the bounds of his traditional and legal powers, doing his will first and waiting (or not) for the courts and the legislatures to catch up.

This captured in small relief the basic difference between Wilson and Teddy Roosevelt, bitter rivals and the only two proudly progressive presidents of the Progressive Era. These were very different men with very similar ideas. Roosevelt was a great actor upon the world stage; Wilson saw himself more as a director. Roosevelt was the "bull moose" who charged into any problem; Wilson was the "schoolmaster" who first drew up a lesson plan. One wanted to lead a band of brothers, the other a graduate seminar. But if the roles they played were different, the moral of the story was the same. While Wilson wrote treatises explaining why Americans should abandon their "blind devotion" to the Constitution, Teddy was rough-riding all over the document, doing what he pleased and giving bellicose speeches about how the courts had sided against "popular rights" and were "lagging behind" the new realities. Indeed, William Howard Taft—Roosevelt's honorable yet overwhelmed successor in the White House—might not have chosen to run for reelection, hence denying Roosevelt the Republican nomination, had he not been convinced that Roosevelt's "impatience with the delay of the law" made him "not unlike Napoleon."[15]

There were many fault lines running through Progressivism. On one side, there were the likes of John Dewey and Jane Addams, who were more socialistic and academic in their approach to politics and policy. On the other were the nationalists who appealed more directly to patriotism and militarism. Wilson and Roosevelt more or less represented the two sides. In much the same way national socialists often split into two camps emphasizing either nationalism or socialism, some progressives concentrated on social reform while others were more concerned with American "greatness."

One might also put it that Roosevelt reflected the masculine side of Progressivism—the daddy party—while Wilson represented the movement's maternal side. Roosevelt certainly trumpeted the "manly virtues" at every opportunity. He wanted a ruling elite drawn from a (metaphorical) warrior caste that embraced the "strenuous life," a meritocracy of vigor dedicated to defeating the decadence of "soft living." Wilson's ruling elite would be drawn from the ranks of "disinterested" technocrats, bureaucrats, and social workers who understood the root causes of social decay.

Few progressives saw these as opposing values. There was no inherent trade-off between militant nationalism and progressive reform; rather, they complemented each other (a similar complementarity existed between the different branches of progressive eugenicists, as we'll see). Consider, for example, Senator Albert J. Beveridge, the most important progressive in the U.S. Senate during the first decade of the twentieth century. When Upton Sinclair's *Jungle* exposed the horrors of the meatpacking industry, it was Beveridge who led the fight for reform, sponsoring the Meat Inspection Act of 1906. He shepherded the fights against child labor and in favor of the eight-hour workday. He was perhaps Teddy Roosevelt's chief senatorial ally in the progressive insurgency against the "conservative" wing of the Republican Party. He was the bane of special interests, railroad magnates, and trusts and the friend of reformers, conservationists, and moderns everywhere. And he was a thoroughly bloodthirsty imperialist. "The opposition tells us we ought not to rule a people without their consent. I answer, the rule of liberty, that all just governments derive their authority from the consent of the governed, applies only to those who are capable of self-government."[16] Indeed, the progressives in Congress actively supported or went along with virtually every major military excursion of the Roosevelt and Taft administrations. Under Wilson, they were decidedly more hawkish than the White House. All the while it fell to the *conservatives* in Congress to fight expenditures on such things as the "big navy," the cornerstone of the imperial project. Indeed, it must be understood that imperialism was as central to Progressivism as efforts to clean up the food supply or make factories safe.[17]

The 1912 election boiled down to a national referendum on the sort of Progressivism America wanted, or at least the sort of Progressivism it would get. The beleaguered incumbent, William Howard Taft, had never wanted to be president. His real dream—which he later accomplished—was to be chief justice of the Supreme Court. Taft meant it when he said he was the conservative in the race. He was a *conservative liberal*—among the last of a dying breed. He believed classical liberalism—or his fairly worldly version of it—needed to be defended against ideologues who would read their own will into the law.

Today the issues in the 1912 campaign seem narrow and distant. Wilson championed the "New Freedom," which included what he called the "second struggle for emancipation"—this time from the trusts and big corporations. Roosevelt campaigned on the "New Nationalism," which took a different view of corporations. Teddy, the famous trustbuster, had resigned himself to "bigness" and now believed the state should use the trusts for its own purposes rather than engage in an endless and fruitless battle to break them up. "The effort at prohibiting all combination has substantially failed," he explained. "The way out lies, not in attempting to prevent such combinations, but in completely controlling them in the interest of the public welfare." Teddy's New Nationalism was equal parts nationalism and socialism. "The New Nationalism," Roosevelt proclaimed, "rightly maintains that every man holds his property subject to the general right of the community to regulate its use to whatever degree the public welfare may require it." This sort of rhetoric conjured fears among classical liberals (again, increasingly called conservatives) that Teddy would ride roughshod over American liberties. "Where will it all end?" asked the liberal editor of the New York *World* about the rush to centralize government power. "Despotism? Caesarism?"[18]

Huey Long famously said—or allegedly famously said—that if fascism ever came to America it would be called "Americanism." It's interesting, then, that this is the name Teddy Roosevelt gave to his new ideology. Not everyone was blind to this distressing side of Roosevelt's personality. The America "that Roosevelt dreamed of was always a sort of swollen Prussia, truculent without and regimented within," declared H. L. Mencken. Deriding Roosevelt as a "Tammany Nietzsche" who'd converted to the "religion of militarists," Mencken scored him for stressing "the duty of the citizen to the state, with the soft pedal upon the duty of the state to the citizen."[19]

In this context, Wilson was perceived as the somewhat more conservative candidate—because, again, he was closer to nineteenth-century laissez-faire liberalism. He promised to limit government's ability to centralize power by corralling industry into the same bed as the state. In a famous campaign speech at the New York Press Club he proclaimed, "The history of liberty is the history of the limitation of government power." Alas, it is difficult to take his liberty-loving rhetoric too seriously. Just two weeks after his Press Club speech, Wilson returned to his progressive antipathy toward individualism: "While we are followers of Jefferson, there is one principle of Jefferson's which no longer can obtain in the practical politics of America. You know that it was Jefferson who said that the best government is that which does as little governing as possible . . . *But that time is passed. America is not now and cannot in the future be a place for unrestricted individual enterprise.*"[20]

Since Wilson ended up governing largely as a New Nationalist, the subtler distinctions between his and Roosevelt's platforms do not matter very much for our purposes. America was going to get a progressive president no matter what in 1912. And while those of us with soft spots for Teddy might like to think things would have turned out very differently had he won, we are probably deluding ourselves.

HOW IT HAPPENED HERE

The prevailing assumption today is that the rise of fascism in Europe transpired on a completely independent track—that due to numerous national and cultural differences between America and Europe, it *couldn't happen here.* But this makes no sense whatsoever. Progressivism and, later, fascism were international movements—and, in their origin, expressions of great hopes—that assumed different forms in different countries but drew on the same intellectual wellsprings. Many of the ideas and thinkers the Fascists and Nazis admired were as influential here as they were in Italy and Germany, and vice versa. For example, Henry George, the radical populist guru of American reform, was more revered in Europe than he was in America. His ideas gave shape to the *völkisch* economic theories on which the Nazi Party was initially founded. Among British Socialists, his *Progress and Poverty* was a sensation. When Marx's son-in-law came to America to proselytize for scientific socialism, he was so enamored of George that he returned to Europe preaching the gospel of American populism.

From the 1890s to World War I, it was simply understood that progressives in America were fighting the same fight as the various socialist and "new liberal" movements of Europe.[21] William Allen White, the famed Kansas progressive, declared in 1911, "We were parts, one of another, in the United States and Europe. Something was welding us into one social and economic whole with local political variations. It was Stubbs in Kansas, Jaurès in Paris, the Social Democrats [that is, the Socialists] in Germany, the Socialists in Belgium, and I should say the whole people in Holland, fighting a common cause." When Jane Addams seconded Teddy Roosevelt's nomination at the Progressive Party Convention in 1912, she declared, "The new party has become the American exponent of a world-wide movement toward juster social conditions, a movement which the United States, lagging behind other great nations, has been unaccountably slow to embody in political action."[22]

Ultimately, however, America was the sorcerer's apprentice to Europe's master. American writers and activists drank from European intellectual wells like men dying of thirst. "Nietzsche is in the air," declared a reviewer in the *New York Times* in 1910. "Whatever one reads of a speculative kind one is sure to come across the name of Nietzsche sooner or later." Indeed, he went on, "[m]uch of the Pragmatism of Prof. [William] James bears auspicious resemblance to doctrines of Nietzsche." Noticing that Roosevelt was always reading German books and "borrowing" from Nietzsche's philosophy, Mencken (a serious, if imperfect, Nietzsche scholar himself) concluded, "Theodore had swallowed Friedrich as a peasant swallows Peruna—bottle, cork, label and testimonials."[23] William James, America's preeminent philosopher, looked to the southern corners of the continent as well. As discussed earlier, James was a close student of the Italian pragmatists who were busy laying the groundwork for Mussolini's Fascism, and Mussolini would regularly acknowledge his debt to James and American Pragmatism.

But no nation influenced American thinking more profoundly than Germany. W. E. B. DuBois, Charles Beard, Walter Weyl, Richard Ely, Nicholas Murray Butler, and countless other founders of modern American liberalism were among the nine thousand Americans who studied in German universities during the nineteenth century. When the American Economic Association was formed, five of the six first officers had studied in Germany. At least twenty of its first twenty-six presidents had as well. In 1906 a professor at Yale polled the top 116 economists and social scientists in America; more than half had studied in Germany for at least a year. By their own testimony, these intellectuals felt "liberated" by the experience of studying in an intellectual environment predicated on the assumption that experts could mold society like clay.[24]

No European statesman loomed larger in the minds and hearts of American progressives than Otto von Bismarck. As inconvenient as it may be for those who have been taught "the continuity between Bismarck and Hitler," writes Eric Goldman, Bismarck's Germany was "a catalytic of American progressive thought." Bismarck's "top-down socialism," which delivered the eight-hour workday, health care, social insurance, and the like, was the gold standard for enlightened social policy. "Give the working-man the right to work as long as he is healthy; assure him care when he is sick; assure him maintenance when he is old," he famously told the Reichstag in 1862. Bismarck was the original "Third Way" figure who triangulated between both ends of the ideological spectrum. "A government must not waver once it has chosen its course. It must not look to the left or right but go forward," he proclaimed. Teddy Roosevelt's 1912 national Progressive Party platform conspicuously borrowed from the Prussian model. Twenty-five years earlier, the political scientist Woodrow Wilson wrote that Bismarck's welfare state was an "admirable system . . . the most studied and most nearly perfected" in the world.[25]

Indeed, few figures represent the foreign, particularly German influence on Progressivism better than Wilson himself. Wilson's faith that society could be bent to the will of social planners was formed at Johns Hopkins, the first American university to be founded on the German model. Virtually all of Wilson's professors had studied in Germany—as had almost every one of the school's fifty-three faculty members. But his most prominent and influential teacher was Richard Ely, the "dean of American economics," who in his day was more vital to Progressivism than Milton Friedman or Friedrich Hayek have been to modern conservatism. Despite his open hostility to private property, and his fondness for what would today be called McCarthyite politics, Ely was not a top-down socialist like Bismarck. Rather, he taught his students to imagine a socialism of spirit that would replace laissez-faire from within men's hearts. Ely eventually moved to the University of Wisconsin, where he helped found the "Wisconsin model"—a system still admired by leftist intellectuals whereby college faculties help run the state. Ely also served as a mentor to Teddy Roosevelt, who said that Ely "first introduced me to radicalism in economics and then made me sane in my radicalism."[26]

Wilson revered Bismarck as much as Teddy Roosevelt or any of the other Progressives did. In college he wrote a fawning essay in which he lavished praise on this "commanding genius" who united the "moral force of Cromwell and the political shrewdness of Richelieu; the comprehensive intellect of Burke . . . the diplomatic ability of Talleyrand, without his coldness." Wilson goes on about the Iron Chancellor's "keenness of insight, clearness of judgement, and promptness of decision," and ends wistfully, "Prussia will not soon find another Bismarck."[27]

Bismarck's motive was to forestall demands for more democracy by giving the people the sort of thing they might ask for at the polls. His top-down socialism was a Machiavellian masterstroke because it made the middle class dependent upon the state. The middle class took away from this the lesson that enlightened government was not the *product* of democracy but an *alternative* to it. Such logic proved disastrous little more than a generation later. But it was precisely this logic that appealed to the progressives. As Wilson put it, the essence of Progressivism was that the individual "marry his interests to the state."[28]

The most influential thinker along these lines—and another great admirer of Bismarck's—was the man who served as the intellectual bridge between Roosevelt and Wilson: Herbert Croly, the author of *The Promise of American Life,* the founding editor of the *New Republic,* and the guru behind Roosevelt's New Nationalism.

After Taft was elected president in 1908, Roosevelt tried to give his protégé a wide berth, first going on a famous African safari, followed by a fact-finding tour of Europe. At some point he picked up a copy of *The Promise of American Life,* which his friend Judge Learned Hand had sent him. The book was a revelation. "I do not know when I have read a book which profited me as much," he wrote to Croly. "All I wish is that I were better able to get my advice to my fellow-countrymen in practical shape according to the principles you set forth."[29] Many people at the time credited Croly's book with convincing Roosevelt to run for president again; more likely, the book provided a marketable intellectual rationale for his return to politics.

Even if Croly's contribution to American liberalism had begun and ended with *The Promise of American Life,* he would rank as one of the most important voices in American intellectual history. When the book came out in 1909, Felix Frankfurter hailed it as "the most powerful single contribution to progressive thinking."[30] The book was praised by dozens of reviewers. More than any other writer, Croly was credited with giving a coherent voice to the progressive movement and, by extension, modern liberalism. It has been celebrated ever since by liberals, even though most of them have probably never read this long, bizarre, often tedious, tortuous tome. Indeed, the fact that it is such a badly written book may be the sign that its appeal rested on something more important than its prose: it gave form to an idea whose time had come.

Croly was a quiet man who'd grown up with noisy parents. His mother was one of America's first female syndicated columnists and a dedicated "feminist." His father was a successful journalist and editor whose friends dubbed him "The Great Suggester." Their home was something of a "European island in New York," according to one historian.[31] The most interesting thing about the senior Croly—if by "interesting" you mean really loopy—was his obsession with Auguste Comte, a semimystical French philosopher whose biggest claim to fame was his coinage of the word "sociology." Comte argued that humanity progressed in three stages and that in the final stage mankind would throw off Christianity and replace it with a new "religion of humanity," which married religious fervor to science and reason—even to the extent of making "saints" out of such figures as Shakespeare, Dante, and Frederick the Great.[32] Comte believed that the age of mass industrialization and technocracy would pluck the human mind from the metaphysical realm for good, ushering in an age where pragmatic managers would improve the plight of all based upon man-made morality. He anointed himself the high priest of this atheistic, secular faith, which he called positivism. The elder Croly made his Greenwich Village home into a positivist temple where he held religious ceremonies for select guests, whom he would try to convert. In 1869 young Herbert became the first and probably last American to be christened in Comte's religion.

Croly attended Harvard University, though due to family and personal problems he was absent for long stints. While there he studied closely under William James as well as Josiah Royce and George Santayana. From James, he learned to think pragmatically. Thanks to Royce he converted from positivism to progressive Christianity. Santayana persuaded him of the need for a "national regeneration" and a new "socialistic aristocracy." The result of all these influences was a brilliant young man who was capable of remarkable hardheadedness while never losing his mystical zeal. He was also a fascist. Or at least he was an exponent of a pre-fascist worldview that would seem prescient just a few years later.

When reading about Herbert Croly, one often finds phrases such as "Croly was no fascist, but . . ." Yet few make the effort to explain *why* he was not a fascist. Most seem to think it is simply self-evident that the founder of the *New Republic* could not have been a disciple of Mussolini's. In reality, however, almost every single item on a standard checklist of fascist characteristics can be found in *The Promise of American Life*. The need to mobilize society like an army? Check! Call for spiritual rebirth? Check! Need for "great" revolutionary leaders? Check! Reliance on manufactured, unifying, national "myths"? Check! Contempt for parliamentary democracy? Check! Non-Marxist Socialism? Check! Nationalism? Check! A spiritual calling for military expansion? Check! The need to make politics into a religion? Hostility to individualism? Check! Check! Check! To paraphrase Whittaker Chambers: from almost any page of *The Promise of American Life,* a voice can be heard, from painful necessity, commanding, "To fascism go!"

Croly was an unabashed nationalist who craved a "national reformer . . . in the guise of St. Michael, armed with a flaming sword and winged for flight," to redeem a decadent America. This secular "imitator of Christ" would bring an end to "devil-take-the-hindmost" individualism in precisely the same manner that the real Jesus closed the Old Testament chapter of human history. "An individual," Croly wrote, sounding very much like Wilson, "has no meaning apart from the society in which his individuality has been formed." Echoing both Wilson and Theodore Roosevelt, Croly argued that "national life" should be like a "school," and good schooling frequently demands "severe coercive measures."[33]

Croly's ideas garnered the attention of Willard Straight, an investment banker with J. P. Morgan and a diplomat, and his wife,

Dorothy, a member of the Whitney family. The Straights were prominent philanthropists and reformers, and they saw in Croly's ideas a map for the transformation of America into a "progressive democracy" (the title of another of Croly's books). They agreed to support Croly in his effort to start the *New Republic,* a journal whose mission was "to explore and develop and apply the ideas which had been advertised by Theodore Roosevelt when he was the leader of the Progressive party."[34] Joining Croly as editors were the self-described socialist-nationalists Walter Weyl and the future pundit extraordinaire Walter Lippmann.

Like Roosevelt, Croly and his colleagues looked forward to many more wars because war was the midwife of progress. Indeed, Croly believed that the Spanish-American War's greatest significance lay in the fact that it gave birth to Progressivism. In Europe wars would force more national unification, while in Asia wars were necessary for imperial expansion and for the powerful nations to let off a little steam. Croly constructed this worldview out of what he deemed vital necessity. Industrialization, economic upheaval, social "disintegration," materialistic decadence, and worship of money were tearing America apart, or so he—and the vast majority of progressives—believed. The remedy for the "chaotic individualism of our political and economic organization" was a "regeneration" led by a hero-saint who could overthrow the tired doctrines of liberal democracy in favor of a restored and heroic nation. The similarities with conventional fascist theory should be obvious.[35]

One might defend Croly by noting that such ideas were simply "in the air" at the end of the nineteenth century, a common set of responses to a common atmosphere of social, economic, and political change. And indeed, *this is part of my argument.* There were of course significant differences between fascism and Progressivism, but these are mainly attributable to the cultural differences between Europe and America, and between national cultures in general. (When Mussolini invited the leader of the Falange Española—the Spanish fascists—to the first Fascist congress, he adamantly refused. The Falange, he insisted, was not fascist, it was Spanish!)

Fascism was one name given to one form of "experimentation" in the 1920s. These experiments were part of the great utopian aspirations of the "world-wide movement" Jane Addams spoke of at the

Progressive Party Convention. There was a religious awakening afoot in the West as progressives of all stripes saw man snatching the reins of history from God's hands. Science—or what they believed to be science—was the new scripture, and one could only perform science by "experimenting." And, just as important, only scientists know how to conduct a proper experiment. "Who will be the prophets and pilots of the Good Society?" Herbert Croly asked in 1925. He noted that for a generation progressive liberals believed that a "better future would derive from the beneficent activities of expert social engineers who would bring to the service of social ideals all the technical resources which research could discover and ingenuity could devise." Five years earlier, Croly noted in the *New Republic* that the practitioners of the "scientific method" would need to join with the "ideologists" of Christ, in order to "plan and effect a redeeming transformation" of society whereby men would look for "deliverance from choice between unredeemed capitalism and revolutionary salvation."[36]

To better understand the spirit of this fascist moment, we need to examine how progressives looked to two other great "experiments" of the age, Italian Fascism and Russian Bolshevism. Some of this was touched upon in Chapter 1, but it's worth repeating: liberals often saw Mussolini's project and Lenin's as linked efforts. Lincoln Steffens referred to the "Russian-Italian" method as if the two things constituted a single enterprise.

The *New Republic* in particular was at times decidedly optimistic about *both* experiments. Some seemed more excited about the Italian effort. Charles Beard, for example, wrote of Mussolini's efforts:

This is far from the frozen dictatorship of the Russian Tsardom; it is more like the American check and balance system; and it may work out in a new democratic direction . . . Beyond question, an amazing experiment is being made here, an experiment in reconciling individualism and socialism, politics and technology. It would be a mistake to allow feeling aroused by contemplating the harsh deeds and extravagant assertions that have accompanied the Fascist process (as all other immense historical changes) to obscure the potentialities and the lessons of the adventure—no, not adventure, but destiny riding without any saddle and bridle across the historic peninsula that bridges the world of antiquity and our modern world.[37]

Such enthusiasm paled in comparison to the way progressives greeted the "experiment" in the Soviet Union. Indeed, many of the remaining left-wing footdraggers on the war became enthusiastic supporters when they learned of the Bolshevik Revolution. Suddenly Wilson's revolutionary rhetoric seemed to be confirmed by the forces of history (indeed, Wilson himself saw the earlier fall of the tsar to the Kerensky government as the last obstacle to U.S. entry into the war, since he would no longer have a despotic regime as an ally). A wave of crusading journalists went to Moscow to chronicle the revolution and convince American liberals that history was on the march in Russia.

John Reed led the charge with his *Ten Days That Shook the World*. Reed was an unreconstructed admirer of the Bolsheviks. He dismissed complaints about the Red Terror and the mass murder of non-Bolshevist socialist revolutionaries easily: "I don't give a damn for their past. I'm concerned only with what this treacherous gang has been doing during the past three years. To the wall with them! I say I have learned one mighty expressive word: '*raztrellyat*' [*sic*] (execute by shooting)." The progressive public intellectual E. A. Ross—who will reappear in our story later—took a common tack and argued that the Bolsheviks had killed relatively few members of the opposition, so it really wasn't a big deal.[38] Reed and Ross at least acknowledged that the Bolsheviks were killing people. Many pro-Bolshevik liberals simply refused to concede that the Red Terror even transpired. This was the beginning of nearly a century of deliberate lies and useful idiocy on the American left.

When the Bolsheviks overthrew the Kerensky government, Wilson's refusal to recognize them—and his subsequent intervention in Siberia and Murmansk—were denounced as "Wilson's stab in Russia's back" because most liberals saw the Bolsheviks as a popular and progressive movement. One British journalist writing in the *New Republic* proclaimed the Bolsheviks "stand for rationalism, for an intelligent system of cultivation, for education, for an active ideal of cooperation and social service against superstition, waste, illiteracy, and passive obedience." As the historian Eugene Lyons noted, these crusaders "wrote as inspired prophets of an embattled revolution . . . they were dazzled by a vision of things to come."[39]

To be sure, not all left-leaning observers were fooled by the Bolsheviks. Bertrand Russell famously saw through the charade, as did the American socialist Charles E. Russell. But most progressives believed that the Bolsheviks had stumbled on the passage out of the old world and that we should follow their lead. When the war ended and Progressivism had been discredited with the American people, the intellectuals looked increasingly to the Soviet Union and Fascist Italy as exemplars of the new path that America had foolishly abandoned after its brilliant experiment with war socialism.

Nearly the entire liberal elite, including much of FDR's Brain Trust, had made the pilgrimage to Moscow to take admiring notes on the Soviet experiment. Their language was both religiously prophetic and arrogantly scientific. Stuart Chase reported after visiting Russia in 1927 that unlike in America, where "hungry stockholders" were making the economic decisions, in the Soviet Union the all-caring state was in the saddle, "informed by battalions of statistics" and heroically aided by Communist Party officials who need "no further incentive than the burning zeal to create a new heaven and a new earth which flames in the breast of every good Communist."[40]

That same year two of America's leading New Deal economists, Rexford Guy Tugwell and Paul Douglas, pronounced themselves awed by the Soviet "experiment." "There is a new life beginning there," Tugwell wrote in his report. Lillian Wald visited Russia's "experimental schools" and reported that John Dewey's ideas were being implemented "not less than 150 per cent." Indeed, the whole country was, for liberals, a giant "Laboratory School." Dewey himself visited the Soviet Union and was much impressed. Jane Addams declared the Bolshevik endeavor "the greatest social experiment in history." Sidney Hillman, John L. Lewis, and most of the other leaders of the American labor movement were effusive in their praise of "Soviet pragmatism," Stalin's "experiment," and the "heroism" of the Bolsheviks.[41]

W. E. B. DuBois was thunderstruck. "I am writing this in Russia," he wrote back to his readers in the *Crisis*. "I am sitting in Revolution Square . . . I stand in astonishment and wonder at the revelation of

Russia that has come to me. I may be partially deceived and half-informed. But if what I have seen with my eyes and heard with my ears in Russia is Bolshevism, I am a Bolshevik."[42]

DuBois offers a good illustration of how fascism and communism appealed to the same progressive impulses and aspirations. Like many progressives, he'd studied in Germany in the 1890s and retained a fondness for the Prussian model. An anti-Semite early in his career—in 1924 his magazines started carrying a swastika on the cover, despite complaints from Jewish progressives—DuBois applied for a grant in 1935 from an organization with known ties to the Nazis that was run by a well-known Jew hater who'd dined with Joseph Goebbels. He truly believed the Nazis had a lot of great ideas and that America had much to learn from Germany's experiment in National Socialism (though later, DuBois denounced Nazi anti-Semitism).

And so it was with other pro-Soviet liberal icons. Recall how a year before Lincoln Steffens announced he'd seen the future in the Soviet Union, he'd said much the same thing about Fascist Italy. The heroic success of fascism, according to Steffens, made Western democracy—run by "petty persons with petty purposes"—look pathetic by comparison. For Steffens and countless other liberals, Mussolini, Lenin, and Stalin were all doing the same thing: transforming corrupt, outdated societies. Tugwell praised Lenin as a pragmatist who was merely running an "experiment." The same was true of Mussolini, he explained.

The *New Republic* defended both fascism and communism on similar grounds throughout the 1920s. How, a correspondent asked, could the magazine think Mussolini's brutality was a "good thing"? Croly answered that it was not, "any more than it was a 'good thing' for the United States, let us say, to cement their Union by waging a civil war which resulted in the extermination of slavery. But sometimes a nation drifts into a predicament from which it can be rescued only by the adoption of a violent remedy."[43]

Charles Beard summed up the fascination well. Il Duce's hostility to democracy was no big deal, he explained. After all, the "fathers of the American Republic, notably Hamilton, Madison, and John Adams, were as voluminous and vehement [in opposing democracy] as any Fascist could desire." Mussolini's dictatorial style was likewise perfectly consistent with the "American gospel of action, action, action." But what really captured Beard's imagination was the economic system inherent to fascism, namely corporatism. According to Beard, Mussolini had succeeded in bringing about "by force of the State the most compact and unified organization of capitalists and laborers into two camps which the world has ever seen."[44]

The key concept for rationalizing progressive utopianism was "experimentation," justified in the language of Nietzschean authenticity, Darwinian evolution, and Hegelian historicism and explained in the argot of William James's pragmatism. Scientific knowledge advanced by trial and error. Human evolution advanced by trial and error. History, according to Hegel, progressed through the interplay of thesis and antithesis. These experiments were the same process on a vast scale. So what if Mussolini cracked skulls or Lenin lined up dissident socialists? The progressives believed they were participating in a process of ascendance to a more modern, more "evolved" way of organizing society, replete with modern machines, modern medicine, modern politics. In a distinctly American way, Wilson was as much a pioneer of this movement as Mussolini. A devoted Hegelian—he even invoked Hegel in a love letter to his wife—Wilson believed that history was a scientific, unfolding process. Darwinism was the perfect complement to such thinking because it seemed to confirm that the "laws" of history were reflected in our natural surroundings. "In our own day," Wilson wrote while still a political scientist, "whenever we discuss the structure or development of a thing . . . we consciously or unconsciously follow Mr. Darwin."[45]

Wilson won the election of 1912 in an electoral college landslide, but with only 42 percent of the popular vote. He immediately set about to convert the Democratic Party into a progressive party and, in turn, make it the engine for a transformation of America. In January 1913 he vowed to "pick out progressives and only progressives" for his administration. "No one," he proclaimed in his inaugural address, "can mistake the purpose for which the Nation now seeks to use the Democratic Party . . . I summon all honest men, all patriotic, all forward-looking men, to my side. I will not fail them, if they will but counsel and sustain me!" But he warned elsewhere, "If you are not a progressive . . . you better look out."[46]

Without the sorts of mandates or national emergencies other liberal presidents enjoyed, Wilson's considerable legislative success is largely attributable to intense party discipline. In an unprecedented move, he kept Congress in continual session for a year and a half, something even Lincoln hadn't done during the Civil War. Sounding every bit the Crolyite, he converted almost completely to the New Nationalism he had recently denounced, claiming he wanted no "antagonism between business and government."[47] In terms of domestic policy, Wilson was successful in winning the support of progressives in all parties. But he failed to win over Roosevelt's followers when it came to foreign policy. Despite imperialist excursions throughout the Americas, Wilson was deemed too soft. Senator Albert Beveridge, who had led the progressives to their greatest legislative successes in the Senate, denounced Wilson for refusing to send troops to defend American interests in China or install a strongman in Mexico. Increasingly, the core of the Progressive Party became almost entirely devoted to "preparedness"—shorthand for a big military buildup and imperial assertiveness.

The outbreak of war in Europe in 1914 distracted Wilson and the country from domestic concerns. It also proved a boon to the American economy, cutting off the flow of cheap immigrant labor and increasing the demand for American exports—something to keep in mind the next time someone tells you that the Wilson era proves progressive policies and prosperity go hand in hand.

Despite Wilson's promise to keep us out of it, America entered the war in 1917. In hindsight, this was probably a misguided, albeit foregone, intervention. But the complaint that the war wasn't in America's interests misses the point. Wilson *boasted* as much time and again. "There is not a single selfish element, so far as I can see, in the cause we are fighting for," he declared. Wilson was a humble servant of the Lord, and therefore selfishness could not enter into it.[48]

Even for ostensibly secular progressives the war served as a divine call to arms. They were desperate to get their hands on the levers of power and use the war to reshape society. The capital was so thick with would-be social engineers during the war that, as one writer observed, "the Cosmos Club was little better than a faculty meeting of all the universities."[49] Progressive businessmen were just as eager, opting to work for the president for next to nothing—hence the phrase "dollar-a-year men." Of course, they were compensated in other ways, as we shall see.

WILSON'S FASCIST POLICE STATE

Today we unreflectively associate fascism with militarism. But it should be remembered that fascism was militaristic because militarism was "progressive" at the beginning of the twentieth century. Across the intellectual landscape, technocrats and poets alike saw the military as the best model for organizing and mobilizing society. Mussolini's "Battle of the Grains" and similar campaigns were publicized on both sides of the Atlantic as the enlightened application of James's doctrine of the "moral equivalent of war." There was a deep irony to America's war aim to crush "Prussian militarism," given that it was Prussian militarism which had inspired so many of the war's American cheerleaders in the first place. The idea that war was the source of moral values had been pioneered by German intellectuals in the late nineteenth and early twentieth centuries, and the influence of these intellectuals on the American mind was enormous. When America entered the war in 1917, progressive intellectuals, versed in the same doctrines and philosophies popular on the European continent, leaped at the opportunity to remake society through the discipline of the sword.

It is true that some progressives thought World War I was not well-advised on the merits, and there were a few progressives— Robert La Follette, for example—who were decidedly opposed (though La Follette was no pacifist, having supported earlier progressive military adventures). But most supported the war enthusiastically, even fanatically (the same goes for a great many American Socialists). And even those who were ambivalent about the war in Europe were giddy about what John Dewey called the "social possibilities of war." Dewey was the *New Republic*'s in-house philosopher during the lead-up to the war, and he ridiculed self-described pacifists who couldn't recognize the "immense impetus to reorganization afforded by this war." One group that did recognize the social possibilities of war were the early feminists who, in the words of Harriot Stanton Blatch, looked forward to new economic opportunities for women as "the usual, and happy, accompaniment of war." Richard Ely, a fervent believer in "industrial armies," was a zealous believer in the draft: "The moral effect of taking boys off street corners and out of saloons and drilling them is excellent, and the economic effects are likewise beneficial." Wilson clearly saw things along the same lines. "I am an advocate of peace," he began one typical declaration, "but there are some splendid things that come to a nation through the discipline of war." Hitler couldn't have agreed more. As he told Joseph Goebbels, "The war . . . made possible for us the solution of a whole series of problems that could never have been solved in normal times."[50]

We should not forget how the demands of war fed the arguments for socialism. Dewey was giddy that the war might force Americans "to give up much of our economic freedom . . . We shall have to lay by our good-natured individualism and march in step." If the war went well, it would constrain "the individualistic tradition" and convince Americans of "the supremacy of public need over private possessions." Another progressive put it more succinctly: "Laissez-faire is dead. Long live social control."[51]

Croly's *New Republic* was relentless in its push for war. In the magazine's very first editorial, written by Croly, the editors expressed their hope that war "should bring with it a political and economic organization better able to redeem its obligations at home." Two years later Croly again expressed his hope that America's entry into the war would provide "the tonic of a serious moral adventure." A week before America joined the war, Walter Lippmann (who would later write much of Wilson's Fourteen Points) promised that hostilities would bring out a "transvaluation of values as radical as anything in the history of intellect." This was a transparent invocation of Nietzsche's call for overturning all traditional morality. Not coincidentally, Lippmann was a protégé of William James's, and his call to use war to smash the old order illustrates how similar Nietzscheans and American pragmatists were in their conclusions and, often, their principles. Indeed, Lippmann was sounding the pragmatist's trumpet when he declared that our understanding of such ideas as democracy, liberty, and equality would have to be rethought from their foundations "as fearlessly as religious dogmas were in the nineteenth century."[52]

Meanwhile, socialist editors and journalists—including many from the *Masses,* the most audacious of the radical journals that Wilson tried to ban—rushed to get a paycheck from Wilson's propaganda ministry. Artists such as Charles Dana Gibson, James Montgomery Flagg, and Joseph Pennell and writers like Booth Tarkington, Samuel Hopkins Adams, and Ernest Poole became cheerleaders for the war-hungry regime. Musicians, comedians, sculptors, ministers—and of course the movie industry—were all happily drafted to the cause, eager to wear the "invisible uniform of war." Isadora Duncan, an avant-garde pioneer of what today would be called sexual liberation, became a toe tapper in patriotic pageants at the Metropolitan Opera House. The most enduring and iconic image of the time is Flagg's "I Want You" poster of Uncle Sam pointing the shaming finger of the state-made-flesh at uncommitted citizens.

Almost alone among progressives, the brilliant, bizarre, disfigured genius Randolph Bourne seemed to understand precisely what was going on. The war revealed that a generation of young intellectuals, trained in pragmatic philosophy, were ill equipped to prevent means from becoming ends. The "peculiar congeniality between the war and these men" was simply baked into the cake, Bourne lamented. "It is," he sadly concluded, "as if the war and they had been waiting for each other."[53]

Wilson the great centralizer and would-be leader of men moved overnight to empower these would-be social engineers, creating a vast array of wartime boards, commissions, and committees. Overseeing it all was the War Industries Board, or WIB, chaired by Bernard Baruch, which whipped, cajoled, and seduced American industry into the loving embrace of the state long before Mussolini or Hitler contemplated their corporatist doctrines. The progressives running the WIB had no illusions about what they were up to. "It was an industrial dictatorship without parallel—a dictatorship by force of necessity and common consent which step by step at last encompassed the Nation and united it into a coordinated and mobile whole," declared Grosvenor Clarkson, a member and subsequent historian of the WIB.[54]

More important than socializing industry was nationalizing the people for the war effort. "Woe be to the man or group of men that seeks to stand in our way," Wilson threatened in June 1917. Harking back to his belief that "leaders of men" must manipulate the passions of the masses, he approved and supervised one of the first truly Orwellian propaganda efforts in Western history. He set the tone himself when he defended the first military draft since the Civil War. "It is in no sense a conscription of the unwilling: it is, rather, selection from a nation which has volunteered in mass."[55]

A week after the war started, Walter Lippmann—no doubt eager to set about the work of unleashing a transvaluation of values—sent a memo to Wilson imploring him to commence with a sweeping propaganda effort. Lippmann, as he argued later, believed that most citizens were "mentally children or barbarians" and therefore needed to be directed by experts like himself. Individual liberty, while nice, needed to be subordinated to, among other things, "order."[56]

Wilson tapped the progressive journalist George Creel to head the Committee on Public Information, or CPI, the West's first modern ministry for propaganda. Creel was a former muckraking liberal journalist and police commissioner in Denver who had gone so far as to forbid his cops from carrying nightsticks or guns. He took to the propaganda portfolio immediately, determined to inflame the American public into "one white-hot mass" under the banner of "100 percent Americanism." "It was a fight for the *minds* of men, for the 'conquest of their convictions,' and the battle line ran through every home in every country," Creel recalled. Fear was a vital tool, he argued, "an important element to be bred into the civilian population. It is difficult to unite a people by talking only on the highest ethical plane. To fight for an ideal, perhaps, must be coupled with thoughts of self-preservation."[57]

Countless other liberal and leftist intellectuals lent their talents and energies to the propaganda effort. Edward Bernays, who would be credited with creating the field of public relations, cut his teeth on the Creel Committee, learning the art of "the conscious and intelligent manipulation of the organized habits and opinions of the masses." The CPI printed millions of posters, buttons, pamphlets, and the like in eleven languages not counting English. The committee eventually had more than twenty subdivisions with offices in America and around the world. The Division of News alone issued more than six thousand releases. Just under one hundred pamphlets were printed with an estimated circulation of seventy-five million. A typical poster for Liberty Bonds cautioned, "I am Public Opinion. All men fear me! . . . [I]f you have the money to buy and do not buy, I will make this No Man's Land for you!" A CPI poster asked, "Have you met the Kaiserite? . . . You find him in hotel lobbies, smoking compartments, clubs, offices, even homes . . . He is a scandal-monger of the most dangerous type. He repeats all the rumors, criticism, he hears about our country's part in the war. He's very plausible . . . People like that . . . through their vanity or curiosity or *treason* they are helping German propagandists sow the seeds of discontent."[58]

One of Creel's greatest ideas—an instance of "viral marketing" before its time—was the creation of an army of nearly a hundred thousand "Four Minute Men." Each was equipped and trained by the CPI to deliver a four-minute speech at town meetings, in restaurants, in theaters—anyplace they could get an audience—to spread the word that the "very future of democracy" was at stake. In 1917–18 alone, some 7,555,190 speeches were delivered in fifty-two hundred communities. These speeches celebrated Wilson as a larger-than-life leader and the Germans as less-than-human Huns. Invariably, the horrors of German war crimes expanded as the Four Minute Men plied their trade. The CPI released a string of propaganda films with such titles as *The Kaiser*, *The Beast of Berlin,* and *The Prussian Cur.* The schools, of course, were drenched in nationalist propaganda. Secondary schools and colleges quickly added "war studies courses" to the curriculum. And always and everywhere the progressives questioned the patriotism of anybody who didn't act "100 percent American."

Another Wilson appointee, the socialist muckraker Arthur Bullard—a former writer for the radical journal the *Masses* and an acquaintance of Lenin's—was also convinced that the state must whip the people up into a patriotic fervor if America was to achieve the "transvaluation" the progressives craved. In 1917 he published *Mobilising America,* in which he argued that the state must "electrify public opinion" because "the effectiveness of our warfare will depend on the ardour we throw into it." Any citizen who did not put the needs of the state ahead of his own was merely "dead weight." Bullard's ideas were eerily similar to the Sorelian doctrines of the "vital lie." "Truth and falsehood are arbitrary terms . . . there are life-less truths and vital lies . . . The force of an idea lies in its inspira-tional value. It matters very little if it's true or false."[59]

The radical lawyer and supposed civil libertarian Clarence Darrow—today a hero to the left for his defense of evolution in the Scopes "Monkey" trial—both stumped for the CPI and defended the government's censorship efforts. "When I hear a man advising the American people to state the terms of peace," Darrow wrote in a government-backed book, "I know he is working for Germany." In a speech at Madison Square Garden he said that Wilson would have been a traitor not to defy Germany, and added, "Any man who re-fuses to back the President in this crisis is worse than a traitor." Darrow's expert legal opinion, it may surprise modern liberals to know, was that once Congress had decided on war, the right to ques-tion that decision evaporated entirely (an interesting standard given the tendency of many to assert that the Bush administration has be-haved without precedent in its comparatively tepid criticism of dis-sent). Once the bullets fly, citizens lose the right even to discuss the issue, publicly or privately; "acquiescence on the part of the citizen becomes a duty."[60] (It's ironic that the ACLU made its name support-ing Darrow at the Scopes trial.)

The rationing and price-fixing of the "economic dictatorship" re-quired Americans to make great sacrifices, including the various "meatless" and "wheatless" days common to all of the industrialized war economies in the first half of the twentieth century. But the tac-tics used to impose these sacrifices dramatically advanced the sci-ence of totalitarian propaganda. Americans were deluged with patriotic volunteers knocking on their doors to sign this pledge or that oath not only to be patriotic but to abstain from this or that "lux-ury." Herbert Hoover, the head of the national Food Administration, made his reputation as a public servant in the battle to get Americans to tighten their belts, dispatching over half a million door knockers for his efforts alone. No one could dispute his gusto for the job. "Supper," he complained, "is one of the worst pieces of extravagance that we have in this country."[61]

Children were a special concern of the government's, as is always the case in totalitarian systems. They were asked to sign a pledge card, "A Little American's Promise":

At table I'll not leave a scrap
Of food upon my plate.
And I'll not eat between meals but
For supper time I'll wait.
I make that promise that I'll do
My honest, earnest part
In helping my America
With all my loyal heart.

For toddlers who couldn't sign a pledge card, let alone read, the Progressive war planners offered a rewritten nursery rhyme:

Little Boy Blue, come blow your horn!
The cook's using wheat where she ought to use corn
And terrible famine our country will sweep,
If the cooks and the housewives remain fast asleep!
Go wake them! Go wake them! It's now up to you!
Be a loyal American, Little Boy Blue![62]

Even as the government was churning out propaganda, it was silencing dissent. Wilson's Sedition Act banned "uttering, printing, writing, or publishing any disloyal, profane, scurrilous, or abusive language about the United States government or the military." The postmaster general was given the authority to deny mailing privileges to any publication he saw fit—effectively shutting it down. At least seventy-five periodicals were banned. Foreign publications were not allowed unless their content was first translated and approved by censors. Journalists also faced the very real threat of being jailed or having their supply of newsprint terminated by the War Industries Board. "Unacceptable" articles included any discussion—no matter how high-minded or patriotic—that disparaged the draft. "There is a limit," Postmaster General Albert Sidney Burleson declared. That limit has been exceeded, he explained, when a publication "begins to say that this Government got in the war wrong, that it is in it for the wrong purposes, or anything that will impugn the motives of the Government for going into the war. They can not say that this Government is the tool of Wall Street or the munitions-makers . . . There can be no campaign against conscription and the Draft Law."[63]

The most famous episode of censorship came with the government's relentless campaign against the *Masses*, the radical literary journal edited by Max Eastman. The postmaster general revoked the magazine's right to be distributed via the mails under the Espionage Act. Specifically, the government charged the magazine with trying to hamper military recruitment. Among the "illegal" contents: a cartoon proclaiming this was a war to make the world "safe for capitalism" and an editorial by Eastman praising the courage of draft resisters. Six editors faced trial in New York but managed to "win" hung juries (jurors and lawyers commented afterward that the defendants would almost certainly have been found guilty if any of them had been German or Jewish).

Of course, the "chilling effect" on the press in general was far more useful than the closures. Many of the journals that were shut down had tiny readerships. But the threat of being put out of business did wonders in focusing the minds of other editors. If the power of example wasn't strong enough, editors received a threatening letter. If that didn't work, they could lose their mail privileges "temporarily." Over four hundred publications had been denied privileges by May 1918. The *Nation* had been suppressed for criticizing Samuel Gompers. The journal *Public* had been smacked for suggesting that the war should be paid for by taxes rather than loans, and the *Freeman's Journal and Catholic Register* for reprinting Thomas Jefferson's views that Ireland should be a republic. Even the pro-war *New Republic* wasn't safe. It was twice warned that it would be banned from the mails if it continued to run the National Civil Liberties Bureau's ads asking for donations and volunteers.

Then there was the inevitable progressive crackdown on individual civil liberties. Today's liberals tend to complain about the McCarthy period as if it were the darkest moment in American history after slavery. It's true: under McCarthyism a few Hollywood writers who'd supported Stalin and then lied about it lost their jobs in the 1950s. Others were unfairly intimidated. But nothing that happened under the mad reign of Joe McCarthy remotely compares with what Wilson and his fellow progressives foisted on America. Under the Espionage Act of June 1917 and the Sedition Act of May 1918, *any* criticism of the government, even in your own home, could earn you a prison sentence (a law Oliver Wendell Holmes upheld years after the war, arguing that such speech could be banned if it posed a "clear and present danger"). In Wisconsin a state official got two and a half years for criticizing a Red Cross fund-raising drive. A Hollywood producer received a ten-year stint in jail for making a film that depicted British troops committing atrocities *during the American Revolution.* One man was brought to trial for explaining in his own home why he didn't want to buy Liberty Bonds.[64]

No police state deserves the name without an ample supply of police. The Department of Justice arrested tens of thousands without just cause. The Wilson administration issued a letter for U.S. attorneys and marshals saying, "No German enemy in this country, who has not hitherto been implicated in plots against the interests of the United States, need have any fear of action by the Department of Justice so long as he observes the following warning: Obey the law; keep your mouth shut."[65] This blunt language might be forgivable except for the government's dismayingly broad definition of what defined a "German enemy."

The Justice Department created its own quasi-official *fascisti,* known as the American Protective League, or APL. They were given badges—many of which read "Secret Service"—and charged with keeping an eye on their neighbors, co-workers, and friends. Used as private eyes by overzealous prosecutors in thousands of cases, they were furnished with ample government resources. The APL had an intelligence division, in which members were bound by oath not to reveal they were secret policemen. Members of the APL read their neighbors' mail and listened in on their phones with government approval. In Rockford, Illinois, the army asked the APL to help extract confessions from black soldiers accused of assaulting white women. The APL's American Vigilante Patrol cracked down on "seditious street oratory." One of its most important functions was to serve as head crackers against "slackers" who avoided conscription. In New York City, in September 1918, the APL launched its biggest slacker raid, rounding up fifty thousand men. Two-thirds were later found to be innocent of all charges. Nevertheless, the Justice Department approved. The assistant attorney general noted, with great satisfaction, that America had never been more effectively policed. In 1917 the APL had branches in nearly six hundred cities and towns with a membership approaching a hundred thousand. By the following year, it had exceeded a quarter of a million.[66]

One of the only things the layman still remembers about this period is a vague sense that something bad called the Palmer Raids occurred—a series of unconstitutional crackdowns, approved by Wilson, of "subversive" groups and individuals. What is usually ignored is that the raids were immensely popular, particularly with the middle-class base of the Democratic Party. Attorney General A. Mitchell Palmer was a canny progressive who defeated the Republican machine in Pennsylvania by forming a tight bond with labor. He had hoped to ride the popularity of the raids straight into the Oval Office, and might have succeeded had he not been sidelined by a heart attack.

It's also necessary to note that the American Legion was born under inauspicious circumstances during the hysteria of World War I in 1919. Although it is today a fine organization with a proud history, one cannot ignore the fact that it was founded as an essentially fascist organization. In 1923 the national commander of the legion declared, "If ever needed, the American Legion stands ready to protect our country's institutions and ideals as the fascisti dealt with the destructionists who menaced Italy."[67] FDR would later try to use the legion as a newfangled American Protective League to spy on domestic dissidents and harass potential foreign agents.

Vigilantism was often encouraged and rarely dissuaded under Wilson's 100 percent Americanism. How could it be otherwise, given Wilson's own warnings about the enemy within? In 1915, in his third annual message to Congress, he declared, "The gravest threats against our national peace and safety have been uttered within our own borders. There are citizens of the United States, I blush to admit, born under other flags . . . who have poured the poison of disloyalty into the very arteries of our national life; who have sought to bring the authority and good name of our Government into contempt, to destroy our industries wherever they thought it effective for their vindictive purposes to strike at them, and to debase our politics to the uses of foreign intrigue." Four years later the president was still convinced that perhaps America's greatest threat came from "hyphenated" Americans. "I cannot say too often—any man who carries a hyphen about with him carries a dagger that he is ready to plunge into the vitals of this Republic whenever he gets ready. If I can catch any man with a hyphen in this great contest I will know that I have got an enemy of the Republic."[68]

This was the America Woodrow Wilson and his allies sought. And they got what they wanted. In 1919, at a Victory Loan pageant, a man refused to stand for the national anthem. When "The Star-Spangled Banner" ended, a furious sailor shot the "disloyal" man three times in the back. When the man fell, the *Washington Post* reported, "the crowd burst into cheering and handclapping." Another man who refused to rise for the national anthem at a baseball game was beaten by the fans in the bleachers. In February 1919 a jury in Hammond, Indiana, took two minutes to acquit a man who had murdered an immigrant for yelling, "To Hell with the United States." In 1920 a salesman at a clothing store in Waterbury, Connecticut, received a six-month prison sentence for referring to Lenin as "one of the brainiest" leaders in the world. Mrs. Rose Pastor Stokes was arrested, tried, and convicted for telling a women's group, "I am for the people, and the government is for the profiteers." The Republican antiwar progressive Robert La Follette spent a year fighting an effort to have him expelled from the Senate for disloyalty because he'd given a speech opposing the war to the Non-Partisan League. The *Providence Journal* carried a banner—every day!—warning readers that any German or Austrian "unless known by years of association should be treated as a spy." The Illinois Bar Association ruled that members who defended draft resisters were not only "unprofessional" but "unpatriotic."[69]

German authors were purged from libraries, families of German extraction were harassed and taunted, sauerkraut became "liberty cabbage," and—as Sinclair Lewis half-jokingly recalled—there was talk of renaming German measles "liberty measles." Socialists and other leftists who agitated against the war were brutalized. Mobs in Arizona packed Wobblies in cattle cars and left them in the desert without food or water. In Oklahoma, opponents of the war were tarred and feathered, and a crippled leader of the Industrial Workers of the World was hung from a railway trestle. At Columbia University the president, Nicholas Murray Butler, fired three professors for criticizing the war, on the grounds that "what had been wrongheadedness was now sedition. What had been folly was now treason." Richard Ely, enthroned at the University of Wisconsin, organized professors and others to crush internal dissent via the Wisconsin Loyalty Legion. Anybody who offered "opinions which hinder us in this awful struggle," he explained, should be "fired" if not indeed "shot." Chief on his list was Robert La Follette, whom Ely attempted to hound from Wisconsin politics as a "traitor" who "has been of more help to the Kaiser than a quarter of a million troops."[70]

Hard numbers are difficult to come by, but it has been estimated that some 175,000 Americans were arrested for failing to demonstrate their patriotism in one way or another. All were punished, many went to jail.

For the most part, the progressives looked upon what they had created and said, "This is good." The "great European war . . . is striking down individualism and building up collectivism," rejoiced the Progressive financier and J. P. Morgan partner George Perkins. Grosvenor Clarkson saw things similarly. The war effort "is a story of the conversion of a hundred million combatively individualistic people into a vast cooperative effort in which the good of the unit was sacrificed to the good of the whole." The regimentation of society, the social worker Felix Adler believed, was bringing us closer to creating the "perfect man . . . a fairer and more beautiful and more righteous type than any . . . that has yet existed." The *Washington Post* was more modest. "In spite of excesses such as lynching," it editorialized, "it is a healthful and wholesome awakening in the interior of the country."[71]

Perhaps some added context is in order. At pretty much the exact moment when John Dewey, Herbert Croly, Walter Lippmann, and so many others were gushing about the "moral tonic" the war would provide and how it was the highest, best cause for all people dedicated to liberal, progressive values, Benito Mussolini was making nearly identical arguments. Mussolini had been the brains of the Italian Socialist Party. He was influenced by many of the same thinkers as the American progressives—Marx, Nietzsche, Hegel, James, and others—and he wanted Italy to fight on the Allied side, that is, the eventual *American* side. And yet Mussolini's support for the war automatically rendered him and his Fascist movement "objectively" right-wing according to communist propaganda.

So does this mean that the editors of the *New Republic*, the progressives in Wilson's government, John Dewey, and the vast majority of self-described American Socialists were all suddenly right-wingers? Of course not. Only in Italy—home of the most radical socialist party in Europe after Russia—did support for the war automatically transform left-wingers into right-wingers. In Germany the socialists in the Reichstag voted in favor of the war. In Britain the socialists voted in favor of the war. In America the socialists and progressives voted in favor of the war. This didn't make them right-wingers; it made them shockingly bloodthirsty and jingoistic left-wingers. This is just one attribute of the progressives that has been airbrushed from popular history. "Perhaps I was as much opposed to the war as anyone in the nation," declared none other than Mother Jones, a champion of "Americanist" socialism, "but when we get into a fight I am one of those who intend to clean hell out of the other fellow, and we have to clean the kaiser up . . . the grafter, the thief, the murderer." She was hardly alone. The pro-war socialist Charles E. Russell declared that his former colleagues should be "driven from the country." Another insisted that antiwar socialists should be "shot at once without an hour's delay."[72]

In the liberal telling of America's story, there are only two perpetrators of official misdeeds: conservatives and "America" writ large. progressives, or modern liberals, are never bigots or tyrants, but conservatives often are. For example, one will virtually never hear that the Palmer Raids, Prohibition, or American eugenics were thoroughly progressive phenomena. These are sins America itself must atone for. Meanwhile, real or alleged "conservative" misdeeds—say, McCarthyism—are always the exclusive fault of conservatives and a sign of the policies they would repeat if given power. The only culpable mistake that liberals make is failing to fight "hard enough" for their principles. Liberals are never responsible for historic misdeeds, because they feel no compulsion to defend the inherent goodness of America. Conservatives, meanwhile, not only take the blame for events not of their own making that they often worked the most assiduously against, but find themselves defending liberal misdeeds in order to defend America herself.

War socialism under Wilson was an entirely progressive project, and long after the war it remained the liberal ideal. To this day liberals instinctively and automatically see war as an excuse to expand governmental control of vast swaths of the economy. If we are to believe that "classic" fascism is first and foremost the elevation of martial values and the militarization of government and society under the banner of nationalism, it is very difficult to understand why the Progressive Era was not also the Fascist Era.

Indeed, it is very difficult not to notice how the progressives fit the objective criteria for a fascist movement set forth by so many students of the field. Progressivism was largely a middle-class movement equally opposed to runaway capitalism above and Marxist radicalism below. Progressives hoped to find a middle course between the two, what the fascists called the "Third Way" or what Richard Ely, mentor to both Wilson and Roosevelt, called the "golden mean" between laissez-faire individualism and Marxist socialism. Their chief desire was to impose a unifying, totalitarian moral order that regulated the individual inside his home and out. The progressives also shared with the fascists and Nazis a burning desire to transcend class differences within the national community and create a new order. George Creel declared this aim succinctly: "No dividing line between the rich and poor, and no class distinctions to breed mean envies."[73]

This was precisely the social mission and appeal of fascism and Nazism. In speech after speech, Hitler made it clear that his goal was to have no dividing lines between rich and poor. "What a difference compared with a certain other country," he declared, referring to war-torn Spain. "There it is class against class, brother against brother. We have chosen the other route: rather than to wrench you apart, we have brought you together." Robert Ley, the head of the Nazis' German Labor Front, proclaimed flatly, "We are the first country in Europe to overcome the class struggle." Whether the rhetoric matched the reality is beside the point; the appeal of such a goal was profound and the intent sincere. A young and ambitious German lawyer who wanted to study abroad was persuaded by his friends to stay home so he wouldn't miss the excitement. "The [Nazi] party was intending to change the whole concept of labour relations, based on the principle of co-determination and shared responsibility between management and workers. I knew it was Utopian but I believed in it with all my heart . . . Hitler's promises of a caring but disciplined socialism fell on very receptive ears."[74]

Of course, such utopian dreams would have to come at the price of personal liberty. But progressives and fascists alike were glad to pay it. "Individualism," proclaimed Lyman Abbott, the editor of the *Outlook,* "is the characteristic of simple barbarism, not of republican civilization."[75] The Wilsonian-Crolyite progressive conception of the individual's role in society would and should strike any fair-minded person of any true liberal sensibility today as at least disturbing and somewhat fascistic. Wilson, Croly, and the vast bulk of progressives would have no principled objection to the Nazi conception of the *Volksgemeinschaft*—"people's community," or national community—or to the Nazi slogan about placing "the common good before the private good." Progressives and fascists alike were explicitly indebted to Darwinism, Hegelianism, and Pragmatism to justify their worldviews. Indeed, perhaps the greatest irony is that according to most of the criteria we use to locate people and policies on the ideological spectrum in the American context—social bases, demographics, economic policies, social welfare provisions—Adolf Hitler was indisputably to Wilson's *left*.

This is the elephant in the corner that the American left has never been able to admit, explain, or comprehend. Their inability and/or refusal to deal squarely with this fact has distorted our understanding of our politics, our history, and ourselves. Liberals keep saying "it can't happen here" with a clever wink or an ironic smile to insinuate that the right is constantly plotting fascist schemes. Meanwhile, hiding in plain sight is this simple fact: it *did* happen here, and it might very well happen again. To see the threat, however, you must look over your left shoulder, not your right.

Franklin Roosevelt's
Fascist New Deal

T HE NATION WAS caught up in a war fever, fomented by the government, even though there was no war. Striking union members were provoked into a riot by government forces. Sixty-seven workers were killed, some shot in the back. A young correspondent reported, "I understood deep in my bones and blood what fascism was." A leading intellectual who'd signed on with the government declared in a lecture to students, "The ordeal of war brings out the magnificent resources of youth."[1]

The British ambassador cabled London to alert his superiors to the spreading hysteria fomented by the nation's new leader. The "starved loyalties and repressed hero-worship of the country have found in him an outlet and a symbol." Visiting the rural hinterlands, an aide reported back on the brewing cult of personality: "Every house I visited—mill worker or unemployed—had a picture of the President . . . He is at once God and their intimate friend; he knows them all by name, knows their little town and mill, their little lives and problems. And though everything else fails, he is there, and will not let them down."[2]

Though the crisis was economic in nature, the new national commander had promised to seek the "power to wage a war against the emergency, as great as the power that would be given to me if we were in fact invaded by a foreign foe . . . I assume unhesitatingly the leadership of this great army of our people dedicated to a disciplined attack upon our common problems."

Presumably some readers already know that the country I'm talking about is America, and the leader FDR. The labor riots took place in Chicago. The wide-eyed young reporter was Eric Sevareid, one of the titans of CBS news. The intellectual who harangued Dartmouth students about the virtues of war was Rexford Tugwell, one of the most prominent of the New Deal's Brain Trusters. And of course the last quotations were from Franklin Delano Roosevelt himself in his first inaugural address.

As liberalism in recent years has fallen into ideological and intellectual disarray, American liberals have crouched into a fetal position around Franklin D. Roosevelt's "legacy." Liberal legal theorists have made the New Deal into a second American founding. Leading journalists have descended into abject idolatry. Indeed, it sometimes seems that all one needs to know about the merits of a policy is whether Roosevelt himself would have favored it. It is a given that Republicans are wrong, even fascistic, whenever they want to "dismantle" FDR's policies.

One of the most poignant ironies here is that a modern-day Hitler or Mussolini would never dismantle the New Deal. To the contrary, he'd redouble the effort. This is not to say that the New Deal was evil or Hitlerian. But the New Deal was a product of the impulses and ideas of its era. And those ideas and impulses are impossible to separate from the fascist moment in Western civilization. According to Harold Ickes, FDR's interior secretary and one of the most important architects of the New Deal, Roosevelt himself privately acknowledged that "what we were doing in this country were some of the things that were being done in Russia and even some of the things that were being done under Hitler in Germany. But we were doing them in an orderly way." It's hard to see how orderliness absolves a policy from the charge of fascism or totalitarianism. Eventually, the similarities had become so transparent that Ickes had to warn Roosevelt that the public was increasingly inclined "to unconsciously group four names, Hitler, Stalin, Mussolini and Roosevelt."[3]

The notion that FDR harbored fascist tendencies is vastly more controversial today than it was in the 1930s, primarily because fascism has come to mean Nazism and Nazism means simply evil. Saying, for example, that FDR had a Hitlerite fiscal policy just confuses people. But the fascist flavor of the New Deal was not only regularly discussed; it was often cited as evidence in Roosevelt's favor. There was an enormous bipartisan consensus that the Depression required dictatorial and fascistic policies to defeat it. Walter Lippmann, serving as an ambassador for America's liberal elite, told FDR in a private meeting at Warm Springs, "The situation is critical, Franklin. You may have no alternative but to assume dictatorial powers."[4] Eleanor Roosevelt, too, believed that a "benevolent dictator" might be the only answer for America. And it was hardly lost on the liberal intellectuals swirling around the Roosevelt administration that the enormously popular Benito Mussolini had used the same methods to whip the unruly Italians into shape. After all, the *New Republic*—the intellectual home of the New Deal—had covered the goings-on in Italy with fascination and, often, admiration.

Indeed, the New Deal was conceived at the climax of a worldwide fascist moment, a moment when socialists in many countries were increasingly becoming nationalists and nationalists could embrace nothing other than socialism. Franklin Roosevelt was no fascist, at least not in the sense that he thought of himself in this way. But many of his ideas and policies were indistinguishable from fascism. And today we live with the fruits of fascism, and we call them liberal. From economic policy, to populist politics, to a faith in the abiding power of brain trusts to chart our collective future—be they at Harvard or on the Supreme Court—fascistic assumptions about the role of the state have been encoded upon the American mind, often as a matter of bipartisan consensus.

This was not FDR's "vision," for he had none. He was the product of an age where collectivism, patriotic exhortations, and a pragmatic rejection of overreliance on principle simply seemed to be the "way of the future." He imbibed these attitudes and ideas from his experience during the Progressive Era and from his advisers who did likewise. If Wilson was an intentional totalitarian, Roosevelt became one by default—largely because he didn't have any better ideas.

PROGRESSIVE FROM THE BEGINNING

Born in 1882, a year before Mussolini, Franklin Delano Roosevelt was hardly raised to be a great man. Indeed, he wasn't raised to be much of anything. A sweet and gentle boy, he was sheltered from anything like what we would today call a normal childhood. Almost smothered with attention from his parents, James Roosevelt and the former Sara Delano, he was expected to emulate their lifestyle as aristocrats. Young FDR had few friends his own age. An only child, he was educated mostly by Swiss tutors at home (recall that Wilson, too, had been homeschooled). In 1891, while his parents visited a spa in Bismarck's Germany, young Franklin—"Franz" to his class-mates—attended a local *Volksschule,* where he studied map reading and military topography. He claimed to remember the experience fondly, particularly his study of German military maps.

Roosevelt's youth laid the foundations of his adult personality. When Franklin was only eight, his father suffered the first of several heart attacks. Franklin responded by resolving to conceal his sorrow and anxiety from his father. This is apparently where FDR first be-gan the practice of masking his real feelings behind a permanently cheery demeanor. For the rest of his life, and particularly when he was president, his friends and enemies alike would complain that they could never trust that Roosevelt was telling them what he really thought. This was a polite way of saying that they could never be sure whether Roosevelt was lying to their face. "When I talk to him, he says 'Fine! Fine! Fine!' " Huey Long lamented. "But Joe Robinson [a political enemy of Long's] goes to see him the next day and again he says 'Fine! Fine! Fine!' Maybe he says 'fine' to every-body."[5]

FDR left his parental cocoon in 1896 to attend Groton. The tran-sition was difficult. Raised speaking German with his German-speaking governess and French with his French-language tutors, and to speak English haughtily in all other circumstances, Roosevelt grated on the other students. Eventually, though, his determination to fit in—almost an obsession with conformity—paid off, and he rose in social status. He was not a particularly gifted student. His highest scores were in punctuality and neatness. Indeed, the consensus is that FDR verged on being an intellectual lightweight. He rarely read books, and those he did read were far from weighty. The historian Hugh Gallagher writes, "He had a magpie mind, and many interests, but he was not deep."[6]

FDR suffered painfully from envy for his cousin Teddy Roosevelt. When Franklin enrolled at Harvard in 1904, he took to mimicking the Bull Moose's mannerisms—in much the same way many baby-boomer liberals, like Bill Clinton and John Kerry, emulated John F. Kennedy in their youth. Young Franklin would over-pronounce "deee-lighted," shout "bully!" and wear knockoffs of his cousin Teddy's iconic pince-nez glasses.

It was also during college that Roosevelt secretly courted his distant cousin Eleanor. The match seemed odd to many but proved to be a powerful political symbiosis. Franklin, smooth and insubstantial, seemed to want a partner who provided attributes he did not have. Eleanor offered conviction, steadfastness, earnestness—and extremely valuable connections. She was ballast for her husband's airiness. Franklin's mother, who retained a tight rein on her son (in part by keeping him on a strict allowance) until she died in 1941, opposed the marriage. But she acquiesced in the face of Franklin's determination, and in 1905 the two were married. Eleanor's uncle Teddy gave her away.

By this time FDR was attending law school at Columbia University. He never received his degree but passed the bar and became a fairly unremarkable lawyer. In 1910 he was invited to run for the New York State Senate from Dutchess County, largely because of his wealth, name, and connections. The county Democratic chairman, Edward E. Perkins, consented to have what he considered to be a young fop on the ticket largely because he expected Roosevelt to contribute to the party treasury and to pay for his own campaign. When FDR met with Perkins and other party bosses, he arrived dressed in his riding clothes. Perkins disliked the young aristocrat but acquiesced, saying, "You'll have to take off those yellow shoes" and "put on some regular pants."[7] FDR eagerly accepted and won the race. Much as at Groton and Harvard, however, he didn't make many friends in the state legislature and was considered a second-rate intelligence. His colleagues often made fun of him, using his initials to call him "Feather Duster" Roosevelt.

Still, Roosevelt performed serviceably as a progressive state senator and won reelection fairly easily in 1912 thanks to his relationship with Louis Howe, a brilliant political fixer who taught him how to appeal to otherwise hostile constituencies. But he never finished his second term. Instead, he was tapped by Woodrow Wilson to serve as assistant secretary of the navy. Franklin was ecstatic about taking the same job "Uncle Teddy" (by marriage) had used to jump-start his own political prospects fifteen years earlier.

Franklin Roosevelt was sworn in on March 17, 1913, his eighth wedding anniversary, at the age of thirty-one. And he immediately dedicated himself to emulating Teddy. His immediate boss, patron, and mentor was the famed progressive newspaperman Josephus Daniels. As both secretary of the navy and a journalist, Daniels represented all of the bizarre contradictions—from today's perspective—of the progressive movement. He was a thoroughgoing racist whose North Carolina newspapers regularly published horrendously offensive cartoons and editorials about blacks. But he was also deeply committed to a host of progressive reforms, from public education to public health to women's suffrage. A longtime political ally of William Jennings Bryan, Daniels could sound both pacifist and belligerent notes, though once ensconced in the Wilson administration, he was a dutiful advocate for "preparedness," expansion of the navy, and, ultimately, war.

Daniels was constantly outflanked by his young assistant secretary's belligerence. FDR proved to be a very capable and astoundingly *political* assistant secretary. "I get my fingers into everything," he liked to say, "and there's no law against it."[8] He particularly relished the fact that when his boss was away, he was the acting secretary. He loved the martial pomp, gushing with pride over the seventeen-gun salutes he received in his honor and taking an enormous amount of interest in designing a military flag for his office. Indeed from day one FDR was one of the "Big Navy Boys"—and he was constantly frustrated with what he perceived to be his boss's slow-footedness when it came to rearmament.

From his first days as assistant secretary, FDR formed a powerful alliance with constituencies deeply invested in the development of a large naval war machine, particularly the Navy League, which was seen by many as little more than a mouthpiece for steel and financial interests. Just a month after his appointment, FDR gave a pro-big-navy speech at the league's annual convention. He even hosted a league planning meeting in his own office. During the months when the United States was officially neutral, FDR opened a channel with Teddy Roosevelt, Henry Cabot Lodge, and other Republican hawks critical of the Wilson administration. He even leaked naval intelligence to the Republicans so they could attack the administration, and Daniels in particular, for "unpreparedness."[9] Today he might be called part of the neocon cabal inside the Wilson administration.

FDR witnessed, approved, and, on occasion, participated in all of the excesses of World War I. There's no record anywhere that he disapproved of George Creel's propaganda ministry or that he had any larger misgivings about the war abroad or at home. He watched as Creel's acolytes actively promoted what they dubbed "the Wilson cult." He approved of the oppression of dissidents and heartily celebrated the passage of the Sedition and Espionage acts. He sent a letter congratulating a U.S. district attorney who'd successfully won a case against four socialists who'd distributed antiwar publications. In speeches he inveighed against slackers who failed to buy Liberty Bonds or fully support the war.[10]

After the Great War, the country slowly regained its sanity. But many liberals remained enamored of war socialism, believing that a peacetime militarization of the society was still necessary. Daniels—partly out of a desire to scare the country into ratifying the Treaty of Versailles—warned that America might need to "become a super-Prussia." The administration—with Daniels and Roosevelt at the forefront—pushed aggressively but unsuccessfully for a peacetime draft. The administration also failed to pass a new peacetime sedition law like the one it imposed on the nation during the war (in 1919–20, Congress considered some seventy such bills). And once Wilson was out of office, the government released its political prisoners, including Eugene V. Debs, who was pardoned by Wilson's Republican successor, Warren Harding. Nonetheless, the nation emerged from "the war to make the world safe for democracy" less free at home and less safe in the world. No wonder Harding's campaign slogan had been "A Return to Normalcy."

In 1920 FDR's backers tried to orchestrate a Democratic presidential ticket with the revered progressive Herbert Hoover at the top and

FDR as vice president. Hoover was open to the idea, but the plan fell apart when he threw his hat in with the Republicans. Roosevelt successfully maneuvered himself onto the Democratic ticket nonetheless as the running mate of James M. Cox of Ohio. FDR ran as a loyal Wilsonian, even if Wilson himself—now bitter and twisted, physically and psychologically—was less than gracious in his support.

Other Wilsonians, however, were ecstatic. Now back at the *New Republic,* Walter Lippmann, who had worked with Roosevelt on the Wage Scale Committee in 1917, sent him a congratulatory note calling his nomination "the best news in many a long day." But the campaign was doomed from the outset due to the deep resentment many Americans felt toward the Wilson administration and Progressives in general.

After a crushing defeat at the polls, FDR went into business. Then, in 1921, he contracted polio. He spent much of the next decade struggling to overcome his disability and planning a political comeback.

Indeed, FDR faced two existential crises that were really one: how to fight the disease and stay politically viable. He bravely fought his condition, most famously at the spa he purchased for that effort at Warm Springs. This kept him out of the limelight most of the time. But he did attend the ill-fated 1924 Democratic National Convention, where he painstakingly walked on crutches to center stage to nominate Al Smith for president. He didn't make another public appearance until 1928, when he gave another convention speech for Smith. In a perverse sense, Roosevelt was lucky. By keeping out of the public eye while working the political angles behind the scenes, he managed to stay untainted, biding his time, during a moment when the services of a progressive party were blessedly unwelcome.

While no intellectual, FDR possessed a certain genius for gauging the political temper of the times. He read people very well and picked up tidbits of information through extensive conversations with a vast range of intellectuals, activists, politicians, and the like. He was a sponge, biographers tell us, absorbing the zeitgeist while almost never concerning himself with larger philosophical conclusions. He was, in the words of the historian Richard Hofstadter, "content in large measure to follow public opinion." In many ways

Roosevelt saw himself as a popularizer of intellectual currents. He spoke in generalities that everyone found agreeable at first and meaningless upon reflection. He could be—or at least sound—Jeffersonian and Hamiltonian, internationalist and isolationist, this and that as well as the other thing. He was like a "chameleon on plaid," groused Herbert Hoover.[11]

Roosevelt's slipperiness stemmed from more than people pleasing. Until late in his presidency, his overriding imperative was to split differences, to claim the "middle way." "I think that you will agree," he wrote a friend about one speech, "that it is sufficiently far to the left to prevent any further suggestion that I am leaning to the right."[12] Once, when he was given two completely opposing policy proposals, he simply ordered his aide and postmaster general, James Farley, to reconcile them. His favorite form of management was to pit two individuals or departments against each other with the same task.

The problem with this sort of triangulation is that you end up moving to whatever you believe is the epicenter between two ever-shifting and hard-to-define horizons. Worse still, Roosevelt translated this approach into a de facto Third Way governing philosophy. This in effect meant that nothing was fixed. No question about the role of government or its powers was truly settled. And it is for this reason that both conservatives and radicals have always harbored feelings ranging from frustration to contempt for FDR. For the radicals FDR wasn't principled enough to commit to lasting change, while for conservatives he wasn't principled enough to stand his ground. He planted his flag atop a buoy at sea, permanently bobbing with the currents. Unfortunately, the currents tended to push him in only one direction: statism, for that was the intellectual tide of the time.

Today many liberals subscribe to the myth that the New Deal was a coherent, enlightened, unified endeavor encapsulated in the largely meaningless phrase "the Roosevelt legacy." This is poppycock. "To look upon these programs as the result of a unified plan," wrote Raymond Moley, FDR's right-hand man during much of the New Deal, "was to believe that the accumulation of stuffed snakes, baseball pictures, school flags, old tennis shoes, carpenter's tools, geometry books, and chemistry sets in a boy's bedroom could have been put there by an interior decorator." When Alvin Hansen, an influential economic adviser to the president, was asked—in 1940!—whether "the basic principle of the New Deal" was "economically sound," he responded, "I really do not know what the basic principle of the New Deal is."[13]

This raises the first of many common features among New Deal liberalism, Italian Fascism, and German National Socialism, all of which shared many of the same historical and intellectual forebears. Fascist and Nazi intellectuals constantly touted a "middle" or "Third Way" between capitalism and socialism. Mussolini zigzagged every which way, from free trade and low taxes to a totalitarian state apparatus. Even before he attained power, his stock response when asked to outline his program was to say he had none. "Our program is to govern," the Fascists liked to say.

Hitler showed even less interest in political or economic theory, fascist or otherwise. He never read Alfred Rosenberg's *Myth of the Twentieth Century* or many of the other "classic" fascist texts. And the inability of numerous Nazis and fascists to plow through the Nazi bible *Mein Kampf* is legendary.

The "middle way" sounds moderate and un-radical. Its appeal is that it sounds unideological and freethinking. But philosophically the Third Way is not mere difference splitting; it is utopian and authoritarian. Its utopian aspect becomes manifest in its antagonism to the idea that politics is about trade-offs. The Third Wayer says that there are no false choices—"I refuse to accept that X should come at the expense of Y." The Third Way holds that we can have capitalism and socialism, individual liberty and absolute unity. Fascist movements are implicitly utopian because they—like communist and heretical Christian movements—assume that with just the right arrangement of policies, all contradictions can be rectified. This is a political siren song; life can never be made perfect, because man is imperfect. This is why the Third Way is also authoritarian. It assumes that the right man—or, in the case of Leninists, the right party—can resolve all of these contradictions through sheer will. The populist demagogue takes on the role of the parent telling the childlike masses that he can make everything "all better" if they just trust him.

FDR's "middle way" had a very specific resonance, seemingly

contradictory to its philosophical assumptions. As many communists were keen to note, it was born of a Bismarckian attempt to forestall greater radicalism. The elites, including business leaders, were for the most part reconciled to the fact that "socialism" of some kind was going to be a permanent feature of the political economy. Middle-way politics was a carefully crafted appeal to the middle class's entirely justifiable fear of the Red menace. Hitler and Mussolini exploited this anxiety at every turn; indeed it was probably the key to their success. The fascist appeal was homegrown socialism, orderly socialism, socialism with a German or Italian face as opposed to nasty "foreign" socialism in much the same way that 100 percent Americanism had been progressive America's counteroffer to Bolshevism.

Time and again, FDR's New Dealers made the very same threat— that if the New Deal failed, what would come next would be far more radical. As we'll see, a great many of FDR's Old Right opponents were actually former progressives convinced that the New Deal was moving toward *the wrong kind of socialism*. That the Third Way could be cast as an appeal to both utopians and anti-utopians may sound implausible, but political agendas need not be logically coherent, merely popularly seductive. And seductiveness has always been the Third Way's defining characteristic.

The German and American New Deals may have been merely whatever Hitler and FDR felt they could get away with. But therein lies a common principle: the state *should* be allowed to get away with anything, so long as it is for "good reasons." This is the common principle among fascism, Nazism, Progressivism, and what we today call liberalism. It represents the triumph of Pragmatism in politics in that it recognizes no dogmatic boundaries to the scope of government power. The leader and his anointed cadres are decision makers above and beyond political or democratic imperatives. They invoke with divine reverence "science" and the laws of economics the way temple priests once read the entrails of goats, but because they have blinded themselves to their own leaps of faith, they cannot see that morals and values cannot be derived from science. Morals and values are determined by the priests, whether they wear black robes or white lab smocks.

AN "EXPERIMENTAL" AGE

Ever since FDR's presidency—when "liberalism" replaced "progressivism" as the preferred label for center-left political ideas and activism—liberals have had trouble articulating what liberalism *is,* beyond the conviction that the federal government should use its power to do nice things wherever and whenever it can. Herbert Croly said it well when he defended the *New Republic* against critics who said the magazine's qualified support for Mussolini violated its liberal principles: "If there are any abstract liberal principles, we do not know how to formulate them. Nor if they are formulated by others do we recognize their authority. Liberalism, as we understand it, is an activity."[14] In other words, liberalism is what liberals *do* or decide is worth doing, period. Faith without deeds is dead, according to the Bible. Pragmatic liberals internalized this while protesting they have no faith. This was at the core of what the German historian Peter Vogt called the progressives' "elective affinity" for fascism. Or as John Patrick Diggins says, "Fascism appealed, first of all, to the pragmatic ethos of experimentation."[15]

As president, Roosevelt bragged that he was married to no preconceived notions. He measured an idea's worth by the results it achieved. "Take a method and try it," he famously declared at Oglethorpe University in May 1932. "If it fails, admit it frankly and try another. But above all, try something." The only coherent policy Roosevelt subscribed to was "bold, persistent experimentation." Conservatives were cast by FDR and his allies as opponents of all change, selfish slaves to the status quo. But stasis is not the American conservative position. Rather, conservatives believe that change for change's sake is folly. What kind of change? At what cost? For the liberals and progressives, everything was expendable, from tradition to individualism to "outdated" conceptions of freedom. These were all tired dogmas to be burned on the altars of the new age.

When FDR was elected president in 1932, three events were viewed as admirable experiments: the Bolshevik Revolution, the Fascist takeover in Italy, and the American "experiment" in war socialism under Wilson. By 1932 admiration for the Russian "social experiment" had become a definitive component of American liberalism—in much the same way that admiration for Prussian top-down socialism had been two decades earlier. Simply, the Soviet Union was the future, and "it worked."

Intermingled in these encomiums to what Lincoln Steffens called the "Russian-Italian method"—signifying that, as far as he was concerned, Bolshevism and Fascism were not opposites but kindred movements—were lusty expressions of nostalgia for the short-lived American "experiment" with war socialism under Woodrow Wilson. "We planned in war!" was the omnipresent refrain from progressives eager to re-create the kind of economic and social control they had under Wilson. The Italians and the Russians were beating America at its own game, by continuing their experiments in war socialism while America cut short its project, choosing instead to wallow in the selfish crapulence of the Roaring Twenties. In 1927 Stuart Chase said it would take five years to see if the "courageous and unprecedented experiment" in the Soviet Union was "destined to be a landmark for economic guidance" of the whole world. Half a decade later he concluded that the evidence was in: Russia was the new gold standard in economic and social policy. So "why," he asked in his 1932 book, *A New Deal*, "should Russians have all the fun of remaking a world?"[16]

Chase's comment is indicative of an important aspect of the progressive mind-set. Anybody who has ever met a student activist, a muckraking journalist, or a reformist politician will notice the important role that boredom and impatience play in the impulse to "remake the world." One can easily see how boredom—sheer, unrelenting ennui with the status quo—served as the oxygen for the fire of progressivism because tedium is the tinder for the flames of mischievousness.[17] In much the same way that Romanticism laid many of the intellectual predicates for Nazism, the impatience and disaffection of progressives during the 1920s drove them to see the world as clay to be sculpted by human will. Sickened by what they saw as the spiritual languor of the age, members of the avant-garde convinced themselves that the status quo could be easily ripped down like an aging curtain and just as easily replaced with a vibrant new tapestry. This conviction often slid of its own logic into anarchism and radicalism, related worldviews which assumed that anything would be better than what we have now.

A deep aversion to boredom and a consequent, indiscriminate love for novelty among the intellectual classes translated into a routinized iconoclasm and a thoroughgoing contempt for democracy, traditional morality, the masses, and the bourgeoisie, and a love for "action, action, action!" that still plagues the left today. (How much of the practiced radicalism of the contemporary left is driven by the childish pranksterism they call being subversive?) Many of George Bernard Shaw's bons mots seem like shots in the dark against the monster of boredom—which could only be conquered by a Nietzschean superman. At one time or another Shaw idolized Stalin, Hitler, and Mussolini as the world's great "progressive" leaders because they "did things," unlike the leaders of those "putrefying corpses" called parliamentary democracies. In like terms, Gertrude Stein praised Huey Long by declaring that he was "not boring."[18]

Or consider H. G. Wells. More than any other figure, his literary escapism and faith in science as the salvation of man were seen as the preeminent antidotes to the disease of Western malaise. In the summer of 1932, Wells delivered a major speech at Oxford University to Britain's Young Liberals organization, in which he called for a " 'Phoenix Rebirth' of Liberalism" under the banner of "Liberal Fascism."[19] Fabian socialism had failed, he explained, because it hadn't grasped the need for a truly "revolutionary" effort aimed at the total transformation of society. His fellow Socialists understood the need for socialism, but they were just too nice about it. Their advocacy of piecemeal "Gas, Water and School-Board socialization" was simply too boring. Conventional democratic governments, meanwhile, were decadent, feeble, and dull. If the liberals in the 1930s were going to succeed where the Fabians had failed—abolishing private property, achieving a fully planned economy, violently crushing the forces of reaction—they'd have to learn that lesson.

Wells confessed that he'd spent some thirty years—since the dawn of the Progressive Era—reworking the idea of liberal fascism. "I have never been able to escape altogether from its relentless logic," he explained. "We have seen the *Fascisti* in Italy and a number of clumsy imitations elsewhere, and we have seen the Russian Communist Party coming into existence to reinforce this idea." And now he was done waiting. "I am asking for a Liberal *Fascisti,* for enlightened Nazis."

"And do not let me leave you in the slightest doubt as to the scope and ambition of what I am putting before you," he continued:

> These new organizations are not merely organizations for the spread of defined opinions . . . the days of that sort of amateurism are over—they are organizations to *replace* the dilatory indecisiveness of [democracy]. The world is sick of parliamentary politics . . . The Fascist Party, to the best of its ability, *is* Italy now. The Communist Party, to the best of its ability, *is* Russia. Obviously the Fascists of Liberalism must carry out a parallel ambition on a still vaster scale . . . They must begin as a disciplined sect, but they must end as the sustaining organization of a reconstituted mankind.[20]

Wells's fiction was so thinly veiled in its praise for fascism that the attentive reader can only squirm. In *The War in the Air,* German airships liquidate New York City's "black and sinister polyglot population." In *The Shape of Things to Come,* veterans of a great world war—mostly airmen and technicians—in black shirts and uniforms fight to impose one-world government on the beaten and undisciplined masses. In Wells's far-flung future, a historian looks back on the twentieth century and finds that the roots of the new, enlightened "Air Dictatorship" lay in Mussolini's Fascism—a "bad good thing," the historian calls it—as well as Nazism and Soviet Communism. In 1927 Wells couldn't help but notice "the good there is in these Fascists. There is something brave and well-meaning about them." By 1941 no less a figure than George Orwell couldn't help but conclude, "Much of what Wells has imagined and worked for is physically there in Nazi Germany."[21]

Wells was an enormous fan of FDR's, and the two met often at the White House, particularly during 1934. Wells pronounced Roosevelt "the most effective transmitting instrument possible for the coming of the new world order." In 1935 and 1936 he briefly switched to Huey Long's and Father Coughlin's more exciting brand of fascism.

(He described the bayou dictator as "a Winston Churchill who has never been at Harrow.")[22] By 1939, however, he was again firmly back in the Roosevelt camp, seeing FDR's brand of "personal government" as indispensable.

Wells's vision neatly captures the sense of excitement that infused the Western left in the 1930s. It should be no surprise that an avant-garde of self-described supermen would welcome an age where supermen would run the world. To be sure, these were on the whole dark and pessimistic times. But the spirit of "the worse the better" served as a wind behind liberals eager to remake the world, to end the days of drift and inaugurate the era of progressive mastery.

STEALING FASCIST THUNDER

Herbert Hoover won the presidential contest of 1928 in no small part on the strength of the international craze for economic planning and collectivization. He was a self-made millionaire, but his chief appeal was his experience as an engineer. In the 1920s and 1930s it was widely believed that engineering was the highest calling, and it was hoped that engineers could clear political mountains the same way they moved real ones.[23]

Hoover failed to deliver as the Great Engineer, ironically because he gave the people too much of what they wanted. Indeed, many economic historians concede that the New Deal was, in significant respects, an accelerated continuation of Hoover's policies rather than a sharp break from them. The lines are even blurrier when one notes that FDR went into office as a budget balancer who cut government pay. Of course, the New Deal was an even greater failure when it came to curing the Great Depression—but Roosevelt had something going for him that Hoover did not: an appreciation of the fascist moment.

Just as progressivism constituted a definite international moment during the second decade of the twentieth century, so in the 1930s the Western world was riding through a storm of collectivist sentiments, ideas, and trends. In Switzerland, Holland, Belgium, and Finland, quasi-fascist parties received their highest share of the votes. Until 1934 it seemed possible that Oswald Mosley, founder of the British Union of Fascists (who, like Mussolini, always considered himself a man of the left), might occupy 10 Downing Street. Meanwhile, in the United States, national socialists or populist progressives such as Huey Long and Father Coughlin were hugely popular, and they, more than any other group, moved the political center of gravity in America to the left.

This is as good a place as any to tackle the enduring myth that Long and Coughlin were conservatives. It is a bedrock dogma of all enlightened liberals that Father Charles Coughlin was an execrable right-winger (Long is a more complicated case, but whenever his legacy is portrayed negatively, he is characterized as right-wing; whenever he is a friend of the people, he's a left-winger). Again and again, Coughlin is referred to as "the right-wing Radio Priest" whom supposedly insightful essayists describe as the ideological grandfather of Rush Limbaugh, Pat Buchanan, Ann Coulter, and other putative extremists.[24] But Coughlin was in no meaningful way a conservative or even a right-winger. He was a man of the left in nearly all significant respects.

Born in 1891 in Hamilton, Ontario, Coughlin was ordained as a priest in 1916. He taught at Catholic schools in Canada for seven years, and then moved to Michigan. He eventually found a spot as a parish priest in the town of Royal Oak, a suburb of Detroit. He named the church the Shrine of the Little Flower after Saint Thérèse. Coughlin's first taste of publicity came when he battled the local Ku Klux Klan, which was at the time harassing Catholics, many of them immigrants. He talked a local radio station into permitting him to deliver sermons over the air. He was a success almost from the outset.

From 1926 until 1929 Coughlin confined himself almost entirely to religious topics, denunciations of the Klan, sermons for children, and diatribes against Prohibition—all for an audience that didn't extend very far outside the Detroit area. His big breakthrough came with the stock market collapse, when he took up populist economics. He shrewdly tapped into popular anxiety and economic discontent, and his broadcasts were picked up by more and more stations as a result. In 1930 he signed a deal with CBS to deliver six months of sermons on sixteen stations across the country on his *Golden Hour of the Little Flower.*

Almost instantly Coughlin became the most successful political commentator of the fledgling mass-media age. With over forty million listeners and a reported million letters a week, he became one of the most powerful voices in American politics.

His first victim was that ostensible conservative, Herbert Hoover. In October 1931, in a fiery speech against laissez-faire economics, Coughlin declared that America's problems couldn't be solved "by waiting for things to adjust themselves and by eating the airy platitudes of those hundreds of so-called leaders who have been busy assuring us that the bottom has been reached and that prosperity and justice and charity are waiting 'just around the corner.' "[25] His favorite villains were "international bankers" and their ilk. Donations and letters poured in.

In November, denouncing Hoover's belief that economic relief was a local matter, Coughlin made an impassioned case for government activism at the national level. He railed against a federal government that could help the starving of Belgium and even pigs in Arkansas but wouldn't feed Americans because of its antagonism to welfare. As the presidential election loomed, Coughlin threw all his weight behind Franklin Delano Roosevelt. The left-wing theocrat swore that the New Deal was "Christ's Deal" and that the choice Americans faced was "Roosevelt or Ruin." Meanwhile, he wrote the Democratic candidate, Roosevelt, grotesquely sycophantic letters explaining that he would change his own positions if that's what the campaign needed.

FDR didn't like Coughlin much, but, true to form, he was glad to let the priest think he did. When FDR won, thanks in part to a successful strategy of going after urban Catholic voters, Coughlin concluded that he had been instrumental in getting him elected. When FDR invited the Radio Priest to attend the inauguration, Coughlin assumed that the president-elect saw things the same way. Over time, he became increasingly convinced that he was an official White House spokesman, often creating serious headaches for the White House even as he celebrated this "Protestant President who has more courage than 90 per cent of the Catholic priests in the country." "Capitalism is doomed and is not worth trying to save," Coughlin pronounced. At other times he advocated "state capitalism"—a phrase rich in both fascist and Marxist associations.[26]

Indeed, Coughlin's economic populism usefully illustrates how ideological categories from the 1930s have been systematically misapplied ever since. As mentioned before, Richard Pipes described Bolshevism and Fascism as twinned heresies of Marxism. Both sought to impose socialism of one sort or another, erase class differences, and repudiate the decadent democratic-capitalist systems of the West. In a sense, Pipes's description doesn't go far enough. While Fascism and Bolshevism were surely heresies of Marxism, virtually all collectivist visions at the end of the nineteenth and beginning of the twentieth centuries were heresies of Marxism in the sense that Marxism itself was heretical. All of these isms, as the philosopher Eric Voegelin argued, were premised on the idea that men could create utopias through the rearrangement of economic forces and political will. Marxism, or really Leninism, was the most influential and powerful of these heresies and came to define the left. But just as Leninism was a kind of applied Marxism, so, too, was Fascism (as well as technocracy, Fabian socialism, corporatism, war socialism, German social democracy, and so on). Collectivism was the "wave of the future," according to the title and argument of a book by Anne Morrow Lindbergh, and it would be known by different names in different places. The fascist moment that gave birth to the "Russian-Italian method" was in reality a religious awakening in which Christianity was to be either sloughed off and replaced or "updated" by the new progressive faith in man's ability to perfect the world.[27]

From the dawn of the Progressive Era through the 1930s, the intellectual and ideological landscape was fractured within this larger camp. The fight between left and right was for the most part between left-wing and right-wing *socialists*. But virtually all camps subscribed to some hybridized version of Marxism, some bastardization of the Rousseauian dream of a society governed by a general will. It was not until the late 1940s, with the revival of classical liberalism led by Friedrich Hayek, that collectivism of all stripes was once again fought from a right that did not share the core assumptions of the left. What is aggravating is that vestigial carbuncles like Coughlin are still counted as figures of the right—because of their anti-Semitism or opposition to FDR, or because they are simply too

embarrassing to the left—even though on the fundamental philosophical and political questions Coughlinites were part of the liberal-
progressive coalition.

Coughlin himself was a darling among Capitol Hill Democrats,
particularly the progressive bloc—the liberals to the left of FDR who
pushed him for ever more aggressive reforms. In 1933 the administration was under considerable pressure to include Coughlin in the
U.S. delegation to a major economic conference in London. Ten senators and seventy-five congressmen sent a petition declaring that
Coughlin had "the confidence of millions of Americans." The vast
majority of the signatories were Democrats. There was even a
groundswell among progressives for FDR to appoint Coughlin treasury secretary.

This was no joke. Indeed, Coughlin was perhaps the foremost
American advocate of what had become an international push
toward economic nationalism. An heir to the Free Silver movement,
he was a classic left-wing populist. The more "dignified" forces of
liberalism embraced him in much the same way today's Democratic
Party embraces Michael Moore. Raymond Moley ran an article on
inflation by Coughlin in the journal he edited. Secretary of
Agriculture Henry Wallace collaborated with Coughlin in an effort
to sway the administration's monetary policy further to the left.
Recall that Wallace (who was Alger Hiss's boss at Agriculture) went
on to become Roosevelt's penultimate vice president, the leading
Soviet "useful idiot" in the United States, the editor of the *New
Republic,* and the Progressive Party's 1948 presidential nominee. In
1933 the League for Independent Political Action, a far-left group of
intellectuals chaired by John Dewey, invited Coughlin to participate
in its summer institute. When William Aberhart, the "radical premier" of Alberta, Canada, visited Coughlin in Detroit in 1935 to discuss his own left-wing economic program, Aberhart explained he
wanted to get "the most expert advice on the continent."[28]

Coughlin was more than willing to roll up his sleeves for the role
of attack dog for the Democratic Party. The centrist Democrat Al
Smith, the first Catholic to win a major party's presidential nomination, had become an increasingly bitter foe of the New Deal and
FDR. This was all the provocation Coughlin needed. After tipping

off FDR in a telegram, Coughlin took to the air to flay his fellow Catholic as a bought-and-paid-for tool of Wall Street.

Liberals often debated among themselves whether Coughlin's contribution was worth the price of his unflinching demagoguery. Until late in 1934 the answer was invariably yes. Chief among his defenders was Monsignor John Ryan, the most respected liberal Catholic intellectual and theologian in America at the time. When Coughlin unfairly and cruelly ripped Al Smith to shreds, many wondered whether it was time to distance themselves from the Radio Priest. Ryan intervened and declared the rabble-rouser was "on the side of the angels." This was the standard liberal defense of the supposedly right-wing Coughlin. He was fighting the good fight, so who cared about his excesses?

At a congressional hearing on FDR's monetary policy, Coughlin offered a two-hour peroration that held the committee transfixed. "If Congress fails to back up the President in his monetary program," he blustered, "I predict a revolution in this country which will make the French Revolution look silly!" "I know the pulse of the Nation," he further declared. "And I know Congress will do nothing but say: 'Mr. Roosevelt, we follow.' " "God is directing President Roosevelt," he added. "He is the answer to our prayers." In his sermons the leader of America's religious left sounded like he'd borrowed Mussolini's talking points: "Our Government still upholds one of the worst evils of decadent capitalism, namely, that production must be only at the profit for the owners, for the capitalist, and not for the laborer."[29]

So how did Coughlin suddenly become a right-winger? When did he become persona non grata in the eyes of liberal intellectuals? On this the historical record is abundantly clear: liberals started to call Coughlin a right-winger when he moved further to the *left*.

This isn't nearly as contradictory as it sounds. Coughlin became a villain in late 1934 almost solely because he had decided that FDR wasn't radical enough. FDR's less than fully national-socialist policies sapped Coughlin's patience—as did his reluctance to make the priest his personal Rasputin. Still, Coughlin managed for most of the year to qualify his support, saying things like "More than ever, I am in favor of *a* New Deal." Finally, on November 11, 1934, he announced he was forming a new "lobby of the people," the National

Union for Social Justice, or NUSJ. He issued sixteen principles of social justice as the platform for the new super-lobby. Among its articles of faith:

- that every citizen willing to work and capable of working shall receive a just and living annual wage which will enable him to maintain and educate his family . . .
- I believe in nationalizing those public necessities which by their very nature are too important to be held in the control of private individuals.
- I believe in upholding the right of private property yet of controlling it for the public good.
- I believe not only in the right of the laboring man to organize in unions but also in the duty of the Government which that laboring man supports to protect these organizations against the vested interests of wealth and of intellect.
- I believe in the event of a war and for the defense of our nation and its liberties, if there shall be a conscription of men let there be a conscription of wealth.
- I believe in preferring the sanctity of human rights to the sanctity of property rights. I believe that the chief concern of government shall be for the poor, because, as is witnessed, the rich have ample means of their own to care for themselves.[30]

The following month Coughlin issued another seven principles, to elaborate exactly how the NUSJ would combat the horrors of capitalism and modern commerce. These were even more explicitly anti-capitalist. Thus it was the government's "duty" to limit the "profits acquired by any industry." All workers must be guaranteed what we would today call a living wage. The government must guarantee the production of "food, wearing apparel, homes, drugs, books and all modern conveniences." "This principle," Coughlin rightly explained, "is contrary to the theory of capitalism."[31]

The program was largely derived from the prevailing views of the liberal wing of the Catholic Church, the Minnesota Farmer-Labor and Wisconsin Progressive labor parties, and Coughlin's own well-worn themes. That his economic doctrine should be influenced from the disparate branches of American populism shouldn't be a surprise. From the outset, Coughlin's ideological roots intermingled with those of many New Dealers and progressives and populists. At no time was he ever associated with classical liberalism or with the economic forces we normally connect with the right.

This returns us to one of the most infuriating distortions of American political debate. In the 1930s, what defined a "right-winger" was almost exclusively opposition to Franklin Roosevelt and the New Deal. The muckraking journalist J. T. Flynn, for example, is often labeled a leading light of the Old Right for no other reason than that he was a relentless FDR critic and a member of America First (indeed, he was one of the most articulate voices decrying the incipient fascism of the New Deal). But Flynn was no classical liberal. He had been a left-leaning columnist for the *New Republic* for much of the 1930s, and he denounced Roosevelt for moving in what he considered a rightward direction. As for his isolationism, he considered himself a fellow traveler with Norman Thomas, head of the American Socialist Party, Charles Beard, and John Dewey.

Senator Huey Long, the archetypal American fascist, is likewise often called a right-winger by his detractors—though his place in the liberal imagination is more complicated. Many Democrats, including Bill Clinton, still admire Long and invoke him very selectively. Long inspired Sinclair's *It Can't Happen Here* as well as the far superior *All the King's Men* by Robert Penn Warren, and his larger-than-life persona elicits an ambivalent reaction from liberals who admire his economic populism but dislike his unrefined demagoguery. But leaving all that aside, what cannot be denied is that Long attacked the New Deal from the *left*. His Share the Wealth plan was pure booboisie socialism. His well-documented opposition to the actual Socialist Party was entirely cultural and pragmatic, not ideological. "Will you please tell me what sense there is in running on a socialist ticket in America today?" Long quizzed a reporter from the *Nation*. "What's the use of being right only to be defeated?" Meanwhile, Norman Thomas was regularly beseeched by his rank and file to show more sympathy to Coughlin and Long. "Now I am a socialist," an Alabama man wrote Thomas in 1935, "have been for thirty five years . . . [Long] is telling the people the things we have been telling them for a generation. They listen to him . . . while they thought we were fools."[32]

What makes Long so recognizable as a fascist was his folksy contempt for the rules of democracy—"the time has come for all good men to rise above principle"—and his absolute faith that he was the authentic voice of the people. His rule over Louisiana certainly transcended that of a mere political boss. He had an authentic organic connection with his constituents that seemed to exceed anything Americans had seen before. "There is no dictatorship in Louisiana. There is a perfect democracy there, and when you have a perfect democracy it is pretty hard to tell it from a dictatorship."[33] Oddly enough, what may have allowed so many liberals and socialists to recognize the fascism in Long's politics was their own elitism and cosmopolitanism. Long had no use for pointy-headed experts and elites. His was an undiluted populism of the sort that throws aside dogma and celebrates the wisdom of the mob above all else. He appealed to the narcissism of the masses, proclaiming that through his own will to power he could make "every man a king." He had a relationship with his folk more akin to Hitler's relationship to the *Volk* than FDR could ever manage. As such, many liberals saw it as threatening, and rightly so.

Within the White House, Long and Coughlin were seen, along with other populist and radical movements and leaders—including Upton Sinclair's 1934 campaign for the governorship of California and Dr. Francis Townsend's bizarre pension movement, which swept the country in the 1930s—as dangerous threats to the control and rule of New Deal planners.[34] But only the most sloppy and circular thinking—the sort that says right-wing equals bad, and had equals right wing—would label such radicals and collectivists as anything but creatures of the left.

In 1935 Roosevelt was sufficiently worried about these various threats from the left that he ordered a secret poll to be conducted. The results scared the dickens out of many of his strategists, who concluded that Long could cost FDR the election if he ran on a third-party ticket. Indeed, Roosevelt confessed to aides that he hoped to "steal Long's thunder" by adopting at least some of his issues.

How did FDR hope to steal the thunder of incipient fascist and collectivist movements in the United States? Social Security, for starters. Although the extent of its influence is hotly debated, few dispute that the national-socialist push from below—represented by

Long, Coughlin, and Townsend—contributed to the leftward tilt of Roosevelt's "Second Hundred Days." FDR the Third Wayer aped the Bismarckian tactic of splitting the difference with the radicals in order to maintain power. Indeed, just when Long's popularity was spiking, Roosevelt unexpectedly inserted a "soak the rich" bill into his list of "must pass" legislative proposals. How things would have played out over time is unknowable because Long was assassinated in September 1935. As for Coughlin, his problems accelerated as he became ever more of an economic radical and ever more sympathetic to the actual, name-brand, foreign fascism of Mussolini and Hitler. His anti-Semitism—evident even when Roosevelt and New Deal liberals welcomed his support—likewise became ever more pronounced. During the war FDR ordered his Justice Department to spy on Coughlin with the aim of silencing him.

How much electoral support Long, the Coughlinites, and the rest would have garnered had Long survived to challenge Roosevelt at the polls remains a matter of academic speculation, but it is somewhat irrelevant to the larger point. These populist leftists framed the public debate. That Coughlin garnered 40 million listeners in a nation of only 127 million and that his audience was largest when he was calling the New Deal "Christ's Deal" should tell us something about the nature of FDR's appeal, and Coughlin's. Even those New Dealers who despised Long and Coughlin believed that if they didn't steal their thunder, "Huey Long and Father Coughlin might take over." What's more, there was precious little daylight between the substantive ideas and motivations of "street" or "country" fascists like Long and Coughlin and those of the more rarefied intellectuals who staffed the Roosevelt administration.

REMEMBERING THE FORGOTTEN MAN

One can easily make too much of the parallel chronology of Hitler's and Roosevelt's tenures. But it is not a complete coincidence that they both came to power in 1933. Though obviously very different men, they understood many of the same things about politics in the mass age. Both owed their elections to the perceived exhaustion of traditional liberal politics, and they were the two world leaders who most successfully exploited new political technologies. Roosevelt most famously utilized the radio—and the Nazis quickly aped the practice. FDR broke with all tradition to fly to the Democratic National Convention to accept his party's nomination. The imagery of him flying—a man of action!—rather than sitting on the porch and waiting for the news was electrifying, as was Hitler's brilliant use of planes, most famously in Leni Riefenstahl's *Triumph of the Will.* Take away the text of New Deal, Soviet, and Nazi propaganda posters and other artwork, and it's almost impossible to tell whether the bulging-biceps laborers are the New Soviet Man, the New Nazi Man, or the New Deal Man. Max Lerner observed in 1934, "The most damning blow that the dictatorships have struck at democracy has been the compliment they have paid us in taking over (and perfecting) our most prized devices of persuasion and our underlying contempt for the credulity of the masses."[35]

Where FDR and Hitler overlapped most was in their fawning over "the forgotten man." Fascism's success almost always depends on the cooperation of the "losers" during a time of economic and technological change. The lower-middle classes—the people who have just enough to fear losing it—are the electoral shock troops of fascism (Richard Hofstadter identified this "status anxiety" as the source of Progressivism's quasi-fascist nature). Populist appeals to resentment against "fat cats," "international bankers," "economic royalists," and so on are the stock-in-trade of fascist demagogues. Hitler and Mussolini were surely more demagogic than FDR, but Roosevelt fully understood the "magic" of such appeals. He saw nothing wrong with ascribing evil motives to those who didn't support him, and he certainly relished his role as the wellborn tribune of the little guy.

Obviously, this wasn't all a cynical act. FDR did care about the little guy, the worker, and the like. But so did Hitler. Indeed, there is a mounting body of scholarship showing that "Hitler's New Deal" (David Schoenbaum's phrase) was not only similar to FDR's but in fact more generous and more successful. Germany prospered under Hitler according to the most basic indicators. The birthrate increased 50 percent from 1932 to 1936; marriages increased until Germany led Europe in 1938–39. Suicide plummeted by 80 percent from 1932 to 1939. A recent book by the German historian Götz Aly calls Hitler the "feel good dictator" because he was so successful in restoring German confidence.[36]

When Hitler became chancellor he focused like a laser on the economy, ending unemployment far faster than FDR. When asked by the *New York Times* if his first priority was jobs, Hitler boisterously responded, "Wholly! I am thinking first of those in Germany who are in despair and who have been in despair for three years . . . What does anything else matter?" Hitler said he was a great admirer of Henry Ford, though he didn't mention Ford's virulent anti-Semitism. What appealed to Hitler about Ford was that he "produces for the masses. That little car of his had done more than anything else to destroy class differences."[37]

Mussolini and Hitler also felt that they were doing things along similar lines to FDR. Indeed, they celebrated the New Deal as a kindred effort. The German press was particularly lavish in its praise for FDR. In 1934 the *Völkischer Beobachter*—the Nazi Party's official newspaper—described Roosevelt as a man of "irreproachable, extremely responsible character and immovable will" and a "warmhearted leader of the people with a profound understanding of social needs." The paper emphasized that Roosevelt, through his New Deal, had eliminated "the uninhibited frenzy of market speculation" of the previous decade by adopting "National Socialist strains of thought in his economic and social policies." After his first year in office, Hitler sent FDR a private letter congratulating "his heroic efforts in the interests of the American people. The President's successful battle against economic distress is being followed by the entire German people with interest and admiration." And he told the American ambassador, William Dodd, that he was "in accord with the President in the view that the virtue of duty, readiness for sacrifice, and discipline should dominate the entire people. These moral demands which the President places before every individual citizen of the United States are also the quintessence of the German state philosophy, which finds its expression in the slogan 'The Public Weal Transcends the Interest of the Individual.' "[38]

Mussolini was even more assiduous in claiming the New Deal as an incipient fascist phenomenon. He reviewed FDR's book *Looking Forward,* saying, in effect, "This guy's one of us": "The appeal to the decisiveness and masculine sobriety of the nation's youth, with which Roosevelt here calls his readers to battle, is reminiscent of the ways and means by which Fascism awakened the Italian people." Mussolini wrote that FDR understood that the economy could not "be left to its own devices" and saw the fascistic nature of how the American president put this understanding into practice. "Without question, the mood accompanying this sea change resembles that of Fascism," he wrote. (He later reviewed a book by Henry Wallace, proclaiming, "Where is America headed? This book leaves no doubt that it is on the road to corporatism, the economic system of the current century.") The *Völkischer Beobachter* also noted that "many passages in his book *Looking Forward* could have been written by a National Socialist. In any case, one can assume that he feels considerable affinity with the National Socialist philosophy."[39]

In a famous interview with Emil Ludwig, Mussolini reiterated his view that "America has a dictator" in FDR. In an essay written for American audiences, he marveled at how the forces of "spiritual renewal" were destroying the outdated notion that democracy and liberalism were "immortal principles." "America itself is abandoning them. Roosevelt is moving, acting, giving orders independently of the decisions or wishes of the Senate or Congress. There are no longer intermediaries between him and the nation. There is no longer a parliament but an 'état majeur.' There are no longer parties, but a single party. A sole will silences dissenting voices. This has nothing to do with any demo-liberal conception of things." In 1933 members of Mussolini's press office recognized that these statements were starting to hurt their putative comrade-in-arms They issued an order: "It is not to be emphasized that Roosevelt's policy is fascist because these comments are immediately cabled to the United States and are used by his foes to attack him." Still, the admiration remained mutual for several years. FDR sent his ambassador to Italy, Breckinridge Long, a letter regarding "that admirable Italian gentleman," saying that Mussolini "is really interested in what we are doing and I am much interested and deeply impressed by what he has accomplished."[40]

Perhaps Norman Thomas, America's leading socialist, put the question best: "To what extent may we expect to have the economics of fascism without its politics?"[41]

But the most glaring similarity between Nazi Germany, New Deal

America, and Fascist Italy wasn't their economic policies. It was their common glorification of war.

THE FASCIST NEW DEALS

The core value of original fascism, in the eyes of most observers, was its imposition of war values on society. (This perception—or misperception, depending on how it is articulated—is so fundamental to the popular understanding of fascism that I must return to it several times in this book.) The chief appeal of war to social planners isn't conquest or death but *mobilization*. Free societies are disorganized. People do their own thing, more or less, and that can be downright inconvenient if you're trying to plan the entire economy from a boardroom somewhere. War brings conformity and unity of purpose. The ordinary rules of behavior are mothballed. You can get things done: build roads, hospitals, houses. Domestic populations and institutions were required to "do their part."

Many progressives probably would have preferred a different organizing principle, which is why William James spoke of the moral *equivalent* of war. He wanted all the benefits—Dewey's "social possibilities" of war—without the costs. Hence, in more recent times, the left has looked to everything from environmentalism and global warming to public health and "diversity" as war equivalents to cajole the public into expert-driven unity. But at the time the progressives just couldn't think of anything else that did the trick. "Martial virtues," James famously wrote, "must be the enduring cement" of American society: "intrepidity, contempt of softness, surrender of private interest, obedience to command must still remain the rock upon which states are built."[42]

In Italy many of the first Fascists were veterans who donned paramilitary garb. The fascist artistic movement Futurism glorified war in prose, poetry, and paint. Mussolini was a true voluptuary of battle, rhetorically and literally. "War alone brings up to its highest tension all human energy and puts the stamp of nobility upon the peoples who have courage to meet it," he declared in a Jamesian spirit in the *Enciclopedia italiana*'s entry on Fascism. Meanwhile, from the movement's origin as the German Fighting League Against

Interest Slavery, the Nazis were always a paramilitary organization, determined to recapture the esprit de corps of the Great War, the socialism of the trenches.

Still, not every Fascist pounding the table about war actually wanted one. Mussolini didn't launch a war until a full sixteen years into his reign. Even his Ethiopian adventure was motivated by a desire to revitalize Fascism's flagging domestic fortunes. Hitler did not commence his military buildup at once, either. Indeed, while solidifying power, he cultivated an image as a peacemaker (an image many Western pacifists were willing to indulge in good faith). But few dispute that he saw war as a means as much as an end.

With the election of Franklin Roosevelt, the progressives who'd sought to remake America through war socialism were back in power. While they professed to eschew dogma, they couldn't be more dogmatically convinced that World War I had been a successful "experiment." Had not the experiences of the Soviet Union and Fascist Italy in the 1920s proved that America had dropped the ball by relinquishing war socialism?

During the campaign FDR promised to use his experience as an architect of the Great War to tackle the Depression. Even before he was nominated, he ordered aides to prepare a brief on presidential war powers. He asked Rexford Tugwell to find out if he could use the 1917 Trading with the Enemy Act to unilaterally embargo gold exports and extracted an assurance from his intended attorney general that no matter what the arguments to the contrary, the Department of Justice would find that Roosevelt had the authority to do whatever he felt necessary in this regard. Roosevelt's inaugural address was famously drenched with martial metaphors: "I assume unhesitatingly the leadership of this great army of our people dedicated to the disciplined attack upon our common problems."

According to a document unearthed by the *Newsweek* columnist Jonathan Alter, FDR's staff prepared a radio address to the American Legion, the first to be delivered after his inaugural, in which FDR was to instruct the veterans that they should become his own "extra-constitutional" "private army" (Alter's words). "A new commander-in-chief under the oath to which you are still bound," Roosevelt's prepared text read, "I reserve to myself the right to command you in any phase of the situation which now confronts us."[43]

While Alter concedes this was "dictator talk—an explicit power grab" and showed that FDR or his minions contemplated forming "a makeshift force of veterans to enforce some kind of martial law," he minimizes the importance of his own discovery.[44] He leaves out the legacy of the American Protective League, which FDR no doubt endorsed. He fails to mention that the American Legion saw itself as an "American Fascisti" for a time. And he leaves out that FDR—who showed no reluctance when it came to using the FBI and other agencies to spy on domestic critics—oversaw the use of the American Legion as a quasi-official branch of the FBI to monitor American citizens.

Almost every program of the early New Deal was rooted in the politics of war, the economics of war, or the aesthetics of war emerging from World War I. The Tennessee Valley Authority, or TVA, the signature public works project of the New Deal, had its roots in a World War I power project. (As FDR explained when he formally asked Congress to create the thing, "This power development of war days leads logically to national planning.") The Supreme Court defended the constitutionality of the TVA in part by citing the president's war powers.

Many New Deal agencies, the famous "alphabet soup," were mostly continuations of various boards and committees set up fifteen years earlier during the war. The National Recovery Administration was explicitly modeled on the War Industries Board of World War I. The Securities and Exchange Commission was an extension of the Capital Issues Committee of the Federal Reserve Board. The Reconstruction Finance Corporation was an updated version of the War Finance Corporation. FDR's public housing initiative was run by the architect of World War I–era housing policies. During the war, public housing had been a necessity for war laborers. Under FDR, everyone became in effect a war laborer.

Presumably it is not necessary to recount how similar all of this was to developments in Nazi Germany. But it is worth noting that for the first two years of the American and German New Deals, it was America that pursued militarism and rearmament at a breakneck pace while Germany spent relatively little on arms (though Hitler faced severe constraints on rearmament). The Public Works Administration paid for the aircraft carriers *Yorktown* and *Enterprise* as well as four cruisers, many smaller warships, and over one hundred army planes parked at fifty military airports. Perhaps one reason so many people believed the New Deal ended the Depression is that the New Deal's segue into a full-blown war economy was so seamless.

Old Wilson hands infested every level of the Roosevelt bureaucracy. This makes sense in that Roosevelt's was the first Democratic administration since Wilson. Even so, the New Dealers weren't looking for mere retreads; they wanted war veterans. When Holger Cahill at first declined the invitation to head the Federal Art Project, a colleague explained, "An invitation from the Government to a job like that is tantamount to an order. It's like being drafted."[45]

Not only did government agencies organize themselves along military lines, but the staffers spoke in military jargon. Field work was work "in the trenches." Junior staffers were called "noncoms." New federal programs went "over the top." And so on.

Perhaps no program better represented the new governmental martial outlook than the Civilian Conservation Corps, or CCC. Arguably the most popular program of the New Deal, the CCC mobilized some 2.5 million young men into what could only be called paramilitary training. CCCers mostly worked as a "forestry army," clearing dead wood and the like. Enlistees met at army recruiting stations; wore World War I uniforms; were transported around the country by troop trains; answered to army sergeants; were required to stand at attention, march in formation, employ military lingo—including the duty of calling superiors "sir"—read a CCC newspaper modeled on *Stars and Stripes;* went to bed in army tents listening to taps; and woke to reveille.

After the CCC was approved by Congress, FDR reported, "It is a pretty good record, one which I think can be compared with the mobilization carried on in 1917." The Speaker of the House boasted of the CCC's success: "They are also under military training and as they come out of it they come out improved in health and developed mentally and physically and are more useful citizens and if ever we should become involved in another war they would furnish a very valuable nucleus for our army."[46] Meanwhile, the Nazis were establishing similar camps for virtually identical reasons.

The chief motive among social planners was to get young men

out of the mainstream workforce. The public arguments tended to emphasize the need to beef up the physical and moral fiber of an embryonic new army. FDR said the camps were ideal for getting youth "off the city street corners." Hitler promised his camps would keep youth from "rotting helplessly in the streets." Mussolini's various "battles"—the "Battle of the Grains" and such—were defended on similar grounds.

A second rationale was to transcend class barriers, an aspect of the program that still appeals to liberals today. The argument, then as now, is that there are no common institutions that foster a sense of true collective obligation. There's merit to this point. But it's interesting that the Nazis were far more convinced of this rationale than the New Dealers, and it informed not only their Labor Service program but their entire domestic agenda.[47]

A far more shocking example of the militarization of American life came in the form of the National Recovery Administration, led by Hugh "Iron Pants" Johnson, *Time*'s Man of the Year for 1933. General Johnson was a pugnacious brawler who threatened that Americans who didn't cooperate with the New Deal would get a "sock in the nose." The military liaison to the War Industries Board and director of America's first military draft during the Great War— which he later called the "great schooling" for the New Deal— Johnson was convinced that what America needed was another injection of wartime fervor and fear. Few public figures—Joseph McCarthy included—were more prone to question the patriotism of their opponents. At every opportunity, Johnson claimed the war on the Depression was indistinguishable from battle. "This is war— lethal and more menacing than any other crisis in our history," he wrote. No sphere of life was out of bounds for the new service. "It is women in homes—and not soldiers in uniform—who will this time save our country," he announced. "They will go over the top to as great a victory as the Argonne. It is zero hour for housewives. Their battle cry is 'Buy now under the Blue Eagle!' "[48]

The Blue Eagle was the patriotic symbol of compliance that all companies were expected to hang from their doors, along with the motto "We do our part," a phrase used by the administration the way the Germans used *"Gemeinnutz geht vor Eigennutz."*[49] Now largely airbrushed from popular awareness, the stylized Indian eagle clutching a band of lightning bolts in one claw and an industrial cogwheel in the other was often compared to the swastika or the German Reich eagle in both American and German newspapers. Johnson demanded that compliance with the Blue Eagle program be monitored by an army of quasi-official informants, from union members to Boy Scouts. His totalitarian approach was unmistakable. "When every American housewife understands that the Blue Eagle on everything that she permits to come into her home is a symbol of its restoration to security, may God have mercy on the man or group of men who attempt to trifle with this bird."[50]

It's difficult to exaggerate the propagandistic importance FDR invested in the Blue Eagle. "In war, in the gloom of night attack, soldiers wear a bright badge on their shoulders to be sure their comrades do not fire on comrades," the president explained. "On that principle those who cooperate in this program must know each other at a glance." In a fireside chat in 1933, Roosevelt called for a great Mussolini-style "summer offensive against unemployment." Hollywood did its part. In the 1933 Warner Brothers musical *Footlight Parade,* starring James Cagney, a chorus line uses flash cards to flip up a portrait of Roosevelt, and then forms a giant Blue Eagle. Will Rogers led a Who's Who roster of stars in Blue Eagle and NRA radio broadcasts.

Johnson's favorite means of promoting compliance with the Blue Eagle were military parades and Nuremberg-style rallies. On September 12, 1933, Johnson harangued an audience of ten thousand at Madison Square Garden, vowing that 85 percent of America's workers were already under the authority of the Blue Eagle. The following day New York was nearly shut down by a Blue Eagle parade in honor of "The President's NRA Day." All Blue Eagle–compliant stores were ordered shut at 1:00 p.m., and the governor declared a half-day holiday for everyone else as well. Under the direction of a U.S. Army major general, the Blue Eagle parade marched from Washington Square up Fifth Avenue to the New York Public Library, where it passed a reviewing stand upon which stood Johnson, the governors from the tristate area, and Eleanor Roosevelt.

This was the biggest parade in New York's history, eclipsing even the ticker-tape parade to celebrate Charles Lindbergh's crossing of the Atlantic. In true corporatist fashion, labor and management alike were expected to participate. The President's NRA Day Parade boasted fifty thousand garment workers, thirty thousand city laborers, seventeen thousand retail workers, six thousand brewery hands, and a Radio City Music Hall troupe. Nearly a quarter-million men and women marched for ten hours past an audience of well over a million people, with forty-nine military planes flying overhead. Because of events like this, writes Arthur Schlesinger Jr., Johnson and Roosevelt achieved their goal of "transforming a government agency into a religious experience."[51] A member of the British Independent Labour Party was horrified by such pageantry, saying it made him feel like he was in Nazi Germany.

The New York parade was no isolated incident. Similar spectacles were held in cities across the country, where marchers typically wore the uniforms of their respective occupations. The Philadelphia Eagles football team was named in honor of the Blue Eagle. A hundred thousand schoolkids were marched onto the Boston Common and forced to swear an oath, administered by the mayor: "I promise as a good American citizen to do my part for the NRA. I will buy only where the Blue Eagle flies."[52] In Atlantic City, beauty pageant contestants had the Blue Eagle stamped on their thighs. In San Francisco, eight thousand schoolchildren were orchestrated to form an enormous Blue Eagle. In Memphis, fifty thousand citizens marched in the city's Christmas parade, which ended with Santa Claus riding a giant Blue Eagle.

Not surprisingly, victims of the Blue Eagle received little sympathy in the press and even less quarter from the government. Perhaps the most famous case was Jacob Maged, the forty-nine-year-old immigrant dry cleaner who spent three months in jail in 1934 for charging thirty-five cents to press a suit, when the NRA had insisted that all loyal Americans must charge at least forty cents. Because one of the central goals of the early New Deal was to create artificial scarcity in order to drive prices up, the Agricultural Adjustment Administration ordered that six million pigs be slaughtered. Bountiful crops were left to rot. Many white farmers were paid not to work their land (which meant that many black tenant farmers went hungry). All of these policies were enforced by a militarized government.

In urban centers the plight of blacks was little better. By granting new collective bargaining powers to unions, FDR also gave them the power to lock blacks out of the labor force. And the unions—often viscerally racist—did precisely that. Hence some in the black press said the NRA really stood for the "Negro Run Around," the "Negro Removal Act," and "Negroes Robbed Again." At a rally in Harlem a protester drew a picture of the Blue Eagle and wrote underneath: "That Bird Stole My Pop's Job."[53] Meanwhile, under Johnson's watchful eye, policemen would break down doors with axes to make sure tailors weren't working at night and—literally—yank newsboys from the street because they didn't work for big corporations.

It should not be surprising to learn that General Johnson was an ardent disciple of Fascism. As head of the NRA, he distributed copies of *The Corporate State* by Raffaello Viglione—an unapologetic Fascist tract by one of Mussolini's favorite economists. He even gave one to Secretary of Labor Frances Perkins, imploring her to hand out copies to the cabinet.

By 1934 Johnson's fascist methods and, more important, his unstable personality had led to his downfall. And while he was undoubtedly the most unrelentingly fascistic and pro-Fascist member of the Roosevelt administration, his ideas and methods were not at all out of the mainstream. When Alexander Sachs, a respected economist who'd grown up in Europe, was invited to consult on the formation of the NRA, he warned that it could only be administered "by a bureaucracy operating by fiat and such bureaucracy would be far more akin to the incipient Fascist or Nazi state than to a liberal republic." No one followed his advice, and he joined the administration anyway. In late 1934 Rexford Tugwell visited Italy and found the Fascist project familiar. "I find Italy doing many of the things which seem to me necessary . . . Mussolini certainly has the same people opposed to him as FDR has. But he has the press controlled so that they cannot scream lies at him daily." The Research and Planning Division of the NRA commissioned a study, *Capitalism and Labor Under Fascism,* which concluded, "The fascist principles are very similar to those which have been evolving in America and so are of particular interest at this time."

It's ironic that in the 1930s it was far from out-of-bounds to call the New Deal or FDR fascist. Yet for the two generations after World

War II it was simply unacceptable to associate the New Deal with fascism in any way. This cultural and political taboo has skewed American politics in profound ways. In order to assert that the New Deal was the opposite of fascism—rather than a kindred phenomenon—liberal intellectuals had to create an enormous straw man out of the modern conservative movement. This was surprisingly easy. Since "right-wing" was already defined as anti-Roosevelt, it did not take much effort to conflate the American right with Nazism and fascism. Thus, for example, liberals portray American "isolationism" as a distinctly conservative tradition, even though most of the leading isolationists associated with America First and similar causes in the 1930s and 1940s were in fact liberals and progressives, including Joe Kennedy, John Dewey, Amos Pinchot, Charles Beard, J. T. Flynn, and Norman Thomas.

The myth of right-wing fascism only began to unravel decades later thanks to an unlikely figure: Ronald Wilson Reagan, a former Roosevelt Democrat. In both 1976 and 1980 Reagan refused to retract his opinion that the early New Dealers looked favorably on the policies of Fascist Italy. In 1981 the controversy was renewed when then-President Reagan stuck to his guns. "Reagan Still Sure Some in New Deal Espoused Fascism," read the headline of a *Washington Post* article.[54] Reagan's refusal to back off this claim was a watershed moment, though the taboo remains largely intact.

But why was the taboo there in the first place? One answer is both obvious and entirely understandable: the Holocaust. As one of the signature evils of human history, the extermination of European Jewry colors everything it touches. But this is terribly inaccurate, in that various other fascist regimes don't deserve to be blamed for the Holocaust, including Fascist Italy. Nowhere here do I suggest that New Dealism was akin to Hitlerism if we are to define Hitlerism solely in terms of the Holocaust. But fascism was already fascism *before* the Holocaust. The Holocaust chronologically and to a certain extent philosophically was the death rattle of fascism in Germany. To use the last chapter of German fascism to explain away the earlier fascisms of Italy, America, and elsewhere is akin to reading the wrong book backward. And to say that the New Deal had nothing in common with fascism because the later New Dealers stood opposed to the Holocaust is to say that there is nothing distinct or significant to fascism save the Holocaust—a position no serious person holds.

Indeed, it seems impossible to deny that the New Deal was objectively fascistic. Under the New Deal, governmental goons smashed down doors to impose domestic policies. G-Men were treated like demigods, even as they spied on dissidents. Captains of industry wrote the rules by which they were governed. FDR secretly taped his conversations, used the postal service to punish his enemies, lied repeatedly to maneuver the United States into war, and undermined Congress's war-making powers at several turns. When warned by Frances Perkins in 1932 that many provisions of the New Deal were unconstitutional, he in effect shrugged and said that they'd deal with that later (his intended solution: pack the Supreme Court with cronies). In 1942 he flatly told Congress that if it didn't do what he wanted, he'd do it anyway. He questioned the patriotism of anybody who opposed his economic programs, never mind the war itself. He created the military-industrial complex so many on the left decry as fascist today.

In 1936 Roosevelt told Congress, "We have built up new instruments of public power. In the hands of a people's government this power is wholesome and proper. But in the hands of political puppets of an economic autocracy such power would provide shackles for the liberties of the people."[55] As Al Smith noted, the upshot of this statement is that Roosevelt didn't mind an authoritarian government, so long as representatives of "the people"—that is, liberals— ran the government. But if anybody "we" dislike gets control of the government, it would constitute tyranny.

This kind of skewed rationale gets to the heart of liberal fascism. Progressivism, liberalism, or whatever you want to call it has become an ideology of power. So long as liberals hold it, principles don't matter. It also highlights the real fascist legacy of World War I and the New Deal: the notion that government action in the name of "good things" under the direction of "our people" is always and everywhere justified. Dissent by the right people is the highest form of patriotism. Dissent by the wrong people is troubling evidence of incipient fascism. The anti-dogmatism that progressives and fascists alike inherited from Pragmatism made the motives of the activist the only criteria for judging the legitimacy of action. "I want to assure you," FDR's aide Harry Hopkins told an audience of New Deal activists in New York, "that we are not afraid of exploring anything within the law, and we have a lawyer who will declare anything you want to do legal."[56]

Today, particularly under Bush, it is precisely this attitude that liberals call fascist. But that yardstick is too short to get the full measure of what made the New Deal fascistic. We render fascism and Nazism into cartoons when we simply say that they were evil. The seduction of Nazism was its appeal to community, its attempt to restore via an all-powerful state a sense of belonging to those lost in modern society. Modernization, industrialization, and secularization sowed doubt and alienation among the masses. The Nazis promised to make people feel they belonged to something larger than themselves. The spirit of "all for one, one for all" suffused every Nazi pageant and parade.

This was the fundamental public philosophy shared by all of FDR's Brain Trust, and they inherited it wholesale from Herbert Croly and his comrades. "At the heart of the New Deal," writes William Schambra, "was the resurrection of the national idea, the renewal of the vision of national community. Roosevelt sought to pull America together in the face of its divisions by an appeal to national duty, discipline, and brotherhood; he aimed to restore the sense of local community, at the national level." Roosevelt himself observed that "we have been extending to our national life the old principle of the local community" in response to the "drastic changes" working their way through American life.[57] Militarism in America, as in Nazi Germany and Fascist Italy, was a means to this end, not the end itself.

This has been the liberal enterprise ever since: to transform a democratic republic into an enormous tribal community, to give every member of society from Key West, Florida, to Fairbanks, Alaska, that same sense of belonging—"we're all in it together!"—that we allegedly feel in a close-knit community. The yearning for community is deep and human and decent. But these yearnings are often misplaced when channeled through the federal government and imposed across a diverse nation with a republican constitution. This was the debate at the heart of the Constitutional Convention and one that the progressives sought to settle permanently in their favor. The government cannot love you, and any politics that works on a different assumption is destined for no good. And yet ever since the New Deal, liberals have been unable to shake this fundamental dogma that the state can be the instrument for a politics of meaning that transforms the entire nation into a village.

We should close this discussion by once again reiterating that whatever the similarities between the three New Deals, the differences between America, Germany, and Italy are more important. FDR's sins were nowhere near those of Hitler or Mussolini. Some of this has to do with the man. FDR believed in America and the American way of life—or at least he firmly believed that he believed in them. He still stood for election, though he did violate the tradition that presidents only serve two terms. He respected the system, though he did try to castrate the Supreme Court. He was not a tyrant, though he did put over a hundred thousand citizens into camps on the theory that their race could not be trusted. There are good arguments to be had on all sides of these and other events. But one thing is clear: the American people could never be expected to countenance tyranny for too long. During wartime this country has historically done whatever it takes to see things through. But in peacetime the American character is not inclined to look to the state for meaning and direction. Liberals have responded to this by constantly searching for new crises, new moral equivalents of war.

The former *New Republic* journalist J. T. Flynn was perhaps the most famous anti-Roosevelt muckraker of the 1930s. He loathed Roosevelt and was convinced that the New Deal was a fascist enterprise. He predicted that proponents of the New Deal and its successors would become addicted to crises to maintain power and implement their agendas. He wrote of the New Deal: "It is born in crisis, lives on crises, and cannot survive the era of crisis. By the very law of its nature it must create for itself, if it is to continue, fresh crises from year to year. Mussolini came to power in the postwar crisis and became himself a crisis in Italian life . . . Hitler's story is the same. And our future is charted out upon the same turbulent road of a permanent crisis."[58]

But Flynn understood that while America might go down a similar road, it needn't be as bumpy a ride. He predicted that American fascism might manifest itself as "a very genteel and dainty and pleas-

ant form of fascism which cannot be called fascism at all because it
will be so virtuous and polite." Waldo Frank made a similar observation in 1934:

> The NRA is the beginning of American Fascism. But unlike
> Italy and Germany, democratic parliamentarianism has for gen-
> erations been strong in the Anglo-Saxon world; *it is a tribal in-
> stitution*. Therefore, a Fascism that disposes of it, rather than
> sharpens and exploits it, is not to be expected in North America
> or Britain. Fascism may be so gradual in the United States
> that most voters will not be aware of its existence. The true
> Fascist leaders will not be present imitators of German Führer
> and Italian condottieri, prancing in silver shirts. They will be
> judicious, black-frocked gentlemen; graduates of the best uni-
> versities; disciples of Nicholas Murray Butler and Walter
> Lippmann.[59]

I think it is clear that to the extent there's any validity to my argument at all—that fascism, shorn of the word, endures in the liberal
mind—this analysis is true. We have been on the road to serfdom, we
may still be on that road, but it doesn't *feel* that way.

The question is why. Why "nice" fascism here and not the nastier
variety? My own answer is: American exceptionalism. This is what
Frank is referring to when he says democracy in America is a "tribal
institution." American culture supersedes our legal and constitutional framework. It is our greatest bulwark against fascism.

Werner Sombart famously asked: "Why is there no socialism in
the United States?" The answer for historians and political theorists
has always been: because America has no feudal past, no class problems of the European sort. This, as Wolfgang Schivelbusch argues,
is also largely the answer to the question: "Why is there no Fascism
in the United States?" But this is the case only if we mean the oppression, cruelty, and tyranny of classical fascism. Nationalism and
fascism can only bring out traits that are already in a society's genetic code. In Germany the blackest parts of the German soul were
unleashed, in Italy the insecurities of a faded star of Western civilization. In America, fascism hit at the beginning of the American century, which meant, among other things, that it was not nearly so dark

a vision. We had no bitter resentments to vindicate, no grievances to avenge. Instead, fascism in America was a more hopeful affair (though let us recall that fascism succeeded at first in Italy and Germany because it offered hope as well).

That doesn't mean we didn't have bleak moments. But these moments could not be sustained. The progressives and liberals had two shots at maintaining real fascistic war crises—during World War I and again during the New Deal and World War II. They couldn't keep it going, because the American system, the American character, and the American experience made such "experiments" unsustainable. As for the genteel fascism Flynn referred to, that's a different story—one that begins in the chapters that follow.

While the cultural left has long seen the outlines of fascism in the alleged conformity of the 1950s, the third fascist moment in the United States actually began in the 1960s. It differed dramatically from the first two fascist moments—those that followed the Progressive Era and the New Deal—largely by virtue of the fact it came after the hard collectivist era in Western civilization. But as with the previous eras, the 1960s represented an international movement. Students launched radical uprisings around the world, in France, Indonesia, Czechoslovakia, Poland, Senegal, South Korea, Mexico, and the United States. Meanwhile, working from within the establishment, a new cohort of liberal activists sought to re-create the social and political dynamics of their parents' generation, to further the legacies and fulfill the promises of the Progressive Era. This two-pronged assault, from above and below, ultimately succeeded in seizing the commanding heights of the government and the culture. The next two chapters will consider each in turn.

· 5 ·

The 1960s:
Fascism Takes to the Streets

T HE SELF-STYLED revolutionaries had grown increasingly
brazen in their campaign to force concessions from the university. Students and professors who were labeled race traitors received death threats. Enemies of the racial nation were savagely
beaten by roaming thugs. Guns were brought onto the campus, and
the students dressed up in military uniforms. Professors were held
hostage, badgered, intimidated, and threatened whenever their teaching contradicted racial orthodoxy. But the university administration,
out of a mixture of cowardice and sympathy for the rebels, refused
to punish the revolutionaries, even when the president was manhan-
dled by a fascist goon in front of an audience made up of the campus community.

The radicals and their student sympathizers believed themselves
to be revolutionaries of the left—the opposite of fascists in their
minds—yet when one of their professors read them the speeches of
Benito Mussolini, the students reacted with enthusiasm. Events
came to a climax when students took over the student union and the
local radio station. Armed with rifles and shotguns, they demanded
an ethnically pure educational institution staffed and run by members of their own race. At first the faculty and administration were
understandably reluctant; but when it was suggested that those who
opposed their agenda might be killed, most of the "moderates"

quickly reversed course and supported the militants. In a mass rally reminiscent of Nuremberg, the professors recanted their reactionary ways and swore fidelity to the new revolutionary order. One professor later recalled how easily "pompous teachers who catechized about academic freedom could, with a little shove, be made into dancing bears."[1]

Eventually, the fascist thugs got everything they wanted. The authorities caved in to their demands. The few who remained opposed quietly left the university and, in some cases, the country, once it was clear that their safety could not be guaranteed.

The University of Berlin in 1932? Milan in 1922? Good guesses. But this all happened at Cornell in the spring of 1969. Paramilitary Black Nationalists under the banner of the Afro-American Society seized control of the university after waging an increasingly aggressive campaign of intimidation and violence.

The public excuse for the armed seizure of the Cornell student union was a cross burning outside a black dorm. This was later revealed to be a hoax orchestrated by the black radicals themselves in order to provide a pretext for their violence—and to overshadow the administration's fainthearted and toothless "reprimands" of six black radicals who'd broken campus rules and state laws. This Reichstag-fire-style tactic worked perfectly, as the gun-toting fascist *squadristi* stormed Straight Hall in the predawn hours, rousting bleary-eyed parents who were staying there for Parents Weekend. These bewildered souls who had the misfortune to bankroll the educations of the very gun-toting scholarship students now calling them "pigs" were forced to jump from a three-foot-high cargo deck into the freezing Ithaca rain. "This is Nazism in its worst form," declared a mother with breathless, if understandable, exaggeration.[2] The university president, James A. Perkins, was required to cancel his morning convocation address, sublimely titled "The Stability of the University."

In popular myth the 1960s was a gentle utopian movement that opposed the colonialist Vietnam War abroad and sought greater social equality and harmony at home. And it is true that the vast majority of those young people who were drawn to what they called the movement were starry-eyed idealists who thought they were ushering in the Age of Aquarius. Still, in its strictly political dimension, there is no denying that the movement's activist core was little more than a fascist youth cult. Indeed the "movement" of the 1960s may be considered the third great fascist moment of the twentieth century. The radicals of the New Left may have spoken about "power to the people" and the "authentic voice of a new generation," but they really favored neither. They were an avant-garde movement that sought to redefine not only politics but human nature itself.

Historically, fascism is of necessity and by design a form of youth movement, and all youth movements have more than a whiff of fascism about them. The exaltation of passion over reason, action over deliberation, is a naturally youthful impulse. Treating young people as equals, "privileging" their opinions precisely because they lack experience and knowledge, is an inherently fascist tendency, because at its heart lies the urge to throw off "old ways" and "old dogmas" in favor of what the Nazis called the "idealism of the deed." Youth politics—like populism generally—is the politics of the tantrum and the hissy fit. The indulgence of so-called youth politics is one face of the sort of cowardice and insecurity that leads to the triumph of barbarism.

While there's no disputing that Nazism's *success* was deeply connected to the privations of the great German Depression, that should not lead one to think that Nazism itself was a product of poverty. Even before World War I, Germany was undergoing a revolution of youth. The war merely accelerated these trends, heightening both idealism and alienation. Klaus Mann, the secular Jew and homosexual novelist, spoke for much of his generation when he wrote in 1927, "We are a generation that is united, so to speak, only by perplexity. As yet, we have not found the goal that might be able to dedicate us to common effort, although we all share the search for such a goal."[3] Mann understated the case. While young Germans were divided about what should replace the old order, they were united by more than mere perplexity. A sort of youthful identity politics had swept through Germany, fired by the notion that the new generation was different and better because it had been liberated from the politics of corrupt and cowardly old men and was determined to create an "authentic" new order.

German youth culture in the 1920s and early 1930s was ripe with rebelliousness, environmental mysticism, idealism, and no small amount of paganism, expressing attitudes that should be familiar to anyone who lived through the 1960s. "They regarded family life as repressive and insincere," writes one historian. They believed sexuality, in and out of marriage, was "shot through with hypocrisy," writes another. They, too, believed you couldn't trust anyone over thirty and despised the old materialistic order in all its manifestations. To them, "parental religion was largely a sham, politics boastful and trivial, economics unscrupulous and deceitful, education stereotyped and lifeless, art trashy and sentimental, literature spurious and commercialized, drama tawdry and mechanical." Born of the middle class, the youth movement rejected, even loathed, middle-class liberalism. "Their goal," writes John Toland, "was to establish a youth culture for fighting the bourgeois trinity of school, home and church."[4]

In cafés they howled at the decadence of German society in cadences reminiscent of Allen Ginsberg. In the woods they'd commune with nature, awaiting "messages from the forest." A führer— or popularly acclaimed "leader"—might read passages from Nietzsche or the poet Stefan George, who wrote: "The people and supreme wisdom yearn for the Man!—The Deed! . . . Perhaps someone who sat for years among your murderers and slept in your prisons will stand up and *do the deed!*" "These young people," Toland writes, "thriving on mysticism and impelled by idealism, yearned for action—any kind of action."[5]

Even before the Nazis seized power, student radicals were eager to challenge the stodgy conservatism of German higher education, which cherished classically liberal academic freedom and the authority of scholars and teachers. A wave of Nietzschean pragmatism (Julien Benda's phrase) had swept across Europe, bringing with it a wind that blew away the stale dogmas of their parents' generation, revealing a new world to be seen with fresh eyes. The Nazis told young people that their enthusiasm shouldn't be restrained through academic study—rather, it should be indulged through political action. The tradition of study for its own sake was thrown aside in the name of "relevance." Let us read no more of Jewish science and foreign abstractions, they cried. Let us learn of Germans and war and what we can do for the nation! Intuition—which young people have in abundance—was more important than knowledge and experience, insisted the radicals. The youth loved how Hitler denounced the theorists—"ink knights," he spat. What was required, according to Hitler, was a "revolt against reason" itself, for "[i]ntellect has poisoned our people!"[6] Hitler rejoiced that he stole the hearts and minds of youth, transforming universities into incubators of activism for the Fatherland.

The Nazis succeeded with stunning speed. In 1927, during a time of general prosperity, 77 percent of Prussian students insisted that the "Aryan paragraph"—barring Jews from employment—be incorporated into the charters of German universities. As a halfway measure, they fought for racial quotas that would limit the number of racially inappropriate students. In 1931, 60 percent of all German undergraduates supported the Nazi Student Organization. Regional studies of Nazi participation found that students generally outpaced any other group in their support for National Socialism.[7]

A key selling point for German youth was the Nazi emphasis on the need for increased student participation in university governance. Nazis believed that the voice of the students needed to be heard and the importance of "activism" recognized as an essential part of higher education. Foreshadowing a refrain common to American student radicals of the 1960s, like Columbia's Mark Rudd, who declared that the only legitimate job of the university was "the creation and expansion of a revolutionary movement," the Nazis believed that the university should be an empowering incubator of revolutionaries first and peddlers of abstraction a very, very distant second.[8]

The Nazis' tolerance for dissident views sharply declined, of course, once they attained and solidified power. But the themes remained fairly constant. Indeed, the Nazis fulfilled their promise to increase student participation in university governance as part of a broader redefinition of the university itself. Walter Schultze, the director of the National Socialist Association of University Lecturers, laid out the new official doctrine in an address to the first gathering of the organization, wherein he explained that "academic freedom" must be redefined so that students and professors alike could work together toward the larger cause. "Never has the German idea of freedom been conceived with greater life and vigor than in our day . . . Ultimately freedom is nothing else but responsible service on behalf of the basic values of our being as a Volk."[9]

Professors who deviated from the new orthodoxy faced all of the familiar tactics of the campus left in the 1960s. Their classrooms were barricaded or occupied, threats were put in their mail, denunciations were posted on campus bulletin boards and published in student newspapers, lecturers were heckled. When administrators tried to block or punish these antics, the students mounted massive protests, and the students naturally won, often forcing the resignation of the administrator.

What cannot be overstated is that German students were first and foremost rebelling against the *conservatism* of both German higher education and the older generation's "bourgeois materialism." The churches, too, were suspect because they had become so closely associated with the old, corrupt World War I regime. The students wanted to run the universities, which to traditional academics was akin to inmates running the asylum. Meanwhile, most of the progressive professors, at least those who weren't Jews or Bolsheviks, gamely went along. Indeed, many such academics—like Hans-Georg Gadamer—who in later years would exploit their victim status under the Nazis, were quite happy to take a better office vacated by a Jewish colleague. Martin Heidegger, the most influential philosopher of the twentieth century, took to the Nazi revolution instantly.

The Cornell takeover echoed these and other fascist themes. Black student radicals, convinced of their racial superiority and the inherent corruption of liberalism, mounted a sustained campaign of intimidation and violence against the very institution that afforded them the luxury of an education. President Perkins himself was a quintessentially progressive educator. With degrees from Swarthmore and Princeton, he cut his teeth as a New Dealer in the Office of Price Administration. Intellectually, Perkins was a product of the progressive-pragmatic tradition of William James and John Dewey, rejecting the idea that universities should be dedicated to the pursuit of eternal truths or enduring questions. He ridiculed the "intellectual chastity" of traditional scholarship and mocked non-pragmatic scholars—modern-day ink knights—who spent their time devoted to "barren discussions of medieval scholasticism." Like so many of the New Deal intellectuals, Perkins was hostile to the idea that the past had much to say about the present. For him, the watchword was "relevance," which in the 1960s quickly led to "empowerment."[10]

Perkins believed that universities should be laboratories for social change, training grounds for "experts" who would parachute into the real world and fix society, like the progressives of Wilson's and FDR's day. For these reasons—plus a decided lack of courage—Perkins prostrated himself to fascist goons while he ruthlessly turned his back on those whose educations, jobs, and even lives were threatened by Black Power radicals. German students insisted that they be taught "German science" and "German logic." The black radicals wanted to be taught "black science" and "black logic" by black professors. They demanded a separate school tasked to "create the tools necessary for the formation of a black nation." They backed up these demands not with arguments but with violence and passionate assertion. "In the past it has been all the black people who have done all the dying," shouted the leader of the black radicals. "Now the time has come when the pigs are going to die." Perkins supinely obliged after only token opposition. After all, he explained, "there is nothing I have ever said or will ever say that is forever fixed or will not be modified by changed circumstances." The first course offered in the new program was Black Ideology.[11]

Since then, what we now call identity politics has become the norm in academia. Whole departments are given over to the exploration and celebration of race and gender differences. Diversity is now code for the immutable nature of racial identity. This idea, too, traces itself back to the neo-Romanticism of the Nazis. What was once the hallmark of Nazi thinking, forced on higher education at gunpoint, is now the height of intellectual sophistication. Andrew Hacker, then a young professor at Cornell, today perhaps the preeminent white liberal writer on racial issues, has written that "historically white" colleges "are white . . . in logic and learning, in their conceptions of scholarly knowledge and demeanor."[12]

Readers of a certain age probably know next to nothing about the Cornell uprising, and an even larger number probably have a hard time reconciling this spectacle with the image of the 1960s conjured by the popular culture. They believe in the Sorelian myth of the 1960s as an age when the "good guys" overturned a corrupt system, rebelled against their "square" parents, and ushered in an age of enlightenment and decency, now under threat from oppressive conservatives who want to roll back its utopian gains. Liberal baby boomers have smeared the lens of memory with Vaseline, depicting the would-be revolutionaries as champions of peace and love—*free* love at that! Communes, hand-holding, marching arm in arm for peace and justice, and singing "Kumbaya" around the campfire: these are the images the New Left wants to put at the front of our collective memory. Some on the left still argue that the 1960s was a period of revolutionary politics, though they are split over the extent of the revolution's failures and triumphs. More mainstream liberals want us to remember John F. Kennedy uniting the nation with his call to "ask not what your country can do for you—ask what you can do for your country." Others emphasize the antiwar or civil rights movements.

Speaking as a presidential candidate in 2003, Howard Dean offered the consensus view when he told the *Washington Post* that the 1960s was "a time of great hope." "Medicare had passed. Head Start had passed. The Civil Rights Act, the Voting Rights Act, the first African American justice [appointed to] the United States Supreme Court. We felt like we were all in it together, that we all had responsibility for this country . . . That [strong schools and communities were] everybody's responsibility. That if one person was left behind, then America wasn't as strong or as good as it could be or as it should be. That's the kind of country that I want back."[13]

There's no reason not to take Dean at his word. Indeed, unlike many liberal Democrats who were products of that time, Dean is admirably willing to admit that he was decisively shaped by the decade—while the Clintons and John Kerry, who were vastly more influenced by radical politics, insist on pretending that the 1960s was little more than a movie playing in the background. In a sense, however, one could say that Dean is the bigger liar. For almost everything about this gauzy rendition of the 1960s is a distortion.

First of all, young people were not uniformly "progressive." Public opinion surveys found that young Americans were often the most pro-military while people over fifty were the most likely to oppose war. Numerous studies also show that radical children were not rebelling against their parents' values. The single best predictor of whether a college student would become a campus radical was the ideology of his or her own parents. Left-leaning parents produced left-leaning children who grew up to be radical revolutionaries. The most significant divide among young people was between those attending college and those not. But even among campus youth, attitudes on Vietnam didn't turn negative until the 1960s were almost over, and even then there was much less consensus than the PBS documentaries would suggest.

Moreover, the student radicals themselves were not quite the antiwar pacifists that John Lennon nostalgists might think. They did not want to give peace a chance when the peace wasn't favorable to their agenda. The Students for a Democratic Society, or SDS, did not start out as an antiwar organization. Indeed, its leader, Tom Hayden, considered the early antiwar activism a distraction from its core mission in the streets. Even after the New Left became chiefly defined by its stance against the war, it was never pacifistic, at least at its most glorified fringes. The Black Panthers, who assassinated police in ambushes and plotted terrorist bombings, were revered by New Left radicals—Hayden called them "our Vietcong." The Weathermen, an offshoot of the SDS, conducted a campaign of domestic terrorism and preached the cleansing value of violence. Vietnam Veterans Against the War, the group John Kerry spoke for and led, internally debated whether or not it should assassinate politicians who supported the war.[14] Gandhis they were not.

This raises an even more fundamentally dishonest aspect of the 1960s myth. Dean, speaking for many, paints the 1960s as a time of great unity. "People my age really felt that way."[15] But this is patent nonsense. "People" didn't feel that way. *The people Howard Dean knew* felt that way—or at least their nostalgia causes them to think they did. It's bizarre how many people remember the 1960s as a time of "unity" and "hope" when it was in reality a time of rampant domestic terrorism, campus tumult, assassinations, and riots. Nostalgia for their own youth can't explain this myopia, since liberals also pine for the 1930s as a time when "we were all in it together." This, too, is a gross distortion. The United States was not unified in the 1930s; it was torn by political unrest, intense labor violence, and the fear that one totalitarianism or another lay just around the corner. If unity alone was the issue, the left would pine for the 1950s or even the 1920s. But the left didn't thrive in these decades, so any unity enjoyed by Americans was illegitimate.

In other words, it is not unity the left longs for but victory; unity on terms not their own (such as the "staid conformity" of the 1950s) is false and misleading. In the 1930s and 1960s, the left's popular-front approach yielded real power—and that is the true object of liberal nostalgia; nothing more, nothing less.

THE NEW LEFT'S FASCIST MOMENT

The elevation of unity as the highest social value is a core tenet of fascism and all leftist ideologies. Mussolini adopted the socialist symbol of the fasces to convey that his movement valued unity over the liberal democratic fetish of debate and discussion. That clanking, unrhymed chant we hear at protest rallies today—"The people *united* will never be defeated!"—is a perfectly fascist refrain. Perhaps it is true that "the people united will never be defeated," but that doesn't mean the people are right (as Calvin Coolidge liked to say, "One with the law on his side is a majority"). We tend to forget that unity is, at best, morally neutral and often a source of irrationality and groupthink. Rampaging mobs are unified. The Mafia is unified. Marauding barbarians bent on rape and pillage are unified. Meanwhile, civilized people have disagreements, and small-*d* democrats have arguments. Classical liberalism is based on this fundamental insight, which is why fascism was always antiliberal. Liberalism rejected the idea that unity is more valuable than individuality. For fascists and other leftists, meaning and authenticity are found in collective enterprises—of class, nation, or race and the state is there to enforce that meaning on everyone without the hindrance of debate.

The first task of any fascist reformation is to discredit the authority of the past, and this was the top priority of the New Left. The Old Left was "suffocating under a blanket of slogans, euphemisms and empty jargon," while the New Left's mission lay in "getting people to think." Received wisdom, dogma, and "ritualistic language," Tom Hayden wrote in his 1961 "Letter to the New (Young) Left," would be swept aside by a revolutionary spirit that "finds no rest in conclusions [and in which] answers are seen as provisional, to be discarded in the face of new evidence or changed conditions." Hayden, like Mussolini, Woodrow Wilson, and the New Dealers, placed his hopes in a pragmatism that would yield a Third Way between the "author-itarian movements both of Communism and the domestic Right." Hayden, of course, also promised that his new movement would transcend labels and take "action."[16]

In academia a parallel revolt was under way. In 1966, at a confer-ence at Johns Hopkins University, the French literary critic Jacques Derrida introduced the word "deconstruction"—a term coined by Nazi ideologues—into the American intellectual bloodstream. Deconstruction—a literary theory which holds that there is no single meaning to any text—caught fire in the minds of academics and stu-dents alike who hoped to be liberated from the dead weight of his-tory and accumulated knowledge. If all texts were diversely interpretable with no "true" meaning at their core, then the important thing—the *only* thing really—was the meaning the reader *imposed* upon the text. In other words, meaning is created through power and will. The right interpretation is the one held by the interpreter who "wins" the academic power struggle. According to Derrida and his acolytes, reason was a tool of oppression. Beneath every seemingly rational decision was pure Nietzschean will to power. Derrida hoped to snatch the veil from the Enlightenment and reveal the tyranny of "logocentrism" beneath (another word with fascist roots).

This, too, was a replay of the pragmatic spirit that had sought to liberate society from the cage of inherited dogma. Pragmatism in-spired Woodrow Wilson, Franklin Roosevelt, and Benito Mussolini, as well as their court intellectuals, to discard the "putrefying corpse" of classical liberalism and parliamentary democracy in order to em-power "men of action" to solve society's problems through bold ex-perimentation and the unfettered power of the state. As one progressive reformer put it, "We were all Deweyites before we read Dewey."[17] Similarly, many in the academy were deconstructionists before they read Derrida.

The literary critic Paul de Man was one such sleeper deconstruc-tionist. De Man, who first met Derrida at the 1966 Johns Hopkins conference, became the foremost champion of deconstruction in the United States and a huge influence on Derrida himself. De Man taught at Cornell in the first half of the 1960s, and then moved to Johns Hopkins and Yale. Derrida's and de Man's writings served as an intellectual warrant for the radicalization of faculty who wanted to find common cause with the marchers in the streets by "speaking truth to power."[18] At Cornell, in the years preceding the takeover, de Man championed the defenestration of the "core curriculum," arguing that nothing worthwhile would be lost if the university turned its back on the traditional benchmarks of a liberal education. How could it be otherwise if all those ancient texts were in effect meaningless?

Such ideas contributed to the implosion of the American university in much the same way that they accelerated the Nazi takeover of German universities. Polite liberals were forced to choose between doing their jobs and siding with the radicals. For the more politicized professors this was no choice at all, since they already agreed with the aims of the revolution. But for individuals like Clinton Rossiter, a decent liberal centrist and one of America's most distinguished historians, the choice was destructive. A professor at Cornell during the uprising, Rossiter at first fought for the ideal of academic freedom along with other threatened faculty, but eventually he threw in his lot with the black fascists. Just two days before he made his decision, he'd told the *New York Times,* "If the ship goes down, I'll go down with it—as long as it represents reason and order. But if it's converted to threats and fear, I'll leave it and take a job as a night watchman at a local bakery." Fine words. But when truly forced to choose between working at a bakery and giving in to threats and intimidation, he turned his back on his friends and his principles.[19]

The parallel between the reformation of American universities in the 1960s and what occurred in Nazi Germany runs even deeper. Deconstruction is a direct and unapologetic offshoot of Heidegger's brand of existentialism, which not only was receptive to Nazism but helped foster it. Heidegger was the great inheritor of Nietzsche's assault on truth and morality, which held that we make our own truth and decide our own morality. For Heidegger and Nietzsche alike, good and evil were childish notions. What matters is will and choice. *Self-assertion* was the highest value. Choices were worthwhile only if they were authentic choices, heedless of conventional morality. This was the ethos of Nazism that Heidegger wholeheartedly embraced and never forthrightly renounced, even decades after the extent of the Holocaust and other Nazi crimes were known. The Nazi critique of Western civilization was total. In his infamous rectorial address, Heidegger looked forward to the time—hastened by Hitler's efforts—"when the spiritual strength of the West fails and its joints crack, when the moribund semblance of culture caves in and drags all forces into confusion and lets them suffocate in madness."[20]

Deconstruction's indebtedness to the fascist avant-garde remains one of the most controversial subjects in academia today, precisely because that debt is so obvious and profound. Paul de Man, for example, was a Nazi collaborator in Belgium who wrote seething pro-Nazi and anti-Semitic articles for a fascist newspaper during the occupation. Herbert Marcuse, a protégé of Heidegger's, became the leader of the New Left's academic brain trust. He attacked Western society mercilessly, arguing that "liberal tolerance" was "serving the cause of oppression"—an argument that echoed the fascist assault of the 1930s almost perfectly. Frantz Fanon, who preached about the "redemptive" power of violence, was widely seen as a direct heir of Georges Sorel, the pre-fascist theorist admired and emulated by Italian Fascists and Bolsheviks alike. The Nietzschean pragmatist Michel Foucault—revered by postmodernists and feminist theorists—set as his North Star the "sovereign enterprise of Unreason."[21] Foucault's hatred for Enlightenment reason was so profound that he celebrated the Iranian revolution of 1979 and the dictatorship of the mullahs precisely because it was a premodern assault on Enlightenment principles. Carl Schmitt, a grotesque Nazi philosopher, is among the most chic intellectuals on the left today. His writings were passed around as samizdat by New Left radicals in Europe, including Joschka Fischer, who spent the 1970s beating up policemen in West German streets and later became foreign minister and vice-chancellor in the government of Gerhard Schröder from 1998 to 2005.

For more than sixty years, liberals have insisted that the bacillus of fascism lies semi-dormant in the bloodstream of the political right. And yet with the notable and complicated exceptions of Leo Strauss and Allan Bloom, no top-tier American conservative intellectual was a devotee of Nietzsche or a serious admirer of Heidegger. All major conservative schools of thought trace themselves back to the champions of the Enlightenment—John Locke, Adam Smith, Montesquieu, Burke—and none of them have any direct intellectual link to Nazism or Nietzsche, to existentialism, nihilism, or even, for the most part, Pragmatism.[22] Meanwhile, the ranks of left-wing intellectuals are infested with ideas and thinkers squarely in the fascist tradition. And yet all it takes is the abracadabra word "Marxist" to absolve most of them of any affinity with these currents. The rest get off the hook merely by attacking bourgeois morality and American values—*even though such attacks are themselves little better than a reprise of fascist arguments.*

In a seminar there may be important distinctions to be made between, say, Foucault's "enterprise of Unreason," Derrida's tyrannical logocentrism, and Hitler's "revolt against reason." But such distinctions rarely translate beyond ivy-covered walls—and they are particularly meaningless to a movement that believes action is more important than ideas. Deconstruction, existentialism, postmodernism, Pragmatism, relativism: all of these ideas had the same purpose—to erode the iron chains of tradition, dissolve the concrete foundations of truth, and firebomb the bunkers where the defenders of the ancien régime still fought and persevered. These were ideologies of the "movement." The late Richard Rorty admitted as much, conflating Nietzsche and Heidegger with James and Dewey as part of the same grand project.

Few were more adept at using the jargon of the "movement" than fascists and pre-fascists. Hitler uses the phrase "the Movement" over two hundred times in *Mein Kampf.* A Nazi Party journal was called *Die Bewegung* (*The Movement*). The word "movement" itself is instructive. Movement, unlike progress, doesn't imply a fixed destination. Rather, it takes it as a given that *any* change is better. As Allan Bloom and others have noted, the core passion of fascism was *self-assertion.* The Nazis may have been striving for a utopian Thousand-Year Reich, but their first instincts were radical: Destroy what exists. Tear it down. Eradicate *"das System"*—another term shared by the New Left and fascists alike. "I have a *barbaric* concept of socialism," a young Mussolini once said. "I understand it as the greatest act of negation and destruction . . . Onward, you new barbarians! . . . Like all barbarians you are the harbingers of a new civilization."[23] Hitler's instincts were even more destructive. Even before he ordered the obliteration of Paris and issued his scorched-earth policy on German soil, his agenda was to rip apart everything the bourgeoisie had created, to destroy the reactionaries, to create new art and architecture, new culture, new religion, and, most of all, new Germans. This project could only commence upon the ashes of *das System*. And if he couldn't create, he could take solace in destroying.

How exactly is this different from the "Burn, baby, burn!" ethos of the late 1960s?

THE ACTION CULT

Five months after the Cornell takeover, the Weathermen gathered in Chicago's Lincoln Park. Armed with baseball bats, helmets, and, in the words of the historian Jim Miller, "apparently bottomless reserves of arrogance and self-loathing," they prepared to "smash through their bourgeois inhibitions and 'tear pig city apart' in a 'national action' they called 'The Days of Rage.' " Like Brownshirts and fascist *squadristi,* they smashed windows, destroyed property, and terrorized the bourgeoisie. They'd already bloodied themselves the previous year at the 1968 Democratic National Convention, where, the Weathermen claimed, their violence had done "more damage to the ruling class . . . than any mass, peaceful gathering this country has ever seen."[24]

The desire to destroy is a natural outgrowth of the cult of action. After all, if you are totally committed to revolutionary change, any boundaries you run into—the courts, the police, the rule of law—must be either converted, co-opted, or destroyed. All fascists are members of the cult of action. Fascism's appeal was that it would get things done. Make the trains run on time, put people to work, get the nation on the move: these are sentiments sewn into the fiber of every fascist movement. The fascist state of mind can best be described as "Enough talk, more action!" Close the books, get out of the library, get moving. Take action! What kind of action? Direct action! Social action! Mass action! Revolutionary action! Action, action, action.

Communists loved action, too. That's not surprising considering the family bonds between communism and fascism. But fascists valued action more. Communism had a playbook. Fascism had a hurry-up offense, calling its plays on the field. Sure, fascism had its theorists, but in the streets, fascists cared about victory more than doctrine. "In a way utterly unlike the classical 'isms,' " writes Robert O. Paxton, "the rightness of fascism does not depend on the truth of any of the propositions advanced in its name. Fascism is 'true' insofar as it helps fulfill the destiny of a chosen race or people or blood." Or as Mussolini himself put it in his "Postulates of the Fascist Program," fascists "do not feel tied to any particular doctrinal form."[25]

The word "activist" enters the English language at the turn of the century with the rise of pragmatic Progressivism. The early fascist intellectuals fancied themselves "activist philosophers." Mussolini, while still a socialist in good standing, wrote in 1908, "The plebs, who are excessively Christianized and humanitarian, will never understand that a higher degree of evil is necessary so that the Superman might thrive . . . The Superman knows revolt alone. Everything that exists must be destroyed." This represented an early marriage of Leninism and Nietzsche. Instead of the individual superman, the vanguard of the revolution would be the new breed of supermen. The Nazis were likewise inspired by Nietzsche but also by the Romantics, who believed that the spirit of the act is more important than the idea behind it. This was the Nazi "Cult of the Deed." The French fascists even dubbed their movement the *Action Française,* putting action on an equal footing with nation. Mussolini defined both socialism and fascism as "movement, struggle, and action." One of his favorite slogans was "To live is not to calculate, but to act!" Hitler mocked those who believed that arguments and reason should trump the naked power of the people. When four renowned economists sent Hitler a letter disputing his socialist schemes, Hitler responded, "Where are your storm troopers? Go on the street, go into folk meetings and try to see your standpoint through. Then we'll see who is right—we or you."[26]

Sixties radicalism was suffused with an identical spirit. The early intellectuals of the SDS—centered on the Institute for Policy Studies (a think tank today closely affiliated with the left wing of the Democratic Party)—were adherents of what they called "existential pragmatism," a blend in equal parts of Jean-Paul Sartre and John Dewey. "I'm a nihilist! I'm proud of it, proud of it!" shrieked a delegate to a 1967 meeting of the Princeton SDS. "Tactics? It's too late . . . Let's break what we can. Make as many answer as we can. Tear them apart."[27]

Mark Rudd, the chairman of the SDS at Columbia University and the leader of the takeover there in 1968, represented the ascendancy of what SDS "moderates" called the "action freaks" or the "action faction." A voluptuary of violence, Rudd subscribed to the Sorelian view that "direct action" would "raise consciousness" (then a freshly minted phrase). When the "moderates" told him the movement needed more organization and outreach, he responded, "Organizing is just another word for going slow."[28] Mussolini, who divided his *squadristi* into "action squads," could certainly sympathize.

As the reader may recall from our earlier discussion, it was Georges Sorel, the French engineer turned intellectual, who pioneered the idea that the masses needed myths to be moved to action. Recognizing that Marxism, like all social science, rarely panned out in real life, Sorel married William James's will to believe to Nietzsche's will to power and applied them to mass psychology. Revolutionaries didn't need to understand the reality of Marxism; they needed to believe in the myth of Marxism (or nationalism, syndicalism, fascism, and so on). "[T]o concern oneself with social science is one thing and to mold consciousness is another," he wrote.[29] Passion, not facts, was the fuel for action. "It is faith that moves mountains, not reason," Mussolini explained in a 1932 interview (echoing Woodrow Wilson's *Leaders of Men*). "Reason is a tool, but it can never be the motive force of the crowd."

As the cross-burning incident at Cornell demonstrated, this preference for arousing passions at the expense of truth and reason defined the agenda of those fighting in the trenches. The practice of "lying for justice"—always acceptable on the communist left—was infused into the American New Left with new potency. The catchphrase at the Columbia uprising was "the issue is not the issue." No wonder, since the actual "issue"—building a gym in adjacent Harlem—was such small beer. For most of the activists, deceit wasn't the point. The point was passion, mobilization, action. As one SDS member proclaimed after he and his colleagues seized a building and kidnapped a dean, "We've got something going on here and now we've just got to find out what it is."[30]

BUILDING A POLITICS OF MEANING

The movement of the 1960s didn't start out destructive. In fact it started out brimming with high-minded idealism and hope. The Port Huron Statement, the signature document of the New Left, was for all its overwrought verbiage a well-intentioned statement of democratic optimism and admirable honesty. The authors—chief among them Tom Hayden—conceded that they were in fact bourgeois radicals, "bred in at least modest comfort." Driven by a sense of alienation from the American way of life, the young radicals craved a sense of unity and belonging, a rediscovery of personal meaning through collective political endeavors. Life seemed out of balance. "It is difficult today to give human meaning to the welter of facts that surrounds us," the authors proclaimed. Their aim was to create a political system that would restore "human meaning" (whatever that is). "The goal of man and society," they insisted, "should be human independence: a concern not with image of popularity but with finding a meaning in life that is personally authentic." This urge for self-assertion should be translated into a politics that could unleash the "unrealized potential for self-cultivation, self-direction, self-understanding, and creativity."[31]

At the time, youth activists found a willing ear in mainstream liberalism, which was preaching more and more about "national service," "sacrifice," and "action." John F. Kennedy—the youngest president ever elected, replacing the oldest president ever elected—simultaneously fed and appealed to this atmosphere at every turn. "Let the word go forth," he declared in his inaugural address with an almost authoritarian tempo, "that the torch has been passed to a new generation of Americans, born in this century, tempered by war, disciplined by a hard and bitter peace." His most famous line, "Ask not what your country can do for you—ask what you can do for your country," resonated with a generation desperate to find collective redemption in peace the way their parents had in war.

A subconscious current ran through the entire society, a quest for community and galvanizing leadership. As Tom Hayden noted in March 1962, "Three out of every four students believe 'that what the nation needs is a strong fearless leader in whom we can have faith.' "

The embryonic youth movement hoped that Kennedy might prove to be that leader. The Peace Corps, and later VISTA, drew volunteers from the same wellspring of youthful activism. The University of California at Berkeley—the home of the first campus revolt of the 1960s—provided "the single most important source of volunteers for the Peace Corps in the early 1960s." When the Student Peace Union, or SPU, protested in front of the White House in February 1962, Kennedy ordered his kitchen to send the picketers coffee while the SPU proudly distributed copies of a *New York Times* article which claimed that the president was "listening" to them.[32]

And then there was the quest for community. The Red Diaper Babies of the 1960s inherited from their parents the same drive to create a new community organized around political aspirations. According to Todd Gitlin, the former president of the SDS, "There was a longing to 'unite the fragmented parts of personal history,' as The Port Huron Statement put it—to transcend the multiplicity and confusion of roles that become normal in a rationalized society: the rifts between work and family, between public and private, between strategic, calculating reason and spontaneous, expressive emotion." Gitlin continues, "At least for some of us, the circle evoked a more primitive fantasy of fusion with a symbolic, all-enfolding mother: the movement, the beloved community itself, where we might be able to find in Yale psychologist Kenneth Keniston's words, 'the qualities of warmth, communion, acceptedness, dependence and intimacy which existed in childhood.' " Mark Rudd likewise reminisced about the glories of the "communes" set up at Columbia: "For many it was the first communal experience of their lives—a far cry from the traditional lifestyle of Morningside Heights [at Columbia], that of individuals retiring into their rooms or apartments. One brother remarked to me, 'The communes are a better high than grass.' "[33]

The SDS's original mission wasn't radical; it was humane: community outreach. The first significant project the group undertook was the Economic Research and Action Project, begun in 1963. SDS members fanned out like knights from the roundtable in search of the grail of self-fulfillment by moving into inner-city ghettos in an earnest effort to politicize the poor, the oppressed, and the criminal underclass. It should tell us something that the most compelling catchphrase for liberals and leftists alike in the 1960s was "community": "community action," "community outreach," "communities of mutual respect."

As Alan Brinkley has noted, most of the protests and conflagrations of the 1960s had their roots in a desire to preserve or create communities. The ostensible issue that launched the takeover of Columbia University in 1968 was the encroachment of the campus into the black *community*. The administration's appeasement of Black Nationalists was done in the name of welcoming blacks to the Cornell *community*, and the Black Nationalists took up arms because they felt that assimilation into the Cornell community, or the white community generally, amounted to a negation of their own community—that is, "cultural genocide."

The Berkeley uprising was sparked in large part by the school's expansion into a tiny park that, at the end of the day, was just a place for hippies to hang out and feel comfortable in their own little community. Hippies may call themselves nonconformists, but as anyone who's spent time with them understands, they prize conformity above most things. The clothes and hair are ways of fitting in, of expressing shared values. Peace signs may symbolize something very different from the swastika, but both are a kind of insignia instantly recognizable to friend and foe alike. Regardless, the Berkeley protesters felt that their world, their folk community, was being destroyed by a cold, impersonal institution in the form of the university and, perhaps, modernity itself. "You've pushed us to the end of your civilization here, against the sea in Berkeley," shouted one of the leaders of the People's Park uprising. "Then you pushed us into a square-block area called People's Park. It was the last thing we had to defend, this square block of sanity amid all your madness . . . We are now homeless in your civilized world. We have become the great American gypsies, with only our mythology for a culture."[34] This is precisely the sort of diatribe one might have heard from a bohemian Berliner in the 1920s.

There is no disputing that Nazism was an evil ideology from the first spark of its inception. But that does not mean that every adherent of Nazism was motivated by evil intent. Germans did not collectively decide to be Hollywood villains for all eternity. For millions of Germans the Nazis seemed to offer hope for community and meaning and authenticity, too. As Walter Laqueur wrote in *Commentary* shortly after the Cornell uprising:

> Most of the basic beliefs and even the outward fashions of the present world-youth movements can be traced back to the period in Europe just before and after the First World War. The German Neue Schar of 1919 were the original hippies: long-haired, sandaled, unwashed, they castigated urban civilization, read Hermann Hesse and Indian philosophy, practiced free-love, and distributed in their meetings thousands of asters and chrysanthemums. They danced, sang to the music of the guitar, and attended lectures on the "Revolution of the Soul." The modern happening was born in 1910 in Trieste, Parma, Milan, and other Italian cities where the Futurists arranged public meetings to recite their poems, read their manifestos, and exhibit their ultra-modern paintings. No one over thirty, they demanded, should in future be active in politics . . .
>
> For the historian of ideas, the back issues of the periodicals of the youth movements, turned yellow with age, make fascinating reading . . . It is indeed uncanny how despite all the historical differences, the German movement preempted so many of the issues agitating the American movement of today, as well as its literary fashions.[35]

Let us return to the example of Horst Wessel, the most famous "youth leader" of the early Nazi movement, "martyred" in his battle against the "Red Front and reactionaries" as immortalized in the Nazi "Horst Wessel Lied" ("Horst Wessel Song"). Wessel fit the 1960s ideal of a youth leader "from the streets" fighting for social justice. The son of a Lutheran pastor, he rebelled against his middle-class upbringing by dropping out of law school at twenty-one and enlisting in the Nazi storm troopers. He moved into a shady working-class part of town and, with his comrades, joined in bloody street battles against the communists. But Wessel also earned a reputation as an idealistic and sensitive proselytizer for the "revolution from below," which would usher in a united racial community transcending class differences. He walked the walk, living among criminals and the struggling proletariat:

Whoever is convinced that the Germany of today is not worthy of guarding the gates of true German culture must leave the theatre . . . the salons . . . the studies . . . their parents' houses . . . literature . . . the concert halls. He must take to the streets, he must really go to the people . . . in their tenements of desperation and woe, of criminality . . . where the SA is protecting German culture . . . Every beer hall brawl is a step forward for German culture, the head of every SA man bashed in by the communists is another victory for the people, for the Reich, for the house of German culture.[36]

An amateur poet, Wessel wrote a small tribute to the cause, "Die Fahne hoch" ("Raise High the Flag"), which promised, "The day breaks for freedom and for bread" and "Slavery will last only a short time longer." Around the same time, he fell in love with Erna Jaenicke, a prostitute whom he first met when she was being beaten up by pimps at a neighborhood bar. The two soon moved into a run-down boardinghouse together, over the protests of his mother. There's some evidence that Wessel grew increasingly disenchanted with the Nazis, realizing that the communists shared many of the same aspirations. He certainly became less active in the ranks of the Brownshirts. But whether he would have broken with them is unknowable because he died at the hands of the communists in 1930.

And that was all that really mattered to Joseph Goebbels, who translated Wessel's death into a propaganda coup. Overnight, Wessel was transfigured into a martyr to the Nazi cause, a Sorellan religious myth aimed at the idealistic and perplexed youth of the interwar years. Goebbels described him as a "Socialist Christ" and unleashed a relentless torrent of hagiography about Wessel's work with the poor. By the beginning of World War II, the places of his life and death in Berlin had been made into stations of the cross, and shrines had been erected at his birthplace in Vienna as well as his various homes in Berlin. His little poem was set to music and became the official Nazi anthem.

In the German feature film *Hans Westmar: One of Many,* the young protagonist, based on Wessel, peers from his fraternity window and declares to his privileged comrades: "The real battle is out there, not here with us. The enemy is on the march . . . I tell you, all of Germany will be won down there, on the street. And that's where we must be—with our people. We can no longer live in our ivory towers. We must join our hands in battle with the workers. There can't be classes anymore. We are workers too, workers of the mind, and our place now is next to those who work with their hands."[37]

Even if the propagandized Wessel were a complete fabrication—though it was not—the mythologized version illustrates the more interesting, and important, truth. Germany was filled with millions of young men who were receptive to the shining ideal that Wessel represented. Of course, the virulent anti-Semitism of the Nazis makes it difficult to see (and impossible to forgive), but the dream of a unified, classless Germany was deeply heartfelt by many Nazi joiners; and if reduced to that alone, it was not an evil dream at all.

But just as the line between "good" totalitarianism and bad is easily crossed, dreams can quickly become nightmares. Indeed, some dreams, given their nature, *must* eventually become nightmares. And for the Horst Wessels of the American New Left, whatever admirable idealism they might have had quickly and unavoidably degenerated into fascist thuggery.

The most famous of these figures was Tom Hayden. The son of middle-class parents in the Detroit suburb of Oak Park (near Father Coughlin's parish) and the chief author of The Port Huron Statement, Hayden played an admirable role in the early civil rights struggle in the South. He certainly believed himself to be a young democrat, but the seeds of a totalitarian bent were evident from his earliest days at the University of Michigan. In a speech delivered to the Michigan Union in 1962—which became a manifesto titled *Student Social Action*—Hayden proclaimed that the youth must wrest control of society from their elders. To this end the universities had to become incubators of revolutionary "social action." Richard Flacks, a young academic who would join Hayden in the new crusade along with his wife, Mickey, was thunderstruck. He went home and told his wife (an activist in a group called Women Strike for Peace), "Mickey, I've just seen the next Lenin!"[38]

By the end of the decade, Hayden had indeed become a forthright advocate of "Leninist" violence and mayhem, glorifying crime as political rebellion and openly supporting Mao, Ho Chi Minh, and, of course, the murderous Black Panthers. He helped write the

"Berkeley Liberation Program." Among the highlights: "destroy the university unless it serves the people"; "all oppressed people in jail are political prisoners and must be set free"; "create a soulful social-ism"; "students must destroy the senile dictatorship of adult teach-ers." His "community outreach" in the slums of Newark preceded and in part fomented the horrific race riots there. "I had been fasci-nated by the simplicity and power of the Molotov cocktail during those days in Newark," he writes in his autobiography. Hayden hoped that with the use of violence, the New Left could create "lib-erated territories" in the ghettos and campus enclaves and use them to export revolution to the rest of the United States. At a 1967 panel discussion with leading New York intellectuals, Hannah Arendt lec-tured Hayden about his defense of bloody insurrection. He snapped in response, "You may put me in the position of a leper, but I say a case can be made for violence in the peace movement." At the Columbia occupation, Hayden explained that the protests were just the start of "bringing the war home." Echoing Che Guevara's chant of "two, three, many Vietnams," Hayden called for "two, three, many Columbias."[39]

One of the most illuminating symptoms of left-wing revolutionary movements is their tendency to blur the difference between common crime and political rebellion. The Brownshirts beat up storekeepers, shook down businessmen, and vandalized property, rationalizing all of it in the name of the "movement." Left-wing activists still refer to the L.A. riots as an "uprising" or "rebellion." A similar moral ob-tuseness plagued the movement in the 1960s. "The future of our struggle is the future of crime in the streets," declared Hayden. The only way to "revolutionize youth," he explained, was to have "a se-ries of sharp and dangerous conflicts, life and death conflicts" in the streets. Hayden was no doubt inspired by (and inspiring to) the Black Panthers, who regularly staged ambushes of police in the streets. At the 1968 Democratic National Convention demonstrations in Chicago his co-organizer Rennie Davis implored the crowd, "Don't vote . . . join us in the streets of America . . . Build a National Liberation Front for America." Hayden was put on trial for his in-citement of violence in Chicago. In June 1969 he pronounced on the "need to expand our struggle to include a total attack on the courts."[40]

Hayden was a moderate, according to Mark Rudd, the leader of the so-called action faction of the SDS. Rudd, who organized the Columbia "rebellion," was born to a middle-class Jewish family in New Jersey, and his parents hardly encouraged his behavior. When he called his father to explain that he "took a building" from the president of Columbia University, his father replied, "Then give it back to him." Rudd's preferred rallying cry at the time was "Up against the wall, motherfucker!" which he used on teachers and administrators with abandon. "Perhaps nothing upsets our enemies more than this slogan," he explained. "To them it seemed to show the extent to which we had broken with their norms, how far we had sunk to brutality, hatred and obscenity. Great!" The term, he explained, clarified that the administrators, faculty, and police who opposed the radicals were "our enemies." "Liberal solutions, restructuring, partial understandings, compromise are not allowed anymore. The essence of the matter is that we are out for social and political revolution, nothing less."[41]

Rudd eventually joined the Weathermen, who, out of deference to the female terrorists in the group, soon changed their name to the Weather Underground (though they sometimes went by the moniker "The Revolutionary Youth Movement"). In 1970 the group declared a "state of war" against the United States of America and commenced a campaign of terrorist attacks. Rudd took the position that the best way to foment revolution was to target military installations, banks, and policemen. One of their first bombings was intended to target a dance for noncommissioned officers at Fort Dix, New Jersey (though another version says that the bomb, wrapped in roofing nails, was intended for Columbia). In any event, the inexperienced bomb makers famously blew themselves up in a Greenwich Village town house, killing three members and leaving the survivors fugitives for life. The explosion was one of the reasons Rudd had to go underground. He did not surface again for several years, eventually turning himself in after technical violations of wiretapping laws made the federal case against him difficult to prosecute. Today he is a math teacher at a community college in Albuquerque, New Mexico. Rudd has expressed remorse for his violent youthful activities, but he is still a passionate opponent of American (and Israeli) foreign policy.

Many of us forget that the Weather Underground bombing campaign was not a matter of a few isolated incidents. From September 1969 to May 1970, Rudd and his co-revolutionaries on the white radical left committed about 250 attacks, or almost one terrorist bombing a day (government estimates put that number much higher). During the summer of 1970, there were twenty bombings a week in California. The bombings were the backbeat to the symphony of violence, much of it rhetorical, that set the score for the New Left in the late 1960s and early 1970s. Rudd captured the tone perfectly: "It's a wonderful feeling to hit a pig. It must be a really wonderful feeling to kill a pig or blow up a building." "The real division is not between people who support bombings and people who don't," explained a secret member of a "bombing collective," but "between people who will *do* them and people who are too hung up on their own privileges and security to take those risks."[42]

Bourgeois self-loathing lay at the very heart of the New Left's hatred of liberalism, its love affair with violence, and its willingness to take a sledgehammer to Western civilization. "We're against everything that's 'good and decent' in honky America," declared one rebel. "We will burn and loot and destroy. We are the incubation of your mother's worst nightmare." The Weathermen became the storm troopers of the New Left, horrifying even those who agreed with their cause. Convinced that all whites were born tainted with the original sin of "skin privilege," the fighting brigade of the New Left internalized racialist thinking as hatred of their own whiteness. "All white babies are pigs," declared one Weatherman. On one occasion the feminist poet Robin Morgan was breast-feeding her son at the offices of the radical journal *Rat*. A Weatherwoman saw this and told her, "You have no right to have that pig male baby." "How can you say that?" Morgan asked. "What should I do?" "Put it in the garbage," the Weatherwoman answered.[43]

Bernardine Dohrn, an acid-loving University of Chicago law student turned revolutionary, reflected the widespread New Left fascination with the serial-killing hippie *Übermensch* Charles Manson. "Dig It! First they killed those pigs, then they ate dinner in the same room with them, they even shoved a fork into a victim's stomach! Wild!" In appreciation, her Weather Underground cell made a three-fingered "fork" gesture its official salute.[44]

Of course, there was a great deal of playacting among the revolutionaries as well. Abbie Hoffman, the co-founder of the yippies (the Youth International Party) along with Jerry Rubin, was the son of prosperous Jewish parents in Worcester, Massachusetts. The product of private schools—where he was a troublemaker from the start, no doubt due in part to his bipolar disorder—Hoffman attended Brandeis University, where he studied under the New Left intellectual icon Herbert Marcuse. Hoffman bought into Marcuse's view that bourgeois America was "radically evil" and that it had to be radically challenged as a result. But Hoffman had something over Marcuse, Rudd, Hayden, and the rest: he could be legitimately funny about his mission (though not nearly as funny as he thought he was). His was a funny fascism, a naughty nihilism. His book titles alone give a good flavor of his approach: *Steal This Book*, *Fuck the System*, and *Revolution for the Hell of It*. "Personally, I always held my flower in a clenched fist," he wrote in his autobiography. He mastered the art of calling anybody he disliked or opposed a "fascist," dubbing Ronald Reagan "the fascist gun in the West." Hoffman, another member of the Chicago Seven, was a fugitive from justice for most of the 1970s, eluding charges that he was a cocaine dealer.

His antics were less an echo of the Nazis—a generally humorless bunch—and more an updating of the Italian Futurists, the artistic auxiliary to Italian Fascism.[45] The Futurists were actors, poets, writers, and other artists determined to bring all of the qualities of youth and revolution into the streets and cafés of Italy. Their fascism was theatrically violent, glorying in shock and disruption. The Futurists embraced the rush of speed and technology, the yippies glorified the rush of drugs. But it was really the same shtick. Hoffman and Rubin, for example, proposed a "Theater of Disruption" during the Chicago convention that would blend "pot and politics into a political grass-leaves movement." Updating Sorel's doctrines of myth and violence—no doubt without credit—Hoffman set out to create a "vast myth" of bloodshed and shock. "We will burn Chicago to the ground!" "We will fuck on the beaches!" "We demand the Politics of Ecstasy!" It may sound funny now, but the intent was to force a confrontation that would spill blood in the streets. In August a yippie underground newspaper, *Seed,* announced it had withdrawn its request for a permit for a youth rock festival. The editorial explained, "Chicago may host a Festival of Blood . . . Don't come to Chicago if you expect a five-day Festival of Life, music and love."[46]

For those willing to look past a lot of meaningless rhetoric about Marxism, the fascist nature of all this was glaringly obvious. Indeed, one could simply take countless radicals at their word when they said they were "beyond ideology" and all about action. One of the most obvious giveaways was the New Left's obsession with the "street." The radicals talked incessantly about "taking it to the streets," of the need for "street theater," street protest, street activism, even "dancing in the street," as the song went. Many of the best books during and about the period use "street" in their titles, James Baldwin's *No Name in the Street*, Jim Miller's *Democracy Is in the Streets,* and Milton Viorst's *Fire in the Streets* being just a few examples.

Fascists were always fixated with the street. Horst Wessel, the martyred street fighter, captured the spirit of the street in the poem that became the Nazi anthem: "Clear the streets for the brown battalions . . . Soon will fly Hitler-flags over every street." The Futurists considered the street the only authentic stage. "The raging broom of madness swept us out of ourselves and drove us through streets as rough and deep as the beds of torrents," declared F. T. Marinetti, the founder of the Futurist movement. The Futurists, according to Marinetti's famous phrase, glorified "the beautiful ideas which kill." "For anyone who has a sense of historical connections, the ideological origins of Fascism can be found in Futurism," wrote Benedetto Croce in 1924, "in the determination to go down into the streets, to impose their own opinions, to stop the mouths of those who disagree, not to fear riots or fights, in this eagerness to break with all tradition, in this exaltation of youth which was characteristic of Futurism."[47]

That violence was central to fascism is often an exaggerated point. Violence has been essential to nearly all revolutionary movements, save the few explicitly nonviolent ones. But the avant-garde fascists idealized violence as an end in itself, seeing it as "redemptive" and "transformative." Mussolini talked about the power and importance of violence but committed far less of it than you might expect. Yes, his goons beat people up and there were a handful of killings, but mostly Mussolini liked the aesthetics of violence, the sound of brutal rhetoric, the poetry of revolutionary bloodshed. "For revolutions are insane, violent, idiotic, bestial," he explained. "They are like war. They set fire to the Louvre and throw the naked bodies of princesses on the street. They kill, plunder, destroy. They are a man-made Biblical flood. Precisely therein consists their great beauty."[48]

Here again, the similarities to the New Left are striking. Violence suffused their political talk; physical violence merely punctuated it. Violence for the New Left and Fascists alike worked on numerous symbolic levels. It elevated the sense of crisis that revolutionaries crave in order to polarize society. Indeed, polarization was an identical strategic objective for the New Left and the Nazis. Forcing mainstream liberals to choose sides on the assumption that most would follow their sympathies to the left was the only way Hayden and others could usher in their revolution. That was what they meant by "bringing the war home." (One of Rudd's comrades who was killed in the Greenwich Village blast, Ted Gold, argued that the only way to radicalize liberals was to "turn New York into Saigon."[49]) The Nazis similarly assumed that Germans who favored socialist economic policies but who rejected the idea of thralldom to Moscow would ultimately side with the *National* Socialists over the *International* ones. German Communists made a similar gamble, believing that Nazism would accelerate the historical march toward Communism. Hence, again, the German socialist mantra "First Brown, then Red."

Somewhat paradoxically, support for violence—even violent rhetoric, as in Rudd's fondness for expletives—helped radicals differentiate themselves from liberals, whom the hard left saw as too concerned with politeness, procedure, and conventional politics. When "moderates" at the Columbia takeover tried to dissuade a member of the "defense committee" at the Math Hall (where the most radical students were holed up), he responded, "You fucking liberals don't understand what the scene's about. It's about power and disruption. The more blood the better." At the march on the Washington Monument to end the war in 1965, Phil Ochs sang his contemptuous "Love Me, I'm a Liberal."[50] Saul Alinsky, whose *Rules for Radicals* served as a bible for the New Left (and who later became one of Hillary Clinton's mentors), shared the fascist contempt for liberals as corrupted bourgeois prattlers: "Liberals in their meetings utter bold words; they strut, grimace belligerently, and then issue a weasel-worded statement 'which has tremendous implications, if read between the lines.' They sit calmly, dispassionately, studying the issue; judging both sides; they sit and still sit."[51]

Substitute the word "fascist" for "radical" in many of Alinsky's statements and it's sometimes difficult to tell the difference: "Society has good reason to fear the Radical . . . He hits, he hurts, he is dangerous. Conservative interests know that while Liberals are most adept at breaking their own necks with their tongues, Radicals are most adept at breaking the necks of Conservatives." And: "The Radical may resort to the sword but when he does he is not filled with hatred against those individuals whom he attacks. He hates these individuals not as persons but as symbols representing ideas or interests which he believes to be inimical to the welfare of the people." In other words, they're not *people* but dehumanized *symbols*. "Change means movement," Alinsky tells us. "Movement means friction. Only in the frictionless vacuum of a nonexistent abstract world can movement or change occur without that abrasive friction of conflict."[52]

New Left violence also supported numerous other fascist themes, from the cult of unreason, the lust for action, the craving for authenticity—talk was cheap—to a sense of shame about the martial accomplishments of the older generation. Just as many Nazi youth missed the Great War and were desperate to prove their mettle to their parents and themselves, many in the New Left had "issues" with their parents' participation in World War II (and for many Jews, their parents' Holocaust ordeal). In addition, many radicals were desperate to prove they weren't cowards for refusing to fight in Vietnam.

Lastly, violence served as an homage to the true radicals and revolutionaries at home and abroad. Black Panther envy is a recurring theme in the history of New Left radicalism. The blacks were the "real thing," and the whites were desperate to gain their approval and support. French intellectuals and Upper West Side liberals achieved new heights of sycophancy in their desire to prove their radical bona fides. They cheered when black athletes at the 1968 Olympics raised their fists in defiance at the American national anthem, not caring (or knowing) that the imagery was entirely derivative of fascist aesthetics. "The fist," an Italian Fascist proclaimed in 1920, "is the synthesis of our theory."[53] And when George Foreman paraded an American flag at the same Olympics, the Norman Mailer crowd called him an Uncle Tom.

You can tell a lot about a movement by its heroes, and here, too, the record reflects very poorly on the New Left. For all their prattle about "participatory democracy" it's shocking how few democrats ranked as heroes to even the "peaceful" members of the movement. At Columbia, Berkeley, and campuses across America, the student activists plastered up posters of Che Guevara, Fidel Castro, Mao Tse-tung, and Ho Chi Minh. Under Rudd's leadership, the SDS formed quasi-official ties with Castro's government. In Chicago and elsewhere, they chanted, "Ho-Ho-Ho-Chi-Minh!" Mao Tse-tung's *Little Red Book* of revolutionary maxims became a huge best seller.

Rather than call these regimes fascist—which I firmly believe they were—we'll merely note the similarities between these Third World movements and regimes and the conventional fascist ones. Mao, Ho, Castro, and even the Panthers were all ethnocentric movements of "national liberation." This is *precisely* how Mussolini and Hitler depicted their causes. Hitler promised to get Germany out from under the thumb of Versailles and "international finance capitalism." Mussolini argued that Italy was a "proletarian nation" deserving, like Germany, its "moment in the sun." Mao's Cultural Revolution, his mixture of socialism and folk Chinese custom, fits perfectly in the fascist wheelhouse. What is Castro but a military dictator (note the constant uniform) who has burnished his leadership cult with socialist economics, nationalist rhetoric, and unending Nuremberg Rally populism?

That Che Guevara has become a chic branding tool is a disgusting indictment of both American consumer culture and the know-nothing liberalism that constitutes the filthy residue of the 1960s New Left. Ubiquitous Che shirts top the list of mass-marketed revolutionary swag available for sale at the nearest bobo chic retailer—including a popular line of children's wear. Here's the text for one ad promoting this stuff: "Featured in *Time* magazine's holiday web shopping guide, 'Viva la revolution!' Now even the smallest rebel can express himself in these awesome baby onesies. This classic Che Guevara icon is also available on a long-sleeve tee in kids' sizes . . .

Long live the rebel in all of us . . . there's no cooler iconic image than Che!"[54]

The Argentine henchman of the Cuban revolution was a murderer and goon. He penned classically fascist apothegms in his journals: "hatred as an element of struggle; unbending hatred for the enemy, which pushes a human being beyond his natural limitations, making him into an effective, violent, selective and cold-blooded killing machine." Guevara was a better writer, but the same muse helped to produce *Mein Kampf.* Guevara reveled in executing prisoners. While fomenting revolution in Guatemala, he wrote home to his mother, "It was all a lot of fun, what with the bombs, speeches and other distractions to break the monotony I was living in." His motto was "If in doubt, kill him," and he killed a great many. The Cuban-American writer Humberto Fontova described Guevara as "a combination of Beria and Himmler."[55] Guevara certainly killed more dissidents and lovers of democracy than Mussolini ever did, and Mussolini's Italy was undoubtedly more "free" than any society Guevara the "freedom fighter" was seeking. Would you put a Mussolini onesie on your baby? Would you let your daughter drink from a Himmler sippy cup?

One can have a Jesuitical argument about the precise political labels these men deserve, but the fact remains that what made these "liberationist" movements so popular were precisely those attributes Guevara, Castro, Mao, and the rest shared with the heroes of fascism. And if you scrub the names Marx and Lenin from their speeches, what remains is the stuff of any diatribe Mussolini delivered from a balcony (indeed, sometimes with Mussolini you don't even need to scrub the Marx and Lenin away). These were all *nationalists* committed to *national socialism* promising to enact a "truer" and more "organic" democracy, one that rejected the "formulaic," "superficial," and "decadent" "sham democracy" of the bourgeois West. Figures like the Congolese nationalist Patrice Lumumba were heroes for no other reason than that they opposed the United States and claimed to represent a racially pure revolutionary cause.[56] The United Nations and affiliated elites adopted the racist stance that when blacks or other oppressed peoples killed each other or killed whites, it was a legitimate expression of Third World will to power. Pan-Africanism, Pan-Arabism, the Chinese way, and anticolonialism generally were recast versions of Hitler's Pan-Germanism and Mussolini's effort to be the ruler of "Latin civilization" and "Italians everywhere." Third Worlders needed lebensraum, too.

Under doctrines of black liberation, "revolutionary" violence was always justified so long as you insisted that the bloodied corpse had somehow been an accomplice to oppression. Whites became the new Jews. "[T]o shoot down a European is to kill two birds with one stone, to destroy an oppressor and the man he oppresses at the same time," observed Jean-Paul Sartre in his preface to one of Frantz Fanon's books. All of this blood chic was retailed in Norman Mailer's *White Negro,* which fetishized black crime as hip, cool, and revolutionary. The New Left not only bought this line; they sold it. A poll found 20 percent of American students identified with Che Guevara—beating out Nixon (19 percent), Humphrey (16 percent), and Wallace (7 percent).[57]

Madness, cruelty, and totalitarianism were "in." Thugs and criminals were heroes, while champions of the rule of law were suddenly "fascists." Almost from the outset, this logic poisoned the civil rights movement's early triumphs. At Cornell most of the black students were admitted on what we'd today call affirmative action, with lower-than-average SAT scores. Particularly revealing is the fact that many of the gun-toting revolutionaries were recruited to the school precisely because they fit Mailer's stereotype of the noble "ghetto youth," the authentic Negro, and as such were given preference over other blacks with higher scores and better qualifications—because more qualified blacks were too "white."[58]

By the end of the decade, the civil rights movement had for all intents and purposes become a Black Power movement. And Black Power, with its clenched fists, Afro-pagan mythology, celebration of violence, emphasis on racial pride, and disdain for liberalism, was arguably America's most authentic indigenous fascism. Stokely Carmichael—at one time the "prime minister" of the Black Panther Party—himself defined Black Power (a term he originated) as "a movement that will smash everything Western civilization has created."[59] Carmichael shared Hitler's dream of building a folkish racial state upon the ashes of the old order.

Indeed, when one reads the racial indoctrination taught to the children of Nazi Germany, it's difficult to see the difference between

Carmichael's black pride and Hitler's German pride. "What is the first Commandment of every National Socialist?" asked a Nazi catechism. "Love Germany above all else and your ethnic comrade as your self!" The connections between Black Nationalism and Nazism, Fascism, and other supposedly right-wing racist groups aren't merely theoretical—or recent. Marcus Garvey, the founder of the Back to Africa movement, admitted in 1922 that his ideology was perfectly simpatico with Mussolini's. "We were the first fascists," he declared. Indeed, his rhetoric was often eerily consonant with German fascism: "Up You Mighty Race, Accomplish What You Will," "Africa for the Africans . . . at Home and Abroad!" and so forth. In the 1960s Elijah Muhammad, the head of the Nation of Islam, formed a cordial relationship with George Lincoln Rockwell, the head of the American Nazi Party. Rockwell was even invited to speak at the Nation of Islam National Convention in 1962, at which he praised Elijah Muhammad as the black Adolf Hitler. On January 28, 1961, Muhammad sent Malcolm X to Atlanta to negotiate an agreement with the Ku Klux Klan whereby the Klan would support a separate black state.[60]

More generally, the Black Power movement became addicted to violence, setting the tone for the white left. H. Rap Brown had exhorted his followers to "do what John Brown did, pick up a gun and go out and shoot our enemy." Malcolm X repeatedly exhorted blacks to employ "any means necessary." James Forman, a leader of the Student Nonviolent Coordinating Committee, declared that if he were assassinated, he'd want in retaliation "10 war factories destroyed . . . one Southern governor, two mayors and 500 racist white cops dead." Good thing he belonged to an avowedly *nonviolent* group! Benjamin Chavis, the future head of the NAACP, first attained national recognition when he was arrested and convicted as a member of the Wilmington Ten, a group that allegedly conspired to firebomb a grocery store and then shoot the police when they responded to the scene.[61] And always and everywhere there were the Panthers, in their paramilitary garb and black shirts sporting fascistic or militaristic ranks and titles (minister of defense, minister of information), robbing banks, calling for the slaughter of "pigs" and honkies, staging ambushes for police, kidnapping judges and children, and calling for a separate black state.

Meanwhile, what of the supposedly fascistic American right? While the New Left relentlessly denounced the founding fathers as racist white males and even mainstream liberals ridiculed the idea that the text of the Constitution had any relevance for modern society, conservatives were launching an extensive project to restore the proper place of the Constitution in American life. No leading conservative scholar or intellectual celebrated fascist themes or ideas. No leading conservative denigrated the inherent classical liberalism of the United States' political system. To the contrary, Barry Goldwater, Ronald Reagan, William F. Buckley, Jr., and the conservatives around *National Review* dedicated themselves to restoring the classically liberal vision of the founders.

What confused the left then and now about American conservatism is that love and support for one's country do not necessarily put one on the road to fascism. Patriotism is not the same thing as extreme nationalism or fascism. The Nazis killed a great many German patriots whose love of their homeland was deep and profound. In a sense, one of the Jews' greatest offenses was that they were patriotic Germans. It was in the 1960s that the left convinced itself that there is something fascistic about patriotism and something perversely "patriotic" about running down America. Anti-Americanism—a stand-in for hatred of Western civilization—became the stuff of sophisticates and intellectuals as never before. Flag burners became the truest "patriots" because dissent—not just from partisan politics, but from the American project itself—became the highest virtue. In 2003 the professor at Columbia who hoped America would face "a million Mogadishus" is a patriot in the eyes of the left. But Americans eager to maintain limited government—of all things!—are somehow creeping fascists.

Witnessing how the brutality and wanton destruction of the Nazis had swept Hitler to power, the novelist Thomas Mann wrote in his diary that this was a new kind of revolution, "without underlying ideas, against ideas, against everything nobler, better, decent, against freedom, truth and justice." The "common scum" had won the day, "accompanied by vast rejoicing on the part of the masses."[62] Liberals in the 1960s who lived through a similar degradation of decency by the same intellectual rot began to rebel. Confronted with an ideology that always assumed America was the problem and never the solution, they chose to mount a counterassault. These patriots in both parties became in large part that band of intellectuals known as neo-conservatives. They were given that name by leftists who thought the prefix "neo" would conjure associations with neo-Nazis.

But since the testimony of neoconservatives counts for nothing in most corners of liberal thought, it's worth noting that even some titans of the left still had the clarity of vision to understand what they were dealing with. Irving Louis Horowitz, a revered leftist intellectual (he was the literary executor of C. Wright Mills) specializing in revolutionary thought, saw in 1960s radicalism a "fanatic attempt to impose a new social order upon the world, rather than await the verdict of consensus-building formulas among disparate individuals as well as the historical muses." And he saw this fanaticism for what it was: *"Fascism returns to the United States not as a right-wing ideology, but almost as a quasi-leftist ideology."*[63]

Peter Berger, a Jewish refugee from Austria and a respected peace activist and left-wing sociologist (he helped popularize the phrase "social construction of reality"), saw much the same thing. When "observing the [American] radicals in action, I was repeatedly reminded of the storm troopers that marched through my childhood in Europe." He explored a long list of themes common to 1960s radicalism and European fascism and concluded they formed a "constellation that strikingly resembles the common core of Italian and German fascism." In 1974 A. James Gregor wrote *The Fascist Persuasion in Radical Politics,* which synthesized and cataloged these trends with sweeping detail and intellectual rigor. "In the recent past," he observed, "student radicals and the 'new left' have legitimized a political style calculated to be maximally serviceable to an American variant of fascism."

Even some in the SDS recognized that the more extreme members were degenerating into fascism. An editorial in the *Campaigner* (published by the New York and Philadelphia Regional Labor Committee of the Students for a Democratic Society) observed of the SDS faction that spawned the Weathermen, "There is a near identity between the arguments of anarchists (around the Columbia strike movement, e.g.) and Mussolini's polemics for action against theory, against program."[64]

The "youth movement" theorizing sparked by Charles Reich's

Greening of America, the indictment of reason, the populist appeals to defeating "the system," the table thumping for a new *Volk*-centric community that would replace capitalism with a more organic and totalitarian approach, was too much for some leftists with a clear understanding of the historical roots of fascism. The fascistic "overtones," Stewart Alsop wrote of *The Greening of America,* "are obvious to anyone who has seen those forests of arms raised in unison by the revolutionary young, or heard their mindless shouted chants. Professor Reich is certainly a good and kindly man, without a fascist bone in his body," Alsop continued, "and most of the 'liberated' young he worships are good and kindly too. But surely anyone with a sense of the political realities can smell the danger that these silly, kind, irrational people, in their cushioned isolation from reality, are bringing upon us all. The danger starts with the universities, but it does not end there. That is what makes the mush so scary." No less a socialist icon than Michael Harrington declared Reich's sweeping indictment of modernity—he called it "elite existentialism"—to have much in common with the Romantic roots of Nazism.

Today the liberal left's version of the 1960s makes about as much sense as it does to remember Hitler as the "man of peace" described by Neville Chamberlain. In its passions and pursuits, the New Left was little more than an Americanized updating of what we've come to call the European Old Right. From *Easy Rider* to *JFK,* Hollywood has been telling us that if only the forces of reaction hadn't killed their Horst Wessels, we would today be living in a better, more just, and more open-minded country. And if only we could rekindle the hope and ambition of those early radicals, "what might have been" will turn into "what could still be." This is *the* vital lie of the left. Western civilization was saved when the barbarians were defeated, at least temporarily, in the early 1970s. We should be not only grateful for our slender victory but vigilant in securing it for posterity.

Such vigilance is impossible without understanding the foundations on which contemporary liberalism stands, and that in turn requires a second look at the 1960s—this time from the top down. For while the radicals in the streets were demanding more power, the progressives already in power were playing their parts as well.

It is understandable that the 1960s is viewed as an abrupt change or turning point in our history, because in many respects the changes were so sudden (and in some cases for the better). But there was also a profound continuity underlying the events of the decade. When Kennedy said that the torch had been passed to a new generation, he was referring in no small part to a new generation of progressives. These men (and a few women) were dedicated to continuing the projects of Wilson and Roosevelt. When the torch is passed, the runner changes, but the race remains the same.

In the chapter that follows, we will show that John F. Kennedy and Lyndon Baines Johnson represented the continuation of the liberal quest begun by Woodrow Wilson and his fellow progressives—the quest to create an all-caring, all-powerful, all-encompassing state, a state that assumes responsibility for every desirable outcome and takes the blame for every setback on the road to utopia, a state that finally replaces God.

· **6** ·

From Kennedy's Myth
to Johnson's Dream:
Liberal Fascism and the
Cult of the State

F OR GENERATIONS, THE central fault line in American politics has involved the growth and power of the state. The conventional narrative has conservatives trying to shrink the size of
government and liberals trying—successfully—to expand it. There's
more than a little evidence to support this understanding. But much
of it is circumstantial. Liberals often argue for restraining government in areas such as law enforcement (the Warren Court's *Miranda*
ruling, for example), national security (opposition to the Patriot Act
and domestic surveillance), and that vast but ill-defined realm that
comes under the rubric of "legislating morality." While disagreements over specific policies proliferate, virtually all conservatives
and most libertarians favor assertiveness in government's traditional
role as the "night-watchman state." Many go further, seeing the government as a protector of decency and cultural norms.

In short, the argument about the *size* of government is often a
stand-in for deeper arguments about the *role* of government. This
chapter will attempt to show that for some liberals, the state is in fact
a substitute for God and a form of political religion as imagined by
Rousseau and Robespierre, the fathers of liberal fascism.

Historically, for many liberals the role of the state has been a matter less of size than of function. Progressivism shared with fascism a
deep and abiding conviction that in a truly modern society, the state

must take the place of religion. For some, this conviction was born of the belief that God was dead. As Eugen Weber writes, "The Fascist leader, now that God is dead, cannot conceive of himself as the elect of God. He believes he is elect, but does not quite know of what—presumably of history or obscure historical forces." This is the fascism that leads to the *Führerprinzip* and cults of personality. But there is a second kind of fascism that sees the state not as the replacement of God but as God's agent or vehicle. In both cases, however, the state is the ultimate authority, the source and maintainer of values, and the guarantor of the new order.

We've already touched on statolatry as a progressive doctrine; later we will examine how this worldview manifests itself in what is commonly called the culture war. The hinge of that story is the 1960s, specifically the administrations of John F. Kennedy and Lyndon B. Johnson.

While not a modern liberal himself, JFK was turned after his death into a martyr to the religion of government. This was due partly to the manipulations of the Kennedy circle and partly to the (much more cynical) machinations of LBJ, who hijacked the Kennedy myth and harnessed it to his own purposes. Those purposes, consistent with the "nice" totalitarian impulse of the progressive movement in which Johnson had cut his political teeth, were nominally secular, but on a deeper, and perhaps unconscious, level fundamentally religious.

• • •

On November 22, 1963, John F. Kennedy was assassinated in Dallas, Texas. As if on cue, Dallas was christened "the city of hate." A young TV reporter named Dan Rather heard a rumor that some Dallas schoolchildren had cheered when they heard the news of Kennedy's death. The rumor wasn't true, and the local Dallas CBS affiliate refused to run the story. Rather made an end run around the network and reported the story anyway.

Rather wasn't the only one eager to point fingers at the right. Within minutes Kennedy's aides blamed deranged and unnamed right-wingers. One headline proclaimed the assassination had taken place "deep in the hate of Texas." But when it became clear that a deranged Marxist had done the deed, Kennedy's defenders were dismayed. "He didn't even have the satisfaction of being killed for civil rights," Jackie lamented to Bobby Kennedy when he told her the news. "It's—it had to be some silly little Communist."[1]

Or maybe not, the Kennedy mythmakers calculated. They set about creating the fable that Kennedy died battling "hate"—established code, then and now, for the political right. The story became legend because liberals were desperate to imbue Kennedy's assassination with a more exalted and politically useful meaning. Over and over again, the entire liberal establishment, led by the *New York Times*—and even the pope!—denounced the "hate" that claimed Kennedy's life. The Supreme Court justice Earl Warren summed up the conventional wisdom—as he could always be counted upon to do—when he theorized that the "climate of hatred" in Dallas—code for heavy right-wing and Republican activity—moved Lee Harvey Oswald to kill the president.[2]

The fact that Oswald was a communist quickly changed from an inconvenience to proof of something even more sinister. How, liberals asked, could a card-carrying Marxist murder a liberal titan on the side of social progress? The fact that Kennedy was a raging anti-communist seemed not to register, perhaps because liberals had convinced themselves, in the wake of the McCarthy era, that the real threat to liberty must always come from the right. Oswald's Marxism sent liberals into even deeper denial, their only choice other than to abandon anti-anti-communism. And so, over the course of the 1960s, the conspiracy theories metastasized, and the Marxist gunman became a patsy. *"Cui bono?"* asked the Oliver Stones then and ever since. Answer: the military-industrial complex, allied with the dark forces of reaction and intolerance, of course. Never mind that Oswald had already tried to murder the former army major general and prominent right-wing spokesman Edwin Walker or that, as the Warren Commission would later report, Oswald "had an extreme dislike of the rightwing."[3]

Amid the fog of denial, remorse, and confusion over the Kennedy assassination, an informal strategic response developed that would serve the purposes of the burgeoning New Left as well as assuage the consciences of liberals generally: transform Kennedy into an all-purpose martyr for causes he didn't take up and for a politics he didn't subscribe to.

Indeed, over the course of the 1960s and beyond, a legend grew up around the idea that if only Kennedy had lived, we would never have gotten bogged down in Vietnam. It is a central conceit of Arthur Schlesinger's *Robert Kennedy and His Times*. Theodore Sorensen, Tip O'Neill, and countless other liberals subscribed to this view. A popular play on Broadway, *MacBird,* suggested that Johnson had murdered JFK in order to seize power. But even Robert F. Kennedy conceded in an oral history interview that his brother never seriously considered withdrawal and was committed to total victory in Vietnam. Kennedy was an aggressive anti-communist and Cold War hawk. He campaigned on a fictitious "missile gap" with the Soviets in a largely successful effort to move to Richard Nixon's right on foreign policy, tried to topple Castro at the Bay of Pigs, brought the world to the brink of nuclear war during the Cuban missile crisis, and got us deep into Vietnam. A mere three and a half *hours* before Kennedy died, he was boasting to the Fort Worth Chamber of Commerce that he had increased defense spending on a massive scale, including a 600 percent increase on counterinsurgency special forces in South Vietnam. The previous March, Kennedy had asked Congress to spend fifty cents of every federal dollar on defense.[4]

The Kennedy myth also veers sharply from reality when it comes to the issue of race. The flattering legend is that Kennedy was an un-alloyed champion of civil rights. Supposedly, if he had lived, the racial turmoil of the 1960s could have been avoided. The truth is far more prosaic. Yes, Kennedy pushed for civil rights legislation, and he deserves credit for it. But he was hardly breaking with the past. In the supposedly reactionary 1950s, Republicans had carried most of the burden of fulfilling the American promise of equality to blacks. Eisenhower had pushed through two civil rights measures over strong opposition from southern Democrats, and in particular Senate Majority Leader Lyndon Johnson, who fought hard to dilute the legislation. Again, Kennedy was on the right side of history, but his efforts were mostly reactive. "I did not lie awake worrying about the problems of Negroes," he confessed.[5]

There is considerable irony in the fact that in the first election to replace Kennedy, Barry Goldwater was roundly hailed as the "fascist" in the race. The bespectacled small-government conservative in funereal suits was about as far from a fascist as one can get in American politics. Meanwhile, the intellectuals denouncing Goldwater as a crypto-Nazi failed to grasp that it was John F. Kennedy who was advancing fascist themes and aesthetics in American politics. FDR had been the first president to use modern technology to construct a mythological narrative about himself, but it was Kennedy who transformed that technique into an art. "Camelot," a phrase never used to describe Kennedy's tenure when he was alive, has become a catchall for every gauzy memory and un-fulfilled wish of the Kennedy presidency. In 1964 James Reston summarized the newly minted liberal nostalgia for America's Greek god of a president. "He was a story-book President, younger and more handsome than mortal politicians, remote even from his friends, graceful, almost elegant with poetry on his tongue and a radiant young woman at his side."[6]

Many elements of the Kennedy myth are as obvious now as they were then. He was the youngest man ever elected president (Teddy Roosevelt had been the youngest to serve). He was the first president born in the twentieth century. He was a man of action—a bona fide war hero. He was also an intellectual—the author of a best-selling book on political courage—who made liberalism cool and glam-orous, but at the same time a pragmatist who would never let the pointy-headed Ivy Leaguers with whom he surrounded himself get in the way of the right course of action. He represented a national yearning for "renewal" and "rebirth," appealing to American ideal-ism and calling for common sacrifice.

Recall the key themes to Mussolini's cult of personality: youth, action, expertise, vigor, glamour, military service. Mussolini cast himself as the leader of a youth movement, a new generation em-powered through intellect and expertise to break with the old cate-gories of left and right. JFK's stirring inaugural spoke of "a new generation of Americans—born in this century, tempered by war, disciplined by a hard and bitter peace, proud of our ancient heritage." Mussolini's entire movement (like Hitler's) was built around the generation of Italians who'd been tempered in World War I and their resentment against the bitter peace of Versailles. The Italian Fascist government, billed as a "regime of youth," sold itself as a techno-cratic marvel in which Mussolini ran many of the ministries himself through force of will and indomitable vigor. Fascist propagandists saturated the media with pictures of Mussolini chopping wood, skiing, running, and standing bare-chested in the Alpine snow. Moreover, Mussolini's reputation as an intellectual and writer was in fact well deserved—unlike Kennedy's.

The Kennedy operation endeavored mightily to send similar messages. Nary a newspaper article could be printed about the new president without references to his love of action, his youth, his vigor. Films of his manly exertions seemed to be everywhere. He could not be so obvious as Mussolini in his womanizing, but his cultivated status as a sex symbol was the product of decided political calculation. Kennedy ran explicitly as a war hero, and his political troops could usually be recognized by their PT-109 insignia pins. His campaign commercials, crammed with images of Kennedy the warrior, boasted that this was a "time for greatness." Kennedy, like Mussolini, promised a national "restoration" and a "new politics" that would transcend old categories of left and right. He insisted that the forceful application of his own will and that of his technocratic aides would be more effective in solving the nation's problems than traditional democratic means.

Indeed, Kennedy was almost literally a superhero. It is a little-known but significant fact that no president has appeared more times in Superman comic books than JFK. He was even entrusted with Superman's secret identity and once pretended to be Clark Kent so as to prevent it from being exposed. When Supergirl debuted as a character, she was formally presented to the Kennedys. (Not surprisingly, the president took an immediate liking to her.) In a special issue dedicated to getting American youth to become physically fit—just like the astronaut "Colonel Glenn"—Kennedy enlists Superman on a mission to close the "muscle gap."[7]

Comic book writers weren't alone in making this connection. In 1960 Norman Mailer wrote a ponderous piece for *Esquire* titled "Superman Comes to the Supermarket." Ostensibly a report from the Democratic National Convention in Los Angeles, the essay was more like a term paper for a Noam Chomsky seminar. But it does give you a sense of how even leading intellectuals like Mailer understood that they were being offered a myth—and were eager to accept it.[8]

The original Kennedy myth did not emphasize Kennedy's progressive credentials. Ted Sorensen recalled that JFK "never identified himself as a liberal; it was only after his death that they began to claim him as one of theirs." Indeed, the Kennedy family had serious trouble with many self-described progressives (who, after World War II, were essentially warmed-over communists) because of its close ties to that other prominent Irish-American politician, Joe McCarthy. After Roy Cohn, Bobby Kennedy was McCarthy's most valued aide. Jack Kennedy never denounced his Senate colleague, who was also a dear friend of his father's. But then, Kennedy was always more of a nationalist than a liberal. While a student at Harvard, he sent the isolationist America First Committee a one-hundred-dollar contribution with a note attached, telling them, "What you are doing is vital."[9]

World War II changed JFK's perspective—as it did for most isolationists. It also amplified Kennedy's fascination with "greatness." He was awed by Churchill and would lip-synch Churchill's oratory on the *I Can Hear It Now* albums narrated by Edward R. Murrow.[10] In later years, staffers knew they could win Kennedy's ear if they could make him think that greatness was in the offing. His entire political career was grounded in the hope and aspiration that he would follow FDR as a lion of the twentieth century.

JFK famously inherited this ambition from his father, Joseph P. Kennedy, the pro-Nazi Democratic Party boss who was desperate to put a son in the White House. In 1946 Joe distributed a hundred thousand copies of John Hersey's article on JFK's PT-109 exploits. Soon an entire team of intellectuals was put to work, transforming JFK into the next great man of action. Kennedy's first book, *Why England Slept,* an expanded version of his undergraduate thesis, was a dish concocted by many chefs. His second, *Profiles in Courage,* about great men who stick to their principles despite adversity, was essentially produced by a committee chaired by Ted Sorensen and only intermittently supervised by Kennedy himself. Of course, Kennedy accepted the Pulitzer alone.

Kennedy was the first modern politician to recognize and exploit the new clout enjoyed by intellectuals in American society. The old Brain Trusters were economists and engineers, men concerned with shaping earth and iron. The new Brain Trusters were image men, historians, and writers—propagandists in the most benign sense—concerned with spinning words and pictures. Kennedy was no dunce, but he understood that in the modern age style tends to trump substance. (An indisputably handsome and charming man, he obviously benefited from the rise of television.) And the Kennedy machine represented nothing if not the triumph of style in American politics.

Kennedy's political fortune also stemmed from the fact that he seemed to be riding the waves of history. Once again, the forces of progressivism had been returned to power after a period of peace and prosperity. And despite the unprecedented wealth and leisure of the postwar years—indeed largely because of them—there was a palpable desire among the ambitious, the upwardly mobile, the intellectuals, and, above all, the activists of the progressive-liberal establishment to get "America moving again." "More than anything else," the conservative publisher Henry Luce wrote in 1960, "the people of America are asking for a clear sense of National Purpose."[11]

This was the dawn of the third fascist moment in American life, which would unfurl throughout the 1960s and into the 1970s, both in the streets and universities—as seen in the previous chapter—and in the halls of government. What ended as bloodshed in the streets began in many respects as a well-intentioned "revolution from above" by heirs to the Wilson-FDR legacy incapable of containing the demons they unleashed.

Perhaps the best expression of this bipartisan-elite clamor for "social change" came in a series of essays on "the national purpose" co-published by the *New York Times* and *Life* magazine. Adlai Stevenson wrote that Americans needed to transcend the "mystique of privacy" and turn away from the "supermarket temple." Charles F. Darlington, a leading corporate executive and former State Department official, explained that America needed to recapture the collective spirit of national purpose it had enjoyed "during parts of the Administrations of Woodrow Wilson and the two Roosevelts" (you can guess which parts). Above all, a reborn America needed to stop seeing itself as a nation of individuals. Once again, "collective action" was the cure. Darlington's call for a "decreased emphasis on private enterprise" amounted to a revival of the corporatism and war socialism of the Wilson and Roosevelt administrations.[12]

On the eve of JFK's inauguration in January 1960, a *Look* report, utilizing data from a special Gallup survey, found that Americans were actually feeling pretty good: "Most Americans today are relaxed, unadventurous, comfortably satisfied with their way of life and blandly optimistic about the future." The trick, then, was to rip Americans' attention away from their TV dinners and fan-tailed cars and get them to follow the siren song of the intellectuals. And that meant Kennedy needed a crisis to bind the public mind to a new Sorelian myth. "Great crises produce great men," Kennedy proclaimed in *Profiles in Courage,* and his entire presidency would be dedicated to the creation of crises commensurate with the greatness he yearned to achieve.[13]

A vast retinue of brains and activists, nostalgic for the excitement of the New Deal and World War II, shared Kennedy's desire to shake America out of its complacency. In the 1950s Arthur Schlesinger Jr. spoke for this entire circle of progressives, young and old, when he lamented the "absent discontents" of the American people.[14]

Kennedy, like FDR, believed he was a true democrat, and it would be unfair to label him a fascist. But his obsession with fostering crises in order to whip up popular sentiments in his favor demonstrates the perils of infatuation with fascist aesthetics in democratic politics. Ted Sorensen's memoirs count sixteen crises in Kennedy's first eight months in office. Kennedy created "crisis teams" that could short-circuit the traditional bureaucracy, the democratic process, and even the law. David Halberstam writes that Johnson inherited from Kennedy "crisis-mentality men, men who delighted in the great international crisis because it centered the action right there in the White House—the meetings, the decisions, the tensions, the power, *they* were movers and activists, and this was what they had come to Washington for, to meet these challenges." Garry Wills and Henry Fairlie—hardly right-wing critics—dubbed the Kennedy administration a "guerilla government" for its abuse of and contempt for the traditional governmental system. In an interview in 1963 Otto Strasser, the left-wing Nazi who helped found the movement, told the scholar David Schoenbaum that Kennedy's abuse of authority and crisis-mongering certainly made him look like a fascist.[15]

Everything about Kennedy's politics conveyed a sense of urgency. He ran on a "missile gap" that never existed and governed based on a heightened state of tension with the Soviets that he labored to create. He constantly spoke the language of "danger" and "sacrifice," "courage" and "crusade." He installed the first "situation room" in the White House. His first State of the Union address, delivered eleven days after his inaugural, was a "wartime speech without a war." Kennedy warned that freedom itself was at its "hour of maximum danger." "Before my term has ended we shall have to test again whether a nation organized and governed such as ours can endure. The outcome is by no means certain."[16]

Kennedy's adrenaline-soaked presidency was infectious, and deliberately so. His administration launched a massive campaign to encourage the construction of fallout shelters, with various agencies competing to spend hundreds of millions of dollars on the conversion of schools and hospitals into nuclear bunkers. We think of those duck-and-cover drills as icons of the 1950s, but it was under Kennedy that they reached the climate of extreme paranoia so often parodied today. The administration distributed fifty-five million wallet-sized cards with instructions on what to do when the nukes started raining from the sky. If, as the New Left so often claimed, the mobilization of "youth" in the 1960s was spurred by the anxiety of living under the shadow of "the bomb," then they have JFK to thank for it.

Even Kennedy's nondefense policies were sold as the moral analogue of war. He justified more education spending—as Johnson would after him—on the explicit grounds that we needed to stay competitive with the Soviets. Kennedy's tax cuts—aimed to counteract the worst stock market crash since the Depression—were implemented not in the spirit of supply-side economics (as some conservatives are wont to insinuate) but as a form of Keynesianism, justified in the language of Cold War competition. Indeed, Kennedy was the first president to explicitly claim that the White House had a mandate to ensure economic growth—because America couldn't ignore Khrushchev's boastful threat that the Soviet Union would soon "bury" the United States economically.[17] His intimidation of the steel industry was a rip-off of Truman's similar effort during the Korean War, itself a maneuver from the playbooks of FDR and Wilson. Likewise, the Peace Corps and its various domestic equivalents were throwbacks to FDR's martial CCC. Even Kennedy's most ambitious idea, putting a man on the moon, was sold to the public as a response to the fact that the Soviet Union was overtaking America in science.

Particularly in response to Kennedy's crackdown on the steel industry, some observers charged that he was making himself into a strongman. The *Wall Street Journal* and the Chamber of Commerce likened him to a dictator. Ayn Rand explicitly called him a fascist in a 1962 speech, "The Fascist New Frontier."

It is not a joyful thing to impugn an American hero and icon with the label fascist. And if by fascist you mean evil, cruel, and bigoted, then Kennedy was no fascist. But we must ask, what made his administration so popular? What made it so effective? What has given it its lasting appeal? On almost every front, the answers are those very elements that fit the fascist playbook: the creation of crises, nationalistic appeals to unity, the celebration of martial values, the blurring of lines between public and private sectors, the utilization of mass media to glamorize the state and its programs, invocations of a new "post-partisan" spirit that places the important decisions in the hands of experts and intellectual supermen, and a cult of personality for the national leader.

Kennedy promised to transcend ideology in the name of what would later be described as cool pragmatism. Like the pragmatists who came before him, he eschewed labels, believing that he was beyond right and left. Instead, he shared Robert McNamara's confidence that "every problem could be solved" by technocratic means. Once again the Third Way defined ideological sophistication. In his 1962 Yale commencement address, President Kennedy explained that "political labels and ideological approaches are irrelevant to the solution" of today's challenges. "Most of the problems . . . that we now face, are technical problems, are administrative problems," he insisted at a press conference in May 1962. These problems "deal with questions which are now beyond the comprehension of most men" and should therefore be left to the experts to settle without subjecting them to divisive democratic debate.[18]

Once again, Kennedy's famous declaration "And so, my fellow Americans: ask not what your country can do for you—ask what you can do for your country" is seen today as a fine patriotic turn of phrase. Liberals in particular see it as an admirable call to service. And it is both of these things. But what is often missed is the historical context and motivation. Kennedy was trying to re-create the unity of World War II in the same way FDR had tried to revive the unity of World War I. His declaration that we should put a man on the moon was not the result of Kennedy's profound farsightedness, nor even of his desire to wallop the Russians. Rather, it was his best option for finding a moral equivalent of war.

HE DIED FOR LIBERALISM

All of this went down the memory hole after Kennedy's murder. Kennedy the nationalistic Third Wayer was replaced by Kennedy the fighting liberal. The JFK of Camelot eclipsed the one who tried to assassinate Patrice Lumumba and Fidel Castro.

Woodrow Wilson's grandson Dean Francis Sayre delivered a sermon at the Washington National Cathedral in homage to the fallen leader. "We have been present at a new crucifixion," he told the assembled dignitaries. "All of us," he explained, "have had a part in the slaying of our President. It was the *good* people who crucified our Lord, and not merely those who acted as executioners." Chief Justice Earl Warren declared that the president had an organic and mystical bond with the people. He is "chosen to embody the ideals of our people, the faith we have in our institutions, and our belief in the fatherhood of God and the brotherhood of man." Five days after Kennedy's death, the new president, Lyndon Johnson, capped his address to a joint session of Congress by asking that Americans "put an end to the teaching and the preaching of hate and evil and violence" and turn away from "the apostles of bitterness and bigotry."[19]

Even after the nature of the assassination was more clear, the notion that "hate" and America's collective sin killed Kennedy endured. Washington's Methodist bishop, John Wesley Lord, declared that the nation needed to "atone" for Kennedy's death. Rather than naming monuments after Kennedy, the nation could more appropriately "thank a martyr for his death and sacrifice" by redoubling its commitment to liberal politics.[20]

Most historians view Kennedy and Johnson as representing the last gasp of traditional progressive politics, ending the era that began with Wilson and ran through the New Deal and the Fair Deal to the New Frontier and the Great Society. Programmatically, that's largely right (though it lets the very liberal Nixon off the hook). But the Kennedy presidency represented something more profound. It marked the final evolution of Progressivism into a full-blown religion and a national cult of the state.

From the beginning, Kennedy's presidency had tapped into a nationalistic and religious leitmotif increasingly central to American liberalism and consonant with the themes of both Progressivism and fascism. The Kennedy "action-intellectuals" yearned to be supermen, a Gnostic priesthood imbued with the special knowledge of how to fix society's problems. JFK's inaugural opened the decade with the proclamation that America was the agent of God and the possessor of godlike powers: "For man holds in his mortal hands the power to abolish all forms of human poverty and all forms of human life." The sociologist Robert Bellah found proof in this address that America already had a civil religion, defined by "the obligation, both collective and individual, to carry out God's will on earth." The *New York Times*'s C. L. Sulzberger wrote that the inaugural appealed to anybody who believed there was "still room on this earth for the kingdom of heaven."[21]

John F. Kennedy represented the cult of personality tradition of American liberalism. He wanted to be a great man in the mold of Wilson and the Roosevelts. He was more concerned with guns than butter. Lyndon Baines Johnson, a southern populist ward heeler born and bred in the New Deal tradition, was, on the other hand, all about the butter. Johnson could neither be a warrior nor a priest. If he couldn't be the liberal lion his predecessor wanted to be, he could embody the maternal aspect of Progressivism as the caring and protective shepherd overseeing his flock. He would transform the Kennedy personality cult into a cult of government. To this end, LBJ, a crafty and clever politician, made shameless use of JFK's assassination, converting it into precisely the sort of transformative national crisis that had always eluded Kennedy himself. His legacy, the modern welfare state, represents the ultimate fruition of a progressive statist tradition going back to Woodrow Wilson.

As we've seen, Wilson and the progressives laid the intellectual foundations for the divinized liberal state. The progressives, it should be remembered, did not argue for totalitarianism because the war demanded it; they argued for totalitarianism and were delighted that the war made it possible. But World War I also proved to be the undoing of the progressive dream of American collectivism. The total mobilization of the war—and the stupidity of the war in the first place—reawakened in its aftermath the traditional American resistance to such tyranny. In the 1920s the progressives sulked while Americans enjoyed remarkable prosperity and the Russians and Italians (in their view) had "all the fun of remaking a world." The Great Depression came along just in time: it put the progressives back in the driver's seat. As we have seen, FDR brought no new ideas to government; he merely dusted off the ideas he had absorbed as a member of the Wilson administration. But he left the state immeasurably strengthened and expanded. Indeed, it is worth recalling that the origins of the modern conservative movement stem from an instinctive desire to shrink the state back down to a manageable size after the war. But the Cold War changed that, forcing many conservatives to support a large national security state in order to defeat communism. This decision on the part of foreign policy hawks created a permanent schism on the American right. Nonetheless, even though Cold War conservatives believed in a limited government, their support for anti-communism prevented any conceivable attempt to actually get one.

Kennedy's contribution to the permanent welfare state was for the most part stylistic, as we've seen. But his "martyrdom" provided a profound *psychological* crisis that proved useful for the promotion of liberal goals and ideas. Johnson used it not just to hijack the national political agenda but to transform Progressivism itself into a full-blown mass political religion. For the first time, the progressive dream could be pursued without reservation during a time of prosperity and relative peace. No longer dependent on war or economic crisis, Progressivism finally got a clean shot at creating the sort of society it had long preached about. The psychological angst and anomie that progressives believed lay at the core of capitalist society could be healed by the ministrations of the state. The moment to create a politics of meaning on its own merits had finally arrived.

In his first speech as president, Johnson signaled his intention to build a new liberal church upon the rock of Kennedy's memory. That church, that sacralized community, would be called the Great Society.

THE BIRTH OF THE LIBERAL GOD-STATE

We have already discussed at some length the personalities driving American liberalism. It is now necessary to take what may seem like a sharp detour to address the cult of the state itself in American liberalism. Without this historical detour, it is difficult to see modern liberalism for what it is: a religion of state worship whose sacrificial Christ was JFK and whose Pauline architect was LBJ.

It's hard to fix a specific starting date for the progressive race for the Great Society, but a good guess might be 1888, the year Edward Bellamy's novel *Looking Backward* burst on the American scene. One of the most influential works of progressive propaganda ever conceived, the book sold hundreds of thousands of copies and was hailed as the biggest publishing sensation since *Uncle Tom's Cabin.* The narrator of the book, which is set in the faraway year 2000, lives in a utopian, militarized society. Workers belong to a unified "industrial army," and the economy is run by all-powerful central planners partly inspired by the successes of German military planning. Citizens are drafted into their occupations, for "every able-bodied citizen [is] bound to work for the nation, whether with mind or muscle." The story's preacher informs us that America has finally created the kingdom of heaven on earth. Indeed, everyone looks back on the "age of individualism" with bemused contempt.[22]

The umbrella in particular is remembered as the symbol of the nineteenth century's disturbing obsession with individualism. In Bellamy's utopia, umbrellas have been replaced with retractable canopies so that everyone is protected from the rain equally. "[I]n the nineteenth century," explains a character, "when it rained, the people of Boston put up three hundred thousand umbrellas over as many heads, and in the twentieth century they put up one umbrella over all the heads."[23]

Bellamy's vision of a militarized, nationalistic, socialist utopia captivated the imagination of young progressives everywhere. Overnight, Bellamite "Nationalist Clubs" appeared across the country dedicated to "the nationalization of industry and the promotion of the brotherhood of humanity." Nationalism in America, as in most of

Europe, meant both nationalism and socialism. Thus Bellamy predicted that individual U.S. states would have to be abolished because
"state governments would have interfered with the control and discipline of the industrial army."[24]

Religion was the glue that held this American national socialism
together. Bellamy believed that his brand of socialist nationalism
was the true application of Jesus' teachings. His cousin Francis
Bellamy, the author of the Pledge of Allegiance, was similarly devoted. A founding member of the First Nationalist Club of Boston
and co-founder of the Society of Christian Socialists, Francis wrote
a sermon, "Jesus, the Socialist," that electrified parishes across the
country. In an expression of his "military socialism," the Pledge of
Allegiance was accompanied by a fascist or "Roman" salute to the
flag in American public schools. Indeed, some contend that the
Nazis got the idea for their salute from America.[25]

Everywhere one looked, "scientific" utopianism, nationalism, socialism, and Christianity blended into one another. Consider the
1912 Progressive Party convention. The *New York Times* described it
as a "convention of fanatics," at which political speeches were punctuated by the singing of hymns and shouts of "Amen!" "It was not a
convention at all. It was an assemblage of religious enthusiasts," the
Times reported. "It was such a convention as Peter the Hermit held.
It was a Methodist camp meeting done over into political terms." The
"expression on every face" in the audience, including that of Jane
Addams, who rose to nominate Teddy Roosevelt for his quixotic last
bid for the presidency, was one "of fanatical and religious enthusiasm." The delegates, who "believed—obviously and certainly believed—that they were enlisted in a contest with the Powers of
Darkness," sang "We Will Follow Jesus," but with the name
"Roosevelt" replacing the now-outdated savior. Among them were
representatives of every branch of Progressivism, including the
Social Gospeller Washington Gladden, happily replacing the old
Christian savior with the new "Americanist" one. Roosevelt told the
rapturous audience, "Our cause is based on the eternal principles of
righteousness . . . We stand at Armageddon, and we battle for the
Lord."[26]

The American Social Gospel and Christian sociology movements
essentially sought to bend Christianity to the progressive social

agenda. Senator Albert Beveridge, the progressive Republican from Indiana who chaired the 1912 convention, summed up the progressive attitude well when he declared, "God has marked us as His chosen people, henceforth to lead in the regeneration of the world."[27]

Walter Rauschenbusch offers the best short explanation of the Social Gospel for our purposes. A professor at the Rochester Theological Seminary and a onetime preacher on the outskirts of New York's Hell's Kitchen, the slender clergyman with a thin goatee had become the informal leader of the movement when he published *Christianity and the Social Crisis* in 1907. "[U]nless the ideal social order can supply men with food, warmth and comfort more efficiently than our present economic order," he warned, "back we shall go to Capitalism . . . 'The God that answereth by low food prices,' " he boomed, " 'let him be God.' " Left-wing clergy like Rauschenbusch were convinced that the state was the instrument of God and that collectivism was the new order sanctioned by Jesus.[28]

Progressive clergy like Rauschenbusch laid the philosophical and theological foundation for statism in ways that the new crop of social scientists never could. They argued from pulpits and political gatherings and in the intellectual press for a total and complete reconception of scripture in which redemption could only be achieved collectively. Conservative theologians argued that only the individual could be born again. The progressive Christians claimed that individuals no longer mattered and that only the state could serve as divine intercessor. The Baptist Social Gospel preacher argued that the state must become "the medium through which the people shall co-operate in their search for the kingdom of God and its righteousness."[29]

Inspiration for such ideas came from an improbable source: Bismarck's Prussia. Bismarck inspired American progressives in myriad ways, some of which have been touched on already. First, he was a centralizer, a uniter, a European Lincoln who brought disparate regions and factions under the yoke of the state, heedless of dissent. Second, he was the innovator of top-down socialism, which pioneered many of the welfare state programs the progressives yearned for: pensions, health insurance, worker safety measures, eight-hour workdays, and so on. Bismarck's efficiency at delivering programs without the messiness of "excessive" democracy set the precedent for the idea that "great men," modernizers, and "men of action" could do what the leaders of decadent and decaying democracies could not.

Moreover, Bismarck's socialism from above gelded classical liberalism in Germany and helped to hobble it around the globe. This was precisely his purpose. Bismarck wanted to forestall greater socialist or democratic radicalism by giving the people what they wanted without having them vote for it. To this end he bought off the left-leaning reformers who didn't particularly care about limited government or liberal constitutionalism. At the same time, he methodically marginalized, and in many cases crushed, the classical or limited-state liberals (a similar dynamic transpired in the United States during World War I). Hence, in Germany, both left and right became in effect statist ideologies, and the two sides fought over who would get to impose its vision on society. Liberalism, defined as an ideology of individual freedom and democratic government, slowly atrophied and died in Germany because Bismarck denied it a popular constituency. In its place was the statist liberalism of Dewey and DuBois, Wilson and FDR, a liberalism defined by economic entitlements and the alleviation of poverty.

Then there was the Kulturkampf—a subject to be discussed at greater length in a later chapter. The important point about the Kulturkampf, lost on so many contemporary commentators, is that it was a liberal phenomenon. German progressives declared war on backward Catholicism, believing that their blending of science and a form of nationalistic Social Gospel was the ideology of the future. It was a model the progressives adapted to American soil.

The godfathers of the liberal God-state were the philosopher G. W. F. Hegel and the scientist Charles Darwin. Hegel had argued that history was an unfolding evolutionary process, and the engine driving that process was the state. The "State is the actually existing, realized moral life . . . The divine idea as it exists on earth," Hegel declared in *The Philosophy of History*. "[A]ll worth which the human being possesses—all spiritual reality, he possesses only through the State."[30] The movement of the state through time was the "march of God on earth." Darwin's theory of evolution seemed to confirm that man was part of a larger organism, governed and directed by the state as the mind guides the body. For the "modern" clergy this meant that politics was a religious calling; after all, politics is nothing less than the effort to define the mission of the state, and the state was the hand of God.

Virtually all of the leading progressive intellectuals shared this "organic" and spiritual understanding of politics—perhaps none more than Richard Ely. "God works through the State in carrying out His purposes more universally than through any other institution," proclaimed the founder of the American Economic Association and the so-called Wisconsin School of progressivism. The state, he insisted, "is religious in its essence," and there is no corner of human existence beyond the scope of its authority. A mentor to Wilson and a great influence on Teddy Roosevelt, Ely was a postmillennialist Christian who defined the state as "a mighty force in furthering God's kingdom and establishing righteous relations."[31] Many of Ely's famous colleagues at the University of Wisconsin saw their advocacy for economic reform, eugenics, war, socialism, Prohibition, and the rest of the progressive agenda as part of a united effort to bring about the "New Jerusalem."

It made little sense to talk about progressives as a group distinct from the theocratic zealots trying to create a new God-state. The American Economic Association, its mission statement dedicated to uniting church, state, and science to secure America's redemption, served as both the intellectual engine of progressive social policy and a de facto organ of the Social Gospel movement. More than sixty clergymen—roughly half the group's roster—counted themselves as members. Later, during World War I, Ely was the most rabid of jingoists, organizing loyalty oaths, hurling accusations of treason, and arguing that opponents of the war should be shot.

With Woodrow Wilson, it is impossible to separate the priest from the professor. From early essays with such titles as "Christ's Army" and "Christian Progress" to his later addresses as president, Wilson made it clear that he was a divine instrument, and the state the holy sword of God's crusade, while at the same time insisting that he represented the triumph of science and reason in politics. Speaking to the Young Men's Christian Association, he told the audience that public servants should be guided solely by the question: What would Christ do in your situation? He then proceeded to explain, "There is a mighty task before us, and it welds us together. It is to make the

United States a mighty Christian Nation, and to Christianize the world."[32]

The war only served to intensify these impulses. "The Past and the Present are in deadly grapple," he declared. His goal was the complete "destruction of *every* arbitrary power anywhere . . . that can disturb the peace of the world" and the "settlement of *every* question" facing mankind. Wilson advocated "Force! Force to the utmost! Force without stint or limit! The righteous and triumphant Force which shall make Right the law of the world, and cast every selfish dominion down in the dust." America was "an instrument in the hands of God," he proclaimed, while his propaganda ministry called World War I a war "to re-win the tomb of Christ."[33]

Wilson shared with other fascist leaders a firm conviction that his organic connection with "the people" was absolute and transcended the mere mechanics of democracy. "So sincerely do I believe these things that I am sure that I speak the mind and wish of the people of America." Many Europeans recognized him as an avatar of the rising socialist World Spirit. In 1919 a young Italian socialist proclaimed, "Wilson's empire has no borders because He [*sic*] does not govern territories. Rather He interprets the needs, the hopes, the faith of the human spirit, which has no spatial or temporal limits."[34] The young man's name was Benito Mussolini.

That Wilson's government intruded deeply into the private sector in unprecedented ways is indisputable. It launched the effort, carried forward by FDR, of turning the economy into a "cooperative" enterprise where labor, business, and government sat around a table and hashed things out on their own. Such a system—they called it syndicalism, corporatism, and fascism in Europe—sounds attractive on paper, but inevitably it serves to benefit the people inside the room and few others. When Wilson's dollar-a-year men weren't rewarding their respective industries, they were subjecting more of the private sector to government control. Wilson's planners set prices on almost every commodity, fixed wages, commandeered the private railroads, created a vast machinery for the policing of thought crimes, and even tried to dictate the menu of every family meal.[35]

Wilson's war socialism was temporary, but its legacy was permanent. The War Industries Board and cartels closed shop after the war, but the precedent they set would prove too attractive for progressives to abandon.

While America was the victor in World War I, Wilson and the progressives lost *their* war at home. The government's deep penetration into civil society seemed forgivable during a war but was unacceptable during peace. Likewise, the artificial economic boom came to an end. Moreover, the Treaty of Versailles, which was supposed to justify every imposition and sacrifice, proved a disappointing riot of hypocrisies and false promises.

But the progressive faith endured. Liberal intellectuals and activists insisted during the 1920s that Wilson's war socialism had been a smashing success and its failures a result of insufficient zeal. "We planned in war" became their slogan. Alas, they couldn't convince the yokels in the voting booths. As a result, they came more and more to admire the Bismarckian approach of top-down socialism. They also looked to Russia and Italy, where "men of action" were creating utopias with the bulldozer and the slide rule. The Marxist emphasis on scientific socialism and social engineering infected American Progressivism. And since science isn't open to democratic debate, an arrogant literal-mindedness took over Progressivism.

It was also around this time that through a dexterous sleight of hand, Progressivism came to be renamed "liberalism." In the past, liberalism had referred to political and economic *liberty* as understood by Enlightenment thinkers like John Locke and Adam Smith. For them, the ultimate desideratum was maximum individual freedom under the benign protection of a minimalist state. The progressives, led by Dewey, subtly changed the meaning of this term, importing the Prussian vision of liberalism as the alleviation of material and educational poverty, and liberation from old dogmas and old faiths. For progressives liberty no longer meant freedom from tyranny, but freedom from want, freedom to be a "constructive" citizen, the Rousseauian and Hegelian "freedom" of living in accord with the state and the general will. Classical liberals were now routinely called conservatives, while devotees of social control were dubbed liberals. Thus in 1935 John Dewey would write in *Liberalism and Social Action* that activist government in the name of the economically disadvantaged and social reconstruction had "virtually come to define the meaning of liberal faith."[36]

Given this worldview, it shouldn't be surprising that so many liberals believed the Soviet Union was the freest place on earth. In a series of articles on the Soviet Union for the *New Republic*, Dewey hailed the grand "experiment" as the "liberation of a people to consciousness of themselves as a determining power in the shaping of their ultimate fate." The Soviet revolution had brought "a release of human powers on such an unprecedented scale that it is of incalculable significance not only for that country, but for the world." Jane Addams also called the Soviets "the greatest social experiment in history."[37] Freed from the dogmas of the past, and adhering to evolutionary imperatives, Pragmatists believed that even states must "learn by doing"—even if that meant, once again, that the new Jacobins had to unleash terror on those who would not comply with the general will.

For a generation progressives had complained that America lacked, in effect, a *Volksgeist*, a singular general will that could fuel this conception of a God-state. When the stock market crashed in 1929, they believed their shining moment had returned.

"[T]he United States in the 1920s," writes William Leuchtenburg, "had almost no institutional structure to which Europeans would accord the term 'the State.' " Beyond the post office, most people had very little interaction with or dependence on "the government in Washington."[38] The New Deal changed all that. It represented the last stage in the transformation of American liberalism, whereby the U.S. government became a European "state" and liberalism a political religion.

As economic policy, the New Deal was a failure. If anything, it likely prolonged the Depression. And yet we are constantly told that the New Deal remains the greatest domestic accomplishment of the United States in the twentieth century and a model liberals constantly wish to emulate, preserve, and restore. In 2007 Nancy Pelosi reportedly said that three words prove the Democrats aren't out of ideas: "Franklin Delano Roosevelt."[39] Why such devotion? The answer most often offered is that the New Deal gave Americans "hope" and "faith" in a "cause larger than themselves." Hope for *what*? Faith in *what*? What "cause"? The answer: the liberal God-state or, if you prefer, the Great Society—which is merely that society governed by the God-state in accordance with the general will.

The New Deal amounted to a religious breakthrough for American liberalism. Not only had faith in the liberal ideal become thoroughly religious in nature—irrational, dogmatic, mythological—but many smart liberals recognized this fact and welcomed it. In 1934 Dewey had defined the battle for the liberal ideal as a "religious quality" in and of itself. Thurman Arnold, one of the New Deal's most influential intellectuals, proposed that Americans be taught a new "religion of government," which would finally liberate the public from its superstitions about individualism and free markets.[40] It was as Robespierre insisted: the "religious instinct" must be cultivated to protect the revolution.

The apotheosis of liberal aspirations under FDR took place not during the New Deal but during World War II. Roosevelt in his 1944 State of the Union address proposed what he called a "second Bill of Rights." But this was really an argument for a *new* Bill of Rights, turning the original on its head. "Necessitous men are not free men," he declared. Therefore the state must provide a "new basis of security and prosperity." Among the new rights on offer were "a useful and remunerative job," "a decent home," "adequate medical care and the opportunity to achieve and enjoy good health," "adequate protection from the economic fears of old age, sickness, accident, and unemployment," and "a good education." This second Bill of Rights remains the spiritual lodestar of liberal aspirations to this day.[41]

PURGING THE DEMONS WITHIN

The war against Hitler was as pristine an example of good versus evil as we've seen in the history of warfare. But that doesn't mean the war (and the New Deal mobilization) had only salutary effects. People grew accustomed to following the exhortations of elites—in the press, at leading institutions, and in government—without much reflection or skepticism. These elites told the American public that the war and state planning had "saved" Western civilization and that it was now America's job to keep it safe.

The postwar environment saw the fusion of any number of

progressive strains into a coherent agenda. Government was now truly run by experts. The public consensus was favorable to liberal ambitions. Classical liberalism seemed permanently discredited. Even the utopian dream of a new world order and, perhaps, a world government envisioned by Wilson, H. G. Wells, and many others was given new life by the creation of the United Nations. The problem for liberalism was that the new enemy on the horizon wasn't from the right but from the left. For liberals in the late 1920s and early 1930s the Soviet Union was like Bismarck's Prussia a generation earlier—a model to be emulated. During the 1930s the Soviets were on the front line fighting the fascist threat. In the 1940s the Soviets were our allies. But after the war it soon became clear that Soviet intentions weren't that honorable and that Soviet methods were embarrassingly difficult to distinguish from Nazi methods.

There is a modern notion that liberals didn't disapprove of or oppose anti-communism; they just opposed McCarthyite excesses. The problem is that communists and liberals have always made allowances for McCarthyite tactics when it is one of their enemies getting grilled. The House Un-American Activities Committee, after all, was founded by a progressive Democrat, Samuel Dickstein, to investigate German sympathizers. During the barely remembered "Brown scare" of the 1940s, everyone from real Nazi supporters— the German-American Bund, for example—to misguided isolationists was targeted and harassed. Much like Wilson, FDR believed that any domestic dissent was treachery and insisted that his Department of Justice persecute his opponents. At the height of the madness, Walter Winchell read the names of isolationists on the radio, calling them "Americans we can do without."[42] American communists in this period readily named names and compiled lists of "German sympathizers."

One might excuse such tactics as a necessary evil in the fight against Nazism. But the more poignant hypocrisy is that American communists *did the same thing to other American communists*. The Smith Act, which made it illegal to belong to an organization that advocated the overthrow of the United States, was a linchpin of American fascism, according to many leftists. But American communists themselves used the Smith Act to get American Trotskyites arrested during the war.

But that was a sideshow far from public eyes. After the war, liberals could not tolerate such tactics when aimed at their own ranks. Their denial that their own ideas and history had any link with totalitarianism was so total that anybody who suggested otherwise had to be destroyed. Whittaker Chambers demonstrated this when he accurately identified Alger Hiss, a scion of American liberalism, as a communist. The establishment rallied around Hiss while it demonized Chambers as a liar, a psychopath, a fascist.[43]

Joseph McCarthy could not be so easily dismissed, largely because he was a U.S. senator. Despite his flaws and unforgivable excesses, he accurately called attention to the fact that much of the liberal establishment had been infested with communists and communist sympathizers. For that crime he, too, was dubbed a fascist.

Ask a liberal today *why* McCarthy was a fascist, and the answers you usually get are that he was a "bully" and a "liar." Bullies and liars are bad, but there's nothing inherently right-wing about them. You will also hear that McCarthyism represents a grotesque distortion of patriotism, jingoism, and the like. This is a more complicated complaint, though it's worth remembering that many on the left think nearly any exhortation to patriotism is fascist. Still, it is true that McCarthyism represented a certain ugly nationalist strain in the American character. But far from being right-wing, this sentiment was in fact a throwback to traditional left-wing populist politics. Red baiting, witch hunts, censorship, and the like were a tradition in good standing among Wisconsin progressives and populists.

Today few remember that McCarthy's political roots lay firmly in the Progressive Era. McCarthy was, after all, a populist progressive from quite arguably the most progressive state in the Union, Richard Ely's and Robert La Follette's Wisconsin. Joe McCarthy was a product of Wisconsin and its traditions. Indeed, the primary reason he ran for the Senate as a Republican is that he'd learned in his first campaign for public office—when he ran as a Democrat—that Wisconsin under La Follette had essentially become a one-party Republican state. In his 1936 bid for district attorney of Shawano County, McCarthy railed against the Republican presidential candidate as a "puppet" of right-wing business interests and fat cats like William Randolph Hearst. When he finally challenged La Follette for his Senate seat, he ran not as a bona fide right-winger but as a populist more in tune with the needs of Wisconsin.

There was much about McCarthy that was fascistic, including his conspiratorialism, his paranoid rhetoric, his bullying, and his opportunism; but those tendencies did not come from the conservative or classical liberal traditions. Rather, McCarthy and McCarthyism came out of the progressive and populist traditions. His followers were mostly middle-class, very often progressive or populist in their assumptions about the role of the state, and in many respects heirs to the Coughlinism of the early New Deal. The most effective such McCarthyite was the four-term Nevada Democratic senator Pat McCarran, author of the Internal Security Act, which required communist-front organizations to register with the attorney general, barred communists from working in defense-related industries, banned immigration of communists, and provided for the internment of communists in case of national emergency.

The point is not that McCarthy was simply a La Follette Progressive. Both La Follettes were honorable and serious men, in many ways among the most courageous politicians of the twentieth century. Nor am I saying that McCarthy was just another liberal, though he continued to use the word positively until as late as 1951. What I am saying is that what it meant to be a liberal was changing very rapidly after World War II. And once again, the losers in a liberal civil war—the right wing *of the left*—were demonized. Liberalism was in effect shedding its unrefined elements, throwing off the husk of the Social Gospel and all of that God talk. Had not the Holocaust proved that God was dead? The old liberals increasingly seemed like the William Jennings Bryan character in *Inherit the Wind*—superstitious, angry, backward. Through the benefit of hindsight one can see how liberals would have invented the cool pragmatist JFK had he not existed. Then again, as we've seen, they largely did invent him.

At the dawn of the 1950s American liberals needed a unified field theory that not only sustained their unimpeachable status as Olympians but also took account of the Holocaust as well as the populist firebrands who'd dared to question the wisdom, authority, and patriotism of the liberal elite. The backward and unsatisfying language of religion increasingly cut off to them, their own legacy of eugenics discredited, and the orthodox Marxist narrative largely un-persuasive to the masses, liberals needed something that could unite and revive this trinity. They found the glue they needed in psychology.

A handful of immensely influential Marxist theorists, mostly Germans from the so-called Frankfurt School (transplanted to Columbia University beginning in the 1930s), married psychology and Marxism to provide a new vocabulary for liberalism. These theorists—led by Theodor Adorno, Max Horkheimer, Erich Fromm, and Herbert Marcuse—tried to explain why fascism had been more popular than communism in much of Europe. Borrowing from Freud and Jung, the Frankfurt School described Nazism and Fascism as forms of mass psychosis. That was plausible enough, but their analysis also held that since Marxism was objectively superior to its alternatives, the masses, the bourgeoisie, and anyone else who disagreed with them had to be, quite literally, mad.

Adorno was the lead author of *The Authoritarian Personality,* published in 1950. The book presented evidence that people holding "conservative" views scored higher on the so-called F-Scale (*F* for "Fascism") and were hence in dire need of therapy. The political scientist Herbert McClosky likewise diagnosed conservatives as a pre-fascist "personality type" comprising mostly "the uninformed, the poorly educated, and . . . the less intelligent." (Lionel Trilling famously reduced conservatism to a series of "irritable mental gestures which seek to resemble ideas.")[44] For McClosky, Adorno, and establishment liberals generally, conservatism was at best the human face of the madness of Nazi-style fascism.

It's tempting to say these theorists merely threw a patina of pseudoscientific psychobabble over the propaganda leaflets of Stalin's Third International. But the tactic was more sophisticated than that. The essential argument was brilliant in its simplicity. The original Marxist explanation of fascism was that it was the capitalist ruling classes' reaction to the threat of the ascendancy of the working classes. The Frankfurt School deftly psychologized this argument. Instead of rich white men and middle-class dupes protecting their economic interests, fascism became a psychological defense mechanism against change generally. Men who cannot handle "progress" respond violently because they have "authoritarian personalities."

So, in effect, anyone who disagrees with the aims, scope, and methods of liberalism is suffering from a mental defect, commonly known as fascism.

The Columbia University historian Richard Hofstadter was the Frankfurt School's most successful publicist. For Hofstadter, American history was a tale of liberals decapitating fascist Hydra heads in every chapter. His work dripped with the language of *The Authoritarian Personality.* In "Pseudo-Conservative Revolt"—which later became part of *The Paranoid Style in American Politics*—Hofstadter used psychological scare words to describe the crypto-fascist menace within: "clinical," "disorder," "complexes," "thematic apperception." As Christopher Lasch writes, *"The Authoritarian Personality* had a tremendous impact on Hofstadter and other liberal intellectuals, because it showed them how to conduct political criticism in psychiatric categories, to make those categories bear the weight of political criticism. This procedure excused them from the difficult work of judgment and argumentation. Instead of arguing with opponents, they simply dismissed them on psychiatric grounds."[45]

It didn't take long for such psychological theorizing to break its banks and become an all-purpose solution to the "social question," as progressives used to put it. Indeed, modern psychology was a perfect substitute for the Social Gospel, militarism, Thurman Arnold's "religion of government," "social control," and even eugenics. Whereas progressives were once determined to weed out the biologically unfit, they now directed the same energies to the psychologically unfit. Some liberal psychiatrists even began describing a new "religion of psychiatry" that would cure society of its "extremist," traditional, backward, *conservative* elements. Adorno and his colleagues had laid the groundwork for this transition by identifying the "authoritarian family" as the locus of evil in the modern world.

A wave of liberal theologians met the psychiatrists halfway, arguing that various neuroses were the product of social alienation and that traditional religion should reorient itself toward healing them. Psychiatry—and "relevance"—became the new standards for clergy everywhere. For Paul Tillich, the source of salvation would be a redefining and recombining of the secular and the sacred, rendering politics, psychiatry, and religion all parts of the same seamless web. Stripped of its jargon, this project was an almost perfect replay of the liberal pattern. Liberals love populism, when it comes from the left. But whenever the people's populist desires are at cross-purposes with the agenda of the left, suddenly "reaction," "extremism," and of course "fascism" are loosed upon the land. Bill Clinton titled his "blueprint" for America *Putting People First,* but when the people rejected his agenda, we were informed that "angry white men" (read white "authoritarian personalities") were a threat to the Republic. Similarly, when the people supported New Deal social planners, one could barely find an inch of daylight between Progressivism and populism. But when the same people had become fed up with social-ism from above, they became "paranoid" and dangerous, susceptible to diseases of the mind and fascistic manipulation. Hence, liberal so-cial planners were all the more justified in their efforts to "fix" the people, to reorient their dysfunctional inner lives, to give them "meaning." It was all reminiscent of Bertolt Brecht's famous quip: "Would it not be easier . . . for the government / To dissolve the peo-ple / And elect another?"[46]

THE GREAT SOCIETY: LBJ'S FASCIST UTOPIA

Much like the Nazi movement, liberal fascism had two faces: the street radicals and the establishment radicals. In Germany the two groups worked in tandem to weaken middle-class resistance to the Nazis' agenda. In the previous chapter we saw how the liberal fas-cists of the SDS and Black Panther movements rose up to terrorize the American middle class. In the remainder of this chapter—and the next—we will explain how the "suit-and-tie radicals" of the 1960s, people like Hillary Clinton and her friends, used this terror to expand the power and scope of the state and above all to change the public attitude toward the state as the agent of social progress and universal caring and compassion.

Lyndon Johnson seems an odd choice for liberalism's deliverer. Then again, he was no one's *choice.* An assassin's bullet anointed him to the job. Still, it's not as if he hadn't prepared for it.

Amazingly, Johnson was the only full-fledged New Dealer to serve as president save FDR himself. Indeed, in many respects LBJ was the ultimate company man of the modern welfare state, the personification of everything the New Deal represented. Despite his large personality, he was in reality the personification of the system he helped to create.

From the beginning, FDR took a shine to LBJ. He told Harold Ickes that Johnson might well be the first southern president of the postwar generation. Johnson was a fanatically loyal FDR man. As a congressional aide, he threatened to resign more than once when his boss contemplated voting contrary to Roosevelt. In 1935 he was the head of the Texas branch of the National Youth Administration, winning the attention of the future Speaker of the House Sam Rayburn and singling himself out as a star among the young New Dealers. In 1937, at the age of twenty-eight, he was elected to represent Texas's Tenth District. He caught FDR's attention while the president was in Texas, where they met and spent considerable time together. When FDR returned to Washington, he called his aide Thomas Corcoran and informed him, "I've just met the most remarkable young man. Now I like this boy, and you're going to help him with anything you can." FDR became Johnson's "political Daddy," in Johnson's own words, and more than any other elected official LBJ mastered the art of working the New Deal. Johnson brought a staggering amount of pork to his constituents in his first year alone. "He got more projects, and more money for his district, than anybody else," Corcoran recalled. He was "the best Congressman for a district that ever was."[47]

However, once elected, Johnson didn't brag about his support for the New Deal. He learned from the defeat of the Texas congressman Maury Maverick that getting praise from East Coast liberals didn't help you much in Texas. When he heard that the *New Republic* was going to profile him along with other influential New Deal congressmen, LBJ panicked. He called a friend at the International Labor Organization and implored her: "You must have some friend in the labor movement. Can't you call him and have him denounce me? [If] they put out that . . . I'm a liberal hero up here, I'll get killed. You've got to find somebody to denounce me!"[48]

When he became president in his own right, he no longer had to keep his true feelings secret. He could finally and unabashedly come out of the closet as a liberal. JFK's death, meanwhile, was the perfect *psychological* crisis for liberalism's new phase. Woodrow Wilson used war to achieve his social ends. FDR used economic depression and war. JFK used the threat of war and Soviet domination. Johnson's crisis mechanism came in the form of spiritual anguish and alienation. And he exploited it to the hilt.

When Johnson picked up the fallen flag of liberalism, he did so with the succinct, almost biblical phrase "let us continue." But continue what? Surely not mere whiz-kid wonkery or touch football games at Hyannis Port. Johnson was tasked with building the church of liberalism on the rock of Kennedy's memory, only he needed to do so in the psychological buzz phrases of "meaning" and "healing." He cast himself—or allowed himself to be cast—as the secular Saint Paul to the fallen liberal Messiah. LBJ's Great Society would be the church built upon the imagined "word" of Camelot.

On May 22, 1964, Johnson offered his first description of the Great Society: "The Great Society rests on abundance and liberty for all. It demands an end to poverty and racial injustice, to which we are totally committed in our time. But that is just the beginning . . . The Great Society is a place where every child can find knowledge to enrich his mind and to enlarge his talents. It is a place where leisure is a welcome chance to build and reflect, not a feared cause of boredom and restlessness. It is a place where the city of man serves not only the needs of the body and the demands of commerce but the desire for beauty and the hunger for community."[49]

It was an ambitious project, to put it mildly. In the Great Society all wants would be fulfilled, all needs satisfied. No good thing would come at the cost of another good thing. The state would foster, nurture, and guarantee every *legitimate* happiness. Even leisure would be maximized so that every citizen would find "meaning" in life.

Johnson conceded that such a subsidized nirvana couldn't materialize overnight. It would require the single-minded loyalty and effort of every American citizen and the talents of a new wave of experts. "I do not pretend that we have the full answer to those problems," he admitted. "But I do promise this: We are going to assemble the best thought and the broadest knowledge from all over the world to find those answers for America."[50] Johnson established some fifteen committees to answer the question, what is the Great Society?

The renaissance in liberal ambition transpired even as America's intrinsic antistatist antibodies were reaching a critical mass. In 1955 *National Review* was born, giving an intellectual home to a heterodox collection of thinkers who would form modern conservatism. It's revealing that while William F. Buckley had always been a classical liberal and Catholic traditionalist, nearly all of the intellectual co-founders of *National Review* were former socialists and communists who'd soured on the god that failed.

In 1964 Senator Barry Goldwater was *National Review*'s candidate of choice rather than of compromise. Goldwater was the first Republican presidential candidate since Coolidge to break with the core assumptions of Progressivism, including what Goldwater called "me-too Republicanism." As a result, Goldwater was demonized as the candidate of "hate" and nascent fascism. LBJ accused him of "preach[ing] hate" and consistently tried to tie him to terrorist "hate groups" like the Klan (whose constituency was, of course, traditionally Democratic). In a speech before steelworkers in September 1964, Johnson denounced Goldwater's philosophy of the "soup line"—as if free-market capitalism's ideal is to send men to the poorhouse—and scorned the "prejudice and bigotry and hatred and division" represented by the affable Arizonan.[51] Needless to say, this was a gross distortion. Goldwater was a champion of limited government who put his faith in the decency of the American people rather than in a bunch of bureaucrats in Washington. His one great mistake, which he later admitted and apologized for, was to vote against the Civil Rights Act.

Few liberals, then or now, would dispute that the Great Society was premised on love and unity. "We will do all these things because we love people instead of hate them . . . because you know it takes a man who loves his country to build a house instead of a raving, ranting demagogue who wants to tear down one. Beware of those who fear and doubt and those who rave and rant about the dangers of progress," Johnson railed. Meanwhile, the establishment worked overtime to insinuate that Goldwater was an architect of the "climate of hate" that had claimed Kennedy's life. As befitted the newly psychologized zeitgeist, Goldwater was denounced as, quite literally, insane. An ad in the *New York Times* reported that 1,189 psychiatrists had diagnosed him as not "psychologically fit" to be president. The charge was then recycled in excessive "free media" coverage. Dan Rather's colleague Daniel Schorr (now a senior correspondent with National Public Radio) reported on the *CBS Evening News,* with no factual basis whatsoever, that candidate Goldwater's vacation to Germany was "a move by Senator Goldwater to link up" with neo-Nazi elements.[52]

Goldwater lost in a landslide. And given LBJ's monumental ego as well as the hubris of his intellectual coterie, it's no wonder that the election results were greeted as an overwhelming endorsement of the Great Society project.

Again, Johnson was in many ways a perfect incarnation of liberalism's passions and contradictions. His first job (tellingly enough) was as a schoolteacher during the rising tide of the Deweyan revolution in education. Indeed, as some observed during the debates over the Great Society, the roots of the phrase stretched back to Dewey himself. The phrase appears over and over in Dewey's 1927 *The Public and Its Problems*.[53] Ultimate credit, however, should properly go to the co-founder of Fabian socialism, Graham Wallas, who in 1914 published *The Great Society*, a book familiar to the two Johnson aides who claimed credit for coining Johnson's "the Great Society."

One of those aides was Richard Goodwin, a golden boy of the Kennedy administration (he graduated first in his class at Harvard Law) who came to JFK's attention for his work as a congressional investigator probing the quiz show scandals of the 1950s. LBJ inherited Goodwin as a speechwriter. In the summer of 1965 Goodwin offered what the *New York Times* called "the most sophisticated and revealing commentary to date" on the question, what is the Great Society? His answer lay in the need for the state to give "meaning" to individuals and "make the world a more enjoyable and above all enriching place to live in." "The Great Society," Goodwin explained, "is concerned not with the quantity of our goods but the quality of our lives." Though he didn't say so directly, it was clear that the Great Society would offer the opposite of the "hate" that killed Kennedy: love.[54]

But it was also to be a tough love. Goodwin made it clear that if the citizenry didn't want to find meaning through state action or measure the quality of their lives on a bureaucratic slide rule, such reluctance would be overcome. But not necessarily via persuasion. Rather, it was the government's task "to spur them into action or the support of action." Here again Dewey's ghost was hard at work.

Goodwin declared that the Great Society must "ensure our people the environment, the capacities, and the social structures which will give them a meaningful chance to pursue their individual happiness." This differed very little from Dewey's version of state-directed democracy. Dewey held that "[n]atural rights and natural liberties exist only in the kingdom of mythological social zoology" and that "organized social control" via a "socialized economy" was the only means to create "free" individuals.[55]

The religious character of modern liberalism was never far from the surface. Indeed, the 1960s should be seen as another in a series of "great awakenings" in American history—a widespread yearning for new meaning that gave rise to a tumultuous social and political movement. The only difference was that this awakening largely left God behind. Paul Goodman, whose 1960 *Growing Up Absurd* helped launch the politics of hope in the first part of the decade, came to recognize in the second half how insufficient his original diagnosis had been: "I . . . imagined that the world-wide student protest had to do with changing political and moral institutions, to which I was sympathetic, but I now saw [in 1969] that we had to do with a religious crisis of the magnitude of the Reformation in the fifteen hundreds, when not only all institutions but all learning had been corrupted by the Whore of Babylon."[56]

This view of the 1960s as essentially a religious phenomenon has gained a good deal of respectability in recent years, and scholars now debate the finer points of its trajectory. The deeply perceptive journalist John Judis, for example, argues that the 1960s revolt had two phases, a postmillennial politics of hope followed by a premillennial politics of despair, the latter ushered in by the escalation of the war, race riots at home, and the assassinations of Robert Kennedy and Martin Luther King, Jr. "Postmillennialism" and "premillennialism" are theologically freighted terms for two related religious visions. Postmillennialists believe that man can create a kingdom of God on earth. The Social Gospellers were mostly postmillennialists in their aspirations; they believed the Hegelian God-state was the kingdom of heaven on earth. Premillennialists believe that the world is coming to an end and can't get better before it gets worse.[57]

Judis's chronological scheme has its merits, but ultimately it makes more sense to see these visions not as distinct *phases* of liberalism but as contending strains within liberalism itself. The left has always had an apocalyptic streak. Lenin argued "the worse the better." Georges Sorel's writings make no sense unless you understand that he saw politics as an essentially religious enterprise. The revolutionary vanguard has always demanded that destruction come before creation. The Futurists, anarchists, vorticists, Maoists, and various other modernist and left-wing avant-gardes believed that hammers were for smashing first, building second. Hitler was, of course, a great believer in the social benefits of destruction (though, as he often explained, he understood that real power came not from destroying but from corrupting institutions).

We should also note the apocalyptic logic of Progressivism generally. If the wheel of history, the state, is moving us forward to the kingdom of heaven, then anytime the "enemy" takes over, we are moving in a metaphysically wrong direction. This is never more transparent than when the mainstream media describe socialistic reforms as a "step forward" and free-market ones as "going backward" or "turning back the clock." And when non-progressives are in charge too long, the demands from the left to "tear the whole thing down" grow louder and louder.

In other words, the apocalyptic fervor Judis identifies in the late 1960s had its roots not just in the disillusion of the Kennedy assassination and the failures of Great Society liberalism but in the pent-up religious impulses inherent to Progressivism generally. The patient reformists had their chance; now it was time to "burn, baby, burn!"

The 1960s wasn't all about "fire in the streets," though—just as the French Revolution wasn't all about the Terror. Complex bureaucracies designed to "rationalize" the economy employed more Jacobins than the guillotine ever did. The born-again spirit of reform provided the drumbeat for the "long march through the institutions." Ralph Nader's consumerist crusade was launched in the 1960s, as was the modern environmental movement. Betty Friedan's *Feminine Mystique* was published in 1963.[58] The Stonewall riots, which gave birth to the gay pride movement, took place in the summer of 1969. Once again, the line between formal religion and Progressive politics was blurred beyond recognition. Once again, religious leaders in the "mainline" churches were seduced by radical politics.[59] The Methodist youth magazine *motive*—a major influence on the young Hillary Clinton—featured a birthday card to Ho Chi Minh in one issue and advice on how to dodge the draft in others. All of these political crusades were grounded in a moralizing fervor and a spiritual yearning for something more than bread alone. Most of the radicals of the New Left later explained that theirs was really a spiritual quest more than a political one. Indeed, that's why so many of them disappeared into the communes and EST seminars, searching for "meaning," "authenticity," "community," and, most of all, "themselves." For the 1960s generation "self-actualization" became the new secular grace.[60]

In 1965 Harvey Cox, an obscure Baptist minister and former Oberlin College chaplain, wrote *The Secular City,* which turned him into an overnight prophet. Selling more than one million copies, *The Secular City* argued for a kind of desacralization of Christianity in favor of a new transcendence found in the "technopolis," which was "the place of human control, of rational planning, of bureaucratic organization." Modern religion and spirituality required "the breaking of all supernatural myths and sacred symbols." Instead, we must spiritualize the material culture to perfect man and society through technology and social planning. In *The Secular City* "politics replaces metaphysics as the language of theology." Authentic worship was done not by kneeling in a church but by "standing in a picket line." *The Secular City* was an important intellectual hinge to the transition of the 1960s (though we should note that Cox recanted much of its argument twenty years later).[61]

Evidence of liberalism's divided nature can be found in the enduring love-hate relationship between "hopeful" liberals and "apocalyptic" leftists. Throughout the 1960s, centrist liberals made allowances and apologies for the radicals to their left. And when push came to shove—as it did at Cornell—they capitulated to the radicals. Even today, mainstream liberals are far more inclined to romanticize the "revolutionaries" of the 1960s, in part because so many of them played that role in their youth. On college campuses today, administrators—often living fossils from the 1960s—applaud the Kabuki dance of left-wing protest as a central part of higher education. The only time they get worried is when the protest comes from the right.

But the most important legacy of the 1960s has to be liberal guilt. Guilt over their inability to create the Great Society. Guilt over leaving children, blacks, and the rest of the Coalition of the Oppressed "behind." Guilt is among the most religious of emotions and has a way of rapidly devolving into a narcissistic God complex. Liberals were *proud* of how guilty they felt. Why? Because it confirmed liberal omnipotence. Kennedy and Johnson represented the belief that an enlightened affluent society could solve every problem, redress every wrong. Normally you don't feel guilty when forces outside your control do evil. But when you have the power to control everything, you feel guilty about everything. Lyndon Johnson not only accelerated Kennedy's politics of expectation when he declared, "We can do it all; we're the richest country in the world," but rendered any shortcomings, anywhere, evidence of sagging commitment, racism, insensitivity, or just plain "hate." Feeling guilty was a sign of grace, for it proved your heart was in the right place.

Conservatives were caught in a trap. If you rejected the concept of the omnipotent state, it was proof that you hated those whom government sought to help. And the only way to prove you didn't hate them—whoever "they" were—was to support government intervention (or "affirmative action," in Kennedy's phrase) on their behalf. The idea of a "good conservative" was oxymoronic. Conservatism by definition "holds us back"—leaves some "behind"—when we all know that the solution to every problem lies just around the corner.

The result was a cleavage in the American political landscape. On one side were the radicals and rioters, who metaphorically—and sometimes literally—got away with murder. On the other were conservatives—hateful, sick, pre-fascist—who deserved no benefit of the doubt whatsoever. Liberals were caught in the middle, and most, when forced to choose, sided with the radicals ("they're too impatient, but at least they care!"). The fact that the radicals despised liberals for not going far enough fast enough only confirmed their moral status in the minds of guilt-ridden liberals.[62]

In this climate, a liberal spending spree was inevitable. Like noblemen of yore purchasing indulgences from the Church, establishment liberals sought to expiate their guilt by providing the "oppressed" with as much swag as possible. Fear, of course, played an important role as well. Pragmatic liberals—while understandably reluctant to admit it publicly—undoubtedly bought into the Bismarckian logic of placating the radicals with legislative reforms and government largesse. For others, the very real threat of radicalism provided precisely the sort of "crisis mechanism" liberals are always in search of. The "race crisis" panic sweeping through liberalism was often cited as a justification to dust off every statist scheme sitting on a progressive shelf.

From cash payments to the poor to building new bridges and community redevelopment, the payout was prodigious even by New Deal standards. The civil rights movement, which had captured the public's sympathies through King's message of equality and color blindness, quickly degenerated into a riot of racially loaded entitlements. George Wiley, the president of the National Welfare Rights Organization, insisted that welfare was "a right, not a privilege." Some even argued that welfare was a form of reparations for slavery. Meanwhile, any opposition to such programs was stigmatized as evidence of bigotry.

The War on Poverty, affirmative action, community redevelopment, and the vast panoply of subsidies that fall under the rubric of welfare—Aid to Families with Dependent Children, housing grants, Medicare, Women, Infants, and Children benefits, food stamps— were churned out by a massively increased administrative state on a scale undreamed of by FDR. But most on the left were not satisfied, in part because these programs proved remarkably ineffective at creating the Great Society or defeating poverty. While even FDR had recognized that the dole could be a "narcotic . . , of the human spirit," in the 1960s such concerns were widely dismissed as rubbish.[63] The *New Republic* argued that Johnson's antipoverty program was fine "as a start" but insisted that there was "no alternative to really large-scale, ameliorative federal social welfare action and payments." Michael Harrington, whose *The Other America* laid the moral groundwork for the War on Poverty, led a group of thirty-two left-wing intellectuals, grandiosely dubbed the "Ad Hoc Committee on the Triple Revolution," which proclaimed that the state should provide "every individual and every family with an adequate income as a matter of right." The committee lamented that Americans were "all too confused and frightened by a bogey we call the 'welfare state,' [a] term of pride in most parts of the world."[64]

Recipients weren't the only ones hooked on the narcotic of "relief"; the pushers were, too. Like a man determined to pound a square peg into a round hole, establishment liberals kept insisting that just a little more money, a little more effort, would produce the social euphoria of the elusive Great Society. As Mickey Kaus argues in *The End of Equality,* the liberal response to every setback could be summarized in one word: "more."[65] When welfare seemed to cause fathers to abandon their families, liberals responded that payments should be extended to families where the father remains at home. But this in turn encouraged recipients to stay or become unemployed. The answer to that? Give money to employed poor fathers, too. But this in turn created an incentive for families to split up the moment the father moved out of poverty, so they wouldn't lose their benefits. Meanwhile, if you criticized any of this, you were a fascist.

The unintended but inevitable consequences of liberal utopianism spilled forth. From 1964 onward, crime in America grew at about 20 percent per year.[66] Liberal court rulings, particularly the Supreme Court's *Miranda* decision, caused clearance rates to plummet in major cities. Welfare had the tendency to encourage family breakdown, illegitimate births, and other pathologies it was designed to cure. The original civil rights revolution—which was largely based on a classically liberal conception of equality before the law—failed to produce the level of integration liberals had hoped for. In 1964 Hubert Humphrey—"Mr. Liberal"—swore up and down in the well of the Senate that the Civil Rights Act could in no way lead to quotas and if anyone could prove otherwise, "I will start eating the pages one after the other, because it is not there." By 1972 the Democratic Party—under the guise of the "McGovern rules"—embraced hard quotas (for blacks, women, and youth) as its defining organizational principle.[67] And it should be no surprise that a Democratic Party determined to do anything it could to make itself "look like America" would in turn be committed to making America look like the Democratic Party. And if you criticized any of *this,* you also were a fascist.

Indeed, even as quintessentially fascist street violence erupted in American cities, white liberals responded by basking in guilt and blaming the right. The Watts riots in 1965 were the real turning point. Not only was the collective liberal intelligentsia determined to blame white America—"the system"—for the violence, but the violence itself became morally admirable "rebellion." Johnson commented that such behavior was to be expected when "people feel they don't get a fair shake." Hubert Humphrey said that if he'd been born poor, he might have rioted also. An entire "riot ideology" unfolded that, in the words of the urban historian Fred Siegel, became a new form of "collective bargaining." Destroy your neighborhood and the government will buy you a better one.[68]

The extent of liberal denial was put on full display when Daniel Patrick Moynihan, then an adviser to Richard Nixon, advocated a policy of "benign neglect" on racial issues. The subject of race, Moynihan had told Nixon in confidence, "has been too much talked about . . . We may need a period in which Negro progress continues and racial rhetoric fades."[69] To this end Moynihan urged the president to avoid confrontations with black extremists and instead invest his energies in an aggressive class-based approach to social policy. To this, liberal editorialists, activists, and academics responded in horror, calling the memo "shameful," "outrageous," and "cruel" on its face. The reaction was instructive. Liberals had so thoroughly imbibed the assumptions of the God-state that to suggest the state could, never mind *should*, turn its back on the chosen people—for who could be more anointed than the poor black victims of slavery and segregation?—was tantamount to saying that God had ceased being God. When it comes to the state, neglect could not be benign, only malign. The state is love.

A more practical irony of the transformation of American liberalism is that it had fallen into the pre-fascist logic of the Bismarckian welfare state. Bismarck had pioneered the concept of liberalism without liberty. In exchange for lavish trinkets from an all-powerful state, Bismarck bought off the forces of democratic revolution. Reform without democracy empowered the bureaucratic state while keeping the public satisfied. Blacks in particular married their interests to the state and its righteous representatives, the Democratic Party. Blacks and the Democrats meet each other service for service, and so ingrained is this relationship that many liberal black intellectuals consider opposition to the Democratic Party to be, quite literally, a form of racism. Liberals also entered a Bismarckian bargain with the courts. Facing mounting disappointments in the democratic arena, liberals made peace with top-down liberalism from activist judges. Today liberalism depends almost entirely on "enlightened" judges who use Wilson's living Constitution to defy popular will in the name of progress.

All of this is traceable back to the Kennedy assassination, in which a deranged communist martyred a progressive icon. In 1983, on the twentieth anniversary of the murder, Gary Hart told *Esquire,* "If you rounded us [Democratic politicians] all up and asked, 'Why did you get into politics?' nine out of ten would say John Kennedy."[70] In 1988 Michael Dukakis was convinced (absurdly enough) that he was the reincarnation of Kennedy, even tapping Lloyd Bentsen as his running mate to re-create the "magic" of the Boston-Austin axis. In 1992 the high-water mark of the Clinton campaign was the Reifenstahlesque film of a teenage Bill Clinton shaking hands with President Kennedy. John Kerry affected a Kennedy accent in school, went by the initials JFK, and tried to model his political career on Kennedy's. In 2004 Howard Dean and John Edwards also claimed to be the true heirs of the Kennedy mantle. As did past candidates, including Bob Kerrey, Gary Hart, and, of course, Ted and Robert Kennedy. In 2007 Hillary Clinton said she was the JFK in the race.

A true indication of how thoroughly the Kennedy myth seeped into the grain of American life can be seen in how Americans greeted the death of his son John F. Kennedy Jr. in 1999. "John-John," as he was endearingly and condescendingly dubbed, was by all accounts a good and decent man. He was certainly very handsome. And he was the son of a beloved president. Yet beyond that, his career and contributions were lackluster at best. He took the New York Bar exam three times. He was an unremarkable prosecutor. He founded a childish magazine, *George,* which intentionally blurred the lines between the personal and the political, substance and celebrity, the trivial and the important. And yet when John Junior died in a tragic plane crash, his death was greeted in abjectly religious terms by a political class entirely convinced that the Son, like the Father, had been imbued with the Kennedy Holy Ghost. The historian Douglas Brinkley wrote in the *New York Times* that JFK Jr. was his generation's "photogenic redeemer." Wall-to-wall coverage portrayed the younger Kennedy as a lost "national savior." Bernard

Kalb summarized the tenor of the coverage: JFK Jr. was being de-picted as "a kind of a secular messiah who would, had he lived, [have] rescued civilization from all its terrible problems."[71]

Today, to deny JFK's status as the martyr to what might have been is to deny the hope of liberalism itself. For more than a generation, liberal politics in America has been premised on the politics of a ghost. The Jack Kennedy whom liberals remember *never existed*. But the Kennedy myth represents not a man but a moment—a mo-ment when liberals hoped to bring about the kingdom of heaven on earth. The times were not as propitious as liberals remember—after all it was only Kennedy's death, not his life, that truly rallied Americans around "Kennedyism" in huge numbers. But that's not the point. What matters is that the people *believe* the myth and there-fore pursue it. Liberals believed for a "brief shining moment" that they could bring about their kingdom of heaven, their Camelot. Ever since, they have yearned to re-create that moment. Looked at from outside, the myth appears to be little more than power worship. But from within, it is gospel. Meanwhile, it's telling that Democrats wish to preserve the substance of the Great Society while maintaining the mythology of Camelot. Every Democrat says he wants to *be* JFK while insisting that he will *do* more or less what LBJ did. No Democrat would dream of saying he wanted to emulate Lyndon Johnson, because the myth is what matters most.

Liberal Racism:
The Eugenic Ghost
in the Fascist Machine

THERE IS NO issue on which modern liberals consider themselves more thoroughly enlightened than that of race. And there is no contentious topic where they are quicker to insist that dissent from liberal orthodoxy is a sign of creeping fascism. In virtually every major racially charged debate over the last forty years, at least some self-righteous liberals have invoked the record of the Holocaust to warn, darkly, that if opponents of racial preferences of one kind or another get their way, we just may find ourselves on the slippery slope to Nazi Germany.

White liberals learned this trick from black liberals. Black civil rights figures love playing the Nazi card. When Newt Gingrich tried to reach out to liberal Democrats by inviting them to social functions, New York representative Major Owens was outraged. "These are people who are practicing genocide with a smile; they're worse than Hitler," Owen said. "Gingrich smiles . . . [and] says they're going to be our friend. We're going to have cocktail-party genocide." The NAACP chairman Julian Bond is supposed to be a moderate in racial politics, but he, too, has a weakness for Nazi analogies. "Their idea of equal rights is the American flag and the Confederate swastika flying side by side," he recently declared. Harry Belafonte smeared conservative blacks—Condoleezza Rice, Colin Powell, and others—in the Bush administration by snorting that Hitler also "had a lot of Jews high up in the hierarchy of the Third Reich" (this is untrue, by the way). Jesse Jackson has never met a *reductio ad Hitlerum* he didn't like. Over the course of his career he has compared Republicans to genocidal Nazis countless times, from decrying the Hitlerian roots of the religious right to denouncing George W. Bush's "Nazi tactics."[1]

The American right is constantly required to own the darkest chapters in the country's history: the accommodation of segregationists, McCarthyite excesses, isolationism prior to World War II, and so on. Rarely mentioned is the liberal side of these stories, in which the Democratic Party was the home to Jim Crow for a century; in which American liberalism was at least as isolationist as American conservatism; in which the progressive Red Scare made McCarthyism look like an Oxford Union debate; in which successive Democratic presidents ordered such things as the detention of Japanese-Americans, sweeping domestic surveillance of political enemies, and the (justified) use of horrific weapons on Japan; and in which Moscow-loyal communists "named names" of heretical Trotskyites.[2]

Perhaps most damning of all is the liberal infatuation with eugenics, which has simply been whitewashed out of existence. Like the editors of the old Soviet encyclopedias who would send out updates to instruct which pages should be torn out, American liberalism has repeatedly censored and rewritten its own history so that the "bad guys" were always conservatives and the good guys always liberals. This revisionism plays a role in our bioethical debates today: liberals still have a soft spot for certain types of eugenics, but they are as blind to their current attraction as they are to their historical one.

In fact, they have blind spots on blind spots. Ignorant of their own history and only vaguely aware of the nature of Nazi eugenics, they work on the assumption that eugenics is something bad that only bad people want to pursue. Like the "liberal" who wants to ban negative political ads and campus hate speech but believes he is a fierce opponent of censorship, the modern liberal retains an attraction for eugenic ideas, but it never dawns on him that what he wants to do might be called by that name.

Meanwhile, in current debates it is typically assumed that conservatives don't mean what they say. Conservative opposition to racial preferences may be defended with high-flying rhetoric about color-blind equality, but beneath the surface, liberals assert, the lofty rhetoric amounts to "coded" appeals to the racism of southern whites and a desire to "turn back the clock" on racial progress.

The controversy over Charles Murray's *Bell Curve* is the most notorious example of this phenomenon in the last twenty years. Upon its release virtually every progressive voice in the country denounced Murray as a "social Darwinist" bent on promoting every reactionary measure from rounding up racial defectives to forced sterilization. America's largest Jewish organization proclaimed, "To take Charles Murray seriously is to endanger more than sixty years of progress towards racial justice by adopting the long disproved and discredited theories of social Darwinism and eugenics." The black scholar Adolph Reed called Murray and his co-author, Richard J. Herrnstein, "intellectual brownshirts" and declared that endorsements of Nazi-like "extermination, mass sterilization and selective breeding" were implicit in the work.[3] But whatever the merits or demerits of *The Bell Curve* may be, the simple fact is that Murray and Herrnstein were making a deeply libertarian case for state *nonintervention*. Yes, they focused on issues of classic concern to eugenicists—the heritability of intelligence and its distribution among races—but their argument was 180 degrees opposite from *real* eugenics, which means using state power to improve the racial, genetic, or biological health of the community.

Liberals constantly expect conservatives to atone for the racism, real and alleged, of various dead conservatives. Meanwhile, in large part because liberals were right about the moral imperative of desegregation, they see no need to explore their own intellectual history. They're the good guys, and that's all they need to know. Left unasked is why Progressivism—*not conservatism*—was so favorably inclined to eugenics. Is there something inherent to a "pragmatic" ideology of do-goodery that makes it susceptible to eugenic ideas? Or is liberalism's ignorance of its own history to blame? I'm not claiming that the editors at the *New Republic* today sympathize with eugenicists simply because previous editors did. But modern liberalism does provide a hospitable, nurturing environment for all sorts of "nice" eugenic and racist notions precisely because liberals haven't taken the sort of intellectual and historical inventory conservatives have. It's high time someone did.

When reading the literature on the subjects of eugenics and race, one commonly finds academics blaming eugenics on "conservative" tendencies within the scientific, economic, or larger progressive communities. Why? Because according to liberals, racism is objectively conservative. Anti-Semitism is conservative. Hostility to the poor (that is, social Darwinism) is conservative. Therefore, whenever a liberal is racist or fond of eugenics, he is magically transformed into a conservative. In short, liberalism is never morally wrong, and so when liberals are morally flawed, it's because they're really conservatives!

In an otherwise thoughtful essay in the *New Republic,* the Yale historian and professor of surgery Sherwin Nuland writes:

Eugenics was a creed that appealed to social conservatives, who were pleased to blame poverty and crime on heredity. Liberals—or progressives, as they were then usually called— were among its most vigorous opponents, considering the inequities of society to be due to circumstantial factors amenable to social and economic reform. And yet some progressive thinkers agreed with the eugenicists that the lot of every citizen would be improved by actions that benefited the entire group. Thus were the intellectual battle lines drawn.[4]

Alan Wolfe, also in the *New Republic*, writes: "Racial conservatism has its roots in biological and eugenicist thought. Liberal theories of racial damage, by contrast, grew out of a twentieth-century concern with the impact of social environments on individuals."[5]

How convenient. Alas, this is simply untrue. In order to see how this conventional wisdom is built upon a series of useful liberal myths, and therefore understand the real lineage of American liberalism, we need to unlearn a lot of false history and categories we take on faith. In particular, we need to understand that American Progressivism shares important roots with European fascism. No clearer or more sinister proof of this exists than the passion with which American and European progressives greeted eugenics— widely seen as *the* answer to the "social question."

Let's review our story so far. The fascist moment at the beginning of the twentieth century was a transatlantic phenomenon.

Intellectuals across the West embraced the idea that nations were organic entities in need of direction by an avant-garde of scientific experts and social planners. Contemptuous of nineteenth-century dogma, this self-anointed progressive elite understood what needed to be done in order to bring humanity to the sunny uplands of utopia. War, nationalism, the quest for state-directed community, economic planning, exaltation of the public, derogation of the private: these are what defined all of the various and competing new isms of the West.

Eugenics fit snugly within this new worldview, for if nations are like bodies, their problems are in some sense akin to diseases, and politics becomes in effect a branch of medicine: the science of maintaining social health. By lending scientific credibility to the Hegelian and Romantic view of nations as organic beings, Darwinism bequeathed to scientists a license to treat social problems like biological puzzles. All the ills of modern mass society—urban crowding, a rising population among the lower classes, poor public hygiene, even the dumbing down of mainstream bourgeois culture—now seemed curable through conscientious application of biological principles.

Indeed, the population explosion, and in particular the explosion of the "wrong" populations, were of a piece with Darwinian thought from the outset. Darwin himself admitted that his ideas were merely an extension of Malthusianism to the natural world. (Thomas Malthus was the economic philosopher who predicted that a natural human tendency to overbreed, coupled with finite natural resources, would yield persistent misery.) Intellectuals feared that modern technology had removed the natural constraints on population growth among the "unfit," raising the possibility that the "higher elements" would be "swamped" by the black and brown hordes below.

Not only was America no exception to this widespread panic among the intellectual and aristocratic classes; it often led the way. American progressives were obsessed with the "racial health" of the nation, supposedly endangered by mounting waves of immigration as well as overpopulation by native-born Americans. Many of the outstanding progressive projects, from Prohibition to the birth control movement, were grounded in this quest to tame the demographic beast. Leading progressive intellectuals saw eugenics as an important, and often indispensable, tool in the quest for the holy grail of "social control."

Scholarly exchanges between eugenicists, "raceologists," race hygienists, and birth controllers in Germany and the United States were unremarkable and regular occurrences. Hitler "studied" American eugenics while in prison, and sections of *Mein Kampf* certainly reflect that immersion. Indeed, some of his arguments seem to be lifted straight out of various progressive tracts on "race suicide." Hitler wrote to the president of the American Eugenics Society to ask for a copy of his *Case for Sterilization*—which called for the forcible sterilization of some ten million Americans—and later sent him another note thanking him for his work. Madison Grant's *Passing of the Great Race* also made a huge impression on Hitler, who called the book his "bible." In 1934, when the National Socialist government had sterilized over fifty thousand "unfit" Germans, a frustrated American eugenicist exclaimed, "The Germans are beating us at our own game."[6]

Of course American progressives are not culpable for the Holocaust. But it is a well-documented fact that eugenics lay at the heart of the progressive enterprise. The eugenic crusade, writes the historian Edwin Black, was "created in the publications and academic research rooms of the Carnegie Institution, verified by the research grants of the Rockefeller Foundation, validated by leading scholars from the best Ivy League universities, and financed by the special efforts of the Harriman railroad fortune."[7] German race science stood on American shoulders.

It would be nice to say that liberals' efforts to airbrush eugenics from their own history and fob it off on conservatives are unacceptable. But of course they *have* been accepted. Most intellectuals, never mind liberal journalists and commentators, don't know much about either conservatism or the history of eugenics, but they take it on faith that the two are deeply entwined. One can only hope that this wrong can be made right with a dose of the truth. A brief review of the progressive pantheon—the intellectual heroes of the left, then and now—reveals how deeply imbued the early socialists were with eugenic thinking.

Just as socialist economics was a specialization within the larger progressive avocation, eugenics was a closely related specialty. Eugenic arguments and economic arguments tracked each other, complemented each other, and, at times, melted into each other.

Sidney Webb, the father of Fabian socialism and still among the most revered British intellectuals, laid it out fairly clearly. "No consistent eugenicist," he explained, "can be a 'Laissez Faire' individualist [that is, a conservative] unless he throws up the game in despair. He must interfere, interfere, interfere!" The fact that the "wrong" people were outbreeding the "right" ones would put Britain on the path of "national deterioration" or, "as an alternative," result "in this country gradually falling to the Irish and the Jews."[8]

Indeed, British socialism, the intellectual lodestar of American Progressivism, was saturated with eugenics. The Fabians Sidney and Beatrice Webb, George Bernard Shaw, Harold Laski, and H. G. Wells were devoted to the cause. John Maynard Keynes, Karl Pearson, Havelock Ellis, Julian and Aldous Huxley, Eden Paul, and such progressive publications as the *New Statesman* (founded by Webb) and the *Manchester Guardian* were also supporters of eugenics to one extent or another.

As discussed earlier, Wells was probably the most influential literary figure among pre–World War II American progressives. Despite his calls for a new "liberal fascism" and an "enlightened Nazism," Wells more than anyone else lent romance to the progressive vision of the future. He was also a keen eugenicist and particularly supportive of the extermination of unfit and darker races. He explained that if his "New Republic" was to be achieved, "swarms of black and brown, and dirty-white and yellow people" would "have to go." "It is in the sterilisation of failures," he added, "and not in the selection of successes for breeding, that the possibility of an improvement of the human stock lies." In *The New Machiavelli,* he asserts that eugenics must be the central tenet of any true and successful socialism: "Every improvement is provisional except the improvement of the race." While Wells could be squeamish about how far the state should go in translating this conclusion into policy, he remained a forceful advocate for the state to defend aggressively its interest in discouraging parasitic classes.[9]

George Bernard Shaw—no doubt because of his pacifist opposition to World War I—has acquired the reputation of an outspoken individualist and freethinker suspicious of state power and its abuses. Nothing could be further from the truth. Shaw was not only an ardent socialist but totally committed to eugenics as an integral part of the socialist project. "The only fundamental and possible socialism is the socialization of the selective breeding of Man," he declared. Shaw advocated the abolition of traditional marriage in favor of more eugenically acceptable polygamy under the auspices of a State Department of Evolution and a new "eugenic religion." He particularly lamented the chaotic nature of a laissez-faire approach to mate selection in which people "select their wives and husbands less carefully than they select their cashiers and cooks." Besides, he explained, a smart woman would be more content with a 10 percent share in a man of good genetic stock than a 100 percent share in a man of undesirable lineage. What was therefore required was a "human stud farm" in order to "eliminate the Yahoo whose vote will wreck the commonwealth." According to Shaw, the state should be firm in its policy toward criminal and genetically undesirable elements. "[W]ith many apologies and expressions of sympathy, and some generosity in complying with their last wishes," he wrote with ghoulish glee, we "should place them in the lethal chamber and get rid of them."[10]

Other liberal heroes shared Shaw's enthusiasm. John Maynard Keynes, the founding father of liberal economics, served on the British Eugenics Society's board of directors in 1945—at a time when the popularity of eugenics was rapidly imploding thanks to the revelation of Nazi concentration camp experiments. Nonetheless, Keynes declared eugenics "the most important, significant and, I would add, *genuine* branch of sociology which exists." Julian Huxley, the founder of the World Wildlife Fund, first director of UNESCO, and revered science popularizer, co-wrote *The Science of Life* with Wells and Wells's son. Huxley, too, was a sincere believer in eugenics. Havelock Ellis, the pioneering sex theorist and early architect of the birth control movement, spoke for many when he proposed a eugenic registry of all citizens, so as to provide "a real guide as to those persons who are most fit, or most unfit to carry on the race." Ellis did not oppose Nazi sterilization programs, believing that good science "need not become mixed up in the Nordic and anti-Semitic aspects of Nazi aspiration." J. B. S. Haldane, the British geneticist, wrote in the *Daily Worker,* "The dogma of human equality is no part of Communism . . . the formula of Communism: 'from each according to his ability, to each according to his needs,' would be nonsense, if abilities were equal."[11]

Harold Laski, to some the most respected British political scientist of the twentieth century (he was Joseph Kennedy Jr.'s tutor and JFK's professor), echoed the panic over "race suicide" (an American term): "The different rates of fertility in the sound and pathological stocks point to a future swamping of the better by the worse." Indeed, eugenics was Laski's first great intellectual passion. His first published article, "The Scope of Eugenics," written while he was still a teenager, impressed Francis Galton, the founder of eugenics. At Oxford, Laski studied under the eugenicist Karl Pearson, who wrote, "Socialists have to inculcate that spirit which would give offenders against the State short shrift and the nearest lamp-post."[12]

Laski, of course, had an enormous impact on American liberalism. He was a regular contributor to the *New Republic*—which in its early years published scores of leading British intellectuals, including Wells.[13] He also taught at Harvard and became friends with Felix Frankfurter, an adviser to FDR and, later, Supreme Court justice. Frankfurter introduced Laski to FDR, and he became one of Roosevelt's most ardent British supporters, despite his strong communist ties. More famously, he became one of Justice Oliver Wendell Holmes's closest friends, despite an age difference of more than five decades. The two maintained a storied correspondence that lasted nearly twenty years.

EUGENICS, AMERICAN-STYLE

American progressives, who took their lead in many ways from their British cousins, shared a similar ardor for racial hygiene. Take Justice Holmes, the most admired jurist of the progressive period and one of the most revered liberal icons in American legal history. It seems that no praise of Holmes can go too far. Felix Frankfurter called him "truly the impersonal voice of the Constitution." "No Justice thought more deeply about the nature of a free society or was more zealous to safeguard its conditions by the most abundant regard for civil liberty than Mr. Justice Holmes." Another observer commented, "Like the Winged Victory of Samothrace, he is the summit of hundreds of years of civilization, the inspiration of ages yet to come." Others have declared that "for the American lawyer he is the beau ideal, and the lawyer quotes his aphorisms as the literate layman quotes Hamlet."[14]

What explains Holmes's popularity with liberals? It's a complicated question. Holmes was hailed by many civil libertarians for his support of free speech during the war. Progressives loved him for holding that their nation-building social welfare programs were constitutional. "If my fellow citizens want to go to hell, I will help them. It's my job," Holmes famously declared. This has caused some conservatives to admire his "judicial restraint." But the truth is he practiced "restraint" mostly because he agreed with the direction the progressives were taking.

In 1927 Holmes wrote a letter to Harold Laski in which he proudly told his friend, "I . . . delivered an opinion upholding the constitutionality of a state law for sterilizing imbeciles the other day—and felt that I was getting near the *first principle of real reform*." He went on to tell Laski how amused he was when his colleagues took exception to his "rather brutal words . . . that made them mad."[15]

Holmes was referring to his decision in the notorious case of *Buck v. Bell*, in which progressive lawyers on both sides hoped to get the Supreme Court to write eugenics into the Constitution. Holmes was eager to oblige. The state of Virginia deemed a young woman, Carrie Buck, "unfit" to reproduce (though she was not, as it turned out, retarded, as the state had contended). She was consigned to the Virginia State Colony for Epileptics and Feebleminded, where she was cajoled into consenting to a salpingectomy, a form of tubal ligation. The case depended in part on a report by America's leading eugenicist, Harry Laughlin of the Eugenics Record Office in Cold Spring Harbor, New York—the RAND Corporation of eugenics research, funded by various leading progressive philanthropists. Without having ever met Buck, Laughlin credited the assessment of a nurse who observed of the Buck family, "These people belong to the shiftless, ignorant, and worthless class of anti-social whites of the South." Hence, Laughlin concluded that eugenic sterilization would be "a force for the mitigation of race degeneracy."

Writing for the majority, Holmes issued a terse opinion barely over a single page long. The decision now ranks as one of the most vilified and criticized examples of legal reasoning in American history. Yet of all his many opinions, it is perhaps the most revealing. Citing only one precedent, a Massachusetts law mandating vaccinations for public school children, Holmes wrote that "the principle that sustains compulsory vaccination is broad enough to cover cutting the Fallopian tubes . . . It is better for all the world, if instead of waiting to execute degenerate offspring for crime, or to let them starve for their imbecility, society can prevent those who are manifestly unfit from continuing their kind." He concluded by declaring, famously: "Three generations of imbeciles are enough." As we will see, this reasoning endures in the often unspoken rationale for abortion.

The opinion tied together many of the major strains in progressive thought at the time. Holmes, a bloody-minded veteran of the Civil War, saw war as a source of moral values in a world without meaning. Given the sacrifice of so many noble characters on the battlefield, requiring degenerates like Carrie Buck to sacrifice their ability to breed—or even their lives—for the greater good seemed entirely reasonable and fair. By citing a public health measure as an adequate precedent, Holmes further underscored how the health of the organic body politic trumped individual liberty. Whether through the prism of mobilization or public health, the project was the same. As Holmes put it in a 1915 *Illinois Law Review* article, his "starting point for an ideal for the law" would be the "co-ordinated human effort . , . to build a race."[16]

Given such rhetoric, it is impossible not to see Progressivism as a fascistic endeavor—at least by the standards we use today.

There's a general consensus among liberal historians that Progressivism defies easy definition. Perhaps that's because to identify Progressivism properly would be too inconvenient to liberalism, for doing so would expose the eugenic project at its core. The most obvious reply—that progressives were merely representing the age they lived in—fails on several levels. For one thing, the progressive eugenicists had non-progressive, anti-eugenic adversaries—premature conservatives, radical libertarians, and orthodox Catholics—whom the progressives considered to be backward and reactionary.

For another, arguing that progressives were a product of their time simply reinforces my larger argument: Progressivism was born of the fascist moment and has never faced up to its inheritance. Today's liberals have inherited progressive prejudice wholesale, believing that traditionalists and religious conservatives are dangerous threats to progress. But this assumption means that liberals are blind to fascistic threats from their own ranks.

Meanwhile, conservative religious and political dogma—under relentless attack from the left—may be the single greatest bulwark against eugenic schemes. Who rejects cloning most forcefully? Who is most troubled by euthanasia, abortion, and playing God in the laboratory? Good dogma is the most powerful inhibiting influence against bad ideas and the only guarantor that men will act on good ones. A conservative nation that seriously wondered if destroying a blastocyst is murder would not wonder at all whether it is murder to kill an eight-and-a-half-month-old fetus, let alone a "defective" infant.

Mainstream liberalism is joined at the hip with racial and sexual-identity groups of one kind or another. A basic premise shared by all these groups is that their members should be rewarded simply by virtue of their racial, gender, or sexual status. In short, the state should pick winners and losers based upon the accidents of birth. Liberals champion this perspective in the name of antiracism. Unlike conservatives who advocate a color-blind state, liberals still believe that the state should organize society on racial lines. We are accustomed to talking about this sort of social engineering as a product of the post-civil-rights era. But the color-blind doctrine championed by progressives in the 1960s was a very brief parenthesis in a very long progressive tradition. In short, there is more continuity between early Progressivism and today's multiculturalism than we think.

Here again, Woodrow Wilson was the pioneer. Wilson's vision of "self-determination" has been retroactively gussied up as a purely democratic vision. It wasn't. It was in important respects an organic, Darwinian-Hegelian vision of the need for peoples to organize themselves into collective spiritual and biological units—that is, identity politics. Wilson was a progressive both at home and abroad. He believed in building up nations, peoples, races into single entities. His racial vision was distinct from Hitler's—and obviously less destructive—but just as inseparable from his worldview.

Wilson's status as the most racist president of the twentieth century is usually attributed to the fact that he was a southerner, indeed the first southern president since Reconstruction. And it is true that he harbored many Dixiecrat attitudes. His resegregation of the federal government, his support for antimiscegenation laws, his antagonism toward black civil rights leaders as well as antilynching laws, and his notorious fondness for D. W. Griffith's *Birth of a Nation* all testify to that. But in fact Wilson's heritage was incidental to his racism. After all, he was in no way a traditional defender of the South. He embraced Lincoln as a great leader—hardly a typical southern attitude. Moreover, as a believer in consolidating federal power, Wilson, in his opinion on states' rights, ran counter to those who complained about the "War of Northern Aggression." No, Wilson's racism was "modern" and consistent both with the Darwinism of the age and with the Hegelianism of his decidedly Germanic education. In *The State* and elsewhere, Wilson can sound downright Hitlerian. He informs us, for example, that some races are simply more advanced than others. These "progressive races" deserve progressive systems of government, while backward races or "stagnant nationalities," lacking the necessary progressive "spirit," may need an authoritarian form of government (a resurgence of this vision can be found among newly minted "realists" in the wake of the Iraq war). This is what offended him so mightily about the post–Civil War Reconstruction. He would never forgive the attempt to install an "inferior race" in a position superior to southern "Aryans."

Wilson was also a forthright defender of eugenics. As governor of New Jersey—a year before he was sworn in as President—he signed legislation that created, among other things, the Board of Examiners of Feebleminded, Epileptics, and Other Defectives. Under the law, the state could determine when "procreation is inadvisable" for criminals, prisoners, and children living in poorhouses. "Other Defectives" was a fairly open category.[17] But Wilson was merely picking up where Teddy Roosevelt left off. The Bull Moose—recently rediscovered by liberal Republicans and "centrist" liberals—regularly decried "race suicide" and supported those "brave" souls who were battling to beat back the tide of mongreliza-tion (although on a personal level Roosevelt was far less of a racist than Wilson).

Roosevelt, like Wilson, was merely demonstrating the attitudes that made him so popular among "modern" progressive intellectuals. In *The Promise of American Life,* Herbert Croly speculated that a "really regenerated state government" would take steps to prevent "crime and insanity" by regulating who could marry and procreate. Such an empowered state, he wrote archly, "might conceivably reach the conclusion that the enforced celibacy of hereditary criminals and incipient lunatics would make for individual and social improvement even more than would a maximum passenger fare on the railroads of two cents a mile." The state, he insisted, must "interfere on behalf of the really fittest."[18]

Still, these thoughts qualified Croly as something of a "dove" on the issue of eugenics. Charles Van Hise, Roosevelt's close adviser, was more emphatic. "He who thinks not of himself primarily, but of his race, and of its future, is the new patriot," explained Van Hise, a founder of the American conservation movement and president of the University of Wisconsin during its glory days as the premier training ground for American progressives.[19] Van Hise summarized the American progressive attitude toward eugenics well when he ex-plained: "We know enough about agriculture so that the agricultural production of the country could be doubled if the knowledge were applied; we know enough about disease so that if the knowledge were utilized, Infectious and contagious diseases would be substan-tially destroyed in the United States within a score of years; we know enough about eugenics so that if the knowledge were applied, the de-fective classes would disappear within a generation."[20]

The key divide among progressives was not between eugenicists and non-eugenicists or between racists and non-racists. It was be-tween advocates of "positive eugenics" and advocates of "negative eugenics," between those who called themselves humanists and those who subscribed to theories of race suicide, between environ-mentalists and genetic determinists. The positive eugenicists ar-gued for merely encouraging, cajoling, and subsidizing the fit to breed more and the unfit to breed less. The negative eugenicists operated along a spectrum that went from forced sterilization to imprisonment (at least during the reproductive years). Environmentalists stressed that improving the material conditions of the degenerate classes would improve their plight (many progressives were really Lamarckians when it came to human evolution). Race suicide theorists believed that whole lines and classes of people were beyond salvation.

For a variety of reasons, those we would today call conservatives often opposed eugenic schemes. The lone dissenter in *Buck v. Bell,* for example, wasn't the liberal justice Louis Brandeis or Harlan Fiske Stone but the "archconservative" Pierce Butler.[21] The Catholic conservative G. K. Chesterton was subjected to relentless ridicule and scorn for his opposition to eugenics. In various writings, most notably *Eugenics and Other Evils: An Argument Against the Scientifically Organized Society,* Chesterton opposed what was held to be the sophisticated position by nearly all "thinking people" in Britain and the United States. Indeed, the foremost institution combating eugenics around the world was the Catholic Church. It was the Catholic influence in Italy—along with the fact that Italians were a genetically polyglot bunch—that made Italian Fascism less obsessed with eugenics than either the American progressives or the Nazis (though Mussolini did believe that over time Fascist government would have a positive eugenic effect on the Italians).

Nonetheless, progressives did come up with a term for conservative opponents of eugenics. They called them social Darwinists. Progressives invented the term "social Darwinism" to describe anyone who opposed Sidney Webb's notion that the state must aggressively "interfere" in the reproductive order of society. In the hothouse logic of the left, those who *opposed* forced sterilization of the "unfit" and the poor were the villains for letting a "state of nature" rule among the lower classes.

Herbert Spencer, the supposed founder of social Darwinism, was singled out as the poster boy for all that was wrong in classical liberalism. Spencer was indeed a Darwinist—he coined the phrase "survival of the fittest"—but his interpretation of evolutionary theory reinforced his view that people should be left alone. In almost every sense, Spencer was a good—albeit classical—liberal: he championed charity, women's suffrage, and civil liberties. But he was the incarnation of all that was backward, reactionary, and wrong according to the progressive worldview, not because he supported Hitlerian schemes of forced race hygiene but because he adamantly *opposed* them. To this day it is de rigueur among liberal intellectuals and historians to take potshots at Spencer as the philosophical wellspring of racism, right-wing "greed," and even the Holocaust.[22]

Thanks to some deeply flawed scholarship by the liberal historian Richard Hofstadter, nearly all of the so-called robber barons of the nineteenth and early twentieth centuries were dubbed social Darwinists, too, even though subsequent historians have demonstrated that Gilded Age industrialists were barely influenced by Darwinism, if at all. Darwinism was a fixation of intellectuals and academics. The so-called robber barons generally lacked formal education. To the extent they grounded their worldview in anything, it was in Christian ethics and the writings of Adam Smith. Moreover, they believed that capitalism was *good* for the poor. Yet selective quotations and sweeping generalizations—usually infused with Marxist clichés—rendered the robber barons ersatz fascists.[23]

A few historians have dealt with these conundrums by labeling the progressives "reform Darwinists." Reform Darwinists were the only real Darwinians as we understand the term today. Almost all the leading progressive intellectuals interpreted Darwinian theory as a writ to "interfere" with human natural selection. Even progressives with no ostensible ties to eugenics worked closely with champions of the cause. There was simply no significant stigma against racist eugenics in progressive circles.[24]

Before we continue, it is important to dispel a misperception that may be building in some readers' minds. While progressive eugenicists were often repugnantly racist, eugenics as a field was not *necessarily* so. Obviously, intermarriage with blacks would be greeted with horror by people already terrified by "Aryans" marrying Slavs or Italians. But W. E. B. DuBois shared many of the eugenic views held by white progressives. His "Talented Tenth" was itself a eugenically weighted term. He defined members of the Talented Tenth as "exceptional men" and the "best of the race." He complained that "the negro has not been breeding for an object" and that he must begin to "train and breed for brains, for efficiency, for beauty." Over his long career he time and again returned to his concern that the worst blacks were overbreeding while the best were underbreeding. Indeed, he supported Margaret Sanger's "Negro Project," which sought to sharply curtail reproduction among "inferior" stocks of the black population.[25]

Perhaps an even better indication of how little modern popular conceptions jibe with the historical reality during this period is the Ku Klux Klan. For decades the Klan has stood as the most obvious candidate for an American brand of fascism. That makes quite a bit of sense. The right-wing label, on the other hand, isn't nearly as clean a fit. The Klan of the Progressive Era was not the same Klan that arose after the Civil War. Rather, it was a collection of loosely independent organizations spread across the United States. What united them, besides their name and absurd getups, was that they were all inspired by the film *The Birth of a Nation*. They were, in fact, a "creepy fan subculture" of the film. Founded the week of the film's release in 1915, the second Klan was certainly racist, but not much more than the society in general. Of course, this is less a defense of the Klan than an indictment of the society that produced it.

For years the conventional view among scholars and laymen alike was that the Klan was rural and fundamentalist. The truth is it was often quite cosmopolitan and modern, thriving in cities like New York and Chicago. In many communities the Klan focused on the reform of local government and on maintaining social values. It was often the principal extralegal enforcer of Prohibition, the consummate progressive "reform." "These Klansmen," writes Jesse Walker in an illuminating survey of the latest scholarship, "were more likely to flog you for bootlegging or breaking your marriage vows than for being black or Jewish."[26]

When modern liberals try to explain away the Klan membership of prominent Democrats—most frequently West Virginia senator Robert Byrd—they cough up a few clichés about how good liberals "evolved" from their southern racial "conservatism." But the Klan of the 1920s was often seen as reformist and modern, and it had a close relationship with some progressive elements in the Democratic Party. The young Harry Truman as well as the future Supreme Court justice Hugo Black were members. In 1924, at the famous "Klanbake"

Democratic convention, the KKK rallied around the future senator William McAdoo, Woodrow Wilson's secretary of the treasury (and son-in-law), a key architect of Wilson's war socialism, and a staunch Prohibitionist.

Moreover, if the Klan was less racist than we've been led to believe, academia was staggeringly more so. Indeed, the modern institution of academic tenure was largely carved out by progressive academia's solidarity with E. A. Ross, the author of the "race suicide" thesis.[27] Simultaneously one of America's leading sociologists, economists, and "raceologists," Ross was the quintessential reform Darwinist. He first became attracted to Progressivism when he saw that one of his conservative professors was horrified by Henry George's *Progress and Poverty*—a tract that inspired American progressives, British socialists, and German national socialists. Ross studied in Germany and then returned to the United States, where he finished his studies among the Germanophiles of Johns Hopkins and under the tutelage of Woodrow Wilson and Richard Ely.

A great bear of a man, Ross was an omnipresent public intellectual, writing for all the right magazines and giving lectures at all the right schools. He served as a tutor on immigration issues to Teddy Roosevelt, who was kind enough to write the introduction to Ross's *Sin and Society*. He shared with Ely, Wilson, and others a conviction that social progress had to take into account the innate differences between the races. Ross also shared Wilson's view, expressed in *The State,* that various races were at different stages of evolution. Africans and South Americans were still close to savages. Other races—mostly Asians—might be more "advanced" but had slid into evolutionary degeneration. Ross believed that America faced similar degeneration through immigration, intermarriage, and the refusal of the state to impose sweeping eugenic reforms. In 1914 he wrote: "Observe immigrants not as they come travel-wan up the gangplank, nor as they issue toil-begrimed from pit's mouth or mill-gate, but in their gatherings, washed, combed, and in their Sunday best . . . [They] are hirsute, low-browed, big-faced persons of obviously low mentality . . . [C]learly they belong in skins, in wattled huts at the close of the Great Ice Age. These ox-like men are descendants of those who always stayed behind."[28]

Such views didn't stop Ross from getting a prominent appointment at Stanford. Stanford's conservative grande dame and benefactor, Jane Lanthrop Stanford, however, disliked not only his politics and his activism but also his increasingly loud and crude denunciations of Chinese "coolies." She forced the president of the school, David Starr Jordan—himself an avid eugenicist—to fire Ross.

The faculty erupted in outrage. Professors resigned. Progressive academics and organizations, led by Richard Ely's American Economic Association, rallied to his cause. The *New York Times* and other prominent newspapers editorialized on Ross's behalf. These efforts came to naught, and Ross left for the University of Nebraska (where he helped Roscoe Pound formulate the doctrine of "sociological jurisprudence"—a bedrock of modern liberalism's "living constitution") and eventually found a home at the University of Wisconsin working alongside Ely under the "race patriot" Charles Van Hise.

It is telling that while we constantly hear about America's racist past and our need to redeem ourselves via racial quotas, slavery reparations, and other overtures toward "historically oppressed groups," it is rare indeed that anyone mentions the founders of American liberalism. Again, when liberals are the historical villains, the crime is laid at the feet of America itself. The crime is considered proof of America's conservative past. When conservatives sin, the sin is conservatism's alone. But never is liberalism itself to blame.

Consider the infamous Tuskegee experiments, where poor black men were allegedly infected with syphilis without their knowledge and then monitored for years. In the common telling, the episode is an example of southern racism and American backwardness. In some versions, black men were even deliberately infected with syphilis as part of some kind of embryonic genocidal program. In fact, the Tuskegee experiments were approved and supported by well-meaning health professionals who saw nothing wrong or racist with playing God. As the University of Chicago's Richard Shweder writes, the "study emerged out of a liberal progressive public health movement concerned about the health and wellbeing of the African-American population." If racism played a part, as it undoubtedly did, it was the racism of liberals, not conservatives. But that's not how the story is told.

I'm not saying that people who once called themselves progressives were racist and therefore those who call themselves progressives today are racist, too. Rather, the point is that the edifice of contemporary liberalism stands on a foundation of assumptions and ideas integral to the larger fascist moment. Contemporary liberals, who may be the kindest and most racially tolerant people in the world, nonetheless choose to live in a house of distinctly fascist architecture. Liberal ignorance of this fact renders this fascist foundation neither intangible nor irrelevant. Rather, it underscores the success of these ideas, precisely because they go unquestioned.

The greatest asset liberalism has in arguments about racism, sexism, and the role of government generally is the implicit assumption that liberalism's intentions are better and more high-minded than conservatism's. Liberals think with their hearts, conservatives with their heads, goes the cliché. But if you take liberalism's history into account, it's clear this is an unfair advantage, an intellectual stolen base. Liberals may be right or wrong about a given policy, but the assumption that they are automatically arguing from the more virtuous position is rubbish.

What is today called liberalism stands, domestically, on three legs: support for the welfare state, abortion, and identity politics. Obviously, this is a crude formulation. Abortion, for example, could be lumped into identity politics, as feminism is one of the creeds extolling the iron cage of identity. Or one could say that "sexual liberty" is a better term than abortion. But I don't think any fair-minded reader would dispute that these three categories nearly cover the vast bulk of the liberal agenda—or at least describe the core of liberal passions today.

In the remainder of this chapter, I propose to look at each area, starting with the least obvious—and perhaps least important—to see how the progressive urge to reengineer society from the bottom up manifests itself in these three pillars of liberalism today.

THE WELFARE STATE

What is the welfare state? The plain meaning is fairly obvious: a social safety net, a system by which the government can address economic inequalities, presumably for the betterment of the whole society, with special emphasis on the least fortunate. The term, and to a significant degree the concept, begins with Bismarck's Prussia. Bismarck's *Wohlfahrtsstaat* included everything from guaranteed pensions and other forms of "social insurance" to a whole constellation of labor reforms. This "state socialism," as we've seen, was an enormous inspiration to progressives, socialists, and social democrats in Britain and America, and, of course, in Germany.

But there were at least two important differences between America and Prussia. First, America was a democratic republic with a firm constitution designed to protect minorities (albeit imperfectly) against the tyranny of the majority. Second, Germans already constituted a "racial nation." American progressives were frustrated by the first point because they were envious of the second. The progressives believed that, in the words of Justice Holmes, the aim of law and social policy was to "build a race." Our democracy, with its inconvenient checks and balances, including a diverse population, made such a project difficult. Nonetheless, progressive social policy—the granite foundation of today's welfare state—was from the outset dedicated to solving this "problem."

The American welfare state, in other words, was in important respects a eugenic racial project from the outset. The progressive authors of welfare state socialism were interested not in protecting the weak from the ravages of capitalism, as modern liberals would have it, but in weeding out the weak and unfit, and thereby preserving and strengthening the Anglo-Saxon character of the American racial community.

"Raceologists" like E. A. Ross dedicated their careers to this effort. At the macro level, Ross described the program as one of "social control." This meant mining the society for its purest elements and forging those elements into a "superior race." For white Anglo Protestants, this would amount to a national "restoration" (the watchword of all fascist movements). For the rest, it meant pruning the American garden of racial "weeds," "defective germ plasm," and other euphemisms for non-Aryan strains. Education, in the broadest sense, required getting the entire society to see the wisdom in this policy. Perhaps in a perfect world, the state wouldn't have to get involved: "The breeding function of the family would be better discharged if public opinion and religion conspired . . . to crush the aspirations of woman for a life of her own."[29] But it was too late for such measures, so the state had to interfere.

Ross was a showman, but his ideas fit squarely within the worldview of progressive economics, on both sides of the Atlantic. Consider the debate over the minimum wage. The controversy centered on what to do about what Sidney Webb called the "unemployable class." It was Webb's belief, shared by many of the progressive economists affiliated with the American Economic Association, that establishing a minimum wage above the value of the unemployables' worth would lock them out of the market, accelerating their elimination as a class. This is essentially the modern conservative argument *against* the minimum wage, and even today, when conservatives make it, they are accused of—you guessed it—social Darwinism. But for the progressives at the dawn of the fascist moment, this was an argument for it. "Of all ways of dealing with these unfortunate parasites," Webb observed, "the most ruinous to the community is to allow them unrestrainedly to compete as wage earners."[30]

Ross put it succinctly: "The Coolie cannot outdo the American, but he can underlive him." Since the inferior races were content to live closer to a filthy state of nature than the Nordic man, the savages did not require a civilized wage. Hence if you raised minimum wages to a civilized level, employers wouldn't hire such miscreants in preference to "fitter" specimens, making them less likely to reproduce and, if necessary, easier targets for forced sterilization. Royal Meeker, a Princeton economist and adviser to Woodrow Wilson, explained: "Better that the state should support the inefficient wholly and prevent the multiplication of the breed than subsidize incompetence and unthrift, enabling them to bring forth more of their kind."[31] Arguments like these turn modern liberal rationales for welfare state wage supports completely on their head.

Few better epitomized the international nature of this progressive-socialist-nationalist consensus than the University of Wisconsin economist John R. Commons. Describing himself as "a socialist, a single-taxer, a free-silverite, a greenbacker, a municipal-ownerist, a member of the Congressional Church," Commons was a lion of the international labor movement and dubbed the "American Sidney

Webb." His seminar room contained a giant chart that tracked the global success of progressive economics.[32] Commons believed that many poor whites could be saved by government intervention and that they should receive the bounty of a lavishly generous welfare state. But he conceded that, by his estimate, nearly 6 percent of the population was "defective" and 2 percent was irretrievably degenerate and in need of "segregation." These estimates didn't even include blacks and other "inferior" races, whom he considered irredeemable, save perhaps through intermarriage with Aryans. Black inferiority was the main reason this champion of the labor movement felt slavery was justified.[33]

Commons and colleagues at Wisconsin laid the foundation for most of the labor reforms we have today, many of them wholly defensible and worthwhile. Others, such as the Davis-Bacon Act, reflect the racial animus of the progressives. The act was passed in 1931 in order to prevent poor black laborers from "taking" jobs from whites. Its authors were honest about it, and it was passed explicitly for that reason; the comparatively narrow issue of cheap black labor was set against the backdrop of the vestigial progressive effort to maintain white supremacy. By requiring that contractors on federal projects pay "prevailing wages" and use union labor, the act would lock black workers out of federal jobs projects. Today the Davis-Bacon Act is as sacred to many labor movement liberals as *Roe v. Wade* is to feminists. Indeed, as Mickey Kaus has observed, devotion to Davis-Bacon is more intense today than it was thirty years ago, when self-described neoliberals considered it a hallmark of outdated interest-group liberalism.

To be fair, not all progressives supported the welfare state on eugenic grounds. Some were *deeply skeptical* of the welfare state—but *also* on eugenic grounds. The Yale economist Henry Farnam cofounded with Commons the American Association for Labor Legislation, the landmark progressive organization whose work laid the foundation for most social insurance and labor laws today. They argued that public assistance was dysgenic—that is, it increased the ranks of the "unfit"—because it afforded the degenerate classes an opportunity to reproduce, whereas in a natural environment such rabble would die off. But Farnam, the protectionist economist Simon Patten, and others didn't therefore *oppose* the welfare state on those grounds. That would be tantamount to social Darwinism! Rather, they argued that the unintended consequences of the welfare state required a draconian eugenics scheme to "weed out" the defective germ plasm bred by the state's largesse. Why should Aryans be denied the benefits of state socialism when you could simply sweep up the unavoidable mess with a eugenic broom?

Perhaps the only unifying political view held by virtually all eugenicists was that capitalism was dysgenic. "Racial hygiene" was a subset of the larger "social question," and the one thing everyone knew was that laissez-faire was not the answer to the social question.

Until the Nazis came along, Germany generally lagged behind the United States and much of Europe when it came to eugenics. When Indiana passed the first sterilization law in 1907—for "confirmed criminals, idiots, imbeciles and rapists"—the West took notice. In the subsequent thirty years, twenty-nine other American states passed similar laws, as did Canada and most of Europe. Yes, the Germans admired America's "fitter family" contests, in which good American Aryans were judged like prized cattle at county fairs, but some Scandinavian nations were years ahead of the Germans when it came to eugenic schemes, and many European countries—and Canadian provinces—remained committed to eugenics decades after the fall of the Third Reich.[34]

Comparisons between the progressives' efforts to "build a race" and the Nazis' efforts to hone or redeem their already homogeneous racial nation can easily become overly invidious because the checks on such programs in America were so much stronger. Thanks to American exceptionalism, progressives were forced to tinker surgically with scalpels—a point they lamented often—while thanks to German exceptionalism, National Socialists had a free hand to use axes, sledgehammers, and bulldozers. In a sense, Germany had been waiting for eugenics to arrive in order to give a scientific rationale to the deep Romantic yearnings in its culture.

Nietzsche himself had pointed the way. In 1880 he wrote, "The tendency must be towards the rendering extinct of the wretched, the deformed, the degenerate." Reproduction, Nietzsche argued, needed to be taken out of the hands of the masses so that "race as a whole [no longer] suffers." "The extinction of many types of people is just as desirable as any form of reproduction." Marriage itself, Nietzsche argued, must be more scrupulously regulated by the state. "Go through the towns and ask yourselves whether these people should reproduce! Let them go to their whores!"[35]

It's almost impossible to talk about the "influence" of eugenic thought on Nazi public policy, since the Nazis conceived of eugenics as the goal of *all* public policy. One of the last things Hitler ever committed to paper was his wish that Germany stay loyal to its race laws. Everything—marriage, medicine, employment, wages—was informed by notions of race hygiene and the eugenic economics pioneered by British and American socialists and progressives. As in America, marriage licenses were a vital tool for eugenic screening. Marriages viewed as "undesirable to the whole national community" were forbidden. Meanwhile, subsidies, travel allowances, bonuses, and the like were doled out to favored racial classes. Forced sterilizations became a standard tool of statecraft.[36]

As we'll see, the Nazis co-opted independent religious and other charities under the auspices of the state. During their rise to power they constructed an alternative charitable infrastructure, offering social services the state couldn't provide. When the Nazis finally took over, they methodically replaced the traditional infrastructure of the state and churches with a Nazi monopoly on charity.

But the more relevant aspect of the Nazi welfare state was how it geared itself entirely toward building a racially defined national community. While it used the standard leftist rhetoric of guilt and obligation typically invoked to justify government aid for the needy and unfortunate, it excluded anyone who wasn't a "national comrade." This points to the unique evil of Nazism. Unlike Italian Fascism, which had less use for eugenics than America or Germany, Nazism was defined as racial socialism. Everything for the race, nothing for those outside it, was the central ethos of Nazism's mission and appeal.

One last point about the interplay of eugenics and the welfare state. In both Germany and America, eugenics gained currency because of the larger faith in "public health." World War I and the great influenza epidemic drafted the medical profession into the ranks of social planners as much as any other. For doctors promoted to the rank of physicians to the body politic, the Hippocratic oath lost influence. The American medical journal *Military Surgeon* stated matter-of-factly, "The consideration of human life often becomes quite secondary . . . The medical officer has become more absorbed in the general than the particular, and the life and limb of the individual, while of great importance, are secondary to measures *pro bono publico* [for the public good]."[37]

The Germans called this sort of thinking *"Gemeinnutz geht vor Eigennutz,"* the common good supersedes the private good. And it was under this banner that Germany took the logic of public health to totalitarian extremes. Prohibition was the premier illustration of how closely American progressives linked moral and physical health, and many Nazis looked favorably upon the American effort. The appreciation was mutual. In 1933 the American *Scientific Temperance Journal* celebrated the election of Hitler, a famous teetotaler. And while the racist undercurrent to Prohibition was always there—alcohol fueled the licentiousness of the mongrel races—in Germany the concern was more that alcohol and the even more despised cigarette would lead to the degeneracy of Germany's Aryan purity. Tobacco was credited with every evil imaginable, including fostering homosexuality.

The Nazis were particularly fixated on cancer—the Germans were the first to spot the link between smoking and the disease, and the word "cancer" soon became an omnipresent metaphor. Nazi leaders routinely called Jews "cancers" and "tumors" on German society. But this was a practice formed from a broader and deeper habit. On both sides of the Atlantic, it was commonplace to call "defectives" and other groups who took more than they gave "cancers on the body politic." The American Eugenics Society was dubbed "The Society for the Control of Social Cancer." In Germany, before the Jews were rounded up, hundreds of thousands of disabled, elderly, and mentally ill "pure" Germans were eliminated on the grounds that they were "useless bread gobblers" or "life unworthy of life" (*lebensunwertes Leben*), a term that first appeared in Germany in 1920. The application of these techniques and ideas to the "Jewish problem" seemed like a rational continuation of eugenic theory in general.

But the Holocaust should not blind us to less significant but more directly relevant repercussions of Progressive Era ideas that have escaped the light of scrutiny. The architects of the New Deal, the Fair Deal, and the Great Society all inherited and built upon the progressive welfare state. And they did this in explicit terms, citing such prominent race builders as Theodore Roosevelt and Woodrow Wilson as their inspirations. Obviously, the deliberate racist intent in many of these policies was not shared by subsequent generations of liberals. But that didn't erase the racial content of the policies themselves. The Davis-Bacon Act still hurts low-wage blacks, for example. FDR's labor and agricultural policies threw millions of blacks out of work and off their land. The great migration of African-Americans to northern cities was in no small part a result of the *success* of progressive policies. Black leaders didn't call the National Recovery Administration, or NRA, the "Negro Run Around" for nothing.

In the previous chapter I noted that liberals cling to the myth of the New Deal out of religious devotion to the idea of the all-caring God-state. Something similar is at work in the liberal devotion to the Great Society. The rationales for the Great Society are almost always suffused with racial guilt and what could only be described as a religious faith in the state's redemptive power. In his book *White Guilt,* Shelby Steele tells of an encounter with a self-described "architect" of the Great Society. "Damn it, we *saved* this country!" the man barked. "This country was about to blow up. There were riots everywhere. You can stand there now in hindsight and criticize, but we had to keep the country together, my friend."[38] Moreover, added the LBJer, you should have seen how grateful blacks were when these programs were rolled out.

Well, the first claim is a falsehood, and the second is damning. While the civil rights acts were obviously great successes, liberals hardly stopped at equality before the law. The Great Society's racial meddling—often under various other guises—yielded one setback after another. Crime soared because of the Great Society and the attitudes of which it partook. In 1960 the total number of murders was lower than it had been in 1930, 1940, and 1950 despite a population explosion. In the decade after the Great Society, the murder rate effectively doubled. Black-on-black crime soared in particular. Riots exploded on LBJ's watch, often with the subtle encouragement of Great Society liberals who rewarded such behavior. Out-of-wedlock births among blacks skyrocketed. Economically, as Thomas Sowell has cataloged, the biggest drop in black poverty took place during the two decades *before* the Great Society.[39] In the 1970s, when the impact of Great Society programs was fully realized, the trend of black economic improvement stopped almost entirely.

One could go on like this for pages. But the facts are of secondary importance. Liberals have fallen in love with the *idea* behind the racial welfare state. They've absorbed the Marxist and fascist conception of "the system" as racist and corrupt and therefore in constant need of state intervention. In particular, as Steele notes, they've convinced themselves that support for such programs is proof of their own moral worth. Blacks were "grateful" to white liberals; therefore, white liberals aren't racist. We return once again to the use of politics to demonize those who fall outside the consensus—that is, conservatives—and to anoint those within it. Whites who oppose the racial spoils system are racists. Blacks who oppose it are self-hating race traitors.

Usually white liberals will simply opt to support black liberals who make such charges, rather than make them themselves. But occasionally they will step up and do so. Maureen Dowd, for example, writes that it is "impossible not to be disgusted" with blacks such as Clarence Thomas. According to Dowd, the Supreme Court justice hates himself for "his own great historic ingratitude" to white liberals or has been "driven barking mad" by it. Take your pick. Steele summarizes the racism of this sort of thinking: "[W]e'll throw you a bone like affirmative action if you'll just let us reduce you to your race so we can take moral authority for 'helping' you. When they called you a nigger back in the days of segregation, at least they didn't ask you to be grateful."[40]

ABORTION

Margaret Sanger, whose American Birth Control League became Planned Parenthood, was the founding mother of the birth control movement. She is today considered a liberal saint, a founder of modern feminism, and one of the leading lights of the progressive pantheon. Gloria Feldt of Planned Parenthood proclaims, "I stand by Margaret Sanger's side," leading "the organization that carries on Sanger's legacy." Planned Parenthood's first black president, Faye

Wattleton—*Ms.* magazine's Woman of the Year in 1989—said that she was "proud" to be "walking in the footsteps of Margaret Sanger."[41] Planned Parenthood gives out annual Maggie Awards to individuals and organizations who advance Sanger's cause. Recipients are a Who's Who of liberal icons, from the novelist John Irving to the producers of NBC's *West Wing.* What Sanger's liberal admirers are eager to downplay is that she was a thoroughgoing racist who subscribed completely to the views of E. A. Ross and other "raceologists." Indeed, she made many of them seem tame.

Sanger was born into a poor family of eleven children in Corning, New York, in 1879. In 1902 she received her degree as a registered nurse. In 1911 she moved to New York City, where she fell in with the transatlantic bohemian avant-garde of the burgeoning fascist moment. "Our living-room," she wrote in her autobiography, "became a gathering place where liberals, anarchists, Socialists and I.W.W.'s could meet."[42] A member of the Women's Committee of the New York Socialist Party, she participated in all the usual protests and demonstrations. In 1912 she started writing what amounted to a sex-advice column for the *New York Call,* dubbed "What Every Girl Should Know." The overriding theme of her columns was the importance of contraception.

A disciple of the anarchist Emma Goldman—another eugenicist—Sanger became the nation's first "birth control martyr" when she was arrested for handing out condoms in 1917. In order to escape a subsequent arrest for violating obscenity laws, she went to England, where she fell under the thrall of Havelock Ellis, a sex theorist and ardent advocate of forced sterilization. She also had an affair with H. G. Wells, the self-avowed champion of "liberal fascism." Her marriage fell apart early, and one of her children—whom she admitted to neglecting—died of pneumonia at age four. Indeed, she always acknowledged that she wasn't right for family life, admitting she was not a "fit person for love or home or children or anything which needs attention or consideration."[43]

Under the banner of "reproductive freedom," Sanger subscribed to nearly all of the eugenic views discussed above. She sought to ban reproduction of the unfit and regulate reproduction for everybody else. She scoffed at the soft approach of the "positive" eugenicists, deriding it as mere "cradle competition" between the fit and the unfit. "More children from the fit, less from the unfit—that is the chief issue of birth control," she frankly wrote in her 1922 book *The Pivot of Civilization.* (The book featured an introduction by Wells, in which he proclaimed, "We want fewer and better children . . . and we cannot make the social life and the world-peace we are determined to make, with the ill-bred, ill-trained swarms of inferior citizens that you inflict on us." Two civilizations were at war: that of progress and that which sought a world "swamped by an indiscriminate torrent of progeny.")[44]

A fair-minded person cannot read Sanger's books, articles, and pamphlets today without finding similarities not only to Nazi eugenics but to the dark dystopias of the feminist imagination found in such allegories as Margaret Atwood's *Handmaid's Tale.*[45] As editor of the *Birth Control Review,* Sanger regularly published the sort of hard racism we normally associate with Goebbels or Himmler. Indeed, after she resigned as editor, the *Birth Control Review* ran articles by people who worked for Goebbels and Himmler. For example, when the Nazi eugenics program was first getting wide attention, the *Birth Control Review* was quick to cast the Nazis in a positive light, giving over its pages for an article titled "Eugenic Sterilization: An Urgent Need," by Ernst Rüdin, Hitler's director of sterilization and a founder of the Nazi Society for Racial Hygiene. In 1926 Sanger proudly gave a speech to a KKK rally in Silver Lake, New Jersey.

One of Sanger's closest friends and influential colleagues was the white supremacist Lothrop Stoddard, author of *The Rising Tide of Color Against White World-Supremacy*. In the book he offered his solution for the threat posed by the darker races: "Just as we isolate bacterial invasions, and starve out the bacteria, by limiting the area and amount of their food supply, so we can compel an inferior race to remain in its native habitat."[46] When the book came out, Sanger was sufficiently impressed to invite him to join the board of directors of the American Birth Control League.

Sanger's genius was to advance Ross's campaign for social control by hitching the racist-eugenic campaign to sexual pleasure and female liberation. In her "Code to Stop Overproduction of Children," published in 1934, she decreed that "no woman shall have a legal right to bear a child without a permit . . . no permit shall be valid for more than one child."[47] But Sanger couched this fascistic agenda in the argument that "liberated" women wouldn't mind such measures because they don't really want large families in the first place. In a trope that would be echoed by later feminists such as Betty Friedan, she argued that motherhood itself was a socially imposed constraint on the liberty of women. It was a form of what Marxists called false consciousness to want a large family.

Sanger believed—prophetically enough—that if women conceived of sex as first and foremost a pleasurable experience rather than a procreative act, they would embrace birth control as a necessary tool for their own personal gratification. She brilliantly used the language of liberation to convince women they weren't going along with a collectivist scheme but were in fact "speaking truth to power," as it were.[48] This was the identical trick the Nazis pulled off. They took a radical Nietzschean doctrine of individual will and made it into a trendy dogma of middle-class conformity. This trick remains the core of much faddish "individualism" among rebellious conformists on the American cultural left today. Nonetheless, Sanger's analysis was surely correct, and led directly to the widespread feminist association of sex with political rebellion. Sanger in effect "bought off" women (and grateful men) by offering tolerance for promiscuity in return for compliance with her eugenic schemes.

In 1939 Sanger created the previously mentioned "Negro Project," which aimed to get blacks to adopt birth control. Through the Birth Control Federation, she hired black ministers (including the Reverend Adam Clayton Powell Sr.), doctors, and other leaders to help pare down the supposedly surplus black population. The project's racist intent is beyond doubt. "The mass of significant Negroes," read the project's report, "still breed carelessly and disastrously, with the result that the increase among Negroes . . . is [in] that portion of the population least intelligent and fit." Sanger's intent is shocking today, but she recognized its extreme radicalism even then. "We do not want word to go out," she wrote to a colleague, "that we want to exterminate the Negro population, and the minister is the man who can straighten out that idea if it ever occurs to any of their more rebellious members."[49]

It is possible that Sanger didn't really want to "exterminate" the Negro population so much as merely limit its growth. Still, many in the black community saw it that way and remained rightly suspicious of the progressives' motives. It wasn't difficult to see that middle-class whites who consistently spoke of "race suicide" at the hands of dark, subhuman savages might not have the best interests of blacks in mind. This skepticism persisted within the black community for decades. Someone who saw the relationship between, for example, abortion and race from a less trusting perspective telegrammed Congress in 1977 to tell them that abortion amounted to "genocide against the black race." And he added, in block letters, "AS A MATTER OF CONSCIENCE I MUST OPPOSE THE USE OF FEDERAL FUNDS FOR A POLICY OF KILLING INFANTS."[50] This was Jesse Jackson, who changed his position when he decided to seek the Democratic nomination.

Just a few years ago, the racial eugenic "bonus" of abortion rights was something one could only admit among those fully committed to the cause, and even then in politically correct whispers. No more. Increasingly, this argument is acceptable on the left, as are arguments in favor of eugenics generally.

In 2005 the acclaimed University of Chicago economist Steven Levitt broke the taboo with his critical and commercial hit *Freakonomics* (co-written with Stephen Dubner). The most sensational chapter in the book updated a paper Levitt had written in 1999 which argued that abortion cuts crime. "Legalized abortion led to less unwantedness; unwantedness leads to high crime; legalized abortion, therefore, led to less crime."[51] *Freakonomics* excised all references to race and never connected the facts that because the aborted fetuses were disproportionately black and blacks disproportionately contribute to the crime rate, reducing the size of the black population reduces crime. Yet the press coverage acknowledged this reality and didn't seem to mind.

In 2005 William Bennett, a committed pro-lifer, invoked the Levitt argument in order to denounce eugenic thinking. "I do know that it's true that if you wanted to reduce crime, you could—if that were your sole purpose—you could abort every black baby in this country, and your crime rate would go down. That would be an impossible, ridiculous, and morally reprehensible thing to do, but your crime rate would go down." What seemed to offend liberals most was that Bennett had accidentally borrowed some conventional liberal logic to make a conservative point, and, as with the social Darwinists of yore, that makes liberals quite cross. According to the *New York Times*'s Bob Herbert, Bennett believed "exterminating blacks would be a most effective crime-fighting tool." Various liberal spokesmen, including Terry McAuliffe, the former head of the Democratic National Committee, said Bennett wanted to exterminate "black babies." Juan Williams proclaimed that Bennett's remarks speak "to a deeply racist mindset."[52]

In one sense, this is a pretty amazing turnaround. After all, when liberals advocate them, we are usually told that abortions do not kill "babies." Rather, they remove mere agglomerations of cells and tissue or "uterine contents." If *hypothetical* abortions committed for allegedly conservative ends are infanticide, how can *actual* abortions performed for liberal ends not be?

Some liberals are honest about this. In 1992 Nicholas Von Hoffman argued in the *Philadelphia Inquirer:*

> Free cheap abortion is a policy of social defense. To save ourselves from being murdered in our beds and raped on the streets, we should do everything possible to encourage pregnant women who don't want the baby and will not take care of it to get rid of the thing before it turns into a monster . . . At their demonstration, the anti-abortionists parade around with pictures of dead and dismembered fetuses. The pro-abortionists should meet these displays with some of their own: pictures of the victims of the unaborted—murder victims, rape victims, mutilation victims—pictures to remind us that the fight for abortion is but part of the larger struggle for safe homes and safe streets.[53]

Later that same year, the White House received a letter from the *Roe v. Wade* co-counsel Ron Weddington, urging the new president-elect to rush RU-486—the morning-after pill—to the market as quickly as possible. Weddington's argument was refreshingly honest:

> [Y]ou can start immediately to eliminate the barely educated, unhealthy and poor segment of our country. No, I'm not advocating

some sort of mass extinction of these unfortunate people. Crime, drugs and disease are already doing that. The problem is that their numbers are not only replaced but increased by the birth of millions of babies to people who can't afford to have babies. There, I've said it. It's what we all know is true, but we only whisper it, because as liberals who believe in individual rights, we view any program which might treat the disadvantaged as discriminatory, mean-spirited and . . . well . . . so Republican.

[G]overnment is also going to have to provide vasectomies, tubal ligations and abortions . . . There have been about 30 million abortions in this country since Roe v. Wade. Think of all the poverty, crime and misery . . . and then add 30 million unwanted babies to the scenario. We lost a lot of ground during the Reagan-Bush religious orgy. We don't have a lot of time left.[54]

How, exactly, is this substantively different from Margaret Sanger's self-described "religion of birth control," which would, she wrote, "ease the financial load of caring for with public funds . . . children destined to become a burden to themselves, to their family, and ultimately to the nation"?[55]

The issue here is not the explicit intent of liberals or the rationalizations they invoke to deceive themselves about the nature of abortion. Rather, it is to illustrate that even when motives and arguments change, the substance of the policy remains in its effects. After the Holocaust discredited eugenics per se, neither the eugenicists nor their ideas disappeared. Rather, they went to ground in fields like family planning and demography and in political movements such as feminism. Indeed, in a certain sense Planned Parenthood is today *more* eugenic than Sanger intended. Sanger, after all, despised abortion. She denounced it as "barbaric" and called abortionists "bloodsucking men with M.D. after their names." Abortion resulted in "an outrageous slaughter" and "the killing of babies," which even the degenerate offspring of the unfit did not deserve.[56]

So forget about intent: look at results. Abortion ends more black lives than heart disease, cancer, accidents, AIDS, and violent crime *combined*. African-Americans constitute little more than 12 percent of the population but have more than a third (37 percent) of abortions. That rate has held relatively constant, though in some regions the numbers are much starker; in Mississippi, black women receive some 72 percent of all abortions, according to the Centers for Disease Control. Nationwide, 512 out of every 1,000 black pregnancies end in an abortion.[57] Revealingly enough, roughly 80 percent of Planned Parenthood's abortion centers are in or near minority communities. Liberalism today condemns a Bill Bennett who speculates about the effects of killing unborn black children; but it also celebrates the actual killing of unborn black children, and condemns him for opposing it.

Of course, orthodox eugenics also aimed at the "feebleminded" and "useless bread gobblers"—which included everyone from the mentally retarded to an uneducated and malnourished underclass to recidivist criminals. When it comes to today's "feebleminded," influential voices on the left now advocate the killing of "defectives" at the beginning of life and at the end of life. Chief among them is Peter Singer, widely hailed as the most important living philosopher and the world's leading ethicist. Professor Singer, who teaches at Princeton, argues that unwanted or disabled babies should be killed in the name of "compassion." He also argues that the elderly and other drags on society should be put down when their lives are no longer worth living.

Singer doesn't hide behind code words and euphemisms in his belief that killing babies isn't always wrong, as one can deduce from his essay titled "Killing Babies Isn't Always Wrong" (nor is he a lone voice in the wilderness; his views are popular or respected in many academic circles).[58] But that hasn't caused the left to ostracize him in the slightest (save in Germany, where people still have a visceral sense of where such logic takes you). Of course, not all or even most liberals agree with Singer's prescriptions, but nor do they condemn him as they do, say, a William Bennett. Perhaps they recognize in him a kindred spirit.

IDENTITY POLITICS

Today's liberals have no particular animus toward racial minorities (majorities are another issue). They may even be prejudiced in favor of racial minorities. They give them *extra credit*. Built into the core of liberal racial views is that it's something of an accomplishment just *being* black.

For the last forty years or so, popular entertainment has glorified what the *National Review* editor Richard Brookhiser calls "the Numinous Negro." Given how blacks were depicted in the past, it's understandable that artists would overcompensate in the other direction. But this is a broader cultural trend, encompassing politics and policy as well. The Congressional Black Caucus, for the most part a motley collection of extreme left-wing politicians, dubs itself the "conscience of the Congress" for no discernible reason other than its members' racial identity. White liberals are perfectly happy to perpetrate this perception, partly out of guilt, partly out of somewhat cynical calculation that allows them to appear noble as the (self-appointed) defenders of black America. But most white liberals, and black ones, too, subscribe to a philosophical orientation which insists that blacks *are* in some significant way "better."

Certainly this is objectively true among such quintessentially fascist black supremacists as Louis Farrakhan and the black "raceologist" Leonard Jeffries. Indeed, across the Afrocentric and Black Nationalist left, bizarre and ahistorical fantasies proliferate about the superiority of ancient African civilization, about white conspiracies to erase black history, and the like. The similarity to Nazi mythology about the mythic Aryan past is not superficial. One of the few places in America where you can be sure to find *The Protocols of the Elders of Zion* is Afrocentrist bookshops. And, again, both the Nation of Islam and the Back to Africa movement expressed some ideological affinity with Nazism and Italian Fascism, respectively.

Even on the liberal left, where these poisonous notions are far more diluted, it's axiomatic that there is something inherently and distinctly good about blacks. How so? Well, it *must* be so. If you buy into the various doctrines of multiculturalism and identity politics you already believe that blackness is distinct, immutable, and unchanging. Once you accept this logic—and the left obviously does—you are then left with a fairly simple choice. If race is *not* neutral, if "race matters," as Cornel West says, then *how* does it matter? Given the choice between assigning a positive value or a negative value, liberals opt for the positive.

Positive discrimination forms the backbone of our racial spoils system. Gone are the days when affirmative action was justified solely on the grounds put forward by Lyndon Johnson of helping blacks or redressing historical injustices.[59] To be sure, these arguments still loom quite large for many liberals, and that is to their credit. But they have been subsumed into a larger creed of multiculturalism, and liberals fall back on the rhetoric of racial damage—that is, affirmative action is necessary to "fix" what's been done to blacks—only when affirmative action is under threat. This is the breakwater for a vast Coalition of the Oppressed that relies on the core logic of black entitlement to empower a sweeping cultural and political agenda under the rubric of diversity. So long as blacks are in need of special treatment, the coalition has the political leverage for us-too politics. In a racial spoils state, this sort of tragedy of the commons was inevitable. Feminists, following in the wake of blacks, also wanted special treatment. Hispanic leftists copied the same model. Now homosexuals argue they are in nearly every meaningful sense the moral equivalent of blacks. Eventually, the ranks of the oppressed swelled to the point where a new argument was needed: "multiculturalism."

Here the similarities with German fascist thought become most apparent. Isaiah Berlin famously argued that fascism was the progeny of the French reactionary Comte Joseph de Maistre. Berlin was clearly exaggerating de Maistre's influence (both Nazis and Italian Fascists explicitly rejected de Maistre), but his argument nonetheless helps us understand how fascism and identity politics overlap and interact.

Inherent to the Enlightenment is the idea that all mankind can be reasoned with. The *philosophes* argued that men all over the world were each blessed with the faculty of reason. It was the European right which believed that mankind was broken up into groups, classes, sects, races, nationalities, and other gradations in the great chain of being. The reactionary de Maistre railed against the notion that there were any "universal rights of man." In his most famous statement on the subject he declared, "Now, there is no such thing as 'man' in this world. In my life I have seen Frenchmen, Italians, Russians, and so on. I even know, thanks to Montesquieu, that one can be Persian. But as for man, I declare I've never encountered him. If he exists, I don't know about it."[60]

De Maistre meant that we are all prisoners of our racial and ethnic identities. (He didn't mention gender, but that likely went without saying.) Indeed, there is less difference between today's identity politics and the identity politics of the fascist past than anyone realizes. As one fascist sympathizer put it in the 1930s, "Our understanding struggles to go beyond the fatal error of believing in the equality of all human beings and tries to recognize the diversity of peoples and races."[61] How many college campuses hear that kind of rhetoric every day?

Today it is the left that says there is no such creature as "man." Instead, there are African-Americans, Hispanics, and Native Americans. Left-wing academics speak of the "permanence of race," and a whole new field of "whiteness studies" has sprouted up at prominent universities and colleges, dedicated to beating back the threat of whiteness in America. The sociologist Andrew Hacker decries "white logic," and a host of other scholars argue that blacks and other minorities underperform academically because the subject matter in our schools represents white-supremacist thinking. Black children reject schoolwork because academic success amounts to "acting white." This welter of nonsense enshrines and empowers a host of collectivist notions that place the state at the center of managing the progress of groups; those who oppose this agenda get clubbed over the head with the charge of racism. For example, the Seattle public school system recently announced that "emphasizing individualism as opposed to a more collective ideology" is a form of "cultural racism." Indeed, the case for Enlightenment principles of individualism and reason itself is deemed anti-minority. Richard Delgado, a founder of critical race theory, writes: "If you're black or Mexican, you should flee Enlightenment based democracies like mad, assuming you have any choice."[62]

In the 1960s, when the civil rights movement still relied on the classically liberal formulation of judging people by the content of their character, enlightened liberals denounced the "one-drop" rule which said that if you had a single drop of "black" blood you were black, a standard transparently similar to National Socialist notions of who counted as a Jew. Now, according to the left, if you have one drop of black blood, you should be counted as black for the purposes of *positive* discrimination. So valuable are the privileges associated with blackness that some black intellectuals want to make "racial fraud" a crime.[63] It's a strange racism problem when people are clamoring to join the ranks of the oppressed and lobbying for laws to make sure "oppressors" don't get to pass themselves off as "victims."

The glorification of racial permanence has caused the left to abandon narrow rationales for affirmative action in favor of the doctrine of multiculturalism. The diversity argument—which, by the way, is only used to defend favored groups; Asians and Jews almost never count toward the goal of diversity—is an argument for the permanence of race and identity. In other words, if the left has its way, racial preferences will no longer have anything to do with redressing past wrongs (except when such preferences are under attack). Rather, the pursuit of diversity will become the permanent license for social-engineering bean counters to discriminate against whatever group they see fit in order to reach the desired "balance." For example, quotas unfairly kept Jews out of universities to help white Protestants. Now quotas unfairly keep Jews (and Asians) out of universities to help blacks and Hispanics. What's different is that now liberals are sure such policies are a sign of racial progress.

Diversity depends on, and therefore ratifies, racial essentialism. Not only do rich (and, increasingly, foreign-born) blacks count as much as poor ones, but the argument now is that mere exposure to blacks is uplifting in and of itself. The policy is condescending and counterproductive because it assumes that blacks come to school not as Tom Smith or Joe Jones but as interchangeable Black-Perspective Student. Professors turn to black students for "the black point of view," and students who don't present the party line are counted as inauthentic by condescending white liberals (that is, most faculty and administrators) or by race-gaming blacks. I've been to dozens of campuses, and everywhere the story is the same: blacks eat, party, and live with other blacks. This self-segregation increasingly manifests itself in campus politics. Blacks become a student body within a student body, a microcosm of the nation within a nation. Ironically, the best way for a white kid to benefit from exposure to a black kid, and vice versa, would be for there to be fewer black students or at least no black dorms. That way blacks would be forced to integrate with the majority culture. But of course, integration is now derided as a racist doctrine.

You might say it's outrageous to compare the current liberal program to help minorities with the poisonous ideology of fascism and Nazism. And I would agree if we were talking about things like the Holocaust or even Kristallnacht. But at the philosophical level, we are talking about categorical ways of thinking. To forgive something by saying "it's a black thing" is philosophically no different from saying "it's an Aryan thing." The moral context matters a great deal. But the excuse is identical. Similarly, rejecting the Enlightenment for "good" reasons is still a rejection of the Enlightenment. And any instrumental or pragmatic gains you get from rejecting the Enlightenment still amount to taking a sledgehammer to the soapbox you're standing on. Without the standards of the Enlightenment, we are in a Nietzschean world where power decides important questions rather than reason. This is exactly how the left appears to want it.

One last point about diversity. Because liberals have what Thomas Sowell calls an "unconstrained vision," they assume everyone sees things through the same categorical prism. So once again, as with the left's invention of social Darwinism, liberals assume their ideological opposites take the "bad" view to their good. If liberals assume blacks—or women, or gays—are inherently good, conservatives must think these same groups are inherently bad.

This is not to say that there are no racist conservatives. But at the philosophical level, liberalism is battling a straw man. This is why liberals must constantly assert that conservatives use code words—because there's nothing obviously racist about conservatism per se. Indeed, the constant manipulation of the language to keep conservatives—and other non-liberals—on the defensive is a necessary tactic for liberal politics. The Washington, D.C., bureaucrat who was fired for using the word "niggardly" correctly in a sentence is a case in point.[64] The ground must be constantly shifted to maintain a climate of grievance. Fascists famously ruled by terror. Political correctness isn't literally terroristic, but it does govern through fear. No serious person can deny that the grievance politics of the American left keeps decent people in a constant state of fright—they are afraid to say the wrong word, utter the wrong thought, offend the wrong constituency.

If we maintain our understanding of political conservatism as the heir of classical liberal individualism, it is almost impossible for a fair-minded person to call it racist. And yet, according to liberals, race neutrality is itself racist. It harkens back to the "social Darwinism" of the past, we are told, because it relegates minorities to a savage struggle for the survival of the fittest.

There are only three basic positions. There is the racism of the left, which seeks to use the state to help favored minorities that it regards as morally superior. There is racial neutrality, which is, or has become, the conservative position. And then there is some form of "classical racism"—that is, seeing blacks as inferior in some way. According to the left, only one of these positions isn't racist. Race neutrality is racist. Racism is racist. So what's left? Nothing except liberalism. In other words, agree with liberals and you're not racist. Of course, if you adopt color blindness as a policy, many fair-minded liberals will tell you that while you're not personally racist, your views "perpetuate" racism. And some liberals will stand by the fascist motto: if you're not part of the solution, you're part of the problem. Either way, there are no safe harbors from liberal ideology. Hence, when it comes to race, liberalism has become a kind of soft totalitarianism and multiculturalism the mechanism for a liberal *Gleichschaltung*. If you fall outside the liberal consensus, you are either evil or an abettor of evil. This is the logic of the *Volksgemeinschaft* in politically correct jargon.

Now, of course you're not going to get a visit from the Gestapo if you see the world differently; if you don't think the good kind of diversity is skin deep or that the only legitimate community is the one where "we're all in it together," you won't be dragged off to reeducation camp. But you very well may be sent off to counseling or sensitivity training.

· 8 ·

Liberal Fascist Economics

IN RECENT YEARS liberals have largely succeeded in defining the conventional wisdom when it comes to economics. "Corporations are too powerful." They have a "stranglehold" on "the system," the entirety of which is now corrupted by the soiled touch of commerce. Every liberal publication in America subscribes to this perspective to some extent, from the *Nation* to the *New Republic* to the *New York Times*. The further you move to the left, the more this conviction becomes a caricature. Thus Bill Maher showed up at the Republican National Convention in 2000 dressed in a NASCAR-style tracksuit festooned with corporate logos to mock how the Republicans were stooges of Wall Street. Arianna Huffington supposedly switched from right to left due to her disgust with corporate "pigs at the trough." William Greider, Kevin Phillips, Robert Reich, Jonathan Chait, and every other would-be Charles Beard on the American left hold similar views. Corporations are inherently right-wing, we are assured, and if left unchecked, these malign and irresponsible entities will bring us perilously close to fascism. The noble fight against these sinister "corporate paymasters" is part of the eternal struggle to keep fascism—however ill defined—at bay.

Ever since the 1930s, there has been a tendency to see big business—"industrialists," "economic royalists," or "financial ruling classes"—as the real wizards behind the fascist Oz. Today's liberals are just the latest inheritors of this tradition. On the conspiratorial left, for example, it is de rigueur to call George W. Bush and Republicans in general Nazis. The case is supposedly bolstered by the widely peddled smear that Bush's grandfather was one of the industrialists who "funded" Hitler.[1] But even outside the fever swamps, the notion that liberals must keep a weather eye on big business for signs of creeping fascism is an article of faith. Robert F. Kennedy Jr. recycles this theme when he writes, "The rise of fascism across Europe in the 1930s offers many lessons on how corporate power can undermine a democracy. Mussolini complained that 'fascism should really be called corporatism.' Today, George Bush and his court are treating our country as a grab bag for the robber barons." Countless others have echoed these sentiments, arguing, in the words of Norman Mailer, that America is already a "pre-fascist" society run by corporations and their lickspittles in the Republican Party. The political scientist Theodore Lowi has said that the Republicans are "friendly fascists, a dominant effort to combine government and corporations." The Canadian novelist John Ralston Saul argues in his book *The Unconscious Civilization* that we live in a corporatist-fascist society but we are unwilling to see it. Corporate CEOs, Saul laments, are "the true descendants of Benito Mussolini."[2]

There is much unintentional truth to this collective diagnosis, but these would-be physicians have misread both the symptoms and the disease. In the left's eternal vigilance to fend off fascism, they have in fact created it, albeit with a friendly face. Like a medieval doctor who believes that mercury will cure madness, they foster precisely the sickness they hope to remedy. Good medicine, like good economics, depends on discarding unproven mythology. Yet for nearly a century the left and liberals have been using textbooks brimming with superstition. These myths are entwined with one another in a magnificent knot of confusion. Among the strands of this knot are the palpably false notions that big business is inherently right-wing or conservative (in the American sense); that European fascism was a tool of big business; and that the way to keep business from corrupting government is for government to regulate business to within an inch of its life.

In reality, if you define "right-wing" or "conservative" in the American sense of supporting the rule of law and the free market, then the more right-wing a business is, the less fascist it becomes. Meanwhile, in terms of economic policy, the more you move to the political center, as defined in American politics today, the closer you get to true fascism. If the far left is defined by socialism and the far right by laissez-faire, then it is the mealymouthed centrists of the Democratic Leadership Council and the Brookings Institution who are the true fascists, for it is they who subscribe to the notion of the Third Way, that quintessentially fascistic formulation that claims to be neither left nor right.[3] More important, these myths are often deliberately perpetuated in order to hasten the transformation of American society into precisely the kind of fascist—or corporatist—nation liberals claim to oppose. To a certain extent we do live in a fascistic "unconscious civilization," but we've gotten here through the conscious effort of liberals who want it that way.[4]

CUI BONO?

The notion that fascism was a tool of big business is one of the most persistent and enduring myths of the past century. It has been parroted by Hollywood, countless journalists, and generations of academics (though not necessarily by historians who specialize in the subject). But as Chesterton said, fallacies do not cease to be fallacies simply because they become fashions.

Doctrinaire Marxism-Leninism defined fascism as "the most reactionary and openly terroristic form of the dictatorship of finance capital, established by the imperialistic bourgeoisie to break the resistance of the working class and all the progressive elements of society." Trotsky, an admirer of Mussolini's, conceded that fascism was a "plebeian movement in origin" but that it was always "directed and financed by big capitalist powers."[5] This interpretation was foreordained because by the 1920s communists were convinced that they were witnessing capitalism's long overdue collapse. Marxist prophecy held that the capitalists would fight back to protect their interests rather than face extinction in the new socialist era. When fascism succeeded in Italy, communist seers simply declared, "This is it!" At the Fourth Congress of the Communist International in 1922, less than a month after the March on Rome—long before Mussolini consolidated power—the assembled communists settled on this interpretation with little debate over the actual facts on the ground.

That the defeated Italian Reds had already spread the rumor that their former comrade had betrayed the movement for his thirty pieces of silver only made this self-serving myth easier to swallow. Convinced that they alone were on the side of the people, the Reds responded to every political defeat by asking, *"Cui bono?"*—"Who benefits?" The answer had to be the ruling capitalists. "Fascism" thus became a convenient label for "desperate capitalists."

Ever since, whenever the left has met with political defeat, it has cried, "Fascism!" and insisted the fat cats were secretly pulling the strings. Max Horkheimer, the Frankfurt School Freudian Marxist, declared that no anticapitalist theories of fascism could even be entertained. "Whoever is not prepared to talk about capitalism should also remain silent about fascism." "Central to all socialist theories of fascism," writes the historian Martin Kitchen, "is the insistence on the close relationship between fascism and industry." Yale's Henry Ashby Turner calls this an "ideological straightjacket" that constrains virtually all Marxist-influenced scholarship. "Almost without exception . . . these writings suffer, as do those of 'orthodox' Marxists, from over-reliance on questionable, if not fraudulent scholarship, and from egregious misrepresentation of factual information."[6] In point of fact, there is zero evidence that Mussolini was the pawn of monolithic "big capitalism." Far from being uniformly supportive of fascism, big business was bitterly divided right up until Mussolini seized power. Fascist intellectuals, moreover, were openly contemptuous of capitalism and laissez-faire economics.

This socialist mythology became even cruder in response to Nazism. Hitler's success horrified the communists, though not because the communists were delicate little flowers. Nazi tactics in the 1920s were no more barbaric than communist tactics. What terrified the Reds was the fact that the Browns were beating them at their own game. Like Macy's bad-mouthing Gimbels, the Bolsheviks and their sympathizers mounted a desperate campaign to discredit Nazism. Marxist prophecy, it turned out, also made for good propaganda. Stalin personally issued orders never to use the word "socialist" when referring to fascists—even when fascists routinely identified themselves as socialists—and later, under the doctrine of social fascism, instructed followers to dub all competing progressive and socialist ideologies "fascist." Meanwhile, the left-wing press in Germany and throughout the West became a transmission belt for one bogus rumor after another that German industrialists were bankrolling the mad corporal and his Brownshirts. The success of this propaganda effort remains the chief reason liberals continue to link capitalism and Nazism, big business and fascism.

This is all nonsense, as we've seen. The National Socialist German Workers' Party was in every respect a grassroots populist party. Party leaders spouted all sorts of socialist prattle about seizing the wealth of the rich. *Mein Kampf* is replete with attacks on "dividend-hungry businessmen" whose "greed," "ruthlessness," and "short-sighted narrow-mindedness" were ruining the country. Hitler adamantly took the side of the trade union movement over "dishonorable employers." In 1941 he was still calling big-business men "rogues" and "cold-blooded money-grubbers" who were constantly complaining about not getting their way. When the left charged that Hitler was being funded by the capitalists, he responded that these were nothing but "filthy lies." In particular, German leftists claimed that the capitalist icon Hugo Stinnes was Hitler's secret patron—a charge for which there is still no evidence. Hitler exploded in rage at the suggestion. After all, he'd demonized Stinnes in speeches and articles for quite some time. Stinnes believed that economic improvement and not political revolution would solve Germany's woes, a view that Hitler considered sacrilegious.[7]

It's also important to recognize that while Hitler was first among equals in the Nazi Party in the 1920s, his comrades spoke for "the movement" as well. And the rank-and-file radicals of the "old fighters" were resolutely anti-big-business populists. Upon seizing power, the radicals in the Nazi Party Labor Union threatened to put business leaders in concentration camps if they didn't increase workers' wages. That is hardly the sort of thing one would expect from a party secretly on the take from big business all along.

According to Henry Ashby Turner's definitive scholarship, throughout the 1920s the Nazis received virtually no significant support from German—or foreign—industrialists. Some successful professionals, merchants, and small-business men did give nominal support, but that was usually driven by noneconomic concerns, such as rank anti-Semitism and populist rage. The Nazis made most of their money from membership dues and small contributions. Much of the rest came from selling the 1920s equivalent of bumper stickers and T-shirts. The Nazis hawked brown shirts and National Socialist flags. They also endorsed products such as cigarettes (despite Hitler's hatred of them) and even margarine. They charged admission to rallies, which were really youth "happenings." The foreign media also paid for interviews with Hitler. "Compared to the sustained intake of money raised by membership dues and other contributions of the Nazi rank and file," Turner explains, "the funds that reached the [party] from the side of big business assume at best a marginal significance."[8]

When Hitler did raise small amounts from wealthy donors, the motivations for such support more often had to do with radical chic than with preserving the capitalist system. Edwin Bechstein and Hugo Bruckmann are often cited as wealthy supporters of Nazism. But they only met Hitler through their wives, Helene and Elsa. Both women were middle-aged, established members of Munich high society, and while they jealously competed with each other, they shared a common love for Wagnerian opera and were united by their crushes on the fiery radical who would titillate the patrons of their respective salons by hanging his holstered gun and bullwhip on the coatrack before entering and expounding on everything from Wagner to Bolshevism to the Jews. Both women were incensed when rumors circulated that Hitler's whip was a gift from the *other* woman. The reality was that Hitler had received bullwhips from both women and let each believe that he only carried hers. Such scenes were more reminiscent of Tom Wolfe's account of Leonard Bernstein's fundraising party for the Black Panthers than of some star chamber where the scions of international capitalism schemed to use Hitler as a sword to beat back the Red menace. Eventually, the husbands offered their wives' pet project some money, but not very much. Hitler still had to ride to many appearances in the back of an old pickup truck.

THE FASCIST BARGAIN

Many liberals are correct when they bemoan the collusion of government and corporations. They even have a point when they decry special deals for Halliburton or Archer Daniels Midland as proof of creeping fascism. What they misunderstand *completely* is that this is the system they set up. This is the system they want. This is the system they mobilize and march for.

Debates about economics these days generally enjoy a climate of bipartisan asininity. Democrats want to "rein in" corporations, while Republicans claim to be "pro-business." The problem is that being "pro-business" is hardly the same thing as being pro–free market, while "reining in" corporations breeds precisely the climate liberals decry as fascistic.

The fascist bargain goes something like this. The state says to the industrialist, "You may stay in business and own your factories. In the spirit of cooperation and unity, we will even guarantee you profits and a lack of serious competition. In exchange, we expect you to agree with—and help implement—our political agenda." The moral and economic content of the agenda depends on the nature of the regime. The left looked at German business's support for the Nazi war machine and leaped to the conclusion that business always supports war. They did the same with American business after World War I, arguing that because arms manufacturers benefited from the war, the armaments industry was therefore responsible for it.

It's fine to say that incestuous relationships between corporations and governments are fascistic. The problem comes when you claim that such arrangements are inherently right-wing.[9] If the collusion of big business and government is right-wing, then FDR was a right-winger. If corporatism and propagandistic militarism are fascist, then Woodrow Wilson was a fascist and so were the New Dealers. If you understand the right-wing or conservative position to be that of those who argue for free markets, competition, property rights, and the other political values inscribed in the original intent of the American founding fathers, then big business in Fascist Italy, Nazi Germany, and New Deal America was not right-wing; it was left-wing, *and* it was fascistic. What's more, it still is.

Since the dawn of the Progressive Era, reformers have constructed an army of straw men, conjured a maelstrom of myths, to justify blurring the lines between business and government. According to civics textbooks, Upton Sinclair and his fellow muckrakers unleashed populist rage against the cruel excesses of the meatpacking industry, and as a result Teddy Roosevelt and his fellow progressives boldly reined in an industry run amok. The same story repeats itself for the accomplishments of other muckrakers, including the pro-Mussolini icons Ida Tarbell and Lincoln Steffens. This narrative lives on as generations of journalism students dream of exposing corporate malfeasance and prompting government-imposed "reform."

The problem is that it's totally untrue, a fact Sinclair freely acknowledged. "The Federal inspection of meat was, historically, established at the packers' request," Sinclair wrote in 1906. "It is maintained and paid for by the people of the United States for the benefit of the packers." The historian Gabriel Kolko concurs: "The reality of the matter, of course, is that the big packers were warm friends of regulation, especially when it primarily affected their innumerable small competitors." A spokesman for "Big Meat" (as we might call it today) told Congress, "We are now and have always been in favor of the extension of the inspection, also to the adoption of the sanitary regulations that will insure the very best possible conditions." The meatpacking conglomerates knew that federal inspection would become a marketing tool for their products and, eventually, a minimum standard. Small firms and butchers who'd earned the trust of consumers would be forced to endure onerous compliance costs, while large firms not only could absorb the costs more easily but would be able to claim their products were superior to uncertified meats.[10]

This story plays itself out again and again during the Progressive Era. The infamous steel industry—heirs to the nineteenth-century robber barons—embraced government intervention on a massive scale. The familiar fairy tale is that the government stepped in to control predatory monopolies. The truth is almost exactly the opposite. The big steel firms were terrified that free competition would undermine their predatory monopolies, so they asked the government to intervene and the government happily obliged. U.S. Steel, which was the product of 138 merged steel firms, was stunned to see its profits decline in the face of stiff competition. In response, the chairman of U.S. Steel, Judge Elbert Gary, convened a meeting of leading steel companies at the Waldorf-Astoria in 1907 with the aim of forming a "gentlemen's agreement" to fix prices. Representatives of Teddy Roosevelt's Justice Department attended the meetings. Nonetheless, the agreements didn't work, as some firms couldn't be trusted not to undersell others. "Having failed in the realm of economics," Kolko observes, "the efforts of the United States Steel group were to be shifted to politics." By 1909 the steel tycoon Andrew Carnegie was writing in the *New York Times* in favor of "Government control" of the steel industry. In June 1911 Judge Gary told Congress, "I believe we must come to enforced publicity [socialization] and government control . . . even as to prices." The Democrats—still clinging to classical liberal notions—rejected the proposal as "semi-socialistic."[11]

One need only look at Herbert Croly's *Promise of American Life* to see how fundamentally fascistic progressive economics were. Croly was contemptuous of competition. Trust-busting was a fool's errand. If a corporation got so big that it became a monopoly, Croly didn't believe it should be broken up; rather, it should be nationalized. Big business "contributed enormously to American economic efficiency," he explained. "Cooperation" was Croly's watchword: "It should be the effort of all civilized societies to substitute cooperation for competitive methods."[12] As a philosophical and practical matter, Croly opposed the very conception of the neutral rule of law for business. Since all legislation was ultimately aimed at discriminating against one interest or another (a view revived by critical legal theorists more than a century later), the state should abandon the charade of neutrality and instead embrace a "national" program that put the good of the collective ahead of the individual.

As we've seen, World War I offered a golden opportunity for Croly's agenda. Big business and the Wilson administration formed the Council of National Defense, or CND, according to Wilson, for the purpose of redesigning "the whole industrial mechanism . . . in the most effective way." "It is our hope," Hudson Motor Car Company's Howard Coffin explained in a letter to the Du Ponts, "that we may lay the foundation for that closely knit structure, industrial, civil, and military, which every thinking American has come to realize is vital to the future life of this country, in peace and in commerce, no less than in possible war."[13]

When the war broke out, the CND was largely folded into the War Industries Board, or WIB. Run by "dollar-a-year men" from the world of finance and business, the WIB set prices, trade quotas, wages, and, of course, profits. Trade associations were formed along vaguely syndicalist lines. "Business willed its own domination, forged its bonds, and policed its own subjection," wrote Grosvenor Clarkson, a WIBer and historian of the effort. The aim was for the "concentration of commerce, industry and all the powers of government." "Historians have generally concluded," writes Robert Higgs, "that these businessmen-turned-bureaucrats used their positions to establish and enforce what amounted to cartel arrangements for the various industries."[14]

Many industrialists wanted to keep the War Industries Board going after World War I, and politicians, including Herbert Hoover, tried to grant their wish. The war, horrible as it was, had proved that national planning worked. Stuart Chase, who coined the phrase "New Deal," explicitly cited two models for what America needed to do, the Soviet *Gosplan* and the war socialism of World War I. Rexford Tugwell gushed that laissez-faire had "melted away in the fierce new heat of nationalistic vision."[15]

The propaganda of the New Deal—"malefactors of great wealth" and all that—to the contrary, FDR simply endeavored to re-create the corporatism of the last war. The New Dealers invited one industry after another to write the codes under which they would be regulated (as they had been begging to do in many cases). The National Recovery Administration, or NRA, was even more aggressive in forcing industries to fix prices and in other ways collude with one another. The NRA approved 557 basic and 189 supplementary codes, covering roughly 95 percent of all industrial workers.

It was not only inevitable but *intended* for big business to get bigger and the little guy to get screwed. For example, the owners of the big chain movie houses wrote the codes in such a way that independents were nearly run out of business, even though 13,571 of the 18,321 movie theaters in America were independently owned. In business after business, the little guy was crushed or at least severely disadvantaged in the name of "efficiency" and "progress." The codes for industries dealing in cotton, wool, carpet, and sugar were—"down to the last comma"—simply the trade association agreements from the Hoover administration. And in almost every case big business came out the winner. In "virtually all the codes we have examined," reported Clarence Darrow in his final report investigating Hugh Johnson's NRA, "one condition has been persistent . . . In Industry after Industry, the larger units, sometimes through the agency of . . . [a trade association], sometimes by other means, have for their own advantage written the codes, and then, in effect and for their own advantage, assumed the administration of the code they have framed." We may believe that FDR fashioned the New Deal out of concern for the "forgotten man." But as one historian put it, "The principle . . . seemed to be: to him that hath it shall be given."[16]

Indeed, FDR's pragmatism and experimentalism, so cherished by liberals then and now, were of a deeply ideological sort: social planners should be given a free rein to do what they like until they get it right. Thurman Arnold, the theorist behind the new "religion of government" and director of FDR's antitrust division, abandoned the standard liberal antipathy for cartels, monopolies, and trusts and instead emphasized consumption.

All this was done with the acquiescence of the liberal establishment, later called the "new class" of managers, experts, and technocrats. The idea was that the smartest people should be immune to the rules of chaotic capitalism and vulgar politics. The "best practices" of business and engineering should be applied to politics. These schemes went by any number of labels—syndicalism, Fordism, Taylorism, technocracy—but the underlying impulse was the same. Businessmen were part of this new conventional wisdom. Gerard Swope, the president of GE, provides a perfect illustration of the business elite's economic worldview. A year before FDR took office, he published his modestly titled *The Swope Plan*. His idea was that the government would agree to suspend antitrust laws so that industries could collude in order to adjust "production to consumption." Industry would "no longer operate in independent units, but as a whole, according to rules laid out by a trade association . . . the whole supervised by some federal agency like the Federal Trade Commission." Under Swopism, as many in and out of government called it, the state would remove the uncertainty for the big-business man so that he could "go forward decisively instead of fearsomely."[17]

As transparently fascistic as all this sounds today, it sounded even more fascistic back then. New Deal staffers studied Mussolini's corporatism closely. *Fortune* and the fairly liberal *BusinessWeek* both devoted considerable space to praising the Italian "experiment." "The Corporate State is to Mussolini what the New Deal is to Roosevelt," proclaimed *Fortune*. During both the Hoover and the early Roosevelt administrations, hosts of independent economists from across the ideological spectrum noted the similarities between Italian and Nazi economic policies and American ones. William Welk, a leading scholar of Italian Fascist economics, wrote in *Foreign Affairs* that the NRA codes seemed like imitations of their Italian counterparts, only the Italian Fascists had paid much more attention to social justice.[18]

The view from abroad was little different. "We have not yet been informed whether, now that Rooseveltism has become openly and unmistakably Fascist, the British Trades Union Council means to withdraw its blessing and support from America's attempt to reform Capitalism," wrote Fenner Brockway, the British pacifist, socialist, and journalist, in the *New Leader*. Giuseppe Bottai, the Fascist minister of corporations until 1932, wrote an essay for *Foreign Affairs*, "Corporate State and the N.R.A.," in which he suggested that while the similarities were real, the Italian system treated labor better.[19]

The Nazis saw the similarities as well. "There is at least one official voice in Europe that expresses understanding of the methods and motives of President Roosevelt," began a *New York Times* report in July 1933. "This voice is that of Germany, as represented by Chancellor Adolf Hitler." The German leader told the *Times*, "I have sympathy with President Roosevelt because he marches straight toward his objective over Congress, over lobbies, over stubborn bureaucracies."[20] In July 1934 the Nazi Party's newspaper, *Der Völkische Beobachter*, described Roosevelt as America's "absolute lord and master," a man of "irreproachable, extremely responsible character and immovable will," and a "warmhearted leader of the people with a profound understanding of social needs." Roosevelt's books *Looking Forward* (which, as mentioned earlier, had been favorably reviewed by Mussolini himself) and *On Our Way* were translated into German and received lavish attention. Reviewers were quick to note the similarities between Nazi and New Deal policies.

So what was the essence of this "revolution from above"? In the economic sphere it was most often called "corporatism," a slippery word for dividing up industry into cooperative units, guilds, and associations that would work together under the rubric of "national purpose." Corporatism simply seemed like a more honest and straightforward attempt at what social planners and businessmen had been groping toward for decades. Other names proliferated as well, from "syndicalism" to "national planning" to, simply, the "Third Way." The new sense of national purpose, it was thought, would allow business and labor to put aside their class differences and hammer out what was best for everyone, in much the same way the war planners had in Germany, America, and throughout the West. The Third Way represented a widespread exhaustion with politics and a newfound faith in science and experts.

The image of the fasces conjures the spirit of the idea: strength in unity. Corporations or syndicates representing different sectors of the economy would, like the sticks around the fasces, bind tightly together for the "public interest."[21] Fascists agreed with Marxists that class conflict was a central challenge of economic life; they merely differed—often only at a theoretical level—on how the conflict should be resolved. By making citizens see themselves as Germans or Italians rather than as workers or bosses, corporatists hoped to make Hitler's declaration "There are no such thing as classes" a reality. Hitler in fact believed in classes—siding culturally and politically with the workers over the rich—but he, like most fascists, believed that class differences could be subordinated to the common good through nationalistic fervor. Under the Third Way, society would get all the benefits of capitalism with none of the drawbacks. The market would exist, but it would be constrained within "healthy" and "productive" borders. As the Italian Fascist procurator general Senator Silvio Longhi put it, "The state recognizes and safeguards individual property rights so long as they are not being exercised in a way which contravenes the prevailing collective interest."[22]

"I believe," proclaimed FDR in 1932, "that the individual should have full liberty of action to make the most of himself; but I do not believe that in the name of that sacred word, a few powerful interests should be permitted to make industrial cannon fodder of the lives of half of the population of the United States." Such Third Way rhetoric had a familiar echo in much Nazi propaganda as well. In a typical editorial, written on May 27, 1929, Goebbels explained that the party "was not against capital but against its misuse . . . For us, too, property is holy. But that does not mean that we sing in the chorus of those who have turned the concept of property into a distorted monstrosity . . . A people of free and responsible owners: that is the goal of German socialism."[23]

THE NAZI *GLEICHSCHALTUNG*

Fascism is the cult of unity, within all spheres and between all spheres. Fascists are desperate to erode the "artificial," legal, or cultural boundaries between family and state, public and private, business and the "public good." Unlike communist Jacobinism (or Jacobin communism, if you prefer), which expropriated property and uprooted institutions in order to remake society from the ground up, fascism pragmatically sought to preserve what was good and authentic about society while bending it to the common good. Interests or institutions that stood in the way of progress could be nationalized, to be sure. But if they worked with the regime, if they "did their part," they could keep their little factories, banks, clubs, and department stores.

It's revealing that corporatism has many of its roots in Catholic doctrine. The 1891 papal encyclical *Rerum novarum* proposed corporatism or syndicalism in response to the dislocations of the Industrial Revolution. In 1931 an updated encyclical, *Quadragesimo anno,* reaffirmed the principles of *Rerum novarum.* The two documents formed the backbone of progressive Catholic social thought. The Church's interest in corporatism stemmed from its belief that this was the best way to revive medieval social arrangements that gave man a greater sense of meaning in his life.

In short, corporatism was in large measure a spiritual project. Both the cold impersonal forces of Marx's history and the unloving dogma of Adam Smith's invisible hand would be rejected in favor of a Third Way that let the "forgotten man" *feel* like he had a place in the grand scheme of things.

The Nazis had a word for this process: *Gleichschaltung.* A political word borrowed—like so many others—from the realm of engineering, it meant "coordination." The idea was simple: all institutions needed to work together as if they were part of the same machine. Those that did so willingly were given wide latitude by the state. "Islands of separateness"—be they businesses, churches, or people—were worn down over time. There could be no rocks in the river of progress. In effect, the entire society agreed to the fascist bargain, in which they bought economic, moral, and political security in exchange for absolute loyalty to the ideals of the Reich. Of course, this was a false security; the fascist bargain is a Faustian bargain. But that is what people thought they were getting.

The Führer Principle was a key mechanism of the *Gleichschaltung.* Under the *Führerprinzip,* all of civil society was supposed to operate like a military unit with each cell reporting loyally to its leader, and those leaders to their leaders, all the way up to Hitler himself. For German businesses this was an easy transition because they already implemented something like a *Führerprinzip* in their organizations. In this sense German business culture contributed to the rise of Nazism, partly by laying the groundwork for a German Swopism, but indirectly as well, by readying the German mind for the sort of social control the Nazis wished to impose.

The Krupp *Konzern*—the reviled armory for the Third Reich—blazed the trail for the fascist bargain in the nineteenth century with Alfred Krupp's General Regulations. In the 1870s Krupp instituted a health service, schools, life insurance, workmen's compensation, a pension scheme, hospitals, even an old-age home for his employees. His General Regulations served as a mini social contract between him and his workers. In return for their loyalty—that is, eschewing labor unions and socialist agitation—Krupp provided all the perks the socialists were fighting for. "What may strike the Ausländer as odd," writes William Manchester, "is that Alfred's General Regulations were regarded—and in Essen are still regarded—as liberal. For the first time a German firm was spelling out its duties to its men."[24] Krupp's General Regulations became one of the central progressive documents for reform in Bismarck's Prussia and, by extension, much of the West. Today companies with similar policies get fawning profiles on *60 Minutes.*

Under the *Gleichschaltung,* the Nazis merely extended and broadened these arrangements. The state demanded loyalty from Krupp and his ilk in return for the protection of the state. This was merely another way of saying that all of society was to be Nazified—that is, politicized—so that every unit of society did its part for the larger cause. As a result, businesses became transmission belts for Nazi propaganda and values. The Nazi "war on cancer" was taken up by firms that banned smoking. The Nazi war on alcoholism and the Hitlerite emphasis on organic foods slowly pushed the beverage industry away from beer and booze and toward natural fruit juices. Children were a special priority. In 1933 the Nazis banned alcohol advertising aimed at children. In 1936 a new certification system was implemented that labeled some beverages and foodstuffs "fit" or "unfit" for children. (Coca-Cola was ruled unfit for kids.) That same year a full quarter of all the mineral water produced in Germany came from breweries. In 1938 the head of the Reich Health Office, Hans Reiter, declared that henceforth sweet cider was the official "people's drink" (*Volksgetränk*) of Germany.

The Nazis—always disproportionately supported by bureaucrats in the "helping professions"—benefited from particularly eager accomplices in the health-care industry. In a nation where democracy and civil liberties were swept aside and experts—doctors, regulators, and "industrial hygienists"—were promoted to positions of unparalleled authority, the Nazis offered a much-yearned-for opportunity to "get beyond politics." For example, the Reich Anticancer Committee proclaimed in its first annual report: "The year 1933 was a decisive one for the war against cancer: the national socialist revolution (*Umwälzung*) has created entirely new opportunities for sweeping measures in an area that until now has been rather limited . . . The energetic and unanimous engagement (*Einsatz*) of the medical profession has shown that new avenues have opened for the struggle against cancer in the new Germany."[25]

Vast public and moral health campaigns were put in place to promote safe working environments, along with the production of wholesome organic foods, anti-animal-cruelty measures, and other progressive advances. While many of these reforms were imposed from above by social engineers with the willing compliance of businessmen now freed from the usual concerns about such costly modifications, the Nazis also worked tirelessly to cultivate and encourage demand from below for these reforms. Everyone from the lowliest worker to the wealthiest baron was encouraged to believe and enforce the idea that if you weren't part of the solution, you were part of the problem. German consumers, too, were hectored relentlessly to buy products that promoted the "common good."

Language itself was bent to what could only be called Nazi political correctness. Victor Klemperer, a professor of Romance languages at the University of Dresden fired for his Jewish ancestry in 1935, dedicated himself to chronicling the subtle transformations of speech and daily life brought about by the *Gleichschaltung*. "The mechanization of the individual," he explained, "first manifested itself in *'Gleichschaltung.'* " He watched as phrases like "Hitler weather"—to describe a sunny day—crept into everyday conversation. The Nazis "changed the values, the frequency of words, [and] made into common property words that had previously been used by individuals or tiny troupes. They confiscated words for the party, saturated words and phrases and sentence forms with their poison. They made the language serve their terrible system. They conquered words and made them into their strongest advertising tools, at once the most public and the most secret."[26]

Popular culture, from television and film to marketing and advertising, was an essential tool for this process. Movie studios in particular were eager to work with the regime and vice versa. Goebbels put a great deal of stock in the medium, believing that "film is one of the most modern and far-reaching means of influencing the masses." But he assured the film industry that the government would not be taking over. Rather, this would be a public-private partnership. "We have no intention of obstructing production," he told studio heads in his first address to the industry, "neither do we wish to hamper private enterprise: On the contrary, this will receive a great deal of impetus through the national movement."[27] The film industry worked with the government, formally and informally, releasing mostly escapist fare for German audiences as well as a steady stream of allegorically worshipful films about Hitler. Movie audiences were subtly encouraged to change their thinking not merely about, say, Jews and foreign policy, but about what it meant to be a human being in the modern world.

Despite the Nazis' complete control of society, many still felt that big business was getting away with murder. Himmler was particularly vexed by the slow pace of his efforts to transform the way Germans ate: "The artificial is everywhere; everywhere food is adulterated, filled with ingredients that supposedly make it last longer, or look better, or pass as 'enriched,' or whatever else the industry's admen want us to believe . . . [W]e are in the hands of the food companies, whose economic clout and advertising make it possible for them to prescribe what we can and cannot eat . . . [A]fter the war we shall take energetic steps to prevent the ruin of our people by the food industries."[28] Here we can see the inexorable undertow of Third Way totalitarianism. Every problem in life must logically be the result of insufficient cooperation by institutions or individuals. If only we could turn the ratchet one more notch, then—click!—everything would fall into place and all contradictions would be eliminated.

Obviously, the Jews bore the brunt of the *Gleichschaltung*. They were the "other" against whom the Nazis defined their organic society. Given Jewish economic success, the business community of necessity played a central role in the "Aryanization" of society—a convenient excuse for businesses to seize Jewish holdings and for German professionals to take Jewish jobs in academia, the arts, and science. A great many Germans simply refused to make good on their debts to Jewish creditors. Banks foreclosed on mortgages. Vultures seized Jewish businesses or offered to pay pennies on the dollar for them, knowing full well that Jews had no recourse. Or they informed on their competitors, charging that Firm X was insufficiently committed to purging the stain of Judaism from its business.

Nothing so horrific happened in the United States, and it's unlikely that it would have, even if Hugh Johnson's darkest fantasies had been realized. But the practices of the Nazis and Johnson's NRA were more similar than different. Johnson's thugs broke down doors and threw people in jail for not participating with the Blue Eagle. Hitler's goons did likewise. "Those who are not with us are against us," Johnson roared, "and the way to show that you are a part of this great army of the New Deal is to insist on this symbol of solidarity." The New Dealers' slogan "We do our part" echoed the Nazi refrain

"The common good before the private good." After all, it was Stuart Chase, not Albert Speer, who argued in his *Economy of Abundance* that what was required was an "industrial general staff with dictatorial powers."[29]

As for popular culture, there isn't enough room to discuss the subject as fully as it deserves. The New Deal invested millions of dollars funding artists and writers who repaid this kindness by generating a vast body of artistic and literary work propping up the New Deal. But one episode in particular may shed light on the true nature of the period.

Like many other leading Americans, the media tycoon William Randolph Hearst believed America needed a dictator. After first backing the America Firster Jack Garner, he switched to FDR (and claimed that he put Roosevelt over the top at the Democratic convention). Deciding that the best way to influence FDR—and the American people—was via Hollywood, he personally reworked a script based on the book *Gabriel Over the White House,* which became a movie of the same name starring Walter Huston as President Judd Hammond.

The propagandistic nature of the film cannot be exaggerated. Hammond, a Hoover-like partisan hack of a president, has a car accident and is visited by the archangel Gabriel. When he recovers, he is reborn with a religious fervor to do good for America. He fires his entire cabinet—big-business lackeys all! Congress impeaches Hammond, and in response he appears before a joint session to proclaim, "We need action—immediate and effective action." After this he suspends Congress, assuming the "temporary" power to make all laws. He orders the formation of a new "Army of Construction" answerable only to him, spends billions on one New Deal–like program after another, and nationalizes the sale and manufacture of alcohol. When he meets with resistance from gangsters, presumably in league with his political enemies, he orders a military trial run by his aide-de-camp. Immediately after the trial, the gangsters are lined up against a wall behind the courthouse and executed. With that victory under his belt, Hammond goes on to bring about world peace by threatening to destroy any nation that disobeys him—or reneges on its debts to America. He dies of a heart attack at the end and is eulogized as "one of the greatest presidents who ever lived."

One of the project's uncredited script doctors was the Democratic presidential nominee, Franklin D. Roosevelt. He took time off from the campaign to read the script and suggested several important changes that Hearst incorporated into the film. "I want to send you this line to tell you how pleased I am with the changes you made in 'Gabriel Over the White House,' " Roosevelt wrote a month into office. "I think it is an intensely interesting picture and should do much to help."[30]

Ever since, Hollywood has been equally eager to help liberal causes and politicians. The movie *Dave,* starring Kevin Kline as a bighearted populist who is asked to impersonate a stricken (conservative) president and engineers a socially conscious coup d'état, is merely an updating of the same premise.

THE LIBERAL FASCIST BARGAIN

Today we still live under the fundamentally fascistic economic system established by Wilson and FDR. We do live in an "unconscious civilization" of fascism, albeit of a friendly sort infinitely more benign than that of Hitler's Germany, Mussolini's Italy, or FDR's America. This is the system I call liberal fascism.

Just because business thrives under capitalism doesn't mean businessmen are necessarily principled capitalists. Businessmen—at least those at the helm of very large corporations—do not like risk, and capitalism by definition requires risk. Capital must be put to work in a market where nothing is assured. But businessmen are, by nature and training, encouraged to beat back uncertainty and risk. Hence, as a group, they aren't principled capitalists but opportunists in the most literal sense.[31]

Most successful businessmen would prefer not to bother with politics. For years both Wal-Mart and Microsoft boasted that they had no interest in Washington. Microsoft's chief, Bill Gates, bragged that he was "from the other Washington," and he basically had one lonely lobbyist hanging around the nation's capital. Gates changed his mind when the government nearly destroyed his company. The Senate Judiciary Committee invited him to Washington, D.C., to atone for his success, and the senators, in the words of the *New York Times,* "took a kind of giddy delight in making the wealthiest man in America squirm in his seat."[32] In response, Gates hired an army of consultants, lobbyists, and lawyers to fight off the government. In the 2000 presidential election, Wal-Mart ranked 771st in direct contributions to federal politicians. In the intervening years, unions and regulators began to drool over the enormous target the mega-retailer had become. In 2004 Wal-Mart ranked as the single largest corporate political action committee. In 2006 it launched an unprecedented "voter education" drive.

There's a special irony to the example of Wal-Mart. One of the Nazis' most salient political issues was the rise of the department store. They even promised in their 1920 party platform to take over the Wal-Marts of their day. Plank 16 reads: "We demand the creation of a healthy middle class and its conservation, immediate communalization of the great [department stores] and their being leased at low cost to small firms, the utmost consideration of all small firms in contracts with the State, county or municipality." Once in power, the Nazis didn't completely make good on their promise, but they did ban department stores from entering a slew of businesses—much as today's critics would like to do with Wal-Mart. In America, too, fascist movements—such as Father Coughlin's National Union for Social Justice—targeted department stores as the engine of community breakdown and middle-class anxiety.[33]

Wal-Mart provides an example, in microcosm, of how liberals use the word "fascist" to describe anything outside the control of the state. For example, the New York *Daily News* columnist Neil Steinberg dubbed the company "an enormous fascist beast rising to its feet and searching for new worlds to conquer."[34] His solution to conquer the fascist beast? Invite it into bed with government, under the sheet of regulation, of course. It's also worth noting that both Wal-Mart and Microsoft found it necessary to protect themselves from Washington, not merely because government couldn't resist meddling, but because their competitors couldn't resist lobbying government to meddle.

This is one of the underappreciated consequences of the explosion in the size of government. So long as some firms are willing to prostitute themselves to Uncle Sam, every business feels the pressure to become a whore. If Acme can convince the government to pick on

Ajax, Ajax has no choice but to pressure the government not to. In effect, politicians become akin to stockbrokers, taking a commission from clients who win and lose alike. Microsoft's competitors were eager to have the government tear it apart for their own benefit. This dynamic was rampant in Nazi Germany. Steel firms, increasingly reluctant to play the Nazis' game, pressed for more protections of their autonomy. As a result, chemical firms leaped up as loyal Nazis and took government contracts away from the steel industry.

Most businesses are like beehives. If government doesn't bother them, they don't bother government. If government meddles with business, the bees swarm Washington. Yet time and again, the liberal "remedy" for the bee problem is to smack the hive with a bigger stick. There are hundreds of medical industry lobbies, for specific diseases, specialties, and forms of treatment, each of which spends a fortune in direct and indirect lobbying and advertising. Do you know which medical profession spends almost nothing? Veterinary care. Why? Because Congress spends almost no time regulating it.[35] Why do pharmaceutical industries spend so much money lobbying politicians and regulators? Because they are so heavily regulated that they cannot make major decisions without a by-your-leave from Washington.

As the size and scope of government have grown, so have the numbers of businesses petitioning the government. In 1956 the *Encyclopedia of Associations* listed forty-nine hundred groups. Today it lists over twenty-three thousand. Keep in mind that John Commons, a titan of liberal economics, believed that the proliferating influence of trade associations rendered us a fascist system nearly seventy years ago! Of course, not all of these groups are formal lobbying organizations, but they all work with—or on—government in some way. Meanwhile, the total number of registered lobbyists in the United States has tripled since 1996, and it has doubled in the last five years alone. As of this writing there were roughly thirty-five thousand registered lobbyists in Washington. From 1970 to 1980, when twenty new federal agencies were born, the number of lawyers in Washington roughly doubled to forty thousand.[36] These numbers don't come close to capturing the full scope of the situation. PR firms, law firms, advocacy groups, and think tanks have exploded across the nation's capital to do "indirect" lobbying of the press,

opinion makers, Congress, and others in order to create a more favorable "issues environment." When one of my lobbyist friends
takes me out for a beer, he calls it "third-party outreach."

Corporations have long had Washington offices, but the tradition
used to be that they were professional backwaters, the place you sent
Ted when his drinking became too much of a problem or where you
let Phil diddle around until he reached retirement age. Now they are
enormous and very professional operations. Between 1961 and 1982
the number of corporate offices in Washington grew tenfold. Salaries
for corporate lobbyists have been rising exponentially over the last
decade.

In Nazi Germany businesses proved their loyalty to the state by
being good "corporate citizens," just as they do today. The means of
demonstrating this loyalty differed significantly, and the moral content of the different agendas was categorical. Indeed, for the sake of
argument let us concede that what the Nazi regime expected of
"good German businesses" and what America expects of its corporate leaders differed enormously. This doesn't change some important fundamental similarities.

Consider, for example, the largely bipartisan and entirely well-
intentioned Americans with Disabilities Act, or ADA, celebrated
everywhere as a triumph of "nice" government. The law mandated
that businesses take a number of measures, large and small, to ac-
commodate customers and employees with various handicaps.
Offices had to be retrofitted to be wheelchair compliant. Various
public signs had to be written in Braille. Devices to aid the hearing
impaired had to be made available. And so on.

Now imagine you are the CEO of Coca-Cola. Your chief objection
to this law is that it will cost you a lot of money, right? Well, not
really. If you know that the CEO of Pepsi is going to have to make
the same adjustments, there's really no problem for you. All you
have to do is add a penny—or really a fraction of a penny—to the
cost of a can of Coke. Your customers will carry the freight, just as
Pepsi's customers will. The increase won't cost you market share,
because your price compared with your competitor's has stayed
pretty much the same. Your customers probably won't even notice
the price hike.

Now imagine that you own a small, regional soft drink company.

You've worked tirelessly toward your dream of one day going eyeball-to-eyeball with Coke or Pepsi. Proportionally speaking, making your factories and offices handicapped-friendly will cost you vastly more money, not just in terms of infrastructure, but in terms of the bureaucratic legal compliance costs (Coke and Pepsi have enormous legal departments; you don't). Plans to expand or innovate will have to be delayed because there's no way you can pass on the costs to your customers. Or imagine you're the owner of an even smaller firm hoping to make a play at your regional competitors. But you have 499 employees, and for the sake of argument, the ADA fully kicks in at 500 employees. If you hire just one more, you will fall under the ADA. In other words, hiring just one thirty-thousand-dollar-a-year employee will cost you millions.

The ADA surely has admirable intent and legitimate merits. But the very nature of such do-gooding legislation empowers large firms, entwines them with political elites, and serves as a barrier to entry for smaller firms. Indeed, the penalties and bureaucracy involved in even trying to fire someone can amount to guaranteed lifetime employment. Smaller firms can't take the risk of being forced to provide a salary in perpetuity, while big companies understand that they've in effect become "too big to fail" because they are de facto arms of the state itself.

Perhaps the best modern example of the fascist bargain at work is the collusion of government and the tobacco companies. Let us recall that in the 1990s the tobacco companies were demonized for selling "the only product which, if used properly, will kill you." Bill Clinton and Al Gore staked vast amounts of political capital in their war against "Big Tobacco." The entire narrative of "right-wing" corporations versus progressive reformers played itself out almost daily on the front pages of newspapers and on the nightly news. The attorney general of Texas proclaimed that "history will record the modern-day tobacco industry alongside the worst of civilization's evil empires." Christopher Lehmann-Haupt suggested in the *New York Times Book Review* that "only slavery exceeds tobacco as a curse on American history." Tobacco executives were "the most criminal, disgusting, sadistic, degenerate group of people on the face of the earth," according to one widely quoted antitobacco activist.[37]

Out of this environment sprang forth the—unconstitutional—

tobacco settlement whereby "Big Tobacco" agreed to pay $246 *billion* to state governments. Why would the tobacco companies agree to a settlement that cost them so much money and that forced them to take out ads disparaging their own product and pay for educational efforts to dissuade children from ever becoming their customers? The reason, quite simply, is that it was in their interests. The tobacco companies not only had their lawsuits settled; they bought government approval of a new illegal cartel. "Big Tobacco" raised prices above the costs imposed by the settlement, guaranteeing a tidy profit. Smaller companies who did not agree to the settlement are still forced to make large escrow payments. When these firms started to thrive, cutting into the market share of the big tobacco companies, state governments jumped in and ordered them to make even larger payments. "All states have an interest in reducing . . . sales [by non-settlement companies] in every state," Vermont's attorney general warned fellow state attorneys general. The government in effect enforces a system by which small businesses are crushed in order to maintain the high profits of "Big Tobacco." Now, you might think this is all fine. But how—exactly—is this a free-market approach? How—exactly—is this unlike the corporatism of Fascist Italy, Nazi Germany, and Hugh Johnson's NRA?[38]

This is the hidden history of big business from the railroads of the nineteenth century, to the meatpacking industry under Teddy Roosevelt, to the outrageous cartel of "Big Tobacco" today: supposedly right-wing corporations work hand in glove with progressive politicians and bureaucrats in both parties to exclude small businesses, limit competition, ensure market share and prices, and generally work as government by proxy. Many of JFK's "action-intellectuals" were businessmen who believed that government should be run by postpartisan experts who could bring the efficiencies of business to government by blurring the lines between business and government. Big business rallied behind LBJ, not the objectively free-enterprise Barry Goldwater. Free marketeers often decry Richard Nixon's wage and price controls, but what is usually forgotten is that big business cheered them. The day after Nixon announced his corporatist scheme, the president of the National Association of Manufacturers declared, "The bold move taken by the President to strengthen the American economy deserves the support and cooperation of all groups."[39] Jimmy

Carter's supposedly prescient efforts to tackle the energy crisis led to the creation of the Energy Department, which became—and remains—a piggy bank for corporate interests. Archer Daniels Midland has managed to reap billions from the environmental dream of "green" alternative fuels like ethanol.

Indeed, we are all Crolyites now. It was Croly's insight that if you aren't going to expropriate private businesses, but instead want to use business to implement your social agenda, then you should want businesses themselves to be as big as possible. What's easier, strapping five thousand cats to a wagon or a couple of giant oxen? Al Gore's rhetoric about the need to "tame Big Oil" and the like is apposite. He doesn't want to nationalize "Big Oil"; he wants to yoke it to his own agenda. Likewise, Hillary Clinton's proposed health-care reforms, as well as most of the proposals put forward by leading Democrats (and a great many Republicans), involve the fusion of big government and big business. The economic ideas in Hillary Clinton's *It Takes a Village* are breathlessly corporatist. "A number of our most powerful telecommunications and computer companies have joined forces with the government in a project to connect every classroom in America to the Internet," she gushes. "Socially minded corporate philosophies are the avenue to future prosperity and social stability."[40] It doesn't take a Rosetta stone to decipher what liberals mean by "socially minded corporate philosophies."

The granddaddy of all such "philosophies" is of course industrial policy, the ghost of corporatism made flesh in modern liberalism. In 1960 President Kennedy called for a "new partnership" with corporate America. In the 1970s Jimmy Carter called for "reindustrialization" under a new "social contract" to deal with the "crisis of competitiveness." A young aide in the Carter administration named Robert Reich launched his career as a buzz-phrase generator, spewing out such impressive-sounding nuggets as "target stimulants" and "indicative planning." Later, the "Atari Democrats" once again claimed that the "future" lay in "strategic partnerships" between the public and the private sectors.

In the 1980s envy for corporatist "Japan Inc." reached delirious proportions. The intellectual descendants of those who worshipped Bismarck's Prussia and Mussolini's Ministry of Corporations now fell under the spell of Japan's Ministry of International Trade and

Industry, which soon became the lodestar of enlightened economic policy. James Fallows led an all-star cast of liberal intellectuals— including Clyde Prestowitz, Pat Choate, Robert Kuttner, Ira Magaziner, Robert Reich, and Lester Thurow—in a quest for the holy grail of government-business "collaboration."

Reich was one of the pioneers of the Third Way movement. Indeed, Mickey Kaus writes that Third Way rhetoric is Reich's "most annoying habit" and his "characteristic mode of argument."[41] In 1983 Reich wrote *The Next American Frontier,* in which he championed "an extreme form of corporatism" (Kaus's words) where in exchange for "restructuring assistance" from the government, businesses would "agree to maintain their old work forces intact." Workers would become de facto citizens of their companies, in a relationship eerily similar to Krupp's General Regulations. And in an even more eerie echo of Italian Fascist corporatist thought, corporations would "largely replace geographic jurisdictions as conduits of government support for economic and human development." Social services—health care, day care, education, and so forth—would all be provided via your employer. This was all not only good but inevitable because "business enterprises," according to Reich, "are rapidly becoming the central mediating structures in American society, replacing geographic communities as the locus of social services and, indeed, social life."[42]

Yet somehow it's the economic *right* that wants corporations to have more control over our lives.

In 1984 the former Republican strategist Kevin Phillips wrote *Staying on Top: The Business Case for a National Industrial Strategy.* "Businessmen," Phillips warned, "must set aside old concepts of laissez-faire . . . it is time for the U.S. to begin plotting its economic future" on a new Third Way course.[43] Amusingly, Phillips has also argued that George W. Bush's great-grandfather S. P. Bush was a war profiteer because he served on Woodrow Wilson's War Industries Board, the very model of the system Phillips advocates.

In 1992 Bill Clinton and Ross Perot both tapped into the widespread craving for a "new alliance" between government and business (in 1991, 61 percent of Americans said they supported some such relationship). "Without a national economic strategy, this country has been allowed to drift," candidate Clinton declared in a typical speech. "Meanwhile, our competitors have organized themselves around clear national goals to save, promote and enhance high-wage, high-growth jobs." Clinton was ultimately foiled by Congress and the federal deficit in his hope to "invest" hundreds of billions of dollars in his strategic plan for industry. But his administration did try very hard to "target" specific industries for help, to very little effect—unless you count Al Gore's "invention" of the Internet. Hillary Clinton's ill-fated health-care plan sought to dragoon the health-care industry into a web where it would be impossible to tell where government began and the private sector left off. Small businesses, like those poor dry cleaners and newspaper boys during the New Deal, simply had to take one for the team. When it was pointed out to her that small businesses would be devastated by her plan, Clinton dismissed the complaints, saying, "I can't save every undercapitalized entrepreneur in America."[44]

Democratic, and most Republican, health-care plans don't call for expropriating the private property of doctors and pharmaceutical companies or even for the cessation of employer-provided health care. Rather, they want to use corporations for government by proxy. There's a reason liberal economists joke that General Motors is a health-care provider that makes cars as an industrial by-product.

GM offers an ironic confirmation of Marxist logic. According to orthodox Marxism, the capitalist system becomes fascist as its internal contradictions get the better of it. As a theory of political economy, this analysis falls apart. But at the retail level, there's an undeniable truth to it. Industries that once had a proudly free-market stance suddenly sprout arguments in favor of protectionism, "industrial policy," and "strategic competitiveness" once they find that they can't hack it in the market. The steel and textile industries, certain automobile companies—Chrysler in the 1980s, GM today—and vast swaths of agriculture claim that the state and business should be "partners" at precisely the moment it's clear they can no longer compete. They quickly become captives of politicians seeking to protect jobs or donations or both. These "last-gasp capitalists" do the country a great disservice by skewing the political climate toward a modified form of national socialism and corporatism. They're *fleeing* the rough-and-tumble of capitalist competition for the warm embrace of *It Takes a Village* economics, and Hillary Clinton calls it "progress."

Look, for example, at which agricultural sectors lobby the government most and which tend to leave it alone. Big sugar growers in the Midwest and Florida have spent millions to protect their industry from foreign—and domestic—competition precisely because they are so uncompetitive. And the return on their investment has been huge. In 1992 a handful of sugar refiners gave then–New York Senator Al D'Amato a mere $8,500 in campaign contributions. In return D'Amato successfully supported a tariff rebate to the sugar industry worth $365 million—a return of about 4 million percent. The sugar industry accounts for 17 percent of all agricultural lobbying in the United States. Meanwhile, apple growers—like most fruit and vegetable farmers—spend relatively little lobbying for subsidies because their industry is competitive. But they do have to lobby the government to keep it from subsidizing uncompetitive farmers who might try to move into the fruit and vegetable market.[45]

There's no sector of the American economy more suffused with corporatism than agriculture. Indeed, both Democrats and Republicans are decidedly fascistic when it comes to the "family farmer," pretending that their policies are preserving some traditional *völkisch* lifestyle while in reality they're subsidizing enormous corporations.

But corporatism is only part of the story. Just as corporations were enmeshed in the larger Nazi *Gleichschaltung,* supposedly right-wing big business is central to the progressive coordination of contemporary society. If big business is so right-wing, why do huge banks fund liberal and left-wing charities, activists, and advocacy groups, then brag about it in commercials and publicity campaigns? How to explain that there's virtually no major issue in the culture wars—from abortion to gay marriage to affirmative action—where big business has played a major role on the American right while there are dozens of examples of corporations supporting the liberal side?

Indeed, the myth of the right-wing corporation allows the media to tighten liberalism's grip on both corporations and the culture. John McCain perfectly symbolizes this catch-22 of modern liberalism. McCain despises the corrupting effect of "big money" in politics, but he is also a major advocate of increased government regulation of business. Apparently he cannot see that the more government regulates business, the more business is going to take an interest in "regulating" government. Instead, he has concluded that he should try to regulate political speech, which is like decrying the size of the garbage dump and deciding the best thing to do is regulate the flies.

These speech regulations in turn give an unfair advantage to some very big businesses—media conglomerates, movie studios, and such—to express their political views in ways exempt from government censorship. It's no surprise that some of these outlets tend to celebrate McCain's genius and courage and use their megaphones to expand on the need for him to go even further and for other politicians to follow his lead. Of course, this dynamic is much larger than mere regulation. The *New York Times* is pro-choice and supports pro-choice candidates—openly on its editorial pages, more subtly in its news pages. Pro-life groups need to *pay* to get their views across, but such paid advertising is heavily regulated, thanks to McCain, at exactly the moment it might influence people—that is, near Election Day. One can replace abortion with gun control, gay marriage, environmentalism, affirmative action, immigration, and other issues, and the dynamic remains the same.

This is how the liberal *Gleichschaltung* works; contrary voices are regulated, barred, banned when possible, mocked and marginalized when not. Progressive voices are encouraged, lionized, amplified—in the name of "diversity," or "liberation," or "unity," and, most of all, "progress."

Go into a Starbucks sometime and pick up one of their brochures highlighting their Corporate Social Responsibility Report. The report covers all the progressive concerns—the environment, trade, sustainable development, and so on. It devotes a whole section to "embracing diversity" in which the huge multinational boasts that it is "striving to increase our diversity in our U.S. workforce." Thirty-two percent of its vice presidents are women and 9 percent people of color. They spend $80 million a year with minority- and women-owned suppliers and provide "extensive diversity training courses to address our partners' relevant business needs. Diversity content is also woven through our general training practices." "Partners," by the way, is the Orwellian term they use for "employees."[46] In the new corporatism, we are all "partners" after all.

Environmentalism in particular offers a number of eerie parallels to fascist practices, including as an overarching rationale for corporatist policies. According to generic fascism, an atmosphere of crisis must be maintained in order to circumvent conventional rules. Today, while Hollywood and the press relentlessly hype the threat of global warming, big business works assiduously to form alliances and partnerships with government as if the fight against global warming were the moral equivalent of war. Indeed, Al Gore—who makes much of such public-private partnerships—claims that global warming is equivalent to the Holocaust and anybody who denies it is the moral equivalent of a Holocaust denier. Meanwhile, one oil company after another markets itself as a vital ally against global warming. British Petroleum runs creepily propagandistic ads in which it assures the viewer that it has enlisted in the environmental crusade and is moving "beyond petroleum." When the late libertarian crusader Julian Simon visited an oil installation in Alaska, he got so sick of hearing managers boast about the "environmental benefits" of their work that he finally asked, "What do you produce here? Oil or environmental benefits?"[47]

GE, the birthplace of Swopism, today spends millions of dollars promoting its "Ecomagination" program, through which it hopes to prove that GE is a progressive company. GE's CEO declared at the launch of his green initiative, "It's no longer a zero-sum game—things that are good for the environment are also good for business." The audience, eating organic hors d'oeuvres and drinking wine from a solar-powered winery, listened enthusiastically as the head of the biggest industrial manufacturer in America explained, "Industry cannot solve the problems of the world alone. We need to work in concert with government,"[48] No surprise, then, that GE's launch party was held at its Washington office. Indeed, the agenda behind "ecomagination" is to invest in "clean" and "green" technologies, and then lobby government to subsidize them through tax cuts or outright grants.

Corporations' power to "switch on" their workers to larger political agendas is a vastly underappreciated aspect of modern American civilization. Diversity is a perfect case in point. Big corporations have a vested interest in supporting diversity for a host of legitimate reasons. No firm wants to appear hostile to potential customers, for example. Nor is it smart to turn away qualified applicants out of racial animus. Moreover, the legal regime *requires* firms to be diverse whenever possible. And just as laws like the ADA help big businesses over small ones, affirmative action has the same effect. According to the Yale Law School professor Peter Schuck, affirmative action programs "also tend to advantage large companies by imposing onerous reporting, staffing, and other compliance costs on smaller competitors who cannot bear them as easily."[49] Survey data confirm that CEOs of large firms are more likely to support mandatory affirmative action programs than the CEOs of small firms.

Such progressive leadership doesn't come without a heavy investment in reeducation. Almost all mid-level and senior executives in corporate America have been through "diversity training" and/or "sexual harassment training," and often they're sent back for further reeducation—usually because the definition of "tolerance" has been ratcheted up. Corporations have accepted the logic of diversity gurus who insist that if you aren't actively promoting diversity—with goals, timetables, and the like—you are actively opposing it. The totalitarian nature of this training has not gotten nearly the attention it deserves—partly because journalists themselves have been so thoroughly reprogrammed by the giant corporations they work for.

Ask yourself this: What would happen to the businessman who simply refused to employ the acceptable number of black—or, one day soon, gay—applicants? Let's assume that this businessman is an evil person, racist, mean, miserly. But there was once a notion that freedom involved the right to be bad. So let's say this businessman refuses to hire blacks, gays, Jews, or members of other "oppressed" groups. What happens next? First he gets a letter from the government saying he has to have a workforce that looks like America. Then he'll get another letter. Perhaps he'll also get a letter from some disappointed job applicant threatening to sue. Eventually, he will be brought before a judge and told he must hire people he doesn't want to hire. If he still refuses, he may lose a lot of money in a civil suit. Or he might have his company taken away from him and put into receivership. If he persists in his stubborn independence, the state will, one way or another, take away his company. No doubt the Robert Reichs of the world will say that you have the right to employ the people you want, so long as your rights don't intrude on the "common good."

We might even agree with Reich because we think discrimination is evil. But is it really any less fascistic than telling a businessman that he must fire the Jews in his employ? Or if that's too dark a rumination, consider this: the restaurant chain Hooters came within a hairbreadth of being forced to hire men as "Hooters girls." It sounds funny, but just because something is done in the name of diversity doesn't make it un-fascist. It just makes it a nicer form of fascism.

· 9 ·

Brave New Village:
Hillary Clinton and the
Meaning of Liberal Fascism

LIBERALISM IS A culture and a dogma, much as conservatism is. Individual liberals may think they've reached their conclusions through careful deliberation—and no doubt many have—but there is no escaping the undertow of history and culture. Ideas and ideology are transmitted in more ways than we can count, and ignorance about where our ideas come from doesn't mean they don't come from somewhere.

Now, of course, this doesn't mean that the past has an iron grip on the present. For example, I am a strong supporter of states' rights. Racists once used support for states' rights as a cover for perpetuating Jim Crow. That does not mean that I am in favor of Jim Crow. But, as discussed earlier, conservatives have had to work very, very hard to explain why states' rights is no longer an argument about preserving Jim Crow. When someone asks me why my support for federalism won't lead to Jim Crow, I have answers at the ready. No such similar intellectual effort exists, or is required, on the left. Liberals are confident they've always been on the right side of history. George Clooney expresses a common sentiment among liberals when he says, "Yes, I'm a liberal, and I'm sick of it being a bad word. I don't know at what time in history liberals have stood on the wrong side of social issues."[1]

This is one of the main reasons I've written this book: to puncture the smug self-confidence that simply by virtue of being liberal one is also virtuous. At the same time, I need to repeat that I am not playing the movie backward. Today's liberals aren't the authors of past generations' mistakes any more than I'm responsible for the callousness of some conservative who championed states' rights for the wrong reason well before I was born. No, the problems with liberalism today reside in liberalism today. The relevance of the past is that unlike the conservative who has wrestled with his history to make sure he does not repeat it, liberals see no need to do anything of the sort. And so, armed with complete confidence in their own good intentions, they happily go marching past boundaries we should stay well clear of. They reinvent ideological constructs we've seen before in earlier times, unaware of their pitfalls, blithely confident that the good guys could never say or do anything "fascist" because fascism is by definition anything not desirable. And liberalism is nothing if not the organized pursuit of the desirable.

Hillary Clinton is a fascinating person, not because of her dull and unremarkable personality, but because she is a looking glass through which we can see liberal continuity with the past and glimpse at least one possible direction of its future. She and her husband have been like Zeligs of the liberal left, appearing everywhere, interacting with everyone who has influenced liberalism over the decades. Because she is smart and ambitious, she has balanced idealism with cynicism, ideology with calculation. This, of course, is true of a great many politicians. But to the extent Hillary Clinton deserves the fame and attention, it is because observers believe she has the insight, advisers, and institutional power to pick the winning combinations.

If Waldo Frank and J. T. Flynn were right that American fascism would be distinct from its European counterparts by virtue of its gentility and respectability, then Hillary Clinton is the fulfillment of their prophecy. But more than that, she is a representative figure, the leading member of a generational cohort of elite liberals who (unconsciously of course) brought fascist themes into mainstream liberalism. Specifically, she and her cohort embody the maternal side of fascism—which is one reason why it is not more clearly recognized as such.

What follows, then, is a group portrait of Hillary and her friends—the leading proponents and exemplars of liberal fascism in our time.

THE POLITICS OF HUMAN RECONSTRUCTION

Hillary Clinton is conventionally viewed by her supporters as a liberal—or by conservative opponents as a radical leftist in liberal sheep's clothing; but it is more accurate to view her as an old-style progressive and a direct descendant of the Social Gospel movement of the 1920s and 1930s.

Nothing makes this clearer than the avowedly religious roots of her political vocation. Born to a Methodist family in Park Ridge, Illinois, she always had a special attachment to the Social Gospel. She was an active member in her church youth group as a teenager and the only one of the Rodham kids to regularly attend Sunday services. "She's really a self-churched woman," the Reverend Donald Jones, her former youth minister and mentor, told *Newsweek*.[2]

Jones was being humble. The truth is that he was a major influence, the most important person in her life outside of her parents, according to many biographers. A disciple of the existential German émigré theologian Paul Tillich, Jones was a radical pastor who eventually lost his ministry for being too political. Hillary wrote to Jones regularly while in college. When she moved to Arkansas, Clinton taught Sunday school and often spoke as a lay preacher on the topic "Why I Am a United Methodist" at Sunday services. Even today, Jones told *Newsweek,* "when Hillary talks it sounds like it comes out of a Methodist Sunday-school lesson."[3]

Jones bought Hillary a subscription to the Methodist magazine *motive* as a graduation present just before she went off to Wellesley. Spelled with a lowercase *m* for reasons no one but the editors probably ever cared about, *motive* in the late 1960s and early 1970s (when it folded) was an indisputably radical left-wing organ, as mentioned earlier.

Three decades later Clinton recalled for *Newsweek* that her thinking about the Vietnam War really changed when she read an essay in *motive* by Carl Oglesby. *Newsweek* chose to portray this as an endearing remembrance by a spiritual liberal, describing Oglesby as a "Methodist theologian." But this description is highly misleading.[4] Oglesby, elected president of the Students for a Democratic Society, or SDS, in 1965, was a leading antiwar activist. His argument against

Vietnam was theological only in the sense that liberal fascism is a political religion. Communist countries were good, according to Oglesby, because they were pragmatically trying to "feed, clothe, house and cure their people" in the face of persecution by a "virulent strain" of American imperialism and capitalism. Violence by oppressed peoples in the Third World or in the American ghetto was entirely rational and even commendable.[5]

Hillary Clinton saw such radical politics as cut from the same cloth as her religious mission. After all, she was reading this material in an official Methodist publication given to her by her minister. "I still have every issue they sent me," she told *Newsweek*.[6]

In 1969 Hillary was the first student in Wellesley's history to give a commencement address at her own graduation. Whether she began to see herself as a feminist leader at this time or whether the experience simply reinforced such aspirations is unknowable. But from that point on, Hillary increasingly draped herself in the rhetoric of the movement—the youth movement, the women's movement, the antiwar movement—and gravitated toward others who believed that both her generation and her gender had a rendezvous with destiny. The speech had such an impact that her photo made it into *Life* magazine, which picked her as one of the new generation's leaders (Ira Magaziner, a student at Brown University and Hillary's future health-care guru, was also highlighted by *Life*).

Trimmed of its New Age hokum, Hillary Clinton's Wellesley commencement address was an impassioned search for meaning, dripping with what by now should be familiar sentiments. "We are, all of us, exploring a world that none of us even understands and attempting to create within that uncertainty. But there are some things we feel, feelings that our prevailing, acquisitive, and competitive corporate life, including tragically the universities, is not the way of life for us. We're searching for a more immediate, ecstatic and penetrating mode of living." She continued: "We're not interested in social reconstruction; it's human reconstruction" they were interested in. College life, she explained, had briefly lifted the "burden of inauthentic reality." It gave the students an opportunity to search for authenticity. "Every protest, every dissent, whether it's an individual academic paper, Founder's parking lot demonstration, is unabashedly an attempt to forge an identity in this particular age."[7] A deep current of longing runs through her relatively short remarks: a longing for unity, for connectedness, for the resolution of "inauthentic" feelings and institutions in a holistic marriage that "*transform[s] the future into the present*" so that "limitations no longer exist" and "hollow men" are made whole.[8] It's fitting that Wellesley's motto is "*Non ministrari sed ministrare*" ("Not to be ministered unto but to minister").

THE TOTALITARIAN TEMPTATION

After graduation, Hillary was offered an internship by her hero Saul Alinsky—famed author of *Rules for Radicals*—about whom she wrote her thesis: "There Is Only the Fight: An Analysis of the Alinsky Model." In an unprecedented move, Wellesley sequestered the thesis in 1992, even refusing to divulge the title until the Clintons left the White House.

Readers familiar with Alinsky and his times will understand what an enormous figure the "Godfather" of community activism was on the left. The son of Russian Jewish immigrants, Alinsky got his start as a criminologist, but in 1936, fed up with the failures of social policy, he committed himself to attacking the supposed root causes of criminality. He eventually became a labor organizer in his native Chicago, working in the real-life neighborhood in which Upton Sinclair's *Jungle* was set. "It was here," writes P. David Finks, "that Saul Alinsky would invent his famous 'method' of community organizing, borrowing tactics from the Catholic Church, Al Capone's mobsters, University of Chicago sociologists and John L. Lewis' union organizers."[9] His violent, confrontational rhetoric often sounded much like that heard from Horst Wessel or his Red Shirt adversaries in the streets of Berlin.

Alinsky joined forces with the churches and the CIO—then chockablock with Stalinists and other communists—learning how to organize in the streets. In 1940 he founded the Industrial Areas Foundation, which pioneered the community activism movement. He became the mentor to countless community activists—most famously Cesar Chavez—laying the foundation for both Naderism and the SDS. He believed in exploiting middle-class mores to achieve his agenda, not flouting them as the long-haired hippies did. Indeed, Alinsky believed that working through friendly or vulnerable institutions in order to smash enemy redoubts was the essence of political organization. And he was, by universal consensus, an "organizational genius." He worked closely with reformist and left-leaning clergy, who were for most of his career his chief patrons. Perhaps as a result, he mastered the art of unleashing preachers as the frontline activists in his mission of "rubbing raw the sores of discontent."[10]

In many respects, Alinsky's methods inspired the entire 1960s generation of New Left agitators (Barack Obama, for years a Chicago community organizer, was trained by Alinsky's disciples). It's worth noting, however, that Alinsky was no fan of the Great Society, calling it "a prize piece of political pornography" because it was simultaneously too timid and too generous to the "welfare industry." Indeed, there was something deeply admirable about Alinsky's contempt for both the statism of elite liberals and the radically chic New Leftists, who spent their days "spouting quotes from Mao, Castro, and Che Guevara, which are as germane to our highly technological, computerized, cybernetic, nuclear-powered, mass media society as a stagecoach on a jet runway at Kennedy airport."[11]

Still, there's no disputing that vast swaths of his writings are indistinguishable from the fascist rhetoric of the 1920s and 1930s. His descriptions of the United States could have come from any street corner Brownshirt denouncing the corruption of the Weimar regime. His worldview is distinctly fascistic. Life is defined by war, contests of power, the imposition of will. Moreover, Alinsky shares with the fascists and pragmatists of yore a bedrock hostility to dogma. All he believes in are the desired ends of the movement, which he regards as the source of life's meaning. "Change means movement. Movement means friction," he writes. "Only in the frictionless vacuum of a nonexistent abstract world can movement or change occur without that abrasive friction of conflict." But what comes through most is his unbridled love of power. Power is a good in its own right for Alinsky. Ours "is a world not of angels but of angles," he proclaims in *Rules for Radicals,* "where men speak of moral principles but act on power principles."[12]

Hillary turned down Alinsky's offer in order to attend Yale Law

School. He told her it was a huge mistake, but Hillary responded that only by marching through America's elite institutions could she achieve real power and change the system from within. This was a typical rationalization of many upper-class college students in the 1960s, who prized their radical credentials but also looked askance at the idea of sacrificing their social advantages. It's significant, however, that one of Hillary's chief criticisms of Alinsky in her thesis was that he failed to build a national movement based on his ideas. But Hillary, more than most, never gave up the faith. She remained true to her radical principles. Thus at Yale—where she eventually met Bill Clinton—she quickly fell in with the leftist fringe.

There is an almost literary synchronicity to the overlapping of narratives and ideas at Yale in the late 1960s and early 1970s. Bill Clinton was taught constitutional law by Charles Reich, the "Level III consciousness" guru. Reich, in turn, had served as a partner to the famed New Deal lawyer and intellectual Thurman Arnold—a disciple of the Crolyite liberals of the *New Republic*—who championed a new "religion of government." In the 1930s critics saw Arnold's work as one of the linchpins of American-style fascism. He went on to co-found the law firm Arnold, Fortas & Porter.[13]

Hillary helped edit the *Yale Review of Law and Social Action,* which at the time was a thoroughly radical organ supporting the Black Panthers and publishing articles implicitly endorsing the murder of police. One article, "Jamestown Seventy," suggested that radicals adopt a program of "political migration to a single state for the purpose of gaining political control and establishing a living laboratory for experiment."[14] An infamous *Review* cover depicted police as pigs, one with his head chopped off. The Panthers had become an issue on campus because the "chairman" of the Panthers, Bobby Seale, was put on trial in New Haven along with some fellow goons for the murder of one of their own. Hillary volunteered to help the Panthers' legal team, even attending the trial to take notes to help with the defense. She did such a good job of organizing the student volunteers that she was offered a summer internship in the Berkeley, California, law offices of Robert Treuhaft, one of Seale's lawyers. Treuhaft was a lifelong member of the American Communist Party who had cut his teeth fighting for the Stalinist faction in the California labor movement.[15]

Hillary's attraction to radical groups and figures such as the Black Panthers, Alinsky, and—according to some biographers—Yasir Arafat is perfectly consistent with liberalism's historic weakness for men of action. Just as Herbert Croly could make allowances for Mussolini and countless others applauded Stalin's "tough decisions," the 1960s generation of liberals had an inherent weakness for men who "transcended" bourgeois morality and democracy in the name of social justice. This love of hard men—Castro, Che, Arafat—is clearly tied to the left's obsession with the fascist values of authenticity and will.[16]

After law school, however, Hillary eschewed such radical authenticity in favor of pragmatism. She worked as a lawyer in Little Rock and as an activist within the confines of the liberal establishment, chairing the state-funded radical organ the Legal Services Corporation, as well as the nonprofit Children's Defense Fund. Before that she'd been a Democratic staffer for the House Judiciary Committee. Her marriage to Bill Clinton, arguably the most relentlessly dissected union in American history, need not occupy much of our time. Whatever their romantic feelings toward each other may have been or continue to be, reasonable people can agree that it was also a deeply political arrangement.

The most revealing aspect of Clinton's career prior to her arrival in Washington was her advocacy for children. Clinton wrote important articles, often denounced by critics as advocating the right of children to "divorce" their parents. She never quite says as much, though it seems undeniable that she was pointing down that road. But the child-divorce debate was always a side issue. What is more important, Hillary Clinton's writings on children show a clear, unapologetic, and principled desire to insert the state deep into family life—a goal that is in perfect accord with similar efforts by totalitarians of the past.

This is hardly a view unique to myself or to the denizens of the American right. As the late Michael Kelly wrote in an influential profile of the then-new First Lady, she is the heir to "the politics of do-goodism, flowing directly from a powerful and continual stream that runs through American history from Harriet Beecher Stowe to Jane Addams to Carry Nation to Dorothy Day . . . [T]he world she wishes to restore . . . [is] a place of security and community and clear moral values."[17]

The late Christopher Lasch came to a similar conclusion. Lasch, one of the most perceptive students of American social policy in the twentieth century, and no partisan right-winger, reviewed all of Clinton's relevant writings for an article in the left-leaning journal *Harper's* in 1992. The result is a sober (and sobering) discussion of Clinton's worldview. Lasch dubs Clinton a modern "child saver," a term critical historians apply to progressives eager to insert the God-state into the sphere of the family. While Clinton cavils that she wants the state to intervene only in "warranted cases," her real aim, as she admits, is to set down a full and universal "theory that adequately explains the state's appropriate role in child rearing." To this end, she advocates the abolition of "minority status"—that is, the legal codification of what distinguishes a child from an adult. This would be a great progressive leap forward in line with—Clinton's words—"the abolition of slavery and the emancipation of married women." Finally, "children, like other persons," would be presumed "capable of exercising rights and assuming responsibilities until it is proven otherwise."[18]

Tellingly, Clinton focuses on *Wisconsin v. Yoder,* a 1972 Supreme Court case that permitted three Amish families to keep their kids out of high school, defying mandatory attendance laws. Justice William O. Douglas dissented, noting that nobody ever asked the kids what they wanted. The "children should be entitled to be heard," he declared. Clinton takes Douglas's dissent and builds an argument claiming children should be "masters of their own destiny." Their voices should be weighted more heavily than the views of parents in the eyes of courts. Observing that in order to become "a pianist or an astronaut or an oceanographer" a child must "break from the Amish tradition," she concludes that a child "harnessed to the Amish way of life" would likely lead a "stunted and deformed" life. Lasch offers a devastating conclusion: "She condones the state's assumption of parental responsibilities . . . because she is opposed to the principle of parental authority in any form." Clinton's writings "leave the unmistakable impression that it is the family that holds children back, the state that sets them free." In Clinton's eyes, Lasch concluded, "the movement for children's rights . . . amounts to another stage in the long struggle against patriarchy."[19]

Since Plato's *Republic*, politicians, intellectuals, and priests have been fascinated with the idea of "capturing" children for social-engineering purposes. This is why Robespierre advocated that children be raised by the state. Hitler—who understood as well as any the importance of winning the hearts and minds of youth—once remarked, "When an opponent says 'I will not come over to your side,' I calmly say, 'Your child belongs to us already . . . You will pass on. Your descendants, however, now stand in the new camp. In a short time they will know nothing but this new community.' " Woodrow Wilson candidly observed that the primary mission of the educator was to make children as unlike their parents as possible. Charlotte Perkins Gilman stated it more starkly. "There is no more brilliant hope on earth to-day," the feminist icon proclaimed, "than this new thought about the child . . . the recognition of 'the child,' children as a class, children as citizens with rights to be guaranteed only by the state; instead of our previous attitude toward them of absolute personal [that is, parental] ownership—the unchecked tyranny . . . of the private home."[20]

Progressive education has two parents, Prussia and John Dewey. The kindergarten was transplanted into the United States from Prussia in the nineteenth century because American reformers were so enamored of the order and patriotic indoctrination young children received outside the home (the better to weed out the un-American traits of immigrants).[21] One of the core tenets of the early kindergartens was the dogma that "the government is the true parent of the children, the state is sovereign over the family." The progressive followers of John Dewey expanded this program to make public schools incubators of a national religion. They discarded the militaristic rigidity of the Prussian model, but retained the aim of indoctrinating children. The methods were informal, couched in the sincere desire to make learning "fun," "relevant," and "empowering." The self-esteem obsession that saturates our schools today harks back to the Deweyan reforms from before World War II. But beneath the individualist rhetoric lies a mission for democratic social justice, a mission Dewey himself defined as a religion. For other progressives, capturing children in schools was part of the larger effort to break the backbone of the nuclear family, the institution most resistant to political indoctrination.

National Socialist educators had a similar mission in mind. And as odd as it might seem, they also discarded the Prussian discipline of the past and embraced self-esteem and empowerment in the name of social justice. In the early days of the Third Reich, grade-schoolers burned their multicolored caps in a protest against class distinctions. Parents complained, "We no longer have rights over our children." According to the historian Michael Burleigh, "Their children became strangers, contemptuous of monarchy or religion, and perpetually barking and shouting like pint-sized Prussian sergeant-majors . . . Denunciation of parents by children was encouraged, not least by schoolteachers who set essays entitled 'What does your family talk about at home?' "[22]

Now, the liberal project Hillary Clinton represents is in no way a *Nazi* project. The last thing she would want is to promote ethnic nationalism, anti-Semitism, or aggressive wars of conquest. But it must be kept in mind that while these things were of enormous importance to Hitler and his ideologues, they were in an important sense secondary to the underlying mission and appeal of Nazism, which was to create a new politics and a new nation committed to social justice, radical egalitarianism (albeit for "true Germans"), and the destruction of the traditions of the old order. So while there are light-years of distance between the *programs* of liberals and those of Nazis or Italian Fascists or even the nationalist progressives of yore, the underlying impulse, the totalitarian temptation, is present in both.

The Chinese Communists under Mao pursued the Chinese way, the Russians under Stalin followed their own version of communism in one state. But we are still comfortable observing that they were both communist nations. Hitler wanted to wipe out the Jews; Mussolini wanted no such thing. And yet we are comfortable calling them both fascists. Liberal fascists don't want to mimic generic fascists or communists in myriad ways, but they share a sweeping vision of social justice and community and the need for the state to realize that vision. In short, collectivists of all stripes share the same totalitarian temptation to create a politics of meaning; what differs between them—and this is the most crucial difference of all—is how they act upon that temptation.

THE FIRST LADY OF LIBERAL FASCISM

When Bill Clinton was elected president, his wife arrived in Washington as arguably the most powerful unelected—and unappointed—social reformer since Eleanor Roosevelt. She admitted to the *Washington Post* that she'd always had a "burning desire" to "make the world . . . better for everybody." She had had this desire ever since the days when Don Jones showed her that the poor and oppressed didn't have it as good as she did. And for Hillary, healing this social discord required power. "My sense of Hillary is that she realizes absolutely the truth of the human condition, which is that you cannot depend on the basic nature of man to be good and you cannot depend entirely on moral suasion to make it good," Jones told Michael Kelly. "You have to use power. And there is nothing wrong with wielding power in the pursuit of policies that will add to the human good. I think Hillary knows this. She is very much the sort of Christian who understands that the use of power to achieve social good is legitimate."[23] The echoes of Alinsky are obvious. Less obvious are the questions of who determines what the social good should be and by what means it should be achieved.

But Hillary didn't frame her mission in overtly Christian terms save, perhaps, when speaking to avowedly Christian audiences. Instead, she fashioned the quintessential expression of liberal fascism in modern times: "the politics of meaning."

Now, when I say that the politics of meaning, and Hillary Clinton's ideas in general, are fascist, I must again be clear that they are not evil. Nor do they sound fascist to modern ears—indeed, that is the whole point. Today we equate fascism with militaristic language and racism, but war in the late nineteenth and early twentieth centuries provided a great many of the metaphors for political discourse and for everyday conversation in general. So many of these words and phrases are part of the vernacular today that we don't even realize their roots in battle and blood ("entrenched positions," "storm fronts," "hot shot," and so on). Liberal fascism isn't militaristic, but the same passions that prompted progressives to talk in terms of "industrial armies" and "going over the top" for the Blue Eagle lurk beneath today's liberal rhetoric. War was seen as a communal, unifying experience that focused the public's mind on the common good and whose passions and discipline could be harnessed to socially "useful" ends. Today the modern left is in many ways openly antiwar and avowedly pacifist. But liberals still yearn nostalgically for the unifying experiences of the labor and civil rights movements. The language is obviously nicer, and the intent is objectively "nicer," too. But at the most substantive level, the politics of meaning stands on Mussolini's shoulders.

As for racism, there is a great deal of racism, or perhaps a more fair word would be "racialism," in liberalism today. The state counts "people of color" in different ways from how it counts white people. Further to the left, racial essentialism lies at the core of countless ideological projects. Anti-Semitism, too, is more prominent on the left today than at any time in recent memory. Obviously, this is not the same kind of racism or anti-Semitism that Nazis subscribed to. But again, Nazi racism does not define fascism. Moreover, Nazi racism—quite in sync with progressive racism, let us remember— was an expression of a deeper impulse to define the individual by his relationship to the collective.

Let me anticipate one last criticism. Some will say that Hillary Clinton's politics of meaning is old hat. Clinton hasn't mentioned the phrase in years, swept under the rug by political expediency like the memory of her disastrous health-care plan. This would be a more salient critique if my aim was to offer anti-Clinton talking points for the 2008 presidential campaign. But that's not my concern. What I find interesting about Clinton is her ability to illuminate the continuity of liberal thought. If what liberals thought and did in the 1920s is relevant today—as I believe it is—then surely what liberals thought and did in the 1990s is relevant as well. Moreover, there is no evidence that she's been chastened ideologically. In her 1996 book, *It Takes a Village,* Clinton hardly backed off her radical views on children, even though those views were a political liability in 1992. She did, however, repackage her message in more palatable ways, thanks to the help of a ghostwriter.

Lastly, Clinton's politics of meaning was arguably the most interesting and serious expression of liberalism in the 1990s, delivered at the apex of liberal optimism. Since Bush's election and the 9/11 attacks, liberalism has been largely reactive, defined by its anti-Bush passions more than anything else. Hence, it seems worthwhile to investigate what liberals were saying when they were dancing to their own tune.

In April 1993 Clinton delivered a commencement address to the University of Texas at Austin in which she declared, "We need a new politics of meaning. We need a new ethos of individual responsibility and caring. We need a new definition of civil society which answers the unanswerable questions posed by both the market forces and the governmental ones, as to how we can have a society that fills us up again and makes us feel that we are part of something bigger than ourselves."[24]

The phrase "fills us up again" is particularly telling—in 1969 she had talked of how we needed a politics to make "hollow men" whole. She seems to be suggesting that without a social cause or mission to "fill" her, Hillary's life (and ours) is empty and purposeless. Hillary has seemingly put pragmatic concerns ahead of everything else her whole life, but whenever she's given a chance to express herself honestly, the same urges come to the fore: meaning, authenticity, action, transformation.

The politics of meaning is in many respects the most thoroughly totalitarian conception of politics offered by a leading American political figure in the last half century. Hillary's views have more in common with the totalizing Christian ideologies of Pat Robertson and Jerry Falwell than they do with the "secular atheism" such Christian conservatives ascribe to her. But they have even more in common with the God-state Progressivism of John Dewey, Richard Ely, Herbert Croly, and Woodrow Wilson and other left-wing Hegelians. Hillary's vision holds that America suffers from a profound "spiritual crisis" requiring the construction of a new man as part of a society-wide restoration and reconstruction effort leading to a new national community that will provide meaning and authenticity to every individual. Hers is a Third Way approach that promises to be neither left nor right, but a synthesis of both, under which the state and big business will work hand in hand. It is a fundamentally religious vision hiding in the Trojan horse of social justice that seeks to imbue social policy with spiritual imperatives.

To better understand the politics of meaning, we should consider the career of Clinton's self-anointed guru, the progressive activist and rabbi Michael Lerner. Lerner was born to nonobservant Jews in New Jersey—his mother was the chairwoman of the state Democratic Party. A graduate of Columbia University in 1964, he received his Ph.D. from Berkeley, where he served as a teaching assistant to Herbert Marcuse and led the SDS. A fan of LSD, a "progressive drug," he believed that taking the hallucinogen was the only way to truly understand socialism (the irony clearly escaped him). When his sister married a successful attorney, a number of prominent politicians attended the wedding. Lerner could not let such an opportunity slip by. He interrupted the festivities with a speech denouncing the guests as "murderers" with "blood on your hands" for not doing more to stop the war in Vietnam.[25]

When Cupid aimed his arrow at him, he told his paramour, "If you want to be my girlfriend, you'll have to organize a guerrilla *foco* first." (A *foco* is a form of paramilitary cadre pioneered by Che Guevara—much cherished in Marxist-Leninist theory—designed for lightning-fast insurrectionary strikes.) When the two were married in Berkeley, they exchanged rings extracted from the fuselage of an American aircraft downed over Vietnam. The wedding cake was inscribed with the Weathermen motto "Smash Monogamy." (The marriage lasted less than a year.) Lerner claims to have been a leader in the nonviolent wing of the New Left. While a professor at the University of Washington, he founded the Seattle Liberation Front, which he later claimed was a nonviolent alternative to the Weathermen. Nonetheless, he was arrested on charges of incitement to riot as one of the members of the "Seattle Seven." The charges were eventually dropped, but not before J. Edgar Hoover dubbed him—no doubt hyperbolically—"one of the most dangerous criminals in America."[26]

In 1973 Lerner wrote *The New Socialist Revolution,* a clichéd ode to the glories of the coming socialist takeover. The rhetoric was quintessentially Mussolinian: "The first task of the revolutionary movement . . . is to destroy bourgeois hegemony and develop a radical consciousness among each of the potential constituencies for revolutionary action."[27]

Over the years, Lerner's thinking evolved. First, he became deeply interested in mass psychology (he's a licensed psychotherapist), imbibing all the Frankfurt School nonsense about fascist personalities (conservatism is a treatable illness in Lerner's view). Second, he became a rabbi. And while his commitment to progressive politics never waned, he increasingly became obsessed with the "spiritual" aspect of politics. Finally, he cast aside dialectical materialism in favor of attacking consumer materialism and the psychic pain it causes. In 1986 he launched *Tikkun,* an odd magazine dedicated in large part to creating a new Social Gospel with heavily Jewish and ecumenical biases.

After Hillary Clinton's politics of meaning speech, which was partly inspired by Lerner (who'd ingratiated himself with then-Governor Clinton), the radical rabbi psychotherapist went into overdrive, promoting himself as the house seer of the Clinton administration. He was to be the Herbert Croly of the new Progressive Era. Though many in the press recognized a hustler when they saw one, he nonetheless got the attention he wanted. The *New York Times* hailed him as "This Year's Prophet." When it became clear, however, that the politics of meaning sounded too much like New Age hokum, the press and the Clintons turned a cold shoulder. In response, Lerner released his opus, *The Politics of Meaning: Restoring Hope and Possibility in an Age of Cynicism.*

The book strikes one fascist chord after another. Lerner cites a long, familiar litany of progressive ideas and causes. He speaks about making the powerless more powerful, about throwing off the baggage of the past, about eschewing dogma and embracing national community, about rejecting the overly rational expertise of doctors and scientists. He waxes eloquent about the various crises—spiritual, ecological, moral, and social—afflicting Western bourgeois democracies that must be remedied through a politics of redemption. He also talks about creating new men and women—rejecting the false dichotomies between work and family, business and government, private and public. Above all, he insists that his new politics of meaning must saturate every nook and cranny of our lives by smashing the compartmentalism of American life. Morality, politics, economics, ethics: none of these things can be separated from anything else. We must have our metaphysics confirmed in every human interaction and encounter.

In this he unwittingly echoes Hitler's belief that "economics is secondary" to the revolution of the spirit. Lerner writes, "If there were a different ethical and spiritual connection between people, there would be a different economic reality . . . And that is why meaning cannot be given lower priority than economics."[28] Needless to say, this is something of a departure from the Marxist materialism of his youth. Lerner's preferred agenda would, of course, echo many of the guarantees from the Nazi Party platform of 1920, including equal rights, guaranteed health care, excessive taxes on the undeserving wealthy, and clampdowns on big corporations. A few relevant items from a 1993 article in *Tikkun:*

> The Department of Labor should mandate that . . . every workplace should provide paid leave for a worker to attend 12 two-hour sessions on stress . . .
>
> The Department of Labor should sponsor "Honor Labor" campaigns designed to highlight the honor due to people for their contributions to the common good . . .
>
> The Department of Labor should create a program to train a corps of union personnel, worker representatives, and psychotherapists in the relevant skills to assist developing a new spirit of cooperation, mutual caring, and dedication to work.[29]

This is precisely the sort of thing that Robert Ley's German Labor Front pioneered. The comparison is more than superficial. The National Socialist state, like the progressive and fascist ones, was based on the Hegelian idea that freedom could only be realized by living in harmony with the state, and it was the state's duty to ensure said harmony. There were no private individuals. (Ley famously said that the only private individual in the Nazi state is a person asleep.) Lerner argues in *The Politics of Meaning* that "the workplace needs to be reconceptualized as a primary locus for human development." In another book, *Spirit Matters,* he writes (in one gargantuan sentence) that under his new "movement for Emancipatory Spirituality" the "government needs to be reconceptualized as the public mechanism through which we all show that we care about everyone else, and government employees should be evaluated, rewarded, and promoted only to the extent that they are able to make the public come away from those interactions with a renewed sense of hope and a deepened conviction that other people really do care, and have shown that by creating such a sensitive and caring government."

Lerner's ideal is the Israeli kibbutz, where even plucking chickens has transcendent meaning for the laborer. He pines for a way to re-create the sense of shared purpose people feel during a crisis like a flood or other natural disaster. Freedom, for Lerner, is reconceived in a Deweyan sense toward communal social "construction." Or, as the Nazis said more pithily, "Work makes you free."[30]

Under the politics of meaning, all of society's institutions are wrapped around the state like sticks around the fascist blade. Every individual is responsible for maintaining not only his own ideological purity but that of his fellow man. Lerner is, in effect, the ideologist of the liberal *Gleichschaltung,* the Nazi idea of coordinating every institution in society. This becomes apparent when he shifts to a discussion of how these reforms are to be implemented. Lerner writes that all government agencies and private businesses should issue "annual ethical-impact reports," which would assess "their effect on the ethical, spiritual, and psychological well-being of our society and on the people who work in and with these institutions."[31] His intent is arguably nicer, but is this really so different from the bureaucratization of ideological loyalty that required German businesses and institutions to constantly provide documentation showing their assertive loyalty to the spirit of the new era? Spiritual slackers in twenty-first-century America would no doubt find such scrutiny fascistic—albeit in a very caring and nurturing way.

Lerner believes it is the job of every profession—coordinating with the state, of course—to "reflect" on its own contribution to the spiritual and psychic health of the national *Volksgemeinschaft.* "Such reflection, for example, has led some lawyers associated with a politics-of-meaning perspective to envision a second stage of trials, in which the adversary system is suspended and the focus is shifted to healing the problems and pain that the initial trial has uncovered in the community."[32] That may sound a little silly to some ears, and it hardly seems to threaten a fascist coup. But if there is ever a fascist takeover in America, it will come not in the form of storm troopers kicking down doors but with lawyers and social workers saying, "I'm from the government and I'm here to help."

Oddly enough, Lerner vaguely comprehends his own ideology's relationship to fascism. In an ironic twist, he admits that he once "could not understand why the European Left had been unable to stem the popularity of the fascists." Fascist "hatred of others was based on the degree to which they had come to believe (usually mistakenly) that the demeaned Others had actually caused the breakdown of their communities of shared meaning and purpose." Lerner notes that many former liberals "have now turned to the Right to find the sense of community and meaning that liberals, social democrats, and the Left always thought was irrelevant or necessarily reactionary."[33] He writes that the 1990s are witnessing the rise of "fascistic" right-wing movements and that they can only be countered by his politics of meaning.

Lerner's analysis breaks down in several parts, largely because of his thumbless grasp of the true nature of fascism.[34] But far more important, he largely concedes that the politics of meaning is in effect an attempt to provide an *alternative* to an imagined *right-wing* politics of meaning that he considers fascistic. He sees a fascistic straw man on the right and in response feels justified in creating an actual—*nice*—fascism of the left. He grounds all of it in vast departures into religious exhortation, arguing that his is a "politics in the image of God," a point he also hammers home relentlessly in his recent books *The Left Hand of God* and *Spirit Matters*.[35]

Defenders of the politics of meaning, such as Cornel West, Jonathan Kozol, and even such mainstream historians as John Milton Cooper, reject or ignore the radical statism of Lerner's project. Still, they defend their political religion with a lot of classical Third Way verbiage about rejecting both free-market anarchy and statism in favor of a new synthesis balancing the community and the individual. "To put it in crude terms," writes Lerner, "neither capitalism nor socialism in the forms that they have developed in the twentieth century seem particularly appealing to me." Rather, what appeals to him are pragmatic approaches "that differ from the typical Left/Right divisions, which must be transcended as we develop a politics for the twenty-first century."[36] It's all so unoriginal. The French Fascist slogan was much catchier: *Ni droite ni gauche!*

As we've seen, ideologically fascist and progressive totalitarianism was never a mere doctrine of statism. Rather, it claimed that the state was the natural brain of the organic body politic. Statism was the route to collectivism. Government was merely the place where the spiritual will of the people would be translated into action (Marxists liked to use the word "praxis" to describe this unity of theory and action). One consequence of this view is that institutions and individuals that stand apart from the state or the progressive tide are inherently suspect and labeled selfish, social Darwinist, conservative, or, most ironically, fascist. The state's role is not so much to make every decision as to be the metronome for the *Gleichschaltung,* ensuring that the decision makers are all in perfect agreement about the direction society needs to take. In a properly ordered progressive society, the state wouldn't take over Harvard or McDonald's, but it would certainly ensure that the Harvards and McDonald's had their priorities straight. The politics of meaning is ultimately a theocratic doctrine because it seeks to answer the fundamental questions about existence, argues that they can only be answered collectively, and insists that the state put those answers into practice.

This liberal fascist thinking was nicely exposed in an exchange between the television producer Norman Lear and the conservative columnist Charles Krauthammer in 1993. Krauthammer called Hillary Clinton's politics of meaning address a "cross between Jimmy Carter's malaise speech and a term paper on Siddhartha" delivered with "the knowing self-assurance, the superior air of a college student manifesto."[37]

Norman Lear leaped into the breach to defend Hillary. The creator of the television shows *All in the Family, Maude, Sanford and Son,* and *Good Times,* Lear was also the founder of People for the American Way, or PFAW, an organization with an ironically conservative sound to it. He launched PFAW in an effort to beat back the religious right, which was allegedly trying to destroy the fabled "wall of separation" between church and state. But in the late 1980s Lear started to show a slight change of heart. In 1989, in an address to the annual meeting of the American Academy of Religion in Anaheim, California, he lamented "the spiritual emptiness in our culture." "Among secularists," he noted, "the aversion toward discussing moral values, let alone religion, can reach absurd extremes."[38]

It's understandable that a left-wing civil libertarian like Lear would greet the arrival of a politics of meaning as nigh on providential. Lear wrote a bitter response in the *Washington Post* denouncing Krauthammer's cynicism in the face of Clinton's brilliant summation of America's spiritual crisis. "The sophisticates of our politics, our culture and the media," Lear opined, "are embarrassed to talk seriously about the life of the spirit." "Our obsession with numbers, the quantifiable, the immediate, has cost us our connection with that place in each of us that honors the unquantifiable and eternal—our capacity for awe, wonder and mystery; that place where acts of faith in a process larger than ourselves, prove ultimately satisfying in the fullness of time."[39]

Lear's cri de coeur is an almost pitch-perfect restatement of the neo-Romantic objections to modern society that inspired fascist movements across Europe and the search for "a cause larger than ourselves" of the American Progressives. He might receive an appreciative hearing from the early Paul de Man, Ezra Pound, and countless other fascist theorists and ideologues who denounced the Western—particularly Jewish—obsession with numbers and technical abstraction. But even more telling is the fact that Lear's People for the American Way is second perhaps only to the ACLU as an enforcer of the liberal *Gleichschaltung*. In lawsuits, campaign contributions, amicus briefs, advertising, and righteous news conferences, People for the American Way serves as a tireless mason in the construction of the wall between church and state, shrinking the public space for traditional religion and building the foundation of a secular counter-church of liberalism.

In other words, Lear is an adamant proponent of spiritualizing politics; but there's no room for traditional religion in his ideal political system, for it is the progressive priesthood—not churches or synagogues—that must sanctify the quest for meaning and spirituality. Independent sources of moral faith are "divisive" and need to be undermined, walled off, excluded from our "common project." This means that liberal churches are fine because they are perceived—rightly or wrongly—to have subordinated religious doctrine to political doctrine. As John Dewey put it in his brief for a secular religion of the state: "If our nominally religious institutions learn how to use their symbols and rites to express and enhance such a faith, they may become useful allies of a conception of life that is in harmony with knowledge and social needs." Hitler was more succinct: "Against a

Church that identifies itself with the State . . . I have nothing to say."[40]

Conservatives are fond of scoring liberals for their cafeteria Christianity, picking those things they like from the religious menu and eschewing the hard stuff. But there's more than mere hypocrisy at work. What appears to be inconsistency is in fact the continued unfolding of the Social Gospel tapestry to reveal a religion without God. Cafeteria liberals aren't so much inconsistent Christians as consistent progressives.

EVERYTHING WITHIN THE VILLAGE . . .

No more thorough explication of the liberal fascist agenda can be found than in Hillary Clinton's best-selling book, *It Takes a Village*. All the hallmarks of the fascist enterprise reside within its pages. Again, the language isn't hostile, nationalistic, racist, or aggressive. To the contrary, it brims with expressions of love and democratic fellow feeling. But this only detracts from its fascist nature if fascism itself means nothing more than hostile or aggressive (or racist and nationalistic). The fascistic nature of *It Takes a Village* begins with the very title. It draws from a mythic and mythical communal past. "It takes a village to raise a child" is supposedly an African proverb whose authorship is lost in the mists of time—from "the ancient African kingdom of Hallmarkcardia," according to P. J. O'Rourke.[41] Clinton invokes this premodern image as a source of authority in order to reorganize modern society. It may not be as powerful as all that Teutonic imagery the National Socialists threw around. But is it any more rational? Any less Romantic? More important, the metaphor of the village is used in precisely the same way that the symbol of the fasces was. The difference is that the fasces were a symbol for a martial age; the village is a symbol for a maternal one.

In Mrs. Clinton's telling, villages are wonderful, supportive, nurturing places where everyone is looking out for one another: from "everything in the State, nothing outside the State" to "everything in the village, nothing outside the village." The village, she writes, "can no longer be defined as a place on a map, or a list of people or organizations, but its essence remains the same: it is the network of values and relationships that support and affect our lives."[42] In Hillary's village, the concept of civil society is grotesquely deformed. Traditionally, civil society is that free and open space occupied by what Burke called "little platoons"—independent associations of citizens who pursue their own interests and ambitions free from state interference or coercion.

That is not Hillary's civil society. In a book festooned with encomiums to every imaginable social work interest group in America, Mrs. Clinton mentions "civil society" just once. In a single paragraph she dispatches the concept as basically another way of describing the village. "[C]ivil society," she writes, is just a "term social scientists use to describe the way we work together for common purposes."[43] *No, no, no.* "Civil society" is the term social scientists use to describe the way various *groups,* individuals, and families work for their own purposes, the result of which is to make the society healthily democratic. Civil society is the rich ecosystem of independent entities—churches, businesses, volunteer and neighborhood associations, labor unions, and such—that helps regulate life outside of state control. Bowling leagues, thanks to the Harvard social scientist Robert Putnam, are the archetypal institution of civil society. Bowling leagues are not mechanisms for working together for "common purposes." The late Seymour Martin Lipset even demonstrated that although many labor unions were corrupt and illiberal, so long as they remained independent of the state—and the state independent of them—they enriched democracy.

In Clinton's village, however, there is no public square where free men and women and their voluntary associations deal with each other on their own terms free from the mommying of the state. There are no private transactions, just a single "spiritual community that links us to a higher purpose" managed by the state.[44] This is the *Volksgemeinschaft* reborn as a Social Gospel day-care center.

Think again of the image of a fasces, its many weak reeds or sticks bundled together to show strength in numbers. The first chapter of Mrs. Clinton's book begins with a quotation from the poet Verna Kelly: "Snowflakes are one of nature's most fragile things, but just look what they can do when they stick together."[45] It's a cute image, but is the message any different? Over and over again, Clinton uses a velvet hammer to beat it into the reader's head that togetherness, partnership, and unity are the only means of America's salvation.

The point where theory and practice most obviously merge is in the area of economic policy. Corporations were among the most important reeds in the fascist bundle. So it is in Hillary Clinton's village. "Community-minded companies are already doing a number of things that citizens should applaud and government should encourage, when possible, with legislative changes to make them more attractive." These include the usual wish list from "no-layoff" policies to employer-provided day care. Again and again, Clinton beams sunshine wherever the lines between corporations, universities, churches, and government are already thin, hoping that the illumination of her gaze will cause even the shadows dividing them to disappear. Defense contractors are working with government to make peaceful products. Hooray. Automobile companies are working with the EPA to build green cars. Huzzah. Such "[s]ocially minded corporate philosophies are the avenue to future prosperity and social stability."[46] Everyone will be secure and happy, nestled in the cozy confines of the village.

This all sounds peachy in the abstract. But when Clinton tried to impose precisely this sort of vision with her health-care plan, she had a harder edge. Recall Hillary's response when it was pointed out to her that her plan would destroy countless small businesses: "I can't save every undercapitalized entrepreneur in America."[47] If they can't be part of the solution, who cares if they have problems?

ETERNAL CORPORATISM

I suppose one cannot talk about Hillary Clinton without mentioning her health-care plan. So much ink has been spilled in that cause it hardly seems worth wading into the details of Clinton's effort to control one-seventh of the U.S. economy. What may be more worthwhile is to see how her health-care plan was the inevitable consequence of liberal empowerment. There was an Aesopian nature to the Clintonites. For example, once Hillary tapped her old friend—and Bill's Rhodes scholar pal—Ira Magaziner to head up her Health

Reform Task Force, it was inevitable that a large, government-run, corporatist product would come out of the sausage maker. Why? Because that's what Magaziner *does*. The scorpion must sting the frog, and Magaziner must propose sweeping new public-private partnerships where experts make all the big decisions.

Magaziner, Hillary's co-leader in *Life* magazine in 1969, was a true phenomenon at Brown University (his senior thesis, he told *Newsweek,* was nothing less than a Comtian "search for a new metaphysics, a new answer to the question, 'Why be good?' "). As a junior, he took it upon himself to study the school's curriculum and propose an alternative that was more "relevant" and pragmatic, leaving it up to the young to design their own educations. He created his own major, "Human Studies," and he produced a nearly five-hundred-page report. The shocking part is that he succeeded in getting his Deweyan curriculum (few grades, lots of self-discovery) accepted. For traditionalists, the curriculum has made Brown the joke of the Ivy League ever since; for progressives, it has made the school its crown jewel.[48]

At Oxford, Magaziner led anti-Vietnam protests and allied himself with a smitten Vanessa Redgrave. James Fallows, a fellow Rhodes scholar and future Carter speechwriter and industrial planning publicist, explained that the main difference between Clinton and Magaziner was "the difference between somebody who planned to run for office and somebody who didn't." When Magaziner moved to Boston, he launched an Alinsky-Hayden-style community organization effort in Brockton, Massachusetts. Later, he went to work for the Boston Consulting Group, or BCG, where he acquired a knack for telling companies how to invest in the technologies of the future. Soon he was taking jobs from foreign governments to give them the same advice. In 1977 he got a gig consulting to Sweden. The final result of his efforts was dubbed "A Framework for Swedish Industrial Policy," in which he called for Sweden to redesign its economy from the top down, discarding old industries and investing heavily in the winners of tomorrow. Even the Swedes (!) rejected it as naive and heavy-handed. The Boston Consulting Group was so embarrassed it tried to make the report disappear.[49]

Told by a red-faced BCG he shouldn't do any more governmental planning, Magaziner decided to start his own firm. In 1979 he founded Telesis, which means "intelligently planned progress"—a nice summation of an attitude described throughout this book. In 1980 Magaziner wrote a book titled *Japanese Industrial Policy.* In 1982 he co-wrote a book on industrial policy with Robert Reich—a Yale Law School classmate of the Clintons as well as a fellow Rhodes scholar. In 1984, at the age of thirty-six, he penned a giant plan for the state of Rhode Island, the most ambitious state-level industrial planning effort in memory. Dubbed the Greenhouse Compact, the plan envisioned the state as a "greenhouse" for the right technologies—that is, technologies the government was smart enough to pick even though the market wasn't. The voters of Rhode Island rejected the measure handily. One could go on, but you get the point.

Now, does it seem likely that the Clintons, who'd known Magaziner for twenty years, expected that he'd come up with anything other than a corporatist strategy for American health care the moment they picked him? All of the studying, the meetings, the towers of briefing books, and the forests of file folders: these were all props in a Kabuki dance that had been scripted and blocked out well in advance.

Or consider fellow Yalie Robert Reich. We've already touched on his views on industrial policy and the Third Way. But it's worth looking at Reich as a true acolyte of the religion of government. I have been openly disdainful of psychological theorizing in earlier chapters, but how can we see Robert Reich as anything but a walking Sorelian myth, a one-man band belting out noble lies for the cause?

In his Clinton administration memoirs, *Locked in the Cabinet,* Reich describes a Thomas Nast cartoon world where he is in constant battle with greedy fat cats, Social Darwinists, and Mr. Monopoly. In one scene he recounts how he told some hard truths to the National Association of Manufacturers, describing a room as billowing with cigar smoke and filled with hostile men whose boos and hisses were punctuated with curses. Jonathan Rauch, one of Washington's best journalists and thinkers, checked the videotape. The audience was polite, even warm. They didn't smoke at all. Plus, the room was one-third female. In another episode Reich reported that a congressman jumped up and down shouting, "Evidence! Evidence!" at Reich during a hostile hearing. Rauch again checked the tape. Instead of an inquisition, it was a typically "dull, earnestly wonkish hearing," and most of the statements Reich attributed to his tormentor were simply "fabricated" by him. Indeed, vast swaths of the book are pure fantasy—but in a very familiar sort of way. At every turn people say things that confirm Reich's cartoon version of reality. Representative Robert Michel, the former House Republican leader, supposedly tells Reich that Newt Gingrich and company "talk as if they're interested in ideas, in what's good for America. But don't be fooled. They're out to destroy. They'll try to destroy anything that gets in their way, using whatever tactics are available." Michel never said any such thing.[50]

When *Slate* asked him about the controversy, Reich said, "Look, the book is a memoir. It's not investigative journalism." When Rauch asked him about his tall tales, "Did you just make them up?" Reich responded, "They're in my journal." Finally, Reich simply fell back on pure relativism. "I claim no higher truth than my own perceptions."[51] In other words, his defense is that this is really the way he sees the world. So again, if Reich is capable of bending reality to fit his political-morality tale, if he is programmed to see the world as a series of vital lies and useful myths, how exactly could the Clintons have expected him to do anything but stay true to form? It's not like the Clintons didn't know what their two old friends believed. Bill Clinton's policy manifesto, *Putting People First,* was essentially a Magaziner-Reich Festschrift.

What seems to motivate people like Reich is an abiding conviction that they are on the right side of history. Their aim is to help the people, and therefore they are not required to play by the rules. Moreover, just as they claim to be secularists, they also claim to be pragmatists, unconstrained by dogma, unlike those hidebound conservatives. Circumstances change, so, too, must our ideas. Or as Jonathan Chait of the *New Republic* puts it, "[I]ncoherence is simply the natural byproduct of a philosophy rooted in experimentation and the rejection of ideological certainty." This is a bit reminiscent of a line from Mussolini, quoted in the same magazine by Charles Beard. "The fascisti," Il Duce announced, "are the gypsies of Italian politics; not being tied down to any fixed principles, they proceed unceasingly toward one goal, the future well-being of the Italian people."[52]

THINK OF THE CHILDREN

Such self-confidence cannot operate in a vacuum. It needs a mechanism to convince or force others to surrender their interests to the greater good. The *New Republic*'s former editor George Soule, the author of *A Planned Society* (which popularized the phrase "we planned in war"), explained it well. The greatest of "the lessons from our war planning" was that "we must have an objective which can arouse general loyalty and enthusiasm." In *It Takes a Village,* Clinton cheers the way crises erase the wall between business and government but laments that the social benefits of natural disasters and wars are temporary. "Why does it take a crisis to open our eyes and hearts to our common humanity?"[53] In response to this problem, liberals have manufactured one "crisis" after another in their quest to find a new moral equivalent to war, from the war on cancer, to global warming, to countless alleged economic crises. Indeed, a brief perusal of the last hundred years of economic journalism from the left would have you believe that the most prosperous century in human history was one long, extended economic crisis.

But we should return to Hillary Clinton's crisis of choice: the children. The very concept of "the children" was designed to circumvent traditional political processes. The giveaway is the prefatory article, which denotes an entire category of human beings for whom all violations of the principle of limited government may be justified.

Constitutionally ordered liberal societies tend to view citizens as adults who are responsible for their own actions. But children are the Achilles' heel of every society (if libertarianism could account for children and foreign policy, it would be the ideal political philosophy). We make allowances for children. We have different rules for them—as well we should—and tend not to hold them accountable for their decisions. The "child savers" of the Progressive Era were brilliant at exploiting this weakness. In the modern era it was Marian Wright Edelman, the founder of the Children's Defense Fund, or CDF, and Hillary Clinton's longtime friend and mentor, who relaunched this tradition.

Edelman is perhaps America's leading liberal scold. *Harper's Bazaar* named her "America's universal mother." Her CV is festooned with honorifics and awards like a Christmas tree bending from the weight of too many ornaments—the presidential Medal of Freedom, a MacArthur Fellowship, the Albert Schweitzer Prize for Humanitarianism, a Robert F. Kennedy Lifetime Achievement Award, and so on. Her organization is showered with contributions from enormous corporations eager to buy grace on the cheap. Edelman got her start working for the NAACP and eventually found her way to Yale Law School and to Washington, D.C., as the policy-entrepreneur founder of the CDF. She is undoubtedly a kind and self-less woman, deeply religious and steeped in the traditions of the Social Gospel. Inspiring quotations from Edelman are so om-nipresent in the welfare, civil rights, and feminist industries—"in-dustries" being the best word for these self-esteem-building, logrolling, black-tie fund-raiser networks—that they could be com-bined into a liberal Maoist *Little Red Book* for earnest social cru-saders. "Service is the rent we pay to be living. It is the very purpose of life and not something you do in your spare time," she proclaims. "Whoever said anybody has a right to give up?" she asks. "No per-son has the right to rain on your dreams," she avers.

While few would question the rectitude of her campaigns for black equality and desegregation, Edelman's greatest influence has been in welfare policy, and there her ideas about how to organize society and American politics have proven to be spectacularly wrong. In many respects Edelman was a basic welfare state liberal, believing no entitlement or transfer payment was too big. Her great innovation was to defend the welfare system from empirical criti-cism—that is, it doesn't work—by hiding behind the image of poor children. "When you talked about poor people or black people you faced a shrinking audience," she has said. "I got the idea that chil-dren might be a very effective way to broaden the base for change." Indeed, Edelman more than anyone else can be blamed for the saccharine omnipresence of "the children" in American political rhetoric.[54]

The problem is that while this tactic was brilliant strategically, the net effect was to make responsible reform impossible. After all, the reason the "audience" was "shrinking" for exhortations to expand the welfare state was that it was becoming increasingly obvious that the welfare state was *causing* dependency among black women and alienation among black men. As a result, defenders of the status quo became ever more shrill in their attacks on opponents. Hence the use and abuse of "the children."

Traditional objections to welfare as a violation of constitutional principles and a corrupter of civic virtue—which only gained respectability in the late 1970s—were suddenly beside the point. Edelman, Clinton, and others transformed the debate to one about children. Who cares if—as FDR also believed—"relief" was ultimately detrimental to adults, sapping their initiative? The effects on adults were irrelevant. Children were the beneficiaries of aid checks, not their parents (even though their parents still cashed them). Indeed, one tragic consequence of this strategy was that the government used child poverty to crush individualism and pride among inner-city blacks. James Bovard notes that when Congress mandated food stamps, welfare "recruiters"—a hundred thousand of them created by the War on Poverty—went into the cities to convince poor people to enroll. An Agriculture Department magazine reported that food stamp workers could often overcome people's pride by telling parents, "This is for your children." It continued: thanks to "intensive outreach efforts, resistance of the 'too prouds' is bending."[55]

Perhaps just as important, this provided vital propaganda value for liberals. Ronald Reagan got traction for attacking "welfare queens." But no one would dare attack the unfortunate offspring of these women. Suddenly to criticize welfare policy made you "anti-child," thus spawning all of those liberal talking points about balancing the budget on the "backs of the children." This fed nicely into the psychological propaganda that conservatives are just bad people and that any break with the welfare state is motivated by "hate." Even Bill Clinton wasn't immune. When he signed the welfare reform bill, Peter Edelman resigned as assistant secretary of Health and Human Services, and Marian Edelman called Clinton's action a "moment of shame." "Never let us confuse what is legal with what is right," she proclaimed, pointedly adding, "Everything Hitler did in Nazi Germany was legal, but it was not right." The CDF denounced the move as an act of "national child abandonment," while Ted Kennedy called it "legislative child abuse." The *New York Times* columnist Anna Quindlen dubbed it "the politics of meanness."[56]

But the CDF and other remoras of the Great Society practiced the true politics of meanness, because at the end of the day their welfare state—based though it may have been on love, concern, and niceness—resulted in more damage to the black family and specifically to black children than much that can be laid at the feet of racist neglect. Today black children are less likely to be raised by two parents than they were during the era of slavery.

While Hillary Clinton may have learned from Edelman how to use children as propaganda tools for her ideological agenda, she far surpassed her teacher in the scope of her ambition. For Clinton, welfare policy was simply one front in a wider war. The crisis facing children wasn't merely an issue for poor denizens of the inner city. For Hillary, childhood *is* a crisis, and the government must come to the rescue. On this she has remained remarkably consistent. In her 1973 article "Children Under the Law" in *Harvard Educational Review,* she criticized the "pretense" that "children's issues are somehow beyond politics" and scorned the idea that "families are private, nonpolitical units whose interests subsume those of children." Fast-forward twenty-three years, to her April 24, 1996, address to the United Methodist General Conference: "As adults we have to start thinking and believing that *there isn't really any such thing as someone else's child* . . . For that reason, we cannot permit discussions of children and families to be subverted by political or ideological debate."[57]

These two quotations sound at odds, but the intent is exactly the same. It's just that Hillary Clinton in 1996 is a politician, whereas in 1973 she's a radical lawyer. What Clinton means when she says we cannot permit ideologues to "subvert" the discussion on children is that there can be no debate about what to do about children. And what must be done is to break the unchecked tyranny of the private home, as the progressive icon Charlotte Perkins Gilman put it.

This "brilliant hope"—as Gilman described it—is only realizable if children are cast as a class in perpetual crisis. Much as the proletariat were portrayed by Marxists as being in a constant state of war, with the nation under deadly siege by classical fascists, Hillary's children are in unimaginable existential peril. Thus she approvingly quotes the Cornell psychologist Urie Bronfenbrenner: "The present state of children and families in the United States represents *the greatest domestic problem our nation has faced since the founding of the Republic.* It is sapping our very roots." She concludes, "At a time when the well-being of children is under unprecedented threat, the balance of power is weighted heavily against them." The government must do everything it can to "reverse the crisis affecting our children," she declares. "Children, after all, are citizens too."[58]

Here at last is a "moral equivalent of war" that modern liberals can rally around, a "crisis mechanism" no one would identify as fascistic because when you say "the children" the last thing you think of are storm troopers. Nobody wants to be seen as anti-child. The "child crisis" needed no definition because it had no boundaries. Even people without children should care about other people's children. Fast foods were targeted because they make children fat—and nutritional decisions can't be left to the parent. "More than the much-reviled products of Big Tobacco, big helpings and Big Food constitute the number-one threat to America's children," the *Nation* warned. The Clinton administration and affiliated activists justified its gun control policies based on the threat to children. "No longer will we be silent as the gun lobby refuses to put our children's health and safety first," Hillary Clinton barked in a senatorial debate in 2000.[59]

It's forgotten now, but the early Clinton administration was saturated with such thinking. Janet Reno, appointed the nation's top law enforcement official as part of a gender quota, defined her primary mission as a protector of children. "I would like to use the law of this land to do everything I possibly can," she declared when nominated, "to give to each of them the opportunity to grow to be strong, healthy and self-sufficient citizens of this country." Reno, it may be forgotten, had come to national attention as a crusading prosecutor who won a number of convictions in a series of high-profile child sex-abuse cases. Many of them, it was later revealed, were fraudulent, and Reno's zealous tactics do not look admirable in hindsight. When she came to Washington, the first woman in one of the big four cabinet positions, she was determined to cast herself as primarily a children's advocate, launching her "national children's agenda." "The children of America, 20 percent of whom live in poverty, have no one to advocate for them," Reno said.[60] Reno's zeal as a protector of children no doubt played a role in her disastrous handling of the Branch Davidian raid in Waco, Texas.

But Janet Reno was precisely the sort of attorney general that, at least in theory, the author of *It Takes a Village* would want. Clinton describes an enormous network of activists, advocates, organizations, associations, busybodies, bureaucrats, and meddlers who make up the army of "qualified citizens" whose task it is to protect the village's interests in our children. "I cannot say enough in support of home visits," she gushes. "[The] village needs a town crier—and a town prodder."[61] Again, scrape the saccharine from the sentiment and look underneath. Imagine if, say, the former attorney general John Ashcroft had said, "I cannot say enough in support of home visits." The shrieks of "fascism" would be deafening.

For Hillary Clinton, the most important front in the "war" to protect children is the first three years of life. These precious moments are so critical that we cannot leave parents to cope with them on their own. Hence a vast array of programs are necessary to plug parents into a social network that alleviates their responsibilities. As Christopher Lasch noted well before she ever wrote *It Takes a Village*, Clinton "puts her faith in 'programs.' The proliferation of children's programs—Head Start, day care, prenatal care, maternal care, baby clinics, programs for assessing standards in public schools, immunization programs, child-development programs—serves her as an infallible index of progress."[62]

The twentieth century gave us two visions of a dystopian future, Aldous Huxley's *Brave New World* and George Orwell's *1984*. For many years it was assumed that *1984* was the more prophetic tale. But no more. The totalitarianism of *1984* was a product of the age of Stalin, Lenin, Hitler, and Mussolini, the dictators of a continent with a grand tradition of political and religious absolutism. *Brave New World* was a dystopia based on an *American* future, where Henry Ford is remembered as a messiah (it's set in the year "632 A.F.," after Ford) and the cult of youth that Huxley so despised defines society. Everything is *easy* under the World State. Everyone is *happy*. Indeed, the great dilemma for the reader of *Brave New World* is to answer the question, what's wrong with it?

There's a second important difference between the two dystopias: *1984* is a masculine vision of totalitarianism. Or rather, it is a vision *of* a masculine totalitarianism. Huxley's totalitarianism isn't a "boot stamping on a human face—for ever," as described in *1984*. It's one of smiling, happy, bioengineered people chewing hormonal gum and blithely doing what they're told. Democracy is a forgotten fad because things are so much easier when the state makes all your decisions. In short, Huxley's totalitarianism is essentially feminine. Orwell's was a daddy-dystopia, where the state is abusive and bullying, maintaining its authority through a permanent climate of war and the manufacture of convenient enemies. Huxley's is a maternal misery, where man is smothered with care, not cruelty. But for all our talk these days about manliness, individualism, and even the "nanny state," we still don't have the vocabulary to fight off *nice totalitarianism,* liberal fascism.

With that distinction in mind, let us revisit *It Takes a Village.* On page after page, Clinton extols the idea that just about everything is a health issue. Divorce should be treated like a "public health issue" because it creates stress in children. The very basics of parenting are health issues because "how infants are held, touched, fed, spoken to, and gazed at" determines whether our brains can be "hijacked" by our emotions, potentially making us murderously violent. Mrs. Clinton tells us that Janet Reno issued a report which found that gang violence and gun use are the products of people with badly imprinted brains who become "emotionally hijacked" with little provocation. Quoting doctors, friendly activists, social workers, and random real Americans, in chapter after chapter she argues for interventions on behalf of children from literally the moment they are born. Children need "[g]entle, intimate, consistent contact" to reduce stress, which can "create feelings of helplessness that lead to later developmental problems." Even well-to-do parents need help because after all everyone feels stress, and "we know that babies sense the stress."[63]

It's fair to say that a state empowered to eliminate parental stress is a state with a Huxleyan mandate. And a state with an extreme mandate must logically go to extremes. Hence Clinton argues for the diffusion of parental training into every nook and cranny of public life. Here's one such suggestion: "Videos with scenes of commonsense baby care—how to burp an infant, what to do when soap gets in his eyes, how to make a baby with an earache comfortable—could be running continuously in doctors' offices, clinics, hospitals, motor vehicle offices, or any place where people gather and have to wait."[64]

Imagine if these sorts of ideas were fully implemented at the Department of Motor Vehicles, the passport office, and other places "where people gather and have to wait." Giant flat screens at the airport pumping breast-feeding advice? The JumboTron at football games? At what point would the Brave New World seem to be heading down the pike?

Then there are the home inspectors, the advisers, the teachers, the social workers. Clinton relies on her loyal army of experts to dispense advice about every jot and tittle of child rearing; no detail is too small, no nudge too condescending. "The Child Care Action Campaign . . . advises that 'jigsaw puzzles and crayons may be fine for preschoolers but are inappropriate for infants.' " The Consumer Product Safety Commission, Clinton helpfully passes on, has concluded that "baby showers with a safety theme are a great way to help new and expectant mothers childproof every room in their homes."[65]

Rousseau wanted to take children away from parents and raise them in state-owned boarding schools. Clinton doesn't go that far, but then again, she believes by the time kids are old enough to go to boarding school, it's too late. Hence her passion for day care. Of course, there is a second agenda here. Day care is also the holy grail for baby-boomer feminists who believe not that children should be liberated from the family but that mothers should be liberated from children.

In order to crack the spine of patriarchy, feminists have had to rely on Sorelian myths, noble lies, and crisis mechanisms to win their battles. For example, in 1998 President Clinton proposed a $22 billion federal day-care scheme to cure what Hillary was calling "the silent crisis" of day care. Clinton also used the "silent crisis" formulation in *It Takes a Village* to describe the plight of children generally. These crises were silent for the same reason unicorns are silent—they don't exist. Except, that is, in the hearts and minds of progressive "reformers." Even though eight out of ten children were cared for by family members, only 13 percent of parents polled said finding child care was a "major problem." Shortly before the White House held its crisis-mongering Conference on Child Care, which was intended to lay the groundwork for Hillary's plan, a mere 1 percent of Americans named child care one of the two or three most pressing problems government should fix. And surveys of women conducted since 1974 have shown that growing majorities of married women want to stay home with their children if they can.

Perhaps one reason women would prefer to raise their own children is that they intuitively understand that, all things being equal, day care is, in fact, not great for children. Dr. Benjamin Spock knew this as early as the 1950s, when he wrote that day-care centers were "no good for infants." But when he reissued his *Baby and Child Care* guide in the 1990s, he removed that advice, caving in to feminist pressures and concerns. "It's a cowardly thing that I did," he admits. "I just tossed it in subsequent editions." If, as liberals often suggest, the suppression of science for political ends is fascistic, then the campaign to cover up the dark side of child care certainly counts as fascism. For example, in 1991 Dr. Louise Silverstein wrote in *American Psychologist* that "psychologists must refuse to undertake any more research that looks for the negative consequences of other-than-mother-care." The traditional conception of motherhood is nothing more than an "idealized myth" concocted by the patriarchy to "glorify motherhood in an attempt to encourage white, middle class women to have more children."[66]

It's not that Clinton and others advocate policies they believe are bad for children. That would make them cartoon villains. Rather, they believe in good faith that society would be much improved if we all looked at everybody's children as our own. They sincerely hold, in the words of the feminist philosopher Linda Hirshman, that women cannot be "fully realized human beings" if they don't make work a bigger priority than mothering. In a sense, Hirshman is a feminist version of Michael Lerner, who sees work as a "locus" of meaning. Her contempt for women who don't completely dedicate themselves to work is palpable.[67] And as other feminists note, if women are made to feel "judged" or shamed by their choice of day care, this negativity will be paid forward in the form of brain-warping stress.

Some couch their progressive utopianism in pragmatic language. Sandra Scarr is possibly the most quoted expert on "other-than-mother" care in America and a past president of the American Psychological Society. "However desirable or undesirable the ideal of fulltime maternal care may be," she says, "it is completely unrealistic in the world of the late 20th century." That sounds defensible enough. But her larger agenda lurks beneath the surface. We need to create the "new century's ideal children." Uh-oh. Beware of social engineers who want to "create" a new type of human being. These new children will need to learn how to love *everybody* like a family member. "Multiple attachments to others will become the ideal. Shyness and *exclusive maternal attachment will seem dysfunctional.* New treatments will be developed for children with exclusive maternal attachments."[68] Can you see the Brave New World over the horizon yet?

Among these "treatments"—another word for propaganda—are books that try to put distance between mothers and children, such as *Mommy Go Away!* and *Why Are You So Mean to Me?* In *It Takes a Village,* Clinton cites the Washington-Beech Community Preschool in Roslindale, Massachusetts, where "director Ellen Wolpert has children play games like Go Fish and Concentration with a deck of cards adorned with images—men holding babies, women pounding nails, elderly men on ladders, gray-haired women on skateboards—that counter the predictable images."[69] This sort of thing is carried into progressive grade schools where gender norms are often attacked, as documented in Christina Hoff Sommers's *War Against Boys.*

In short, day care is not bad for children. Rather, the traditional bourgeois standards by which we judge what is good for children are bad. This trick is a genteel replay of the Nazi effort to steal the young away from the hidebound traditions of their parents. The Nazis brilliantly replaced traditional stories and fairy tales with yarns of Aryan bravery, the divinity of Hitler, and the like. Math problems became mechanisms for subliminal indoctrination; kids would still learn math, but the word problems were now about artillery trajectories and the amount of food being wasted on defectives and other minorities. Christian morality was slowly purged from the schools, and teachers were instructed to base their moral teaching on "secular" patriotic ideas. "The idea of loyalty was very important to the Germanic *Volk,* as it is for us today," teachers told their students. Indeed, loyalty to Hitler and the state was drilled into children, while loyalty to one's own parents was discouraged in myriad ways. The children were going to become new men and new women for the new age.

Obviously, the content of the saccharine liberalism children are indoctrinated into today is very different. But there are disturbing similarities, too. Good children will be those who are less attached to their parents and more attached to the "community." The fascist quest for the new man, living in a new, totalitarian society in which every individual feels the warm and loving embrace of the state, once again begins in the crib.

The last step toward the Huxleyan future for Hillary Clinton is philosophical, perhaps even metaphysical. Clinton's views of children are more universal than she seems to realize. Mrs. Clinton says, "I have never met a stupid child," and attests that "some of the best theologians I have ever met were five-year-olds."[70] Don't let the namby-pamby sentiment blind you to what is being said here. By defining the intellectual status of children *up,* she is simultaneously defining *down* the authority and autonomy of adults. In a world where children are indistinguishable from grown-ups, how distinct can grown-ups be from children?

The liberal cult of the child is instructive in its similarities to fascist thought. Children, like youth, are driven by passion, feelings, emotion, will. These are among the fascist virtues as well. Youth represents the glories of "unreason." These sentiments, in turn, are deeply tied to the narcissistic populism that celebrates the instincts of the masses. "I want it now and I don't care if it's against the rules" is the quintessentially childlike populist passion. Fascism is a form of populism because the leader forges a parental bond with his "children." Without the emotional bond between the leader and "the people," Führer and *Volk,* fascism is impossible. "I'm on your side," "I'm one of you," "we're in this together," "I know what it's like to be you," constitutes the sales pitch of every fascist and populist demagogue. Or as Willie Stark says to the nurturing crowd in *All the King's Men:* "Your will is my strength. Your need is my justice." Arguments, facts, *reason:* these are secondary. "The people of Nebraska are for free silver and I am for free silver," proclaimed William Jennings Bryan, America's most beloved populist. "I will look up the arguments later."[71]

Bill Clinton campaigned relentlessly on his ability to "feel our pain." Countless observers marveled at his ability to "feed" off the crowd, to draw energy from the masses. Journalists often called him an "empath" for his ability to intuit what an audience wanted to hear.

This is a great skill in a politician, but one should never forget that demagogues are first and foremost masterful politicians.

Of course, Clinton's demagoguery was of a decidedly feminine nature. He promised hugs, to feel your pain, and to protect you from those mean boys (Republicans and "angry white males"). His watchword was "security"—economic security, social security, security from globalization, crime, job losses, whatever. He was the "first female president," according to the feminist novelist Mary Gordon. When he was accused of failure or error, his reflexive response was that of an overwhelmed single mother: "I've been working so hard," as if that were an adequate substitute for being right or effective. His defenders essentially claimed that he was above the law because he was, as Stanford's Kathleen Sullivan put it, the only person who works for all of us twenty-four hours a day. In other words, he wasn't a person; he was the state in its maternal incarnation. Sure, many Americans liked his policies—or thought they did because the economy was doing well—but they liked *him* because of his oddly maternal *concern*. The political aesthetics here were nothing new. As Goebbels noted of his Führer's popularity, "The entire people loves him, because it feels safe in his hands like a child in the arms of its mother."[72]

Was Bill Clinton a fascist president? Well, he certainly believed in the primacy of emotion and the supremacy of his own intellect. He spun noble lies with reckless abandon. An admirer of Huey Long's, he shared the cornpone dictator's contempt for the rules and had the same knack for demagogic appeals. He was a committed Third Wayer if ever there was one, and he devoutly shared JFK's new politics. But I think if we are going to call him a fascist, it must be in the sense that he was a sponge for the ideas and emotions of liberalism. To say that he was a fascist himself is to credit him with more ideology and principle than justified. He was the sort of president liberal fascism could only produce during unexciting times. But most important, if he was fascist, it was because that's what we as Americans wanted. We craved empathy, because we felt we deserved someone who cared about Me.

Hillary Clinton learned that lesson well when she decided to run for office for the first time. Mrs. Clinton will never have her husband's raw political talent. She's too cold, too cerebral for his style of backslapping, lip-biting politics. Instead, she translated Bill Clinton's political instincts into an ideological appeal. In 2000, when she ran as a carpetbagger for Senate in New York, Mrs. Clinton's track record was a problem. She essentially had none—at least not as a New Yorker. So she crafted a brilliant campaign slogan and rationale: she was the candidate who was "more concerned about the issues that concern New Yorkers." Her discipline in sticking to this message awed veteran political observers. The issues weren't the issue, as they said in the 1960s. *The issue of who was more concerned about the issues was the issue.* "I think that the real issue ought to be who cares about the children of New York City," she said in a typical utterance.[73]

One might ask, since when did "concern" count as the greatest of qualifications? A plumber might well be more concerned about how to successfully remove your spleen than a surgeon would. Does that mean a sane man would prefer a plumber to a doctor? Do banks give loans to the applicants most *concerned* with running a successful business or to those most likely to pay back the loan? Should the student most concerned with getting good grades get straight As?

The response to all this is simple: concern is what children (and the rest of us) look for in parents. In the liberal fascist view, children are citizens and citizens are children (a chapter of Hillary's book is titled "Children Are Citizens Too"), so it follows that leaders should behave like parents. "I think my job is to lead," Bill Clinton remarked while in office, "and take care of the country. And I suppose the older I get, the more it becomes the role of a father figure instead of an older brother."[74]

Under this vision, even your own money is not yours. It's an *allowance.* When asked what his problem was with letting local school districts spend tax dollars the way they saw fit, Bill Clinton snapped back: "Because it's not their money." In 1997 he ridiculed Virginia voters who wanted tax cuts as "selfish," and then chided them like children: "And think how you felt every time in your life you were tempted to do something that was selfish and you didn't do it, and the next day you felt wonderful." In 1999, when the government was running a surplus, many taxpayers felt that getting back some of their money was a reasonable policy. When asked about this, President Clinton responded, "We could give it all back to you and hope you spend it right." Senator Clinton was more straightforward. Talking about George W. Bush's tax cuts, which did return that surplus to the people who created it, Mrs. Clinton—speaking in the classic argot of the Social Gospel—said that those cuts had to be done away with. "We're going to take things away from you on behalf of the common good."[75]

Hillary is no führer, and her notion of the "common good" doesn't involve racial purity or concentration camps. But she indisputably draws her vision from the same eternal instinct to impose order on society, to create an all-encompassing community, to get past endless squabbles and ensconce each individual in the security blanket of the state. Hers is a political religion, an updated Social Gospel—light on the Gospel, heavy on the Social—spoken in soothing tones and conjuring a reassuring vision of cooperation and community. But it remains a singular vision, and there's no room in it for those still suffering from the "stupidity of habit-bound minds," to borrow Dewey's phrase. The village may have replaced "the state," and it in turn may have replaced the fist with the hug, but an unwanted embrace from which you cannot escape is just a nicer form of tyranny.

· 10 ·

The New Age:
We're All Fascists Now

It is generally thought that National Socialism stands only for
brutishness and terror. But this is not true. National Socialism—
more broadly, fascism—also stands for an ideal or rather ideals that
are persistent today under other banners: the ideal of life as art, the
cult of beauty, the fetishism of courage, the dissolution of alienation
in ecstatic feelings of community, the repudiation of the intellect,
the family of man (under the parenthood of leaders). These ideals
are vivid and moving to many people . . . because their content is a
romantic ideal to which many continue to be attached and which is
expressed in such diverse modes of cultural dissidence and
propaganda for new forms of community as the youth/rock culture,
primal therapy, anti-psychiatry, Third-World camp-following, and
belief in the occult.
—Susan Sontag, "Fascinating Fascism"

LIBERALS CONSTANTLY COMPLAIN that conservatives
are trying to impose their cultural vision on the rest of the
country. In contrast, they themselves only care about the "real" issues of class and economics. Thomas Frank, author of the best-
selling *What's the Matter With Kansas?*, leads a whole school of
liberals who argue that middle-class GOP voters have been hood-
winked by Republican strategists pushing manufactured "values" is-

sues. Frank's argument boils down to the old Marxist doctrine of false consciousness, which says that to disagree with the left about the nature of political and economic self-interest is a form of brainwashing or dementia.

But are liberals and leftists really dedicated to economic justice rather than divisive issues like gay marriage or partial-birth abortion? If you look closely, you'll see that liberals object to "values issues" in politics only when they expose liberal weaknesses. When liberals are on the defensive, they use Marxist or, if you prefer, socialistic arguments to delegitimize the opposition's cultural agenda. When conservatives have the upper hand on a cultural issue, liberalism is all about "solving problems" for the average Joe, about paychecks and health care. But on offense, it's about racial quotas, mainstreaming gay culture, scrubbing the public square of Christianity, and a host of explicitly cultural ambitions.

This socialist-parry, cultural-thrust tactic mirrors Nazi maneuvers in interesting ways. When the Nazis were debating traditionalists, monarchists, and the few classical liberals left in Germany, they sounded much like generic socialists lamenting how "big capitalism" was screwing the little guy. Hitler charged that other parties were dividing Germans along sectarian and class lines, while he wanted to focus like a laser on the economy. It was only when the National Socialists had the upper hand that they dropped their economic arguments in favor of imposing a new cultural order.

This economics-on-defense, culture-on-offense approach remained an important tactic for Hitler even after his consolidation of power. For example, in 1938, when he realized that the Nazi cultural agenda was starting to alienate significant segments of the population, he explained in a speech, "National Socialism is a cool, reality-based doctrine, based upon the sharpest scientific knowledge and its mental expression. As we have opened the people's heart to this doctrine, and as we continue to do so at the present, we have no desire to instill in the people a mysticism that lies outside the purpose and goals of our doctrine." Such language should be familiar to liberals who like to call themselves members of the "reality-based community."[1]

There is simply no denying that liberalism is deeply committed to the creation and imposition of culture. Indeed, it's transparently obvious that liberals care primarily about culture. During the 1990s, for example, liberalism dove headlong into the culture-formation business, from Hillary Clinton's politics of meaning to the gender norming of college sports, to gays in the military, to the war on smoking. In 2007, to pick an offbeat recent example, a progressive child-care center in Seattle banned LEGOs because "the children were building their assumptions about ownership and the social power it conveys—assumptions that mirrored those of a class-based, capitalist society—a society that we teachers believe to be unjust and oppressive." In response, they created a playtime that reflected the morally superior standards of "collectivity."[2]

The simple fact of the matter is this: liberals are the aggressors in the culture wars. Why this should seem a controversial point is somewhat baffling. It is manifestly clear that traditionalists are defending their way of life against the so-called forces of progress. When feminist groups finally persuaded the courts to force the Virginia Military Institute to accept women, who was the aggressor? Whose values were being imposed? Which side's activists boast of being "agents of change"? My point is not that the forces of change are always wrong. Far from it. My point is that the left is dishonest when it pretends that it is not in the business of imposing its values on others.

We've discussed how, in the 1950s, the left updated the traditional Marxist critique of capitalism by arguing that fascist reaction was really a psychological response to progress. Whereas once the left argued that fascism was the *political* reaction of economic ruling *classes* against the revolutionary workers, now fascism is expressed as one of many "phobias," or simply "rage," aimed at the advancement of certain groups and causes. These rages and phobias are felt almost exclusively by white male heterosexuals (and the women who love them), the scions of those evil "Dead White European Males." In the 1930s the left claimed that fascists wanted to protect their factories and titles of nobility; now we are told that the fascists—a.k.a. "angry white males"—want to preserve their unfair "privilege." Homophobia, racism, nativism, and, in a neat moral equivalence, both Islamic extremism and Islamophobia are the white male power structure's instinctive fascistic response to the shock of the new.

These kinds of arguments, to borrow a phrase from Carl von

Clausewitz, represent the continuation of war by cultural means. And indeed, nowhere is this logic more visibly on display than in popular culture.

Take the movie *Pleasantville.* An imaginary Mayberry of a town seemingly frozen in the repressive, white-male-dominated 1950s is shaken up by the introduction of freedom-loving, sexually liberated young people from the 1990s. It's the 1960s all over again. The town elders can't handle the challenge—their liberated wives no longer have martinis and slippers waiting for them at the end of the day. In response, the white male elite—led by the Chamber of Commerce, of course—becomes increasingly fascistic. One of the film's clever conceits is that the tradition-bound people of Pleasantville are filmed in black and white while the fully realized human beings are portrayed in living color. This prompts the monochromatic fascists to start treating the "coloreds" as second-class citizens.

A similar theme can be found in the playfully fascistic film *Falling Down,* in which a white middle-class defense contractor played by Michael Douglas becomes violent when he is downsized and thrown out of work. In *American Beauty,* Kevin Spacey's sexually confused ex-marine neighbor snaps and becomes a murderer when he can't handle the idea that his son might be gay. It isn't surprising that Hollywood keeps churning out these chestnuts, but it is amazing that each time it does, so many critics hail them as novel and pathbreaking interpretations, when they are really just a series of recycled clichés.

But there's a larger point behind the effort to cast opponents of change as fascists: to make change itself the natural order by ridiculing the very notion of a natural order. The underlying dogma of these movies is that social and gender roles are not fixed, that tradition, religion, and natural law have no binding power or authority over the individual's will to power, and that the day we made the mistake of thinking otherwise was the day we took a tragic Wrong Turn.

THE KULTURKAMPF, THEN AND NOW

The phrase "culture war" is traceable to two very different thinkers. The more recent is the Marxist Antonio Gramsci, who argued that the only way to throw off the old order was to launch a "long march" through elite cultural institutions. This was the strategy taken by the New Left insurgents of the 1960s, who in short order conquered English departments, editorial boards, movie studios, and the like. But the earlier and more relevant wellspring was Otto von Bismarck's Kulturkampf.

It is common among educated liberals to use the term "Kulturkampf" in referring to the supposed efforts of the right to impose its values on the rest of the country by demonizing liberals. The Germanic overtones are obviously meant to evoke a Hitlerian parallel. Quite the contrary, however, the original Kulturkampf was not a right-wing crackdown on liberal dissenters or imperiled minorities but an onslaught from the *left* against the forces of traditionalism and conservatism. Ostensibly, the Kulturkampf was a war against German Catholics, absorbed for the first time into greater Germany. Bismarck feared that they might not be sufficiently loyal to a Germany led by Prussia, and even more pragmatically, he wanted to avoid the formation of a German Catholic political party.

Bismarck's intentions were grounded in realpolitik and political triangulation. It was the progressive forces in the Reichstag who were the true believers. Catholicism was seen by progressive Germans as foreign, antiquated, backward, and un-German. It stood in the way of nationalism, scientism, and progress. The word "Kulturkampf" itself was coined by the influential scientist Rudolf Virchow, a renowned liberal who hoped the Kulturkampf would liberate men from the clutches of Christian superstition and wed them to progressive principles. Behind that impulse, however, lay a desire to impose a new religion, a progressive religion of the *Volk*-state.

The first Kulturkampf laws, passed with great fanfare in 1873, were hailed as enormous progressive strides in the separation of church and state. Emil Friedberg, a liberal architect of the anti-Catholic "May Laws," explained the state's obligations toward the Catholic Church: "to suppress it, to destroy it, to crush it with violence." In a riot of neo-Jacobinism, liberals harassed and shut down Catholic schools. Mandatory civil marriages weakened the power and influence of the Church. The state claimed the right to appoint, promote, discipline, and even deport Church officials. Most of

Germany's Catholic bishops were either thrown in jail, hounded from office, or chased into exile. Eventually the Kulturkampf exhausted itself; but the idea that traditional Christianity was a threat to national progress took permanent root.[3]

In the 1870s the acid predictably worked its way through the body politic and transformed itself into anti-Semitism. Indeed, the word "anti-Semitism" was coined in 1879 by the atheist and radical leftist Wilhelm Marr in his tract *The Way to Victory of Germanicism over Judaism*. Marr's contribution was to transform hatred of Jews from a theological passion into a "modern" racial and cultural one (he hated assimilated Jews more than orthodox ones, for example). "Anti-Semitism"—as opposed to the more theological *Judenhass*—was intended to ground hatred of Jews in the progressive language of scientific eugenics.

During his rise to power Hitler—in many respects the heir of the Bismarckian progressives—could hardly launch an all-out attack on Christianity. National Socialism, after all, was supposed to unite all Germans. It's "not opportune to hurl ourselves now into a struggle with the Churches. The best thing is to let Christianity die a natural death," Hitler explained to his aides. "A slow death has something comforting about it. The dogma of Christianity gets worn away before the advances of science. Religion will have to make more and more concessions. Gradually the myths crumble. All that's left is to prove that in nature there is no frontier between the organic and the inorganic."[4]

In 1937 the German Social Democratic Party, operating in exile in Prague, enlisted a spy to report from Germany on Nazi progress. The reporter, working in secret, offered a crucial insight into what the Nazis were really up to. The National Socialist German Workers' Party was constructing a new religion, a "counter-church," complete with its own priests, dogmas, holidays, rituals, and rites. The agent used a brilliant metaphor to explain the Nazi effort. The counter-church was being built like a new railway bridge. When you build a new bridge, you can't just tear down the old one willy-nilly. Traffic and commerce will be snarled. The public will protest. Instead, you need to slowly but surely replace the bridge over time. Swap out an old bolt for a new one. Quietly switch the ancient beams for fresh ones, and one day you will have a completely different structure and barely anyone will have noticed.

Like the engineers of that proverbial railway bridge, the Nazis worked relentlessly to replace the nuts and bolts of traditional Christianity with a new political religion. The shrewdest way to accomplish this was to co-opt Christianity via the *Gleichschaltung* while at the same time shrinking traditional religion's role in civil society. To this end, Hitler was downright Bismarckian. The German historian Götz Aly explains how Hitler purchased popularity with lavish social welfare programs and middle-class perks, often paid for with stolen Jewish wealth and high taxes on the rich. Hitler banned religious charity, crippling the churches' role as a counterweight to the state. Clergy were put on government salary, hence subjected to state authority. "The parsons will be made to dig their own graves," Hitler cackled. "They will betray their God to us. They will betray anything for the sake of their miserable little jobs and incomes."[5]

Following the Jacobin example, the Nazis replaced the traditional Christian calendar. The new year began on January 30 with the Day of the Seizure of Power.[6] Each November the streets of central Munich were dedicated to a Nazi Passion play depicting Hitler's Beer Hall Putsch. The martyrdom of Horst Wessel and his "old fighters" replaced Jesus and the apostles. Plays and official histories were rewritten to glorify pagan Aryans bravely fighting against Christianizing foreign armies. Anticipating some feminist pseudo history, witches became martyrs to the bloodthirsty oppression of Christianity.

Under the progressives, the Christian God had been transformed into the God of lower food prices. Under the Nazis, the Christian God would be transformed into an Aryan SS officer with Hitler his right hand. The so-called German Christian pastors preached that "just as Jesus liberated mankind from sin and hell, so Hitler saves the German *Volk* from decay." In April 1933 the Nazi Congress of German Christians pronounced that all churches should catechize that "God has created me a German; Germanism is a gift of God. God wills that I fight for Germany. War service in no way injures the Christian conscience, but is obedience to God."[7]

When some Protestant bishops visited the Führer to register complaints, Hitler's rage got the better of him. "Christianity will disappear from Germany just as it has done in Russia . . . The German race has existed without Christianity for thousands of years . . . and will continue after Christianity has disappeared . . . We must get used to the teachings of blood and race." When the bishops objected that they supported Nazism's secular aims, just not its religious innovations, Hitler exploded: "You are traitors to the Volk. Enemies of the Vaterland and destroyers of Germany."[8]

In 1935 mandatory prayer in school was abolished, and in 1938 carols and Nativity plays were banned entirely. By 1941 religious instruction for children fourteen years and up had been abolished altogether, and Jacobinism reigned supreme. A Hitler Youth song rang out from the campfires:

> *We are the happy Hitler Youth;*
> *We have no need for Christian virtue;*
> *For Adolf Hitler is our intercessor*
> *And our redeemer.*
> *No priest, no evil one*
> *Can keep us*
> *From feeling like Hitler's children.*
> *No Christ do we follow, but Horst Wessel!*
> *Away with incense and holy water pots.*[9]

Meanwhile, the orphans were given new lyrics to "Silent Night":

> *Silent night! Holy night! All is calm, all is bright,*
> *Only the Chancellor steadfast in fight,*
> *Watches o'er Germany by day and night,*
> *Always caring for us.*

In like manner, the American Kulturkampf of the 1960s begins not with the hippies, the Vietnam War, or even civil rights. As befits an attempt to clear the way for a new political religion, it starts with the effort to eliminate prayer in school. As Jeremy Rabkin has argued, the school prayer decisions of the 1960s should be seen as the beginning of the Supreme Court's role as the primary engine of the American Kulturkampf.

Consider abortion. The fundamental logic of the Supreme Court cases legalizing abortion hinges not on the "right to choose" but on the idea that religion and religiously informed morality have no place in public affairs. *Roe v. Wade* and its companion case, *Doe v. Bolton,* stemmed directly from the 1965 case *Griswold v. Connecticut,* in which the Court invalidated a ban on birth control (almost never enforced) on the grounds that the right to privacy can be found in the emanation of a penumbra to the Constitution. But the Court's underlying motivation stemmed from a conviction that religiously inspired laws (Connecticut has a large Catholic population) are suspect. Just two years before *Roe,* in a Pennsylvania case, the Court quashed state aid to Catholic parochial schools on the grounds that it would divide the public along sectarian lines. Moreover, the Court held, religious concerns "tend to confuse and obscure other issues of great urgency." When *Roe v. Wade* finally appeared before the Court, the justices had already concluded that traditional religious concerns can have little weight in public affairs. Laurence Tribe, America's leading liberal constitutional lawyer, argued in the *Harvard Law Review* in 1978 that religious views were inherently superstitious and hence less legitimate than "secular" ones.

In 1987 the Supreme Court ruled that moments of silence at the beginning of the school day constituted a government endorsement of prayer. In 1992 it held that a nonsectarian prayer at a school graduation (offered by a Reform rabbi) was an impermissible endorsement of religion. In 1995 the Ninth Circuit Court of Appeals ruled that the "right to die" could not be hindered simply "in order to satisfy the moral or religious precepts of a portion of the population." Never mind that laws against murder, theft, and perjury can be traced directly back to the same "religious precepts."

More recently, we've seen courts rule that the Pledge of Allegiance, displays of the Ten Commandments, and Christmas crèches are unconstitutional anywhere near a public facility. Justice Antonin Scalia had it right in 1996 in the *Romer v. Evans* case (dealing with the public accommodation of homosexuality in Colorado). "The Court has mistaken a *Kulturkampf* for a fit of spite," he declared. He went on to castigate his colleagues for "taking sides" in the "culture wars."

Why belabor this point about religion? Because it is impossible to understand liberalism's cultural agenda without understanding that modern liberalism is building its own railway bridge, replacing the bricks and beams of traditional American culture with something else. I do not claim that everything in the new liberal structure is bad or wrong. But I reject the clever argumentation of liberals who claim that their effort is merely "pragmatic" or piecemeal. "Oh, just this one brick. What's wrong with this brick?" is how liberals argue about every stage of their project. But it's not just one brick. Nor should conservatives believe it is merely a slippery slope. That image suggests forces outside of our control pulling us in a direction not of our choosing. If society is moving in a direction not of its choosing, it is often because it is being *pushed* by the self-appointed forces of progress.

Tom Wolfe, in his essay "The Great Relearning," details how the counterculture, inspired by the German Bauhaus, wanted to start over, to declare a new Year Zero (much as the Jacobins and Nazis did), to go back to the fork in the road where Western civilization allegedly took the wrong path. The counterculture author Ken Kesey even organized a pilgrimage to the pagan mecca of Stonehenge, believing that this was the last place Western man was on the right track and, presumably, took a wrong turn by leaving his paganism behind. In the remainder of this chapter we will look at how this overarching vision informed the movements and ideas both of classical fascism and of today's cultural left in a few discrete areas of culture: identity, morality, sex, and nature.

THE LIBERAL FASCIST KULTURKAMPF

Isaiah Berlin summarized the neo-Romantic outlook that gave rise to Nazism: "If I am German I seek German virtues, I write German music, I rediscover ancient German laws, I cultivate everything within me which makes me as rich, as expressive, as many-sided, as full a German as it is possible for me to be . . . That is the romantic ideal at its fullest." Such thinking led inexorably to the Nazi conception of right and wrong. "Justice," explained Alfred Rosenberg, "is what the Aryan man deems just. Unjust is what he so deems."[10]

This vision most concretely manifested itself in the effort to purge the influence of the Jewish mind from Nazi Germany. The Jew symbolized everything that kept the German people back. Even "conscience," according to Hitler, "is a Jewish invention" to be discarded in an act of self-liberation. As a result, the Nazis played the same games against the Jews that today's left plays against "Eurocentrism," "whiteness," and "logocentrism." When you hear a campus radical denounce "white logic" or "male logic," she is standing on the shoulders of a Nazi who denounced "Jewish logic" and the "Hebrew disease." While still a Nazi collaborator, Paul de Man—the revered postmodern theorist who eventually taught at Yale and Cornell—wrote of the Jews, "Their cerebralness, their capacity to assimilate doctrines while maintaining a cold detachment from them," is one of "the specific characteristics of the Jewish mind."[11]

The white male is the Jew of liberal fascism. The "key to solving the social problems of our age is to abolish the white race," writes the whiteness studies scholar and historian Noel Ignatiev. Whiteness studies is a cutting-edge academic discipline sweeping American higher education. Some thirty universities have WS departments, but many more schools teach the essentials of whiteness studies in other courses. The executive director of the Center for the Study of White American Culture explains, "There is no crime that whiteness has not committed against people of color . . . We must blame whiteness for the continuing patterns today . . . which damage and prevent the humanity of those of us within it."[12] The journal *Race Traitor* (ironically, a Nazi term) is dedicated "to serve as an intellectual center for those seeking to abolish the white race." Now, this is not a genocidal movement; no one is suggesting that white people be rounded up and put in camps. But the principles, passions, and argumentation have troubling echoes.

First, there is the left's shocking defense of black riot ideology and gangsterism. The glorification of violence, the romance of the street, the denunciations of "the system," the conspiratorialism, the exaltation of racial solidarity, the misogyny of hip-hop culture: all of these things offer a disturbing sense of déjà vu. Hip-hop culture has incorporated a shocking number of fascist themes. On college campuses, administrators routinely look the other way at classically fascist behavior, from newspaper burnings to the physical intimidation of dissident speakers. These attitudes ultimately stem from the view that the white man, like the Jew, represents every facet of what is wrong and oppressive to humanity. As Susan Sontag proclaimed in 1967, "The white race is the cancer of human history." Meanwhile, Enlightenment notions of universal humanity are routinely mocked on the academic left as a con used to disguise entrenched white male privilege.

Just as the Nazi attack on Christianity was part of a larger war on the idea of universal truth, whole postmodern cosmologies have been created to prove that traditional religious morality is a scam, that there are no fixed truths or "natural" categories, and that all knowledge is socially constructed. Or as the line goes in *The Da Vinci Code*, "So Dark, the Con of Man."

The "con" in question is, in effect, a conspiracy by the Catholic Church to deceive the world about Jesus' true nature and his marriage to Mary Magdalene. The book has sold some sixty million copies worldwide. The novel, and movie, have generated debates, documentaries, companion books, and the like. But few have called attention to the ominous roots and parallels with Nazi thought.

Dan Brown should have dedicated his book to "Madame" Helena Blavatsky, the theosophist guru who is widely considered the "mother" of New Age spirituality as well as a touchstone in the development of Nazi paganism and the chief popularizer of the swastika as a mystical symbol. Her theosophy included a grab bag of cultish notions, from astrology to the belief that Christianity was a grand conspiracy designed to conceal the true meaning and history of the supernatural. Her 1888 book, *The Secret Doctrine*, attempted to prove the full extent of the grotesque Western conspiracy that *The Da Vinci Code* only partially illuminates. Christianity was to blame for all the modern horrors of capitalism and inauthentic living, not to mention the destruction of Atlantis.

Alfred Rosenberg's *Myth of the Twentieth Century*, the second most important book in the Nazi canon, borrowed ideas wholesale from Blavatsky. Rosenberg lays out one Christian conspiracy after another. "Before it could fully blossom, the joyous message of German mysticism was strangled by the anti-European church with all the means in its power," he insists. Like Blavatsky and Brown, he suggests the existence of secret Gospels, which, had they not been concealed by the Church, would debunk the "counterfeit of the great image of Christ" found in Matthew, Mark, Luke, and John.

"Christianity," writes Hitler in *Mein Kampf,* "was not content with erecting an altar of its own. It had first to destroy the pagan altars." It was "the advent of Christianity" that first unleashed the "spiritual terror" upon "the *much freer ancient world.*"[13]

Large segments of the cultural left today subscribe to similar notions. For example, Wicca and paganism constitute the fastest-growing religion and religious category in America, with adherents numbering anywhere from 500,000 to 5 million depending on whose numbers you accept. If you add "New Age spirituality," the number of Americans involved in such avocations reaches 20 million and growing. Feminists in particular have co-opted Wicca as a religion perfectly suited to their politics. Gloria Steinem is rhapsodic about the superior political and spiritual qualities of "pre-Christian" and "matriarchal" paganism. In *Revolution from Within* she laments in all earnestness the "killing of nine million women healers and other pagan or nonconforming women during the centuries of change-over to Christianity."[14]

The SS chief, Heinrich Himmler, was convinced that the anti-witch craze was an anti-German plot concocted in large part by the Catholic Church: "The witch-hunting cost the German people hundreds of thousands of mothers and women, cruelly tortured and executed."[15] He dedicated considerable resources for the SS to investigate the witch hunts and prove they were attempts to crush Aryan civilization and the true German faith. The SS put together what amounted to their own X-Files unit—dubbed Special Unit H (for *Hexen,* or "witches")—to ferret out the truth of over thirty-three thousand cases of witch burning, in countries as far away as India and Mexico.

Indeed, most of the founders of National Socialism would be far more comfortable talking witchcraft and astrology with a bunch of crystal-worshipping vegans than attending a church social. Consider the Thule Society, named after a supposed lost race of northern peoples hinted at in ancient Greek texts. The society was founded as the Munich chapter of the German Order, and while its occult and theosophical doctrines were nominally central to its charter, the glue that held it together was racist anti-Semitism. Anton Drexler was encouraged by his mentor Dr. Paul Tafel, a leader of the Thule Society, to found the German Workers' Party, which would soon become the

National Socialist German Workers' Party. Its membership was a veritable Who's Who of founding Nazis, according to Hitler's biographer Ian Kershaw.

Dietrich Eckart, a poet, painter, occultist, morphine addict, playwright, fancier of magic, and devotee of the racial mysticism of Houston Stewart Chamberlain, was a major force in this bohemian circle. Eckart was a father figure and mentor to Hitler, teaching him about public speaking, giving him his first trench coat, and introducing him to leading members of Munich society. As an editor, Eckart transformed the Thule Society's newspaper into the official Nazi Party paper and wrote the anthem "Germany, Awake!" Hitler dedicated *Mein Kampf* to him, writing in the epilogue that he was "a man who devoted his life to reawakening his and our people."

The myth of the Wrong Turn at the heart of liberal fascist ideology doesn't merely generate exotic conspiracy theories and pseudo history, but, as suggested above, it promotes a profound moral relativism. Indeed, feminism's embrace of Wicca is a perfect illustration of the pagan narcissism mentioned earlier. Many Wicca ceremonies conclude with the invocation "Thou Art Goddess." There are no explicit rules to Wicca, merely exhortations to cultivate "the Goddess within," to create the spirituality that best conforms to your already-formed prejudices, desires, and instincts.

Heidegger, the Nazi philosopher, and Thomas Mann, the literary giant—who became a passionate and perceptive anti-fascist but was an early dabbler in fascism's themes—represented the philosophical and literary sides of the push to throw off the chains of bourgeois morality and custom. Heidegger (echoing Nietzsche) argued that a truly authentic individual chooses his own path, whether it conforms with conventional morality or with some individually manufactured morality. Even the right choice is wrong if it is made under the influence of others. To "forgo normal choice and to adopt those offered me by the world or other people," writes Heidegger, is the essence of "inauthenticity." Mann located fascism's appeal to the artist in its invitation to the "self-abandonment to the instincts." Hitler's favorite sculptor explained that his nude works display "the pure air of instinctive drives" and show the "revolutionary youth of today, which tears the veil from the body hidden in shame."[16]

HOLLYWOOD FASCISTS

These once-radical notions now saturate mainstream popular culture. A brief survey serves to illustrate how pervasive their influence has become among the scriptwriters and producers of films coming out of Hollywood, the most powerful de facto propaganda agency in human history.

In the five-Oscar-winning film *American Beauty,* as mentioned above, Kevin Spacey plays Lester Burnham, a bourgeois professional with a bourgeois-professional wife and a conventionally alienated daughter. Lester suddenly realizes that he hates his conventional life when he becomes sexually obsessed with a friend of his teenage daughter. "I feel like I've been in a coma for the past twenty years. And I'm just now waking up," he declares. He then commences a campaign of "self-improvement" that involves a narcissistic obsession with his own body, flipping off all social conventions, and indulging every desire in defiance of reason.

"Janie, today I quit my job. And then I told my boss to go fuck himself, and then I blackmailed him for almost sixty thousand dollars. Pass the asparagus," Lester tells his daughter at the dinner table.

"Your father seems to think this type of behavior is something to be proud of," Lester's controlling, materialistic wife explains.

"And your mother seems to prefer I go through life like a fucking prisoner while she keeps my dick in a mason jar under the sink," he replies.

This sort of thing, where the "real" person is to be found not in the head or the heart but in the crotch, seems to pass for high wisdom in Hollywood.

Of course, sometimes it is not a psychosexual breakthrough that redeems the white man but a physical abnormality or injury usually resulting in the suppression of his ability to reason. In *Forrest Gump* a retarded white man is the only reliably moral force during the chaos of the 1960s and 1970s. In *Regarding Henry,* Harrison Ford plays a career-minded, philandering corporate lawyer with no time for his family who is redeemed with the help of a bullet in his frontal lobe and the sagacity of a black physical therapist who helps the lobotomized Ford discover that it's morally preferable to be a child. In *As Good as It Gets,* Jack Nicholson is a vicious bigot until he starts taking powerful psychotropic drugs, which in effect cure him of his whiteness (Adorno might call it the "anti-fascism pill") and make him tolerant of gays and blacks and able to love. In the Sean Penn vehicle *I Am Sam,* we are told that intelligence, knowledge, and basic coping skills are all irrelevant to good parenting so long as even a severely retarded parent loves his child. Talk to people with severely retarded children or siblings, and they will tell you how pernicious this message can be.

The recurring theme is that men must be awakened from the comfortable nightmare we call life, or what Hillary Clinton in her youth described as "the sleeping sickness of our soul." We are all "slaves" to the "IKEA nesting instinct," according to the protagonist of *Fight Club,* a film whose fascist pretensions have been so well discussed there's no need to revisit them here. The idea that the slumbering masses must be roused from their doldrums is central to Fascism. Marinetti's first Futurist manifesto begins, "Up to now, literature has exalted a pensive immobility, ecstasy, and sleep. We intend to exalt aggressive action, a feverish insomnia, the racer's stride, the mortal leap, the punch and the slap."[17] The pamphlet that first attracted a young Adolf Hitler to National Socialism was titled "My Political Awakening." Pro-Nazi and pre-fascist films and novels often shared a common premise of somnolent young men roused from their passive acceptance of the machine of Western bourgeois democracy.

Is there any doubt that a young Hitler would have given *Dead Poets Society* a standing ovation? The film begins with the students learning poetry by formula, plotting its "perfection along the horizontal of a graph" and its "importance" on the vertical in order to find the "measure of its greatness." You can almost hear Hitler denouncing such a "Jewish" way of gauging art. Along comes Mr. Keating, played by Robin Williams, who tells his students simply to rip those pages from the book! Mr. Keating encourages the students to do even more violence to convention, exhorting them to stand on the *teacher's* desk in a simultaneous display of superiority and contempt for traditional roles.

One boy in particular, Todd, is afraid of Mr. Keating's new approach. But Mr. Keating browbeats the lad to release his "barbaric yawp." Holding his eyes shut, he forces the lad to craft a poem from the bowels of his soul. Todd conjures the image of a "sweaty-toothed madman," and with Mr. Keating's encouragement he gives him form and function. "His hands reach out and choke me . . . Truth . . . Truth is like a blanket that always leaves your feet cold."

Keating encourages his yawping barbarians to live by the maxim "Seize the day!" in a glorious cult of action. Following his example, the truly "free" students join a secret society where they adopt pagan names and meet in an old Indian cave to "suck the marrow out of life," make new gods, and read Romantic poetry.

Neil, another student, is awakened by Mr. Keating and rebels against his bourgeois father's pressure to become a doctor. He wants to live a life of *passion* as an actor. "For the first time in my life, I know what I want to do!" he shouts. "And for the first time, I'm going to *do it!* Whether my father wants me to or not! *Carpe diem!"* The boy finds his true calling playing the pagan fairy of the forest Puck in *A Midsummer Night's Dream.* When his father forbids him to indulge his passions any further, Neil chooses suicide over compromise—a similar ending to Hitler's favorite play, *Der König* (as mentioned earlier, Hitler saw the play seventeen times in three years). Neil is depicted as Christlike, despite his selfishness.

The tragedy of Neil's suicide shatters the school, and Mr. Keating is fired. The surviving members of the Dead Poets Society risk expulsion if they even look at Mr. Keating; yet they cannot resist his charisma. One by one, they stand on their desks, defiant of their new teacher. These beautiful young overmen, united in their will, look to their "captain" and away from traditional authority. All that was missing were the Nazi salutes.

In *The Matrix,* a thoroughly fascistic allegory (with some Marxist notes as well), Keanu Reeves plays a trapped, bourgeois cubicle dweller. His "handle" as a computer hacker, Neo, not only represents his truer party name, as it were, but also encapsulates his status as a New Man, an *Übermensch* who can bend the world to his will and eventually even fly. The falseness of his worker-drone lifestyle is revealed to him when he awakes, as if from a dream, and realizes that what he thought was his real life was a prison, a cage, where parasitic and manipulative forces literally fed on him. Instead of blood-sucking Jews, the enemy is what nineteenth- and twentieth-century

New Agers called the Machine, or *das System*. What awakes him from his nightmare is his authentic choice, which he makes solely so he can be true to himself. Afterward, he joins a pagan secret society, Zion, where the only authentic vestiges of mankind live in Dionysian glory in the warm bowels of Mother Earth, wholly dedicated to awakening the worthy few among their slumbering brethren. The parasitic, puppet-string-pulling "agents" of the system may look human, but are anything but. Colorless, austere white men dressed in dark business suits, they reject the authenticity of human life for cold logic and mechanistic priorities. They are literally rootless, not merely prone to abstraction but *actual* abstractions. There seem to be few of them, but they're everywhere, can take human form, and run everything. In short, they are comic-book versions of everything the Nazis said about the Jews.

It's important to recognize that we are talking not so much about left-wing culture or liberal culture as about *American* culture. In many respects, Hollywood's addiction to fascist aesthetics is non-ideological. *Gladiator* used fascistic imagery because that was the best way to tell the story. In other cases, Hollywood exhibits a deeper fascination with fascism. In films like *V for Vendetta,* the envy for the cool aesthetics of well-dressed cruelty and violence is palpable. The villains and the hero alike are all fascists.

Conservatives are hardly immune to the allure of fascism. Left-wing cultural critics were not wrong to spot fascistic themes in the vigilante films of the 1970s. In the *Death Wish* and *Dirty Harry* movies, for example, unlawful violence was glorified on the grounds that "the system" was irredeemably corrupt, swamped by the usually dark-skinned criminal classes and the clever lawyers who protected them. Pauline Kael of the *New Yorker* dubbed *Dirty Harry* a brand of "fascist medievalism."[18] And if you look at the evolving themes in Clint Eastwood's work, you can tease out a thread of nihilism culminating in the bleakness of *Unforgiven* and his ode to euthanasia in *Million Dollar Baby* (both Academy Award–winning films).

Just because I am noting the fascistic themes in these films doesn't necessarily mean they are *bad*. *Triumph of the Will* was a masterpiece (so the critics tell us). Similarly, I am a fan of the *Dirty Harry* films (as well as many others discussed in this chapter). I would even argue that as a form of artistic protest, those vigilante films had many redeeming qualities. But there's no denying that conservatives are just as willing to embrace fascistic films if they come from the right. Consider such popular films as *Braveheart, The Last Samurai,* and *300.* Many conservatives loved them because they depicted resistance to tyranny and celebrated "freedom." But the "liberty" of these films was not individual liberty per se so much as the freedom of the tribe to behave according to its own relativistic values. The clans of the Scottish Highlands were hardly constitutional republics. Tom Cruise portrays the proto-fascist culture of the Meiji-era samurai as morally superior to that of the decadent West, echoing the German fascination with the Orient. And the Spartans of *300* are a eugenic (and vaguely homoerotic) warrior caste that would have had Hitler applauding in the aisle, despite valiant efforts to Americanize them.

There are defenses to be made of all these films, in that they represent forward progress in the unfolding Western tradition of liberty—and are also good fun. But the simple fact is that fascism is good box office and conservatives, with a few exceptions, are powerless to combat it because they don't even know what they are seeing. Liberals, for their part, are quick to label any "glorification" of war or battle as fascistic, but they cheer nihilism and relativism in the name of individual freedom and rebellion at every turn. This is where conservatives should mount their counterattack, on the prevalent notion that we are all our own priests, and so long as we are faithful to our inner gods, we are authentic and good. Nonetheless, there's no avoiding the fact that in terms of what we like on both big screens and small, we are all fascists now.

THE POLITICS OF SEX

Almost inexplicably, the popular perception these days is that Nazism was a kind of prudery run amok. Ken Starr, John Ashcroft, Laura Schlessinger, and Rick Santorum are just the latest symbols of a supposedly fascistic judgmentalism and hypocritical piety on the American right. In order to make these arguments stick, the debate is skewed so as to paint the champions of traditional morality as crypto-fascists, incapable of thinking maturely about sex.

Arthur Miller's propagandistic play *The Crucible* has become a classic statement of the left's obsession with the "sex panic" of the right. Originally a thinly veiled indictment of McCarthyism, the story is now seen as one of puritanical Comstockery leading to an outbreak of murderous political paranoia. Powerful men who can't handle sexually autonomous women use the tools of the state to launch a witch hunt. This tiresome meme has conquered the liberal imagination. J. Edgar Hoover is now universally depicted as a drag queen despite the flimsiest of evidence. Sidney Blumenthal has argued that anti-communism in the United States was little more than an example of homophobic panic by closeted gay right-wingers. Tim Robbins echoes a similar idea in his film *The Cradle Will Rock,* in which anti-communists and New Deal opponents are little more than sexually repressed fascists. Advocates of family values are now associated with fascism across the international left. "To favor the traditional family over here is to open oneself to the charge of being a Nazi," explains a member of the Swedish parliament.

There's only one problem: none of this has anything to do with Nazism or fascism.

The idea that "family values" are philosophically linked to fascism actually has a long pedigree, going back, again, to the Frankfurt School. Max Horkheimer argued that the root of Nazi totalitarianism was the family. But the truth is as close to the opposite as one can get. While Nazi rhetoric often paid homage to the family, the actual practice of Nazism was consonant with the progressive effort to invade the family, to breach its walls and shatter its autonomy. The traditional family is the enemy of all political totalitarianisms because it is a bastion of loyalties separate from and prior to the state, which is why progressives are constantly trying to crack its outer shell.

Let us start with the obvious. It would be funny were it not tragically necessary to note that the Nazis were not "pro-life." Long before the Final Solution, the Nazis cast the aged, the infirm, and the handicapped onto the proverbial Spartan hillside. It is true that women were second-class citizens in the Nazi worldview, relegated to the status of breeders of the master race. But prudery and Judeo-Christian morality were hardly the justification for these policies.

Nazi attitudes toward sexuality were grounded in unremitting hostility to Christianity and Judaism, both of which rejected the pagan view of sex as gratification, imbuing it instead with deep moral significance. Indeed, if you read Hitler's *Table Talk,* it is almost impossible not to see him as an open-minded freethinker. "Marriage, as it is practiced in bourgeois society, is generally a thing against nature. But a meeting between two beings who complete one another, who are made for one another, borders already, in my conception, upon a miracle." "Religion," Hitler explains, "is in perpetual conflict with the spirit of free research." "The catastrophe, for us, is that of being tied to a religion that rebels against all the joys of the senses." Der Führer talks at length about his contempt for the social prejudices that look down on out-of-wedlock birth. "I love to see this display of health around me."[19]

Recall that Hitler dreamed of transforming Germany into a warrior nation led by cadres of black-garbed Aryan Spartans loyal to him alone. Heinrich Himmler created the SS in the hope of making Hitler's dream come true. He ordered his men "to father as many children as possible without marrying." To this end Himmler created Lebensborn (Wellspring of Life) homes in Germany and occupied Scandinavia, where children sired by SS men and racially pure women would be raised by the state, fulfilling a dream (minus the racial angle) of Robespierre's. After a racial background check, a baby was admitted through a ceremony where an SS dagger was held over the child while the mother took an oath of loyalty to the Nazi cause.

Nazi attitudes toward homosexuality are also a source of confusion. While it is true that some homosexuals were sent to concentration camps, it is also the case that the early Nazi Party and the constellation of Pan-German organizations in its orbit were rife with homosexuals. It's well-known, for example, that Ernst Röhm, the head of the SA, and his coterie were homosexuals, and openly so. When jealous members of the SA tried to use this fact against him in 1931, Hitler had to remonstrate that Röhm's homosexuality was "purely in the private sphere." Some try to suggest that Röhm was murdered on the Night of the Long Knives because he was gay. But the Röhm faction posed the greatest threat to Hitler's consolidation of power because they were, in important respects, the most ardent and "revolutionary" Nazis. Scott Lively and Kevin Abrams write in *The Pink Swastika* that "the National Socialist revolution and the Nazi Party were animated and dominated by militaristic homosexuals, pederasts, pornographers, and sadomasochists." This is surely an overstatement. But it is nonetheless true that the artistic and literary movements that provided the oxygen for Nazism before 1933 were chockablock with homosexual liberationist tracts, clubs, and journals.[20]

The journal *Der Eigene* (meaning "self-aware" or "self-owner") had some 150,000 subscribers—more than twice the *New Republic*'s readership today in a population roughly a fifth the size of that in the United States. The journal was dedicated to men who "thirst for a revival of Greek times and Hellenic standards of beauty after centuries of Christian barbarism." *Der Eigene*—virulently anti-Semitic and nationalistic—grew into an actual movement for homosexual rights demanding the repeal of laws and social taboos against pederasty. The Viennese journal *Ostara*—which surely influenced a young Adolf Hitler—extolled a Spartan male ethic where women and Christianity alike were shackles on the Teutonic male warrior's will to power.

What ties these threads together was the idea of the Wrong Turn. Men were freer before they were caged by bourgeois norms, traditional morality, and logocentrism. Keep this in mind the next time you watch *Brokeback Mountain,* one of the most critically acclaimed and celebrated films of the last decade. Two perfect male specimens are at home only in the pastoral wild, away from the bourgeois conventions of modern life. At home in nature, they are finally free to give themselves over to their instinctual desires. But they cannot live in the hills, indulging their instincts. So they spend the rest of their lives trapped in soul-crippling traditional marriages, their only joy their annual "fishing trips," where they try to re-create the ecstasy of their authentic encounter, the only thing that can liberate them from bourgeois domesticity.

According to a secular liberal analysis, if traditional morality was ever necessary at all (a dubious proposition for many), it has outgrown its utility. In a premodern age when venereal disease was a death sentence and out-of-wedlock birth a calamity, rules and norms for governing personal behavior had their place. But today, conventional morality is merely a means by which the ruling classes oppress women, homosexuals, and other sexually nonconforming rebels. Tom Wolfe's essay "The Great Relearning" begins by recounting how, in 1968, doctors at the Haight-Ashbury Free Clinic discovered diseases "no living doctor had ever encountered before, diseases that had disappeared so long ago they had never even picked up Latin names, diseases such as the mange, the grunge, the itch, the twitch, the thrush, the scroff, the rot."[21] Why were these maladies springing up? The hippie communards, much like the bohemians of Weimar Germany, believed that traditional morality was an antiquated husk with as much relevance as the divine right of kings. They discovered otherwise; we have rules and customs for a reason.

Liberals dismiss abstract arguments involving universal moral principles almost as cavalierly as hippies did in the 1960s. One can argue that abortion might have a downside because it can lead to higher rates of breast cancer, but complaints that it takes a human life or displeases God, we are told, have no place in reasonable discourse. This poses a dilemma for conservatives. For some this means only arguing about what the data show. The problem is that resorting to regression analysis is another way of conceding that notions of right and wrong have no place in public debate. Meanwhile, conservatives of a religious bent hurl charges and epithets that do nothing to persuade the opposition.

Moreover, the culture is so shot through with narcissism and populism that even progressive arguments are denied to the conservative. Thus we are told it is elitist to argue that celebrities and rich people can afford to indulge loose morals in ways the poor cannot. If you're a millionaire, you can handle divorce, out-of-wedlock birth, or drug abuse with little risk to your quality of life and social status. If you are working class, the same behaviors can be destructive. But to point these things out violates today's egalitarian-populist ethos: What's good enough for Paris Hilton must be good enough for us all.

Fascism was a human response to a rapidly unfolding series of technological, theological, and social revolutions. Those revolutions are still playing themselves out, and since the left has defined fascism as conservative opposition to change, it's unlikely we'll ever stop being fascists by that definition. But conservatives aren't reactionaries. Few conservatives today would—or should—try to put the entire sexual revolution back in the bottle. Women's suffrage, birth control, civil rights, these are now part of the classically liberal order, and that's a good thing. Homosexuality is a fresher, and therefore tougher, issue for conservatives. But at least at the elite level, there are few conservatives who want to criminalize homosexuality. My guess is that gay marriage in some form is inevitable, and that may well be for the best. Indeed, the demand for gay marriage is in some respects a hopeful sign. In the 1980s and 1990s gay radicals sounded far more fascistic than the "radicals" of the early twenty-first century who ostensibly *want* to subject themselves to the iron cage of bourgeois matrimony.

The relevant question for conservatives hinges on the sincerity of the left, which is impossible to gauge because they have internalized an incremental approach to their Kulturkampf. Is gay marriage an attempt to blend homosexuals into a conservative—and conservatizing—institution? Or is it merely a trophy in their campaign for acceptance? In the 1990s "queer theorists" declared war on marriage as an oppressive force. The ACLU has already taken up polygamy as a civil rights issue. Al and Tipper Gore wrote a book arguing that families should be viewed as any group of individuals who love each other. These are echoes of ideas found in the fascist past, and conservatives can hardly be blamed for distrusting many on the left when they say they just want marriage and nothing more.

GREEN FASCISM

Nowhere is the idea of the Wrong Turn more starkly expressed in both National Socialist and contemporary liberal thought than in environmentalism. As many have observed, modern environmentalism is suffused with dark Rousseauian visions about the sickness of Western civilization. Man has lost his harmony with nature, his way of life is inauthentic, corrupting, unnatural.

Perhaps the most prominent exponent of this vision is the ubiquitous Al Gore, arguably the most popular liberal in America. As he writes in his thoroughly postmodern manifesto, *Earth in the Balance*, "We retreat into the seductive tools and technologies of industrial civilization, but that only creates new problems as we become increasingly isolated from one another and disconnected from our roots." Gore relentlessly sanctifies nature, arguing that we have been "cut off" from our authentic selves. "The froth and frenzy of industrial civilization mask our deep loneliness for that communion with the world that can lift our spirits and fill our senses with the richness and immediacy of life itself."[22] Of course, one can find similar statements from all sorts of Romantics, including Henry David Thoreau. But let us remember that German fascism was born out of a Romantic revolt against industrialization that philosophically mirrored aspects of transcendentalism. The difference is that while Thoreau sought to separate himself from modernity, Gore seeks to translate his Romantic animosity to modernity into a governing program.

The idea that environmentalism is itself a religion has been much discussed elsewhere. But it is telling how many of these New Age faiths define themselves as nature cults. As the National Public Radio correspondent (and committed witch) Margot Adler explains, "This is a religion that says the world, the earth, is where holiness resides." Joseph Sax, a giant in the field of environmental law and a pioneering activist, describes his fellow environmentalists as "secular prophets, preaching a message of secular salvation." Representative Ed Markey hailed Gore as a "prophet" during his congressional testimony on climate change in early 2007.[23] An environmentally themed hotel in California has replaced the Bible in all its rooms with Gore's *An Inconvenient Truth.* Anyone with kids certainly understands how the invocations to "reduce, reuse, recycle" are taught like catechisms in schoolrooms across the country.

Ultimately, however, environmentalism is fascistic not because of its airy and obscure metaphysical assumptions about the existential plight of man. Rather, its most tangible fascistic ingredient is that it is an invaluable "crisis mechanism." Al Gore constantly insists that global warming is the defining crisis of our time. Skeptics are called traitors, Holocaust deniers, tools of the "carbon interests." Alternately, progressive environmentalists cast themselves in the role of nurturing caregivers. When Gore appeared before Congress in early 2007, he proclaimed that the world has a "fever" and explained that when your baby has a fever, you "take action." You do whatever your doctor says. No time to debate, no room for argument. We must get "beyond politics." In practical terms this means we must surrender to the global nanny state and create the sort of "economic dictatorship" progressives yearn for.

The beauty of global warming is that it touches everything we do—what we eat, what we wear, where we go. Our "carbon footprint" is the measure of man. And it is environmentalism's ability to provide meaning that should interest us here. Almost all committed environmentalists subscribe to some variant of the Wrong Turn thesis. Gore is more eloquent than most in this regard. He rhapsodizes about the need for authenticity and meaning through collective action; he uses an endless series of violent metaphors in which people must be "resistance fighters" against the putatively Nazi regime responsible for the new Holocaust of global warming (again, on the left, the enemy is always a Nazi). Gore alternately blames Plato, Descartes, and Francis Bacon as the white male serpents who tempted mankind to take the wrong turn out of an Edenic past. What is required is to reunite our intellects, our spiritual impulses, and our animalistic instincts into a new holistic balance. Nothing could be more fascistic.

Of course, the greener you get, the more the argument shifts from the white man to mankind in general as the source of the problem. A perverse and bizarre form of self-hatred has infected certain segments of the eco-left. The old critique of the Hebrew disease has metastasized into an indictment of what could be called the human disease. When Charles Wurster, the chief scientist for the Environmental Defense Fund, was told that banning DDT would probably result in millions of deaths, he replied, "This is as good a way to get rid of them as any." The Finnish environmental guru Pentti Linkola argues that the earth is a sinking ship, and a chosen remnant must head to the lifeboats. "Those who hate life try to pull more people on board and drown everybody. Those who love and respect life use axes to chop off the extra hands hanging on the gunwale."[24]

These nominally "fringe" ideas have saturated the mainstream. "Us *Homo sapiens* are turning out to be as destructive a force as any asteroid," proclaimed the *Today Show*'s Matt Lauer in a TV special. "The stark reality is that there are simply too many of us. And we consume way too much . . . The solutions are not a secret: control population, recycle, reduce consumption." Lauer's emphasis on population control should remind us that the progressive eugenic obsession with controlling the population has never disappeared and still lurks behind many environmental arguments.[25]

One reason there is so much overlap between Nazi environmental thought and contemporary liberalism is that the environmental movement predates Nazism and was used to expand its base of support. The Nazis were among the first to make fighting air pollution, creating nature preserves, and pushing for sustainable forestry central planks in their platform. Ludwig Klages's *Man and Earth* was a manifesto for the idea that man had chosen the wrong path. Klages, a wild-eyed anti-Semite, decried the loss of species, the killing of whales, the clearing of forests, disappearing indigenous peoples, and other familiar concerns as symptoms of cultural rot. In 1980, to celebrate the founding of the German Green Party, the Greens reissued the essay.

Even though free-market conservatives have a great deal to offer when it comes to the environment, they are permanently on the defensive. Americans, like the rest of the Western world, have simply decided that the environment is an area where markets and even democracy should have little sway. To approach environmental questions as if they were economic questions—which they ultimately are—seems sacrilegious. Much as liberals have painted themselves as "pro-child" and their opponents as "anti-child," to disagree with liberals on statist remedies to environmental issues makes you "against" the environment and a craven lickspittle of robber barons and industrial fat cats.

Everyone cares about "the environment," just as everyone cares about "the children." For ideological environmentalists that means buying into a holistic vision of the earth and of humans as just another species. For conservatives, we are stewards of the earth, and that means making informed choices between competing goods. Many so-called environmentalists are in fact conservationists, using property rights and market mechanisms to conserve natural resources for posterity. Many on the left believe we must romanticize nature in order to create the political will to save it. But when such romanticism becomes a substitute religion and dissenters heretics, conservatives need to make it clear that environmental utopianism is as impossible as any other attempt to create a heaven on earth.

THE NAZI CULT OF THE ORGANIC

Unlike Marxism, which declared much of culture and humanity ir-relevant to the revolution, National Socialism was holistic. Indeed, "organic" and "holistic" were the Nazi terms of art for totalitarian-ism. The Mussolinian vision of everything inside the state, nothing outside the state, was organicized by the Nazis. In this sense the Bavarian cabinet minister Hans Schemm was deadly serious when he said, "National Socialism is applied biology."[26]

Nazi ideologues believed that the Aryans were the "Native Americans" of Europe, colonized by Romans and Christians and hence deprived of their "natural" symbiosis with the land. Hitler himself was a devoted fan of the novels of Karl May, who romanti-cized the Indians of the American West. The Nazi ideologue Richard Darré summarized much of Nazi *Volk* ideology when he said, "To re-move the German from the natural landscape is to kill him." Ernst Lehmann, a leading Nazi biologist, sounded much like Mr. Gore: "We recognise that separating humanity from nature, from the whole of life, leads to humankind's own destruction and to the death of na-tions."[27]

The Nazi cult of the organic was not some fringe view; it lay at the cutting edge of "enlightened" thought. German historicism had pioneered the organic conception of society and state tied together. The state, wrote Johann Droysen, is "the sum, the united organism, of all the moral partnerships, their common home and harbor, and so far their end." Nor were these ideas uniquely German. Droysen was Herbert Baxter Adams's mentor, and Adams in turn was Woodrow Wilson's. Droysen's work is cited throughout Wilson's writings. The law that established our national park system was dubbed the "Organic Act" of 1916.

Consider two spheres of concern that dominate vast swaths of our culture today: food and health. The Nazis took food very, very seri-ously. Hitler claimed to be a dedicated vegetarian. Indeed, he could talk for hours about the advantages of a meatless diet and the imper-ative to eat whole grains. Himmler, Rudolf Hess, Martin Bormann, and—maybe—Goebbels were vegetarians or health food fetishists of one kind or another. Nor was this mere sucking up to the boss (a real problem, one might imagine, in Nazi Germany). According to Robert Proctor, Hess would bring his own vegetarian concoctions to meetings at the Chancellery and heat them up like the office vegan with some macrobiotic couscous. This annoyed Hitler to no end. Hitler told Hess, "I have an excellent dietician/cook here. If your doctor has prescribed something special for you, she could certainly prepare it. You cannot bring your own food in here." Hess responded that his food had special biodynamic ingredients. Hitler suggested to Hess in return that maybe he might rather stay home for lunch from now on.[28]

Hitler often claimed his vegetarianism was inspired by Richard Wagner, who, in an 1891 essay, argued that meat eating and race mixing were the twin causes of man's alienation from the natural world. Therefore he called for a "true and hearty fellowship with the vegetarians, the protectors of animals, and the friends of temperance." He would also wax eloquent on the vegetarian diets of Japanese sumo wrestlers, Roman legionnaires, Vikings, and African elephants. Hitler believed that man had mistakenly acquired the habit of eating meat out of desperation during the Ice Age and that vegetarianism was the more authentic human practice. Indeed, he often sounded like an early spokesperson for the raw food movement, which is becoming ever more fashionable. "The fly feeds on fresh leaves, the frog swallows the fly as it is and the stork eats the living frog. Nature thus teaches us that a rational diet should be based on eating things in their raw state."[29]

Many leading Nazi ideologues also shared today's deep-seated commitment to animal *rights* as opposed to animal welfare. "How can you find pleasure in shooting from behind cover at poor creatures browsing on the edge of a wood, innocent, defenseless, and unsuspecting?" asked Heinrich Himmler. "It's really pure murder." A top priority of the Nazis upon attaining power was to implement a sweeping animal rights law. In August 1933 Hermann Göring barred the "unbearable torture and suffering in animal experiments," threatening to commit to concentration camps "those who still think they can treat animals as inanimate property."

For anyone with a functioning moral compass, this can only seem like barbaric cognitive dissonance. But for the Nazis it all made sense. The German needed to reconnect with nature, restore his organic purity, find holistic balance. Animals have exactly such a balance because they are immune to reason. Hence, the ideologues believed they were virtuous and deserving of respect. Jews, on the other hand, were alien and deracinating. They were the reason the "biotic community" of Germany was out of balance.

Animal rights advocates correctly note that animal rights activism was a major concern in pre-Nazi Germany and that the animal rights movement shouldn't be associated with Nazism. But as with environmentalism, this is less of a defense than it sounds. It is fine to say that many of Nazism's concerns were held by people who were not Nazis. But the fact that these conventionally leftist views were held by Nazis suggests that Nazism isn't as alien to mainstream progressive thought as some would have us believe.

Ingrid Newkirk, the president of People for the Ethical Treatment of Animals, famously declared, "When it comes to feelings, a rat is a pig is a dog is a boy. There is no rational basis for saying that a human being has special rights."[30] Few sentiments could be more fascist. First there is the emphasis on "feelings"—not thought or reason—as the defining characteristic of life. Second is the assumption that the higher "feelings"—those associated with conscience—are of such little consequence that they don't enter into the equation. When Newkirk says there's no "rational" basis for distinguishing between vermin and humans, what she really means is that there is no legitimate distinction between them, which is why PETA felt no compunction in comparing the slaughter of pigs, cows, and chickens to the slaughter of Jews in their infamous "Holocaust on your plate" campaign.

We joke a lot about "health fascists" these days. The government—partly driven by creeping national-socialist health-care costs—is increasingly fixated on our health. Children's shows on state-run television have been instructed to propagandize for healthier living, so much so that Cookie Monster's "C is for Cookie" has been demoted by the new jingle "Cookies Are a Sometimes Food." This of course is nothing new. Herbert Hoover, Woodrow Wilson's food administrator, required children to sign a loyalty pledge to the state that they wouldn't eat between meals. What we do not understand is that the citizen hectored and hounded by the state to quit smoking has as much right to complain about fascism as an author would if his book was banned. As Robert Proctor was the first to fully catalog in his magisterial work *The Nazi War on Cancer,* obsession with personal and public health lay at the core of the Nazi *Weltanschauung.* The Nazis, according to Proctor, were convinced that "aggressive measures in the field of public health would usher in a new era of healthy, happy Germans, united by race and common outlook, cleansed of alien environmental toxins, freed from the previous era's plague of cancers, both literal and figurative." Hitler loathed cigarettes, believing they were the "wrath of the Red Man against the White Man, vengeance for having been given hard liquor."

The Nazis used the slogan *"Gemeinnutz geht vor Eigennutz"*— "the common good supersedes the private good"—to justify policing individual health for the sake of the body politic. This is the same rationale used today. As one public health advocate wrote in the *New England Journal of Medicine,* "Both health care providers and the commonweal now have a vested interest in certain forms of behavior, previously considered a person's private business, if the behavior impairs a person's 'health.' Certain failures of self-care have become, in a sense, crimes against society, because society has to pay for their consequences . . . In effect, we have said that people owe it to society to stop misbehaving."[31]

In 2004 Hillary Clinton insisted that we look at children's entertainment "from a public health perspective." Subjecting "our children to so much of this unchecked media is a kind of contagion," a "silent epidemic" threatening "long term public health damage to many, many children and therefore to society." Richard Carmona, Bush's surgeon general in 2003, led a long list of public figures who believed "obesity has reached epidemic proportions." His "simple prescription" for ending America's obesity epidemic? "Every American needs to eat healthy food in healthy portions and be physically active every day." This sort of thing changes the meaning of an epidemic from a public health threat that puts people in danger against their will—typhoid, poisoned food, bear attacks—and replaces it with the danger of people doing things they want to do. Just look at how the war on smoking has institutionalized hysteria. Free speech for anything even remotely "pro-tobacco" has been culturally banned and almost totally abolished by law. Tobacco companies themselves have been forced to ritualistically—and expensively—denounce their own products. Free association of smokers has been outlawed in much of America. In addition, the fixation with children allows social planners to intervene to stop "child abusers" who might smoke near children, even outdoors.

Compare all this with a typical admonition found in a Hitler Youth health manual: "Food is not a private matter!" Or, "You have the duty to be healthy!" Or as another uniformed health official put it: "The government has a perfect right to influence personal behavior to the best of its ability if it is for the welfare of the individual and the community as a whole." That last official was C. Everett Koop.[32]

Vegetarianism, public health, and animal rights were merely different facets of the obsession with the organic order that pervaded the German fascist mind then, and the liberal fascist mind today. Again and again Hitler insisted that there "is no gap between the organic and inorganic worlds." Oddly, this fueled the Nazis' view of the Jew as the "other." As I mentioned earlier, in a widely read book on nutrition, Hugo Kleine blamed "capitalist special interests" and "masculinized Jewish half-women" for the decline in the quality of German foods, which contributed to the rise in cancer. Himmler hoped to switch the SS entirely to organic food and was dedicated to making the transition for all of Germany after the war. Organic food was seamlessly linked to the larger Nazi conception of the organic nation living in harmony with a pre- or non-Christian ecosystem.

Many Americans today are obsessed with the organic. Whole Foods has become a franchise of cathedrals to this cult, and even Wal-Mart has succumbed to it. The essence of Whole Foods—where I shop frequently, by the way—is, in the words of the *New York Times,* to provide "premodern authenticity," or the "appearance of premodern authenticity," in order to provide people with "meaning." Walk the aisles of Whole Foods and you'll be amazed by what you find. "In our every deliberation, we must consider the impact of our decisions on the next seven generations." So sayeth the great law of the Iroquois Confederacy—and the label on every roll of Seventh Generation–brand toilet paper. The company promises "affordable, high quality, safe and environmentally responsible" toilet tissue that helps "keep you, your home and our planet healthy." But fear not, Seventh Generation also promises to "get the job done."

Then there's EnviroKidz cereal. Read the box and you learn that "EnviroKidz chooz organic food. Organic agriculture respects the land and the wild creatures who live on it." It concludes, "So if you want the kind of planet where bio-diversity is protected and human beings tread more softly upon the Earth, then chooz certified organic cereals from EnviroKidz. *Wouldn't it be nice if all the food we ate was certified organic?*" The company Gaiam sells a wide array of products at Whole Foods and similar stores. Their literature explains that "Gaia, mother Earth, was honored on the Isle of Crete in ancient Greece 4,000 years ago by the Minoan civilization . . . The concept of Gaia stems from the ancient philosophy that the Earth is a living entity. At Gaiam, we believe that all of the Earth's living matter, air, oceans and land form an interconnected system that can be seen as a single entity."[33]

None of this is evil, and it is certainly well-meaning. But what's fascinating about Whole Foods and the culture it represents is how dependent it is on concocting what amounts to a new pan-human ethnicity. Over thirty years ago, Daniel Patrick Moynihan and Nathan Glazer wrote in *Beyond the Melting Pot*, "To name an occupational group or a class is very much the same thing as naming an ethnic group." That's no longer true, and in response the left and the market are creating faux ethnicities grounded in imagined or romantic pasts from the Rousseauian noble savages of pre-Columbian North America to the fanciful imagined societies of pre-Christian Europe or ancient Greece. I await the release of Thule Society Sugar Pops.

· AFTERWORD ·

The Tempting of Conservatism

The past shows unvaryingly that when a people's freedom
disappears, it goes not with a bang, but in silence amid the comfort
of being cared for. That is the dire peril in the present trend toward
statism. If freedom is not found accompanied by a willingness to
resist, and to reject favors, rather than to give up what is intangible
but precarious, it will not long be found at all.
—Richard Weaver, 1962

I N THIS BOOK I have argued that modern liberalism is the offspring of twentieth-century progressivism, which in turn shares
intellectual roots with European fascism. I have further argued that
fascism was an international movement, or happening, expressing itself differently in different countries, depending on the vagaries of
national culture. In Europe this communitarian impulse expressed itself in political movements that were nationalist, racist, militarist,
and expansionist. In the United States the movement known elsewhere as fascism or Nazism took the form of progressivism—a
softer form of totalitarianism that, while still nationalistic, and militarist in its crusading forms and outlook, was more in keeping with
American culture. It was, in short, a kind of liberal fascism.

After the Holocaust, and in haste after the Kennedy assassination,
nationalistic passions were inverted. A "punitive liberalism" emerged

(in James Piereson's words), in which Herbert Croly's "promise" of American life became the curse of American life. Progressivism's age-old yearning to fix America became a religious crusade to cleanse it, often through self-flagellation, of the nation's myriad sins. In short, liberalism in this country succumbed to the totalitarian temptation: the belief that there is a priesthood of experts capable of redesigning society in a "progressive" manner. That progressive priesthood brooks no opposition, and it is in the ascendant today on many fronts.

So far, so good. However, insofar as this has been a long book that insistently hammers on the danger of allowing these liberal fascist themes and tendencies to percolate unopposed through our politics, economics, and culture, it is perhaps incumbent on me to anticipate a few of the objections that might be raised by even the most well-disposed and open-minded reader. To wit: Aren't you overstating the problem—trying to pin the brown shirt on your opponents in the same way you claim they have done to you? Besides, who cares about the origin of these ideas if the way they are being applied is benign and even beneficial? What's so bad about a little progress and pragmatism, taken in moderation? And if, as you repeatedly state, there is no real prospect of a fascist coup today, why sound the alarm? More to the point, perhaps, why make so much of the Clintons, Kennedy, FDR, and Wilson but so little of, say, Nixon and George W. Bush? If one is looking for evidence of incipient fascism in the United States, shouldn't you be more concerned with the Bush administration's fearmongering, jingoism, and arrogation of executive privilege? Isn't that the real fascist threat today, and not Whole Foods' promotion of organic toilet paper and Hillary Clinton's campaign on behalf of children?

Let's begin at the beginning. Ever since I joined the public conversation as a conservative writer, I've been called a fascist and a Nazi by smug, liberal know-nothings, sublimely confident of the truth of their ill-informed prejudices. Responding to this slander is, as a point of personal privilege alone, a worthwhile endeavor. More important, as a conservative I actually *believe* that conservative policies will be better for America. From school choice to free markets to advancing democracy around the world, I believe that conservatives are, for the most part, correct. When conservative proposals are rebuffed with insinuations of fascist motives, it not only cheapens public discourse but also helps beat back much-needed reforms, and it does so not through argument but through intimidation. Surely, it is no small matter that our public discourse is corrupted in this way, and I have written this book largely to set the record straight and to educate myself—and others—about the real meaning and nature of fascism.

As to whether I am overstating the problem: I have repeatedly made it clear that modern liberals are not cartoonish Nazi villains. These people aren't storm troopers or commissars; they're campus student-life directors and diversity managers, child psychologists and antismoking crusaders. The danger they pose isn't existential or Orwellian, save perhaps in the sense that they might inure Americans to social control from above. The real threat is that the promise of American life will be frittered away for a bag of magic beans called security. No, I don't mean that as an indictment of the Bush administration or the war on terror. There is a difference between literal security—defending the public against external or illegal violence—and the figurative, quasi-religious security promised by the Third Way. Many progressives seem to think we can transform America into a vast college campus where food, shelter, and recreation are all provided for us and the only crime is to be mean to somebody else, particularly a minority.

So of course you will find me guilty of overstatement if you take me to be claiming that liberalism is a Trojan horse for Nazism. And while I have no doubt some hostile critics will assert I am making that case, I am not. But they will have to say so, because to do otherwise is to concede that Hillary Clinton's brave new village is *bad enough*. Of course, you can live a happy life in a medicalized, psychologized society where the state is your mommy. But only if you have been conditioned to find joy in such a society, and that is the aim of many liberal institutions: to rewrite the habits of our hearts. But of course, while I would view it as tragic to lose the America of individualism and freedom, I can certainly imagine worse horrors. Living in some vast North American Belgium, after all, surely has its pleasures.

I did not set out to write a modern version of *The Road to Serfdom* (would that I could). Nor do I have any desire to be a right-wing Joe

Conason, obsessively pecking away at the keyboard in an attempt to translate every partisan objection into some frightening omen of lost liberties. But if you are still vexed by the question "So what?" there is a larger danger to keep in mind. The cliché that the road to hell is paved with good intentions has more than its fair share of truth. I do not dispute that liberals have what they believe are the best of intentions as they push for a "modern" European welfare state. But it's worth keeping in mind that a Europeanized America would not only stop being America; there's also no reason to believe it would stop at merely being Europeanized. To paraphrase Chesterton: the danger of an America which stops believing in itself isn't that it will believe in nothing but that it can believe in anything. And that's where the darker dystopian visions start becoming plausible. Like useful idiots of yore, today's liberals want nothing but the best, but by pushing open the door to get it, they may well let in something far worse.

As for why I didn't spend a lot of time on the fascinating case of Richard Nixon, or (say) Truman and Eisenhower, the answer is simple: I told the story I thought needed to be told. These presidents were, in some respects, like LBJ, caretakers of the welfare state, extending the assumptions of the New Deal and the Great Society rather than questioning them. As for Ronald Reagan, he is enjoying what may be the most remarkable rehabilitation in modern American history—as is Barry Goldwater, who all of a sudden has become a hero to the liberal establishment. It seems that American liberals can appreciate dead conservatives when they become useful cudgels to beat up on living ones. Regardless, the story of Ronald Reagan seemed too fresh and too repetitive of the discussion of Goldwater— champions of liberty get called fascists by champions of statism—so it seemed best to leave the Gipper out.

But the current president is a special case, isn't he? George W. Bush has probably been called a fascist more than any other U.S. president. Leading politicians from around the world have compared him to Hitler. A cottage industry of cranks has tried to blame the Bush family for helping to create Hitler in the first place. Bush's democracy agenda—which I support—has become synonymous with a kind of neo-fascism around the globe and in many quarters at home. It's a curious irony that the most Wilsonian president in a generation is seen as a fascist by many people who would bristle at the suggestion that Wilson himself was a fascist.

When I said in the previous chapter, "We're all fascists now," I meant that it is impossible to drain entirely the fascist toxins from our culture. Truth be told, that's not so worrisome. The lethality of a poison depends on the dosage, and a little fascism, like a little nationalism or a little paternalism, is something we can live with—indeed, it may even be considered normal. But there is a yeastiness to such things, a potential for growth that can quickly become deadly. So in response to the reader who asks, "What about Bush? What about the conservatives?" let me close by examining the fascist tendencies that exist today on the American right.

COMPASSIONATE FASCISM

Throughout this book I have focused on the totalitarian tendencies of the left. This was important because of the hardened dogma that fascism is a right-wing phenomenon. But because the longing for community is written in the human heart, the totalitarian temptation can also be found on the right.

People across the ideological spectrum have a tendency to romanticize tribalism under different names, and hence yearn to re-create it. This is, by definition, a reactionary tendency because it attempts to restore an imagined past or satisfy an ancient yearning. Communism was reactionary because it tried to make a tribe of the working class. Italian Fascism tried to make a tribe of the nation. Nazism tried to make a tribe of the German race. Multicultural identity politics is reactionary because it sees life as a contest between different racial or sexual tribes. Similarly, Hillary Clinton's village is reactionary because it tries to restore the tribal comforts of small-town life on a national and even universal level (her American village eventually melts into the global village). But conservatives are just as prone to this human yearning, and while it manifests itself in different ways, I'll concentrate on three.

The first is nostalgia, a dangerous emotion in politics. American conservatives have long cast themselves as champions of hearth and home, traditional virtues, and, of course, family values. I have no objection when conservatives champion these virtues and values in the cultural sphere. Nor do I object when such concerns translate themselves into political efforts to beat back the liberal statist Kulturkampf. But conservatives get into trouble when we try to translate these sentiments into political programs at the national level. The beauty of American conservatism has been that it is an alloy of two very different metals, cultural conservatism and (classical) political liberalism. Whenever it is willing to sacrifice its political liberalism in the name of implementing its cultural conservatism, it flirts with a right-wing socialism all its own.

The second area where conservatism can run off the rails is when, out of a certain desperation to seem relevant, modern, or even progressive, it ventures into me-too conservatism, which is no kind of conservatism at all. American civilization is fundamentally liberal in the classical sense, and the ever-broadening reach of its principles of equality and liberty is both inevitable and desirable. Most conservatives share these underlying liberal values. What they reject are the totalitarian assumptions imported into American liberalism by twentieth-century progressives. The problem is, we now live in a world conditioned by the progressive outlook. People understand things in progressive terms. Even if you are skeptical about such notions, you cannot convince others of the rightness of your own positions if you do not speak the lingua franca. If you believe that abortion is evil, you will not convince someone who rejects moral categories like good and evil.

Lastly, there is the siren song of identity politics. White people are not above tribalism. It is right and good to oppose racial quotas and the balkanizing logic of multiculturalism. It is also worthwhile to defend the broad outlines of American culture, which multiculturalists deride as "white culture" in order to delegitimize and, ultimately, destroy it. But it is dangerously corrupting to fight fire with fire. It is not that "white Christian America" is a bad or oppressive thing. Far from it. Rather, it is the desire to *impose* a vision of white Christian America that is dangerous, for in the effort to translate such a vision into a government program, an open society must become a closed one. Rousseau was right about one thing: censorship is useful for preserving morals but useless for restoring them. A Department of

Judeo-Christian Culture would only succeed in creating a parody of real culture. In Europe the churches are subsidized by the state, and the pews are empty as a result. The problem with values relativism—the notion that all cultures are equal—is that important questions get decided via a contest of political power rather than a contest of ideas, and every subculture in our balkanized society becomes a constituency for some government functionary. The result is a state-sanctioned multicultural ethos where Aztecs and Athenians are equal—at least in the eyes of public school teachers and multicultural gurus. In an open society, best practices win. And the conservative case is that best practices are best not because they are white or Christian but because they are plainly best.

Of course, the danger posed by the multicultural welfare state is that by subscribing to values relativism it creates a climate where white Christians would be fools not to compete for control. For example, if the public schools are going to indoctrinate children to a moral vision, parents cannot be blamed for wanting that vision to be theirs. Much as with state interference in business or other realms of life, once the classical liberal vision of the state as a dispassionate arbiter and adjudicator is discarded in favor of a mommy state that plays favorites, it is only reasonable for people, groups, and businesses to compete for Mother's love.

All three of these impulses have been on ample display among conservatives over the last two decades. There is perhaps no better illustration of this than Patrick J. Buchanan—the leading living exemplar of what liberals mean when they speak of an incipient American fascism.

Born into an Irish Catholic household in Washington, D.C., Buchanan began his career as an editorialist for the *St. Louis Globe-Democrat*. In the 1960s he signed on with Richard Nixon to help with the former vice president's political comeback. A nominal Goldwaterite, Buchanan served as Nixon's ambassador to the conservative movement and vice versa, defending the all-too-progressive Nixon to the conservatives and defending the conservatives to Nixon. After the 1968 election Buchanan served as an adviser and speechwriter for both Nixon and Vice President Spiro Agnew.

Even before he was dubbed "Pitchfork Pat," Buchanan had earned a reputation as a populist. He helped coin the phrase "silent majority" for Nixon and pushed his boss to attack East Coast elites and, often in code, Jews. In a series of memos in 1972 he advised Nixon that the president "should move to re-capture the anti-Establishment tradition or theme in American politics." Nixon should paint George McGovern "as the Candidate of the *New York Times,* the Ford Foundation, elitist left-wing professors, snot-nosed demonstrators, black radicals and the whole elitist gang," Buchanan advised, while Nixon should assume the mantle of "the Candidate of the Common Man, the working man." Liberal commentators repeatedly compare Buchanan to Father Coughlin.[1] And while it is true that Buchanan seems to have a dismaying problem with Jews, this attitude stems not so much from his relationship with conservatism as from his vestigial 1930s-style populism. Buchanan has written glowingly about the America First Committee, and, like Charles Lindbergh, he suggests that America was orchestrated into World War II by groups that did not have America's interests at heart.

In the 1990s liberal anger about Buchanan's "right-wing" fascism reached a fever pitch. As Molly Ivins wrote in response to Buchanan's 1992 Republican National Convention speech: "It probably sounded better in the original German."[2] The irony here is that Buchanan was actually moving to the *left*. For years Buchanan's opponents called him a crypto-Nazi for his defense of Ronald Reagan and the GOP. In reality, the only thing that kept his fascist instincts in check was his loyalty to the GOP and the conservative movement. After Reagan and the Cold War, Buchanan abandoned both in a leftward search for his true principles.

Buchanan calls himself a "paleoconservative," but in truth he's a neo-progressive. During the 2000 election he denounced free marketeers and flat taxers, saying that they spent too much time with "the boys down at the yacht basin."[3] He came out in favor of capping executive pay, in support of higher unemployment benefits, and against any kind of free-market Medicare reform and backed a "Third Way" approach to government activism. Buchanan's neo-Progressivism has even caused the onetime Reagan aide to rail against the social Darwinism of the free market.

Culturally, Buchanan's "lock-and-load" populism was a throwback to William Jennings Bryan and Joe McCarthy. He also represents a resurgence of Progressive Era theories of "race suicide." In

The Death of the West, Buchanan argues that the white race is becoming an "endangered species" about to be swallowed up by Third World hordes. He suggests that the Russian ultranationalist demagogue Vladimir V. Zhirinovsky may have been onto something when he proposed a Russian Lebensborn program whereby Russians would accept polygamy. A proud Irish brawler, Buchanan always took ethnic pride very seriously. Thus rather than opposing left-wing multiculturalism, he embraced it, arguing that elite colleges should take steps to "look more like America" by enforcing quotas for "non-Jewish whites" or "Euro-Americans."[4]

The marriage of statism and eugenic racism motivated Progressive Era thinkers like Woodrow Wilson, Teddy Roosevelt, E. A. Ross, and Richard Ely. Conservatives should ask themselves how such sentiments are any different coming from Buchanan. Meanwhile, liberals who think such ideas earn Buchananites the fascist label need to explain why progressives are absolved from that charge when they believed precisely the same things.

Foreign policy considerations have made it seem like Buchanan and George W. Bush are light-years apart. Indeed, Buchanan's isolationism and harsh views on Israel have earned him a strange new respect from some on both the left and the right. But it should be remembered that Buchanan was the first "compassionate conservative." "I may charge him with plagiarism," Buchanan complained when asked his opinion of George W. Bush's slogan.[5]

Now, Bush's compassionate conservatism differs dramatically in key respects. Buchanan is an immigration restrictionist horrified by the influx of Hispanics into the United States. Bush is famously pro-immigration, arguing that "family values don't end at the Rio Grande." Bush is a free trader, a tax cutter, and a moderate on affirmative action. He is eager to bring minorities into the GOP fold. Also unlike Buchanan, he is an internationalist foreign policy hawk with deep sympathy for Israel.

But there is real commonality between them. First, Bush's politics likewise represents a kind of capitulation to a social base. Bush is a representative of "red state" America in much the way Bill Clinton and, more acutely, John Kerry represent "blue state" America. In many respects, Bushism is merely a concession to reality. In a polarized political culture, presidents must choose sides to get elected.

But such pragmatic concessions do not erase the fact that a politics based on taking care of a constituency with trinkets from the public fisc does profound violence to conservative principles.

Second, both men are products of a new progressive spirit in American politics. After the fall of the Berlin Wall, liberals believed that the demise of national security as a defining issue would allow them to revive the progressive agenda. They hoped to invest the "peace dividend" in all manner of Third Way schemes, including neo-corporatist public-private partnerships, emulating the more enlightened industrial policies of Europe and Japan. Bill Clinton borrowed liberally from Kennedy and FDR, melding populist rhetoric ("putting people first") with the new-politics themes of the Kennedy era. The climax of all this was Hillary Clinton's attempt to take over American health care, which in turn released largely libertarian antibodies in the form of the Contract with America and the, alas short-lived, Gingrich revolution. Some very welcome policies and even more encouraging rhetoric—such as welfare reform and Bill Clinton's January 1996 declaration that "the era of big government is over"—emerged from this tension. But soon enough, the libertarian fever broke when the public sided with President Clinton over the ill-fated government shutdown launched by Newt Gingrich.

Gingrich himself, who'd tried to scuttle various cabinet agencies, was at the same time proclaiming that his speakership represented the dawn of a new Progressive Era, and he has always spoken fondly of earlier generations of liberals. Indeed, throughout the 1990s, Republicans and conservative writers became enthralled with Progressivism. A veritable personality cult developed around Teddy Roosevelt, with one politician after another claiming his mantle— chief among them John McCain, whose fondness for Roosevelt-style regulation borders on legendary.

In the 1990s the *Weekly Standard* launched a crusade for "National Greatness" in the tradition of the Rough Rider. David Brooks quoted approvingly Roosevelt's warning that Americans risk getting "sunk in a scrambling commercialism, heedless of the higher life, the life of aspiration, of toil and risk." What was needed to fight off such decay? Roosevelt's "muscular Progressivism," of course. If Americans "think of nothing but their narrow self-interest, of their commercial activities," Brooks warned, "they lose a sense of grand aspiration and noble purpose." Translation: Americans need a politics of meaning. Meanwhile, the *Standard*'s editor, William Kristol, took to denouncing reflexive antigovernment conservatism as immature and counterproductive while his magazine rattled sabers at China and Iraq.[6]

It was from this milieu that "compassionate conservatism" emerged. Bush's adviser Karl Rove, an ardent fan of Teddy Roosevelt's, offered compassionate conservatism not as an alternative to Clinton's Third Way politics but as a Republican version of the same thing. In 2000 George W. Bush proudly ran as a different kind of conservative, claiming education, single motherhood, and national unity as his themes. Borrowing from Marvin Olasky, the adroit Christian intellectual who coined the phrase "compassionate conservative," the Bush team set out to make it clear that they saw the government as an instrument of love, Christian love in particular.

The very adjective "compassionate" echoes progressive and liberal denunciations of limited government as cruel, selfish, or social Darwinist. In other words, as a marketing slogan alone, it represented a repudiation of the classical liberalism at the core of modern American conservatism because it assumed that limited government, free markets, and personal initiative were somehow "uncompassionate."

Nonetheless, conservatives who complain about Bush's "big-government conservatism" as if it were some great betrayal ignore the fact that they were warned. When Bush responded in a presidential debate in 2000 that his favorite political philosopher was "Jesus Christ," small-government conservatives should have sensed the ghost of the Social Gospel. Michael Gerson, Bush's longtime speechwriter and adviser, is unapologetic about his belief that the federal government should be suffused with the spirit of Christian charity. After he left the White House, he wrote a piece for *Newsweek*, "A New Social Gospel," in which he describes the new evangelicals as "pro-life and pro-poor." In another *Newsweek* essay he railed against small-government conservatism, wrung his hands about "unfettered individualism," and concluded that "any political movement that elevates abstract antigovernment ideology above human needs is hardly conservative, and unlikely to win."[7]

There's no doubt that President Bush believes much of this. In

2003 he proclaimed that "when somebody hurts," it's the government's responsibility to "move." And under Bush, it has. A new cabinet agency has been created, Medicare has increased nearly 52 percent, and spending on education went up some 165 percent. From 2001 to 2006 antipoverty spending increased 41 percent, and overall spending reached a record $23,289 per household. Federal antipoverty spending has surpassed 3 percent of GDP for the first time ever. Total spending (adjusted for inflation) has grown at triple the rate under Clinton. Moreover, Bush created the largest entitlement since the Great Society (Medicare Part D).

This is not to say that Bush has completely abandoned limited-government conservatism. His judicial appointments, tax cuts, and efforts to privatize Social Security represent either a vestigial loyalty to limited government or a recognition that limited-government conservatives cannot be ignored entirely. But Bush really is a different kind of conservative, one who is strongly sympathetic to progressive-style intrusions into civil society. His faith-based initiative was a well-intentioned attempt to blur the lines between state and private philanthropy. In an interview with the *Weekly Standard*'s Fred Barnes, Bush explained that he rejected William F. Buckley's brand of reactionary, limited-government conservatism; instead, the president told Barnes that conservatives had to "lead" and to be "activist." This is of a piece with Bush's misunderstanding of conservatism as support for the social base that calls itself "conservative."[8]

Bush was not always a captive of his base, of course. Much like his progressive forebears—Clinton, Nixon, FDR, and Wilson—when his agenda differs from that of his most loyal constituents, on immigration or education, he questions their motives as "uncompassionate."[9]

What many conservatives, including Bush and Buchanan, fail to grasp is that conservatism is neither identity politics for Christians and/or white people nor right-wing Progressivism. Rather, it is opposition to all forms of political religion. It is a rejection of the idea that politics can be redemptive. It is the conviction that a properly ordered republic has a government of limited ambition. A conservative in Portugal may want to conserve the monarchy. A conservative in China is determined to preserve the prerogatives of the Communist Party. But in America, as Friedrich Hayek and others have noted, a conservative is one who protects and defends what are considered *liberal* institutions in Europe but largely conservative ones in America: private property, free markets, individual liberty, freedom of conscience, and the rights of communities to determine for themselves how they will live within these guidelines.[9] This is why conservatism, classical liberalism, libertarianism, and Whiggism are different flags for the only truly radical political revolution in a thousand years. The American founding stands within this tradition, and modern conservatives seek to advance and defend it. American conservatives are opposed on principle to neither change nor progress; no conservative today wishes to restore slavery or get rid of paper money. But what the conservative understands is that progress comes from working out inconsistencies within our tradition, not by throwing it away.

Conservatives today are constantly on the defensive to prove that they "care" about some issue or group, and often they just throw in the towel on the environment, campaign finance reform, or racial quotas in order to prove that they're good people. Even more disturbing, some *libertarians* are abandoning their historic dedication to negative liberty—preventing the state from encroaching on our freedoms—and embracing a new positive liberty whereby the state does everything it can to help us reach our full potential.[10]

Perhaps the gravest threat is that we are losing sight of where politics begins and ends. In a society where the government is supposed to do everything "good" that makes "pragmatic" sense, in a society where the refusal to validate someone else's self-esteem borders on a hate crime, in a society where the personal is political, there is a constant danger that one cult or another will be imbued with political power. It may be disturbing that in the United Kingdom there are more self-proclaimed Jedis than Jews. I may roll my eyes at Wicca practitioners, couples who wed in Klingon marriage ceremonies, queer theorists, Druids, and Earth Firsters, but so long as this sort of thing doesn't translate itself into a political movement, one can tolerate it with a sense of bemusement. But cults often have a will to power all their own, which is one reason why Germany still bans the Church of Scientology along with the Nazi Party. Already it is becoming difficult to question the pagan assumptions behind environmentalism without seeming like a crackpot. My hunch is it will only get harder. Liberals and leftists for the most part seem incapable of dealing with jihadism—a quintessentially fascist political religion—for fear of violating the rules of multicultural political correctness.

Ultimately the issue here is that of dogma. We are all dogmatic about something. We all believe that there are some fundamental truths or principles that demarcate the acceptable and the unacceptable, the noble and the venal. One root of dogma derives from the Greek for "seems good." Reason alone will not move men. As Chesterton noted, the merely rational man will not marry, and the merely rational soldier will not fight. In other words, good dogma is the most powerful inhibiting influence against bad ideas and the most powerful motive for good deeds. As William F. Buckley put it in 1964 when discussing the libertarian idea to privatize lighthouses, "If our society seriously wondered whether or not to denationalize the lighthouses, it would not wonder at all whether to nationalize the medical profession." The liberal fascist project can be characterized as the effort to delegitimize good dogma by claiming *all* dogma is bad.

This has put conservatives and right-wingers of all stripes at a disadvantage because we have made the "mistake" of writing down our dogma. Indeed, as much as I think it is misguided, at least right-wing Progressivism is honest about where its dogma comes from. One can reject or accept the Bible (or the writings of Marvin Olasky) as the inspiration for a program or policy. Similarly, one can argue with the ideas of Friedrich Hayek and Milton Friedman. Conservatives—unlike purist libertarians—are not opposed to government activism. But we share with libertarians the common dogma that as a general rule, it is a bad idea. That doesn't mean there aren't exceptions to the rule. We dogmatically believe that theft is bad, but we all can imagine hypotheticals wherein stealing might be morally defensible. Similarly, conservatism believes that the role of the state should be limited and its meddling should be seen as an exception. If conservatism loses this general rule—as it has under George W. Bush—it ceases to be conservatism properly understood.

The unique threat of today's left-wing political religions is precisely that they claim to be free from dogma. Instead, they profess to be champions of liberty and pragmatism, which in their view are self-evident goods. They eschew "ideological" concerns. Therefore they make it impossible to argue with their most basic ideas and exceedingly difficult to expose the totalitarian temptations residing in their hearts. They have a dogma, but they put it out of bounds. Instead, they force us to argue with their intentions, their motives, their feelings. Liberals are right because they "care," we are told, making "compassion" the watchword of American politics. Liberals therefore control the argument without either explaining where they want to end up or having to account for where they've been. They've succeeded where the fascist intellectuals ultimately failed, making passion and activism the measure of political virtue, and motives more important than facts. Moreover, in a brilliant rhetorical maneuver they've managed to do this in large part by claiming that their *opponents* are the fascists.

In 1968, in a televised debate on *ABC News* during the Chicago Democratic National Convention, Gore Vidal continually goaded William F. Buckley, eventually calling him a "crypto-Nazi." Vidal himself is an open homosexual, a pagan, a statist, and a conspiracy theorist. Buckley, a patriotic, free-market, antitotalitarian gentleman of impeccably good manners, could take it no more and responded: "Now listen, you queer, stop calling me a crypto-Nazi or I'll sock you in the goddamn face and you'll stay plastered."

It is one of the few times in Buckley's long public life that he abandoned civility, and he instantly regretted it. Nonetheless, having been on the receiving end of many similar insults and diatribes, I have deep sympathy for Buckley's frustration. For at some point it is necessary to throw down the gauntlet, to draw a line in the sand, to set a boundary, to cry at long last, "Enough is enough." To stand athwart "progress" and yell, "Stop!" My hope is that this book has served much the same purpose as Buckley's intemperate outburst while striving for his more typical civility.

· ACKNOWLEDGMENTS ·

My father, Sidney Goldberg, died before I could complete this book. In ways large and small, tangible and intangible, this book would be impossible without him.

My daughter, Lucy, was born while I was working on this book, and without her everything else would be pointless.

My wife, Jessica Gavora, a brilliant writer, editor, and critic, is the love and light of my life who allows me to see all of this, and so much else, clearly.

Adam Bellow, my editor and friend, was an indispensable shepherd and co-pilot throughout this process, and my gratitude for his insight, patience, and encouragement is boundless.

Joni Evans, my super-agent at William Morris, retired from the business while I was working on the book, but I am grateful for all of the effort and wisdom she contributed at the outset. Jay Mandel ably stepped into her elegant shoes, and I am grateful for that as well.

Several young people helped me with research along the way. Alison Hornstein, my first researcher, was stolen away from me too soon by a promising career as an academic. Lyle Rubin, an acutely bright young man, spent a summer swimming in liberal fascism and has remained a valuable sounding board even as he is now serving in the U.S. Marines. Windsor Mann has likewise proven to be an invaluable researcher with a first-rate, inquisitive mind and a very bright future ahead of him.

Working on this book while writing a regular syndicated column and contributing to *National Review* has been a far more arduous experience than I imagined. But then *National Review,* my home, has proven to be more accommodating and encouraging than I could ever have expected. Rich Lowry, my boss and friend, has been unflappably supportive. My brilliant colleague Ramesh Ponnuru has been an irreplaceable source of insights and editorial judgment, for this and almost everything I do. Kate O'Beirne, my savior Kathryn Lopez, John Miller, Michael Potemra, Ed Capano, Jack Fowler, John Derbyshire, Jay Nordlinger, Mark Steyn, and Byron York have made working for *National Review* a joy. John Podhoretz helped me greatly by reading chapters and providing support. Andrew Stuttaford read the entire book at the wire and came through with some invaluable corrections and questions.

My friends Scott McLucas, Tevi Troy, Vin Cannato, Ronald Bailey, Pam Friedman, and Douglas Anderson were, as always, supportive and valuable sounding boards. I would thank my friend Peter Beinart, but he had nothing to do with this book save to provide reassurance, by example, that some liberals still exemplify the intellectual integrity and patriotism that make even modern liberalism merely the loyal opposition, not the enemy. Cosmo, my canine sidekick, cared about none of this, which was what I wanted from him.

Others looked at early drafts of chapters or otherwise helped me think through my arguments. Charles Murray offered valuable guidance very early on. Nick Schulz, my intellectual partner in crime, was a constant source of encouragement and insight. Yuval Levin, Steven Horwitz, and Bradford Short made helpful suggestions, and Bill Walsh offered both crucial editorial guidance and extremely valuable German translations. John Williamson was immensely helpful finding obscure documents and publications. Kevin Holtsberry also provided some much needed editorial criticism. Steven Hayward, Ross Douthat, Christine Rosen, and Brian M. Riedl offered valuable suggestions. Of course, all errors are my own.

And as unorthodox as this may be, I need to thank the readers of *National Review Online.* For years an army of unseen friends and critics have helped me track down and understand everything from facts and figures to ephemera. They've pointed me in interesting directions, corrected my ignorance, and served as my muse on countless occasions. They are the smartest and best readers a writer could ask for.

Lastly, there's Mom. I am grateful to her for getting it. Always.

· APPENDIX: THE NAZI PARTY PLATFORM ·

The program is the political foundation of the NSDAP and accordingly the primary political law of the State. It has been made brief and clear intentionally.

All legal precepts must be applied in the spirit of the party program.

Since the taking over of control, the Fuehrer has succeeded in the realization of essential portions of the Party program from the fundamentals to the detail.

The Party Program of the NSDAP was proclaimed on the 24 February 1920 by Adolf Hitler at the first large Party gathering in Munich and since that day has remained unaltered. Within the national socialist philosophy is summarized in 25 points·

1. We demand the unification of all Germans in the Greater Germany on the basis of the right of self-determination of peoples.
2. We demand equality of rights for the German people in respect to the other nations; abrogation of the peace treaties of Versailles and St. Germain.
3. We demand land and territory (colonies) for the sustenance of our people, and colonization for our surplus population.
4. Only a member of the race can be a citizen. A member of the race can only be one who is of German blood, without

consideration of creed. Consequently no Jew can be a member of the race.

5. Whoever has no citizenship is to be able to live in Germany only as a guest, and must be under the authority of legislation for foreigners.

6. The right to determine matters concerning administration and law belongs only to the citizen. Therefore we demand that every public office, of any sort whatsoever, whether in the Reich, the county or municipality, be filled only by citizens. We combat the corrupting parliamentary economy, office-holding only according to party inclinations without consideration of character or abilities.

7. We demand that the state be charged first with providing the opportunity for a livelihood and way of life for the citizens. If it is impossible to sustain the total population of the State, then the members of foreign nations (non-citizens) are to be expelled from the Reich.

8. Any further immigration of non-citizens is to be prevented. We demand that all non-Germans, who have immigrated to Germany since the 2 August 1914, be forced immediately to leave the Reich.

9. All citizens must have equal rights and obligations.

10. The first obligation of every citizen must be to work both spiritually and physically. The activity of individuals is not to counteract the interests of the universality, but must have its result within the framework of the whole for the benefit of all. Consequently we demand:

11. Abolition of unearned (work and labour) incomes. Breaking of rent-slavery.

12. In consideration of the monstrous sacrifice in property and blood that each war demands of the people personal enrichment through a war must be designated as a crime against the people. Therefore we demand the total confiscation of all war profits.

13. We demand the nationalization of all (previous) associated industries (trusts).

14. We demand a division of profits [profit sharing] of heavy industries.

15. We demand an expansion on a large scale of old age welfare.

16. We demand the creation of a healthy middle class and its conservation, immediate communalization of the great warehouses and their being leased at low cost to small firms, the utmost consideration of all small firms in contracts with the State, county or municipality.

17. We demand a land reform suitable to our needs, provision of a law for the free expropriation of land for the purpose of public utility, abolition of taxes on land and prevention of all speculation in land.

18. We demand struggle without consideration against those whose activity is injurious to the general interest. Common national criminals, usurers, Schieber and so forth are to be punished with death, without consideration of confession or race.

19. We demand substitution of a German common law in place of the Roman Law serving a materialistic world-order.

20. The state is to be responsible for a fundamental reconstruction of our whole national education program, to enable every capable and industrious German to obtain higher education and subsequently introduction into leading positions. The plans of instruction of all educational institutions are to conform with the experiences of practical life. The comprehension of the concept of the State must be striven for by the school [Staatsbuergerkunde] as early as the beginning of understanding. We demand the education at the expense of the State of outstanding intellectually gifted children of poor parents without consideration of position or profession.

21. The State is to care for the elevating national health by protecting the mother and child, by outlawing child-labor, by the encouragement of physical fitness, by means of the legal establishment of a gymnastic and sport obligation, by the utmost support of all organizations concerned with the physical instruction of the young.

22. We demand abolition of the mercenary troops and formation of a national army.

23. We demand legal opposition to known lies and their promulgation through the press. In order to enable the provision of a German press, we demand, that: a. All writers and

employees of the newspapers appearing in the German language be members of the race: b. Non-German newspapers be required to have the express permission of the State to be published. They may not be printed in the German language: c. Non-Germans are forbidden by law any financial interest in German publications, or any influence on them, and as punishment for violations the closing of such a publication as well as the immediate expulsion from the Reich of the non-German concerned. Publications which are counter to the general good are to be forbidden. We demand legal prosecution of artistic and literary forms which exert a destructive influence on our national life, and the closure of organizations opposing the above made demands.

24. We demand freedom of religion for all religious denominations within the state so long as they do not endanger its existence or oppose the moral sense of the Germanic race. The Party as such advocates the standpoint of a positive Christianity without binding itself confessionally to any one denomination. It combats the Jewish-materialistic spirit within and around us, and is convinced that a lasting recovery of our nation can only succeed from within on the framework: common utility precedes individual utility.

25. For the execution of all of this we demand the formation of a strong central power in the Reich. Unlimited authority of the central parliament over the whole Reich and its organizations in general. The forming of state and profession chambers for the execution of the laws made by the Reich within the various states of the confederation. The leaders of the Party promise, if necessary by sacrificing their own lives, to support by the execution of the points set forth above without consideration.

Source: Document as translated at the Nuremberg Trials: *Nazi Conspiracy and Aggression, Volume IV,* Office of the United States Chief Counsel for Prosecution of Axis Criminality (Washington, D.C.: Government Printing Office, 1946), found at Yale University Avalon Project: www.yale.edu/lawweb/avalon/imt/document/nca_vol4/1708-ps.htm (accessed March 13, 2007).

Note: This translation differs in significant respects from other translations. For example, it uses the word "warehouses" where most other translations use "department stores" or "big department stores." But since the Nuremberg translation probably has more credibility with skeptical readers than one more convenient to my thesis, I chose to use this one. Any Internet search engine will yield other translations.

• NOTES •

INTRODUCTION: EVERYTHING YOU KNOW ABOUT
FASCISM IS WRONG

1. *Real Time with Bill Maher,* HBO, Sept. 9, 2005.
2. Roger Griffin, *The Nature of Fascism* (New York: St. Martin's, 1991),
   p. 26; Roger Eatwell, "On Defining the 'Fascist Minimum': The Centrality
   of Ideology," *Journal of Political Ideologies* 1, no. 3 (1996), p. 313;
   Gentile is quoted in Stanley G. Payne, *A History of Fascism, 1914–1945*
   (Madison: University of Wisconsin Press, 1995), p. 5 n. 6.
3. Griffin, *Nature of Fascism,* p. 1, quoting R. A. H. Robinson, *Fascism in
   Europe* (London: Historical Association, 1981), p. 1; the dictionary definition is quoted in Richard Griffiths, *An Intelligent Person's Guide to
   Fascism* (London: Duckworth, 2000), p. 4; Payne, *History of Fascism,*
   p. 3; Gilbert Allardyce, "What Fascism Is Not: Thoughts on the Deflation
   of a Concept," *American Historical Review* 84, no. 2 (April 1979), p. 367
4. George Orwell, "Politics and the English Language," *Horizon,* April 1946,
   in *Essays* (New York: Random House, 2002), p. 959.
5. Michele Parente, "Rangel Ties GOP Agenda to Hitler," *Newsday,* Feb. 19,
   1995, p. A38; Bill Clinton, Remarks to the Association of State Democratic
   Chairs in Los Angeles, June 24, 2000, *Public Papers of the Presidents,* 36
   Weekly Comp. Pres. Doc. 1491; for a typical *Times* article, see Alexander
   Stille, "The Latest Obscenity Has Seven Letters," *New York Times,* Sept.
   13, 2003.
6. Rick Perlstein, "Christian Empire," *New York Times,* Jan. 7, 2007, sec. 7,
   p. 15; Jesse Jackson, interview, "Expediency Was Winner Over Right,"
   Chicago Sun-Times, Dec. 3, 1994, p. 18.
7. In America "social Darwinism" means "survival of the fittest" in an anar-
   chic free-for-all of capitalist predation. This is the tradition of Herbert
   Spencer, a radical freethinker and individualist. By that definition, Nazism

is the opposite of social Darwinism. As we shall see, the Nazis were Darwinists, but they were reform Darwinists, believing that the state should actively pick winners and losers and lavish the winners with social benefits, welfare, and other forms of government largesse—exactly the opposite position of those we call social Darwinists.

8. John Patrick Diggins, *Mussolini and Fascism: The View from America* (Princeton, N.J.: Princeton University Press, 1972), p. 215.

9. One correspondent for the *New York Times* was an enthusiastic supporter of Italian Fascism for many years, writing that fascism was both good for Italy and good for the Abyssinians Mussolini tried to conquer. That reporter, Herbert Matthews, later recanted his support for fascism when it came into conflict with his support for the communists in the Spanish civil war. But years later he found another revolutionary "man of action" he could support with gusto: Fidel Castro.

10. DuBois eventually condemned Nazi anti-Semitism, but often through clenched teeth as he was more than a little resentful of the special attention the plight of Jews was receiving in America. In September 1933 he editorialized in *Crisis:* "Nothing has filled us with such unholy glee as Hitler and the Nordics. When the only 'inferior' peoples were 'niggers,' it was hard to get the attention of the *New York Times* for little matters of race, lynchings and mobs. But now that the damned include the owner of the *Times,* moral indignation is perking up." Harold David Brackman, " 'Calamity Almost Beyond Comprehension': Nazi Anti-Semitism and the Holocaust in the Thought of W. E. B. DuBois," *American Jewish History* 88, no. 1 (March 2000), citing W. E. B. DuBois, "As the Crow Flies," *Crisis* 40 (Sept. 1933), p. 97.

11. See John Garraty, James Q. Wilson, David Schoenbaum, Alonzo Hamby, Niall Ferguson, and, most powerfully, the German historian Wolfgang Schivelbusch.

12. Wolfgang Schivelbusch, *Three New Deals: Reflections on Roosevelt's America, Mussolini's Italy, and Hitler's Germany, 1933–1939* (New York: Metropolitan Books, 2006), pp. 32, 29.

13. Ironically, the liberal historian Richard Hofstadter made a similar, if dramatically more understated, argument about the progressives and populists in *The Age of Reform* and elsewhere. But he intimated that progressives and populists were essentially right-wing forces, an argument I don't believe can be sustained.

14. The national leaders would be "pure and sensitive souls," according to Robespierre, imbued with the ability to do what destiny demanded in "the people's name" and blessed with the "enlightenment" to determine which "enemies within" required execution. See J. M. Thompson, *Robespierre* (New York: Appleton-Century, 1936), p. 247. As Robespierre put it, "The people is sublime, but individuals are weak" or expendable. Gertrude Himmelfarb, "The Idea of Compassion: The British vs. the French Enlightenment," *Public Interest,* no. 145 (Fall 2001), p. 20. See also Simon Schama, *Citizens: A Chronicle of the French Revolution* (New York: Vintage, 1990), p. 836; John Kekes, "Why Robespierre Chose Terror," *City Journal* (Spring 2006). Robespierre explained the need for terror: "If the spring of popular government in time of peace is virtue, the

springs of popular government in revolution are at once virtue and terror: virtue, without which terror is fatal; terror, without which virtue is powerless. Terror is nothing other than justice, prompt, severe, inflexible; it is therefore an emanation of virtue; it is not so much a special principle as it is a consequence of the general principle of democracy applied to our country's most urgent needs."

15. Thomas R. DeGregori, "Muck and Magic or Change and Progress: Vitalism Versus Hamiltonian Matter-of-Fact Knowledge," *Journal of Economic Issues* 37, no. 1 (March 2003), pp. 17–33.

16. Seymour Martin Lipset and Earl Raab, *The Politics of Unreason: Right Wing Extremism in America, 1790–1970* (New York: Harper and Row, 1970), p. 95, citing *New York Sun,* July 23, 1896, p. 2, as reported in Edward Flower, "Anti-Semitism in the Free Silver and Populist Movements and the Election of 1896" (master's thesis, Columbia University, 1952), pp. 27–28.

17. As Robert Proctor writes, "Public health initiatives were pursued not just in spite of fascism, but also in consequence of fascism." The National Socialist "campaign against tobacco and the 'whole-grain bread operation' are, in some sense, as fascist as the yellow stars and the death camps." Robert N. Proctor, *The Nazi War on Cancer* (Princeton, N.J.: Princeton University Press, 2000), pp. 124, 249, 278.

18. Here is a list of the things the New York City Council tried to ban—not all successfully—in 2006 alone: pit bulls; trans fats; aluminum baseball bats; the purchase of tobacco by eighteen- to twenty-year-olds; foie gras; pedicabs in parks; new fast-food restaurants (but only in poor neighborhoods); lobbyists from the floor of council chambers; lobbying city agencies after working at the same agency; vehicles in Central and Prospect parks; cell phones in upscale restaurants; the sale of pork products made in a processing plant in Tar Heel, North Carolina, because of a unionization dispute; mail-order pharmaceutical plans; candy-flavored cigarettes; gas-station operators adjusting prices more than once daily; Ringling Bros. and Barnum & Bailey Circus; Wal-Mart. "Whatever It Is, They're Against It," *New York Post,* Dec. 29, 2006, p. 36.

19. Greenpeace International, "Getting It On for the Good of the Planet: The Greenpeace Guide to Environmentally Friendly Sex," Sept. 10, 2002, www.greenpeace.org/international/news/eco-sex-guide (accessed March 15, 2007).

20. Alexis de Tocqueville, *Democracy in America* (New York: Knopf, 1994), vol. 2, p. 320.

21. Philip Coupland, "H. G. Wells's 'Liberal Fascism,' " *Journal of Contemporary History* 35, no. 4 (Oct. 2000), p. 549.

22. Wells's theology was, to put it mildly, heretical. He argued that God was not all-powerful but rather an ally of man "struggling and taking a part against evil." H. G. Wells, *God, the Invisible King* (New York: Macmillan, 1917), p. xiv. His was also a God of imperialism and conquest.

1. MUSSOLINI: THE FATHER OF FASCISM

1. Many authors have referenced these lyrics to demonstrate Mussolini's widespread popularity, but it is a common mistake to ascribe these lyrics to Cole Porter, the original author of the musical *Anything Goes.* Porter almost certainly did not write these lyrics. Rather, they were probably added by P. G. Wodehouse when he helped adapt the musical for the British stage. It also appears that there were multiple versions of the song with the Mussolini lyric, which hopscotched back and forth across the Atlantic.

2. Roberto Benigni's *Life Is Beautiful* (1998) won Oscars for Best Foreign Language Film and Best Actor and was nominated for Best Director. The title of the film, ironically enough, derives from Leon Trotsky. According to Benigni, shortly before the exiled Bolshevik was to be assassinated in Mexico, he supposedly looked at his wife in their garden and said, "Life is beautiful anyway."

3. John Patrick Diggins, *Mussolini and Fascism: The View from America* (Princeton, N.J.: Princeton University Press, 1972), p. 245; *Letters of Wallace Stevens,* ed. Holly Stevens (New York: Knopf, 1966), p. 295.

4. "Calls Mussolini Latin Roosevelt," *New York Times,* Oct. 7, 1923, p. E10.

5. Diggins, *Mussolini and Fascism,* p. 206; Norman Hapgood, *Professional Patriots* (New York: Boni, 1927), p. 62.

6. "Hughes a Humorist, Will Rogers Says," *New York Times,* Sept. 28, 1926, p. 29; Diggins, *Mussolini and Fascism,* p. 27, citing Will Rogers, "Letters of a Self-Made Diplomat to His President," *Saturday Evening Post,* July 31, 1926, pp. 8–9, 82–84.

7. Toscanini's relationship with the Mussolini regime was turbulent. For reasons probably more artistic than political, he refused to perform the fascist national anthem, "Giovinezza."

8. *The Autobiography of Lincoln Steffens, Volume II: Muckraking/Revolution/ Seeing America at Last* (New York: Harcourt, Brace and World, 1931), p. 799; McClure's view can be found in Diggins, *Mussolini and Fascism,* pp. 28–29.

9. Diggins, *Mussolini and Fascism,* pp. 255, 257.

10. Those numbers evened out a bit as Americans became increasingly interested in the Soviets' five-year plan. Simonetta Falasca-Zamponi, *Fascist Spectacle: The Aesthetics of Power in Mussolini's Italy* (Berkeley: University of California Press, 2000), p. 51.

11. Diggins, *Mussolini and Fascism,* p. 244.

12. La Follette's son, Philip, the famously progressive governor of Wisconsin, kept a picture of Mussolini in his office as late as 1938. Ibid., pp. 220–21.

13. Benito Mussolini, *My Rise and Fall* (New York: Da Capo, 1998), p. 3.

14. Paul Johnson, *Modern Times: The World from the Twenties to the Nineties* (New York: Perennial, 1991), p. 96. Here's how Mussolini describes one incident in his autobiography: "I caught her on the stairs, throwing her into a corner behind a door, and made her mine. When she got up weeping and humiliated she insulted me by saying that I had robbed her of her honor and it is not impossible that she spoke the truth. But I ask you, what kind of honor could she have meant?"

15. Falasca-Zamponi, *Fascist Spectacle,* p. 43.

16. Found in ibid., p. 224, n. 61.

17. The historian Hugh Gallagher writes of Roosevelt, he "was no Thomas Jefferson, and neither a scholar nor an intellectual in the usual sense of the word. He had a magpie mind, and many interests, but he was not deep." William E. Leuchtenburg, *The FDR Years: On Roosevelt and His Legacy* (New York: Columbia University Press, 1995), p. 27, quoting Hugh Gregory Gallagher, *FDR's Splendid Deception: The Moving Story of Roosevelt's Massive Disability—and the Intense Efforts to Conceal It from the Public* (New York: Dodd, Mead, 1985), p. 160.

18. Ivone Kirkpatrick, *Mussolini* (London: Odhams, 1964), p. 47.

19. Ibid., p. 49.

20. Mussolini wrote in a review of Sorel's *Reflections on Violence,* "That which I am . . . I owe to Sorel . . . He is an accomplished Master who, with his sharp theories on revolutionary formations, contributed to the molding of the discipline, the collective energy, the power of the masses, of the Fascist cohorts." A. James Gregor, *The Ideology of Fascism: The Rationale of Totalitarianism* (New York: Free Press, 1969), p. 116. In 1913 Sorel said, "Mussolini is no ordinary Socialist. One day you will see him at the head of a consecrated battalion, greeting the Italian banner with his dagger. He is an Italian of the 15th century, a *condottiere.* You do not know it yet. But he is the one energetic man who has the capacity to correct the weaknesses of the government." Kirkpatrick, *Mussolini,* p. 159.

21. Joshua Muravchik, *Heaven on Earth: The Rise and Fall of Socialism* (San Francisco: Encounter Books, 2002), p. 146; Joseph Husslein, *The Catholic Encyclopedia* (New York: Robert Appleton Company, 1912, p. 386; Roger Eatwell, *Fascism: A History* (New York: Penguin, 1995), p. 11.

22. If all the workers were already dedicated socialists, there would be no need for a general strike because the society would have already made the transition to socialism. Neil McInnes, *Encyclopedia of Philosophy* (New York: Macmillan Publishing Company, 1973). For the Mussolini interview, see Kirkpatrick, *Mussolini*, p. 159. For the quotation from Sharpton, see John Cassidy, "Racial Tension Boils Over as Rape Case Is Branded a Hoax," *Times* (London), June 19, 1988.

23. Zeev Sternhell, *The Birth of Fascist Ideology,* trans. David Maisel (Princeton, N.J.: Princeton University Press, 1994), p. 56.

24. Gregor, *Ideology of Fascism,* p. 116.

25. Gertrude Himmelfarb, "The Idea of Compassion: The British vs. the French Enlightenment," *Public Interest,* no. 145 (Fall 2001).

26. Jean-Jacques Rousseau, *The Social Contract and Discourses,* trans. G. D. H. Cole (New York: Dutton, 1950), p. 297.

27. For example, in 1924 the Italian Fascist theorist Giuseppe Bottai declared in a lecture, "Fascism as Intellectual Revolution": "If by democracy one understands the possibility granted all citizens of actively participating in the life of the state, then nobody will deny democracy's immortality. The French Revolution rendered this possibility historically and ethically concrete, so much so that an ineradicable right was born that exercises a tenacious hold on individual consciousness, independent of abstract invocations of immortal principles or developments in modern philosophy." Reprinted in: Jeffrey T. Schnapp, ed., *A Primer of Italian Fascism* (Lincoln: University of Nebraska Press, 2000), p. 82.

28. See George L. Mosse, *The Nationalization of the Masses: Political Symbolism and Mass Movements in Germany from the Napoleonic Wars Through the Third Reich* (New York: Fertig, 2001); George L. Mosse, "Fascism and the French Revolution," *Journal of Contemporary History* 24, no. 1 (Jan. 1989), pp. 5–26.

29. The observation that Rousseau's state is the most "powerful to be found anywhere in political philosophy" is Robert Nisbet's. Robert Nisbert, *The Present Age: Progress and Anarchy in Modern America* (New York: Harper & Row, 1988), p. 52.

30. Fascism, according to the fascist theorist Giuseppe Bottai, "was, for my comrades or myself, nothing more than a way of continuing the war, of transforming its values into a civic religion." "Fascism as Intellectual Revolution," p. 20. Augusto Turati, a party secretary and self-proclaimed "new apostle of the Fatherland's religion," explained to massive rallies of Italian Youth that the new "fascist religion" demanded "the need to believe absolutely; to believe in Fascism, in the *Duce,* in the Revolution. Just as one believes in God . . . we accept the Revolution with pride, just as we accept these principles—even if we realize they are mistaken, and we accept them without discussion."

31. "Pope in Encyclical Denounces Fascisti and Defends Clubs," *New York Times*, July 4, 1931; "Everything Is Promised," *Time*, July 13, 1931. See also Emilio Gentile, *Politics as Religion*, trans. George Staunton (Princeton, N.J.: Princeton University Press, 2006), p. 95.

32. David Nicholls, *God and Government in an "Age of Reason"* (London: Routledge, 1995), p. 80.

33. The law was passed by the Convention but was never fully implemented. Himmelfarb, "Idea of Compassion." The Tocqueville quotation is from *The Old Régime and the French Revolution* (New York: Anchor, 1955), p. 156, found in ibid.

34. Robespierre, speech of Feb. 5, 1794, in *Modern History Sourcebook,* www.fordham.edu/halsall/mod/robespierre-terror.html.

35. Marisa Linton, "Robespierre and the Terror," *History Today,* Aug. 1, 2006.

36. R. J. B. Bosworth, *The Italian Dictatorship: Problems and Perspectives in the Interpretation of Mussolini and Fascism* (London: Arnold, 1998), p. 104.

37. David Ramsay Steele, "The Mystery of Fascism," *Liberty,* www.la-articles.org.uk/fascism.htm (accessed March 13, 2007).

38. Muravchik, *Heaven on Earth,* p. 148, citing Margherita G. Sarfatti, *The Life of Benito Mussolini,* trans. Frederic Whyte (New York: Stokes, 1925), p. 263.

39. Mussolini, *My Rise and Fall,* p. 36.

40. Muravchik, *Heaven on Earth,* p. 149, citing Jasper Ridley, *Mussolini: A Biography* (New York: St. Martin's, 1997), p. 71.

41. Jeffrey T. Schnapp, pp. 3–6; Charles F. Delzell, *Mediterranean Fascism, 1919–1945* (New York: Harper and Row, 1970), pp. 12–13.

42. Robert O. Paxton, "The Five Stages of Fascism," *Journal of Modern History* 70, no. 1 (March 1998), p. 15.

43. Robert O. Paxton, *The Anatomy of Fascism* (New York: Vintage, 2004),

p. 17; Bosworth, *The Italian Dictatorship*, p. 39. According to Hannah Arendt, Mussolini "was probably the first party leader who consciously rejected a formal program and replaced it with inspired leadership and action alone." Hannah Arendt, *The Origins of Totalitarianism,* rev. ed. (New York: Harcourt, 1966), p. 325 n. 39.

44. Falasca-Zamponi, *Fascist Spectacle,* p. 72.

45. Arnaldo Cortesi, "Mussolini, on Radio, Gives Peace Pledge," *New York Times,* Jan. 2, 1931; W. Y. Elliott, "Mussolini, Prophet of the Pragmatic Era in Politics," *Political Science Quarterly* 41, no. 2 (June 1926), pp. 161–92.

46. Muravchik, *Heaven on Earth,* pp. 170, 171.

2. ADOLF HITLER: MAN OF THE LEFT

1. Adolf Hitler, *Mein Kampf,* trans. Ralph Manheim (repr., Boston: Houghton Mifflin, 1999), p. 533.

2. According to Robert O. Paxton, the first example of "national socialism" as an ideological label and political precursor to fascism was the Cercle Proudhon in France in 1911, a club of intellectuals who aimed to "unite nationalists and left-wing anti-democrats" to mount an attack on "Jewish capitalism." Its founder, Georges Valois, worked tirelessly to convert the working class away from Marxist internationalism to a nation-based socialism. Robert O. Paxton, *The Anatomy of Fascism* (New York: Vintage, 2004), p. 48.

3. Denis Mack Smith, *Mussolini: A Biography* (New York: Vintage, 1983), p. 185; Stanley G. Payne, *A History of Fascism, 1914–1945* (Madison: University of Wisconsin Press, 1995), p. 232; Paul Johnson, *Modern Times: The World from the Twenties to the Nineties* (New York: Perennial, 1991), p. 319; Susan Zuccotti, *The Italians and the Holocaust: Persecution, Rescue, and Survival* (repr., Lincoln: University of Nebraska Press, 2006), p. 30.

4. Joachim Fest, *Hitler* (New York: Harcourt Brace Jovanovich, 1974), p. 203.

5. Claudia Koonz, *The Nazi Conscience* (Cambridge, Mass.: Harvard University Press, 2003), p. 18.

6. This might be a little unfair to Chamberlain in that his appeasement was based in no small part on realpolitik while Western pacifists were often Hitler's useful idiots.

7. William L. Shirer, *The Rise and Fall of the Third Reich* (New York: Touchstone, 1990), p. 205.

8. John Lukacs, *The Hitler of History* (New York: Vintage, 1997), p. 84.

9. David Schoenbaum, *Hitler's Social Revolution: Class and Status in Nazi Germany, 1933–1939* (New York: Norton, 1980), p. 19; Michael Burleigh, *The Third Reich: A New History* (New York: Hill and Wang, 2000), p. 245.

10. Hitler, *Mein Kampf,* p. 406.

11. Ron Rosenbaum, *Explaining Hitler: The Search for the Origins of His*

Evil (New York: Random House, 1998), p. xii; Robert G. L. Waite, *The Psychopathic God: Adolf Hitler* (New York: Da Capo, 1993), p. 20; Eugene H. Methvin, "20th Century Superkillers," *National Review,* May 31, 1985, pp. 22–29.

12. Hitler, *Mein Kampf,* p. 195.

13. Schoenbaum, *Hitler's Social Revolution,* p. 62.

14. Roger Griffin, ed., *Fascism* (New York: Oxford University Press, 1995), p. 123.

15. Hitler, *Mein Kampf,* pp. 484, 496–97.

16. Ibid., p. 484.

17. Burleigh, *Third Reich,* pp. 132–33.

18. Schoenbaum, *Hitler's Social Revolution,* p. 59; Burleigh, *Third Reich,* p. 105.

19. Theodore Abel, *Why Hitler Came Into Power* (Cambridge, Mass.: Harvard University Press, 1938), pp. 135–39; Eugen Weber, *Varieties of Fascism: Doctrines of Revolution in the Twentieth Century* (Malabar, Fla.: Kriegler, 1982), p. 55, quoting Abel, *Why Hitler Came Into Power,* pp. 203–301.

20. Richard Pipes, *Russia Under the Bolshevik Regime, 1919–1924* (New York: Vintage, 1995), p. 253.

21. Erik von Kuehnelt-Leddihn, *Leftism: From de Sade and Marx to Hitler and Marcuse* (New Rochelle, N.Y.: Arlington House, 1974), p. 136; Burleigh, *Third Reich,* p. 55.

22. John Patrick Diggins, *Mussolini and Fascism: The View from America* (Princeton, N.J.: Princeton University Press, 1972), p. 217 n. 19.

23. Ibid., p. 215.

24. Sidney Hook, "The Fallacy of the Theory of Social Fascism," in *American Anxieties: A Collective Portrait of the 1930s,* ed. Louis Filler (Somerset, N.J.: Transaction, 1993), p. 320.

3. WOODROW WILSON AND THE BIRTH OF
LIBERAL FASCISM

1. Fred Siegel, " 'It Can't Happen Here,' " *Weekly Standard,* Aug. 14, 2006, p. 40. Amusingly, one of the most devastating critics of the book was in fact Lewis himself. At a left-wing event held to honor the book and its author, Lewis said, "Boys, I love you all. And a writer loves to have his latest book praised. But let me tell you, it isn't a very good book."

2. Sinclair Lewis, *It Can't Happen Here* (New York: New American Library, 2005), p. 46.

3. Ibid., pp. 16, 17.

4. Woodrow Wilson, "The Ideals of America," *The Atlantic Monthly,* December 1902. See also Tony Smith, *America's Mission: The United States and the Worldwide Struggle for Democracy in the Twentieth Century* (Princeton, N.J.: Princeton University Press, 1994), p. 63; Jan Willem, *Woodrow Wilson: A Life for World Peace,* trans. Herbert H. Rowen (Los Angeles, Calif.: University of California Press 1991), p. 37.

5. Walter McDougall, *Promised Land, Crusader State: The American Encounter with the World Since 1776* (Boston: Houghton Mifflin, 1997), p. 128.
6. George Orwell, "Review of *Power: A New Social Analysis*," *Adelphi,* Jan. 1939, in *Essays* (New York: Random House, 2002), p. 107.
7. Woodrow Wilson, *Constitutional Government in the United States* (New York: Columbia University Press, 1908, 1961).
8. Ronald J. Pestritto, "Why Progressivism Is Not, and Never Was, a Source of Conservative Values," *Claremont Review of Books,* Aug. 25, 2005, www.claremont.org/publications/pubid.439/pub_detail.asp (accessed March 14, 2007). Woodrow Wilson, *The New Freedom* (New York: Doubleday, Page, 1913).
9. Michael McGerr, *A Fierce Discontent: The Rise and Fall of the Progressive Movement in America, 1870–1920* (New York: Free Press, 2003), pp. 66, 59.
10. Ibid., p. 111.
11. McDougall, *Promised Land, Crusader State,* p. 127.
12. John G. West, *Darwin's Conservatives: The Misguided Quest* (Seattle: Discovery Institute, 2006), p. 61.
13. Woodrow Wilson, *Leaders of Men,* ed. T. H. Vail Motter (Princeton, N.J.: Princeton University Press, 1952), pp. 20, 25–26.
14. Eric F. Goldman, *Rendezvous with Destiny: A History of Modern American Reform* (Chicago: Ivan R. Dee, 2001), p. 165.
15. John Milton Cooper Jr., *The Warrior and the Priest: Woodrow Wilson and Theodore Roosevelt* (Cambridge, Mass.: Harvard University Press, 1983), pp. 150–51.
16. Beveridge boasted that the Meat Inspection Act constituted "THE MOST PRONOUNCED EXTENSION OF FEDERAL POWER IN EVERY DIRECTION EVER ENACTED." McGerr, *Fierce Discontent,* p. 163. For the quotation, see William E. Leuchtenburg, "Progressivism and Imperialism: The Progressive Movement and American Foreign Policy, 1898–1916," *Mississippi Valley Historical Review* 39, no. 3 (Dec. 1952), p. 484.
17. Walter McDougall's *Promised Land, Crusader State* is invaluable for understanding this point. McDougall writes:

> Historians stress the dynamic crosscurrents in turn-of-the-century American society. Foster Rhea Dulles thought the era "marked by many contradictions." Richard Hofstadter identified "two different moods" one tending toward protest and reform, the other toward national expansion. Frederick Merk wrote of Manifest Destiny contesting with mission, and Ernest May of "cascades of imperialistic and moralistic oratory." But the contradictions are only a product of our wish to cleanse the Progressive movement of its taint of imperialism abroad. For at bottom, the belief that American power, guided by a secular and religious spirit of service, could remake foreign societies came as easily to the Progressives as trust-busting, prohibition of child labor, and regulation of interstate commerce, meatpacking, and drugs. Leading imperialists like Roosevelt, Beveridge, and Willard Straight were all Progressives; leading Progressives like Jacob Riis,

Gifford Pinchot, and Robert La Follette all supported the Spanish war and the insular acquisitions. (p. 120)

And in a famous 1952 essay, the historian William Leuchtenburg wrote that "imperialism and progressivism flourished together because they were both expressions of the same philosophy of government, a tendency to judge any action not by the means employed but by the results achieved, a worship of definitive action for action's sake, as John Dewey has pointed out, and an almost religious faith in the democratic mission of America." Leuchtenburg, "Progressivism and Imperialism," p. 500.

18. Goldman, *Rendezvous with Destiny,* p. 209; Arthur A. Ekrich Jr., *The Decline of American Liberalism* (New York: Atheneum, 1967), p. 193.

19. Long also said that it would come to America as "anti-Fascism," a fairly prophetic analysis since the left has long considered itself the fighting wedge of "anti-Fascism." For the Mencken quotations, see H. L. Mencken, "Roosevelt: An Autopsy," in *Prejudices: Second Series* (New York: Knopf, 1920), pp. 112, 114.

20. Ronald J. Pestritto, *Woodrow Wilson and the Roots of Modern Liberalism* (Lanham, Md.: Rowman and Littlefield, 2005), p. 255. Emphasis mine.

21. Progressives didn't start widely using the word "progressive" to describe themselves until 1909. In England progressives might be called "Tory democrats," "Labour imperialists," "new liberals," "Fabians," or "collectivists." In America progressives might go by "reformer" or even "radical" and, of course, Republican or Democrat (the widespread use of the word "liberal" to describe progressives didn't fully catch on until the 1920s). In France and Germany many of these labels were in play, too, as were such monikers as *interventionnistes*. Some cited Nietzsche, others Marx, others William James. Many—as Mussolini and Georges Sorel would—claimed all three as influences. Indeed, there's little doubt that some Italian socialist bands called *fascios* in Italy at the time fell squarely in the "progressive" camp. And we know that the nationalist intellectuals who laid the groundwork for fascism in Italy were heavily influenced by William James's pragmatism, just as James was influenced by them.

22. Daniel T. Rodgers, *Atlantic Crossings: Social Politics in a Progressive Age* (Cambridge, Mass.: Harvard University Press, 1998), pp. 57, 74.

23. Joseph Jacobs, "Works of Friedrich Nietzsche," *New York Times,* May 7, 1910; Mencken, "Roosevelt: An Autopsy," p. 111. Indeed, Richard Hofstadter, the iconic liberal historian, saw Teddy Roosevelt as a thinly veiled fascist. In the words of David Brown, Hofstadter's biographer, Roosevelt's defining characteristic was a "Mussolini lite" and his politics, marked by a "stern dedication to nationalism, martial values, and a common spirit of racial identity and destiny" were "a slight variation of the fascist politics that poisoned Europe following Roosevelt's death." David S. Brown, *Richard Hofstadter: An Intellectual Biography* (Chicago: University of Chicago Press, 2006), pp. xvi, 60.

24. Rodgers, *Atlantic Crossings,* pp. 86–87.

25. Goldman, *Rendezvous with Destiny*, p. 102; Charles A. Beard and James Harvey Robinson, *The Development of Modern Europe: An Introduction to the Study of Current History,* vol. 2 (Boston: Ginn & Company, 1907), p. 141; Frederic C. Howe, *Socialized Germany* (New York: C. Scribner's

Sons, 1915), p. 166; Fareed Zakaria, *The Future of Freedom: Illiberal Democracy at Home and Abroad* (New York: W. W. Norton, 2004), p. 66.

26. Murray N. Rothbard, "World War I as Fulfillment: Power and the Intellectuals," *Journal of Libertarian Studies* 9, no. 1 (Winter 1989), p. 103.

27. Woodrow Wilson, *The Papers of Woodrow Wilson,* vol. 1 (New York: Harper, 1927), pp. 6–10.

28. James Bovard, *Freedom in Chains: The Rise of the State and the Demise of the Citizen* (New York: St. Martin's, 2000), p. 8.

29. Charles Forcey, *The Crossroads of Liberalism: Croly, Weyl, Lippmann, and the Progressive Era, 1900–1925* (New York: Oxford University Press, 1961), pp. 124–25.

30. Wilfred M. McClay, "Croly's Progressive America," *Public Interest,* no. 137 (Fall 1999).

31. Goldman, *Rendezvous with Destiny,* p. 192.

32. Charles Forcey, *The Crossroads of Liberalism,* p. 15; Goldman, *Rendezvous with Destiny,* p. 191.

33. Bovard, *Freedom in Chains,* p. 8.

34. Leuchtenburg, "Progressivism and Imperialism," p. 490.

35. Herbert Croly, *The Promise of American Life* (New York: Macmillan, 1911), p. 14.

36. Herbert Croly, "Regeneration," *New Republic* (June 9, 1920), pp. 40–44; originally found in Sydney Kaplan, "Social Engineers as Saviors: Effects of World War I on Some American Liberals," *Journal of the History of Ideas* (June 1956), pp. 347–69.

37. John Patrick Diggins, "Flirtation with Fascism: American Pragmatic Liberals and Mussolini's Italy," *American Historical Review* 71, no. 2 (Jan. 1966), p. 494.

38. "No doubt there were single hours in the world war," Ross wrote in *The Russian Soviet Republic,* "when more Russian lives were consumed than the Red Terror ever took . . . it accomplished its purpose in that the bourgeoisie suddenly ceased to plot." Dimitri von Mohrenschildt, "The Early American Observers of the Russian Revolution, 1917–1921," *Russian Review* 3, no. 1 (Autumn 1943), p. 67. *Razstrellyat* misspelled in original.

39. Ibid., p. 69.

40. Lewis S. Feuer, "American Travelers to the Soviet Union, 1917–32: The Formation of a Component of New Deal Ideology," *American Quarterly* 14, no. 2, pt. 1 (Summer 1962), p. 125; Stuart Chase, Robert Dunn, and Rexford Guy Tugwell, eds., *Soviet Russia in the Second Decade* (New York: John Day, 1928), pp. 49–50, 54.

41. Feuer, "American Travelers to the Soviet Union," pp. 102, 128, 126, 119–49.

42. Ibid., p. 132.

43. The March 2, 1927, issue of the *New Republic* informed readers that "the more liberal attitude is to regard Fascism in Italy, like Communism in Russia, as a political and social experiment which has a function in Italian political development and which cannot be understood and appraised from the formulas either of its friends or enemies."

44. Diggins, "Flirtation with Fascism," p. 494, citing Charles A. Beard, "Making the Fascist State," *New Republic,* Jan. 23, 1929, pp. 277–78.

45. West, *Darwin's Conservatives,* p. 60.

46. It was around this time that the *New Republic* became akin to an intellectual PR firm for the Wilson administration. Teddy Roosevelt was so frustrated that his former cheering section had switched loyalties he proclaimed the *New Republic* a "negligible sheet run by two anemic Gentiles and two uncircumcised Jews." Goldman, *Rendezvous with Destiny*, p. 194.

47. Woodrow Wilson, Address to a Joint Session of Congress on Trusts and Monopolies, Jan. 20, 1914, www.presidency.ucsb.edu/ws/?pid=65374 (accessed March 14, 2007).

48. Wilson's conviction that he was the messianic incarnation of world-historical forces was total. Time and again he argued that he was the instrument of God or history or both. He concluded a famous speech to the League to Enforce Peace:

> But I did not come here, let me repeat, to discuss a program. I came only to avow a creed and give expression to the confidence I feel that the world is even now upon the eve of a great consummation, when some common force will be brought into existence which shall safeguard right as the first and most fundamental interest of all peoples and all governments, when coercion shall be summoned not to the service of political ambition or selfish hostility, but to the service of a common order, a common justice, and a common peace. God grant that the dawn of that day of frank dealing and of settled peace, concord, and cooperation may be near at hand!

Full text can be found at www.presidency.ucsb.edu/ws/index.php?pid =65391. Woodrow Wilson, *The Messages and Papers of Woodrow Wilson*, vol. 1, ed. Albert Shaw (New York: Review of Reviews Corporation, 1924), p. 275. See also "Text of the President's Speech Discussing Peace and Our Part in a Future League to Prevent War," *New York Times*, May 28, 1916, p. 1.

49. William E. Leuchtenburg, *The FDR Years: On Roosevelt and His Legacy* (New York: Columbia University Press, 1995), p. 39.

50. For the Dewey quotation, see www.fff.org/freedom/fd0203c.asp; for the Blatch, see McGerr, *Fierce Discontent,* p. 282, and John M. Barry, *The Great Influenza: The Epic Story of the Deadliest Plague in History* (New York: Penguin, 2004), p. 127; for the Ely, see Murray N. Rothbard, "Richard T. Ely: Paladin of the Welfare-Warfare State," *Independent Review* 6, no. 4 (Spring 2002), p. 587; for the Wilson, see "Gov. Wilson Stirs Spanish Veterans," *New York Times,* Sept. 11, 1912, p. 3; for the Hitler, see *The Goebbels Diaries, 1942–1943,* ed. Louis P. Lochner (New York: Doubleday, 1948), p. 314.

51. McGerr, *Fierce Discontent,* p. 282.

52. For the Croly quotations, see "The End of American Isolation," editorial, *New Republic,* Nov. 7, 1914, quoted in John B. Judis, "Homeward Bound," *New Republic,* March 3, 2003, p. 16; and Ekirch, *Decline of*

American Liberalism, p. 202. For the Lippmann quotations, see Ronald Steel, "The Missionary," *New York Review of Books,* Nov. 20, 2003; and Heinz Eulau, "From Public Opinion to Public Philosophy: Walter Lippmann's Classic Reexamined," *American Journal of Economics and Sociology,* vol. 15, no. 4 (July 1956), p. 441.

53. Leuchtenburg, *FDR Years,* p. 39; David M. Kennedy, *Over Here: The First World War and American Society* (New York: Oxford University Press, 1982), p. 52.

54. Grosvenor Clarkson, *Industrial America in the World War: The Strategy Behind the Line, 1917–1918* (Boston: Houghton Mifflin, 1923), p. 292.

55. McGerr, *Fierce Discontent,* p. 289; Woodrow Wilson, A Proclamation by the President of the United States, as printed in *New York Times,* May 19, 1917, p. 1.

56. Walter Lippmann, *Public Opinion* (New York: Harcourt, Brace, 1922).

57. McGerr, *Fierce Discontent,* p. 288; Barry, *Great Influenza,* p. 127.

58. For the Bernays quotation, see Michael Kazin, *The Populist Persuasion: An American History* (Ithaca, N.Y.: Cornell University Press, 1998), p. 70. For the CPI posters, see Barry, *Great Influenza,* p. 127.

59. Barry, *Great Influenza,* p. 126.

60. "Charges Traitors in America Are Disrupting Russia," *New York Times,* Sept. 16, 1917, p. 3; Stephen Vaughn, "First Amendment Liberties and the Committee on Public Information," *American Journal of Legal History* 23, no. 2 (April 1979), p. 116.

61. McGerr, *Fierce Discontent,* p. 293.

62. Ibid., pp. 293, 294.

63. H. W. Brands, *The Strange Death of American Liberalism* (New Haven, Conn.: Yale University Press, 2001), p. 40. In all of the cases of Burleson's clamping down on the press, there are only two instances when Wilson disagreed with his postmaster enough to redress the situation. In all the others Wilson steadfastly supported the government's largely un-limited right to censor the press—including one instance when Burleson used his powers to harass a local Texas journal that criticized his decision to evict sharecroppers from his property. In a letter to one congressman, Wilson declared that censorship is "absolutely necessary to the public safety." John Sayer, "Art and Politics, Dissent and Repression: *The Masses Magazine* Versus the Government, 1917–1918," *American Journal of Legal History* 32, no. 1 (Jan. 1988), p. 46.

64. Sayer, "Art and Politics, Dissent and Repression," p. 64 n. 99; Ekirch, *Decline of American Liberalism,* pp. 216–17.

65. Carl Brent Swisher, "Civil Liberties in War Time," *Political Science Quarterly* 55, no. 3 (Sept. 1940), p. 335.

66. See Howard Zinn, *The Twentieth Century: A People's History* (New York: HarperCollins, 2003), pp. 89–92.

67. Norman Hapgood, *Professional Patriots* (New York: Boni, 1927), p. 62. See also John Patrick Diggins, *Mussolini and Fascism: The View from America* (Princeton, N.J.: Princeton University Press, 1972), p. 206. About a decade later, a legion representative from Texas pinned a legion button on Mussolini's lapel, making him an honorary member. In return,

Mussolini posed for a photograph wearing a Texas cowboy hat with the legion colonel.

68. "Congress Cheers as Wilson Urges Curb on Plotters," *New York Times,* Dec. 8, 1915, p. 1; Charles Seymour, *Woodrow Wilson and the World War: A Chronicle of Our Own Times* (New Haven, Conn.: Yale University Press, 1921), p. 79; "Suggests Canada Might Vote with US," *New York Times,* Sept. 26, 1919, p. 3.

69. "President Greets Fliers," *Washington Post,* Sept. 10, 1924; Ekirch, *Decline of American Liberalism,* p. 217; Barry, *Great Influenza,* p. 125.

70. For Butler, see Ellen Nore, *Charles A. Beard: An Intellectual Biography* (Carbondale: Southern Illinois University Press, 1983), p. 80; and Kennedy, *Over Here,* p. 74. To his eternal credit, the historian Charles Beard resigned his teaching position in protest. Few of his colleagues followed his example. For Ely, see Rothbard, "Richard T. Ely," p. 588, citing Carol S. Gruber, *Mars and Minerva: World War I and the Uses of the Higher Learning in America* (Baton Rouge: Louisiana State University Press, 1975), p. 207.

71. McGerr, *Fierce Discontent,* p. 299; "Stamping Out Treason," editorial, *Washington Post,* April 12, 1918.

72. Kazin, *Populist Persuasion,* p. 69; John Patrick Diggins, *The Rise and Fall of the American Left* (New York: Norton, 1992), p. 102.

73. McGerr, *Fierce Discontent,* p. 290.

74. David Schoenbaum, *Hitler's Social Revolution: Class and Status in Nazi Germany, 1933–1939* (New York: Norton, 1980), p. 63; Michael Mann, *Fascists* (New York: Cambridge University Press, 2004), p. 146.

75. McGerr, *Fierce Discontent,* p. 59.

4. FRANKLIN ROOSEVELT'S FASCIST NEW DEAL

1. Michael A. Bernstein, *The Great Depression: Delayed Recovery and Economic Change in America, 1929–1939* (New York: Cambridge University Press, 1987), p. 273; William E. Leuchtenburg, *The FDR Years: On Roosevelt and His Legacy* (New York: Columbia University Press, 1995), p. 50.

2. Leuchtenburg, *FDR Years,* pp. 10–11.

3. Lewis S. Feuer, "American Travelers to the Soviet Union, 1917–32: The Formation of a Component of New Deal Ideology," *American Quarterly* 14, no. 2, pt. 1 (Summer 1962), p. 148, citing Harold L. Ickes, *The Secret Diary of Harold L. Ickes: The First Thousand Days* (New York: Simon and Schuster, 1953), p. 104; Alan Brinkley, *The End of Reform: New Deal Liberalism in Recession and War* (New York: Vintage, 1996), p. 22; Ickes, *Secret Diary,* vol. 2, pp. 325–26.

4. The best single treatment of FDR's policies as dictatorial and fascistic can be found in William E. Leuchtenburg's essay "The New Deal as the Moral Analogue of War," in *FDR Years,* pp. 35–75. On Lippmann, see Jonathan Alter, *The Defining Moment: FDR's Hundred Days and the Triumph of*

Hope (New York: Simon and Schuster, 2006), p. 5; Ronald Steel, *Walter Lippmann and the American Century* (Boston: Little, Brown, 1980), p. 300.

5. Alan Brinkley, *Liberalism and Its Discontents* (Cambridge, Mass.: Harvard University Press, 1998), p. 17.

6. Leuchtenburg, *FDR Years,* p. 27, citing Hugh Gregory Gallagher, *FDR's Splendid Deception: The Moving Story of Roosevelt's Massive Disability—and the Intense Efforts to Conceal It from the Public* (New York: Dodd, Mead, 1985), p. 160.

7. Kenneth S. Davis, *FDR: The New Deal Years, 1933–1937* (New York: Random House, 1986), p. 223.

8. James MacGregor Burns, *Roosevelt: The Lion and the Fox, 1882–1940* (New York: Harcourt, Brace, 1984), p. 50.

9. Ibid., pp. 52, 61.

10. However, this attitude didn't extend to his own interests. He told his mother she should not go overboard by following the government mantra that one should buy Liberty Bonds "until it hurts." The man who would later decry "economic royalists" told the woman controlling his purse strings not to sell off any of the family's more valuable assets in order to buy more patriotic—but less lucrative—securities. Davis, *FDR,* pp. 512–13.

11. Richard Hofstadter, *The American Political Tradition and the Men Who Made It* (New York: Vintage, 1989), p. 412; Leuchtenburg, *FDR Years,* p. 2.

12. Burns, *Roosevelt,* p. 144.

13. Brinkley, *Liberalism and Its Discontents,* pp. 18, 37; Alvin H. Hansen, "Toward Full Employment," speech at the University of Cincinnati, March 15, 1949, quoted in Brinkley, *End of Reform,* p. 5.

14. "Liberalism vs. Fascism," editorial, *New Republic,* March 2, 1927, p. 35. It is impossible not to detect the fascist obsession with unity and action in Croly's defense of Mussolini. In another editorial he declared, "Whatever the dangers of Fascism, it has at any rate substituted movement for stagnation, purposive behavior for drifting, and visions of great future for collective pettiness and discouragement." Brinkley, *End of Reform,* p. 155; John Patrick Diggins, *Mussolini and Fascism: The View from America* (Princeton, N.J.: Princeton University Press, 1972), p. 204.

15. John Patrick Diggins, "Flirtation with Fascism: American Pragmatic Liberals and Mussolini's Italy," *American Historical Review* 71, no. 2 (Jan. 1966), p. 495.

16. Stuart Chase, *A New Deal* (New York: Macmillan, 1932), p. 252.

17. The Marquis de Sade considered himself a great revolutionary and *philosophe*. But in reality he was a bored pervert who came up with elaborate rationales to poke and scratch people for the fun of it. Lenin was bored to nausea by anything but constant agitation for revolution. Martin Heidegger taught an entire course on boredom, calling it the "insidious creature [that] maintains its monstrous essence in our [Being]." It's been speculated that Heidegger signed up with the Nazis at least in part to cure himself of boredom.

18. James R. Mellow, *Charmed Circle: Gertrude Stein and Company* (New York: Henry Holt, 2003), p. 416.

19. "We who are over sixty," Sinclair Lewis observed on the occasion of Wells's death in 1946, "have remembered all that he meant to us . . . For here was a man who, more than any other of this century, suggested to our young minds the gaudy fancy (which conceivably might also be fact) that mankind can, by taking thought," refuse "to make our lives miserable and guilty just to please some institution that for a century has been a walking and talking corpse." Eric F. Goldman, *Rendezvous with Destiny: A History of Modern American Reform* (Chicago: Ivan R. Dee, 2001), p. 178. I did not get the title of this book from Wells's speech, but I was delighted to discover the phrase has such a rich intellectual history. See Philip Coupland, "H. G. Wells's 'Liberal Fascism,' " *Journal of Contemporary History* 35, no. 4 (Oct. 2000), pp. 541–58.

20. Coupland, "H. G. Wells's 'Liberal Fascism,' " p. 543.

21. H. G. Wells, *The War in the Air* (New York: Penguin Classics, 2005), p. 128. When the film version opened in theaters, a letter appeared in the British Union of Fascists party newspaper, *Action*, asking, "Is Mr. Wells a Secret Fascist?" The correspondent noted, "The supermen all wore the black shirt and broad shiny belt of Fascism! The uniforms were identical, and their wearers moved and bore themselves in the semi-military manner of fascists." Coupland, "H. G. Wells's 'Liberal Fascism,' " p. 541. H. G. Wells, "What Is Fascism—and Why?" *New York Times Magazine,* Feb. 6, 1927, p. 2; George Orwell, "Wells, Hitler, and the World State," *Horizon,* Aug. 1941, in *Essays* (New York: Knopf, 2002), p. 371.

22. H. G. Wells, *Experiment in Autobiography: Discoveries and Conclusions of a Very Ordinary Brain Since 1866* (New York: Macmillan, 1934), p. 682; William E. Leuchtenburg, *The FDR Years: On Roosevelt and His Legacy* (New York: Columbia University Press, 1995), p. 93.

23. In the 1920s and 1930s various fascist-like intellectual cults popped up based on the idea that engineers should rule, the most famous of which was Thorstein Veblen's "technocracy" fad.

24. As a writer for the *Village Voice* puts it, Coughlin was the leader of a "group of right-wing Christian political losers." James Ridgeway, "Mondo Washington," *Village Voice,* March 14, 2000, p. 41. A writer for the *New York Times* simply declared Pat Buchanan the "Father Coughlin of 1996." Samuel G. Freedman, "The Father Coughlin of 1996," *New York Times,* Feb. 25, 1996. The historian Michael Kazin told *BusinessWeek,* "Buchanan hearkens back to Father Coughlin's 1930s isolationist-conservatism." Lee Walczak, "The New Populism," *BusinessWeek,* March 13, 1995, p. 72. A professor writing for *Foreign Policy* expresses shock that "the contemporary Christian Right have been staunch supporters of Israel," which he says should be a "surprise to observers familiar with the anti-Semitic virulence of such pre–World War II Christian conservatives as radio commentator Father Charles." William Martin, "The Christian Right and American Foreign Policy," *Foreign Policy,* no. 114 (Spring 1999), p. 72. *Newsweek* counts Father Coughlin and Ronald Reagan as two "con-servatives" who really got radio. Howard Fineman, "The Power of Talk," *Newsweek,* Feb. 8, 1993, p. 24. And on and on.

25. Marshall William Fishwick, *Great Awakenings: Popular Religion and Popular Culture* (Binghamton, N.Y.: Haworth, 1995), p. 128.

26. "Lays Banks' Crash to Hoover Policies," *New York Times,* Aug. 24, 1933, p. 7; "State Capitalism Urged by Coughlin," *New York Times,* Feb. 19, 1934, p. 17.

27. A wide range of observers understood that communism was a new religion. John Maynard Keynes began his brilliant 1925 essay "A Short View of Russia" by declaring, "Leninism is a combination of two things which Europeans have kept for some centuries in different compartments of the soul—religion and business. We are shocked because the religion is new, and contemptuous because the business, being subordinated to the religion instead of the other way round, is highly inefficient."

28. Alan Brinkley, *Voices of Protest: Huey Long, Father Coughlin, and the Great Depression* (New York: Vintage, 1983), p. 122.

29. " 'Roosevelt or Ruin,' Asserts Radio Priest at Hearing," *Washington Post,* Jan. 17, 1934, pp. 1–2; Brinkley, *Voices of Protest,* p. 126. See also Father Coughlin, Address, National Union for Social Justice, Nov. 11, 1934, www.ssa.gov/history/fcspeech.html (accessed Feb. 20, 2007).

30. Principles of the National Union for Social Justice, quoted in Brinkley, *Voices of Protest,* pp. 287–88.

31. Coughlin went on: "We maintain the principle that there can be no lasting prosperity if free competition exists in any industry. Therefore, it is the business of government not only to legislate for a minimum annual wage and maximum working schedule to be observed by industry, but also to curtail individualism that, if necessary, factories shall be licensed and their output shall be limited." Charles A. Beard and George H. E. Smith, eds., *Current Problems of Public Policy: A Collection of Materials* (New York: The Macmillan Company, 1936), p. 54.

32. Brinkley, *Voices of Protest,* p. 239.

33. *Wordsworth Dictionary of Quotations* (Ware: Wordsworth Editions, 1998, p. 240); Arthur M. Schlesinger, *The Politics of Upheaval: 1935–1936,* vol. 3 of *The Age of Roosevelt* (Boston: Houghton Mifflin, 2003), p. 66.

34. Sinclair was the muckraking journalist who most famously wrote *The Jungle,* the story of an exploited immigrant in the Chicago meatpacking industry who ultimately finds salvation through socialism. Sinclair himself was formally a member of the Socialist Party until World War I, when he broke with it in favor of intervention (which would have made him a Fascist in Italy). Sinclair remained an ideological socialist (and food faddist) for the rest of his days. Dr. Townsend is an even odder duck. In September 1933 he wrote a letter to his local California newspaper claiming that America's economic problems could be solved if only the federal government gave two hundred dollars to all people over the age of sixty, so long as they promised to spend the money within thirty days. This alone would jump-start the economy and pull the elderly out of poverty. Within three months of that letter to the editor, there were three thousand Townsend clubs across the country, as well as a weekly national newspaper. By the summer of 2005, there were an estimated 2.25 million members across the country. The Townsend movement, which *Today* dubbed "easily the outstanding political sensation of 1935," ended up winning numerous seats in state legislatures and even two governorships. William E.

Leuchtenburg, *Franklin D. Roosevelt and the New Deal* (New York: Harper & Row, 1963), p. 180.

35. Wolfgang Schivelbusch, *Three New Deals: Reflections on Roosevelt's America, Mussolini's Italy, and Hitler's Germany, 1933–1939* (New York: Metropolitan Books, 2006), p. 73.

36. Götz Aly, *Hitler's Beneficiaries: Plunder, Racial War, and the Nazi Welfare State,* trans. Jefferson Chase (New York: Holt, 2007). A discerning reader might ask, "Why was Hitler's Germany so much more successful than America if the Third Reich was more socialist?" It's an excellent question and one that I've asked several economists. The short answer is "real wages." See Jody K. Biehl, "How Germans Fell for the 'Feel-Good' Fuehrer," *Spiegel Online,* March 22, 2005, http://www.spiegel.de/international/0,1518,347726,00.html (accessed June 26, 2007).

37. Anne O'Hare McCormick, "Hitler Seeks Jobs for All Germans," *New York Times,* July 10, 1933, p. 6.

38. John A. Garraty, "The New Deal, National Socialism, and the Great Depression," *American Historical Review* 78, no. 4 (Oct. 1973), pp. 933–34; Schivelbusch, *Three New Deals,* pp. 19–20.

39. Schivelbusch, *Three New Deals,* pp. 23, 24, 19.

40. Benito Mussolini, "The Birth of a New Civilization," in *Fascism,* ed. Roger Griffin (New York: Oxford University Press, 1995), p. 73; Schivelbusch, *Three New Deals,* p. 31.

41. Alonzo L. Hamby, *For the Survival of Democracy: Franklin Roosevelt and the World Crisis of the 1930s* (New York: Free Press, 2004), p. 146.

42. Interestingly, James engages the German philosopher S. R. Steinmetz in his essay. And while he disagrees with Steinmetz on several substantial points, it's worth noting that he says Steinmetz is "a conscientious thinker" and "moral" militarist. Steinmetz, now widely forgotten, was a very prominent German social Darwinist and eugenicist. William James, *Memories and Studies* (New York: Longmans, Green and Co., 1934), p. 281.

43. Alter, *Defining Moment,* p. 4.

44. Ibid., p. 5.

45. Leuchtenburg, *FDR Years,* p. 63.

46. Ibid., pp. 55, 56.

47. Schoenbaum, *Hitler's Social Revolution,* p. 63. Konstantin Hierl, the head of the Labor Service, explained that there was no better way to overcome class differences than to dress "the son of the director and the young worker, the university student and the farmhand, in the same uniform, to set them the same table in common service to *Volk* and *Vaterland.*" Comparing Germany to Spain, Hitler proclaimed in 1936, "What a difference compared with a certain other country. There it is class against class, brother against brother. We have chosen the other route: rather than to wrench you apart, we have brought you together."

48. Hugh S. Johnson, *The Blue Eagle, from Egg to Earth* (Garden City, N.Y.: Doubleday, Doran, 1935), p. 264.

49. Colloquially, this is "All for one, one for all," but its closer translation would be "The community over self-interest."

50. Otto Friedrich, "F.D.R.'s Disputed Legacy," *Time,* Feb. 1, 1982.

51. Hamby, *For the Survival of Democracy,* p. 164.

52. "Not Since the Armistice," *Time,* Sept. 25, 1933, http://www.time .com/time/magazine/article/0,9171,882190,00.html (accessed February 7, 2007); T. H. Watkins, "The Bird Did Its Part," *Smithsonian,* vol. 30, no. 2, May 1999.

53. "Red Rally Dimmed by Harlem Fervor," *New York Times,* Aug. 5, 1934, p. N3.

54. Lee Lescaze, "Reagan Still Sure Some in New Deal Espoused Fascism," *Washington Post,* Dec. 24, 1981, p. A7. Reagan was even more straightforward the previous August: "Anyone who wants to look at the writings of the Brain Trust of the New Deal will find that President Roosevelt's advisers admired the fascist system . . . They thought that private ownership with government management and control a la the Italian system was the way to go, and that has been evident in all their writings." See Steven F. Hayward, *The Age of Reagan: The Fall of the Old Liberal Order, 1964–1980* (Roseville, Calif.: Prima, 2001), p. 681; Robert G. Kaiser, "Those Old Reaganisms," *Washington Post,* Sept. 2, 1980, p. A2.

55. Franklin D. Roosevelt, Annual Message to U.S. Congress, Jan. 3, 1936, quoted in James Bovard, *Freedom in Chains: The Rise of the State and the Demise of the Citizen* (New York: St. Martin's, 2000), p. 17.

56. William E. Leuchtenburg, *Franklin D. Roosevelt and the New Deal* (New York: Harper and Row, 1963), p. 340.

57. William A. Schambra, "The Quest for Community, and the Quest for a New Public Philosophy," paper presented at the American Enterprise Institute's Public Policy Week, Washington, D.C., Dec. 5–8, 1983, quoted in Robert Nisbet, *The Present Age: Progress and Anarchy in Modern America* (New York: HarperCollins, 1988), p. 51; text of President Roosevelt's Speech to His Neighbors, *New York Times,* Aug. 27, 1933, p. 28.

58. Schivelbusch, *Three New Deals,* p. 186.

59. Ibid., p. 37. Emphasis mine.

5. THE 1960s: FASCISM TAKES TO THE STREETS

1. Allan Bloom, *The Closing of the American Mind* (New York: Simon and Schuster, 1987), p. 315.

2. Donald Alexander Downs, *Cornell '69: Liberalism and the Crisis of the American University* (Ithaca, N.Y.: Cornell University Press, 1999), p. 172. I am aware that responsibility for the Reichstag fire is a subject of considerable debate among historians. But the Nazis did not care who was actually responsible for the fire. Rather, they exploited the fire for their own purposes. Some of the Black Nationalists at Cornell surely believed the cross was burned by white racists, but the leadership knew this was not the case and seized on the opportunity.

3. Gordon A. Craig, *Germany, 1866–1945* (Oxford: Clarendon, 1978), p. 478.

4. John Toland, *Adolf Hitler: The Definitive Biography* (New York: Anchor Books, 1992), p. 75.

5. Ibid.

6. Miriam Beard, "The Tune Hitlerism Beats for Germany," *New York Times,* June 7, 1931.

7. Richard Grunberger, *The 12-Year Reich: A Social History of Nazi Germany, 1933–1945* (New York: Da Capo, 1995), p. 306.

8. Terry H. Anderson, *The Movement and the Sixties* (New York: Oxford University Press, 1996), p. 200.

9. Walter Schultze, "The Nature of Academic Freedom," in *Nazi Culture: Intellectual, Cultural, and Social Life in the Third Reich,* ed. George L. Mosse (Madison: University of Wisconsin Press, 1966), p. 316.

10. Downs, *Cornell '69,* p. 9; Rowland Evans and Robert Novak, " 'New Order' at Cornell and the Academic Future," *Los Angeles Times,* May 5, 1969, p. C11.

11. Walter Berns, "The Assault on the Universities: Then and Now," in *Reassessing the Sixties: Debating the Political and Cultural Legacy,* ed. Stephen Macedo (New York: Norton, 1997), pp. 158–59.

12. Dinesh D'Souza, *The End of Racism: Principles for a Multiracial Society* (New York: Free Press, 1995), p. 339.

13. Paul Farhi, "Dean Tries to Summon Spirit of the 1960s," *Washington Post,* Dec. 28, 2003, p. A05.

14. Kerry denies attending the session when the issue was debated. Some claim he was there but voted against the idea. Nobody credibly alleges that he supported such a policy.

15. Farhi, "Dean Tries to Summon Spirit of the 1960s," p. A05.

16. Richard J. Ellis, "Romancing the Oppressed: The New Left and the Left Out," *Review of Politics* 58, no. 1 (Winter 1996), pp. 109–10; James Miller, *Democracy Is in the Streets: From Port Huron to the Siege of Chicago* (New York: Simon and Schuster, 1987), pp. 30–31; Tom Hayden, "Letter to the New (Young) Left," in *The New Student Left: An Anthology,* ed. Mitchell Cohen and Dennis Hale, rev. and expanded ed. (Boston: Beacon, 1967), pp. 5–6. The article originally appeared in the *Activist* (Winter 1961).

17. Eric F. Goldman, *Rendezvous with Destiny: A History of Modern American Reform* (Chicago: Ivan R. Dee, 2001), p. 159.

18. Peggy Kamuf, an American translator of many of Derrida's books, recalls that reading his work in 1970, while a graduate student at Yale, offered a way of finding solidarity with radicals in the streets. Deconstruction, she said, offered a way to do academic work while maintaining "that urgency of response to the abuses of power" that fed political engagement. In short, it let radical academics keep their jobs while turning the universities into incubators for radicalism. Quoted in Scott McLemee, "Derrida, a Pioneer of Literary Theory, Dies," *Chronicle of Higher Education,* Oct. 22, 2004, p. A1, chronicle.com/free/v51/i09/09a00101.htm (accessed Jan. 4, 2007).

19. Downs, *Cornell '69,* p. 232. See also "The Agony of Cornell," *Time,* May 2, 1969; Homer Bigart, "Cornell Faculty Reverses Itself on Negroes," *New York Times,* April 24, 1969. The trauma over the climate of betrayal and bitterness Rossiter both endured and fostered—academic, professional, and personal—doubtless contributed to his tragic decision to kill himself

the following year. Caleb Rossiter, Clinton's son, discounts this view in two vivid chapters in his autobiography. However, it is difficult to read his account without concluding that the stress of these events—particularly the extreme radicalism of his own sons—played some role.

20. Gunther Neske and Emil Kettering, eds., *Martin Heidegger and National Socialism: Questions and Answers* (New York: Paragon House, 1990), p. 6.

21. Richard Wolin, *The Seduction of Unreason: The Intellectual Romance with Fascism* (Princeton, N.J.: Princeton University Press, 2004), pp. 6–7.

22. The relationship between Pragmatism and conservatism is a bit more complicated. William James was a great American philosopher, and there is much in his work that conservatives admire. And if by Pragmatism you simply mean realism or practicality, then there are a great many conservative pragmatists. But if by Pragmatism one means the constellation of theories swirling among the progressives or the work of John Dewey, then conservatives have been at the forefront of a century-long critique of Pragmatism. However, it should be said that both James and Dewey are thoroughly American philosophers whose influence in a wide range of matters defies neat categorization along the left-right axis.

23. Wolin, *Seduction of Unreason,* p. 60.

24. Miller, *Democracy Is in the Streets,* p. 311.

25. Robert O. Paxton, *The Anatomy of Fascism* (New York: Vintage, 2004), pp. 16, 17; R. J. B. Bosworth, *The Italian Dictatorship: Problems and Perspectives in the Interpretation of Mussolini and Fascism* (London: Arnold, 1998), p. 39.

26. Wolin, *Seduction of Unreason,* p. 61; Beard, "The Tune Hitlerism Beats for Germany."

27. See Miller, *Democracy Is in the Streets,* p. 169. The SDS itself started as an offshoot of the League for Industrial Democracy, an anti-communist socialist organization briefly headed by John Dewey. Alan Brinkley, *Liberalism and Its Discontents* (Cambridge, Mass.: Harvard University Press, 1998), p. 232.

28. Todd Gitlin, *The Sixties: Years of Hope, Days of Rage* (New York: Bantam, 1993), p. 337.

29. Zeev Sternhell, *The Birth of Fascist Ideology: From Cultural Rebellion to Political Revolution,* trans. David Maisel (Princeton, N.J.: Princeton University Press, 1994), p. 56.

30. Gitlin, *Sixties,* p. 283.

31. *The Port Huron Statement,* in *Takin' It to the Streets: A Sixties Reader,* ed. Alexander Bloom and Wini Breines (New York: Oxford University Press, 1995), p. 61; Tom Hayden, *The Port Huron Statement: The Visionary Call of the 1960s Revolution* (New York: Avalon, 2005), pp. 97, 52; Brinkley, *Liberalism and Its Discontents,* pp. 229, 233.

32. Gitlin, *Sixties,* p. 101; Maurice Isserman and Michael Kazin, *America Divided: The Civil War of the 1960s,* 2nd ed. (New York: Oxford University Press, 2004), pp. 173, 174. See also W. J. Rorabaugh, *Berkeley at War: The 1960s* (New York: Oxford University Press, 1989), p. 8; Tom Wells, *The War Within: America's Battle Over Vietnam* (New York: Holt, 1994), pp. 117–18, 427; Maurice Isserman, *If I Had a Hammer: The*

Death of the Old Left and the Birth of the New Left (New York: Basic Books, 1987), pp. 196–97.

33. Gitlin, *Sixties,* p. 107; Miller, *Democracy Is in the Streets,* p. 291.
34. Brinkley, *Liberalism and Its Discontents,* p. 235. See also Godfrey Hodgson, *America in Our Time* (Garden City, N.Y.: Doubleday, 1976), pp. 300–5.
35. Walter Laqueur, "Reflections on Youth Movements," *Commentary,* June 1969.
36. Jay W. Baird, "Goebbels, Horst Wessel, and the Myth of Resurrection and Return," *Journal of Contemporary History* 17, no. 4 (Oct. 1982), p. 636.
37. Ibid., pp. 642–43.
38. Miller, *Democracy Is in the Streets,* p. 102.
39. Gitlin, *Sixties,* pp. 359–60; Tom Hayden, *Reunion: A Memoir* (New York: Collier, 1989), p. 247; Henry Raymont, "Violence as a Weapon of Dissent Is Debated at Forum in 'Village'; Moderation Criticized," *New York Times,* Dec. 17, 1967, p. 16; Tom Hayden, "Two, Three, Many Columbias," *Ramparts,* June 15, 1968, p. 40, in *America in the Sixties—Right, Left, and Center: A Documentary History,* ed. Peter B. Levy (Westport, Conn.: Praeger, 1998), pp. 231–33. See also Miller, *Democracy Is in the Streets,* p. 292.
40. Miller, *Democracy Is in the Streets,* p. 310; Jeff Lyon, "The World Is Still Watching after the 1968 Democratic Convention, Nothing in Chicago Was Quite the Same Again," *Chicago Tribune Magazine,* July 24, 1988. See also James W. Ely Jr., "The Chicago Conspiracy Case," in *American Political Trials,* ed. Michael R. Belknap (Westport, Conn.: Praeger, 1994), p. 248; Tom Hayden, *Rebellion and Repression* (New York: World, 1969), p. 15. For the recollections of the defendants and defense attorneys, see "Lessons of the '60s," *American Bar Association Journal* 73 (May 1987), pp. 32–38.
41. Vincent J. Cannato, *The Ungovernable City: John Lindsay and His Struggle to Save New York* (New York: Basic Books, 2001), p. 243.
42. Gitlin, *Sixties,* pp. 399, 401.
43. Ibid., pp. 399, 400. This account, as well as many of the accounts in this chapter, is derived from ibid. as well as Miller's *Democracy Is in the Streets.*
44. Gitlin, *Sixties,* p. 399. Dohrn spent a decade in hiding after her involvement in the "Days of Rage" assault on Chicago, where she now works as the director of the Children and Family Justice Center at Northwestern University. In 1993 she told the *New York Times,* "I was shocked at the anger toward me." She blamed part of the reaction to sexism—because she refused to behave like a "good girl." Susan Chira, "At Home With: Bernardine Dohrn; Same Passion, New Tactics," *New York Times,* Nov. 18, 1993, sec. C, p. 1.
45. The Nazis were pranksters of a sort as well. When *All Quiet on the Western Front* opened in Germany, Goebbels bought up huge numbers of tickets, ordering his storm troopers to heckle the movie and then release hundreds of white mice into the theater.
46. Abbie Hoffman, *The Best of Abbie Hoffman* (New York: Four Walls Eight Windows, 1990), p. 62; Miller, *Democracy Is in the Streets,* pp. 285–86; Gitlin, *Sixties,* p. 324.

47. Richard Jensen, "Futurism and Fascism," *History Today* 45, no. 11 (Nov. 1995), pp. 35–41.
48. Wolin, *Seduction of Unreason,* p. 62.
49. Gold believed that an "agency of the people" would have to take over the United States once imperialism had been dismantled. When someone said his idea sounded like a John Bircher's worst dream, Gold replied, "Well, if it will take fascism, we'll have to have fascism." Gitlin, *Sixties,* p. 399.
50. *I vote for the Democratic Party*
    They want the UN to be strong
    I attend all the Pete Seeger concerts,
    He sure gets me singing those songs.
    And I'll send all the money you ask for
    But don't ask me to come along.
    So love me, love me, love me—
    I'm a liberal.
    (Gitlin, *Sixties,* p. 183.)
51. Saul D. Alinsky, *Rules for Radicals: A Pragmatic Primer for Realistic Radicals* (New York: Vintage, 1972), pp. 120–21.
52. Ibid., p. 21.
53. Paxton, *Anatomy of Fascism,* p. 17.
54. Jay Nordlinger, "Che Chic," *National Review,* Dec. 31, 2004, p. 28.
55. Paul Berman, "The Cult of Che," *Slate,* Sept. 24, 2004, www.slate.com/id/2107100/ (accessed March 15, 2007); Nordlinger, "Che Chic," p. 28.
56. Lumumba, contrary to what I was taught in school, was assassinated not by the CIA but by opposing Congolese forces in a nasty civil war (though the CIA did have a plan in the works to get rid of him). He was handed over to his enemies by his former handpicked chief of staff Mobutu Sese Seko, who eventually took over the country and became a fascistic dictator whose ruthlessness didn't dissaude the American left, particularly the black left, from making him into a Pan-African hero.
57. Jean-Paul Sartre, preface to *The Wretched of the Earth,* by Frantz Fanon, trans. Constance Farrington (New York: Grove, 1963), p. 22; Gitlin, *Sixties,* p. 344.
58. When the black *fascisti* took over Straight Hall, one desperate parent called campus security. The first question the security dispatcher asked the man was whether the perpetrators were white or black. When the father responded they were black, "I was told that there was nothing that could be done for us." Regarding black students and SAT scores, Thomas Sowell writes: "Most of the black students admitted to Cornell had SAT scores above the national average—but far below the averages of other Cornell students. They were in trouble because they were at Cornell—and, later, Cornell would also be in trouble because they were there . . . [S]ome academically able black applicants for admission were known to have been turned away, while those who fit the stereotype being sought were admitted with lower qualifications." See Thomas Sowell, "The Day Cornell Died," *Weekly Standard,* May 3, 1999, p. 31. Also see Berns, "Assault on the Universities."
59. Michael T. Kaufman, "Stokely Carmichael, Rights Leader Who Coined 'Black Power,' Dies at 57," *New York Times,* Nov. 16, 1998.

60. D'Souza, *End of Racism,* pp. 398–99. See also W. E. B. DuBois, "Back to Africa," *Century,* Feb. 1923, cited by John Henrik Clarke, ed., *Marcus Garvey and the Vision of Africa* (New York: Vintage, 1974), pp. 101, 117, 134; John Hope Franklin and August Meier, eds., *Black Leaders of the Twentieth Century* (Urbana: University of Illinois Press, 1982), pp. 132–34. Today, much like in the 1960s, Black Nationalist groups, journals, and "intellectuals" frequently find common cause with white supremacists. The Third World Press, run by the Black Nationalist Haki Madhubuti, typically bars white authors but makes allowances for such anti-Semitic scribblers as Michael Bradley, whose theories about the Jews are perfectly consistent with *The Protocols of the Elders of Zion.*

61. For the Forman quotation, see Nina J. Easton, "America the Enemy," *Los Angeles Times Magazine,* June 18, 1995, p. 8. Chavis was released after the governor of North Carolina caved to international pressure—including from the Soviet Union—alleging an unfair trial.

62. Paxton, *Anatomy of Fascism,* p. 7.

63. Morris L. Fried, "The Struggle Is the Message: The Organization and Ideology of the Anti-war Movement, by Irving Louis Horowitz," *Contemporary Sociology* 1, no. 2 (March 1972), pp. 122–23, citing Irving Louis Horowitz, *The Struggle Is the Message: The Organization and Ideology of the Anti-war Movement* (Berkeley, Calif.: Glendessary, 1970), pp. 122–23.

64. Seymour Martin Lipset, *Rebellion in the University* (Boston: Little, Brown, 1972), p. 115; Robert Soucy, "French Fascist Intellectuals in the 1930s: An Old New Left?" *French Historical Studies* (Spring 1974).

6. FROM KENNEDY'S MYTH TO JOHNSON'S DREAM:
LIBERAL FASCISM AND THE CULT OF THE STATE

1. Max Holland, "After Thirty Years: Making Sense of the Assassination," *Reviews in American History* 22, no. 2 (June 1994), pp. 192–93; "Chapter II—or Finis?" *Time,* Dec. 30, 1966; Philip Chalk, "Wrong from the Beginning," *Weekly Standard,* March 14, 2005; Mimi Swartz, "Them's Fightin' Words," *Texas Monthly,* July 2004.

2. "Pope Paul Warns That Hate and Evil Imperil Civil Order," *New York Times,* Nov. 25, 1963, p. 1; Wayne King, "Dallas Still Wondering: Did It Help Pull the Trigger?" *New York Times,* Nov. 22, 1983, p. A24. The "city of hate" designation remains one of the more bizarre episodes in American mass psychology. It seemed to be pegged largely to the rough treatment LBJ got in his home state from some protesting Republican women during the 1960 election, as well as an anti-UN protest in 1963 that resulted in Adlai Stevenson—then the U.S. ambassador to the UN—getting bonked on the head with an anti-UN placard.

3. Warren Commission, *The Warren Commission Report: Report of the President's Commission on the Assassination of President John F. Kennedy* (New York: St. Martin's, 1992), p. 416.

4. On *MacBird,* see Arthur Herman, *Joseph McCarthy: Reexamining the Life and Legacy of America's Most Hated Senator* (New York: Free Press,

2000), p. 13. Kennedy requested $52.3 billion in military spending plus an additional $1.2 billion for the space program—which he indisputably saw as a defense-related investment—out of a total budget of $106.8 billion. Derek Leebaert, *The Fifty-Year Wound: How America's Cold War Victory Shapes Our World* (Boston: Little, Brown, 2003), p. 267; Aaron L. Friedberg, *In the Shadow of the Garrison State: America's Anti-statism and Its Cold War Grand Strategy* (Princeton, N.J.: Princeton University Press, 2000), p. 140.

5. Steven F. Hayward, *The Age of Reagan: The Fall of the Old Liberal Order, 1964–1980* (Roseville, Calif.: Prima, 2001), p. 23; Todd Gitlin, *The Sixties: Years of Hope, Days of Rage* (New York: Bantam, 1993), pp. 136–37. Kennedy's reaction to the Freedom Rides in the spring of 1961 was hardly unequivocal. He did the right thing by offering federal re-sources to stem the violence, but he was privately furious with the Congress of Racial Equality for creating strife while he was trying to fo-cus on the Vienna summit with Khrushchev. "Can't you get your friends off those goddamned buses?" he implored Harris Wofford, his civil rights adviser. "Stop them," he pleaded. He and Bobby also fought hard to pre-vent Martin Luther King's March on Washington. When they failed, they worked closely with civil rights leaders to spin the message of the famous rally in the administration's favor. What became the 1964 Civil Rights Act was hopelessly bogged down in Congress when Kennedy was murdered, and it's unlikely that he would have pressed for its passage in his reelec-tion campaign.

6. The Camelot appellation hangs on some fairly fragile hooks. Jackie Kennedy recalled that her husband liked the soundtrack to the popular Broadway musical *Camelot,* which had opened a month after Kennedy's election. Theodore White, a Kennedy chronicler, convinced *Life* magazine to run with the idea. The musical's tagline, "for that brief shining mo-ment," became an overnight cliché to describe Kennedy's "thousand days," itself a clever bit of wordplay designed to make the Kennedy moment seem all the more precious and fleeting. See also James Reston, "What Was Killed Was Not Only the President but the Promise," *New York Times Magazine,* Nov. 15, 1964, p. SM24.

7. It's widely believed that the character of Superman was inspired by Nietzsche's doctrine of the *Übermensch,* which can be translated as both "overman" and "superman." But it's worth noting that the actual character was an inversion of the Nietzschean idea—and the Nazified concept. Nietzsche's superman owes no loyalty to conventional morality and le-galisms because he is above such petty concerns. The comic Superman bound himself to such customs even more than normal men. There is a certain nationalistic conceit to the character in that he was born in the American heartland and imbibed all that was good of Americanism. But this manifested itself in benign or beneficial patriotism more than anything else.

At the end of the issue on physical fitness, Superman and Supergirl lead a parade of Americans waving flags and holding signs supporting the president. One marcher carries a placard that reads, "OBSERVE THE PRESIDENT'S PHYSICAL FITNESS PROGRAM AND THE 'WEAK-

LING' AMERICANS WILL BE THE STRONG AMERICANS!" The comic was supposed to appear in early 1964, but the assassination post-poned it. LBJ eventually asked DC Comics to run the issue as a tribute. Kennedy remained a recurring character after his death. In one comic Jimmy Olsen travels to the future and identifies alien villains because they are the only people who didn't observe a moment of silence for the slain president. See http://www.dialbforblog.com/archives/166/ for images from the comic and commentary (accessed July 10, 2007).

8. The election would decide, Mailer wrote, "if the desire of America was for drama or stability, for adventure or monotony." Mailer hoped Americans would choose Kennedy "for his mystery, for his promise that the country would grow or disintegrate by the unwilling charge he gave to the inten-sity of the myth." Norman Mailer, "Superman Comes to the Supermarket," *Esquire,* Nov. 1960, in *Pols: Great Writers on American Politicians from Bryan to Reagan,* ed. Jack Beatty (New York: Public Affairs, 2004), p. 292.

9. Herbert S. Parmet, "The Kennedy Myth and American Politics," *History Teacher* 24, no. 1 (Nov. 1990), p. 32, citing "What JFK Meant to Us," *Newsweek,* Nov. 28, 1983, p. 72; Jonah Goldberg, " 'Isolationism!' They Cried," *National Review,* April 10, 2006, p. 35; Alan McConnaughey, "America First: Attitude Emerged Before World War II," *Washington Times,* Dec. 12, 1991, p. A3.

10. Louis Menand, "Ask Not, Tell Not: Anatomy of an Inaugural" *New Yorker,* Nov. 8, 2004, p. 110.

11. John W. Jeffries, "The 'Quest for National Purpose' of 1960," *American Quarterly* 30, no. 4 (Autumn 1978), p. 451, citing John K. Jessup et al., *The National Purpose* (New York: Holt, Rinehart and Winston, 1960), p. v. *Newsweek* had noted the previous year that "thoughtful men" were worried America had lost its "boldness and imagination, the sense of mis-sion and dedication." Chief among these was Walter Lippmann, an elder statesman of liberalism who had led the march to war in 1917 in the hope that it would bring about a "transvaluation of values." Once again, Lippmann hoped Americans would embrace a collective mission, this time in the face of the Soviet challenge. Jeffries, " 'Quest for National Purpose' of 1960," p. 454, citing "An Unwitting Paul Revere?" *Newsweek,* Sept. 28, 1959, pp. 33–34.

12. Adlai E. Stevenson, "National Purpose: Stevenson's View," *New York Times,* May 26, 1960, p. 30; Charles F. Darlington, "Not the Goal, Only the Means," *New York Times,* July 3, 1960, p. 25; Charles F. Darlington, letter, *New York Times,* May 27, 1960, p. 30.

13. Jeffries, " 'Quest for National Purpose' of 1960," p. 462, citing William Attwood, "How America Feels as We Enter the Soaring Sixties," *Look,* Jan. 5, 1960, pp. 11–15; Leebaert, *Fifty-Year Wound,* p. 261.

14. William F. Buckley, "Mr. Goodwin's Great Society," *National Review* (September 7, 1965), p. 760.

15. Garry Wills, *The Kennedy Imprisonment: A Meditation on Power* (Boston: Houghton Mifflin, 2002), pp. 170, 171; David Schoenbaum, *Hitler's Social Revolution: Class and Status in Nazi Germany, 1933–1939* (New York: Norton, 1980), p. xv n. 4.

16. Leebaert, *Fifty-Year Wound,* p. 263; Wills, *Kennedy Imprisonment,* p. 171.
17. H. W. Brands, *The Strange Death of American Liberalism* (New Haven, Conn.: Yale University Press, 2001), pp. 87–88.
18. Christopher Lasch, *Haven in a Heartless World: The Family Besieged* (New York: Norton, 1995), p. 218 n. 55, citing David Eakins, "Policy-Planning for the Establishment," in *A New History of Leviathan,* ed. Ronald Radosh and Murray Rothbard (New York: Dutton, 1972), p. 198.
19. James Reston, "A Portion of Guilt for All," *New York Times,* Nov. 25, 1963; Tom Wicker, "Johnson Bids Congress Enact Civil Rights Bill with Speed; Asks End of Hate and Violence," *New York Times,* Nov. 28, 1963.
20. "When JFK's Ideals Are Realized, Expiation of Death Begins, Bishop Says," *Washington Post,* Dec. 9, 1963, p. B7.
21. Robert N. Bellah, "Civil Religion in America," *Daedalus* 96, no. 1 (Winter 1967), pp. 1–21; C. L. Sulzberger, "A New Frontier and an Old Dream," *New York Times,* Jan. 23, 1961, p. 22.
22. Bill Kauffman, "The Bellamy Boys Pledge Allegiance," *American Enterprise* 13, no. 7 (Oct./Nov. 2002), p. 50.
23. Edward Bellamy, *Looking Backward, 2000–1887* (New York: New American Library, 1960), p. 111.
24. Nicholas P. Gilman, " 'Nationalism' in the United States," *Quarterly Journal of Economics* 4, no. 1 (Oct. 1889), pp. 50–76; Bellamy, *Looking Backward,* p. 143.
25. The story of the Pledge of Allegiance and its National Socialist roots is a fascinating one. Rex Curry, a passionate libertarian, has made the issue his white whale. See rexcurry.net/pledgesalute.html.
26. "Hail New Party in Fervent Song," *New York Times,* Aug. 6, 1912, p. 1.
27. Senator Albert Beveridge, *Congressional Record,* Senate, Jan. 9, 1900, pp. 704–11, quoted in *The Philippines Reader: A History of Colonialism, Neocolonialism, Dictatorship, and Resistance,* ed. Daniel B. Schirmer and Stephen Rosskamm Shalom (Boston: South End Press, 1987), p. 23.
28. Walter Rauschenbusch, *Christianizing the Social Order* (New York: Macmillan, 1912), p. 330. The Social Gospel journal *Dawn,* founded in 1890, was intended "to show that the aim of socialism is embraced in the aims of Christianity and to awaken members of Christian churches to the fact that the teachings of Jesus Christ lead directly to some specific form or forms of socialism." William G. McLoughlin, *Revivals, Awakenings, and Reform: An Essay on Religion and Social Change in America, 1607–1977* (Chicago: University of Chicago Press, 1980), p. 175.
29. Charles Howard Hopkins, *The Rise of the Social Gospel in American Protestantism, 1865–1915* (New Haven, Conn.: Yale University Press, 1940), p. 253.
30. James Bovard, *Freedom in Chains: The Rise of the State and the Demise of the Citizen* (New York: St. Martin's, 2000), p. 4, quoting G. W. F. Hegel, *The Philosophy of History* (New York: Collier & Son, 1902), p. 87.
31. Murray N. Rothbard, "Richard T. Ely: Paladin of the Welfare-Warfare State," *Independent Review* 6, no. 4 (Spring 2002), p. 586, citing Sidney Fine, *Laissez Faire and the General-Welfare State: A Study of Conflict in American Thought, 1865–1901* (Ann Arbor: University of Michigan Press, 1956), pp. 180–81; John R. Commons, "The Christian Minister and

Sociology" (1892), in *John R. Commons: Selected Essays,* ed. Malcolm Rutherford and Warren J. Samuels (New York: Routledge, 1996), p. 20; Eldon J. Eisenach, *The Lost Promise of Progressivism* (Lawrence: University Press of Kansas, 1994), p. 60 n. 21.

32. John Lukacs, *Remembered Past: John Lukacs on History, Historians, and Historical Knowledge* (Wilmington, Del.: ISI Books, 2005), p. 305.

33. Woodrow Wilson, "Force to the Utmost," speech at the opening of the Third Liberty Loan Campaign, delivered in the Fifth Regiment Armory, Baltimore, April 6, 1918, in *The Messages and Papers of Woodrow Wilson,* ed. Albert Shaw (New York: Review of Reviews Corporation, 1924), vol. 1, p. 484; Woodrow Wilson, Address to Confederate Veterans, Washington, D.C., June 5, 1917, in ibid., p. 410; Ronald Schaffer, *America in the Great War: The Rise of the War Welfare State* (New York: Oxford University Press, 1991), p. 10.

34. R. J. B. Bosworth, *Mussolini's Italy: Life Under the Fascist Dictatorship, 1915–1945* (New York: Penguin, 2006), p. 97.

35. An ad in a newspaper at the time gives a sense of how far the government intruded.

> Here is your schedule for eating for the next 4 weeks which must be rigidly observed, says F. C. Findley, County Food Commissioner:
>
> *Monday:* Wheatless every meal.
> *Tuesday:* Meatless every meal.
> *Wednesday:* Wheatless every meal.
> *Thursday:* Breakfast, meatless; supper wheatless.
> *Friday:* Breakfast, meatless; supper wheatless.
> *Saturday:* Porkless every meal, meatless breakfast.
> *Sunday:* Meatless breakfast; wheatless supper.
>
> Sugar must be used very sparingly at all times. Do not put sugar in your coffee unless this is a long habit, and in that case use only one spoonful. (Robert Higgs, *Crisis and Leviathan: Critical Episodes in the Growth of American Government* [New York: Oxford University Press, 1987], p. 137)

36. John Dewey, *Liberalism and Social Action* (Amherst, N.Y.: Prometheus Books, 2000), p. 30. See also Alex Viskovatoff, "A Deweyan Economic Methodology," in *Dewey, Pragmatism, and Economic Methodology,* ed. Elias L. Khalil (New York: Routledge, 2004), p. 293; Virgil Michel, "Liberalism Yesterday and Tomorrow," *Ethics* 49, no. 4 (July 1939), pp. 417–34; Jonah Goldberg, "The New-Time Religion: Liberalism and Its Problems," *National Review,* May 23, 2005.

37. Lewis S. Feuer, "American Travelers to the Soviet Union, 1917–32: The Formation of a Component of New Deal Ideology," *American Quarterly* 14, no. 2, pt. 1 (Summer 1962), pp. 122, 126.

38. William E. Leuchtenburg, *The FDR Years: On Roosevelt and His Legacy* (New York: Columbia University Press, 1995), p. 284. A. J. P. Taylor made a similar observation about people's interaction with the federal government:

Until August 1914 a sensible, law-abiding Englishman could pass
through life and hardly notice the existence of the state beyond the
post office and the policeman . . . He could travel abroad or leave his
country forever without a passport or any sort of official permission.
He could exchange his money without restriction or limit. He could
buy goods from any country in the world on the same terms as he
bought goods at home. For that matter a foreigner could spend his
life in the country without permit and without informing the
police . . . All this was changed by the impact of the Great War . . .
The state established a hold over its citizens which though relaxed in
peace time, was never to be removed and which the Second World
War was again to increase. The history of the English people and the
English State merged for the first time. (A. J. P. Taylor, *English
History, 1914–1945* [New York: Oxford University Press, 1965],
p. 1)

39. Quoted in Scott Yenor, "A New Deal for Roosevelt," *Claremont Review of
Books* (Winter 2006).

40. Thurman Arnold, *The Folklore of Capitalism* (New Haven, Conn.: Yale
University Press, 1937), p. 389.

41. Leuchtenburg, *FDR Years,* p. 20.

42. Walter Winchell, "Americans We Can Do Without," *Liberty,* Aug. 1,
1942, p. 10.

43. See Sam Tanenhaus, *Whittaker Chambers: A Biography* (New York:
Random House, 1997), pp. 179, 561.

44. Herbert McClosky, "Conservatism and Personality," *American Political
Science Review* 52, no. 1 (March 1958), p. 35; Lionel Trilling, *The Liberal
Imagination: Essays on Literature and Society* (New York: Viking, 1950),
p. ix.

45. David S. Brown, *Richard Hofstadter: An Intellectual Biography* (Chicago:
University of Chicago Press, 2006), p. 90; Casey Blake and Christopher
Phelps, "History as Social Criticism: Conversations with Christopher
Lasch," *Journal of American History* 80, no. 4 (March 1994),
pp. 1310–32.

46. Bertolt Brecht, "The Solution," in *Poems, 1913–1956,* ed. John Willett
and Ralph Manheim (New York: Routledge, 1987), p. 440.

47. Robert Dallek, *Lyndon B. Johnson: Portrait of a President* (New York:
Oxford University Press, 2004), p. 29; Jordan A. Schwarz, *The New
Dealers: Power Politics in the Age of Roosevelt* (New York: Vintage,
1994), p. 276.

48. Schwarz, *The New Dealers,* p. 267.

49. Lyndon B. Johnson, "Commencement Address—the Great Society,"
University of Michigan, Ann Arbor, May 22, 1964, in *Public Papers of the
Presidents of the United States, Lyndon B. Johnson, 1963–64*
(Washington, D.C.: Government Printing Office, 1965), pp. 704–7;
America in the Sixties—Right, Left, and Center: A Documentary History,
ed. Peter B. Levy (Westport, Conn.: Praeger, 1998), pp. 106–7. See also
Hayward, *Age of Reagan,* p. 21.

50. Johnson, "Commencement Address—the Great Society," p. 108.

51. Charles Mohr, "Johnson, in South, Decries 'Radical' Goldwater Ideas,"

New York Times, Oct. 27, 1964; Cabell Phillips, "Johnson Decries Terrorist Foes of Negro Rights," *New York Times,* July 19, 1964; "Transcript of President's News Conference on Foreign and Domestic Affairs," *New York Times,* July 19, 1964.

52. Charles Mohr, "Johnson Exhorts Voters to Reject Demagogic Pleas," *New York Times,* Sept. 23, 1964; advertisement, *New York Times,* Sept. 12, 1964, p. 26; Ralph D. Barney and John C. Merrill, eds., *Ethics and the Press: Readings in Mass Media Morality* (New York: Hastings House, 1975), p. 229. See also Jack Shafer, "The Varieties of Media Bias, Part 1," *Slate,* Feb. 5, 2003, www.slate.com/id/2078200/ (accessed March 19, 2007); Jonah Goldberg, "Hold the Self-Congratulation," *National Review,* Oct. 24, 2005; Jeffrey Lord, "From God to Godless: The Real Liberal Terror," *American Spectator,* June 12, 2006, www.spectator.org/dsp _article.asp?art_id=9943 (accessed Jan. 16, 2007).

53. However, in this work Dewey called the existing society the Great Society. He hoped that the state could transform the Great Society into what he called the "Great Community." But Dewey's Great Community sounds much closer to what Johnson had in mind with his Great Society.

54. Robert R. Semple Jr., "Nation Seeks Way to Better Society," *New York Times,* July 25, 1965.

55. Dewey, *Liberalism and Social Action,* pp. 15, 76. The lineage of the War on Poverty was similarly transparent. Just as the New Deal was sold in the language of war, the War on Poverty was another chapter in the Progressive effort to invoke the "moral equivalent of war." Indeed, most of the Great Society programs were merely greatly expanded versions of New Deal programs, such as Aid to Families with Dependent Children, which started as an insurance plan for the widows of coal miners. Those programs, in turn, were born out of a desire to re-create the "successes" of Wilson's war socialism. See also the chapter on John Dewey by Robert Horwitz, in *The History of Political Philosophy,* ed. Leo Strauss and Joseph Cropsey (Chicago, Ill.: University of Chicago Press, 1987).

56. McLoughlin, *Revivals, Awakenings, and Reform,* p. 207.

57. John B. Judis, "The Spirit of '68: What Really Caused the Sixties," *New Republic,* Aug. 31, 1998.

58. *The Feminine Mystique* is an excellent example of how powerfully the Holocaust had distorted the liberal mind. A longtime communist journalist and activist, Friedan cast herself in *The Feminine Mystique* as a conventional housewife completely ignorant of politics. In a disturbing extended metaphor she argued that housewives were victims of Nazi-like oppression. The "women who 'adjust' as housewives, who grow up wanting to be 'just a housewife,' are in as much danger as the millions who walked to their own death in the concentration camps," she wrote. The home, Friedan wrote in direct echoes of Horkheimer, was a "comfortable concentration camp." The analogy is sufficiently grotesque, intellectually and morally, to merit further dissection.

59. This in turn led to another front of the great awakening: a fight to religious orthodoxy among Christian conservatives and others who rejected the politicization of their faiths.

60. For many, drugs became the new sacrament. After the New Left im-

ploded, Tom Hayden went into hiding "among the psychedelic daredevils of the counterculture," believing that drugs were a way of "deepening self awareness" and helping him to find spiritual meaning and authenticity. Even the most ardent exponents of the drug culture grounded their defense of drugs in explicitly religious terms. Self-proclaimed gurus such as Timothy Leary, a Harvard professor who became a "spiritual guide" with tabs of acid as his Communion wafers, spoke incessantly about how drugs lead to a "religious experience." William Braden, a reporter for the *Chicago Sun-Times,* wrote *The Private Sea: LSD and the Search for God,* one of countless books and tracts that tried to update the new counterculture with the "New Theology," as it was called.

61. William Braden, "The Seduction of the Spirit," *Washington Post,* Sept. 9, 1973, pp. BW1, BW13.

62. The Reverend Martin Marty, an academic theologian and editor at the *Christian Century,* proclaimed in a series of speeches in 1965 that the radicals were "moral agents" and described writers such as James Baldwin as "charismatic prophets." Marty made these remarks at a speech at Columbia University. In response, a student radical challenged him: "What you say is meaningless because the Great Society is basically immoral and rotten." Marty responded that such comments were typical of those who chose to be "morally pure" instead of politically relevant. In other words, moral purity lay at the radicals' end of the political spectrum. "Radicals Called 'Moral Agents,' " *New York Times,* July 26, 1965, p. 19.

63. The famous passage is from FDR's 1935 State of the Union address: "The lessons of history, confirmed by the evidence immediately before me, show conclusively that continued dependence upon relief induces a spiritual disintegration fundamentally destructive to the national fiber. To dole out relief in this way is to administer a narcotic, a subtle destroyer of the human spirit. It is inimical to the dictates of a sound policy. It is in violation of the traditions of America. Work must be found for able-bodied but destitute workers."

64. Hayward, *Age of Reagan,* p. 20, citing "T.R.B. from Washington," *New Republic,* March 14, 1964, p. 3, and citing Gareth Davies, *From Opportunity to Entitlement: The Transformation and Decline of Great Society Liberalism* (Lawrence: University Press of Kansas, 1996), p. 18.

65. Mickey Kaus, *The End of Equality* (New York: Basic Books, 1995).

66. Hayward, *Age of Reagan,* p. 124. A demographic surge in male baby boomers is partly to blame for the rise in crime, but the cultural, legal, and political climate was undoubtedly the chief culprit. In the 1960s policy intellectuals believed that "the system" itself caused crime, and virtually all of the legal reforms of the day pushed in the direction of giving criminals more rights and making the job of police more difficult. Culturally, a wide array of activists and intellectuals had proclaimed that crime—especially black crime—was morally warranted political "rebellion."

67. Ibid., p. 26, citing Richard Epstein, *Forbidden Grounds: The Case Against Employment Discrimination Laws* (Cambridge, Mass.: Harvard University Press, 1992), pp. 186–88; Penn Kemble and Josh Muravchik, "The New Politics & the Democrats" *Commentary,* Dec. 1972, pp. 78–84.

McGovern later joked that his rules opened the doors to the Democratic Party and "twenty million people walked out."

68. Hayward, *Age of Reagan,* pp. 90–92.

69. "Text of the Moynihan Memorandum on the Status of Negroes," *New York Times,* March 1, 1970. See also Peter Kihss, " 'Benign Neglect' on Race Is Proposed by Moynihan," *New York Times,* March 1, 1970, p. 1.

70. Parmet, "Kennedy Myth and American Politics," p. 35, citing Randall Rothenberg, "The Neoliberal Club," *Esquire,* Feb. 1982, p. 42.

71. Douglas Brinkley, "Farewell to a Friend," *New York Times,* July 19, 1999, p. A17; *Reliable Sources,* CNN, July 24, 1999. See also Tim Cuprisin, "Few Shows, Cost Blurring Appeal of Digital TV," *Milwaukee Journal Sentinel,* July 27, 1999, p. 8.

7. LIBERAL RACISM: THE EUGENIC GHOST IN THE FASCIST MACHINE

1. Michele Parente, "Rangel Ties GOP Agenda to Hitler," *Newsday,* Feb. 19, 1995, p. A38; Bond is quoted in "Washington Whispers," *U.S. News & World Report,* July 28, 2003, p. 12; Marc Morano, "Harry Belafonte Calls Black Republicans 'Tyrants,' " Cybercast News Service, Aug. 8, 2005; Steve Dunleavy, "There's Nothing Fascist About a Final Verdict," *New York Post,* Dec. 13, 2000, p. 6.

2. And to the extent these various dark chapters of liberalism are ever mentioned, they are mentioned by hard-left critics of America itself. The net effect is that whenever conservatives commit an alleged evil, it is the result of conservatism. Whenever liberals commit an alleged evil, it is the result either of liberals' insufficiently severe liberalism or of America itself. In short, liberalism is never to blame and conservatives always are.

3. Adolph Reed Jr., "Intellectual Brownshirts," *Progressive,* Dec. 1994.

4. Sherwin B. Nuland, "The Death of Hippocrates," *New Republic,* Sept. 13, 2004, p. 31.

5. Alan Wolfe, "Hidden Injuries," *New Republic,* July 7, 1997.

6. A former adviser to Teddy Roosevelt, and an extremist even by the standards of many eugenicists, Grant wrote, "Mistaken regard for what are believed to be divine laws and a sentimental belief in the sanctity of human life tend to prevent both the elimination of defective infants and the sterilization of such adults as are themselves of no value to the community. The laws of nature require the obliteration of the unfit and human life is valuable only when it is of use to the community or race." Quoted in Richard Weikart, *From Darwin to Hitler: Evolutionary Ethics, Eugenics, and Racism in Germany* (New York: Palgrave Macmillan, 2004), p. 10. See also Robert Jay Lifton, *The Nazi Doctors: Medical Killing and the Psychology of Genocide* (New York: Basic Books, 2000), p. 24; Edwin Black, *War Against the Weak: Eugenics and America's Campaign to Create a Master Race* (New York: Four Walls Eight Windows, 2003), p. 291.

7. Black, *War Against the Weak,* p. xviii.

8. Charles Murray, "Deeper into the Brain," *National Review,* Jan. 24, 2000, p. 49; Thomas C. Leonard, " 'More Merciful and Not Less Effective': Eugenics and American Economics in the Progressive Era," *History of Political Economy* 35, no. 4 (Winter 2003), p. 707.

9. Diane Paul, "Eugenics and the Left," *Journal of the History of Ideas* 45, no. 4 (Oct.–Dec. 1984), p. 586 n. 56, citing H. G. Wells, *Sociological Papers* (London, 1905), p. 60; William J. Hyde, "The Socialism of H. G. Wells in the Early Twentieth Century," *Journal of the History of Ideas* 17, no. 2 (April 1956), p. 220; H. G. Wells, *The New Machiavelli* (New York: Duffield, 1910), p. 379. In *A Modern Utopia* (1905), Wells wrote:

> The State is justified in saying, before you may add children to the community for the community to educate and in part to support, you must be above a certain minimum of personal efficiency . . . and a certain minimum of physical development, and free of any transmissible disease . . . Failing these simple qualifications, if you and some person conspire [note the use of the criminal "conspire"] and add to the population of the State, we will, for the sake of humanity, take over the innocent victim of your passions, but we shall insist that you are under a debt to the State of a peculiarly urgent sort, and one you will certainly pay, even if it is necessary to use restraint to get the payment out of you. (H. G. Wells, *A Modern Utopia* [London, 1905], pp. 183–84, quoted in Michael Freeden, "Eugenics and Progressive Thought: A Study in Ideological Affinity," *Historical Journal* 22, no. 3 [Sept. 1979], p. 656)

10. George Bernard Shaw, *Man and Superman: A Comedy and a Philosophy* (Cambridge, Mass.: University Press, 1903), p. 43; Paul, "Eugenics and the Left," p. 568, citing George Bernard Shaw, *Sociological Papers* (London, 1905), pp. 74–75; Shaw, *Man and Superman,* pp. 45, 43; George Bernard Shaw, preface to *Major Barbara* (New York: Penguin, 1917), p. 47.

11. Freeden, "Eugenics and Progressive Thought," p. 671; Chris Nottingham, *The Pursuit of Serenity: Havelock Ellis and the New Politics* (Amsterdam: Amsterdam University Press, 1999), pp. 185, 213; Paul, "Eugenics and the Left," p. 567, citing J. B. S. Haldane, "Darwin on Slavery," *Daily Worker* (London), Nov. 14, 1949.

12. Paul, "Eugenics and the Left," pp. 568, 573.

13. In its first year of publication, a full quarter of the magazine's contributions came from the British Isles. Daniel T. Rodgers, *Atlantic Crossings: Social Politics in a Progressive Age* (Cambridge, Mass.: Harvard University Press, 1998), p. 276.

14. For more of such encomiums, see Yosal Rogat, "Mr. Justice Holmes: A Dissenting Opinion," *Stanford Law Review* 15, no. 1 (Dec. 1962), pp. 3–44.

15. William E. Leuchtenburg, *The Supreme Court Reborn: The Constitutional Revolution in the Age of Roosevelt* (New York: Oxford University Press, 1995), p. 19. Emphasis mine.

16. Robert J. Cynkar, "Buck v. Bell: 'Felt Necessities' v. Fundamental Values?" *Columbia Law Review* 81, no. 7 (Nov. 1981), p. 1451.

17. In 1911 Wilson asked Edwin Katzen-Ellenbogen, the state's leading eugenicist and an expert on epilepsy, to draft the law. A Polish Catholic of Jewish extraction and American citizenship, Katzen-Ellenbogen has a story too lengthy to recount here. But it is worth noting that this profoundly evil man later found himself a doctor to the SS in France and ultimately a "prisoner" who ended up working with the butchers of Buchenwald. He personally murdered thousands—often in the name of eugenic theories he developed in American psychiatric hospitals—and tortured countless more. The "science" he learned in America was quite warmly received by the SS. In a grotesque miscarriage of justice, he escaped execution at Nuremberg. See Edwin Black, "Buchenwald's American-Trained Nazi," *Jerusalem Report,* Sept. 22, 2003.

18. Herbert Croly, *The Promise of American Life* (New York: Macmillan, 1911), pp. 345, 191.

19. Charles Richard Van Hise, *The Conservation of Natural Resources in the United States* (New York: Macmillan, 1910), p. 378.

20. Scott Gordon, *The History and Philosophy of Social Science* (New York: Routledge, 1993), p. 521; Daniel Kevles, *In the Name of Eugenics: Genetics and the Uses of Human Heredity* (Cambridge, Mass.: Harvard University Press, 1986), p. 68.

21. Justice Butler did not offer a written opinion, but there are two (compatible) possible explanations for his dissent. One, Butler *was* a social Darwinist in the sense that he didn't believe the state should "interfere, interfere, interfere!" as Sidney Webb had put it. Two, he was the Court's only Catholic at the time, and the Church was resolute in its teachings against anything that smacked of eugenics.

22. Edward Pearce, writing in the British *Guardian,* calls Spencer "a downright evil man . . . whose passion for eugenics and elimination made him the daydreamer of things to come." Edward Pearce, "Nietzsche Is Radically Unsound," *Guardian,* July 8, 1992, p. 20. Edwin Black, author of *War Against the Weak,* claims that eugenics was born of Spencer's ideas and that Spencer "completely denounced charity" in *Social Statics.* Black clearly has not read the book; neither of these things is true. See Roderick T. Long, "Herbert Spencer: The Defamation Continues," Aug. 28, 2003, www.lewrockwell.com/orig3/long3.html (accessed March 13, 2007).

23. Part of the problem is that Hofstadter simply got much of the history wrong (a point even the left-wing historian Eric Foner is forced to concede in his introduction to the 1992 edition of *Social Darwinism in American Thought*). Fifteen years after the publication of Hofstadter's book, Irvin Wyllie of the University of Wisconsin demonstrated that almost none of the Gilded Age industrialists expressed themselves in Darwinian terms or took much notice of the Darwin fad among the intellectual classes. Even the phrase "social Darwinism" was almost unknown during the so-called age of the robber barons. In one egregious example, Hofstadter erroneously attributed a statement about the "survival of the fittest" to John D. Rockefeller. Rather, it was Rockefeller's college-educated son, John D.

Rockefeller Jr., who offered the throwaway line in 1902 in an address at Brown University. Irvin G. Wyllie, "Social Darwinism and the Businessman," *Proceedings of the American Philosophical Society,* Oct. 15, 1959, p. 632, citing Raymond B. Fosdick, *John D. Rockefeller, Jr.: A Portrait* (New York: Harper, 1956), pp. 130–31.

24. The progressive Jane Addams worked closely with the Chicago judge Harry Olson, the founder of the American Eugenics Society and onetime president of the Eugenics Research Association. As a pioneer of juvenile courts in America, Olson was dedicated to weeding out "the cheaper races." He advocated sterilization when necessary, but his preferred remedy was to set up a psychiatric gulag where the unfit could live out their lives segregated from the better human stocks. In 1916 the *New Republic* demonstrated the spirit of compromise among progressives in an editorial (almost surely written by Croly):

> Laissez-faire as a policy of population leads straight to perdition . . . *Imbecility breeds imbecility as certainly as white hens breed white chickens; and under laissez-faire imbecility is given full chance to breed, and does so in fact at a rate far superior to that of able stocks* . . . We may suggest that a socialized policy of population cannot be built upon a laissez-faire economic policy. So long as the state neglects its good blood, it will let its bad blood alone . . . *When the state assumes the duty of giving a fair opportunity for development to every child, it will find unanimous support for a policy of extinction of stocks incapable of profiting from their privileges.* (*New Republic,* March 18, 1916; emphasis mine)

Translation: Cast the social safety net as far and as wide as possible, and all good progressives will agree that whoever's left out of the net will be a candidate for "extinction."

25. Daylanne English, "W. E. B. DuBois's Family Crisis," *American Literature* 72, no. 2 (June 2000), pp. 297, 293; Charles Valenza, "Was Margaret Sanger a Racist?" *Family Planning Perspectives* 17, no. 1 (Jan.–Feb. 1985), pp. 44–46.
26. Jesse Walker, "Hooded Progressivism," *Reason,* Dec. 2, 2005.
27. Rexford Tugwell, FDR's Brain Truster, claims, to the contrary, that it was *his* mentor Simon Patten who deserves the honor of coining the phrase. Leonard, " 'More Merciful and Not Less Effective,' " pp. 693–94, 696 n. 13.
28. David M. Kennedy, "Can We Still Afford to Be a Nation of Immigrants?" *Atlantic Monthly,* Nov. 1996, pp. 52–68.
29. Edward Alsworth Ross, *Social Control: A Survey of the Foundations of Order* (New York: Macmillan, 1901), p. 418.
30. Sidney Webb, "The Economic Theory of a Legal Minimum Wage," *Journal of Political Economy* 20, no. 10 (Dec. 1912), p. 992, quoted in Leonard, " 'More Merciful and Not Less Effective,' " p. 703.
31. Edward Alsworth Ross, *Seventy Years of It* (New York: Appleton-Century, 1936), p. 70, quoted in Leonard, " 'More Merciful and Not Less Effective,' " p. 699; Royal Meeker, "Review of *Cours d'économie politique,*" *Political Science Quarterly* 25, no. 3 (1910), p. 544, quoted in Leonard, " 'More Merciful and Not Less Effective,' " p. 703.

32. Commons is rightly a member of the "Labor Hall of Fame." For a glowing summary of his accomplishments, see Jack Barbash, "John R. Commons: Pioneer of Labor Economics," *Monthly Labor Review* 112, no. 5 (May 1989), pp. 44–49, available at www.bls.gov/opub/mlr/1989/05/art4full.pdf (accessed March 16, 2007). The historian Joseph Dorfman writes, "More than any other economist [Commons] was responsible for the conversion into public policy of reform proposals designed to alleviate defects in the industrial system." Joseph Dorfman, *The Economic Mind in America, 1918–1933* (New York: Viking, 1959), vols. 4–5, p. 377, quoted in Barbash, "John R. Commons," p. 44.

A onetime president of the American Economic Association, Commons complained in his influential *Races and Immigrants in America* that "competition has no respect for superior races," which was why "the race with lowest necessities displaces others." Hence, "the Jewish sweat-shop is the tragic penalty paid by that ambitious race." John R. Commons, *Races and Immigrants in America* (New York: Macmillan, 1907), pp. 151, 148.

33. "The negro could not possibly have found a place in American industry had he come as a free man . . . [I]f such races are to adopt that industrious life which is a second nature to races of the temperate zones, it is only through some form of compulsion." Leonard, " 'More Merciful and Not Less Effective,' " p. 701.

34. Christine Rosen, *Preaching Eugenics: Religious Leaders and the American Eugenics Movement* (New York: Oxford University Press, 2004), p. 47. The Swedes—long the model of humane Third Way economics—had passed eugenics laws around the same time as the Nazis. Even more disturbing, the Swedes continued the practice well into the mid-1970s. Over sixty thousand Swedes were forcibly sterilized. Or, to be more fair, some were given the option of being locked up until their child-bearing years were over instead of going under the knife. Among those who received "treatment" were children of racially mixed parents, Swedes with "gypsy features," unwed mothers with "too many" children, habitual criminals, and even a boy deemed "sexually precocious." The Danes passed similar eugenics laws in 1929, even before the Nazis. They sterilized eleven thousand and kept their laws on the books until the late 1960s. In Finland eleven thousand people were sterilized, and four thousand involuntary abortions were performed between 1945 and 1970. Similar revelations came from Norway, France, Belgium, and other quarters of enlightened Europe. A year earlier, Alberta, Canada, went through a similar controversy when it was revealed that nearly three thousand people were sterilized for all the usual reasons. Some were told they were being admitted for appendectomies and left the hospital barren. Adrian Wooldridge, *Cleveland Plain Dealer,* Sept. 15, 1997.

35. Michael Burleigh and Wolfgang Wippermann, *The Racial State: Germany, 1933–1945* (New York: Cambridge University Press, 1991), pp. 34, 35.

36. As Michael Burleigh and Wolfgang Wippermann note, after 1935 Nazi "social policy was indivisible from the 'selection' of 'alien' races and those of 'lesser racial value.' " Ibid., p. 48

37. John M. Barry, *The Great Influenza: The Epic Story of the Deadliest Plague in History* (New York: Penguin, 2004), p. 144.
38. Shelby Steele, *White Guilt: How Blacks and Whites Together Destroyed the Promise of the Civil Rights Era* (New York: HarperCollins, 2006), p. 124.
39. Thomas Sowell, *Civil Rights: Rhetoric or Reality?* (New York: William Morrow, 1984), p. 84.
40. Maureen Dowd, "Could Thomas Be Right?" *New York Times,* June 25, 2003, p. A25; Steele, *White Guilt,* p. 174.
41. David Tell, "Planned Un-parenthood: Roe v. Wade at Thirty," *Weekly Standard,* Jan. 27, 2003, pp. 35–41; Gloria Feldt, *Behind Every Choice Is a Story* (Denton: University of North Texas Press, 2002), pp. xix, xvi; Faye Wattleton, "Humanist of the Year Acceptance Speech," *Humanist,* July–Aug. 1986.
42. *Margaret Sanger: An Autobiography* (New York: Norton, 1938), p. 70.
43. Daniel J. Kevles, "Sex Without Fear," *New York Times,* June 28, 1992.
44. Valenza, "Was Margaret Sanger a Racist?" p. 45, citing David M. Kennedy, *Birth Control in America: The Career of Margaret Sanger* (New Haven, Conn.: Yale University Press, 1970), p. 115; H. G. Wells, introduction to *The Pivot of Civilization,* by Margaret Sanger (Amherst, N.Y.: Humanity Books, 2003), p. 42.
45. While Sanger cast herself as a champion of female liberation, her arguments nonetheless elevated the private realm of procreation to the public agenda. In Sanger's vision women would be "freed" from the reproductive tyranny of the family, but in order for this to happen, women—particularly *certain women*—would be subjected to a new tyranny of the eugenic planner. Marie Stopes, the British Margaret Sanger (that is, the mother of the British birth control movement), was of similar temperament. "Utopia," she explained, "could be reached in my life time had I the power to issue inviolable edicts." Quoted in Mukti Jain Campion, *Who's Fit to Be a Parent?* (New York: Routledge, 1995), p. 131.
46. Quoted in Black, *War Against the Weak,* p. 133. Also quoted in Rosen, *Preaching Eugenics,* p. 216.
47. Steven W. Mosher, "The Repackaging of Margaret Sanger," *Wall Street Journal,* May 5, 1997, p. A18
48. "Birth control is no negative philosophy concerned solely with the number of children brought into this world," she writes. "It is not merely a question of population. Primarily it is the instrument of liberation and of human development." Sanger, *Pivot of Civilization,* p. 224.
49. Valenza, "Was Margaret Sanger a Racist?" p. 45, citing Linda Gordon, *Woman's Body, Woman's Right* (New York: Grossman, 1976), p. 332; Margaret Sanger to C. J. Gamble, Dec. 10, 1939, quoted in Valenza, "Was Margaret Sanger a Racist?" p. 46.
50. Colman McCarthy, "Jackson's Reversal on Abortion," *Washington Post,* May 21, 1988, p. A27.
51. Steven D. Levitt and Stephen J. Dubner, *Freakonomics: A Rogue Economist Explores the Hidden Side of Everything* (New York: HarperCollins, 2005), p. 139.
52. Bill Bennett, *Morning in America,* Sept. 28, 2005; for transcript, see

mediamatters.org/items/200509280006 (accessed March 16, 2007); see also Brian Faler, "Bennett Under Fire for Remark on Crime and Black Abortions," *Washington Post,* Sept. 30, 2005, p. A05. Bob Herbert, "Impossible, Ridiculous, Repugnant," *New York Times,* Oct. 6, 2005, p. A37; *The Big Story with John Gibson,* Fox News Channel, Sept. 30, 2005; see also Jonah Goldberg, " 'Ridiculous,' " *National Review Online,* Oct. 7, 2005; *Fox News Sunday,* Fox News Channel, Oct. 2, 2005; "Talk-Back Live," editorial, *Washington Times,* Oct. 5, 2005, p. A16.

53. Ramesh Ponnuru, *The Party of Death: The Democrats, the Media, the Courts, and the Disregard for Human Life* (Washington, D.C.: Regnery, 2006), p. 65.

54. "The Clinton RU-486 Files: The Clinton Administration's Radical Drive to Force an Abortion Drug on America," Judicial Watch Special Report, 2006, available at www.judicialwatch.org/archive/2006/jw-ru486-report .pdf (accessed March 16, 2007).

55. Steven W. Mosher, "The Repackaging of Margaret Sanger," *Wall Street Journal,* May 5, 1997.

56. Tell, "Planned Un-parenthood," p. 40.

57. Sheryl Blunt, "Saving Black Babies," *Christianity Today,* Feb. 1, 2003.

58. Peter Singer, "Killing Babies Isn't Always Wrong," *Spectator,* Sept. 16, 1995, pp. 20–22.

59. Lyndon Johnson laid out the rationale in his 1965 speech introducing affirmative action when he proclaimed, "You do not take a person who, for years, has been hobbled by chains and liberate him, bring him up to the starting line of a race and then say, 'you are free to compete with all the others,' and still justly believe that you have been completely fair." Rhetorically, this was very Wilsonian in that it translated an entire people into a single collective "person." Lyndon B. Johnson, "To Fulfill These Rights," remarks at the Howard University commencement, June 4, 1965. For full text, see www.lbjlib.utexas.edu/johnson/archives.hom/speeches .hom/650604.asp (accessed May 8, 2007).

60. Joseph de Maistre, *Considerations on France,* trans. Richard A. Lebrun (New York: Cambridge University Press, 1994), p. xxiii.

61. Gene Edward Veith Jr., *Modern Fascism: The Threat to the Judeo-Christian Worldview* (St. Louis: Concordia, 1993), p. 134.

62. Andrew J. Coulson, "Planning Ahead Is Considered Racist?" *Seattle Post-Intelligencer,* June 1, 2006; Debera Carlton Harrell, "School District Pulls Web Site After Examples of Racism Spark Controversy," *Seattle Post-Intelligencer,* June 2, 2006. The guideline was withdrawn in response to protests. But one can be sure the attitudes that spawned it are intact. Richard Delgado, "Rodrigo's Seventh Chronicle: Race, Democracy, and the State," 41 *UCLA Law Review* 720, 734 (1994), cited in Daniel A. Farber and Suzanna Sherry, *Beyond All Reason: The Radical Assault on Truth in American Law* (New York: Oxford University Press, 1997), p. 29.

63. The law professor Luther Wright Jr. suggests that America adopt more rigid racial classifications for all of its citizens and that racial impostors be subjected to "fines and immediate job or benefit termination." Luther Wright Jr., "Who's Black, Who's White, and Who Cares: Reconceptualizing the United States's Definition of Race and Racial Classifications,"

Vanderbilt Law Review, March 1995, p. 513. A similar phenomenon is at work with American Indians. The Native American population in the United States has been growing enormously over the last two decades, far in excess of what is mathematically possible given their fertility rate and death rates. And since, by definition, it's impossible for Native Americans to immigrate to America, the only possible explanation is that more people find it advantageous to call themselves Indians, thanks to our spoils system.

64. Yolanda Woodlee, "Williams Aide Resigns in Language Dispute," *Washington Post,* Jan. 27, 1999, p. B1.

8. LIBERAL FASCIST ECONOMICS

1. Kevin Phillips, a former aide to Richard Nixon, has turned himself into a cottage industry as the voice of "real" conservatism and the "real" Republican Party. He is in fact the voice of the old socially meddling Progressivism that used to mark the bipartisan consensus between the Democrats and the Republicans. As for the charge that George W. Bush's grandfather was a Nazi collaborator of some sort, put forward in Phillips's book *American Dynasty,* Peter Schweizer demonstrates why this is such a bad-faith slander:

> One of Phillips's most attention-grabbing chapters posits the theory that the Bushes were involved in the rise of Adolf Hitler. While he correctly notes that Brown Brothers Harriman, an investment-banking firm employing Prescott Bush and George H. Walker (George W.'s great-grandfather), invested in Nazi-era German companies, Phillips fails to note that it was Averell Harriman, later FDR's ambassador to Moscow and Truman's commerce secretary, who initiated these investments (and some in Soviet Russia) before either of the Bushes joined the firm. Prescott Bush did not oversee these investments; the reality is that he was involved almost exclusively in managing the firm's domestic portfolio. It was Harriman who largely managed the foreign investments and, accordingly, it was he who met German and Soviet leaders. (Peter Schweizer, "Kevin Phillips's Politics of Deceit," *National Review Online,* March 30, 2004, www.nationalreview.com/comment/schweizer200403300 907.asp [accessed Jan. 23, 2007])

2. Robert F. Kennedy Jr., "Crimes Against Nature," *Rolling Stone,* Dec. 11, 2003; Rebecca Shoval, "Al Franken Airs Show at Ithaca College," *Cornell Daily Sun,* April 26, 2006, www.cornellsun.com/node/17563 (accessed Jan. 23, 2007); John Ralston Saul, *The Unconscious Civilization* (New York: Simon and Schuster, 1999), p. 120.

3. Jeffrey T. Schnapp writes, "The notion that fascism represented a 'third way' with respect to capitalist and communist development was a key feature of the movement's self-definition. In contrast to the democratic leveling and standardization of life attributed to capitalism, and to the

collectivism and materialism attributed to bolshevism, fascism claimed to be able to provide all of the advantages of accelerated modernization, without the disadvantages such as the loss of individuality and nationality, or of higher values such as the pursuit of heroism, art, tradition, and spiritual transcendence." Jeffrey T. Schnapp, "Fascinating Fascism," in "The Aesthetics of Fascism," special issue, *Journal of Contemporary History* 31, no. 2 (April 1996), p. 240.

4. Over and over again, in popular articles about fascism, serious authors routinely assert that fascism constitutes "the rejection of both liberalism and socialism," as Alexander Stille wrote in the *New York Times*. Now, it is true that fascists opposed both socialism and liberalism. But these words had specific connotations during the era of classical fascism. Socialism in this context means Bolshevism, an internationalist ideology that called for the complete abrogation of private property and decried other socialist ideologies as "fascist." Liberalism in the 1920s and 1930s was defined as free-market laissez-faire. Translated into contemporary categories, fascism was a rejection of both free-market capitalism and totalitarian communism. That means something slightly different from "the rejection of both liberalism and socialism." Alexander Stille, "The Latest Obscenity Has Seven Letters," *New York Times,* Sept. 13, 2003, sec. B, p. 9.

5. A. James Gregor, *The Ideology of Fascism: The Rationale of Totalitarianism* (New York: Free Press, 1969), p. 12; Robert S. Wistrich, "Leon Trotsky's Theory of Fascism," in "Theories of Fascism," special issue, *Journal of Contemporary History* 11, no. 4 (Oct. 1976), p. 161, citing Leon Trotsky, *Fascism: What It Is and How to Fight It* (New York: Pathfinder, 1972), p. 5.

6. Peter Davies and Derek Lynch, eds., *The Routledge Companion to Fascism and the Far Right* (New York: Routledge, 2002), p. 52; Palmiro Togliatti, *Lectures on Fascism* (London: Lawrence and Wishart, 1976), pp. 1–10; Martin Kitchen, *Fascism* (London: Macmillan, 1982), p. 46; Henry Ashby Turner Jr., ed., *Reappraisals of Fascism* (New York: New Viewpoints, 1975), p. xi.

7. Henry Ashby Turner Jr., *German Big Business and the Rise of Hitler* (New York: Oxford University Press, 1987), p. 75.

8. Ibid., p. 347.

9. In the European tradition, one could quite easily make the case that these arrangements are right-wing, historically speaking, though that is not an open-and-shut case, since even in Europe today free-market economics is described as an ideology of the right. In mid-century Germany, things get even more confusing because, thanks to Bismarck, classical liberalism was extinguished in the 1870s, and what was called liberalism there was in fact statism. In other words, both left and right were left-wing as we understand the terms in America.

10. "Packers Face Report Music," *Washington Post,* June 7, 1906, p. 4; Timothy P. Carney, *The Big Ripoff: How Big Business and Big Government Steal Your Money* (Hoboken, N.J.: Wiley & Sons, 2006), pp. 37–38. See also Gabriel Kolko, *The Triumph of Conservatism: A Reinterpretation of American History, 1900–1916* (New York: Free Press, 1963), pp. 103, 107.

11. Carney, *Big Ripoff,* p. 40; Kolko, *Triumph of Conservatism,* pp. 39, 174.

12. Herbert Croly, *The Promise of American Life* (New York: Macmillan, 1911), pp. 202, 359.

13. Carney, *Big Ripoff,* p. 42, citing Murray Rothbard, "War Collectivism in World War I," in *A New History of Leviathan,* ed. Ronald Radosh and Murray Rothbard (New York: Dutton, 1972), p. 70; Paul A. C. Kostinen, "The 'Industrial-Military Complex' in Historical Perspective: World War I," *Business History Review* (Winter 1967), p. 381.

14. Grosvenor Clarkson, *Industrial America in the World War: The Strategy Behind the Line, 1917–1918* (Boston: Houghton Mifflin, 1923), p. 63; Robert Higgs, "Crisis and Quasi-Corporatist Policy-Making: The U.S. Case in Historical Perspective," *The World & I,* Nov. 1988, reprinted by the Independent Institute, www.independent.org/publications/article.asp?id=312 (accessed Jan. 24, 2007).

15. While in the 1920s, particularly under Calvin Coolidge, the state unraveled some—but by no means all—of the corporatist excess of Wilson's war socialism, many in the government continued to advance the cause. One of them was the secretary of commerce from 1921 to 1928, Herbert Hoover. Contrary to the absurd propaganda that Hoover was some starry-eyed free marketeer, the director of the Food Administration in Woodrow Wilson's cabinet was committed to "organizing" American business to co-operate with government hand in hand. Most economic historians see more continuity than "revolution" in FDR's 1932 economic policies. It was FDR's politics that constituted the real break with the past. He militarized corporatism—just as his overseas counterparts had done—making the New Deal the "moral equivalent of war." The segue to real war was nearly as seamless for Americans as it was for Germans, though the economy was permanently transformed, much to the liking of liberals and business, even before the war began. William E. Leuchtenburg, *The FDR Years: On Roosevelt and His Legacy* (New York: Columbia University Press, 1995), p. 41.

16. Eric F. Goldman, *Rendezvous with Destiny: A History of Modern American Reform* (Chicago: Ivan R. Dee, 2001), pp. 347, 348, 349; William E. Leuchtenburg, *Franklin D. Roosevelt and the New Deal* (New York: Harper and Row, 1963), p. 87.

17. Carney, *Big Ripoff,* p. 46; Alan Brinkley, *The End of Reform: New Deal Liberalism in Recession and War* (New York: Vintage, 1996), p. 37.

18. John Patrick Diggins, *Mussolini and Fascism: The View from America* (Princeton, N.J.: Princeton University Press, 1972), p. 164; William G. Welk, "Fascist Economic Policy and the N.R.A.," *Foreign Affairs,* Oct. 1933, pp. 98–109. I have refrained from recounting the literally numberless similar comments from communists and hard socialists in the United States because the view that New Dealism was fascist was so widespread. Also, thanks to the Stalinist doctrine of social fascism, it was official policy among Reds and other socialists in America to say it was so, even if they didn't think it was. But suffice it to say everyone from Norman Thomas on down repeatedly and cavalierly referred to Hoover and FDR as fascists at one point or another.

19. When Brockway visited the United States, he became even more convinced that Rooseveltism was fascism. He was particularly horrified by the

Civilian Conservation Corps work camps, which "remind one immediately of the Labour Service Camps in Fascist Germany. One has an uneasy feeling that the American camps, no less than the German, would be transferred from civilian to military purposes immediately war or a social uprising threatened, and that behind the mind of the military authorities in charge of them their potential military value is dominant." Barbara C. Malament, "British Labour and Roosevelt's New Deal: The Response of the Left and the Unions," *Journal of British Studies* 17, no. 2 (Spring 1978), pp. 137, 144. See also Giuseppe Bottai, "Corporate State and the N.R.A.," *Foreign Affairs,* July 1935, pp. 612–24.

20. Anne O'Hare McCormick, "Hitler Seeks Jobs for All Germans," *New York Times,* July 10, 1933, pp. 1, 6.
21. In his 1929 "state of the nation" address, Mussolini boasted of his success in implementing the corporate state:

> The employed are integrated within the institutions of the regime: syndicalism and corporatism enable the whole nation to be organized. The system is based on the legal recognition of professional unions, on collective contracts, on the prohibition of strikes and lock-outs . . . [This approach] has already borne fruit. Labour and capital have ceased to consider their antagonism an inexorable fact of history: the conflicts which inevitably arise are solved peacefully thanks to an increasing degree of conscious class collaboration. The social legislation of Italy is the most advanced in the world: it ranges from the law on the eight-hour day to compulsory insurance against tuberculosis. (Benito Mussolini, "The Achievements of the Fascist Revolution," in *Fascism,* ed. Roger Griffin [Oxford: Oxford University Press, 1995], pp. 63–64)

22. R. J. B. Bosworth, *Mussolini's Italy: Life Under the Fascist Dictatorship, 1915–1945* (New York: Penguin, 2006), p. 311.
23. Frank Kingdon, *That Man in the White House: You and Your President* (New York: Arco, 1944), p. 120; Helen M. Burns, *The American Banking Community and New Deal Banking Reforms, 1933–1935* (Westport, Conn.: Greenwood, 1974), p. 100; David Schoenbaum, *Hitler's Social Revolution: Class and Status in Nazi Germany, 1933–1939* (New York: Norton, 1980), pp. 25–26.
24. William Manchester, *The Arms of Krupp: The Rise and Fall of the Industrial Dynasty That Armed Germany at War* (New York: Back Bay Books, 2003), p. 152.
25. Robert N. Proctor, *The Nazi War on Cancer* (Princeton, N.J.: Princeton University Press, 2000), p. 38.
26. Claudia Koonz, *The Nazi Conscience* (Cambridge, Mass.: Harvard University Press, 2003), p. 73.
27. Jay W. Baird, "From Berlin to Neubabelsberg: Nazi Film Propaganda and Hitler Youth Quex," in "Historians and Movies: The State of the Art: Part 1," special issue, *Journal of Contemporary History* 18, no. 3 (July 1983), p. 495; Peter Goddard, "The Subtle Side of Nazi Propaganda Machine," *Toronto Star,* Jan. 19, 1996, p. D4.
28. Proctor, *Nazi War on Cancer,* p. 138.

29. Stuart Chase, *The Economy of Abundance* (New York: Macmillan, 1934), p. 313. The progressive economist John Commons said that the new system of pressure groups and trade associations created by the New Deal amounted to "an occupational parliament of the American people, more truly representative than the Congress elected by territorial divisions. They are the informal American counterparts of Mussolini's 'corporate state,' the Italian occupational state." Abram L. Harris, "John R. Commons and the Welfare State," *Southern Economic Journal* 19, no. 2 (Oct. 1952), pp. 222–33; Higgs, "Crisis and Quasi-Corporatist Policy-Making."

30. Jonathan Alter, *The Defining Moment: FDR's Hundred Days and the Triumph of Hope* (New York: Simon and Schuster, 2006), p. 185.

31. When it was still unclear whether the Nazis would attain power in Germany, Gustav Krupp, the patron of the enormous and infamous arms manufacturer, gave specific instructions to his chauffeur. When leaving meetings with various political leaders, he explained, he told his driver to pay careful attention to which hand he carried his gloves in. If Krupp emerged with his gloves in his right hand, the driver was to give him the traditional Prussian greeting (clicked heels and a tap of the hat). If Krupp had his gloves in his left hand, the chauffeur was instructed to give him the full "Heil Hitler" salute, which Gustav would return with equal gusto. Krupp, like most of Germany's leading businessmen and industrialists, did not like Hitler or the Nazis. Indeed, Krupp—who was rightly tried for war crimes at Nuremberg—had joined other business leaders in trying to prevent Hitler's appointment to the chancellorship. But when it was clear that history was on the side of Nazism, German business started to fall in line.

32. Lizette Alvarez, "An 'Icon of Technology' Encounters Some Rude Political Realities," *New York Times,* March 4, 1998, p. D4.

33. For the Nazi Party platform, see www.hitler.org/writings/programme. Alan Brinkley's *Voices of Protest* has an outstanding discussion of the sources of anti-department-store rage. The chief problem was that the big chains put local general stores out of business. These stores were important cultural and financial institutions in rural America, providing, among other things, credit to farmers during bad seasons. See Alan Brinkley, *Voices of Protest: Huey Long, Father Coughlin, and the Great Depression* (New York: Vintage, 1983), p. 198.

34. Neil Steinberg, *New York Daily News,* Feb. 13, 2005.

35. Roughly 40 percent (or slightly over forty million) of American households own at least one dog, and roughly 35 percent of households contain a cat (and half of them have more than one). The vast majority of pet owners pay for veterinary services in cash with almost no paperwork and no long waits and with a high quality of service. Competition to get into veterinary school is tougher than it is to get into medical school. Why? Because Congress stays out of it (and because they haven't allowed the trial lawyers to get into it). And because government leaves the vets alone, the vets leave government alone.

36. As state governments get involved in more regulatory issues, the numbers of lobbyists at the state level have exploded as well. New York State, for example, has nearly four thousand registered lobbyists.

37. Christopher Lehmann-Haupt, "A Tale of Tobacco, Pleasure, Profits and Death," *New York Times,* April 15, 1996.

38. Christine Hall, "Unholy Alliance," *National Review Online,* April 12, 2006.

39. The *New York Times* reported, "Business leaders applauded yesterday, with varying degrees of enthusiasm, the sweeping proposals announced by President Nixon Sunday night." Robert D. Hershey Jr., "Psychological Lift Seen," *New York Times,* Aug. 17, 1971, p. 1.

40. Hillary Rodham Clinton, *It Takes a Village* (New York: Simon and Schuster, 1996), p. 301.

41. Kaus (who once worked for Reich at the Federal Trade Commission— charged with figuring out how to rule that closing a factory was an "unfair trade practice") offers a few examples from Reich's writings. "But must we choose between zero-sum nationalism and impassive cosmopolitanism?" Reich asks. No! There is "a third, superior position: a positive economic nationalism." "American political rhetoric often frames the decision in the dramatic terms of myth: either we leave the market free, or the government controls it," Reich complains. "There is a third alternative, however." "Two fictions confound discussions of economic change in America. The first is the fiction of automatic adjustment," where layoffs have little negative impact. The "other, opposite fiction," according to Reich, is that people "never adjust to change but simply suffer." Reich claims for himself a "middle, messier ground" in which "[t]here are many options" for pragmatic, expert-driven control of the economy, using capitalism and socialism together. Mickey Kaus, "The Policy Hustler," *New Republic,* Dec. 7, 1992, pp. 16–23.

42. Ibid., p. 20.

43. When Reagan left office, President George H. W. Bush was ill equipped philosophically to deal with the rising clamor for a more planned economy, particularly when the recession hit (which the media exaggerated to great political effect). Once again, advocates of industrial policy dusted off arguments for a planned prosperity grounded in the moral equivalents of war. "Our principal rivals today are no longer military," George Fisher, the chairman of the Council on Competitiveness under Bush, offered in a widespread refrain. "They are those who pursue economic, technology, and industrial policies designed to expand their shares of global markets. This is the way it is. U.S. policy must reflect this reality if we are to remain a world leader and a role model." The former defense secretary Harold Brown called for "a new alliance between government and industry" to develop new technologies. See Kevin Phillips, "U.S. Industrial Policy: Inevitable and Ineffective," *Harvard Business Review,* July/August 1992.

44. Hobart Rowan, "Clinton's Approach to Industrial Policy," *Washington Post,* Oct. 11, 1992, p. H1; Paul A. Gigot, "How the Clintons Hope to Snare the Middle Class," *Wall Street Journal,* Sept. 24, 1993, p. A10.

45. This sort of interference has a cascading effect throughout the economy, creating even more perverse incentives for government and business to get in bed together. Because American companies are required to pay twice

the global market price for sugar, most big sugar consumers—Coca-Cola, for example—use corn sweeteners in their soft drinks instead of sugar. Archer Daniels Midland makes a lot of corn sweetener, which is why it gives a lot of money to politicians who support sugar subsidies.

46. Obviously, much of this is marketing. Starbucks customers, according to a survey by Zogby International, are more likely to be liberal (and female) by a margin of roughly two to one (Republicans and men prefer Dunkin' Donuts). But one shouldn't overlook the point that if "liberals" prefer Starbucks, it is in Starbucks' interest that more people become liberal, which is why it spends so much money on what amounts to public education. Zogby Consumer Profile Finding, "Starbucks Brews Up Trouble for Dunkin' Donuts: Seattle Chain's Coffee Preferred by 34% to 30%; 'Starbucks Divide' Evident in Age, Politics of Coffee's Drinkers," August 8, 2005, http://www.zogby.com/news/ReadNews.dbm?ID=1016 (accessed June 26, 2007).

47. Conversation with Ronald Bailey, science correspondent, *Reason* magazine.

48. Ned Sullivan and Rich Schiafo, "Talking Green, Acting Dirty," *New York Times,* June 12, 2005, p. 23; "The Profiteer: Jeff Immelt," *Rolling Stone,* www.rollingstone.com/politics/story/8742315/the_profiteer/ (accessed March 18, 2007).

49. See www.ceousa.org/pdfs/eeoctestimony5=06.pdf (accessed May 8, 2007).

9. BRAVE NEW VILLAGE: HILLARY CLINTON AND THE MEANING OF LIBERAL FASCISM

1. Interview on *Fresh Air,* National Public Radio, Oct. 18, 2005.

2. Kenneth L. Woodward, "Soulful Matters," *Newsweek,* Oct. 31, 1994, p. 22.

3. Ibid. Jones has stayed involved in her life. During the Lewinsky scandal he reacquainted Clinton with a sermon of Tillich's—"Faith in Action"—and served as a spiritual adviser during her 2000 Senate campaign.

4. I can find no reference to Oglesby being a theologian of any kind. The title of his article, according to *Newsweek,* was "Change or Containment." But it was actually "World Revolution and American Containment" and came from the SDS pamphlet by the same name. Oglesby co-wrote a book with an expert in liberation theology, Richard Shaull, called *Containment and Change,* which may be a source of the confusion. Clinton told *Newsweek,* "It was the first thing I had ever read that challenged the Vietnam War." This seems unlikely since even if she'd been reading *motive* and nothing else, Oglesby's article was hardly the first anti-Vietnam piece to appear in that magazine (it became known for advising young people on how to escape to Sweden to avoid the draft). In time Oglesby became something of a New Left libertarian, believing that the New Left and the Old Right were kindred spirits—or at least should be.

5. "I can no more condemn the Andean tribesmen who assassinate tax collectors than I can condemn the rioters in Watts or Harlem or the Deacons for

Defense and Justice. Their violence is reactive and provoked, and it remains culturally beyond guilt at the very same moment that its victims' personal innocence is most appallingly present in our imaginations." It was Oglesby's idea for the SDS to send "Brigades" to Cuba in solidarity with the regime. David Brock, *The Seduction of Hillary Rodham* (New York: Free Press, 1996), p. 18.

6. Woodward, "Soulful Matters," p. 22.

7. Hillary D. Rodham, 1969 Student Commencement Speech, Wellesley College, May 31, 1969, www.wellesley.edu/PublicAffairs/Commencement/1969/053169hillary.html (accessed March 19, 2007).

8. These last comments came from a poem written by a fellow student:
My entrance into the world of so-called "social problems"
Must be with quiet laughter, or not at all.
The hollow men of anger and bitterness
The bountiful ladies of righteous degradation
All must be left to a bygone age.
And the purpose of history is to provide a receptacle
For all those myths and oddments
Which oddly we have acquired
And from which we would become unburdened
To create a newer world
To transform the future into the present.
See www.wellesley.edu/PublicAffairs/Commencement/1969/053169
hillary.html.

9. P. David Finks, "Organization Man," *Chicago Tribune Magazine,* May 26, 1985, p. 21.

10. "Strength Through Misery," *Time,* March 18, 1966.

11. Saul D. Alinsky, *Rules for Radicals: A Pragmatic Primer for Realistic Radicals* (New York: Vintage, 1972), p. xxi.

12. Ibid., pp. 4, 21, 13.

13. A precocious legal theorist, Reich became a professor at Yale Law School at the impressive age of thirty-two, where he taught Hillary and Bill Clinton, among others, constitutional law. Approaching his fortieth birthday, he accepted a student's invitation to spend a summer at Berkeley in 1967, which just happened to be the Summer of Love. He returned to Yale a long-haired, bell-bottom-wearing guru who wouldn't be caught dead without a string of beads around his neck. He gave up all the tradition-directed dogmas, including academic rigor. The students called one of his courses Kindergarten II because you could read or do anything you wanted. His 1970 book, *The Greening of America,* was not an environmental work, as the title might imply, but a quasi-religious tract on the need for American society to evolve to "Level III consciousness." *Greening* considered political change to be the end stage of the Level III consciousness "revolution." Change had to occur within the culture before politics could change, and within the individual before the culture could. For Reich himself, individual transformation required dropping out of the Yale faculty and wandering around as a self-described "Sorcerer" in search of meaning and authenticity amid the sketchier backwaters of the California counterculture. Much of the New Left followed in his footsteps.

14. It continued: "Now a new frontier must be found to foster further experimentation, an environment relatively unpolluted by conventional patterns of social and political organization. Experimentation with drugs, sex, individual lifestyles or radical rhetoric and action within the larger society is an insufficient alternative. Total experimentation is necessary. New ideas and values must be taken out of heads and transformed into reality." Daniel Wattenberg, "The Lady Macbeth of Little Rock," *American Spectator* 25, no. 8 (Aug. 1992).

15. Treuhaft's wife, Jessica Mitford, was a muckraking communist journalist most famous for writing *The American Way of Death,* an exposé of the American funeral industry. Born to an aristocratic British family, she was a classic girl of privilege who fell in with rebellious radicalism. Several of her sisters were equally radical. Unity Mitford was a famous friend of Hitler's, and Diana Mitford married Oswald Mosley, the founder of the British Union of Fascists. Unity Mitford had to leave the country, incensed that Britain would fight such a progressive leader as Hitler. Diana and Oswald were jailed for the duration of the war. Oswald, of course, always considered himself a man of the left: "I am not, and never have been, a man of the right," Mosley proclaimed in 1968. "My position was on the Left and is now in the centre of politics." Jessica Mitford, meanwhile, remained committed to Stalinism her entire life. When Hungarian freedom fighters were mowed down by Soviet tanks, she argued that the "fascist traitors" got what they deserved.

16. As Allan Bloom wrote, "I have seen young people, and older people too, who are good democratic liberals, lovers of peace and gentleness, struck dumb with admiration for individuals threatening or using the most terrible violence for the slightest and tawdriest of reasons." He continued: "They have a sneaking suspicion that they are face to face with men of real commitment, which they themselves lack. And commitment, not truth, is believed to be what counts." Allan Bloom, *The Closing of the American Mind* (New York: Simon and Schuster, 1987), p. 221.

17. Michael Kelly, *Things Worth Fighting For: Collected Writings* (New York: Penguin, 2004), p. 170. This profile, "Saint Hillary," first appeared in the May 23, 1993, *New York Times Magazine.* For reasons that may strike some as suspicious, it is impossible to find in the Lexis-Nexis database, in professional academic databases, or on the *New York Times* Web site. Fortunately, it appears in Kelly's posthumous *Things Worth Fighting For.* Sadly, and oddly, the *New York Times* does not consider this historic essay to be something worth saving.

18. Christopher Lasch, "Hillary Clinton, Child Saver," *Harper's,* Oct. 1992.

19. Ibid.

20. Michael Burleigh, *The Third Reich: A New History* (New York: Hill and Wang, 2000), p. 235; Christopher Lasch, *Haven in a Heartless World: The Family Besieged* (New York: Norton, 1995), p. 14. While she summarized the environmental position well, it's worth noting that Gilman herself was an unreconstructed racist eugenicist.

21. John Taylor Gatto writes:

A small number of very passionate American ideological leaders including Horace Mann of Massachusetts, Calvin Stowe of Ohio,

Barnas Sears of Connecticut, and others visited Prussia in the first half of the 19th century, fell in love with the order, obedience, and efficiency they saw there, attributed the well-regulated, machine-like society to its educational system, and campaigned relentlessly upon returning home to bring the Prussian vision to these shores . . . So at the behest of Horace Mann and other leading citizens, without any national debate or discussion, we adopted Prussian schooling or rather, most had it imposed upon them . . . The one- and two-room schoolhouses, highly efficient as academic transmitters, breeders of self-reliance and independence, intimately related to their communities, almost exclusively female-led, and largely un-administered, had to be put to death. (Charlotte A. Twight, *Dependent on D.C.: The Rise of Federal Control over the Lives of Ordinary Americans* [New York: Palgrave Macmillan, 2002], p. 138.)

22. Burleigh, *Third Reich,* p. 236.
23. Martha Sherrill, "Hillary Clinton's Inner Politics," *Washington Post,* May 6, 1993, p. D1; Kelly, *Things Worth Fighting For,* p. 172.
24. First Lady Hillary Rodham Clinton, Remarks at University of Texas, Austin, April 7, 1993, clinton4.nara.gov/WH/EOP/First_Lady/html/generalspeeches/1993/19930407.html (accessed March 18, 2007).
25. David Horowitz, *Radical Son: A Generational Odyssey* (New York: Free Press, 1997), p. 175.
26. Tom Gottlieb, "Book Tour Includes a Political Lesson," *Roll Call,* May 16, 2006.
27. Lee Siegel, "All Politics Is Cosmic," *Atlantic Monthly,* June 1996, pp. 120–25.
28. Michael Lerner, *The Politics of Meaning: Restoring Hope and Possibility in an Age of Cynicism* (Cambridge, Mass.: Perseus Books, 1997), pp. 13–14.
29. *Tikkun,* May–June 1993.
30. Lerner, *Politics of Meaning,* p. 226; Michael Lerner, *Spirit Matters* (Charlottesville, Va.: Hampton Roads, 2000), p. 325.
31. Lerner, *Politics of Meaning,* p. 58.
32. Ibid., p. 59.
33. Ibid., pp. 88, 91.
34. Among the points he fails to grasp is the fact that the left has always been about constructing communities; that the right-wing movements he identifies are not necessarily fascistic; or that he is employing the classic liberal tactic of calling the "other" "fascist." Indeed Lerner writes, "The delegitimization of the notion of a possible 'we,' who could act from shared high moral purpose and could achieve morally valuable results, is the number-one goal of the conservative forces in America's elites of wealth and power." Ibid., p. 318.
35. In the former he offers an interesting interpretation of liberal history in order to persuade liberals to reconnect with the old Progressive Social Gospel mission. "With the rise of fascism," he writes, "the American religious Left abandoned the Social Gospel of its pre–World War II past, with its cheery hope of steady progress toward the Kingdom of God." He identifies the theologian Reinhold Niebuhr as the culprit behind this move be-

cause he convinced liberals to take seriously the threat of Nazism. "For Niebuhr and the Christian realists who rallied around his writings, sinfulness required recognizing the limitations of any politics aimed at fundamental social change, accommodating the inequities of their own capitalist societies and championing the Cold War. The Christian 'realists' helped reinforce individualism when they focused religious energy away from social movements." Michael Lerner, *The Left Hand of God: Taking Back Our Country from the Religious Right* (New York: HarperCollins, 2006), p. 164.

36. Lerner, *Politics of Meaning,* pp. 219, 283.
37. Charles Krauthammer, "Home Alone 3: The White House," *Washington Post,* May 14, 1993, p. A31.
38. "By the Dawn's Early Light," *National Review,* Jan. 22, 1990, p. 17.
39. Norman Lear, "A Call for Spiritual Renewal," *Washington Post,* May 30, 1993, p. C7.
40. John Dewey, "What I Believe," *Forum* 83, no. 3 (March 1930), pp. 176–82, in *Pragmatism and American Culture,* ed. Gail Kennedy (Boston: Heath, 1950), p. 28; Adolf Hitler, *Hitler's Table Talk,* trans. Norman Cameron and R. H. Stevens, introduction and preface by Hugh Trevor Roper (New York: Enigma Books, 2000), p. 143.
41. Indeed, O'Rourke argued that *It Takes a Village* is a fascist tract in 1996. He wrote:

    If a name must be put to these stupid politics, we can consult the *Columbia Encyclopedia* under the heading of that enormous stupidity, fascism: "totalitarian philosophy of government that glorifies state and nation and assigns to the state control over every aspect of national life." Admittedly, the fascism in *It Takes a Village* is of a namby-pamby, eat-your-vegetables kind that doesn't so much glorify the state and nation as pester the dickens out of them. Ethnic groups do not suffer persecution except insofar as a positive self-image is required among women and minorities at all times. And there will be no uniforms other than comfortable, durable clothes on girls. And no concentration camps either, just lots and lots of day care. (P. J. O'Rourke, "Mrs. Clinton's Very, Very Bad Book," *Weekly Standard,* Feb. 19, 1996, p. 24)

42. Hillary Rodham Clinton, *It Takes a Village* (New York: Simon and Schuster, 1996), p. 13.
43. Ibid., p. 14.
44. Lear, "Call for Spiritual Renewal," p. C7.
45. Clinton, *It Takes a Village,* p. 20.
46. Ibid., pp. 299, 301.
47. Paul A. Gigot, "How the Clintons Hope to Snare the Middle Class," *Wall Street Journal,* Sept. 24, 1993, p. A10.
48. Howard Fineman, "Clinton's Brain Trusters," *Newsweek,* April 19, 1993, p. 26.
49. Jacob Weisberg, "Dies Ira: A Short History of Ira Magaziner," *New Republic,* Jan. 24, 1994, p. 18. Even the Swedish embassy couldn't get a copy when it asked for one on behalf of *Fortune* magazine.
50. Jonathan Rauch, "Robert Reich, Quote Doctor," *Slate,* May 30, 1997,

www.slate.com/?id=2447 (accessed Jan. 19, 2007). See also Robert Scheer, "What's Rotten in Politics: An Insider's View," *Los Angeles Times,* April 29, 1997.

51. Rauch, "Robert Reich, Quote Doctor." See also Robert Reich, "Robert Reich Replies," *Washington Post,* June 5, 1997, p. A21; Thomas W. Hazlett, "Planet Reich: Thanks for the Memoirs," *Reason,* Oct. 1997, p. 74.

52. Jonathan Chait, "Fact Finders: The Anti-dogma Dogma," *New Republic,* Feb. 28, 2005; Herbert W. Schneider, *Making the Fascist State* (New York: Oxford University Press, 1928), p. 67.

53. Walter Lippmann, *The Good Society* (New Brunswick, N.J.: Transaction, 2004), p. 92; Clinton, *It Takes a Village,* p. 200.

54. Mickey Kaus, "The Godmother," *New Republic,* Feb. 15, 1993, p. 21; Kay S. Hymowitz, "The Children's Defense Fund: Not Part of the Solution," *City Journal* 10, no. 3 (Summer 2000), pp. 32–41.

55. James Bovard, *Freedom in Chains: The Rise of the State and the Demise of the Citizen* (New York: St. Martin's, 2000), p. 68, citing U.S. Department of Agriculture, *Food and Nutrition,* Feb. 1972.

56. Hymowitz, "Children's Defense Fund," pp. 32–41.

57. Lasch, "Hillary Clinton, Child Saver"; Hillary Rodham Clinton, Address to the General Conference, April 24, 1996, www.gcah.org/GC96/hilltext .html (accessed Feb. 6, 2007).

58. Clinton, *It Takes a Village,* pp. 314, 315. Emphasis mine.

59. Ian Williams, "Big Food's Real Appetites," *Nation,* May 6, 2002; *Tim Russert,* CNBC, June 10, 2000.

60. Nomination of Janet Reno, White House, Feb. 11, 1993, www.presidency .ucsb.edu/ws/index.php?pid=47044&st=&st1 (accessed Feb. 6, 2007); Janet Reno, Remarks to Justice Department Employees, Washington, D.C., April 6, 1993.

61. Clinton, *It Takes a Village,* pp. 82, 113.

62. Lasch, "Hillary Clinton, Child Saver."

63. Clinton, *It Takes a Village,* pp. 45, 63, 88–89.

64. Ibid., p. 83.

65. Ibid., pp. 233, 132.

66. Kate O'Beirne, "The Kids Aren't Alright," *National Review,* Sept. 1, 2003; Kate O'Beirne, *Women Who Make the World Worse: And How Their Radical Feminist Assault Is Ruining Our Schools, Families, Military, and Sports* (New York: Penguin, 2006), pp. 36–38.

67. Gretchen Ritter, director of the Women's Studies Program at the University of Texas, likewise writes that mothers who stay home to take care of their children are the equivalent of slackers who refuse "to con- tribute as professionals and community activists." Gretchen Ritter, "The Messages We Send When Moms Stay Home," *Austin American-Statesman,* July 6, 2004, p. A9.

68. O'Beirne, *Women Who Make the World Worse,* p. 40.

69. Clinton, *It Takes a Village,* p. 189.

70. Ibid., pp. 239, 169.

71. William Jennings Bryan, *Omaha World-Herald,* Sept. 23, 1892, quoted in Paolo E. Coletta, *William Jennings Bryan: Volume 1* (Lincoln: University

of Nebraska Press, 1964), p. 75; H. Wayne Morgan, *From Hayes to McKinley: National Party Politics, 1877–1896* (Syracuse, N.Y.: Syracuse University Press, 1969), p. 496.

72. Ian Kershaw, *The "Hitler Myth": Image and Reality in the Third Reich* (New York: Oxford University Press, 1987), p. 73.

73. Elizabeth Kolbert, "Running on Empathy," *New Yorker,* Feb. 7, 2000, p. 36.

74. Bovard, *Freedom in Chains,* p. 19.

75. "The Real Hillary Just Stood Up," *New York Post,* June 30, 2004, p. 30; Amy Fagan, Inside Politics, *Washington Times,* June 30, 2004, p. A07.

10. THE NEW AGE: WE'RE ALL FASCISTS NOW

1. "Reality-based community" became a slogan for left and liberal bloggers starting in 2004. The phrase is generally used as a form of derision for President George W. Bush and his policies. It comes from an October 17, 2004, *New York Times Magazine* article by Ron Suskind, quoting an unnamed aide to George W. Bush:

> The aide said that guys like me were "in what we call the reality-based community," which he defined as people who "believe that solutions emerge from your judicious study of discernible reality" . . . "That's not the way the world really works anymore," he continued. "We're an empire now, and when we act, we create our own reality. And while you're studying that reality—judiciously, as you will—we'll act again, creating other new realities, which you can study too, and that's how things will sort out. We're history's actors . . . and you, all of you, will be left to just study what we do."

Hitler's speech is quoted in Richard J. Evans, *The Third Reich in Power, 1933–1939* (New York: Penguin, 2005), p. 257.

2. John J. Miller, "Banning Legos," *National Review Online,* March 27, 2007.

3. It's interesting to note that during the height of the *Kulturkampf,* America's president, Ulysses S. Grant, lobbied for a constitutional amendment banning the teaching of "sectarian tenets" in any school receiving any amount of public assistance—and mandating that "all church property" be subject to taxation. See Jeremy Rabkin, "The Supreme Court in the Culture Wars," *Public Interest* (Fall 1996), pp. 3–26.

It's important to understand how Protestantism in Germany became corrupted by both nationalist and socialist agendas, in much the same way it had been in America by the progressives. Surveys in 1898 and 1912 revealed that a majority of German workers did not believe in God, but nearly all of them believed that Jesus was a "true workers' friend." If Jesus were alive today, surmised one worker, "he would certainly be a social Democrat, maybe even a leader and a Reichstag deputy." (Michael Burleigh, *Earthly Powers: The Clash of Religion and Politics in Europe from the French Revolution to the Great War* [New York: HarperCollins,

2005], p. 268.) For non-Marxists, the emphasis was less on class and more on the nation as the subject of religious ardor. Adolf Stoecker, the court preacher to Wilhelm II, helped lead the charge and was a direct influence on Hitler and National Socialism. Stoecker denounced capitalism—in part because of its alleged inherent "Jewishness." He advocated workers' communes and a lavish welfare state. He also demanded racial quotas for universities and other professions and went on to found one of the first anti-Semitic parties in Germany, the Christian Socialist Workers' Party. The process of turning Germanism into a religion became symbolically complete when another party came along and changed the word "Christian" to "National"—the Nazis.

4. *Hitler's Table Talk*, p. 59.
5. Hermann Rauschning, *The Voice of Destruction* (New York: Putnam, 1940), p. 50.
6. Other official holy days included Heroes' Memorial Day, Reich Party Day, the Führer's Birthday (of course), and the National Festival of the German People. Winter solstice, brimming with *völkisch* tributes to Germanic superiority, replaced Christmas. Commemoration of the movement's fallen replaced the old Remembrance Day and was drenched with pagan rituals.
7. William E. Drake, "God-State Idea in Modern Education," *History of Education Quarterly* 3, no. 2 (June 1963), p. 90.
8. J. S. Conway, *The Nazi Persecution of the Churches, 1933–45* (New York: Basic Books, 1968), pp. 76–77; Claudia Koonz, *Mothers in the Fatherland: Women, the Family, and Nazi Politics* (New York: St. Martin's, 1987), p. 230.
9. The song continues:
    Singing we follow Hitler's banners;
    Only then are we worthy of our ancestors.
    I am no Christian and no Catholic.
    I go with the SA through thick and thin.
    The Church can be stolen from me for all I care.
    The swastika makes me happy here on earth.
    Him will I follow in marching step;
    Baldur von Schirach take me along.
    (Gene Edward Veith Jr., *Modern Fascism: The Threat to the Judeo-Christian Worldview* [St. Louis: Concordia, 1993], p. 67)
10. Ibid., pp. 94, 102.
11. Ibid., p. 138.
12. Joyce Howard Price, "Harvard Professor Argues for 'Abolishing' White Race," *Washington Times,* Sept. 4, 2002, p. A05.
13. Alfred Rosenberg, *The Myth of the Twentieth Century*. See http://web.archive.org/web/20020603084225/www.ety.com/HRP/books online/mythos/mythosb1chap03.htm (accessed July 10, 2007). Timothy W. Ryback, "Hitler's Forgotten Library," *Atlantic Monthly,* May 2003; Adolf Hitler, *Mein Kampf,* trans. Ralph Manheim (Boston: Houghton Mifflin, 1999), p. 454.
14. Gloria Steinem, *Revolution from Within: A Book of Self-Esteem* (Boston: Little, Brown, 1993), p. 133; see also David Rieff, "Designer Gods," *Transition,* no. 59 (1993), pp. 20–31.

15. Adam LeBor and Roger Boyes, *Seduced by Hitler* (Naperville, Ill.: Sourcebooks, 2001), p. 119.

16. E. F. Kaelin, *Heidegger's "Being and Time": A Reading for Readers* (Tallahassee: University Presses of Florida, 1988), p. 58; Veith, *Modern Fascism,* pp. 119, 124.

17. Zeev Sternhell, *The Birth of Fascist Ideology: From Cultural Rebellion to Political Revolution,* trans. David Maisel (Princeton, N.J.: Princeton University Press, 1994), p. 28.

18. Quoted in Richard Harrington, "The Good, the Bad, and the Bee-Bop," *Washington Post,* Oct. 17, 1988, p. B1.

19. *Hitler's Table Talk,* p. 353.

20. Ian Kershaw, *Hitler, 1889–1936: Hubris* (New York: Norton, 2000), p. 348; Scott Lively and Kevin Abrams, *The Pink Swastika: Homosexuality in the Nazi Party* (Keizer, Ore.: Founders, 1995), p. vii.

21. Tom Wolfe, *Hooking Up* (New York: Picador, 2000), p. 140.

22. Albert Gore, *Earth in the Balance: Ecology and the Human Spirit* (Boston: Houghton Mifflin, 2000), pp. 336, 220–21.

23. See Michael Crichton's Commonwealth Club speech in 2003: www.crichton-official.com/speeches/speeches_quote05.html. Also see Steven Landsburg's *Armchair Economist: Economics and Everyday Life* (New York: Free Press, 1993); Eric Goldscheider, "Witches, Druids, and Other Pagans Make Merry Again," *New York Times,* May 28, 2005, p. B7; Robert H. Nelson, "Tom Hayden, Meet Adam Smith and Thomas Aquinas," *Forbes,* Oct. 29, 1990; Dana Milbank, "Some Heated Words for Mr. Global Warming," *Washington Post,* March 22, 2007, p. A02.

24. William Rees-Mogg, "And Yet the Band Plays On," *Times* (London), May 26, 1994.

25. Matt Lauer, *Countdown to Doomsday,* Sci-Fi Channel, June 14, 2006.

26. See Peter Staudenmaier, "Fascist Ecology: The 'Green Wing' of the Nazi Party and Its Historical Antecedents," www.spunk.org/texts/places/germany/sp001630/peter.html (accessed May 8, 2007).

27. Ibid.

28. Robert N. Proctor, *The Nazi War on Cancer* (Princeton, N.J.: Princeton University Press, 2000), p. 139.

29. Prominent raw foodists (or members of the living food movement) include Demi Moore, Woody Harrelson, Edward Norton, and Angela Bassett; *Hitler's Table Talk,* p. 443.

30. See, for example, www.peta.org/about/whyanimalrights.asp and Charles Oliver, "Don't Put Animal Rights Above Humans," *USA Today,* June 11, 1990, p. 10A.

31. See Jacob Sullum, "What the Doctor Orders," *Reason,* Jan. 1996; Jacob Sullum, "An Epidemic of Meddling," *Reason,* May 2007.

32. Proctor, *The Nazi War on Cancer,* p. 120; Jacob Sullum, "To Your Health!" *National Review,* Sept. 13, 1999.

33. Jon Gertner, "The Virtue in $6 Heirloom Tomatoes," *New York Times Magazine,* June 6, 2004; Jonah Goldberg, "Gaiam Somebody!" *National Review,* March 19, 2001.

AFTERWORD: THE TEMPTING OF CONSERVATISM

1. The Princeton historian Sean Wilentz writes:

> At heart, Buchanan is a man of the old Catholic right—echoing the anti–New Deal catechism popularized by the "radio priest," Father Charles Coughlin, and the muscular, pietistic, corporatist anti-communism that found a hero in Generalissimo Francisco Franco during the Spanish Civil War . . . He detests the welfare state, which he sees as an intrusive secularist force. He regards the world beyond our shores as a tempest of savage tribalism, and he would like, on that account, both to halt immigration and to pull the United States out of the United Nations. He has a penchant for conspiratorial thinking, illustrated by his remarks about the devilish "foreign policy elites" and the pro-Israel "amen corner" that supposedly control our policies abroad and corrupt our politics at home. ("Third Out," *New Republic,* Nov. 22, 1999)

There's much truth here, but what Wilentz gets flatly wrong is that Buchanan does not, in fact, "detest" the welfare state and never has. This is not an insignificant distortion.

2. Molly Ivins, "Notes from Another Country," *Nation,* Sept. 14, 1992.
3. These and other quotations are from Ramesh Ponnuru's "A Conservative No More," *National Review,* Oct. 11, 1999. I'm indebted to Ponnuru in general and to this article in particular for many insights into Buchanan.
4. For Buchanan on Zhirinovsky, see *The Death of the West* (New York: St. Martin's, 2002), p. 18. On Euro-Americans, see "The Disposition of Christian Americans," Nov. 27, 1998, www.buchanan.org/pa-98-1127 .html; and "Un-American Ivy League," *New York Post,* Jan. 2, 1999.
5. See Ponnuru, "A Conservative No More."
6. See David Brooks, "Politics and Patriotism: From Teddy Roosevelt to John McCain," *Weekly Standard,* April 26, 1999; Richard Lowry, "TR and His Fan," *National Review,* Feb. 7, 2000; David Brooks, "A Return to National Greatness: A Manifesto for a Lost Creed," *Weekly Standard,* March 3, 1997; John B. Judis, "Are We All Progressives Now?" *American Prospect,* May 8, 2000.
7. Ramesh Ponnuru, "Swallowed by Leviathan: Conservatism Versus an Oxymoron: 'Big-Government Conservatism,' " *National Review,* Sept. 29, 2003.
8. Fred Barnes, *Rebel-in-Chief: Inside the Bold and Controversial Presidency of George W. Bush* (New York: Three Rivers Press, 2006); see also interview with Tim Russert, CNBC, Jan. 28, 2006.
9. See Samuel Huntington, "Conservatism as an Ideology," *American Political Science Review* 51 (June 1957); and Friedrich Hayek, "Why I Am Not a Conservative," in *The Constitution of Liberty* (Chicago: University of Chicago Press, 1960).
10. See: Jonah Goldberg, "A Lib-Lib Romance," *National Review,* Dec. 31, 2006.

· INDEX ·